2001-2002

STANDARD LESSON COMMENTARY

King James Version

International Sunday School Lessons

Edited by

Ronald G. Davis, Douglas Redford,
Ronald L. Nickelson, and Jonathan Underwood

Published by
STANDARD PUBLISHING
Mark A. Taylor, *Publisher*
Jonathan Underwood, *Senior Editor of Adult Curriculum*
Cheryl Frey, *Office Editor*

Forty-ninth Annual Volume

©2001
STANDARD PUBLISHING
A division of STANDEX INTERNATIONAL Corporation
8121 Hamilton Avenue, Cincinnati, Ohio 45231
Printed in U. S. A.

In This Volume

Artists

TITLE PAGES: James E. Seward

Cover design by DesignTeam

CD-ROM AVAILABLE

The *Standard Lesson Commentary* is available in an electronic format in special editions of the *Standard Lesson Commentary* (King James edition) and *The NIV® Standard Lesson Commentary*. These editions (order # 20002 for KJV and 30002 for NIV®) contain a compact disk for use with Windows®-based computers.

System Requirements: Windows 2000/ME/98/95/3.1; 32 Meg RAM; 25 Meg Available Hard Drive Space; 2x or better CD-ROM drive.

If you have any questions regarding the use or content of this CD-ROM, please contact Technical Support by telephone at 800-446-5564 or 630-789-0710, by fax at 630-789-0997, or by email at techsup@isgrupe.com. Technical Support is available from 9:00 am to 5:00 pm (CST), Monday through Friday.

Index of Printed Texts, 2001-2002

The printed texts for 2001-2002 are arranged here in the order in which they appear in the Bible.
Opposite each reference is the number of the page on which it appears in this volume.

Cumulative Index

A cumulative index for the Scripture passages used in the STANDARD LESSON COMMENTARY *for the years September, 1998—August, 2002, is provided below.*

V

Standard Lesson Commentary
Customer Survey

As part of Standard Publishing's commitment to provide you excellent Christian education resources, we would appreciate your comments about this product: 2001-02 Standard Lesson Commentary. Please take a moment and complete the survey below, detach and mail promptly. Your input is valuable as we develop products for your future use. Thank you for taking time to participate and for purchasing the **Standard Lesson Commentary.**

User Profile (check one response for each item)

1. Gender: ❑ male ❑ female
2. Age: ❑ under 20 ❑ 20—39 ❑ 40—59 ❑ 60 +
3. Education: ❑ High School ❑ Some College ❑ College Graduate ❑ Graduate School
4. Residence: City _____ State _____
5. Church affiliation:
   ❑ Assembly of God ❑ Lutheran
   ❑ Baptist ❑ Methodist
   ❑ Christian Churches / Churches of Christ ❑ Presbyterian
   ❑ Christian Church (Disciples) ❑ Pentecostal
   ❑ Church of God ❑ Roman Catholic
   ❑ Churches of Christ (a cappella) ❑ Other_____
   ❑ Episcopal
6. Purchased by: ❑ Individual User ❑ Church ❑ As gift

7. What is the primary use for your Standard Lesson Commentary? (Check one.)
   ❑ Teacher resource for Sunday school lesson preparation
   ❑ Student resource for Sunday school
   ❑ Devotions
   ❑ Personal study
   ❑ Group Bible study
   ❑ Reference
   ❑ Other_____

8. Features. (Please circle the number that indicates your assessment of the feature indicated.)
   1 unacceptable 2 below average 3 average 4 above average 5 excellent

Feature	1	2	3	4	5	
Lesson Development	1	2	3	4	5	
Graphics	1	2	3	4	5	
Ease of Use	1	2	3	4	5	
CD Rom	1	2	3	4	5	NA
Index	1	2	3	4	5	
Pronunciation Guide	1	2	3	4	5	
Activities	1	2	3	4	5	
Discussion Questions	1	2	3	4	5	

(Continued on back.)

BUSINESS REPLY MAIL
FIRST-CLASS MAIL   PERMIT NO. 760   CINCINNATI OH

POSTAGE WILL BE PAID BY ADDRESSEE

**DIRECTOR OF MARKETING
STANDARD PUBLISHING
8121 HAMILTON AVE
CINCINNATI OH 45231-9943**

‑‑‑‑‑‑‑‑‑‑‑‑‑‑‑‑‑‑‑‑‑‑‑‑ FOLD HERE ‑‑‑‑‑‑‑‑‑‑‑‑‑‑‑‑‑‑‑‑‑‑‑‑

9. Factors influencing purchase decision. (Circle the number that indicates the importance of each factor in the purchase decision.)

    1 not at all   2 slightly   3 somewhat   4 very   5 extremely

Price	1	2	3	4	5
Advertising	1	2	3	4	5
King James Version	1	2	3	4	5
New International Version	1	2	3	4	5
CD ROM availability	1	2	3	4	5
Companion to Standard Publishing Curriculum	1	2	3	4	5
Standard Publishing reputation	1	2	3	4	5
Recommended by church/friend	1	2	3	4	5
Product features	1	2	3	4	5

10. Which other Standard Publishing products do you use? (Check all that apply.)

❏ Christian Standard Magazine
❏ The Lookout Magazine
❏ Standard Publishing Sunday school Curriculum
❏ Vacation Bible School program

❏ Children's ministry resources
❏ Solid Foundation Bible Studies
❏ Other adult ministry resources

*Thank you for taking time to complete this survey
and for purchasing the Standard Lesson Commentary!*

PLEASE TAPE OR GLUE ENDS TOGETHER BEFORE MAILING.

Fall Quarter, 2001

Jesus' Ministry
(Miracles, Parables, the Sermon on the Mount)

About These Lessons

These lessons will focus on the life of Jesus. Rather than examine texts from one Gospel, the lessons of the current quarter will draw from all four of the Gospel records. Together, these four witnesses will provide a unified composite of the life of our Lord, particularly in His wonderful miracles and His powerful teaching. May we follow in the path He has set.

Sep 2

Sep 9

Sep 16

Sep 23

Sep 30

Oct 7

Oct 14

Oct 21

Oct 28

Nov 4

Nov 11

Nov 18

Nov 25

Blessed to Bless Others

WHEN GOD CALLED ABRAM, He said, "I will bless thee, . . . and thou shalt be a blessing" (Genesis 12:2). Abram's blessings were not to be an end in themselves; they would be a blessing to "all families of the earth" (v. 3).

The lessons for the coming year call attention to our privilege and our purpose as "Abraham's seed" (Galatians 3:29). The fall quarter focuses on Jesus' miracles, which distinguish Him as the Son of God, and on His teachings, which define the way of life that should distinguish His followers.

The winter quarter features lessons drawn from the Old Testament, particularly Isaiah. These studies remind us that God has always had a heart for the nations—and so must His people.

The lessons for the spring quarter are taken from Romans and Galatians. Of all Paul's writings, these letters especially resonate with the themes of God's grace in Jesus Christ and the responsibility of His people to live by grace.

The summer quarter brings us back to the Old Testament with the theme, "Worship and Wisdom for Living." Using texts from Psalms and Proverbs, these studies will encourage us to see life the way God sees it. No matter how much knowledge we acquire, without God we are never truly wise—an apt message for our "information age."

May these lessons help us in fulfilling our mission as "children of Abraham"—blessed to bless others!

International Sunday School Lesson Cycle
September, 1998—August, 2004

YEAR	FALL QUARTER (Sept., Oct., Nov.)	WINTER QUARTER (Dec., Jan., Feb.)	SPRING QUARTER (Mar., Apr., May)	SUMMER QUARTER (June, July, Aug.)
1998-1999	God Calls a People to Faithful Living (Old Testament Survey)	God Calls Anew in Jesus Christ (New Testament Survey)	That You May Believe (John)	Genesis: Beginnings (Genesis)
1999-2000	From Slavery to Conquest (Exodus, Leviticus, Numbers, Deuteronomy, Joshua)	Immanuel: God With Us (Matthew)	Helping a Church Confront Crisis (1 and 2 Corinthians)	New Life in Christ (Ephesians, Philippians, Colossians, Philemon)
2000-2001	Rulers of Israel (Judges, 1 and 2 Samuel, 1 Kings 1-11)	Good News of Jesus (Luke)	Continuing Jesus' Work (Acts)	Division and Decline (1 Kings 12-22, 2 Kings 1-17, Isaiah 1-39, Hosea, Amos, Micah)
2001-2002	Jesus' Ministry (Miracles, Parables, Sermon on the Mount)	Light for All People (Isaiah 9:1-7; 11:1-9; 40-66; Ruth, Jonah)	The Power of the Gospel (Romans, Galatians)	Worship and Wisdom for Living (Psalms, Proverbs)
2002-2003	Judgment and Exile (2 Kings 18-25, Jeremiah, Lamentations, Ezekiel, Habakkuk, Zephaniah)	Portraits of Faith (Personalities in the New Testament)	Jesus: God's Power in Action (Mark)	God Restores a Remnant (Ezra, Nehemiah, Daniel, Joel, Obadiah, Haggai, Zechariah, Malachi)
2003-2004	Faith Faces the World (James, 1 and 2 Peter, 1, 2, 3 John, Jude)	A Child Is Given (Samuel, John the Baptist, Jesus) / Lessons From Life (Esther, Job, Ecclesiastes, Song of Solomon)	Jesus Fulfills His Mission (Death, Burial, and Resurrection Texts) / Living Expectantly (1, 2 Thessalonians, Revelation)	Hold Fast to the Faith (Hebrews) / Guidelines for the Church's Ministry (1, 2 Timothy, Titus)

Learning From Jesus

by Orrin Root

JESUS IS OUR MASTER TEACHER and our perfect example. More than that, He is our Lord and our King. It should be our duty and our pleasure to learn what He teaches and follow His example.

In our Sunday school studies, then, it is fitting to spend about a quarter of each year focusing on the life and teachings of Jesus. Within our current six-year cycle, one quarter is devoted to a study of each of the four Gospels—Matthew, Mark, Luke, and John. During the last year of the cycle (2003-2004), portions of two quarters will be devoted to studies from the Gospels. (See the chart on the opposite page.)

For the three months ahead (September, October, and November of 2001), we shall draw material from all four of the Gospels to form a series of lessons arranged by topics. In September we shall study some of Jesus' miracles, in October we shall consider some of His parables, and in November we shall examine four lessons from His Sermon on the Mount.

What follows are brief previews of the lessons to be covered during the next three months.

Unit 1: September
Performing Miracles

Lesson 1: Jesus Works His First Miracle. There was a small emergency at a wedding feast in Cana of Galilee: the wine was all gone. Compassionate Jesus solved the problem by turning approximately one hundred fifty gallons of water into superior wine. Thus He saved the host from embarrassment and, more important, He strengthened His earliest disciples' faith in Him. It should strengthen the faith of modern disciples as well.

Lesson 2: Jesus Displays Power Over Nature. Only a preacher knows how exhausting it is to preach for hours, and only a doctor knows how wearying it is to care for the seriously ill. Jesus had been doing both—though no doctor or preacher is comparable to Jesus. Still, He was so exhausted that He went to sleep in a little boat as it crossed the Sea of Galilee. He continued to sleep, even when a terrific storm arose and threatened to overturn the boat. The frightened disciples awakened Jesus. At His rebuke the wind stopped blowing and the sea was calm. Thus the disciples' faith in Jesus was fortified yet more.

Lesson 3: Jesus Displays Power Over Disease. Jesus quickly became the most popular teacher in Galilee, making the established teachers wild with jealousy. They wanted to accuse Him of breaking the law when He healed on the Sabbath, but His questions left them speechless. So they plotted to kill Him.

The established teachers in Jerusalem were as envious as those in Galilee. When Jesus gave sight to a blind man on the Sabbath, they claimed that He was a sinner. But the man who received his sight resisted their harassment and declared his faith in Jesus.

Lesson 4: A Mother Persists in Faith. Jesus traveled north from Galilee to the area around Tyre and Sidon. Even in that foreign territory His reputation was known. Soon He was recognized by a woman who pleaded for help on behalf of her daughter, who was troubled by a demon. Jesus initially ignored the woman's request because, as He explained to the disciples, His personal mission was only to the people of Israel. When she kept on asking, Jesus told the woman the same thing, noting that it was not proper to give the children's food to the dogs. Humbly she replied that dogs eat crumbs that fall from the children's table. Jesus then praised the woman's faith and set her daughter free from the demon. This reminds us that Jesus' salvation is meant for all the people of the world.

Lesson 5: Lazarus Is Raised. Mary and Martha and their brother Lazarus were dear friends of Jesus. They lived in Bethany, just east of Jerusalem. When Lazarus became very sick, his sisters sent word to Jesus; but Jesus delayed His response to their message. He arrived in Bethany four days after Lazarus had died and had been entombed in a cave. Still, when Jesus called him, the dead man came forth! Jesus' power is stronger than death.

Unit 2: October
Truth in Parables

Lesson 6: Jesus Teaches in Parables. When asked why He used parables in His teaching, Jesus replied that by parables He revealed the truth about His kingdom to those disciples who cared enough to seek it. His answer implied that the truth would remain hidden to hearers who cared only about seeing the miracles that Jesus could do.

One parable described a man who sowed good seed throughout his field, yet the harvest was different because the soil was different in various parts of the field. As Jesus explained the parable, He Himself was the sower, the truth He taught was the seed, and the hearers were the field. The same truth produced different results because the hearers were different. Each of us must ask himself or herself, "What kind of soil am I?" All of us can be better soil than we are now.

Lesson 7: The Good Samaritan. "Who is my neighbor?" asked a lawyer. Jesus answered the question with the story of a good Samaritan who spent time and money to help a wounded stranger. That Samaritan showed himself to be a good neighbor, though he neither lived near the man he helped nor had any acquaintance with him. "Go, and do thou likewise," said Jesus to the lawyer—and to you and me.

Lesson 8: Parables on Prayer. To teach us to be persistent in prayer, Jesus told of a widow who kept on presenting her plea until an unjust judge finally issued a just decision. To teach us to be humble in prayer, He contrasted two men: a proud Pharisee's prayer was devoted to bragging about himself; a humble publican's prayer was a fervent plea for mercy.

Lesson 9: The Sheep and the Goats. Jesus said that at the final judgment He will separate the people of all nations as a shepherd separates sheep from goats. Strictly speaking, this story is a simile rather than a parable; but it resembles a parable in that people are compared with lesser things. Some people will be invited to the kingdom long prepared for them, for they have been kind and helpful to Jesus. Others will be consigned to everlasting fire because they have ignored Jesus in His needs.

When were these people either kind or unkind to Jesus? The answer: when they were kind or unkind to some of His people. Thus, even now you and I are choosing our eternal destiny.

Unit 3: November
The Sermon on the Mount

Lesson 10: Blessed Are You. Jesus' Sermon on the Mount begins with a series of blessings pronounced on people in circumstances that would seem to produce only unhappiness. Thus are we encouraged to walk with Jesus day by day, trusting Him to bless us in any situation. By doing this we become the salt of the earth, improving its flavor and preserving it. According to another metaphor, we become the light of the world, helping all its people to find the right way.

Lesson 11: Jesus Fulfills the Law. Before giving some teaching that appeared to be quite different from the law, Jesus announced that He had not come to destroy the law, but to fulfill it. His fuller teaching covers thoughts, motives, and emotions, as well as acts. He teaches us to be generous rather than merely just, to love even the enemies who hate us, and to do good to those who do only evil to us. Thus do we show ourselves to be children of our Father in Heaven, for He provides rain and sun for the evil people as well as the good.

Lesson 12: Storing Treasures in Heaven. Jesus advised His hearers to lay up treasures in Heaven rather than on earth. To do this, we must not be anxious about our physical needs such as food and clothing. God provides food for the birds; will He not provide for us as well? He provides clothing for the wildflowers; will He not do as much for us? Our first aim is to be ruled by God, to do His will, to be righteous in His sight. Then our physical needs will be supplied.

Lesson 13: Living by the Law of Love. The law said, "Thou shalt love thy neighbor as thyself" (Leviticus 19:18). Our text for this lesson presents the same truth in the form of the well-known Golden Rule: "All things whatsoever ye would that men should do to you, do ye even so to them" (Matthew 7:12). Among other things, this means that we will not be harsh and merciless in judging others, but will first seek out and correct our own faults. We judge a tree correctly by observing what kind of fruit it bears, and we judge a person fairly when we see the results of what he says and does.

What will these thirteen lessons do for us? That depends on what we do with them. If we learn them well, they will increase our understanding of Jesus and His will. If we follow their teaching in our daily living, they will make us better people.

Answers to Quarterly Quiz
on page 8

Lesson 1—1. false. 2. His mother. 3. six. **Lesson 2**—1. faith. 2. five, two, twelve. **Lesson 3**—1. a synagogue. 2. the Herodians. 3. the pool of Siloam. **Lesson 4**—1. cast out a devil. 2. dogs. **Lesson 5**—1. Bethany. 2. two days. 3. Martha. **Lesson 6**—1. by the wayside, stony places, thorns, good ground. 2. true. **Lesson 7**—1. "Master, what shall I do to inherit eternal life?" 2. Jerusalem, Jericho. 3. a priest and a Levite. **Lesson 8**—1. pray, faint. 2. "God be merciful to me a sinner." **Lesson 9**—1. false. 2. devil, angels. **Lesson 10**—1. they shall see God. 2. they shall be called the children of God. 3. salt, light. **Lesson 11**—1. the scribes and Pharisees. 2. go with him twain (two). **Lesson 12**—1. "there will your heart be also." 2. Solomon. **Lesson 13**—1. beam, mote. 2. "Therefore all things whatsoever ye would that men should do to you, do ye even so to them." 3. "ye shall know them."

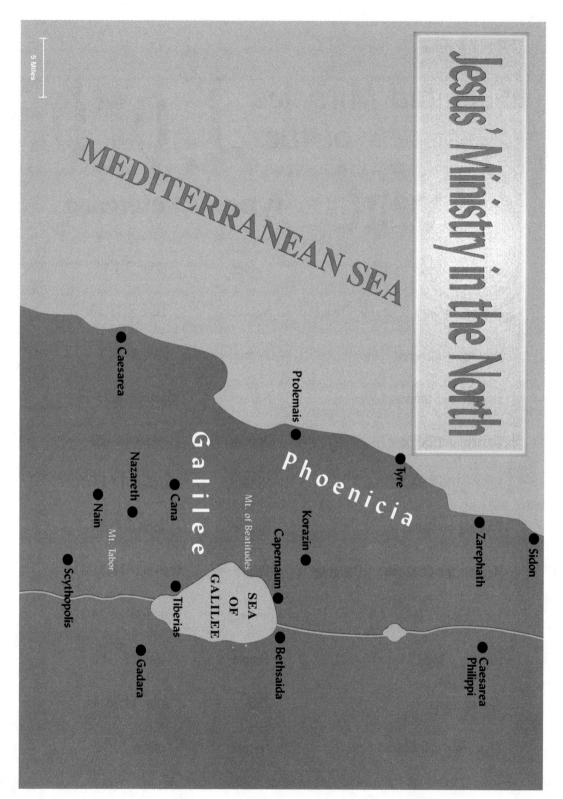

Jesus' Ministry in the North

5 Miles

MEDITERRANEAN SEA

Caesarea

Ptolemais

Tyre

Galilee

Phoenicia

Zarephath

Sidon

Nazareth

Cana

Mt. of Beatitudes

Korazin

Capernaum

Nain

Mt. Tabor

SEA OF GALILEE

Bethsaida

Caesarea Philippi

Scythopolis

Tiberias

Gadara

Selected Miracles of the Lord

Event	Type	Reference
Changing Water to Wine	Nature	John 2:1-11
Passing Through a Hostile Crowd	Nature	Luke 4:28-30
Healing a Withered Hand	People	Mark 3:1-6
Stilling the Storm and Sea	Nature	Matthew 8:23-27
Casting out Demons	Demons	Mark 5:1-20
Feeding the Five Thousand	Nature	Matthew 14:14-21
Walking on Water	Nature	John 6:15-21
Healing the Canaanite s Daughter	People	Matthew 15:21-31
Predicting a Coin in a Fish	Knowledge	Matthew 17:24-27
Healing a Blind Man	People	John 9:1-12
Raising Lazarus	People	John 11:38-44
Appearing in a Closed Room	Nature	John 20:19

Jesus Is in Control

by Roger W. Thomas

DOES IT EVER SEEM THAT YOUR LIFE is totally out of control? That your time, your money, and your circumstances have a life of their own, and that there is very little you can do about them? Most likely, we all have "been there, done that!"

Several factors can lead us to feeling this way. Time—or, rather, a perceived *lack* of time—is probably the main one. We have more labor-saving devices at our disposal than ever before, yet we always seem to be pressed for time. Money is also a major concern and remains so regardless of how much one has. Family problems surface even after the children are grown. And if these aren't enough, the health problems that we often associate with aging actually can develop at any time, sometimes striking even the young. All these circumstances remind us how little real control we have over our lives.

Miracles With a Message

What does this have to do with our lessons for the coming quarter? Quite a bit, actually! Among the lessons you will explore this fall is a unit of studies on the miracles of Jesus. Each miracle will spotlight a time when Jesus' divine power and grace confronted and met a human need.

The first five lessons examine seven of Jesus' miracles. John's Gospel, our source for four of the seven, has an interesting way of viewing these dramatic events. John concludes his account of Jesus' life by saying, "And many other signs truly did Jesus in the presence of his disciples, which are not written in this book: but these are written, that ye might believe that Jesus is the Christ, the Son of God; and that believing ye might have life through his name" (John 20:30, 31).

Clearly Jesus performed many supernatural acts. John could have included more of these than he did (John 21:25), but he chose only certain ones and termed them "signs." As a result of reading about these miracles, John's readers were expected to learn something about Jesus that would lead them to faith in Him. This faith, in turn, would result in eternal life.

It is important to understand that by "eternal life," John meant much more than spending an eternity with God in Heaven. He was describing a relationship with God that first makes the present life satisfying and meaningful and then continues into eternity. This is clear from Jesus' words in John 17:3: "This is life eternal, that they might know thee the only true God, and Jesus Christ, whom thou hast sent." Jesus not only adds years to one's life; He adds life to one's years!

For many today, the lack of quality in life contributes to their sense that life seems out of control. In spite of being alive, they feel lifeless. What they yearn for is what Jesus termed having life "more abundantly" (John 10:10).

Specific Examples

Merrill Tenney, in his *Survey of the New Testament* (page 190), includes this helpful observation on the miraculous signs of Jesus recorded by John: "These . . . miracles operated precisely in the areas where man is unable to effect any change of laws or conditions which affect his life. In these areas Jesus proved himself potent where man is impotent, and the works that He did testify to His supernatural ability."

This may be one of the truths about Jesus that John wanted his readers to understand. Jesus was (and is) the One who controls life—even when it seems out of control. Jesus' first miracle (turning water into wine, John 2:1-11) and His feeding of the five thousand (John 6:1-14) are examples. Both miracles demonstrate how Jesus, as Creator of all (John 1:3), can take what is given Him and use it in remarkable, God-glorifying ways. That is the difference that Jesus can make in our lives as well when we turn them over to Him.

Jesus' raising of Lazarus from the dead (John 11:38-44) confronted the "last enemy" (1 Corinthians 15:26) on its own terrain. Jesus came before a tomb and called a friend to come forth from the clutches of death—and he did! Human ingenuity can, at best, postpone death, but it can never defeat death. Only Jesus does that—a truth that was later made even more apparent through Jesus' own resurrection.

As you consider these and other miracles of our Lord in the lessons that follow, always be on the lookout for evidence provided by these miracles as to who Jesus is. These are not simply stories about what Jesus did "once upon a time." Each miracle points to something that Jesus can still do in the lives of those who sometimes find life out of control, but are willing to relinquish control of their lives to Him.

The promise of John 1:12 still holds: "As many as received him, to them gave he power to become the sons of God, even to them that believe on his name."

Quarterly Quiz

The questions on this page may be used in several ways: as a pretest at the beginning of the quarter; as a review at the end of the quarter; or as a review after each lesson. The questions are based on the Scripture text of each lesson (King James Version). **The answers are on page 4.**

Lesson 1

1. Jesus' disciples were not invited to the wedding at Cana. T/F *John 2:2*
2. To whom did Jesus say, "Woman, what have I to do with thee"? *John 2:3, 4*
3. How many waterpots were used in the miracle at Cana? *John 2:6*

Lesson 2

1. During the storm on the Sea of Galilee, Jesus referred to the disciples as "ye of little _____." *Matthew 8:26*
2. After Jesus provided food for the crowd, using _____ loaves and _____ fishes, _____ baskets of food remained. *Matthew 14:19, 20*

Lesson 3

1. In what place did Jesus heal the man with a withered hand? (a house, a synagogue, or the temple?) *Mark 3:1*
2. Following this miracle, with what group did the Pharisees collaborate to kill Jesus? *Mark 3:6*
3. Where did Jesus tell the man born blind to go wash? *John 9:7*

Lesson 4

1. What did the Canaanite woman want Jesus to do for her daughter? (cast out a devil, heal her leprosy, or give her sight?) *Matthew 15:22*
2. The woman told Jesus that the _____ eat of the crumbs that fall from the table. *Matthew 15:27*

Lesson 5

1. In what town did Lazarus live? *John 11:1*
2. Upon hearing of Lazarus's illness, how long did Jesus stay in the area where He was? *John 11:6*
3. Who said, "Lord, by this time he stinketh: for he hath been dead four days"? *John 11:39*

Lesson 6

1. Name the four types of soil where the seed fell in Jesus' parable. *Matthew 13:4-8*
2. Jesus' use of parables was foretold in the Old Testament. T/F *Matthew 13:34, 35*

Lesson 7

1. A lawyer "tempted" Jesus by asking a certain question. What was it? *Luke 10:25*

2. The man in the parable of the good Samaritan traveled from _____ to _____. *Luke 10:30*
3. What two men passed by the wounded man and did nothing? *Luke 10:31, 32*

Lesson 8

1. Jesus told the parable of the unjust judge so that we should always _____ and not _____. *Luke 18:1*
2. In Jesus' parable of two men praying, what did the publican say in his prayer? *Luke 18:13*

Lesson 9

1. In the final judgment, Jesus will put the sheep on His left hand and the goats on His right. T/F *Matthew 25:33*
2. Jesus described the place of everlasting fire as prepared for the _____ and his _____. *Matthew 25:41*

Lesson 10

1. What reward is promised to the pure in heart? *Matthew 5:8*
2. What reward is promised to the peacemakers? *Matthew 5:9*
3. Jesus calls His followers to be the _____ of the earth and the _____ of the world. *Matthew 5:13, 14*

Lesson 11

1. In the Sermon on the Mount, Jesus said that our righteousness should exceed that of two groups. Which two? *Matthew 5:20*
2. How did Jesus tell us to respond if someone compels us to go a mile? *Matthew 5:41*

Lesson 12

1. Complete this statement of Jesus: "For where your treasure is, ..." *Matthew 6:21*
2. What king, said Jesus, was not "arrayed," or dressed, like one of the lilies of the field? *Matthew 6:29*

Lesson 13

1. Jesus described a man with a _____ in his own eye trying to remove a _____ from his brother's eye. *Matthew 7:3*
2. Quote the Golden Rule. *Matthew 7:12*
3. Complete this statement of Jesus: "Wherefore by their fruits . . . ." *Matthew 7:20*

Jesus Works His First Miracle

DEVOTIONAL READING: Psalm 77:11-15.

BACKGROUND SCRIPTURE: John 2:1-11.

PRINTED TEXT: John 2:1-11.

John 2:1-11

1 And the third day there was a marriage in Cana of Galilee; and the mother of Jesus was there:

2 And both Jesus was called, and his disciples, to the marriage.

3 And when they wanted wine, the mother of Jesus saith unto him, They have no wine.

4 Jesus saith unto her, Woman, what have I to do with thee? mine hour is not yet come.

5 His mother saith unto the servants, Whatsoever he saith unto you, do it.

6 And there were set there six waterpots of stone, after the manner of the purifying of the Jews, containing two or three firkins apiece.

7 Jesus saith unto them, Fill the waterpots with water. And they filled them up to the brim.

8 And he saith unto them, Draw out now, and bear unto the governor of the feast. And they bare it.

9 When the ruler of the feast had tasted the water that was made wine, and knew not whence it was, (but the servants which drew the water knew,) the governor of the feast called the bridegroom,

10 And saith unto him, Every man at the beginning doth set forth good wine; and when men have well drunk, then that which is worse: but thou hast kept the good wine until now.

11 This beginning of miracles did Jesus in Cana of Galilee, and manifested forth his glory; and his disciples believed on him.

GOLDEN TEXT: This beginning of miracles did Jesus in Cana of Galilee, and manifested forth his glory; and his disciples believed on him.—John 2:11.

Jesus' Ministry
Unit 1: Performing Miracles
(Lessons 1-5)

Lesson Aims

After participating in this lesson, a student should be able to:

1. Give the details and result of the miracle that Jesus performed at the wedding feast in Cana of Galilee.

2. Explain the role of Jesus' miracles in establishing His identity as the Son of God.

3. Give thanks for the many miracles that provide solid evidence for believing in Jesus as the Son of God.

Lesson Outline

INTRODUCTION
  A. Feeling Helpless
  B. Lesson Background
I. EMBARRASSING SITUATION (John 2:1-5)
  A. The Occasion (vv. 1, 2)
    A Cause for Celebration
  B. The Need (v. 3)
  C. The Plan (vv. 4, 5)
II. MIRACLE (John 2:6-10)
  A. The Material (vv. 6, 7)
  B. The Product (v. 8)
  C. The Result (vv. 9, 10)
III. EPILOGUE (John 2:11)
  A. The Beginning of Miracles (v. 11a)
  B. The Glory of Jesus (v. 11b)
  C. The Believing Disciples (v. 11c)
    When God Speaks
CONCLUSION
  A. Ancient Unbelievers
  B. Modern Unbelievers
  C. The Word of God
  D. Prayer
  E. Thought to Remember

Introduction

A. Feeling Helpless

One wintry night a carload of friends from another town dropped in to attend the evening service at our church. My wife and I greeted them with joy, but there was no time for us to talk. The prelude was already sounding, so we hurried to our seats. After the benediction, I urged our friends, "Come on over to the house. We'll have ice cream."

Ice cream was an ever-present delight at our house. It was always in the freezer—usually in two or three flavors—ready to be served as a favorite bedtime snack, a ready dessert for any meal, or an impromptu refreshment for unexpected guests.

The guests that evening had eaten ice cream at our house before, and they happily followed us home. As we all trooped into the house, I told my wife, "I promised ice cream."

Her reply nearly floored me: "We don't have any." The unthinkable had happened. For the first time since we had obtained a home freezer, we were out of ice cream—and the house was full of expectant guests. I knew then how the host must have felt at that wedding celebration in Cana of Galilee when a servant whispered nervously, "We're running out of wine." I was speechless, helpless.

Fortunately, my wife was not so helpless. We had milk in the refrigerator, bread in the breadbox, and able helpers among the guests. In just a few minutes we had an ample supply of cinnamon toast and hot chocolate, which proved to be an even better treat than ice cream for that wintry night.

B. Lesson Background

In our lesson text we read of "a marriage in Cana"; however, at a first-century wedding the guests did not see the happy pair stand together and promise to love, cherish, and protect each other "till death do us part." The equivalent of such promises occurred at the "betrothal," when a man and a woman became engaged. The "marriage" was more similar to what we call a wedding reception—simply a glad celebration and a time to rejoice with the happy couple and wish them well in their life together.

More details about the marriage customs of the time are revealed in Jesus' parable of the ten virgins (Matthew 25:1-13). There the festivities began with a party for the groom and his friends at the groom's home, while the bride's girlfriends got together at her home. At a time not announced in advance, the groom went to get his bride and took her to his home. In Jesus' parable the bridegroom did not come until midnight. Probably the celebration then continued for some time, perhaps until dawn. It is not hard to imagine that such an extended party might easily consume more refreshments than the host had provided.

Yet note that there is no suggestion of drunkenness, either in the parable or in today's text. The wine used in such celebrations was usually so diluted with water that its alcoholic content was slight.

I. Embarrassing Situation
(John 2:1-5)

Our text begins by setting the stage for a crisis that must have made the host feel as I did when I had no ice cream for the guests I had invited to our home. We have no hint of how long the wedding feast had been going on before the crisis occurred. Perhaps it had continued for hours.

A. The Occasion (vv. 1, 2)

1. And the third day there was a marriage in Cana of Galilee; and the mother of Jesus was there.

The chapter before this had its setting by the Jordan River, where John the Baptist was preaching. John announced that Jesus was "the Lamb of God, which taketh away the sin of the world" (John 1:29). Several of John's disciples then accompanied Jesus when He left the Jordan to return to Galilee (John 1:43). (He may have led them to His boyhood home in Nazareth.) *The third day* in our text should be counted from the day Jesus left the Jordan.

This group of disciples probably included Peter and Andrew (John 1:40-42), John (most likely the other disciple mentioned in John 1:35-40), and Philip and Nathanael (John 1:43-51). Many students suggest that John's brother James was present as well at this point, making a total of six disciples who went to Galilee with Jesus.

Cana was a small town near Nazareth, though its exact location remains a matter of speculation. Most likely *the mother of Jesus* was a relative or close friend of the bridegroom's family. Perhaps she was helping with some of the details of the gathering.

2. And both Jesus was called, and his disciples, to the marriage.

Jesus had been away from home for nearly two months. During that time, He had been baptized by John the Baptist; He had spent forty days in the desert without human companionship, but tempted by the devil; and He had returned to the Jordan and recruited His first disciples from among the disciples of John (Matthew 3:13—4:11; John 1:29-51). Now He came home to Galilee just in time for the wedding in Cana, and a quick invitation was given to Him and His six new disciples. Such an invitation is another reason for supposing that Jesus' family and the bridegroom's family were either relatives or close friends. [See question #1, page 16.]

A CAUSE FOR CELEBRATION

You can find almost anything on the Internet these days: vitamins, automobiles, exercise equipment—even a wife! At least that's what Rod Barnett thought, when, in 1998, he launched his World Wide Web site with an offer of ten thousand dollars to anyone who would introduce him to the woman whom he would eventually marry.

During the first year of his offer, Barnett received thousands of responses, ranging from children suggesting that he marry their single moms to proposals for immoral liaisons. After about a year had passed, Barnett's unique approach to searching for a wife had resulted in only one "serious relationship," and that lasted just a couple of months. Up to that point he had found nothing to celebrate.

The way one finds a spouse today is certainly different from the custom in Jesus' day. What hasn't changed is the expectation that one's wedding will be a cause for celebration. Jesus was probably invited to the wedding at Cana because He was the kind of person who enjoyed such occasions. He wasn't the dour, lonely, religiose person-who-never-had-much-fun whom some have associated with Jesus.

Perhaps Jesus chose to begin His ministry of miracles at a wedding feast in order to show us that piety shouldn't keep us from celebrating even the intimately physical delights that God has created us to enjoy.   —C. R. B.

B. The Need (v. 3)

3. And when they wanted wine, the mother of Jesus saith unto him, They have no wine.

Here *wanted* means "lacked" rather than "desired," though of course they desired what they lacked. The problem was that the *wine* provided for the party was all gone, or nearly all gone, and the party was not nearly at an end. The reason for the lack is unknown and is not important. The lack itself was terribly embarrassing.

Why did *the mother of Jesus* take this distressing news to Him? Jesus had done no miracles to this point. Mary wouldn't have been expecting that, would she? On the other hand, Mary knew that her son was also God's Son, destined to rule forever (Luke 1:31-33). Now He was approximately thirty years old (Luke 3:23). He had been baptized. He had gathered a few disciples. All of these events might have been taken to indicate that Jesus was about to assert Himself and begin

---

How to Say It

CANA. *Kay*-nuh.
FIRKINS. *fir*-kins.
GALILEE. *Gal*-uh-lee.
NATHANAEL. Nuh-*than*-yull.
NAZARETH. *Naz*-uh-reth.

the promised rule. Was Mary hoping He would do so by working a miracle in order to produce more wine? We can only wonder. [See question #2, page 16.]

C. The Plan (vv. 4, 5)

4. Jesus saith unto her, Woman, what have I to do with thee? mine hour is not yet come.

To address Mary as *Woman* may sound to us as though Jesus was being rude to His mother, but Mary would not have taken it that way. Note that it is the way Jesus spoke to Mary as He tenderly provided for her care while He was dying (John 19:26). Still, a son's addressing his mother in this way is not found in any Greek or Hebrew literature outside the Gospel of John. We wonder about the significance of the address, no matter how tender. Some have suggested that Jesus was asserting His independence from family ties, signaling that Mary's role as His mother was now to be considered less significant than her position as His disciple.

"What to me and to you?" is a literal translation of *what have I to do with thee?* The words seem to say that the shortage of wine was none of Jesus' business or of Mary's. The reason follows: *mine hour is not yet come.* References to Jesus' "hour" or "time" occur elsewhere in John's Gospel (7:6, 8, 30; 8:20). It is clear from later usage of this language in John that Jesus' "hour" described His crucifixion (12:23, 27; 13:1; 16:32; 17:1). Mary was mistaken if she thought this was the time for Jesus to fulfill His mission as the Son of God.

5. His mother saith unto the servants, Whatsoever he saith unto you, do it.

Mary did not beg or plead with Jesus. She simply told the *servants* present to *do* whatever Jesus told them to do. She did not try to tell Jesus what to do, but it is clear that she hoped He would do something. [See question #3, page 16.]

Home Daily Bible Readings

Monday, Aug. 27—The Word in the Beginning (John 1:1-5)

Tuesday, Aug. 28—The Word Became Flesh (John 1:9-14)

Wednesday, Aug. 29—John's Testimony (John 1:15-23)

Thursday, Aug. 30—"This Is the Son of God" (John 1:29-34)

Friday, Aug. 31—"Come and See" (John 1:35-42)

Saturday, Sept. 1—"You Will See Greater Things" (John 1:43-51)

Sunday, Sept. 2—Water Into Wine (John 2:1-11)

II. Miracle
(John 2:6-10)

Perhaps something in Jesus' manner told Mary that He was not flatly refusing to help in this crisis. We can imagine how eagerly she waited to see what would happen.

A. The Material (vv. 6, 7)

6. And there were set there six waterpots of stone, after the manner of the purifying of the Jews, containing two or three firkins apiece.

The *six waterpots* may have contained water that had been used for washing the guests' feet as they came in from the dusty street. The word for *purifying* literally means "cleansing." But this word often suggests a ceremonial or ritual cleansing. *The purifying of the Jews* may, then, mean the water had been for the traditional washing of the guests' hands before they ate (Matthew 15:1, 2). *Two or three firkins* is estimated to be about twenty to thirty gallons. Such a large amount of water suggests that there were many guests.

7. Jesus saith unto them, Fill the waterpots with water. And they filled them up to the brim.

Easily we imagine that all available servants were summoned to help carry out Jesus' command. Perhaps some took a smaller jar and hurried to the town well or spring. Soon the six big *waterpots* were *filled . . . up to the brim.*

B. The Product (v. 8)

8. And he saith unto them, Draw out now, and bear unto the governor of the feast. And they bare it.

Dippers were at hand to fill cups from the big jars. At Jesus' word, the first cupful was taken to *the governor of the feast*, whom we would be more likely to call the master of ceremonies or the toastmaster.

C. The Result (vv. 9, 10)

9. When the ruler of the feast had tasted the water that was made wine, and knew not whence it was, (but the servants which drew the water knew,) the governor of the feast called the bridegroom.

At some point before the master of ceremonies tasted it, *the water . . . was made wine.* In fact, it was such excellent wine that the taster thought it merited special praise. He *called the bridegroom* to hear the praise. Of course, he did not know where the wine came from, *but the servants which drew the water knew.* [See question #4, page 16.]

10. And saith unto him, Every man at the beginning doth set forth good wine; and when men have well drunk, then that which is worse: but thou hast kept the good wine until now.

"Everyone serves the best wine first." So said the master of ceremonies. "Then he serves a cheaper wine—an inferior wine—when those drinking are too drunk to know the difference." Whether this was true or false, whether it was spoken in earnest or in jest, the praise that followed was certainly sincere: *Thou hast kept the good wine until now.*

Again, we see no evidence that anyone was drunk at this celebration. The master of ceremonies did not find his taste dulled. With his first sip, he knew that the wine from the water jar was the best he had tasted that evening. And we suppose that every guest agreed with him.

III. Epilogue
(John 2:11)

Three important statements concerning Jesus' ministry of miracles are evident in this short verse that concludes John's record of an amazing event.

A. The Beginning of Miracles (v. 11a)

11a. This beginning of miracles did Jesus in Cana of Galilee.

John notes that this was the *beginning*, or the first, of Jesus' *miracles*. Thus he implies that others followed. Reading through Matthew, Mark, Luke, and John, we see miracles of four kinds.

1. Miracles in nature. In today's lesson we have seen Jesus change water into wine. In another such miracle, He multiplied a boy's lunch to make a meal for five thousand men, plus some women and children (John 6:1-14). In another, He walked calmly on the surface of the sea (John 6:16-21). In yet another, His command stopped a raging storm (Mark 4:35-41). In these miracles, objects with no sense of hearing obeyed Jesus' command, and objects without a mind obeyed His will.

2. Miracles with people. In countless cases, Jesus healed "all manner of sickness and all manner of disease among the people" (Matthew 4:23, 24). He even restored life to some who had died (Luke 7:11-17; 8:41, 42, 49-56; John 11:38-44).

3. Miracles with demons. Evil spirits sometimes took control of people, causing them to suffer various physical and mental disorders. At Jesus' command, those demons had to release their victims (Luke 7:21; 8:26-39; 9:37-43).

4. Miracles of knowledge. Jesus knew what people were thinking (Luke 5:22; 6:8; 9:47; 11:17; John 2:24, 25). He knew what was happening far away (John 11:14). He did not know when He would come again (Mark 13:32), but He knew He would come (Mark 13:26, 27).

Like the first miracle, all of these miracles demonstrated the glory of Jesus and led others to believe in Him.

Selected Miracles of the Lord

Event	Type	Reference
Changing Water to Wine	Nature	John 2:1-11
Passing Through a Hostile Crowd	Nature	Luke 4:28-30
Healing a Withered Hand	People	Mark 3:1-6
Stilling the Storm and Sea	Nature	Matthew 8:23-27
Casting out Demons	Demons	Mark 5:1-20
Feeding the Five Thousand	Nature	Matthew 14:14-21
Walking on Water	Nature	John 6:15-21
Healing the Canaanite's Daughter	People	Matthew 15:21-31
Predicting a Coin in a Fish	Knowledge	Matthew 17:24-27
Healing a Blind Man	People	John 9:1-12
Raising Lazarus	People	John 11:38-44
Appearing in a Closed Room	Nature	John 20:19

Visual for lesson 1

This poster is a chart of Jesus' miracles. You will find it useful throughout the quarter.

B. The Glory of Jesus (v. 11b)

11b. And manifested forth his glory.

Sometimes the word *glory* means praise or honor. That is its meaning when we say, "Give glory to God." But in this verse the word *glory* means those attributes of Jesus that are worthy of honor and praise. Several of them are shown clearly in His first miracle.

1. His creative power. Without so much as a word or a touch, Jesus transformed six jars of water into jars of excellent wine. Impossible as this would be for any human, it was not difficult at all for the Lord of creation (John 1:3). The heavens and the earth are the handiwork of the One who made six jars of wine at Cana.

2. His compassion. As noted above, Jesus first seemed to say that the shortage of wine was no concern of His. It was a concern of the host. He had made a mistake. He had not provided enough wine. He would be ashamed and embarrassed—but why should anyone else care?

But Mary did care, not because of any failure of her own, but because she shared the feelings of the host. And Jesus cared. He shared the feelings of His mother and His friend. So the creative power of the Almighty was used to supply refreshments for a wedding reception. [See question #5, page 16.]

3. His flexibility. Jesus' time had not yet come (v. 4). But He was willing to adjust His schedule at the request of His mother in order to meet the need of a friend.

C. The Believing Disciples (v. 11c)

11c. And his disciples believed on him.

Jesus' *disciples believed on him* before they came to Cana. The first two of them had followed Him because John the Baptist pointed Him out as "the Lamb of God" (John 1:35-37). These men had been disciples of John. No doubt they had heard John say much more about the greater One who was to come (Luke 3:15-17; John 1:26-34). Philip was convinced that Jesus was the One foretold by the law and the prophets; Nathanael exclaimed, "Rabbi, thou art the Son of God; thou art the King of Israel" (John 1:43-49).

But the faith of these men grew even stronger and deeper when they saw water poured into six jars and wine dipped out. They knew that the power of God was in what Jesus did; how could they ever doubt that the truth of God was in what He said?

WHEN GOD SPEAKS

In Christian circles, one occasionally hears someone say, "The Lord told me . . ." or "The Lord showed me . . ." such-and-such. Some Christians wonder whether this kind of "message" is really God speaking or simply a feeling prompted by the person's own desires.

Other people hear "divine messages" that are clearly *not* from God. For example, Brandon Wilson claimed that God had told him to murder a nine-year-old boy in an Oceanside, California, beachfront rest room in 1998. Wilson, a drifter, said he began to have murderous thoughts as a result of hearing the "shock-rock" music of Marilyn Manson and reading the writings of the German philosopher, Nietzsche (*Nee*-cheh). After his arrest, Wilson said God had told him to start killing people so that the world would come to an end: "There was a part of me that was evil and God had put it there for a reason—to use me."

The incident at the wedding feast in Cana offers a striking contrast to such twisted thinking as Wilson's. At Cana those who obeyed the voice of Jesus found delight and satisfaction for themselves and others, rather than suffering and grief.

So how do *we* determine whether someone's words really represent the voice of God? First, we must measure any alleged "message" by what Scripture teaches. And second, we must examine the "fruits" of the people who claim to have heard from God. If chaos and destruction follow their words and actions, we do well to question the source of their message.   —C. R. B.

VISUALS FOR THESE LESSONS

The visual pictured in each lesson (e.g., page 13) is a small reproduction of a large, full-color poster included in the *Adult Visuals* packet for the Fall Quarter. The packet is available from your supplier. Order No. 192.

Conclusion

Jesus' first miracle was followed by miracles innumerable and undeniable. Day after day Jesus "manifested forth his glory": He showed His divine power, His tender compassion, and His eagerness to help the needy. How could anyone in that time fail to believe in Him? How can anyone in our time doubt that He is the Son of God?

A. Ancient Unbelievers

The priests and Pharisees would not believe in Jesus because He was not one of them. They could not believe that God had chosen a carpenter of Galilee to be the Messiah. They could not deny that Jesus' miracles were done by superhuman power, so they claimed that He did them by the power of Satan (Matthew 12:22-24).

B. Modern Unbelievers

Modern unbelievers are often vocal in denying the miracles of Jesus. They say that every false religion is supported by myths and that Christianity is like all the rest.

But Christianity is supported by facts, not myths. Matthew and John reported what they saw and heard. According to ancient testimony, Mark was taught by Peter. Luke was a careful investigator. He learned from numerous witnesses (Luke 1:1-4). For example, he may have heard the nativity stories from Mary and learned of the plotting of the priests against Jesus from priests who later became Christians (Acts 6:7).

C. The Word of God

Besides having a thorough knowledge of the facts they recorded, the Gospel writers were inspired by the Holy Spirit. Jesus promised that guidance to Matthew and John (John 14:26). There is no reason to deny that Mark and Luke had the same divine leading. Their accounts of Jesus are truly the Word of God, and they all serve the same purpose: "that ye might believe that Jesus is the Christ, the Son of God; and that believing ye might have life through his name" (John 20:31).

D. Prayer

Father, thank You for the solid foundation of facts that supports our faith. Thank You for sending Jesus with the kind of power that convinces us that He is more than human. Thank You for the inspired record that tells of Him. May we have wisdom to understand that record, and courage to follow it. In Jesus' name, amen.

E. Thought to Remember

Jesus served with God's power and spoke with God's truth.

Learning by Doing

This page contains an alternate lesson plan emphasizing learning activities.
Classes desiring such student involvement will find these suggestions helpful.

Learning Goals

After participating in this lesson, each student will be able to:

1. Give the details and result of the miracle that Jesus did at the wedding in Cana of Galilee.

2. Explain the role of Jesus' miracles in establishing His identity as the Son of God.

3. Give thanks for the many miracles that provide solid evidence for believing in Jesus as the Son of God.

Into the Lesson

Begin this week's lesson by asking the learners to recall as many of Jesus' miracles as they can. State: "When you think of a specific miracle, call it out, and we'll make a list." Answers may include the following: feeding the five thousand (John 6:1-14), walking on water (John 6:16-21), raising the widow of Nain's son (Luke 7:11-16), casting out demons from the Gadarene demoniac (Luke 8:26-39), and knowing that Nathanael was sitting under a fig tree (John 1:47, 48).

After a few minutes, state: "Jesus' miracles can be categorized into at least four kinds: miracles in nature, miracles with people, miracles with demons, and miracles of knowledge." Ask the class to identify an example of each kind. State: "Jesus performed many miracles. But what were His purposes? Today's lesson focuses on His first miracle and helps us answer this question."

Into the Word

Ask a class member to read aloud John 2:1-11. After the reading ask the following questions:

1. Who attended this wedding in Cana? *(Jesus' mother, Jesus, His disciples, others, vv. 1, 2.)*

2. How did Jesus find out that there was no more wine? *(His mother told Him, v. 3.)*

3. Since Jesus had not performed any miracle prior to this event, what do you suppose His mother expected Him to do after being told there was no more wine? Why? *(Perhaps she thought He would demonstrate His power. She knew He was God's Son, Luke 1:31-33. Jesus' response, "Mine hour is not yet come," v. 4, assumes she expected Him to act in power.)*

4. What did Jesus tell the servants to do? *(Fill six waterpots with water; later, take some to the governor of the feast, vv. 7, 8.)*

5. What is meant by the phrase, "after the manner of the purifying of the Jews" in v. 6? *(Jewish hospitality included washing people's feet when they entered a house; the Jews also ceremonially washed their hands before eating. See page 12.)*

6. How did the wine Jesus created compare with the wine previously served? *(His wine was excellent; the other was mediocre by comparison, v. 10.)*

7. What was the result of this miracle? *(It established Jesus' identity as the Son of God and promoted the disciples' belief in Him, v. 11.)*

8. What is the meaning of the word *glory* in verse 11? *(It refers not to praise or honor, but to attributes of Jesus worthy of praise.)*

9. What attributes of Jesus do you find in this first miracle? *(His power; His compassion; His willingness to get involved in others' situations.)*

Into Life

State: "The facts of Jesus' first miracle, though important, cannot be applied to our lives. However, several principles that can be applied are woven through this passage. For the next few minutes discuss this question with a person sitting next to you: 'What principles can we derive from this first miracle of Jesus?'" After giving the class time to reflect, ask for the principles to be shared aloud. Write the principles on the board when they are suggested. Though other principles may be suggested, make certain the following ones are presented: (1) God is personally concerned about the individual circumstances of our lives, whether we face a personal sorrow, discouragement, failure, or crisis of any kind. (2) God responds to us when we ask Him for help. The individual circumstances of our situations need to be brought to Jesus as well. (3) Faith grows when God actively intervenes in our daily lives. The disciples recognized Jesus' glory and believed in Him when they witnessed His miracle. When God answers our prayers, even in seemingly small circumstances, our faith grows.

Ask the class to move into groups of three. State: "When we reflect on the miracles Jesus performed, which gave testimony to His identity as the Son of God, our natural response is to thank Him for making Himself known to us. In your groups of three tell of a circumstance or situation that needs to be brought to Jesus; then pray for one another, thanking God for the solid evidence in Jesus' miracles for believing in Him as the Son of God."

Let's Talk It Over

The questions on this page are designed to encourage review of the lesson Scriptures and to promote discussion of the lesson by the class. The answers provided are only discussion starters. Let your class talk it over from there.

1. Jesus' attendance at a wedding feast surprises some people. Is it hard for you to imagine Jesus having fun at a party? Why or why not?

Jesus probably attended the wedding because family was involved; honoring family with one's presence at an important event is proper. Jesus certainly knew in advance what was going to happen, so He went because of the opportunity to display His power. We don't know the future, but we, too, can be alert to opportunities to glorify God in a variety of settings. And Jesus certainly knew the value of recreation. He urged His disciples to "come . . . apart . . . and rest a while" (Mark 6:31) when the press of the crowd was intense. His promise of rest to the heavy laden (Matthew 11:28) is also evidence of His appreciation for recreation. The important thing is keeping one's purpose in focus. Frivolity is never endorsed by Jesus, but well-timed periods of rest and relaxation to improve one's efficiency in ministry are.

2. Mary's appeal to Jesus when the wine ran out indicates a high level of faith. How do you express faith in Jesus?

No human being knew Jesus better than Mary did. The wondrous events preceding and immediately following Jesus' birth, as recorded in the Gospels, made a lasting impression on her (Luke 2:19). When Jesus commenced His ministry, Mary experienced some difficulty in understanding it (see Mark 3:20, 21, 31-35). But her faith in Him, demonstrated at Cana, remained steadfast.

We, too, may have difficulty with certain aspects of our faith as we grow in our discipleship. Still, we can demonstrate faith by trusting God even when we cannot understand all the details. Allow students to tell specific acts they have done or stands they have taken out of their faith in the Lord.

3. The lesson writer notes that Jesus' response to Mary, "Woman, what have I to do with thee?" is not as stark or even rude as it seems to us. Still, it surely was not what Mary expected. Yet her faith did not waver. How do we maintain faith in spite of unexpected events?

The suggestion is made that Jesus' address to Mary was intended to shift her focus from being Jesus' mother to being His disciple. If we, too, will

focus on being Jesus' disciples, whatever happens to us along the way, then we will find faithfulness easier. If, on the other hand, we are determined to figure out how everything should happen and base our faithfulness on that, then we will surely be disappointed. Mary seemed to anticipate Romans 8:28, and she trusted Jesus to make things right. Can we not similarly trust Him?

4. The servants at the wedding feast did as Jesus instructed them. How important do you think their testimony regarding the miracle might later have proved? (Note verse 9: "the servants . . . knew.")

It is easy to imagine skeptics' questioning the servants afterward as to exactly what happened. All the servants, no doubt, would have been consistent in affirming that the jars had never held anything but water. The skeptics were therefore unable to claim that a small amount of wine remaining in the bottom of the jars imparted a wine-like taste. The servants would have pointed out that they filled the jars with nothing but water. In no way could Jesus have come up with a secret supply of wine and arranged for that to be put in the jars. The servants would have declared that they promptly took a sample from the filled jars to the master of ceremonies. No one had time to tamper with them. The servants' testimony would have been impossible for the skeptics to dismiss.

5. Jesus used His miracle-working power to save a family from embarrassment during a wedding banquet. What does that indicate about His compassion toward us?

What causes us embarrassment? Jesus cares about it. What brings us discouragement and distress? Jesus cares about it. What grieves and saddens us? Jesus cares about it. No problem is too trivial for His interest. No crisis is too small or too big for Him to share with us. If the supply of wine for a wedding banquet was a matter of concern to Him, then the troubles we face also touch Him. And His power to overcome these troubles is surely available. We must echo the words of Frank E. Graeff's chorus: "O yes, He cares; I know He cares, His heart is touched with my grief; When the days are weary, the long nights dreary, I know my Savior cares."

Jesus Displays Power Over Nature

DEVOTIONAL READING: John 6:28-40.

BACKGROUND SCRIPTURE: Matthew 8:23-27; 14:1-21.

PRINTED TEXT: Matthew 8:23-27; 14:14-21.

Matthew 8:23-27

23 And when he was entered into a ship, his disciples followed him.

24 And, behold, there arose a great tempest in the sea, insomuch that the ship was covered with the waves: but he was asleep.

25 And his disciples came to him, and awoke him, saying, Lord, save us: we perish.

26 And he saith unto them, Why are ye fearful, O ye of little faith? Then he arose, and rebuked the winds and the sea; and there was a great calm.

27 But the men marveled, saying, What manner of man is this, that even the winds and the sea obey him!

Matthew 14:14-21

14 And Jesus went forth, and saw a great multitude, and was moved with compassion toward them, and he healed their sick.

15 And when it was evening, his disciples came to him, saying, This is a desert place, and the time is now past; send the multitude away, that they may go into the villages, and buy themselves victuals.

16 But Jesus said unto them, They need not depart; give ye them to eat.

17 And they say unto him, We have here but five loaves, and two fishes.

18 He said, Bring them hither to me.

19 And he commanded the multitude to sit down on the grass, and took the five loaves, and the two fishes, and looking up to heaven, he blessed, and brake, and gave the loaves to his disciples, and the disciples to the multitude.

20 And they did all eat, and were filled: and they took up of the fragments that remained twelve baskets full.

21 And they that had eaten were about five thousand men, beside women and children.

GOLDEN TEXT: The men marveled, saying, What manner of man is this, that even the winds and the sea obey him!—Matthew 8:27.

Jesus' Ministry
Unit 1: Performing Miracles
(Lessons 1-5)

Lesson Aims

After this lesson a student should be able to:

1. Describe how Jesus displayed His power over nature in the miracles mentioned in today's texts.

2. Tell how these miracles demonstrate not only Jesus' power but also His compassion.

3. Suggest one way we can act with the same compassion Jesus demonstrated.

Lesson Outline

INTRODUCTION
   A. Weather Watching
   B. Lesson Background
 I. A TROUBLED SEA (Matthew 8:23-27)
   A. Sudden Storm (vv. 23, 24)
   B. Great Calm (vv. 25, 26)
     Nature and Nature's God
   C. Disciples' Response (v. 27)
II. A HUNGRY MULTITUDE (Matthew 14:14-21)
   A. Change of Plan (v. 14)
   B. Puzzling Problem (v. 15)
   C. Miraculous Solution (vv. 16-21)
     Unaware of the Power at Hand
CONCLUSION
   A. Power
   B. Compassion
   C. Prayer
   D. Thought to Remember

Introduction

A. Weather Watching

Weather forecasting is a sophisticated and technical science these days. With radar, satellite images, and computerized models, meteorologists are able to track approaching tornadoes, hurricanes, and other storms so that residents in an affected area can take cover.

In spite of these advances, weather watchers—even the most capable—are by no means infallible. Sometimes a tornado will develop so fast that no one has an opportunity to be given sufficient warning. Or the strength of a particular snowstorm may be misjudged so that it produces much more snow than had been predicted.

There were no weather watchers with Doppler radar and computer models in Jesus' day. When a storm arose on the Sea of Galilee, it often came without warning. Descending from the surrounding hills, an intense storm might develop so swiftly that only boats near the shore could elude it. The water was whipped to a fury by the raging winds. Every boat was endangered; every man caught in a boat became terrified.

B. Lesson Background

During this month of September (the first unit of this quarter's lessons) all of our lessons deal with miracles of Jesus. Last week we considered the first one. Today (in the first portion of our printed text) we move ahead toward the middle of Jesus' three-and-a-half year ministry. Jesus had become the best-known person in Galilee. Crowds gathered wherever He went. They were attracted by His marvelous miracles and His astounding teaching (Matthew 4:23-25; 7:28, 29).

I. A Troubled Sea
(Matthew 8:23-27)

Perhaps to escape the constant pressure of the crowds, Jesus planned to cross to the eastern side of the Sea of Galilee (Mark 4:35). He needed to rest after an especially strenuous day of teaching (Mark 4:1-34).

A. Sudden Storm (vv. 23, 24)

23. And when he was entered into a ship, his disciples followed him.

In today's English, we would probably describe the *ship* mentioned in this verse as a *boat*. At least four of Jesus' *disciples* (Peter, Andrew, James, and John) had been fishermen on the Sea of Galilee. Probably they now *entered* one of the boats they had used in fishing. Apparently the boat was big enough to carry thirteen men without crowding them, but it was likely not much bigger than that.

With some disciples rowing, the boat moved out to the east. Unwilling to lose sight of Jesus, some of the crowd got into other "little ships" and went along (Mark 4:36).

24. And, behold, there arose a great tempest in the sea, insomuch that the ship was covered with the waves: but he was asleep.

Only minutes after the approaching storm could be seen, it was on them with a fury. High *waves* entered the boat. Being made of wood, it would float even if filled with water; but what if a wave lifted and overturned it, throwing the passengers into the turbulent *sea*?

While all this was taking place, Jesus *was asleep*. The boat was tossing wildly, and the waves were splashing water on the sleeper; yet He slept on. How tired He must have been from His day of teaching!

B. Great Calm (vv. 25, 26)

25. And his disciples came to him, and awoke him, saying, Lord, save us: we perish.

Even seasoned fishermen were helpless against such a tempest as this. The *disciples* realized that they were in grave danger. Yet Jesus could turn water into wine; He could heal all kinds of diseases; He could banish demons from the individuals under their control. If anyone could *save* them from their predicament, surely Jesus could. Growing increasingly hopeless, they *awoke him.*

26. And he saith unto them, Why are ye fearful, O ye of little faith? Then he arose, and rebuked the winds and the sea; and there was a great calm.

The disciples did have a *little faith*—enough to make them hope that Jesus could save them, but not enough to keep them from being terrorized by their surroundings. Shouldn't they have known that Jesus was in control, whether awake or asleep? The frightened men soon learned that Jesus' mastery included *the winds and the sea.* At His rebuke the winds stopped blowing and the waves stopped rolling. In contrast to the great storm that had threatened their lives just moments ago, now *there was a great calm.* [See question #1, page 24.]

NATURE AND NATURE'S GOD

On a calm April 14, 1912, the *RMS Titanic* struck an iceberg on her maiden voyage and took two-thirds of her passengers and crew to an icy grave. Human vanity conspired with imperfect engineering in the building and outfitting of the ship in such a way as to court disaster. Watertight bulkheads rose only partway through the hull of the ship. Only half the necessary lifeboats were provided. Those in charge, hoping to make headlines by crossing the Atlantic Ocean in record time, pressed the ship forward at high speed through iceberg-filled waters.

In our text today, we see a picture quite the opposite of the Titanic's final night. Just a few people in a small boat were in danger of drowning in a storm-tossed sea. On this occasion, those on board humbly recognized their frailty before the forces of nature; and the Captain of the vessel took control of those forces. As a result, all on board were saved.

Comparing these two events provides an insightful reminder of a fact of life: our vanity can lead us into foolish schemes that can destroy us and others, but yielding ourselves in trust to the power of God brings salvation.   —C. R. B.

C. Disciples' Response (v. 27)

27. But the men marveled, saying, What manner of man is this, that even the winds and the sea obey him!

Of course, no *manner of man* could command *the winds and the sea.* Only God can do that. The disciples' "little faith" (v. 26) was being guided into learning even greater truth about Jesus: this man was also God. Before Him they were right to marvel. [See question #2, page 24.]

II. A Hungry Multitude (Matthew 14:14-21)

Some time after the tempest was stilled, Jesus gave His twelve disciples miraculous power like His own and sent them out in pairs to preach as He had been preaching (Matthew 10:1-8). The second part of our printed text takes up the story as the Twelve came together with their Teacher once again (Mark 6:30). By this time, approximately four months had passed since the stilling of the tempest.

The joy of this reunion was mixed with grief, however, for just at that time came news that John the Baptist had been put to death by Herod Antipas (Matthew 14:1-12). Jesus told the disciples to "come . . . apart" from the clamoring crowds, perhaps for a time of mourning for John and certainly for a little rest after their strenuous preaching tour (Mark 6:31). So they boarded a boat (probably near Capernaum) and set out to go across to the eastern side of the Sea of Galilee. (This time no storm disturbed them as they made their way across the sea.)

However, the only time the men had for rest was during their journey in the boat. A crowd of people saw them leave. Unwilling to miss any of Jesus' miracles or any of His teaching, many of that throng hurried around the north end of the sea. These were joined by people from the villages that they passed. Thus, by the time Jesus

"What manner of man is this, that even the winds and the sea obey him!"
Matthew 8:27

Visual for lesson 2

Use this visual to illustrate verses 26 and 27 of today's text.

and the disciples arrived at the eastern shore an even larger gathering was waiting for Jesus (Matthew 14:13; Mark 6:32, 33).

A. Change of Plan (v. 14)

14. And Jesus went forth, and saw a great multitude, and was moved with compassion toward them, and he healed their sick.

Jesus *went forth* from the boat, but not to a secluded area where He and His disciples could relax and talk about what they had done on their preaching tour. He *saw a great multitude* eager for His attention. A less compassionate man might have climbed back into the boat and gone in search of a quieter place where he could rest. But Jesus *was moved with compassion toward them.* It must have been difficult for some of the sick people to come to that remote area far from their homes. In some cases, they would have required assistance from family members or friends. All had made the effort because they believed that Jesus could make them well, and they were not disappointed: *he healed their sick.*

Jesus also had compassion for the people who were not sick. They were in distress because they were without good spiritual leaders—"as sheep not having a shepherd" (Mark 6:34). Abandoning His plan for a time of rest and mourning, Jesus led the multitude up the hill (John 6:3), "and he began to teach them many things" (Mark 6:34). [See question #3, page 24.]

B. Puzzling Problem (v. 15)

15. And when it was evening, his disciples came to him, saying, This is a desert place, and the time is now past; send the multitude away, that they may go into the villages, and buy themselves victuals.

If Jesus and *his disciples* started across the Sea of Galilee early in the morning, they must have arrived before noon. People who came on foot were there ahead of them. Now afternoon was turning into *evening.* Many must have been getting hungry.

Matthew, Mark, Luke, and John all record this incident, and they record different details. Perhaps Jesus Himself was the first to mention the problem. He interrupted His teaching for an aside to Philip: "Whence shall we buy bread, that these may eat?" (John 6:5). Of course, Philip was stumped. "Two hundred pennyworth of bread"

How to Say It

ANTIPAS. *An*-tih-pus.
CAPERNAUM. Kuh-*per*-nay-um.
GALILEE. *Gal*-uh-lee.
KOPHINOS (Greek). *kaw*-fin-awss.

(v. 7) would hardly be enough to feed such a crowd. The *New International Version* interprets that as "eight months' wages."

Perhaps Jesus continued with His teaching while Philip quietly consulted the other disciples. To them, Jesus' suggestion seemed quite impractical. Even if they had enough money, any place where bread could be purchased was miles away. So the disciples came to Jesus with the suggestion we see in the verse before us: Jesus should simply dismiss the *multitude* so that the people could *go* and *buy* food (the meaning of *victuals*) for *themselves.* That suggestion was not very practical either. The place where they were situated was *desert,* which implies *deserted*: no one lived there, though the region included splendid grazing land for sheep or cattle (note the reference to "much grass" in John 6:10). There were *villages* only a few miles away, but did all of them together have enough bread for sale to feed that hungry crowd? And how many in the crowd had come with no money?

C. Miraculous Solution (vv. 16-21)

16. But Jesus said unto them, They need not depart; give ye them to eat.

In response to Jesus' suggestion, the disciples could only shake their heads. Perhaps that was when Jesus sent them to see how much bread was available within the crowd (Mark 6:38). So the disciples searched, and Andrew found one boy who had "five barley loaves, and two small fishes" (John 6:8, 9). [See question #4, page 24.]

UNAWARE OF THE POWER AT HAND

The Yates Pool, an oil field in western Texas, got its name from a sheep rancher who owned the property when the Great Depression began. Mr. Yates could not pay his mortgage and was living on government relief. He was faced with foreclosure and with the loss of his land and livelihood.

One day, Yates gave an oil company crew permission to drill for oil on his ranch. Soon after drilling began, a large oil reserve was tapped. The first well started out producing eighty thousand barrels of crude oil a day. Some thirty years later, this huge reserve was yielding even more oil than it had at the beginning.

Before the oil was discovered, Mr. Yates was living in poverty, unaware of the source of wealth that lay so close at hand. He was much like the disciples when confronted with a hungry multitude. Unaware that Jesus Himself was able to solve the dilemma, they were ready to send the crowd away with empty stomachs. Then Jesus gave them a command that caused them to examine their abilities and resources before He stepped in to meet the need.

God may well lead us through a similar process. When we face a difficult circumstance, He may wait until we have tested our own strength and resources before He shows us the way to solve our dilemma.

Like Mr. Yates and like Jesus' disciples, we too can be unaware of the power so close at hand.

—C. R. B.

17. And they say unto him, We have here but five loaves, and two fishes.

No other food was found among the huge crowd. The *loaves* were flat and round, not at all like the loaves of bread we buy today. We might call them rolls or biscuits instead of loaves. That they were made of barley (John 6:9) indicates a cheaper kind of bread; the boy may have been from a poor family.

The Greek word for *fishes* indicates "small fishes" (John 6:9), possibly like the sardines that are available in little flat cans. Apparently the boy was willing to contribute the meal he had brought along, but he must have wondered, as Andrew did, "What are they among so many?" (John 6:9).

18. He said, Bring them hither to me.

In the hands of the boy who brought them, those loaves and fishes could have satisfied one boy's hunger. In the hands of Jesus, they could do whatever Jesus wanted them to do. So Jesus called for them to be brought to Him.

19a. And he commanded the multitude to sit down on the grass.

Mark and Luke provide additional details about this. Jesus had the disciples organize the crowd, and the people were then told to *sit down* in groups of about fifty or a hundred (Mark 6:39, 40; Luke 9:14, 15). Most likely there would have been aisles between the groups, making it easy to distribute the food that soon would be available. This grouping would have alerted the people, making them expectant. They would watch and listen intently when Jesus spoke again.

19b. And took the five loaves, and the two fishes, and looking up to heaven, he blessed, and brake, and gave the loaves to his disciples, and the disciples to the multitude.

With the crowd watching eagerly, Jesus *took* the small food supply in His hands. Raising His eyes toward *heaven*, He gave thanks for the food (John 6:11) and asked God's blessing.

Then Jesus began to break the bread. How we would like to have a fuller description of that! Perhaps He broke a fragment from a loaf, and the fragment was as big as the loaf. Then both fragment and loaf could be broken and rebroken into pieces increasing in size and number. Jesus handed the pieces to His *disciples*, and the disci-

ples carried them to the people. The next verse speaks of twelve baskets of fragments. Perhaps the same twelve baskets were used to take the food to the hungry people.

20. And they did all eat, and were filled: and they took up of the fragments that remained twelve baskets full.

Anyone could have a second helping if he wanted it, or even a third. Any leftovers were not thrown away. Jesus told the disciples to gather up any uneaten *fragments* so that nothing would be wasted (John 6:12), and they gathered *twelve baskets full*.

Where did the baskets come from? Those people had rushed after Jesus impulsively, without planning to go where He would eventually stop. Did some of them just happen to have baskets?

Perhaps they did. Those who read and know Greek tell us that the word used here for *basket* is *kophinos*, which *Young's Analytical Concordance* defines as "a wicker traveling basket." Wickerwork was much less expensive than leather. A traveler might use it for the equivalent of a backpack or valise.

Note that we are reading of a time when the Passover Feast was near (John 6:4). The crowd on this occasion may have included many people on the way from northern Galilee to Jerusalem for the feast. A person on that trip may well have carried a *kophinos* with some clean clothing or other items in it, and may have been eager to lay the contents out on the grass in order to lend the container to one of Jesus' disciples.

Another suggestion is that each of the twelve disciples had such a basket and carried it as he traveled with Jesus about the country. True, the Twelve had just finished a preaching tour during which they took no such item (Matthew 10:5-10); but if they usually carried traveling baskets, they could have left them in Capernaum and picked them up when they finished their tour. [See question #5, page 24.]

21. And they that had eaten were about five thousand men, beside women and children.

We can only guess how many *women and children* ate along with the *five thousand men*. Regardless of the specific number, Jesus had worked yet another unforgettable miracle.

Conclusion

Both this lesson and the previous one have featured two important truths: the unlimited divine power of Jesus and the godly compassion that guided what He did with that power.

A. Power

The power of Almighty God worked in Jesus, and still does. "All things were made by him" (John 1:3). Even today, Jesus is "upholding all things by the word of his power" (Hebrews 1:3). It would seem that Jesus needs no help from us.

Here, then, is a marvel that ranks with the greatest marvels of all time: Jesus wants our help. He values our help. He does marvelous things with our help. Last week we read that Jesus made six big jars of superior wine. He could have made it from nothing, but He chose to make it with water carried by household servants. This week we read that He made a meal for more than five thousand hungry people. That too He could have done from nothing, but He chose to do it with the food contributed by a willing boy.

Never think your tithe is unimportant. Never think the Lord does not appreciate the hours you spend teaching a Sunday school class, or practicing with the church choir, or encouraging the despondent, or cleaning up the kitchen after a fellowship dinner at church. Jesus is using you for the good of His people and the glory of His kingdom. That's wonderful!

And how the Lord multiplies the value of your small help! Through months or years you keep on telling your friend of the joy you find in Christ, and you demonstrate what you say by joyous Christian living. Then one happy day your friend is born again and destined to live forever. How much is that worth?

Regretfully you decide to keep the old car another year, or three years if necessary, so that you can make a large contribution to the fund to acquire property and double the size of the church parking lot. When the lot is ready, church attendance promptly begins to grow. In a few months, church membership also begins to grow. Nearly every week sees people responding to Christ's call and being baptized into Him.

See what the Lord has made of your contribution? Aren't you glad you decided to keep that old car?

B. Compassion

Jesus' compassion is scarcely less notable than His power. Why should He care if the host at a wedding was embarrassed? But He did care, as we saw last week. Why should He care if a crowd was hungry? But He did care, as we saw today.

"Being in the form of God" amid the glories of Heaven, why should Jesus care if men were dying on earth? It was their own fault. But He did care. He exchanged the wealth of Heaven for poverty on earth and for the agonizing death of the old rugged cross (Philippians 2:4-8).

Yes, Jesus cares, and His people care. Our hearts are wrenched when we see pictures of children starving because of tragic circumstances. But what can we do? We cannot feed everyone; should we therefore feed no one?

Paul outlines the activity of our compassion: "As we have therefore opportunity, let us do good unto all men, especially unto them who are of the household of faith" (Galatians 6:10).

1. As we have therefore opportunity. Our opportunity is often limited by our ability and by our resources. It will make matters worse if we recklessly give all we have, and thus make ourselves dependent on the charity of others. We can give generously, even sacrificially, but we need to know when to stop giving.

2. Let us do good unto all men. Yes, and women and children too! No one on earth should be outside the scope of Christian compassion. But we cannot end the distress of all who are in distress. To which appeals must we respond? To which must we say, regretfully, no?

3. Especially unto them who are of the household of faith. This sets our priority. We cannot feed all the starving orphans, but we can feed all those in our own church—and perhaps help with another church as well. In that way we show the kind of love that Jesus said must be our "trademark" to the world (John 13:35).

Are we really doing all we can for others?

C. Prayer

Gracious Father, since we cannot emulate the miracles of Jesus, may we emulate the goodwill and good sense of the boy who put what he had in Jesus' hands. Help us to see and use our opportunities to do good to all men, especially to those who are of the household of faith. In Jesus' name. Amen.

D. Thought to Remember

Count your blessings—and share them.

Learning by Doing

This page contains an alternate lesson plan emphasizing learning activities.
Classes desiring such student involvement will find these suggestions helpful.

Learning Goals

After this lesson each student will be able to:

1. Describe how Jesus displayed His power over nature in the two miracles mentioned in today's texts.

2. Tell how these miracles demonstrate not only Jesus' power but also His compassion.

3. Suggest one way we can act with the same compassion Jesus demonstrated.

Into the Lesson

Prior to class prepare a poster as follows: write the scrambled word "A C I M N O P S O S" on the top line; below that write the following message:
"_ _ _ _ _ _ _ _ _ _ leads to action!"
Begin class by revealing the poster and stating, "Unscramble the word and reveal the message of today's lesson." (The answer is "Compassion leads to action!") When the answer is given correctly, write the word "Compassion" on the ten spaces for the letters. State: "Today we look at two of Jesus' miracles that demonstrate not only His power over nature but also His compassion."

Into the Word

Each of the miracles of Jesus studied today receives additional attention in Gospels other than Matthew. Calming the storm is found in Mark and Luke. Feeding the five thousand is in all three other Gospels. Having your learners compare and contrast the different records is an excellent way to teach their basic content.

For a look at Jesus' calming the storm, assign three sections of your class to examine the three related texts: Matthew 8:23-27; Mark 4:35-41; Luke 8:22-25. Give time for each group to skim its assigned text, and then ask for a show of hands as a response to the question, "Which of the Gospels includes a reference to . . .?" List these events or elements one at a time: ships other than Jesus' ship; the disciples' calling, "Master, Master" (two times); the "calm" that came at Jesus' word; fear in the apostles *after* the miracle; a rebuke of Jesus for "not caring"; being "in jeopardy"; Jesus' words, "Peace, be still"; mention of water filling the boat; the fact that Jesus was asleep; Jesus' use of a "pillow" for His sleep; apostles' affirmation, "What manner of man is this"; Jesus' word that the apostles have "little faith." Pause after each to allow the group to look around at the hands; pause also to let learners note phrasing differences (for example, Matthew says, "little faith," v. 26; Mark says, "no faith," v. 40; Luke says, "Where is your faith?" v. 25).

Re-divide your class into four groups and assign these texts on the feeding of the five thousand: Matthew 14:13-21; Mark 6:30-44; Luke 9: 10-17; John 6:1-14. Prepare a list of events and phrases such as those in the preceding activity and repeat the reading and showing of hands.

Into Life

State: "Genuine compassion always leads to action. When Jesus recognized the two circumstances of fear and hunger, He acted. Though we cannot perform a miracle, compassion for people can lead us to act. But first, we have to recognize people's needs."

Ask the following questions and list the answers on the board or an overhead transparency.

1. What situations in people's lives today cause them to be fearful? *(Possible answers: facing surgery or a terminal illness; taking a major examination; losing a job; having an opportunity to share one's faith; making decisions during or after a divorce; awaiting medical test results.)*

2. In what situations do people today have a physical need? *(Hunger; heating or cooling for comfort; shelter and clothing following a disaster; protection from an abusive family member.)*

Ask, "Having identified a number of situations and circumstances that cause people to have emotional and physical needs, whom do we know who is facing one of these emotional or physical needs?" Prepare a "Compassion Leads to Action" worksheet for this activity. Make three columns on a sheet of paper and label the columns, "Name," "Situation," and "Action." Hand out the worksheet to your students and ask them to move into groups of three. Under each column heading, ask each group to fill in the name of the person(s) needing help, the situation, and some action that will demonstrate compassion for the person. Allow several minutes to complete the worksheet. Then ask each small group to decide (either as a group or as individuals) how to respond to at least one individual listed on the worksheet. Ask some to relate their decisions to the whole class. Conclude the lesson with a prayer of commitment to act in a spirit of compassion for someone this week.

Let's Talk It Over

The questions on this page are designed to encourage review of the lesson Scriptures and to promote discussion of the lesson by the class. The answers provided are only discussion starters. Let your class talk it over from there.

1. "Why are ye fearful?" Jesus asked His disciples. The point is often made that they should not have been fearful since Jesus was with them—and that we should not fear either. But how should we take that? Should we *never* have any fear for personal safety? If so, is this a blanket statement that Christians will never suffer harm? Then what of the many who do suffer harm by storms or other accidents—are they weak in faith? What does it mean to have no fear in a dangerous world?

If Jesus is with us and we are with Him, then we have no reason to be gripped by fear. He is powerful enough and wise enough to handle any danger we may face. And yet, Christians are often held in bondage by various kinds of fear. Some may wrestle with fear of storms. Others may dread the possibility of being a victim of crime or an accident. Still others may have a phobia regarding heights or closed-in places. Jesus' "Lo, I am with you alway" should resound in our hearts and minds to bring us confidence in the face of fear. Like Paul we should be able to declare, "I can do all things through Christ which strengtheneth me" (Philippians 4:13).

2. When Jesus calmed the storm, the disciples marveled at His power. We have read this story so many times that we sense no surprise, but shouldn't we still "marvel"? How can we maintain a reverent sense of awe at the "marvelous" power of Jesus?

"Familiarity breeds contempt," according to an old proverb, and it behooves us to take active measures against that tendency. To that end, we must be sure our participation in worship is never mere ritual or going through the motions, but is heartfelt and sincere. Reading the Bible must not be allowed to become routine, but must be accompanied by an anticipation of discerning God's will. The way we treat others becomes a means of expressing God's love to them—and even of expressing love to Him (Matthew 25:40).

3. Jesus was moved with compassion at the sight of the crowds, so He healed their sick and taught them. How can we show compassion?

Jesus needed time alone with His twelve disciples. They needed rest and time to deal with their grief over John the Baptist's tragic death. But they put all that aside and ministered to the needs of the crowd. With whatever specific means of showing compassion your students may suggest, be sure this emphasis on putting the needs of others ahead of one's own is not lost.

4. When Jesus told the disciples, "Give ye them to eat," the disciples thought He had given them an impossible task. But Jesus had the situation in hand and, with His help, the disciples were indeed able to feed the crowd. Have you ever had an "impossible" task to do? How did you respond? How did you find God's strength sufficient for the task?

This question may produce some inspiring testimonies from your students. Encourage wide participation, and affirm each one who has a story to tell. Some may report on making big changes in their lives, such as overcoming a bad habit. Others may tell about taking on a new role, perhaps a ministry role of some sort, that they had not formerly anticipated. Discuss what leads a person to accept an impossible task—to believe God is in it, wanting them to do it and working in them to succeed in it. Be prepared to tell your own story of how God is at work in you!

5. It may surprise the first-time reader to note that Jesus commanded that the fragments of food be collected (John 6:12). Why is this surprising, and what should we learn from it?

We can imagine the disciples asking one another, "Why should we bother to do this? He has the power to take any one of these fragments and multiply it into enough food to feed a crowd." We know that later Jesus did repeat this miracle by feeding a crowd of more than four thousand people. But He did not do this as a normal practice. This should impress us with the fact that God wants us to make the best possible use of the resources that we possess. We are inclined to pray for special provision or for remarkable displays of His power when we face a challenge. But He may expect us to press on using the talents and opportunities He has already given.

One might wonder, in the course of this discussion, what was done with all those leftovers! Probably they were distributed to poor people in the area. So, again, the issue of using one's resources to the best advantage is paramount.

Jesus Displays Power Over Disease

September 16
Lesson 3

Devotional Reading: John 4:46-54.

Background Scripture: Mark 3:1-6; John 9.

Printed Text: Mark 3:1-6; John 9:1-12, 35-38.

Mark 3:1-6

1 And he entered again into the synagogue; and there was a man there which had a withered hand.

2 And they watched him, whether he would heal him on the sabbath day; that they might accuse him.

3 And he saith unto the man which had the withered hand, Stand forth.

4 And he saith unto them, Is it lawful to do good on the sabbath days, or to do evil? to save life, or to kill? But they held their peace.

5 And when he had looked round about on them with anger, being grieved for the hardness of their hearts, he saith unto the man, Stretch forth thine hand. And he stretched it out: and his hand was restored whole as the other.

6 And the Pharisees went forth, and straightway took counsel with the Herodians against him, how they might destroy him.

John 9:1-12, 35-38

1 And as Jesus passed by, he saw a man which was blind from his birth.

2 And his disciples asked him, saying, Master, who did sin, this man, or his parents, that he was born blind?

3 Jesus answered, Neither hath this man sinned, nor his parents: but that the works of God should be made manifest in him.

4 I must work the works of him that sent me, while it is day: the night cometh, when no man can work.

5 As long as I am in the world, I am the light of the world.

6 When he had thus spoken, he spat on the ground, and made clay of the spittle, and he anointed the eyes of the blind man with the clay,

7 And said unto him, Go, wash in the pool of Siloam, (which is by interpretation, Sent.) He went his way therefore, and washed, and came seeing.

8 The neighbors therefore, and they which before had seen him that he was blind, said, Is not this he that sat and begged?

9 Some said, This is he: others said, He is like him: but he said, I am he.

10 Therefore said they unto him, How were thine eyes opened?

11 He answered and said, A man that is called Jesus made clay, and anointed mine eyes, and said unto me, Go to the pool of Siloam, and wash: and I went and washed, and I received sight.

12 Then said they unto him, Where is he? He said, I know not.

. . . .

35 Jesus heard that they had cast him out; and when he had found him, he said unto him, Dost thou believe on the Son of God?

36 He answered and said, Who is he, Lord, that I might believe on him?

37 And Jesus said unto him, Thou hast both seen him, and it is he that talketh with thee.

38 And he said, Lord, I believe. And he worshipped him.

Golden Text: (Jesus) saith unto the man, Stretch forth thine hand. And he stretched it out: and his hand was restored whole as the other.—Mark 3:5.

Jesus' Ministry
Unit 1: Performing Miracles
(Lessons 1-5)

Lesson Aims

After this lesson a student should be able to:
1. Summarize the accounts of the miracles recorded in today's texts and the reaction of the Pharisees to them.
2. Contrast how Christians and non-Christians tend to view the evidence concerning Jesus found in the Gospels.
3. Prepare a presentation of the gospel (one that anticipates questions non-Christians may ask) and plan to share it soon with a friend.

Lesson Outline

INTRODUCTION
  A. Just Imagine
  B. Lesson Background
I. WITHERED HAND MADE WHOLE (Mark 3:1-6)
  A. The Critics (vv. 1, 2)
  B. The Issue (vv. 3, 4)
  C. The Miracle (v. 5)
  D. The Reaction (v. 6)
    "That's Not How We Do Things Here"
II. BLIND EYES GIVEN SIGHT (John 9:1-12, 35-38)
  A. Disciples' Question (vv. 1, 2)
  B. Answer by Words (vv. 3-5)
  C. Answer by Actions (vv. 6, 7)
  D. Storm of Questions (vv. 8-12)
  E. No Longer Alone (vv. 35-38)
    Willing to Find the Truth
CONCLUSION
  A. Conclusion of the Pharisees
  B. Conclusion of the Man Given Sight
  C. Conclusion of an Agnostic
  D. Conclusion of an Egotist
  E. Conclusion of a Materialist
  F. Conclusion of a Christian
  G. Prayer
  H. Thought to Remember

Introduction

A. Just Imagine

Can you imagine how hard it would be to eat a steak if you had only one hand? That piece of meat seems alive. It refuses to lie still under the knife unless you hold it down with a fork. So you ask a friend to cut the meat for you. (Or maybe you decide to order meat loaf instead!)

But that is only the beginning of your troubles. A broom is designed for two hands. How can you sweep the autumn leaves from the deck of your house? If you call a motel to reserve a room, you had better ask if you can open the door with one hand. A lady I know who likes to travel and has only one hand said that in some motels you can't.

Perhaps the worst part is knowing that very little can be done about your predicament. You can hide the condition with a costly prosthesis, but the result is not really a hand.

Jesus, the Great Physician, specialized in situations like this—severe cases of affliction that no one else could do anything about. This week's lesson calls attention to two examples.

B. Lesson Background

Our printed text begins with an incident from Jesus' busy ministry in Galilee. It took place earlier than the calming of the storm at sea (at the beginning of last week's lesson), but already Jesus was famous for His miracles and His teaching. For the second incident in our text we go to a later time, when Jesus was in Jerusalem only a few months before His death.

I. Withered Hand Made Whole (Mark 3:1-6)

Jesus' custom was to go to a synagogue meeting every Sabbath (Luke 4:16), and it was a Jewish custom to invite visiting teachers to speak at such meetings (Acts 13:15). However, the Pharisees (who were the regular teachers) were not pleased with Jesus. They resented the intrusion of a teacher who was not one of them, and they envied Jesus because He was more popular than they were. They watched Him constantly and listened to Him intently, not hoping to learn from Him but hoping to find fault with Him.

A. The Critics (vv. 1, 2)

1. And he entered again into the synagogue; and there was a man there which had a withered hand.

There was nothing unusual in Jesus' presence at a *synagogue*, but the presence of a *man* with a *withered hand* made some especially watchful, as we see in the next verse.

2. And they watched him, whether he would heal him on the sabbath day; that they might accuse him.

These careful watchers are identified as Pharisees in verse 6. Like nearly everyone in Galilee, they knew that Jesus had been healing "all manner of sickness and all manner of disease" (Matthew 4:23). If He healed this man's hand, they would *accuse him* of working *on the sabbath day*.

On another Sabbath the Pharisees had criticized Jesus' disciples about their actions in the grain fields (Mark 2:23-28). Jesus defended the disciples on that occasion. He obeyed the divine law concerning the Sabbath, but not all the traditions of the Pharisees. [See question #1, page 32.]

B. The Issue (vv. 3, 4)

3. And he saith unto the man which had the withered hand, Stand forth.

Matthew records an interesting piece of information that Mark omits. The Pharisees raised the Sabbath question by asking Jesus, "Is it lawful to heal on the sabbath days?" (Matthew 12:10). Jesus chose to face the issue squarely. He focused attention by asking *the man which had the withered hand* to *stand* up and be seen by all. Here was a living visual aid that could be used to address the question raised by the Pharisees.

4. And he saith unto them, Is it lawful to do good on the sabbath days, or to do evil? to save life, or to kill? But they held their peace.

Instead of answering the Pharisees with a plain yes or no, Jesus chose a way that was more thoughtful and more challenging. Before them all stood a man with his right hand (Luke 6:6) hanging limp and useless. It certainly would be good to repair that hand, to make it strong and useful like the other. Therefore, wouldn't it be bad to leave that hand limp and useless when it could be repaired? Which would be better on a *sabbath day—to do good . . . or to do evil?*

To the crowd it must have seemed that Jesus was expanding the principle to a more severe case than the one before them. Suppose this man were on the verge of death. To heal him would be *to save life*; to do nothing would be, in effect, *to kill* him. Should a man be killed simply because it was the Sabbath? But perhaps what Jesus really had in mind was the contrast between His doing good—as He would shortly heal the man's hand—and the Pharisees' doing evil—they would depart to plan Jesus' death (v. 6).

But they held their peace. The Pharisees could not deny that doing good was better than doing evil, saving life better than killing. But they stubbornly refused to concede that Jesus was right and they had been wrong. They remained silent.

C. The Miracle (v. 5)

5. And when he had looked round about on them with anger, being grieved for the hardness of their hearts, he saith unto the man, Stretch forth thine hand. And he stretched it out: and his hand was restored whole as the other.

We wonder how long Jesus *looked round about on them*—looking from one Pharisee to another. *Anger* showed on His face, but it was an anger

Jesus saith unto the man, Stretch forth thine hand . . . and his hand was restored whole as the other.

Mark 3:5

Visual for lesson 3. *This poster, illustrating Jesus' healing of the man with the withered hand, can be found in the* Adult Visuals *packet.*

mixed with grief at the *hardness of their hearts.* Then Jesus put the truth into action: He did good and not evil, and the withered *hand was restored whole as the other.* [See question #2, page 32.]

D. The Reaction (v. 6)

6. And the Pharisees went forth, and straightway took counsel with the Herodians against him, how they might destroy him.

The Pharisees proceeded to join forces with *the Herodians*, who were supporters of Herod Antipas, king of Galilee. The corruption in the Herod family made the Herodians unlikely allies with the Pharisees, who prided themselves on their avoidance of anything or anyone sinful. That the Pharisees were willing to seek such assistance shows the intensity of their desire to *destroy* Jesus. [See question #3, page 32.]

"THAT'S NOT HOW WE DO THINGS HERE"

Robert Pipes is an eighty-three-year-old preacher with an unconventional approach to evangelism. Every Saturday afternoon for twenty-five years he has driven his motor home through some of the most dangerous housing projects in Los Angeles. Wherever he sees a group of people, he stops and starts preaching through a loudspeaker on top of the vehicle.

Pipes can't say whether anyone has ever been converted by his unusual method, but he perseveres anyway. Drug dealers have thrown rocks at him, the police have given him tickets, and other ministers have criticized him. In essence each was saying, "That's not how we do things here."

Sometimes we object to those who do things differently because we fear that their success might make our conventional methods look bad in comparison. Sometimes it's just stubbornness on our part: we don't like anyone to force change on us and upset the status quo.

Both of those reasons probably led to the Pharisees' objections to Jesus' healing ministry. Of course, they cloaked their jealousy and stubbornness in theological robes, claiming that it was not "lawful" to heal on the Sabbath. It's an ancient (but also very up-to-date) technique for avoiding a confrontation with some tough questions and issues that we would rather not face. —C. R. B.

II. Blind Eyes Given Sight
(John 9:1-12, 35-38)

For the next portion of our text we go to Jerusalem, the capital of Judea, and to a later time, only a few months before Jesus was crucified. The Pharisees there opposed Jesus as bitterly as did those of Galilee. So did the priests, who for the most part were Sadducees. The closing verses of John 8 record that those vindictive enemies, unable to debate with Jesus, picked up stones to kill Him; but He slipped away from them.

A. Disciples' Question (vv. 1, 2)

1. And as Jesus passed by, he saw a man which was blind from his birth.

We are not told just where this *man* was seen. He may have been begging in the street.

2. And his disciples asked him, saying, Master, who did sin, this man, or his parents, that he was born blind?

The disciples held the popular belief that such afflictions as blindness, deafness, and lameness were punishment for *sin*. When one was *born blind*, that raised perplexing questions. Could he possibly have sinned before he was born? Could he be punished from birth for sins he would commit later? Or was he being punished for the sins of *his parents*? If so, where was the justice in that?

B. Answer by Words (vv. 3-5)

3. Jesus answered, Neither hath this man sinned, nor his parents: but that the works of God should be made manifest in him.

This does not mean that the *man* and *his parents* had lived sinless lives; it means that his

---

How to Say It

ANTIPAS. *An*-tih-pus.
HERODIANS. Heh-*roe*-dee-unz.
JUDEA. Joo-*dee*-uh.
PHARISEES. *Fair*-ih-seez.
SADDUCEES. *Sad*-you-seez.
SILOAM. Sigh-*lo*-um.
SYNAGOGUE. *sin*-uh-gog.

---

blindness was not caused by the sins of any of them. Neither should we think that God had caused the blindness in order to have a setting in which to show His *works*. Instead, Jesus turned the disciples' thinking from cause to effect. Because this man was blind, God's work was about to be *made manifest*, or shown, *in him*.

4. I must work the works of him that sent me, while it is day: the night cometh, when no man can work.

Jesus' time on earth was growing short. In a few months He would be crucified. He would rise from the dead and go back to Heaven, but He would no longer do God's *work* on earth with His own hands and feet and voice. In those few months before His death, He must not be diverted from doing His Father's work.

5. As long as I am in the world, I am the light of the world.

For nearly three years Jesus had been giving the *light* of truth to those around Him. Now He was about to symbolize this work by bringing literal light to a man who had spent his entire life in darkness.

C. Answer by Actions (vv. 6, 7)

6, 7. When he had thus spoken, he spat on the ground, and made clay of the spittle, and he anointed the eyes of the blind man with the clay, and said unto him, Go, wash in the pool of Siloam, (which is by interpretation, Sent.) He went his way therefore, and washed, and came seeing.

The *pool of Siloam* was located on the southeastern end of the city of Jerusalem. While we are not told exactly how far the man had to go until he came to the pool, it should be noted that the pool was not far from the temple area, where the incidents recorded in chapter 8 took place.

Jesus could give sight with a touch (Matthew 9:27-30) or a mere word (Mark 10:46-52), so why this elaborate ritual? Jesus did not give a reason, and neither does John. Perhaps it was to teach the man (and us) that some of God's blessings depend on the faith and obedience of the receiver as well as on the power and goodness of the Giver. What we do know is that the man did as he was told, and for the first time in his life he could see.

D. Storm of Questions (vv. 8-12)

8. The neighbours therefore, and they which before had seen him that he was blind, said, Is not this he that sat and begged?

Naturally enough, *the neighbors* were amazed. They took a second look and gasped, *Is not this he that sat and begged?*

9. Some said, This is he: others said, He is like him: but he said, I am he.

There was an immediate difference of opinion about the question asked in verse 8. Some said that this man was the one who had "sat and begged." Others claimed that he was someone else who only looked like the blind man. The man himself settled the question: *I am he.*

10. Therefore said they unto him, How were thine eyes opened?

When the first question was answered, the second followed naturally. How did a blind man become a seeing one?

11. He answered and said, A man that is called Jesus made clay, and anointed mine eyes, and said unto me, Go to the pool of Siloam, and wash: and I went and washed, and I received sight.

Point by point the man told precisely what had happened. But he did not believe that the miracle had been done either by the mud on his eyes or by the water in the *pool of Siloam*. He understood that *Jesus* had done it, and later he said, "He hath opened mine eyes" (v. 30). He understood further that Jesus had done this miracle by divine power: "If this man were not of God, he could do nothing" (v. 33).

12. Then said they unto him, Where is he? He said, I know not.

The man's answer in verse 11 had turned attention from the miracle to the one who had done it—"a man that is called Jesus." Of course, the man did not know *where* Jesus was. He had never seen Jesus, and at this point he would not know Him if he did see Him.

When the Pharisees learned of this miracle, there quickly arose a dispute among their ranks. Some were sure that Jesus was a sinner because He did such an act on the Sabbath. Others asked how a sinner could do such a miracle. As a result, "there was a division among them," verse 16 tells us.

The Pharisees then turned their attention to the man who had received his sight. They tried to prove that no miracle had been done, but the evidence proved even more undeniable. Finally, angered by the man's firm stand, the Pharisees cast him out of the synagogue. To be thus "excommunicated" was a most shameful punishment. Now the Jews would not recognize the man as a Jew, but neither would the Gentiles recognize him as a Gentile. He was a man alone. [See question #4, page 32.]

E. No Longer Alone (vv. 35-38)

35. Jesus heard that they had cast him out; and when he had found him, he said unto him, Dost thou believe on the Son of God?

This outcast was not alone for long. Soon Jesus *found him.* We wonder if anything was spoken between the two before Jesus asked the

---

Home Daily Bible Readings

Monday, Sept. 10—Healed Because of Friends' Faith (Mark 2:1-12)

Tuesday, Sept. 11—Wanting to Be Healed (John 5:2-9a)

Wednesday, Sept. 12—Healing the Gadarene Demoniac (Mark 5:1-15)

Thursday, Sept. 13—Healing Jairus's Daughter (Mark 5:21-24a, 35-43)

Friday, Sept. 14—The Faith That Makes You Whole (Mark 5:24b-34)

Saturday, Sept. 15—"Help Thou Mine Unbelief" (Mark 9:17-29)

Sunday, Sept. 16—Healing a Man With a Withered Hand (Mark 3:1-6)

---

momentous question recorded here: *Dost thou believe on the Son of God?*

36. He answered and said, Who is he, Lord, that I might believe on him?

In the face of angry opposition by eminent scholars, this man already had declared Jesus to be a prophet and a man of God (vv. 17, 33). He was eager to *believe* whatever that prophet told him; but what did Jesus mean by "Son of God"? And of whom did He speak? The man needed more information. [See question #5, page 32.]

37. And Jesus said unto him, Thou hast both seen him, and it is he that talketh with thee.

In the plainest terms, Jesus said that He Himself is the Son of God. *Thou hast . . . seen him* was a reminder that this man had seen nothing at all until the Son of God had given him sight. *It is he that talketh with thee* was a suggestion that the man could learn much more from God's Son.

38. And he said, Lord, I believe. And he worshipped him.

At this point, the man could not have known all the significance in that phrase "Son of God." But he believed what Jesus said, *and he worshipped him.* Like any follower of Jesus, he could spend the rest of his life learning more and more about God's Son.

Isn't our experience like this man's? On the basis of ample evidence we believe that Jesus is "the Christ, the Son of the living God" (Matthew 16:16). We declare our faith in Him; we worship Him; we take our place in the fellowship of believers; as long as we live we keep on learning about His power, His goodness, His grace, His love, and His companionship in our daily walk.

WILLING TO FIND THE TRUTH

John Archibald Wheeler is the physicist who proved that "black holes" exist out in the far reaches of space. A more important fact about him is that he keeps asking questions that many of his fellow scientists are uncomfortable with—questions about creation, about meaning in life, and about why the universe exists.

Wheeler asks, "How could the universe exist and make sense unless it were guaranteed to give rise at some point to life and mind and meaning?" And again, "Is man an unimportant bit of dust on an unimportant planet in an unimportant galaxy somewhere in the vastness of space? No! The necessity to produce life lies at the center of the universe's whole machinery and design." These are really theological issues, but Wheeler raises them as a scientist who sees a logic in the creation with which some scientists are not willing to grapple.

The blind man at first had expressed ignorance of Jesus' identity. Later, when confronted by Jesus about his belief in the Son of God, it became apparent that the man was not an agnostic. Far from it—he expressed an active interest in coming to faith.

John Wheeler and the blind man may be considered brothers in the quest for truth. There is no shame in being ignorant, if we also possess a desire to know the truth and a willingness to ask the right questions, no matter how difficult or unpopular they may be.   —C. R. B.

Conclusion

In the Scripture we have read today, we see two very different conclusions about Jesus. Let's summarize the conclusions along with the presuppositions and evidence on which they were based. Then let's consider some of the conclusions of people today.

A. Conclusion of the Pharisees

1. Presuppositions. We Pharisees are the best of God's people, the wisest and most obedient.

2. Evidence. Jesus is not a Pharisee. He does not honor our traditions. He does not respect our authority. He heals people on the Sabbath.

3. Conclusion. "We know that this man is a sinner" (v. 24).

B. Conclusion of the Man Given Sight

1. Presuppositions. "If [he] were not of God, he could do nothing" (v. 33).

2. Evidence. Jesus gave me my sight.

3. Conclusion. "He is a prophet" (v. 17).

C. Conclusion of an Agnostic

1. Presuppositions. The laws of nature are changeless, and the working of nature is uniform. There are no miracles, and there never were.

2. Evidence. The Gospels tell of many miracles done by Jesus.

3. Conclusion. Those books are mythical, not factual. We don't know whether Jesus was a real person or just a mythical one.

D. Conclusion of an Egotist

1. Presuppositions. I am number one. What I like is good.

2. Evidence. Jesus taught His people to love their neighbors as themselves, even to make sacrifices for the good of others.

3. Conclusion. That's not for me.

E. Conclusion of a Materialist

1. Presuppositions. The "scientific method" is the only avenue for learning. We cannot know much about anything unless we can see it, hear it, touch it, taste it, or smell it.

2. Evidence. Jesus and His followers thought that "the things which are seen are temporal; but the things which are not seen are eternal" (2 Corinthians 4:18).

3. Conclusion. Jesus was a dreamer. I am awake. I give first attention to things I know are real, like money in the bank.

F. Conclusion of a Christian

1. Presuppositions. Some people who are now Christians held very different presuppositions before they looked at the evidence about Jesus. Those who grew up in devout Christian homes learned that the Bible is true and that Jesus is the Son of God. When they began to examine the evidence, they discovered that the facts supported their presuppositions. But those who were reared in non-Christian homes held the exact opposite presuppositions and, upon objective examination of the evidence, found that it disproved those presuppositions.

2. Evidence. The books of Matthew, Mark, Luke, and John have the earmarks of true records. They were written by Jesus' contemporaries. These credible books proclaim that Jesus is the Son of God.

3. Conclusion. Jesus is all the Bible says He is: the Savior and Lord of those who believe Him and follow Him. He is worthy of full allegiance, and I will follow Him today and always.

G. Prayer

Thank You, Father, for the clear record of Your Son. We believe it, Lord, and we want to follow Him faithfully. May we have the wisdom and courage to do so. In Jesus' name. Amen.

H. Thought to Remember

Jesus Christ is Lord.

Learning by Doing

This page contains an alternate lesson plan emphasizing learning activities. Classes desiring such student involvement will find these suggestions helpful.

Learning Goals

After participating in this lesson, each student will be able to:

1. Summarize the accounts of the miracles recorded in today's texts and the reaction of the Pharisees to them.

2. Contrast how Christians and non-Christians tend to view the evidence concerning Jesus found in the Gospels.

3. Prepare a presentation of the gospel (one that anticipates questions non-Christians may ask) and plan to share it soon with a friend.

Into the Lesson

Prepare a poster or a transparency with the following uncompleted simile: "Diseases are to Jesus as _____ are to _____." As class begins, state: "The New Testament describes many diseases and conditions that Jesus healed. Today we start the lesson by completing a simile about Jesus and His power over diseases." Show the simile; then continue: "Work with one sitting next to you to complete this simile. You have three minutes." *(A sample answer: "grains of salt are to a mountain climber.")* State: "All these similes show how easy it is for Jesus to make people whole or well. Today we find two such cases: Jesus healing a withered hand and restoring sight to the blind."

Into the Word

Prior to class prepare the following quiz on a handout. State: "To review these miracles we will take this true/false test." After about a minute, review the answers.

1. Jesus met a man with a withered hand in the temple. *(False–in the synagogue)*

2. The Pharisees watched to see if Jesus would "violate" the Sabbath and heal the man. *(True)*

3. The Pharisees asked Jesus who had sinned to cause the second man's blindness—the man or his parents. *(False–the disciples asked.)*

4. The Herodians plotted with the Sadducees as to how they might destroy Jesus. *(False–with the Pharisees)*

5. Jesus called Himself Son of man. *(False–Son of God)*

6. After spitting on the man's eyes, Jesus told the man to wash in the pool of Siloam. *(False–Jesus spat on the ground.)*

7. Some people thought the man that could see only looked like the blind beggar. *(True)*

8. Jesus became angry with the hardness of the Pharisees' hearts. *(True)*

9. After the man was healed, Jesus was cast out of the synagogue. *(False–the blind man was.)*

10. When Jesus revealed Himself to the man who could see, the man worshiped Jesus. *(True)*

Say: "Notice the different reactions of people to these miracles. Turn the quiz sheet over and you'll find a chart to complete." Make certain this chart is prepared prior to class and copied on the sheet. There are two columns labeled: "Person/Group" and "Reaction." Down the first column list the following six entries: 1. Man with a withered hand, 2. Pharisees, 3. Herodians, 4. Man born blind, 5. Neighbors, 6. Blind man's parents.

Then say, "Work with a person sitting next to you to complete the right-hand column. What are the revealed and/or possible reactions of these people to Jesus' miracles?" After a few minutes, discuss the answers. *(1. Gratitude, 2. Anger, 3. Revenge, 4. Worship, 5. Doubt/Confusion, 6. Fear)*

Into Life

State: "There were different reactions recorded in the New Testament to Jesus' miracles; there are different reactions today. Consider these three areas: Jesus' identity, Jesus' miracles, and Jesus' teaching. How do Christians and non-Christians view the evidence concerning these three issues differently?"

Lead a discussion of contrasting points of view. Jesus' identity: Son of God vs. a "prophet"; God in the flesh vs. a good moral man. Jesus' miracles: supernatural demonstrations of God's power vs. mythical stories in a non-credible book. Jesus' teaching: God's truth for wholesome living in an inspired book vs. a mythical collection of stories.

State: "Many of us know non-Christians who have asked pointed questions about the Bible, Biblical teaching, and the identity of Jesus. What questions do the non-Christians ask?" Write these questions on the board or overhead transparency. *(Possible questions: Why is there evil in the world? If God is love, why doesn't He heal my friend's terminal illness?)* Say: "In groups of three or four, select one of these questions. Then prepare a presentation of the gospel in response to that question." Close the lesson with a prayer requesting opportunities to share these presentations.

Let's Talk It Over

The questions on this page are designed to encourage review of the lesson Scriptures and to promote discussion of the lesson by the class. The answers provided are only discussion starters. Let your class talk it over from there.

1. The Pharisees were very interested in what Jesus said and did, but their interest was for the purpose of finding fault. How should we deal with people who continually find fault with us?

Jesus' example is instructive for us. First, He did not let public opinion determine His actions. He did what was right even when it "offended" the fault-finders. He did not set out to offend them, but He did not let their critical view keep Him from doing God's will.

Then He gave a reasoned explanation for His actions. Many in the crowd would be swayed by the Pharisees' judgment because of their position in society. If Jesus had to oppose them, then He would give sound reasons for doing so.

2. Seldom do we read of Jesus' being angry, but Mark 3:5 is one instance. Note that He was grieved at the Pharisees' hardness of heart. What is it that grieves us when we get angry? What do you think we can learn from Jesus' anger here?

When we get angry, we are usually grieved at the way someone treated us. We've been misunderstood, maligned, or ignored. Worse yet, sometimes we get angry because our own wrong actions or feelings have been exposed and we would rather retaliate than repent!

Jesus' anger was not self-serving. He cared for every person, even His enemies. It grieved Him to see the Pharisees heading down the wrong path. It especially hurt to see that they would deny a person with disabilities the opportunity to be made whole just so they could keep their pretense of holiness. Part of seeking first the Lord's kingdom and His righteousness (Matthew 6:33) must surely include cultivating this same attitude that Jesus had.

3. The Pharisees were bent on destroying Jesus. How do Jesus' enemies attempt to destroy Him in our times? What can we do about it?

Some of Jesus' enemies labor to reduce Him to nothing more than a mythological character. Others admit that there was a "historical Jesus," but they are quick to explain that He was nothing like the "legendary Jesus" portrayed in the Gospels. Such so-called scholars endeavor especially to explain away Jesus' miracles, in particular His literal resurrection from the dead and any self-affirmation of His deity. Others among Jesus'

enemies utilize the weapon of ridicule. In print, film, and video media they frequently make Him and His followers the target of irreverent and uncharitable humor. Perhaps the most common attack today is effected by keeping His name and deeds out of the public arena.

Your students may have many ideas about what we can do to counter these attacks. Some may suggest boycotting sponsors of profane or irreverent portrayals of Him. Some may suggest going to court to allow expressions of faith in the public arena. Whatever ideas are shared, do not overlook the power of a transformed life!

4. The man whom Jesus had healed was questioned about his new condition. While he did not know all the answers, he told what he knew—he told what had happened to him. How can we use his example to encourage Christians today to share the good news of Christ?

Many believers think they have to be able to recite verse after verse of Scripture to share the gospel with another. While it certainly helps to know the Bible, and those who can recite many passages from memory have an advantage in sharing the gospel, every Christian can help another person to find the Lord. Just telling what we know will help another. There is no shame in saying, when someone asks a question we cannot answer, "I'll have to get back to you on that." But if we know the truth, and if we share it in love and with a passion that comes from an appreciation of our own salvation, then God will use us to help others.

5. The man healed of his blindness thrills us with his question about the Son of God: "Who is he, Lord, that I might believe on him?" How do we find people with a similar eagerness to believe the truth about Jesus Christ?

Only God knows the heart, so we need first to pray that God will lead us to receptive hearts. But we can also be observant. One who has been through a humbling experience is often more receptive to the gospel; whom do we know who has had such an experience as illness, financial problems, marital crises, and the like? Also, children often have an eagerness to learn Biblical truths. We should use every means possible to lead children—especially our own—to Christ.

A Mother Persists in Faith

DEVOTIONAL READING: Luke 4:16-21.

BACKGROUND SCRIPTURE: Matthew 15:21-31.

PRINTED TEXT: Matthew 15:21-31.

Matthew 15:21-31

21 Then Jesus went thence, and departed into the coasts of Tyre and Sidon.

22 And, behold, a woman of Canaan came out of the same coasts, and cried unto him, saying, Have mercy on me, O Lord, thou Son of David; my daughter is grievously vexed with a devil.

23 But he answered her not a word. And his disciples came and besought him, saying, Send her away; for she crieth after us.

24 But he answered and said, I am not sent but unto the lost sheep of the house of Israel.

25 Then came she and worshipped him, saying, Lord, help me.

26 But he answered and said, It is not meet to take the children's bread, and to cast it to dogs.

27 And she said, Truth, Lord: yet the dogs eat of the crumbs which fall from their masters' table.

28 Then Jesus answered and said unto her, O woman, great is thy faith: be it unto thee even as thou wilt. And her daughter was made whole from that very hour.

29 And Jesus departed from thence, and came nigh unto the sea of Galilee; and went up into a mountain, and sat down there.

30 And great multitudes came unto him, having with them those that were lame, blind, dumb, maimed, and many others, and cast them down at Jesus' feet; and he healed them:

31 Insomuch that the multitude wondered, when they saw the dumb to speak, the maimed to be whole, the lame to walk, and the blind to see: and they glorified the God of Israel.

GOLDEN TEXT: Jesus answered and said unto her, O woman, great is thy faith: be it unto thee even as thou wilt. And her daughter was made whole from that very hour.
—Matthew 15:28.

Jesus' Ministry
Unit 1: Performing Miracles
(Lessons 1-5)

Lesson Aims

After this lesson a student should be able to:
1. Tell how Jesus' love and power were manifested outside Jewish territory.
2. Explain why Jesus expanded His ministry beyond "the lost sheep of the house of Israel."
3. Suggest a specific way to reach beyond one's usual circle to share Christ's love.

Lesson Outline

INTRODUCTION
  A. A Proud People
  B. Lesson Background
 I. JESUS IN THE NORTH (Matthew 15:21-28)
  A. Desperate Plea (vv. 21, 22)
  B. First Response (vv. 23, 24)
    When God Doesn't Hear Us
  C. Persistent Plea (vv. 25-27)
  D. Request Granted (v. 28)
    Whose Side Is God On?
II. JESUS IN THE EAST (Matthew 15:29-31)
  A. More Miracles (vv. 29, 30)
  B. Marveling Multitude (v. 31)
CONCLUSION
  A. Shining Lights
  B. Caution Without Compromise
  C. Prayer
  D. Thought to Remember

Introduction

Where did national pride and prejudice come from? Possibly their origin can be traced to that long-ago day when the builders of the tower of Babel found that they could not understand one another. The resulting confusion must have been extremely frustrating. It was reduced when the people were scattered over the earth, thus separating the different language groups from each other (Genesis 11:1-9). Perhaps, as time passed, the people of each group looked down on those who did not understand their language.

A. A Proud People

The ancient Israelites were called to be God's people—"a kingdom of priests, and a holy nation" (Exodus 19:6). As such, they were commanded by God to destroy certain nations that were too wicked to live (Deuteronomy 7:1-5). At the same time, they were to obey God's laws so that other nations would witness their obedience and say, "Surely this great nation is a wise and understanding people" (Deuteronomy 4:6).

Though warned not to become proud or arrogant about their status, the Israelites often forgot their God-given duties and responsibilities. They seemed to think that God would protect and bless them regardless of how they lived. The Old Testament records several occasions when they were either oppressed or taken captive by pagan foreigners because they failed to follow the Lord God faithfully.

By the time of Christ, God's people were but a tiny part of the great Roman Empire. But they still had their pride as "Abraham's seed" (John 8:33), and they despised their Roman masters. Many saw the promised Messiah as someone who would deliver Israel from its oppressors and restore its national greatness.

B. Lesson Background

Soon after His miraculous feeding of the five thousand, Jesus withdrew from the crowded centers of Galilee. Perhaps He was trying to find time for some private teaching with His twelve disciples. He had desired such an occasion just before the feeding of the five thousand occurred (Mark 6:30-34). Perhaps Jesus also meant to frustrate the plotting of the Pharisees against His life (Mark 3:6). Whatever His reasons, He was clearly seeking to avoid public notice (Mark 7:24).

I. Jesus in the North
(Matthew 15:21-28)

Looking for privacy, Jesus first traveled northward, beyond the border of Jewish territory.

A. Desperate Plea (vv. 21, 22)

21. Then Jesus went thence, and departed into the coasts of Tyre and Sidon.

Tyre and Sidon were the principal cities of Phoenicia, which was located to the north of Galilee. Both of these cities were situated on the Mediterranean coast; however, the word *coasts* here does not mean seacoasts. It means the territory around these two cities.

22. And, behold, a woman of Canaan came out of the same coasts, and cried unto him, saying, Have mercy on me, O Lord, thou Son of David; my daughter is grievously vexed with a devil.

Jesus had never been to this region before, but people from here were among the crowds that had followed Him in Galilee (Mark 3:7, 8). Evidently they had filled Phoenicia with reports of the wonders Jesus had done. Thus, when He entered their country, some of them recognized Him and spread the word that He was there. Apparently *a woman of Canaan* had heard that Jesus could subdue the demons that sometimes took control of people, so she came to ask Him to help her afflicted *daughter*. Her use of the title *Son of David* indicates that she was aware of the Jews' messianic expectations and believed that Jesus was the fulfillment of those hopes.

It should be noted that while the term *Canaan* is used many times in the Old Testament, this is the only time it is used in the New Testament. Some believe that this was the Jewish manner of describing the people of this territory.

B. First Response (vv. 23, 24)

23. But he answered her not a word. And his disciples came and besought him, saying, Send her away; for she crieth after us.

Apparently this woman repeated her plea for help. Her cries would attract attention at a time when Jesus and His *disciples* wanted to avoid attention, so the disciples told Him, *Send her away.* Did they mean that He should send her away with a refusal, or grant her request and send her away? Jewish prejudice might suggest the former, but Jesus' reply (in the next verse) seems to indicate the latter. [See question #1, page 40.]

24. But he answered and said, I am not sent but unto the lost sheep of the house of Israel.

Jesus came to seek and save *the lost* (Luke 19:10), but His personal mission was to *Israel* only. He gave similar instructions to His disciples when He sent them out to preach during His own ministry (Matthew 10:5, 6). Later they would be sent to all nations (Matthew 28:19, 20); but during the brief three and a half years when Jesus was among them in visible form, it was better to center His attention on the people best prepared to hear His message and pass it on. [See question #2, page 40.]

WHEN GOD DOESN'T HEAR US

Teen-age suicide has been called the "unheard cry for help." It is a subject we don't like to think about, yet it is the second leading cause of death among adolescents. The fifteen-to-twenty-four-year-old age group is the only American age cohort whose death rate has not declined in the last twenty years. This is due primarily to suicide.

Many causes for this tragedy have been suggested: easy availability of alcohol and drugs; a society that glamorizes violence; high family mobility; the demise of the two-parent family; the availability of guns, etc. These all play a part, no doubt, but a major factor may be that many young people have concluded that they are not

important to anyone: no one cares what happens to them or hears them when they cry for help.

The Canaanite woman in today's text may have wondered whether anyone—even God— cared about her plight. When she begged Jesus to heal her daughter, He at first seemed to ignore her; and then He gave an answer that seemed quite abrupt.

But what Jesus was doing was challenging this woman's faith: was she willing to trust Him implicitly? When it seems that God isn't listening to our prayers, is it possible that He is challenging us to trust Him regardless of what happens?

Are we willing to choose a life of faith rather than risk the death of faith? It is only by stretching our faith that we grow.   —C. R. B.

C. Persistent Plea (vv. 25-27)

25. Then came she and worshipped him, saying, Lord, help me.

Now the woman *came* closer to Jesus *and worshipped him.* Perhaps she knelt at His feet; perhaps she praised His power and mercy. But she repeated her plea: *Lord, help me.*

26. But he answered and said, It is not meet to take the children's bread, and to cast it to dogs.

Not meet means not suitable, not fitting, not proper. Jesus said it is not good *to take . . . bread* away from the children and give it to *dogs.* His comment startles us. Did Jesus share the Jewish national pride? Did He really think that Jews were God's children and all other people were dogs?

Two factors may have softened the seeming harshness of Jesus' words. First, the Greek word for *dogs* may well be translated *puppies.* It describes well-loved pets in the home rather than the half-wild dogs that roamed the streets and scrounged for food among the garbage. Taking a

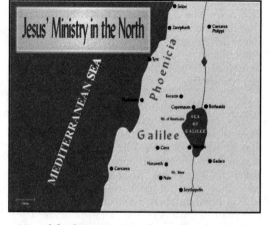

Visual for lesson 4. *Use this map to locate the events of the lessons covered in this quarter.*

cue from that milder word, many students believe that Jesus spoke to this woman in a gentle tone that robbed the comment of its presumed sting. Whether that supposition is correct or not, the woman answered with humble persistence instead of taking offense.

27. And she said, Truth, Lord: yet the dogs eat of the crumbs which fall from their masters' table.

A woman with more pride and less wisdom and faith might have felt insulted at Jesus' comment or would have turned away with a curse. But this woman was content to be a "puppy"—if only she might be given a scrap of the leftovers from the blessings Jesus had been distributing freely among the Jews. Perhaps some Phoenicians had been present when Jesus fed the five thousand and had reported that the leftovers from that miracle had filled twelve baskets. Certainly they had reported that Jesus had healed every illness and freed every person afflicted by a demon. Surely, the woman thought, surely there was more of that divine power than was needed by Jews alone. And how she needed a bit of that power—not for herself, but to set her daughter free from that demon! [See question #3, page 40.]

D. Request Granted (v. 28)

28. Then Jesus answered and said unto her, O woman, great is thy faith: be it unto thee even as thou wilt. And her daughter was made whole from that very hour.

Now the expression on Jesus' face and the tone of His voice must have emphasized the approval spoken by His words. Here was a woman with *faith* enough to be sure of the Master's ability, humility enough to accept a rebuff without anger or despair, and hope enough to keep on pressing her plea.

And her daughter was made whole from that very hour. Mark's account (Mark 7:30) indicates that the daughter was not there with her mother when this miracle occurred. In some way beyond our understanding, Jesus' command reached the evil spirit. He got the message, and he left. The girl was set free.

WHOSE SIDE IS GOD ON?

The National Football Conference "wild card" playoff game between the San Francisco 49ers and the Green Bay Packers on January 3, 1999, was won by the 49ers, apparently because God liked the 49ers best. After all, the touchdown pass that won the game was caught by born-again Christian receiver Terrell Owens. After the touchdown, Owens yelled, "Thank You, Jesus!"

But wait a minute. Some of the five Packer defenders who surrounded Owens when he caught

---

How to Say It
DECAPOLIS. Dee-*cap*-uh-lis.
GALILEE. *Gal*-uh-lee.
HERMES. *Her*-meez.
JUDEA. Joo-*dee*-uh.
MEDITERRANEAN. *Med*-uh-tuh-*ray*-nee-un (strong accent on *ray*).
PHARISEES. *Fair*-ih-seez.
PHOENICIA. Fuh-*nish*-uh.
SIDON. *Sigh*-dun.
TYRE. Tire.
ZEUS. Zoose.

---

the pass were also Christians. And Green Bay defensive end Reggie White said that God had called him out of retirement to play one more season. But to end it like this?

During that same 1998-1999 National Football League season, Minnesota Vikings' quarterback Randall Cunningham, who won his conference's Most Valuable Player award, said, "I can't go out and win unless I do it through Christ. Does God care? Evidently He's cared, because of the success we've had this year." (The Vikings won fifteen of sixteen regular season games that year.)

It has been estimated that as many as forty percent of professional football players claim to be born-again Christians, which leads to the question in the title of this essay: *Whose side is God on?* Or is it possible that God doesn't really care much about who wins a football game?

The Jews in Jesus' day (including His disciples) thought that God was on the side of the "home team" (them) and could not possibly care about a Canaanite woman. But Jesus' words and actions show us that His concern is for all of any race or social class who trust Him. Have we learned this lesson yet?

—C. R. B.

II. Jesus in the East (Matthew 15:29-31)

Jesus did not stay long in the region of Tyre and Sidon, but neither did He return quickly to Galilee. He went to another place where the population was largely Gentile. Again He found that even among foreigners His reputation was well known.

A. More Miracles (vv. 29, 30)

29. And Jesus departed from thence, and came nigh unto the sea of Galilee; and went up into a mountain, and sat down there.

Jesus left Phoenicia, the region where Tyre and Sidon were located. He *came nigh unto the sea of Galilee*, but not to the area called Galilee.

He journeyed to the east side of the sea, to the area called Decapolis (Mark 7:31). The name *Decapolis* means "ten cities." East and southeast of the Sea of Galilee, ten cities had banded together, with the region surrounding them, to form what might be called a "league" of cities. Only one of the ten was located west of the Jordan River. Like Galilee and Judea, this territory was not independent, but was a part of the Roman Empire.

Mark tells us more about the beginning of Jesus' ministry in this area. It seems that He was recognized quickly, and people began to gather about Him. Some of them brought a deaf man who had an impediment in his speech. Still trying to avoid publicity, Jesus took the man away from the gathering crowd and gave him normal hearing and speech. Jesus then asked the man and those present not to tell others about it; but they disregarded that request (Mark 7:32-37). No doubt the crowd grew rapidly.

Perhaps after a large crowd had gathered, Jesus *went up into a mountain, and sat down there.* In today's English we would call this a hill rather than a mountain. We wonder if Jesus found a place where He could sit comfortably and teach such a crowd, as He had done in the famous Sermon on the Mount (Matthew 5:1, 2). The people of Decapolis had not come to listen to a sermon, however. They had other concerns on their minds, as we see in the next verse.

30. And great multitudes came unto him, having with them those that were lame, blind, dumb, maimed, and many others, and cast them down at Jesus' feet; and he healed them.

Great multitudes who had physical problems were brought to Jesus—*and he healed them.* No patient was told to stay in bed; no medicine was given; no one was told to come back in a week or a month. Healing was quick, complete, and permanent. That was plain to the witnesses.

B. Marveling Multitude (v. 31)

31. Insomuch that the multitude wondered, when they saw the dumb to speak, the maimed to be whole, the lame to walk, and the blind to see: and they glorified the God of Israel.

The *multitude* in Decapolis had never seen anything like this. They *wondered,* as you and I would do if we could see the Lord in human form giving such a demonstration of His power and grace. Probably most of the people in Decapolis (being Gentiles) gave nominal worship to the mythical gods of the Greeks: Zeus, Hermes, and the rest. But they knew whom Jesus represented, *and they glorified the God of Israel.* On an earlier occasion, Jesus said to His followers, "Let your light so shine before men, that they may see your good works, and glorify your Father which

is in heaven" (Matthew 5:16). And Jesus practiced what He preached. He Himself was honored, yes; but He managed His miracle working so that the observers also gave glory to His Father in Heaven. [See question #4, page 40.]

Conclusion

"What would Jesus do?" Often that question is asked by one who is not sure what he himself ought to do. In many cases it is an excellent question to ask. All Christians ought to be followers of Jesus, becoming more and more like Him. But our lessons during this month remind us that in some cases the question of what Jesus would do is not pertinent. Jesus could turn water into wine, stop a raging wind from blowing, feed thousands with one boy's lunch, rebuild a withered hand, give sight to a blind man and hearing to a deaf one, and drive a demon away from an afflicted girl. We cannot do any of these. Rather than, "What would Jesus do?" we often need to ask, "What does Jesus want me to do?"

All of us want to obey Jesus' commands and follow His example, don't we? We want to conduct ourselves so that the people around us will not only see us doing good, but will give God credit for the good we do (Matthew 5:16). Here are some examples to think about.

A. Shining Lights

1. To pray or not to pray. While this lesson was being prepared, the TV news told of a Texas high school that had prayer before every game on its athletic schedule. But someone objected vigorously, and a court ordered the custom discontinued. That prayer violated the constitutional separation of church and state, said the court. If a majority of teachers, trustees, and students are Christians, how can they best let their lights shine for the glory of God in such a situation? Consider which of the following options would accomplish this goal most effectively.

a. Accept the ruling of the court and stop having prayer before games. Christians ought to obey the officials of their government (Romans 13:1, 2).

b. Defy the court and continue to have prayer before games. Christians ought to obey God rather than men (Acts 5:27-29).

c. Have a minute of silence in which anyone can pray if he wants to. Christians ought to pray without ceasing (1 Thessalonians 5:17), but try to live peaceably with all men (Romans 12:18).

d. Let the team have prayer in the locker room. Jesus told us to pray in private (Matthew 6:6).

2. Beer in the woods. In our suburb, the "woods" are a little patch of trees down by the railroad track. Boys too young to drink beer legally sometimes hide there to drink beer illegally. Even Christian boys sometimes do this. After all, no Christian wants to seem too pious, does he?

Jim got an older cousin to buy some beer for him, and he was inviting some high school friends to share it. In the following scenario, which boys, if any, show a gleam of Christian light?

Jim: I've got a six-pack in my locker, and some of us are going to the woods after school. Want to come?

Tom: Sure, count me in.

Dick: Not me. You know that's against the law. Do you want all of us to go to jail?

Harry: How many guys will be there?

Jim: I don't know. If more than six come, two or three can share a can.

Harry: OK, I'll be there, and I'll bring my own beer.

When the little group gathered in the woods, Harry's beer turned out to be root beer.

Tom: Hey, look what he's got. That's sissy stuff. You're chicken!

Harry: OK, I'm chicken, but I'm a legal chicken. Besides, this sissy stuff tastes better.

Tom: You've got a point there. In fact, you've got two points. It's legal, and it tastes better. How about sharing your sissy stuff with me? [See question #5, page 40.]

B. Caution Without Compromise

Jesus spent much time in Galilee because leaders of the Jews in Judea were plotting to kill Him (John 5:18). Then the Pharisees of Galilee began plotting to kill Him (Mark 3:6). That may have been one reason for His leaving Galilee and going to Phoenicia and Decapolis. Jesus intended to give His life, but not until the time chosen by His

Home Daily Bible Readings

Monday, Sept. 17—"Come Unto Me, All Ye That Labor" (Matthew 11:25-30)
Tuesday, Sept. 18—A Son Raised From the Dead (Luke 7:11-17)
Wednesday, Sept. 19—Cured, But Don't Tell (Matthew 12:15-21)
Thursday, Sept. 20—Healing by What Authority? (Matthew 12:22-28)
Friday, Sept. 21—Breaking the Tradition of the Elders (Matthew 15:1-9)
Saturday, Sept. 22—Things That Defile (Matthew 15:10-20)
Sunday, Sept. 23—A Woman of Great Faith (Matthew 15:21-31)

Father. He postponed this time by moving away from a dangerous place, but never by leaving the truth behind. Attacked in Galilee because He healed on the Sabbath, He exposed the hypocrisy of the Pharisees who would do a bit of work on the holy day for the comfort of a sheep, but would permit no work at all for the welfare of a man (Matthew 12:9-14). Even more devastating was His denunciation of the hypocritical scribes and Pharisees of Jerusalem (Matthew 23:1-36), which was spoken only days before they had Him crucified.

If we are trying to be like Jesus, surely we must take a firm stand for truth. In places where these Sunday school lessons are used, opposition to truth is not often life-threatening. We have no need to flee our country to escape death. So is there anything we can do to dull the fury of opposition?

Consider our *manner* of telling the truth. We are Christian soldiers, yes. We are to "put on the whole armor of God" (Ephesians 6:11) and "fight the good fight of faith" (1 Timothy 6:12). But that does not cancel our instruction to talk and act "with all lowliness and meekness" (Ephesians 4:2) and "with meekness of wisdom" (James 3:13). Some of the most faithful, earnest, and vigorous preachers of the Word sound as if they are egotistical, arrogant, and vindictive. Of one such preacher a listener commented, "He sounds like he's glad some people are going to Hell."

Very plainly Jesus said, "How can ye escape the damnation of hell?" (Matthew 23:33). But no hearer thought He was glad about that. In fact, Jesus was overcome with grief (Matthew 23:37-39). His grief is pictured poignantly in the record of His triumphal entry into Jerusalem. Multitudes were shouting His praises and calling, "Blessed be the King that cometh in the name of the Lord" (Luke 19:37, 38). But the King they were praising looked down on Jerusalem and burst into tears (Luke 19:41-44).

There is a beautiful little phrase in Ephesians 4:15: "speaking the truth in love." That is a part of our growing into the likeness of Christ. When love shines through the truth we tell and the work we do, hateful opposition is put to shame.

C. Prayer

Thank You, Father, for the truth set forth so plainly in Your Word. From Him who verified it by divine power may we learn to speak it plainly; from Him who wept because of its rejection may we learn to speak it in love. In His name we ask, amen.

D. Thought to Remember

Tell the truth, and tell it with love.

Learning by Doing

This page contains an alternate lesson plan emphasizing learning activities.
Classes desiring such student involvement will find these suggestions helpful.

Learning Goals

After this lesson each student will be able to:

1. Tell how Jesus' love and power were manifested outside Jewish territory.

2. Explain why Jesus expanded His ministry beyond "the lost sheep of the house of Israel."

3. Suggest a specific way to reach beyond one's usual circle to share Christ's love.

Into the Lesson

Begin class today by writing the word "persistence" on the chalkboard or an overhead transparency. State: "When you think of this word, you probably think of someone not giving up—sticking to a particular task. Think about a time in your life when you were the most persistent. Complete this sentence and share it with someone next to you: 'The time in my life when I was most persistent was when _____.'" After a few minutes of sentence completions, ask if there are any who will share their examples of persistence with the class. Then state: "In our text today, we have another example of persistence. Turn to Matthew 15:21-31 and read about a persistent woman said by Jesus to have great faith."

Into the Word

Prior to class, prepare six copies of the lesson text. Label the first copy "Jesus," and use a highlighter to mark all the words spoken by Jesus. Label the second copy "Woman," and highlight the woman's words. Label three copies "Disciples" and another copy "Narrator," and highlight the text accordingly. Select six students, and assign each one to read the part highlighted on his or her copy of the text. Ask the students to stand in front of the class to present this reading. After the reading, ask the following questions:

1. What did this woman of Canaan—outside of Jewish territory—believe about Jesus? *(He is the promised Son of David; the Lord; the one who could cast out the evil spirit from her daughter.)*

2. Why did Jesus not give her an answer when she asked (v. 24)? *(He was sent to the lost sheep of Israel; He was testing the depth of her faith.)*

3. Why did Jesus expand His ministry beyond Israel? *(Because of the faith of this woman of Canaan; because He came to save all people.)*

4. When Jesus went up into the mountain near the Sea of Galilee, what miracles did He perform? *(He caused the lame to walk, the blind to see, the dumb to speak, the maimed to be made whole, and many others, vv. 30, 31.)*

5. How did the people react to Jesus' miracles? *(They wondered and glorified God, v. 31.)*

Into Life

State: "Once again we see Jesus' love and power reaching out to people in need. But there's a basic difference from the other miracles we've studied. Here, Jesus reaches beyond His usual circle to share God's love. If we were to reach beyond our usual circle to share Christ's love, whom would we reach?" As answers are given, write them on the chalkboard or transparency.

Say: "We cannot perform miracles to show Christ's love, but there are other ways Christ's love can be shown. Move into groups of three or four and develop a list of at least seven ways we can show Christ's love to these people." After a few minutes, ask for each group to share its list of suggested ways. *(Answers may include: provide food for those who are hungry, donate clothes to those who need them, provide transportation to church or the doctor, read to the blind, go shopping with/for the individual with a mobility impairment, invite the lonely into one's home, spend time with children of single parents, pay for special events for disadvantaged children, and others.)* Write these on the chalkboard or transparency sheet for all to see.

After listing the suggestions so that all can see them, state: "Here are many ways that we can share Christ's love with those beyond our usual circle. Jesus expanded His ministry beyond the Jews. We need to expand our ministry beyond our own church family." Encourage those in each group to select one way to reach beyond their usual circle of relationships this week.

Learners in each group should decide what they will do as a group to show Christ's love, to whom Christ's love will be shown, and when they will show it. Allow several minutes for these decisions. Then pass out markers and ask each group to write on a sheet of newsprint the answers to these "what," "to whom," and "when" questions. Use masking tape to mount these sheets on the wall as a public commitment to reach beyond the normal circle of friends. Close the class session by asking each group to have a brief prayer of commitment on behalf of the person or group who will be reached this week.

Let's Talk It Over

The questions on this page are designed to encourage review of the lesson Scriptures and to promote discussion of the lesson by the class. The answers provided are only discussion starters. Let your class talk it over from there.

1. The lesson writer suggests the disciples wanted Jesus to heal the woman to get rid of her. That seems like a case of doing the right thing with wrong motives. How can we today maintain a right attitude in ministry even when we are tired or frustrated?

Any person who comes to Christ believing that he is worthy or that she deserves the blessings God has promised comes in vain. We all must come honestly seeking no more than "crumbs" from our Father's table. He, of course, will give us much more than that, but not because we are deserving of it. The woman was humble enough that she did not react in anger to Jesus' apparent rebuff. She did not turn away in indignation. Instead, she accepted the implication that the richest blessings were not for her, and she asked for just a tiny bit of those benefits. She offers us a shining example of the truth found in James 4:10: "Humble yourselves in the sight of the Lord, and he shall lift you up."

2. Jesus had a clear concept of who it was to whom He had been "sent." How can we have such an assurance, to know when to accept a ministry opportunity and when to defer?

Jesus has sent His disciples to "the uttermost part of the earth" (Acts 1:8), but He has not sent every disciple to every place. Each of us must determine which specific part of the earth is the place to which we have been sent. Is the opportunity unique, to us alone, or will there be many who will take advantage of it? Is it an opportunity for which we are specially gifted or otherwise qualified, or will we be outside our area of expertise? Is it an opportunity that will vanish in a short time, or is it regularly available? These questions and others may help us determine to where we have been "sent."

3. A proud person might have been insulted by Jesus' remark. We could say this woman's faith was greater than her pride. What are some ways we today can overcome pride?

Along with her faith, this woman was motivated by love—love for her daughter. If we will truly act in love for those to whom we minister, we will keep pride in check, for love "seeketh not her own" (1 Corinthians 13:5). If we have a passion for spreading the gospel of Christ, then we will put Christ and His message of salvation first and not ourselves. Like Paul, we can then rejoice at the spread of the gospel even if the motives of others are less than honorable and even directed at harming our own reputations (Philippians 1:15-18). Appreciating the value of every member of the body of Christ is also helpful in this matter—see Romans 12:3-8.

4. The crowds beheld Jesus' miracles of healing, "and they glorified the God of Israel." How can we make such glorifying of God our aim?

Paul set forth an important principle for Christian living in Colossians 3:17: "Whatsoever ye do in word or deed, do all in the name of the Lord Jesus, giving thanks to God and the Father by him." Our choices are not always between the right and the wrong or the good and the bad. Very often the Christian finds that he or she must choose between the good and the better or the better and the best. When one makes it a habit to speak and to act in a way that can be said to be dedicated to God, then he or she will bring glory to God. Paul told the Corinthians, "All things are lawful for me, but all things are not expedient: all things are lawful for me, but all things edify not" (1 Corinthians 10:23). When we choose the things that edify, not just what is "lawful," we will honor God. So Paul concludes, "Whatsoever ye do, do all to the glory of God" (v. 31).

5. How can we express to non-Christians our disapproval of their sinful lifestyle without appearing to be harsh and judgmental?

We want to keep the lines of communication open with these people. If they perceive us as merely criticizing and condemning them, they will shut us out. Perhaps the best approach is to show them a better way. Do we have an acquaintance who is living with a friend of the opposite sex? We should be able to demonstrate that Christian marriage is far superior to that arrangement. Do we know someone who seeks thrills through drugs and alcohol? We should be able to point out that nothing is more satisfying than worshiping and serving God. Do we associate with a person who makes a habit of using profane and obscene language? We should be able to describe the advantages of a tongue yielded to God, a tongue dedicated to building others up.

Lazarus Is Raised

DEVOTIONAL READING: John 11:17-27.

BACKGROUND SCRIPTURE: John 11:1-44.

PRINTED TEXT: John 11:1-7, 11b-15, 38-44.

John 11:1-7, 11b-15, 38-44

1 Now a certain man was sick, named Lazarus, of Bethany, the town of Mary and her sister Martha.

2 (It was that Mary which anointed the Lord with ointment, and wiped his feet with her hair, whose brother Lazarus was sick.)

3 Therefore his sisters sent unto him, saying, Lord, behold, he whom thou lovest is sick.

4 When Jesus heard that, he said, This sickness is not unto death, but for the glory of God, that the Son of God might be glorified thereby.

5 Now Jesus loved Martha, and her sister, and Lazarus.

6 When he had heard therefore that he was sick, he abode two days still in the same place where he was.

7 Then after that saith he to his disciples, Let us go into Judea again.

. . . .

11b He saith unto them, Our friend Lazarus sleepeth; but I go, that I may awake him out of sleep.

12 Then said his disciples, Lord, if he sleep, he shall do well.

13 Howbeit Jesus spake of his death: but they thought that he had spoken of taking of rest in sleep.

14 Then said Jesus unto them plainly, Lazarus is dead.

15 And I am glad for your sakes that I was not there, to the intent ye may believe; nevertheless let us go unto him.

. . . .

38 Jesus therefore again groaning in himself cometh to the grave. It was a cave, and a stone lay upon it.

39 Jesus said, Take ye away the stone. Martha, the sister of him that was dead, saith unto him, Lord, by this time he stinketh: for he hath been dead four days.

40 Jesus saith unto her, Said I not unto thee, that, if thou wouldest believe, thou shouldest see the glory of God?

41 Then they took away the stone from the place where the dead was laid. And Jesus lifted up his eyes, and said, Father, I thank thee that thou hast heard me.

42 And I knew that thou hearest me always: but because of the people which stand by I said it, that they may believe that thou hast sent me.

43 And when he thus had spoken, he cried with a loud voice, Lazarus, come forth.

44 And he that was dead came forth, bound hand and foot with graveclothes; and his face was bound about with a napkin. Jesus saith unto them, Loose him, and let him go.

GOLDEN TEXT: Jesus said . . . I am the resurrection, and the life: he that believeth in me, though he were dead, yet shall he live: and whosoever liveth and believeth in me shall never die.—John 11:25, 26.

Lesson Aims

After this lesson a student should be able to:
1. Relate the details surrounding Jesus' raising of Lazarus from the dead.
2. Describe some ways in which people worked with Jesus in doing His miracles, and some ways in which we can work with Jesus today.
3. Express a commitment to work with God in Jesus' life-giving ministry.

Lesson Outline

INTRODUCTION
  A. Misconceptions
  B. Lesson Background
  I. SICKNESS (John 11:1-7)
    A. News of Lazarus (vv. 1-3)
    B. Jesus' First Response (v. 4)
    C. Waiting, Then Going (vv. 5-7)
  II. DEATH (John 11:11b-15)
    A. Figurative Words (vv. 11b-13)
    B. Plain Words (vv. 14, 15)
      A Delayed Blessing
  III. RESURRECTION (John 11:38-44)
    A. The Tomb (v. 38)
    B. Jesus' Request (vv. 39, 40)
      What Does the Future Hold?
    C. Calling to God (vv. 41, 42)
    D. Calling to the Dead Man (v. 43)
    E. Lazarus's Response (v. 44)
CONCLUSION
  A. Human Helpers
  B. Prayer
  C. Thought to Remember

Introduction

A story worth repeating has come down to us from the troubled centuries in Palestine just before the time of Christ. During a portion of those centuries, Israel was under the barbarous rule of Syrians who were determined to wipe out the Jewish religion. They defiled the temple in Jerusalem, using the sacred altar to sacrifice swine to pagan gods. Jews known for their devotion to God were summoned before the authorities and ordered to renounce their faith or die.

One of the Syrians' "tools" for persuading people to comply with their demands was a man-

sized frying pan under which a huge fire burned. Any Jew who refused to give up his faith was tossed into the pan, where he suffered horribly before he died.

One day three brothers were brought in for questioning. Their widowed mother was summoned as well. The Syrians hoped that she would plead with her sons to renounce their faith rather than leave her desolate. But the mother disappointed her captors. Passionately she urged her sons to cling to their faith regardless of the cost.

The oldest son then was thrown into the frying pan, where the others could watch him writhe until he died. White-faced but resolute, the second son reaffirmed his faith and was also thrown into the pan. The Syrians then urged the remaining son to think of his mother. Without him she would have no means of support. She would live in abject poverty—if she lived. She might starve to death.

With that, the young man broke from his captors, ran swiftly, and leaped into the pan.

A. Misconceptions

Two misconceptions about death have been held by thousands through the centuries and are held by thousands now.

One misconception is that death is the worst thing that can happen to someone. Many a person would lie, steal, kill, betray a friend, or even deny Christ if that would save his own life. What is left, he asks, if life is gone?

That misconception was courageously refuted by the Jewish heroes whose story is told above. They were convinced that giving up their faith in God was worse than dying. That conviction was strongly affirmed by Jesus: "Fear not them which kill the body, but are not able to kill the soul: but rather fear him which is able to destroy both soul and body in hell" (Matthew 10:28).

A second misconception is the belief that death is final and irreversible—that dead people stay dead forever. The text of today's lesson records a time when Jesus disproved that fallacy. Not much later He disproved it again when He Himself arose from the dead and ascended into Heaven. And one day all of us will see Him disprove it again (John 5:28, 29).

What comes after death is far more important than death itself.

B. Lesson Background

John 7:1 notes that Jesus had purposely stayed away from "Jewry" (a reference to Judea) because the Jewish leaders there were plotting to kill Him. However, verse 2 records that "the Jews' feast of tabernacles was at hand." Jesus proceeded to go to Jerusalem to observe that autumn feast (John 7:10). It seems that He stayed in that vicinity for more than two months, until the winter "feast of the dedication" (John 10:22, 23).

Within the record of what occurred during these two months, we are introduced to two sisters who lived in Bethany, a village just over the hill east of Jerusalem. Busy housekeepers can sympathize with practical Martha, who was overworked with "much serving" when she had to provide for a houseful of company. But Jesus said that the better choice was made by Mary, who found her delight in sitting at His feet and listening to Him (Luke 10:38-42).

The hostility of Jesus' enemies in Jerusalem increased during the time that He was there to observe the aforementioned feasts. Twice they picked up stones to stone Him, but He escaped (John 8:59; 10:31, 39). Following the second incident, Jesus went across the Jordan beyond their jurisdiction (John 10:40). During this period of withdrawal from the tension in Jerusalem, the incident mentioned in today's text occurred.

I. Sickness
(John 11:1-7)

While Jesus was staying east of the Jordan, the sisters from Bethany enter the story again. This time we also meet their brother, Lazarus.

A. News of Lazarus (vv. 1-3)

1. Now a certain man was sick, named Lazarus, of Bethany, the town of Mary and her sister Martha.

The nature of Lazarus's sickness is not mentioned, but the rest of the account indicates that it was a very serious one. His life was in danger.

2. (It was that Mary which anointed the Lord with ointment, and wiped his feet with her hair, whose brother Lazarus was sick.)

This anointing was done some time later (John 12:1-8). John mentions it here to help the readers identify *Mary*. The anointing was already known to many readers, for Matthew and Mark recorded it long before John wrote this record (Matthew 26:6-13; Mark 14:3-9). Those earlier writers did not mention Mary's name, however. John now reveals that she was the one whom the others wrote about. In this verse he also reveals that the *sick* man *Lazarus* was a *brother* of Mary and Martha.

3. Therefore his sisters sent unto him, saying, Lord, behold, he whom thou lovest is sick.

Lazarus's *sisters sent* word to Jesus of his illness, apparently dispatching a messenger to carry the news. It would be easy to find Jesus, for most likely there would be a crowd with Him.

John 10:41 and 42 note that "many resorted unto him" and "believed on him" while He was residing east of the Jordan.

The message conveyed to Jesus was simple: *Lord, behold, he whom thou lovest is sick.* We do not know whether the messenger proceeded to give details as to the identity of the sick person and the seriousness of his illness. *He whom thou lovest* may have been enough to identify the person as Lazarus, indicating the close friendship that existed between him and Jesus. [See question #1, page 48.]

The text does not report that the sisters asked Jesus to come and heal their brother. Perhaps they were afraid to ask, knowing Jesus' life would be in danger if He came anywhere near Jerusalem. Still, it seems obvious that they hoped He would come. Note how they both almost chided Jesus for not being there when Lazarus died (vv. 21, 32).

B. Jesus' First Response (v. 4)

4. When Jesus heard that, he said, This sickness is not unto death, but for the glory of God, that the Son of God might be glorified thereby.

The disciples probably also counted Lazarus a dear friend. Jesus assured them that *this sickness* would not bring *death* to Lazarus; it would bring *glory*, honor, and praise to *God* and to God's *Son*, Jesus. The disciples had seen many of Jesus' miracles and the praise that followed, so they must have taken Jesus' statement to mean that He was going to receive more praise by healing Lazarus.

C. Waiting, Then Going (vv. 5-7)

5. Now Jesus loved Martha, and her sister, and Lazarus.

All of these three were very dear friends of Jesus. John wanted his readers to be sure of that. Wouldn't such a fact prompt Jesus to get to Bethany as fast as He could to heal His friend? No, strange as it seems, it did not make Him hurry to the rescue. See the next verse.

6. When he had heard therefore that he was sick, he abode two days still in the same place where he was.

We are not told what Jesus did during these *two days*; we suppose that He continued the ministry that He had begun there (John 10:41, 42). It seemed that He was simply ignoring the urgent

---

How to Say It

BETHANY. *Beth*-uh-nee.
JUDEA. Joo-*dee*-uh.
LAZARUS. *Laz*-uh-rus.
SYRIANS. *Sear*-ee-uns.

message from Bethany. That did not appear to be the action one would expect of a dear friend, so John prefaced it with the assurance we saw in verse 5. [See question #2, page 48.]

7. Then after that saith he to his disciples, Let us go into Judea again.

The *disciples* must have been stunned to hear these words. If Jesus was going to *Judea* in response to the message from Bethany, why hadn't He gone when the message arrived? If the sickness was not going to be fatal, why go there at all? The disciples protested, reminding Jesus that some in Jerusalem were about to stone Him before He had left. But Jesus insisted that He must go on with His work, regardless of any danger (vv. 8-10).

II. Death
(John 11:11b-15)

Sometime between the time the messenger was sent to tell Jesus of Lazarus's condition and the time Jesus started toward Judea, Lazarus died. (Since the delay was only two days, but Lazarus had been dead four days when Jesus arrived [v. 39], Lazarus may already have been dead when the messenger reached Him.) Jesus knew of His friend's death, but the disciples did not. So Jesus told them the sad news.

A. Figurative Words (vv. 11b-13)

11b. He saith unto them, Our friend Lazarus sleepeth; but I go, that I may awake him out of sleep.

Many speakers and writers, both ancient and modern, have referred to death as *sleep*. But no one else could use that metaphor as appropriately as Jesus did, for no one else could wake the dead as easily as we can wake a sleeper.

12. Then said his disciples, Lord, if he sleep, he shall do well.

A person who is seriously ill may be kept awake by pain through long days and sleepless nights. When he relaxes and goes to *sleep*, we may first check his pulse to see if he is alive. But if pulse and breathing are normal, we breathe a sigh of relief. We know the crisis is past. The patient is getting better. That is what the *disciples* thought concerning Lazarus. If he was sleeping, he would be all right. There was no need to go back to Bethany—so close to Jerusalem, where vindictive enemies desired to kill Jesus (and perhaps His disciples as well).

13. Howbeit Jesus spake of his death: but they thought that he had spoken of taking of rest in sleep.

Carefully John explained the misunderstanding for his readers. Jesus had spoken figuratively, using *sleep* to mean *death*. But the disciples had taken the Lord's words literally, thinking Lazarus had fallen into a restful *sleep*.

B. Plain Words (vv . 14, 15)

14. Then said Jesus unto them plainly, Lazarus is dead.

Jesus then corrected the disciples' misunderstanding. Lazarus was *dead*.

15. And I am glad for your sakes that I was not there, to the intent ye may believe; nevertheless let us go unto him.

Jesus knew, not only that Lazarus was dead, but also that He was going to restore him to life. That resurrection would strengthen the disciples' belief more than a healing would have. For that Jesus was *glad*, because soon their belief would be severely tested by His own death.

Jesus had brought at least two persons back from death before this incident: the widow's son at Nain (Luke 7:11-17) and the daughter of Jairus (Luke 8:41-56). Perhaps the disciples should have realized that He intended to bring Lazarus back, but their minds were on something else when He spoke of going to Bethany. See verse 16, which is not included in our printed text. It shows that Thomas, and possibly the other disciples as well, were afraid that Jesus and all of them would be killed if they returned to Bethany. Still, they went, though probably with some apprehension.

A DELAYED BLESSING

The Owens River runs along the eastern side of California's Sierra Nevada range. In 1903 Los Angeles callously diverted the river southward, enabling the growth of Los Angeles into what eventually became today's megalopolis. Population growth in the valley was stifled, and Owens Lake dried up, becoming a source of occasional dust storms.

In effect, the Owens Valley "died" and became a relatively unpopulated area of America's most populous state. Recently, however, the courts have forced Los Angeles to give back some of the water to Owens Valley residents; yet there is still not much impetus for growth. Most of the current valley residents are quite happy with this situation. By causing the valley to "die," Los Angeles enabled it to stay isolated from the urban sprawl and pollution that characterizes much of southern California. In a sense, Owens Valley was given a new (and arguably better) life—it is still pristine, scenic, and undeveloped.

Jesus' delay in going to Bethany might have seemed callous at the time—as though it were a selfish refusal to respond immediately when a friend needed Him. However, it provided an opportunity for Lazarus and his family to enjoy the wonderful grace of his being brought back to life.

Sometimes, when God delays in answering our cries for help, the result can be blessings that we did not foresee—including the opportunity to grow into new levels of spiritual health. —C. R. B.

III. Resurrection
(John 11:38-44)

Verses 17-37 of this chapter record that Jesus arrived at Bethany and talked first with Martha, then with Mary. When Jesus asked where Lazarus was buried, Mary led Him and a throng of friends to the place. There Jesus wept along with the others. Though He knew Lazarus soon would be alive again, He shared the grief of the mourners.

A. The Tomb (v. 38)

38. Jesus therefore again groaning in himself cometh to the grave. It was a cave, and a stone lay upon it.

Jesus felt a new surge of grief *in himself* as He approached the burial place along with the other mourners. *It was a cave,* with *a stone* placed across the entrance. Among people who could afford it, the preferred burial place was not a *grave* dug in the ground and then filled with earth to cover the dead body. It was either a natural cave or a small chamber cut into solid limestone by stonecutters. Usually the stone around the entrance was cut to make a vertical face, resembling a wall. Then a large flat slab of stone was cut into a circular shape, like a wheel. This was rolled across the entrance to close the tomb (or rolled aside to open it). A groove wide enough to match the thickness of the wheel was cut in the ground to provide a track for the stone when it closed the entrance. [See question #3, page 48.]

B. Jesus' Request (vv. 39, 40)

39. Jesus said, Take ye away the stone. Martha, the sister of him that was dead, saith unto him, Lord, by this time he stinketh: for he hath been dead four days.

We do not know exactly how many people were present at this moment, but there were many (vv. 19, 31). There was no lack of manpower to move the heavy *stone.* However, practical *Martha* objected. After *four days* the body would be starting to decay. The smell would be offensive. Wouldn't this cause a fresh outburst of grief from the mourners? [See question #4, page 48.]

40. Jesus saith unto her, Said I not unto thee, that, if thou wouldest believe, thou shouldest see the glory of God?

This saying is not recorded in the account of Jesus' talk with Martha a little earlier, but He may have said more than is recorded. It seems that Martha was having an inner struggle between the

knowledge that dead people stay dead and the hope that Lazarus would rise that very day.

Her struggle is seen in verses 21-27. Martha believed that God could do anything Jesus asked (v. 22); but when Jesus promised that Lazarus would rise again, she thought He was speaking of the future day when all the dead will rise. She believed Jesus was the Christ, the Son of God (v. 27); so she believed whatever He said. But since He did not specifically say Lazarus would rise that day, it was hard for her to *believe* that he would.

Thus, when Jesus spoke of opening the grave, Martha's first thought was of a rotting corpse. Jesus promised that faith and hope would be rewarded with a glimpse of *the glory of God.* Did Martha dare believe that meant God would show His glory by bringing Lazarus back to life then and there? No doubt her inner struggle persisted.

WHAT DOES THE FUTURE HOLD?

"The man who saw the future" was an accolade given to R. Buckminster Fuller (1895-1983). This American inventor, engineer, and architect was compared to Leonardo da Vinci, the fifteenth-century Italian genius. On one occasion, Albert Einstein—a genius in his own right—said to Fuller, "Young man, you amaze me!" In the 1920s Fuller conceived of a house that would have solar power, television, air-conditioning, "seeing eye" doors, and a vacuum-cleaning system—none of which had yet been invented!

In his early years, Fuller was thought by many people to be a "crackpot" because his ideas seemed so far-fetched. However, with his 1952 invention of the geodesic dome, this all changed. Today Fuller's domes have a wide range of uses, including housing businesses, radar facilities, and private homes.

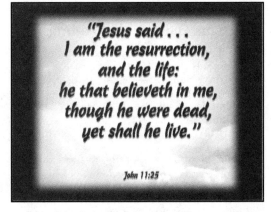

"Jesus said . . . I am the resurrection, and the life: he that believeth in me, though he were dead, yet shall he live."

John 11:25

Visual for lesson 5. *Use this attractive poster to illustrate today's Golden Text. You might also want to display it even after today's lesson is over.*

Lazarus's sister, Martha, believed that when Jesus told her that Lazarus would live again, He was referring to the final resurrection. But Jesus was someone who knew the future, both the long-term and (as seen in this incident) the short-term as well. Others may speculate on what the future holds (some, like da Vinci and Fuller, may do so quite well), but God alone holds the future in His hands. For those who believe in Him, it will be a blessed one.   —C. R. B.

C. Calling to God (vv. 41, 42)

41. Then they took away the stone from the place where the dead was laid. And Jesus lifted up his eyes, and said, Father, I thank thee that thou hast heard me.

The entrance to the cave was opened as Jesus had asked (v. 39). Then Jesus looked up to His *Father* in Heaven and gave thanks that His prayer had been *heard*—which seems to mean both *heard and answered*. Jesus was certain of the miracle that was about to take place.

42. And I knew that thou hearest me always: but because of the people which stand by I said it, that they may believe that thou hast sent me.

Jesus expressed His thanks for answered prayer *because of the people* who were hearing Him. In the next few minutes those people would see the answer to Jesus' prayer, and they would witness new evidence that God had *sent* Jesus and that Jesus was doing God's work.

D. Calling to the Dead Man (v. 43)

43. And when he thus had spoken, he cried with a loud voice, Lazarus, come forth.

No doubt *Lazarus* would have responded to Jesus' call if it had been expressed in a whisper or only in a thought. Like the thanks for answered prayer (v. 41), the *loud voice* was for the

benefit of the people standing by. They heard Jesus speak, and they would see Lazarus obey, though he had been dead for four days.

E. Lazarus's Response (v. 44)

44. And he that was dead came forth, bound hand and foot with graveclothes; and his face was bound about with a napkin. Jesus saith unto them, Loose him, and let him go.

At Jesus' command *he that was dead came forth*. Lazarus was *bound hand and foot with graveclothes* so that he could not walk, yet he *came forth*. His face was *bound about with a napkin* so that he could not see the door, yet he *came forth*. Can you imagine the stunned silence among the onlookers? But then Jesus issued a command to them: *Loose him, and let him go.* So some of those near Lazarus stepped forward to remove the graveclothes. Perhaps one of them took off his own outer garment to clothe the man once dead—now alive! [See question #5, page 48.]

Conclusion

A. Human Helpers

Jesus could do anything He wanted to do, but notice how often He asked humans to help Him. Sometimes He opened blind eyes with a touch or a word, but once He let a blind man stay blind until he found a pool and washed his sightless eyes. He could have given Lazarus clothing along with life, but He left that for bystanders to do.

It is not hard to think of modern examples of how God works with human helpers. God makes the wheat grow, but man plants the seed, harvests the crop, grinds the flour, and bakes the bread. God puts stone in the mountains, trees in the forests, and iron in the ground; but a house does not stand until men quarry the stone, cut the trees into lumber, make the iron into nails, and drive the nails with man-made hammers.

God made the many wonders of this fascinating world, and He designed mankind to use them. How wise we are when we cherish His gifts, conserve them, and use them well! We are winners when we work with God, and we are losers when we work against Him.

B. Prayer

What a wonderful world You have given us, O God, and how wonderfully You have equipped us to use it! Today we pledge ourselves anew to seek Your will in all we do, with both the material things around us and the people around us. May we daily work with You. In Jesus' name, amen.

C. Thought to Remember

Work with God, not against Him.

Home Daily Bible Readings

Monday, Sept. 24—Healed by Sinner or Prophet? (John 9:13-17)

Tuesday, Sept. 25—Once Blind, Now I See (John 9:18-25)

Wednesday, Sept. 26—Who Sees? Who Is Blind? (John 9:26-41)

Thursday, Sept. 27—Lazarus Dies (John 11:1-16)

Friday, Sept. 28—"I Am the Resurrection" (John 11:17-27)

Saturday, Sept. 29—"If You Had Been Here . . ." (John 11:28-37)

Sunday, Sept. 30—The Dead Man Came Forth (John 11:38-44)

Learning by Doing

This page contains an alternate lesson plan emphasizing learning activities.
Classes desiring such student involvement will find these suggestions helpful.

Learning Goals

After this lesson each student will be able to:

1. Relate the details surrounding Jesus' raising of Lazarus from the dead.

2. Describe some ways in which people worked with Jesus in doing His miracles, and some ways in which we can work with Jesus today.

3. Express a commitment to work with God in Jesus' life-giving ministry.

Into the Lesson

Prior to class prepare a large poster board with the following stimulus statement written on it: "Death is . . . ." Attach two markers on a string to the poster and place the poster where it will be easily seen near the door to the classroom. As students arrive, ask them to write a one- to three-word response to the phrase on the poster. *(Possible answers: "final, permanent, scary, fearful, unwelcome, overcome by Jesus.")* When all the students arrive, move the poster to the front for all to see. Review the graffiti statements. Say: "Death does elicit many different reactions. Today we see several in our lesson text. Open your Bibles to John 11, and let's read about these reactions."

Into the Word

Ask three students to read the three sections of the text, John 11:1-7, 11b-15, 38-44. Then review this miracle by asking the following questions:

1. After hearing that Lazarus was sick, how long did Jesus delay? *(Two days, v. 6.)*

2. Who would be glorified through this illness? *(God; God's Son, v. 4.)*

3. Why did Martha resist the command to take away the stone from Lazarus's grave? *(By this time "he stinketh," v. 39.)*

4. How many days had Lazarus been dead when Jesus arrived? *(Four days, v. 39.)*

5. What effect was this miracle of raising Lazarus from the dead meant to have on the disciples? *(To increase their belief in Jesus, v. 15.)* What effect on those who witnessed this miracle? *(To lead them to believe that God sent Jesus to the world, v. 42.)*

Say: "This miracle involved more than Jesus' just speaking a word. Others were involved in working with Jesus to complete this miracle. How did Jesus involve others in this miracle? *(Some removed the stone from the cave, v. 41;*

some removed the graveclothes, v. 44). Let's review four of the miracles we've studied to discover other ways people worked with Jesus when He performed miracles." Divide the class into four groups, and assign each group one of these passages: John 2:1-11, water into wine; Matthew 14:14-21, feeding of the five thousand; Mark 3:1-6, man with withered hand; John 9:1-12, man born blind. After giving several minutes to read and to list the ways others were involved in helping Jesus, ask for each group to report its findings.

State: "Several Scriptures also illustrate this 'working with Jesus.'" Ask volunteers to read 1 Corinthians 3:9; 2 Corinthians 5:18-20; 6:1. After this reading, point out that we are God's fellow workers in a ministry of reconciliation.

Into Life

Say, "We have the privilege of working with Jesus in His life-giving ministry. Let's take a few minutes to consider the ways we can work with Jesus today." As ideas are suggested, write them on the chalkboard or overhead transparency so that all can see the many ways available. *(Some possibilities: invite someone to church, conduct a Bible study, pray daily for someone who is outside of Christ, greet and get acquainted with visitors at church, share the message of salvation).*

Have the class evaluate your church on the extent to which you work with Jesus in the ministry of reconciliation. Ask, "Where would you place us on a scale of 1 (no effort) to 10 (regular effort)?" Ask for suggested answers. Then ask each class member to evaluate himself in the matter of being God's fellow-worker.

Say: "As you can see, there is room for improvement in our working with Jesus. Now I'd like for you to look at the list of possible ways we noted on the board (or overhead) and select one in which you are not currently involved. Then I want to encourage you to complete a commitment worksheet expressing your decision to get involved in Jesus' life-giving ministry." Prior to class, put the following commitment on a sheet of paper and make a copy for each student. "Dear Father, In recognition of Jesus' desire that we work with Him in His life-giving ministry, I now commit myself to _____ during the next four weeks." Ask your students to complete the statement and date it for later personal reference.

Let's Talk It Over

The questions on this page are designed to encourage review of the lesson Scriptures and to promote discussion of the lesson by the class. The answers provided are only discussion starters. Let your class talk it over from there.

1. Lazarus could be identified to Jesus as "he whom thou lovest." What is the value of such endearing friendships among believers? How can we cultivate such a relationship?

God's declaration concerning Adam, "It is not good that the man should be alone" (Genesis 2:18), indicates that people have a social nature. We are made to interact with one another. Even Jesus felt the need for a few close friends to minister to His social needs. Having an especially close friend is important for the times when we need someone in whom we can confide. Such a one can hold us accountable for our behavior and help to pick us up when we fall.

The fellowship of the church helps us to meet that need today. One way to cultivate such friendships is simply to be present where other committed believers assemble. Regular Sunday school and worship attendance, then, is important for social reasons as well as spiritual. Involvement in a small group is also important.

2. When we read John 11, we are initially puzzled by Jesus' slowness in responding to Mary and Martha's message regarding the illness of Lazarus. But later we see how perfect Jesus' timing was. What does this indicate to us about God's responses to our prayers?

How slowly do the answers come to some of our prayers! We wait and wait, and we are tempted to give up; but we hold on to our confidence that the answer will ultimately come. Several of your students can probably recall some previous prayer experiences in which the answer arrived at just the right time. The new job one needed, the improvement in an area of family conflict for another, victory over another's troublesome temptation, the surge of growth in our church—whatever it was, it came to fruition in an unexpected but timely manner. Discuss how often it seemed as if the one praying was at a "dead end" just before experiencing the victorious outcome.

3. When Jesus approached the tomb of Lazarus, He was "groaning in himself." Since Jesus knew He would raise Lazarus to life, why was He so emotionally moved?

Perhaps He was affected less by the reality of death than He was by the sorrow that accompanies the death of a loved one. The first mention of His emotional response to this circumstance occurs in John 11:33. It was when He saw Mary and her friends weeping that "he groaned in the spirit, and was troubled." And two verses later we find that brief, but touching, statement: "Jesus wept." So it seems to have grieved and disturbed Him to see so much sorrow in His friends' hearts. If we would follow Jesus' example, we will connect emotionally to others and "rejoice with them that do rejoice, and weep with them that weep" (Romans 12:15).

4. With His divine power Jesus could have moved the stone from the entrance to the tomb before calling Lazarus back to life. Instead, He asked for men to remove the stone. Suggest some possible reasons why He did this.

The moving of the stone with a mere command would have been an impressive miracle, but the raising of Lazarus was a greater one. Jesus wanted to focus people's attention on that. Also, this miracle is similar to others Jesus performed in which He required some step of obedience from the persons involved. Had Martha continued her objection to opening the tomb and had the men refused to do what Jesus commanded, there may have been no miracle. But they cooperated with Jesus, and something tremendous took place.

5. Jesus claimed to be the Son of God, and He proved that claim through His miracles. How can our familiarity with these claims help us?

Many people today follow a Jesus whom they see as merely human. He was, according to their thinking, an extraordinary man, an exceptional teacher, and an influential religious leader—but still just a man. We know that such a viewpoint is flawed. Unless Jesus was and is the Son of God, His death has nothing to do with our sins. Unless He was and is the Son of God, His promises to be with His church throughout history and to return ultimately in judgment are pointless. So we must be very clear as to His deity. We must join Peter in an intelligent and bold proclamation of Him as "the Christ, the Son of the living God" (Matthew 16:16). We must thrill to Paul's assertion in Romans 1:4 that Jesus was "declared to be the Son of God with power, according to the Spirit of holiness, by the resurrection from the dead."

Jesus Teaches in Parables

DEVOTIONAL READING: Matthew 13:18-23.

BACKGROUND SCRIPTURE: Matthew 13:1-35.

PRINTED TEXT: Matthew 13:1-13, 16, 34, 35.

Matthew 13:1-13, 16, 34, 35

1 The same day went Jesus out of the house, and sat by the sea side.

2 And great multitudes were gathered together unto him, so that he went into a ship, and sat; and the whole multitude stood on the shore.

3 And he spake many things unto them in parables, saying, Behold, a sower went forth to sow;

4 And when he sowed, some seeds fell by the wayside, and the fowls came and devoured them up:

5 Some fell upon stony places, where they had not much earth: and forthwith they sprung up, because they had no deepness of earth:

6 And when the sun was up, they were scorched; and because they had no root, they withered away.

7 And some fell among thorns; and the thorns sprung up, and choked them:

8 But other fell into good ground, and brought forth fruit, some a hundredfold, some sixtyfold, some thirtyfold.

9 Who hath ears to hear, let him hear.

10 And the disciples came, and said unto him, Why speakest thou unto them in parables?

11 He answered and said unto them, Because it is given unto you to know the mysteries of the kingdom of heaven, but to them it is not given.

12 For whosoever hath, to him shall be given, and he shall have more abundance: but whosoever hath not, from him shall be taken away even that he hath.

13 Therefore speak I to them in parables: because they seeing see not; and hearing they hear not, neither do they understand.

. . . .

16 But blessed are your eyes, for they see: and your ears, for they hear.

. . . .

34 All these things spake Jesus unto the multitude in parables; and without a parable spake he not unto them:

35 That it might be fulfilled which was spoken by the prophet, saying, I will open my mouth in parables; I will utter things which have been kept secret from the foundation of the world.

GOLDEN TEXT: Therefore speak I to them in parables: because they seeing see not; and hearing they hear not, neither do they understand.—Matthew 13:13.

Jesus' Ministry
Unit 2: Truth in Parables
(Lessons 6-9)

Lesson Aims

After this lesson a student should be able to:
1. Give the important details of the parable of the sower, and tell what Jesus said about why He taught in parables.
2. Explain the significance of the different kinds of soil in the parable of the sower.
3. Suggest one way he or she can be a better "hearer."

Lesson Outline

INTRODUCTION
  A. Hidden Truth
  B. Lesson Background
  I. PARABLE OF THE SOWER (Matthew 13:1-9)
  A. The Setting (vv. 1, 2)
  B. The Parable (vv. 3-9)
    Spiritual Gardens
  II. PURPOSE OF PARABLES (Matthew 13:10-13, 16)
  A. Disciples' Question (v. 10)
  B. Jesus' Answer (vv. 11-13, 16)
  III. PROPHECY OF PARABLES (Matthew 13:34, 35)
  A. Sermon in Parables (v. 34)
  B. Prediction From Psalms (v. 35)
    More Than a Fad
CONCLUSION
  A. The Hard-packed Path
  B. The Stony Ground
  C. The Thorns
  D. The Good Ground
  E. The Crucial Question
  F. Prayer
  G. Thought to Remember

Introduction

"Hide and Go Seek" was the name we gave to a favorite game at our country school. Shrubbery and outbuildings provided wonderful hiding places near "home base" and far away. To find a hidden child and then win the race to "home base" was a joyous triumph for the one who was designated "it."

A. Hidden Truth

Certainly Jesus did not want to prevent anyone from learning the truth. Like His Father in Heaven, He "will have all men to be saved, and to come unto the knowledge of the truth" (1 Timothy 2:3, 4). Yet, just as healthy, active children find joy in "Hide and Go Seek," adults of strong and healthy minds find joy in seeking after truth; and they value truth all the more when they have searched diligently for it. So to make the truth more interesting, more effective, and more memorable, Jesus sometimes hid it in a parable.

The degree of "seeking" necessary to find the truth in Jesus' parables varies. Matthew 13:31-33 presents the short parables of the mustard seed and of the leaven. In each of these the hidden truth is not hard to find, and Jesus left us to seek it without any help. Next week we shall consider a longer parable—the parable of the good Samaritan (Luke 10:25-37). Jesus followed it with a simple question that led one of His adversaries to acknowledge the lesson Jesus wanted to teach.

In today's lesson we consider the parable of the sower (Matthew 13:3-9). Its message was well hidden, but Jesus unveiled it plainly to seekers who cared enough to ask (Matthew 13:18-23; Mark 4:10).

B. Lesson Background

Our text from Matthew 13 describes an incident that took place a little past the midpoint of Jesus' three-and-a-half-year ministry. In it the word *parables* appears for the first time in Matthew's Gospel. This does not mean that Jesus had never used a parable before, but it does seem that He increased His use of parables at this time. Both Matthew and Mark note that on this occasion Jesus taught only in parables (Matthew 13:34; Mark 4:34). In particular, the parable of the sower so caught the disciples' attention that they asked Jesus why He was using parables in His teaching (Matthew 13:10).

"Repent: for the kingdom of heaven is at hand" (Matthew 4:17). Thus did Matthew summarize Jesus' early teaching in Galilee. Jesus, in His Sermon on the Mount, spoke plainly about the attitudes, the thinking, and the conduct appropriate for people who belong to God's kingdom. Sincere disciples drew closer to Jesus as they tried to follow His instructions, but it appears that more of the hearers liked their selfish way of living and saw no need to repent. Many of them thronged about Jesus solely to be entertained and amazed by His miracles. Many of them seem to have followed Jesus in the hope that He would organize an armed rebellion and throw off the rule of Rome; but they too had no thought of repenting and changing their way of living.

As we shall see in today's study, Jesus used parables as a means of separating true seekers from those interested only in the excitement created by His miracles. Sadly, most of those in the multitudes that thronged about Jesus were not interested in doing His will, but in getting Him to do their will. They missed the real message of His parables. Genuine seekers after truth did not.

I. Parable of the Sower (Matthew 13:1-9)

For about a year Jesus had been teaching in Galilee. He was by far the most popular teacher there. People gathered about Him by the thousands, but they came with different attitudes, different intentions, and different hopes.

A. The Setting (vv. 1, 2)

1. The same day went Jesus out of the house, and sat by the sea side.

Mark's account notes that Jesus had gone into a *house* (Mark 3:19). However, the people who were gathering about Him were so numerous that He and they needed more space. So Jesus moved outside to the wide shore *by the* Sea of Galilee.

2. And great multitudes were gathered together unto him, so that he went into a ship, and sat; and the whole multitude stood on the shore.

Even on the open shore the people pressed so closely about Jesus that only those very near Him could see Him at all. Jesus solved that problem by getting into a boat and pushing out from the shore. Thus separated from the crowd, He could be seen by most of the people.

Contrary to modern custom, this preacher *sat* down while the audience remained standing. We wonder if some or all of the twelve disciples were in the boat with Jesus, but we are not told.

B. The Parable (vv. 3-9)

3. And he spake many things unto them in parables, saying, Behold, a sower went forth to sow.

Most of Matthew 13 is filled with some of the *parables* Jesus used in teaching *many things* that day. The first parable—about a farmer sowing seed—is the one we are studying this week. Probably most of Jesus' hearers knew how sowing seed was done. Holding a bag or basket of seed in front of him, the *sower* would walk across a field, taking handful after handful of the seed and scattering (or "broadcasting") it on the earth. Some students suggest that a farmer in the distance may have been doing this as Jesus began to speak, thus giving the Master Teacher a visual aid.

4. And when he sowed, some seeds fell by the wayside, and the fowls came and devoured them up.

The wayside was not a berm by a highway; it was a footpath through the fields. In the process of a farmer's random sowing, *some seeds fell* on this ground, which was trodden hard by many passing feet. On it the seeds lay exposed, and *fowls* (birds) soon ate them.

Jesus' explanation of this parable is omitted from our printed text in order to make room for a discussion of why Jesus used parables; but we can read it in verses 18-23 of this chapter. The hard path represented an individual who heard Jesus' message with his ears, but did not take it into his mind and heart. As birds soon took seed from the path, "the wicked one" (the devil) quickly snatched Jesus' teaching from the memory of a hearer and it was forgotten (v. 19). [See question #1, page 56.]

5, 6. Some fell upon stony places, where they had not much earth: and forthwith they sprung up, because they had no deepness of earth: and when the sun was up, they were scorched; and because they had no root, they withered away.

The *stony places* were not places with scattered stones on or near the surface; they were places with solid rock not far below the surface. The shallow soil was warm and—in the first few weeks after the rainy season had ended—moist. The seed sprouted quickly and tiny green plants soon appeared. But days of sunshine soon dried all the moisture out of that shallow soil, and the plants *withered*. This soil represented a person who responded enthusiastically to Jesus' call to repent, and began a new and better way of living. But when he found that the better way was not always easy or convenient, his shallow devotion withered (vv. 20, 21). [See question #2, page 56.]

7. And some fell among thorns; and the thorns sprung up, and choked them.

The seed that *fell among thorns* was not sown among thorn bushes, but among thorns that were only seeds hidden in the ground. When the seed started to sprout and grow, so did the thorns. They grew faster, thicker, and stronger than whatever was sown, and soon the desired growth was *choked* and crowded out.

This represented a person in whom Jesus' preaching was unfruitful because that individual was preoccupied by "the care of this world, and the deceitfulness of riches" (v. 22). [See question #3, page 56.]

8. But other fell into good ground, and brought forth fruit, some a hundredfold, some sixtyfold, some thirtyfold.

The *good ground* was not all alike. The more fertile soil produced a hundred times as much as was sown; some less fertile soil produced only thirty times as much. But all the good soil produced as much as it could. This soil represented the people who heard Jesus' message, took it to heart, and lived by it. The fact that some did more good than others reflects the different abilities that different individuals possess, but all of them did what they could (v. 23).

9. Who hath ears to hear, let him hear.

Thus Jesus challenged the people to *hear* and understand and obey, so that they would produce the fruit of godly living.

SPIRITUAL GARDENS

Henry Beard and Roy McKie wrote a book entitled, *Gardening: A Gardener's Dictionary*. To anyone who has battled bugs and dreaded drought in hopes of getting some homegrown vegetables, their tongue-in-cheek definitions have the ring of truth.

Here are some of them. *Garden*: "A free outdoor restaurant operated by the charity-minded to provide meals for insects, birds, and animals." *Annual*: "Any plant that dies before blooming." *Perennial*: "Any plant which, had it lived, would have bloomed year after year." *Nursery*: "The only known place where money grows on trees." *Seed*: "Highly nutritious form of bird food sold in handsome packets."

Jesus' listeners knew about such matters as these. Many or most of them "gardened," but not as a pastime or an amusement. It was their primary means of putting food on their tables. They had no difficulty understanding the vital importance of good soil. They knew how birds, weeds, and hard ground could severely limit an anticipated harvest.

Even if we aren't farmers or gardeners, Jesus' words are clear enough that we should have no difficulty applying them to our circumstances. We should be moved to ask, "What kind of soil and growing conditions does my soul offer for God's Word?" —C. R. B.

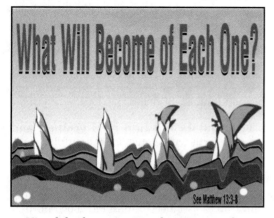

Visual for lesson 6. *Use this poster to discuss the potential of each seedling—each disciple. Note that a good beginning is not enough.*

II. Purpose of Parables
(Matthew 13:10-13, 16)

Both Matthew and Mark tell of this occasion when Jesus used a number of parables in teaching a multitude, and "without a parable spake he not unto them" (Matthew 13:34; Mark 4:33, 34). The twelve disciples did not interrupt that continued teaching, but saved their questions until Jesus was alone with them and some others (Mark 4:10). Matthew includes one of these questions immediately after his record of the first parable. It appears in the next section of our printed text.

A. Disciples' Question (v. 10)

10. And the disciples came, and said unto him, Why speakest thou unto them in parables?

The *disciples* were puzzled. With a huge crowd listening, Jesus did not teach as He had done in the Sermon on the Mount. All He did was tell a lot of simple little stories about ordinary happenings. Even His closest followers did not understand the lessons that those stories were intended to teach. It looked to them as if a great opportunity was being wasted. *Why* did Jesus teach this way?

B. Jesus' Answer (vv. 11-13, 16)

11. He answered and said unto them, Because it is given unto you to know the mysteries of the kingdom of heaven, but to them it is not given.

In the language of the New Testament, *mysteries* are not puzzling situations to be solved by clever detective work. They involve matters that can be known only by God's revealing them. No one can search them out; one must be told or he will never know. Jesus was revealing great truths about the *kingdom of heaven* to His disciples, but not to the multitudes of people who cared little or nothing about those truths. Knowledge of the kingdom's mysteries was *given* to the disciples because they wanted it, not because they were Jesus' "favorites." It was *not given* to most of the people in the crowds because they were not interested in it.

12. For whosoever hath, to him shall be given, and he shall have more abundance: but whosoever hath not, from him shall be taken away even that he hath.

The disciples had a genuine interest in Jesus' teaching; thus they had a growing knowledge of matters pertaining to the kingdom of Heaven. The parables would add to that knowledge, and the disciples would *have more abundance*. Most of the people who heard Jesus were more impressed with His manner of teaching (Matthew 7:28, 29) than with His message. Since they cared little about the truth He taught, whatever they heard was soon *taken away*, or forgotten.

13. Therefore speak I to them in parables: because they seeing see not; and hearing they hear not, neither do they understand.

These words describe those who were part of the careless, curious crowd that came to Jesus to see the miracles He did rather than to learn the truth He taught. They were like the hard-packed soil "by the wayside" (v. 4). The priceless truth of Jesus fell on their ears, but did not sink into their minds and hearts; so it was soon forgotten. [See question #4, page 56.]

16. But blessed are your eyes, for they see: and your ears, for they hear.

The disciples resembled the good ground in Jesus' parable (v. 8). They received Jesus' example and His teachings into their minds and hearts. They shaped their lives by what they learned, and they became fruitful in their service to the Master. They did not understand all that Jesus meant by the parable of the sower; but they were willing to ask Him about it (Luke 8:9), and He explained it to them (Matthew 13:18-23).

Such a blessing was not given to the twelve disciples alone; others were with them to ask and receive the explanation of the parable of the sower from Jesus (Mark 4:10). It seems, then, that anyone who cared enough to seek further instruction from Jesus could share the blessing of understanding the truth of His message.

III. Prophecy of Parables (Matthew 13:34, 35)

Jesus' use of parables was not an afterthought. The Spirit of God foretold it in the words of Psalm 78:2. This is a psalm of Asaph, one of David's chief musicians (1 Chronicles 16:4, 5; 2 Chronicles 5:12).

A. Sermon in Parables (v. 34)

34. All these things spake Jesus unto the multitude in parables; and without a parable spake he not unto them.

Again we are reminded that on this occasion Jesus' teaching was solely *in parables*. Matthew records eight of them. Mark records only four, but two of the four are not found in Matthew. Mark ends this part of his account by saying, "With many such parables spake he the word unto them" (Mark 4:33). Thus Jesus used more parables than are recorded in the Scriptures.

B. Prediction From Psalms (v. 35)

35. That it might be fulfilled which was spoken by the prophet, saying, I will open my mouth in parables; I will utter things which

---

> **How to Say It**
> ASAPH. *Ay*-saff.
> GALILEE. *Gal*-uh-lee.
> SAMARITAN. Suh-*mare*-uh-tun.

have been kept secret from the foundation of the world.

The lines quoted from Psalm 78:2 are Asaph's promise of what he was going to do in that psalm. But at this point Asaph was a *prophet* inspired by God: these lines were also a prophecy of what Jesus would do centuries later by teaching *in parables*. In the chapter we are reading this week, Matthew gives a partial record of how this prophecy was *fulfilled*.

MORE THAN A FAD

Tamagotchis (Tam-uh-*got*-cheez) were a short-lived fad among the younger generation during the late 1990s. You may have missed them if you didn't have children or grandchildren in the right age group at the time. A Tamagotchi was one of several forms of electronic "pets" that needed "feeding" and other forms of attention lest it "die" a "virtual" death (in computer talk).

When the fad died, a Web site opened on the Internet, offering white satin-lined caskets in which to bury the "virtual pets." For a total of twenty dollars, one could also add a tiny tombstone with the "animal's" name on it! Included with the casket and tombstone was a suggested eulogy for an appropriate burial ceremony.

Some of us may find ourselves confessing that the meaning of this phenomenon was (and remains) a mystery to us. Or, if there is a meaning there, it is a very obscure one!

Matthew explains Jesus' use of parables as more than just a "fad" that distinguished His teaching style. By using parables, Jesus was fulfilling a prophecy in the Psalms. Although the meaning of His parables was hidden from the spiritually blind, it was available to those who were sincere seekers after spiritual truth.

Two millennia separate us from Jesus' earthly ministry, but His message is still clear to those who seek, not just "virtual" life, but *eternal* life.

—C. R. B.

Conclusion

Many students have noted that the parable of the sower might fittingly be called the parable of the soils. The sower did his work well, but the results depended on the ground that received the seed. This means little to us unless we take it personally. What kind of soil are you?

A. The Hard-packed Path

George has been going to church regularly ever since he was a baby. He enjoys it. Sunday is his favorite day of the week. He never would have guessed that he was not a good listener. But then his wife was seriously injured in an accident and was unable to leave the house for a month.

Soon after George came home from church one Sunday, his wife asked him what the sermon had been about. To his surprise, George did not know. He remembered a joke the preacher told, but that was all.

"I guess I wasn't listening," George confessed ruefully. "I'm like that hard-packed dirt in the parable. The message just didn't sink in."

The next week, George took a pocket notebook to church. He wrote the sermon title, the main points, and a summary of what the preacher said about each point. He even recorded the joke. When he went home, his report to his wife was nearly as long as the preacher's sermon.

Only three weeks later, George gave the same kind of report without even looking at his notebook. Better than that, he thought of the sermon every day that week. Often it helped him decide what to do. George had become good ground.

B. The Stony Ground

A Sunday school class of young couples without children decided they had more leisure time than most parents had, so they ought to be helping other people. They announced in some of the other adult classes that they were available for baby-sitting, for visiting the sick (to help with housework and yard work), and for maintenance work with the church house and grounds.

Soon calls for help were coming to the class secretary, and she was passing them on to class members. They were delighted. They were helping people, and it felt good!

Six months later, the secretary complained in a class meeting. Too often the members found it inconvenient to answer calls for help. Too often the secretary and her husband had to respond themselves. They were becoming overburdened. Upon hearing this, class members were ashamed. They knew they had been refusing many calls for help. Their helpfulness was like the seed on stony ground. After a glorious start, it had withered.

The class project had been great fun in the beginning, so, they reasoned, the thing to do was to begin again every week. They tried that, and the project became fun again.

C. The Thorns

Is that a thorn? When John and Mary became Christians, they asked that question about some of their activities. Their weekly evening at the tavern was a thorn, they decided. The more they learned of Christian activities, the more that evening disgusted them. So they eliminated it from their lives.

Tennis did not appear to be a thorn. It provided clean fun, good exercise, and pleasant companionship. But John and Mary's tennis club became a thorn when it began to meet on Sunday morning. So they rooted it out of their lives. When they began to play tennis with Christian friends, they found the same fun and exercise and even more pleasant companionship. [See question #5, page 56.]

D. The Good Ground

John and Mary were delighted to find themselves surrounded by Christians who were growing and producing the fruit of Christian service. Mary soon found her field of service in the nursery. John was a construction worker, and his expertise helped maintain the large church building. They both applied themselves to Bible study, and in a few years they became joint teachers of a class of young people.

E. The Crucial Question

Now comes the crucial question, and it is a personal one: *what kind of ground are you?* You can be good ground if you want to.

F. Prayer

Our Father in Heaven, how good it is that Your Son has taught us the difference between good ground and bad. Grateful for His leading, today and every day we promise our best efforts to follow Him and to produce fruit that will bring glory to You. In the Master's name. Amen.

G. Thought to Remember

You can be better than you are.

Home Daily Bible Readings

Monday, Oct. 1—Parable of Tares Among Wheat (Matthew 13:24-30)
Tuesday, Oct. 2—Parable of Wheat and Tares Explained (Matthew 13:36-43)
Wednesday, Oct. 3—Kingdom of Heaven Is Like . . . (Matthew 13:31-33, 44-46)
Thursday, Oct. 4—More Kingdom Parables (Matthew 13:47-53)
Friday, Oct. 5—Ears to Hear (Mark 4:21-29)
Saturday, Oct. 6—Parable of the Sower Explained (Matthew 13:18-23)
Sunday, Oct. 7—So He Told a Parable (Luke 15:1-10)

Learning by Doing

This page contains an alternate lesson plan emphasizing learning activities.
Classes desiring such student involvement will find these suggestions helpful.

Learning Goals

After participating in this lesson, each student will be able to:

1. Give the important details of the parable of the sower and tell what Jesus said about why He taught in parables.

2. Explain the significance of the different kinds of soil in the parable of the sower.

3. Suggest one way he or she can be a better "hearer."

Into the Lesson

Prepare a copy of the following word-find activity for each student. State: "Today we begin class with a word-find puzzle. Four words of at least four letters are hidden. Find all four."

```
S G A W N T A L
I E Z S E S E U
G P L A F O D P
U J N B K W E F
S E H C A E T V
O S X D O R E E
Q U I G R H A J
M S Z A U N B P
```

After a time, ask the class to identify the words: *Jesus, teaches, parables, sower.* Say: "Many people like puzzles and the challenge of solving them. Today's lesson is, 'Jesus Teaches in Parables.' In a sense, Jesus' parables were puzzles. Let's turn to Matthew 13."

Into the Word

Ask a class member to read the lesson text aloud. Then ask the following questions:

1. What were the four types of ground where the seed fell? *(Wayside; Stony; Thorny; Good.)*

2. What happened to the seed in each type of ground? *(Wayside—birds ate the seed; stony—scorched and withered away; thorny—choked out; good—bore fruit.)*

3. What were the differences within the good soil? *(The same seed produced more in some good soil than in other good soil.)*

4. Why did Jesus teach in parables? *(Fulfillment of prophecy, v. 35; mysteries of the kingdom were given to the disciples, not to the crowds, v. 11.)*

State: "Now let's read Jesus' interpretation of this parable in Matthew 13:18-23." Ask for a vol-unteer to read the passage. Discuss the following questions:

5. What are the similarities among the four soils in Jesus' interpretation? *(All hear the Word; the Word and the kingdom are the same; the Word is sown.)*

6. What does a person's understanding of the Word have to do with the kingdom? *(Understanding is necessary for faith and for bearing fruit, vv. 19, 23. See also Romans 10:17.)* State: "Using this parable, Jesus communicated the importance of understanding the Word of God."

7. What factors hindered or eliminated the possibility of the seed bearing fruit? *(Failure to understand the Word; tribulation or persecution; care of this world; the deceitfulness of riches.)*

Into Life

Ask the class to move into groups of three. State: "Now that we have studied the text and understood it, we need to think about its application to our lives. Without giving any names, think of someone you know, perhaps from another congregation, who can be identified with one of the four soils indicated here. Tell your group something about the person and how you see a similarity with a particular type of ground." After several minutes, ask and discuss the following questions:

1. What types of "tribulation or persecution" arise today because of the Word? *(Answers may include: lawsuits prohibiting prayer or religious symbols in school; rejection from peers; ridicule of a person's faith.)*

2. How do the "care of this world" and the "deceitfulness of riches" choke the Word? *(Distraction to hearing and understanding.)*

3. What different results did hearing the Word produce? *(Understanding; depth of faith; fruit-bearing.)*

State: "As you clearly see, hearing the Word is only the first step. Yet, it is a vital step to bearing fruit. The question we want to reflect upon is: How can people become better hearers of the Word today?" As answers are suggested, write them on the board or an overhead transparency sheet. Ask the class, "What do you need to do to improve your hearing of the Word? Spend the next few minutes reflecting upon this question, and then share your decision with someone sitting next to you." Close the lesson in prayer.

Let's Talk It Over

The questions on this page are designed to encourage review of the lesson Scriptures and to promote discussion of the lesson by the class. The answers provided are only discussion starters. Let your class talk it over from there.

1. The "wayside" hearer is easily distracted when listening to sermons or Bible lessons. Thinking about events that follow the service or noticing the antics of a nearby child, the odd way another worshiper is dressed, or some peculiar mannerisms of the speaker can cause a person to lose sight of the message being communicated. How can we make sure we are being good listeners and not being distracted by such matters?

One of the most important things we should do in this pursuit—and one often overlooked—is to come to worship or Sunday School well rested. Drowsiness is one of the most common reasons worshipers and class members are unable to stay focused on the message. We need to make our participation in the Lord's Day activities enough of a priority that we get a good night's rest the night before. Another helpful way to stay focused is to take notes. It may seem futile at first, as it is difficult to catch all the salient points of a message. But with a little persistence, one will find that he or she learns how to listen for key points and can thus produce a fairly detailed outline.

2. The hearers represented by the stony places are prone to hearing only part of what is being taught. They love to hear messages on love, peace, and joy, but not about commitment, sacrificial service, or perseverance in the face of trial. How can we be sure we are not acting like the "stony" hearers? How can such hearers be challenged to listen to the more "difficult" messages?

When we find we do not "like" a particular message, we need to examine ourselves and determine why not. Is the message unbiblical? Was the presentation disorganized and incoherent? These are valid reasons for not liking a message, and they may provide a good reason to discuss it, in the spirit of love and edification, with the speaker. But if we don't like the message because it challenges our comfort zone or exposes our own shortcomings, then we need to repent and ask God to help us make our "soil" a little deeper!

3. The hearers represented by the thorny soil are people who need to do some weeding in their spiritual gardens. How can we do this?

This idea is suggested in James Allen's famous book, *As a Man Thinketh*. In a garden we quickly recognize any weeds that have sprung up near our vegetables. We employ our hoe or our hand to uproot the undesirable plant. Similarly we should be able to recognize any unholy thought, motive, or attitude that springs up in our mind. Bible study helps to make us alert to the appearance of sin. Once we make this identification, we can uproot the offensive thought, banish it from our mind, and plant a wholesome, Christlike thought in its place (Philippians 4:8).

4. Compare Jesus' reason for using parables (v. 13) with the idea of preaching so-called "seeker-sensitive" sermons—messages aimed especially at those who do not have a church background and know little about the Bible.

To some, this concept means preaching that does not offend or challenge unbelievers. It is the religious counterpart to political correctness. Jesus did not practice such a plan. His messages were challenging; only the most discerning and interested really understood them. At one point, virtually all His followers left Him because His message was too difficult (John 6:60, 66). But Jesus was truly "seeker" sensitive. Only those who really were seeking the truth would catch it. But these seekers had to be actively pursuing the truth, not just sitting comfortably hoping to be entertained.

5. The thorns that interfere with our understanding and applying God's Word may be things that are innocent in themselves. How can we learn to eliminate such things in order to leave ourselves adequate time and energy for what is most important?

Many forms of recreation are legitimate and wholesome: reading, attending good films or concerts, playing games, etc. Christians can also profitably participate in various kinds of volunteer service: at crisis pregnancy centers or nursing homes, in organizations that combat pornography or drug abuse, or with missionary support groups. But we dare not let these keep us from our involvement with God's Word. The key to working this out is to plan our schedules by first allotting time for public and private worship. Then we can set aside reasonable segments of time for recreation and for service. Of course, we will probably be faced with saying "no" to friends and associates who endeavor to draw us back into schedule-straining activities.

The Good Samaritan

DEVOTIONAL READING: Deuteronomy 15:7-11.

BACKGROUND SCRIPTURE: Luke 10:25-37.

PRINTED TEXT: Luke 10:25-37.

Luke 10:25-37

25 And, behold, a certain lawyer stood up, and tempted him, saying, Master, what shall I do to inherit eternal life?

26 He said unto him, What is written in the law? how readest thou?

27 And he answering said, Thou shalt love the Lord thy God with all thy heart, and with all thy soul, and with all thy strength, and with all thy mind; and thy neighbor as thyself.

28 And he said unto him, Thou hast answered right: this do, and thou shalt live.

29 But he, willing to justify himself, said unto Jesus, And who is my neighbor?

30 And Jesus answering said, A certain man went down from Jerusalem to Jericho, and fell among thieves, which stripped him of his raiment, and wounded him, and departed, leaving him half dead.

31 And by chance there came down a cer-tain priest that way; and when he saw him, he passed by on the other side.

32 And likewise a Levite, when he was at the place, came and looked on him, and passed by on the other side.

33 But a certain Samaritan, as he jour-neyed, came where he was; and when he saw him, he had compassion on him,

34 And went to him, and bound up his wounds, pouring in oil and wine, and set him on his own beast, and brought him to an inn, and took care of him.

35 And on the morrow when he departed, he took out two pence, and gave them to the host, and said unto him, Take care of him: and whatsoever thou spendest more, when I come again, I will repay thee.

36 Which now of these three, thinkest thou, was neighbor unto him that fell among the thieves?

37 And he said, He that showed mercy on him. Then said Jesus unto him, Go, and do thou likewise.

GOLDEN TEXT: [Jesus asked] Which now of these three, thinkest thou, was neighbor unto him that fell among the thieves? And he said, He that showed mercy on him.
—Luke 10:36, 37.

Lesson Aims

After participating in this lesson, a student should be able to:

1. Describe the occasion for the parable of the good Samaritan and retell the parable.

2. Contrast the lawyer's desire to identify his neighbor with Jesus' command to *be* a neighbor.

3. Identify one person to whom he or she can be a neighbor, and state one specific act of kindness that will be done this week.

Lesson Outline

INTRODUCTION
  A. A Real Neighbor
  B. Lesson Background
 I. OPENING QUESTION (Luke 10:25-28)
  A. "What About Eternal Life?" (v. 25)
  B. Jesus' Question (v. 26)
  C. Correct Answer (vv. 27, 28)
    Rightness or Relationship?
 II. HARDER QUESTION (Luke 10:29-35)
  A. "Who Is My Neighbor?" (v. 29)
  B. Answer in a Parable (vv. 30-35)
III. CLOSING QUESTION (Luke 10:36, 37)
  A. "Who Was the Neighbor?" (v. 36)
  B. Correct Answer (v. 37a)
  C. Application (v. 37b)
    And Then Came the Hard Part
CONCLUSION
  A. The Broadening Field
  B. Selectivity
  C. Another Kind of Choice
  D. Prayer
  E. Thought to Remember

Introduction

When at last the county paved the dirt road by our farm, that road had to be closed for a long time. When we wanted to leave the farm, we had to drive to the end of our lane and then half a mile across the fields to a neighbor's drive that led us to another road.

That was the route my brother and I took early one evening when we started out to a young people's party at church. Carefully we had kept the irrigating water off the field that we would cross, but our neighbor had not been so careful. Not long after reaching his field, we found our wheels spinning in deep mud.

We broke branches from the cottonwood trees and pushed them under the wheels, hoping for traction enough to get us to solid ground; but progress was very slow. Soon it was apparent that we were going to miss the party. My brother was expected to direct some of the activities there, so he hiked half a mile back home to make his excuses by telephone.

I was still working to no avail with the branches when my brother returned. Close behind him came a neighbor with a team of horses to pull our car out of the mud. How did he know about our predicament? His wife had been eavesdropping on the party line. She had heard my brother's telephoned excuse. Just at that moment her husband had come in from the field, his team still harnessed after the day's work. Without hesitation, he had hurried to help us.

A. A Real Neighbor

That man who helped my brother and me out of the mud lived up to the Old Testament meaning of *neighbor*. In New Testament Greek, as in English, the word *neighbor* is related to the word *near*. A neighbor is one who lives nigh, or nearby. But in Old Testament Hebrew, the word *neighbor* is related to the verb that describes what a shepherd does for his sheep. Our English version often translates that verb *feed*, but a shepherd does far more than feed his sheep. He leads them to still waters as well as green pastures. He gives them periods of rest after feeding (Psalm 23:1, 2). He carries lambs too young to keep up with the flock; he takes care to keep pregnant ewes from overexertion (Isaiah 40:11). If necessary, he risks his life to protect the sheep from predators such as lions and bears (1 Samuel 17:34-36). From that same verb comes the name of one who gives similar care to people. That is the word that we usually translate *neighbor*.

The farmer who was neighbor to our family lived up to that name, and he lived near us as well. In the text of today's lesson Jesus tells a story about a man who lived up to that Hebrew name, though he did not live near the man he helped.

B. Lesson Background

At the time Jesus spoke the parable of the good Samaritan, He was in or near Jerusalem. For a long time He had avoided that area because the opposition of scholars and politicians was most fierce there (John 7:1). But about six months before He was to be crucified, Jesus came boldly into that hotbed of hostility to attend the autumn Feast of Tabernacles (John 7:2, 14). It seems that

He stayed in that vicinity for more than two months, observing the winter Feast of Dedication (John 10:22, 23). During those months, Jesus evaded attempts to arrest Him (John 7:32, 45, 46; 10:39) and to stone Him (John 8:59; 10:31). But there was no evasion when some of the nation's most skilled debaters stood up to challenge Him. Jesus met each challenge and won each debate. One of those challenges is recorded in our text.

I. Opening Question
(Luke 10:25-28)

A. "What About Eternal Life?" (v. 25)

25. And, behold, a certain lawyer stood up, and tempted him, saying, Master, what shall I do to inherit eternal life?

Seldom do we see the word *lawyer* in the New Testament. More often the scholars well-versed in the law are called *scribes*. Perhaps the lawyers were scribes who specialized in debate, in controversy, or in especially difficult cases.

Our text says that this lawyer *tempted* Jesus. In today's English we could say *tested* instead of *tempted*. The lawyer was testing Jesus to see how well He knew the Scriptures and the Jewish traditions. No doubt he was hoping to catch Jesus saying something erroneous or questionable so he could accuse Him of ignorance or untruth.

What shall I do to inherit eternal life? That was the lawyer's question. The Old Testament is not very clear about this matter, but there are a few plain indications that the dead will rise (Job 19:25, 26; Isaiah 26:19; Daniel 12:2, 3). From these arose a belief in resurrection and eternal life, which was denied by the Sadducees but affirmed by the Pharisees (Acts 23:8) and the common people (John 11:24). The lawyer asked what he should do to have eternal life after his death.

B. Jesus' Question (v. 26)

26. He said unto him, What is written in the law? how readest thou?

Jesus answered the lawyer's question by asking a question in return. It was reasonable to ask

---

How to Say It

DENARII (Greek). dih-*nair*-ee or dih-*nair*-eye.
GALILEE. *Gal*-uh-lee.
JERICHO. *Jair*-ih-ko.
JUDEA. Joo-*dee*-uh.
LEVITE. *Lee*-vite.
PHARISEES. *Fair*-ih-seez.
SADDUCEES. *Sad*-you-seez.
SAMARITAN. Suh-*mare*-uh-tun.

---

such a question, for the lawyer prided himself on his knowledge of *the law*. What answer did he find *written* there for the question he had asked?

C. Correct Answer (vv. 27, 28)

27. And he answering said, Thou shalt love the Lord thy God with all thy heart, and with all thy soul, and with all thy strength, and with all thy mind; and thy neighbor as thyself.

Eternal life depended on keeping God's commandments—all of them. Apparently this lawyer and his fellow lawyers had concluded that all the commandments were summed up in the two commandments he quoted—from Deuteronomy 6:5 and Leviticus 19:18. In other words, one who fully kept those two commandments would keep all the others as well. That was a valid conclusion. Jesus Himself affirmed it a little later in answer to another lawyer's question (Matthew 22:34-40).

28. And he said unto him, Thou hast answered right: this do, and thou shalt live.

Regardless of the answer the lawyer expected or hoped for, he must have been surprised to hear a reply so brief, so approving, so conclusive. All he had to do to inherit eternal life was what he himself knew and believed—what he had learned from the law he cherished. All he had to *do* was to keep God's commandments.

We Christians may be just as surprised by Jesus' reply. Don't we come to eternal life by God's grace and our faith rather than by what we do (Ephesians 2:8, 9)? Isn't it true that no one is justified by keeping God's commandments (Romans 3:20)? Haven't we all failed in keeping His commandments (Romans 3:23)?

Yes, that is true. But Jesus and the lawyer were talking during a time before that was revealed—before Jesus died in our place. Before offering the gift of eternal life, God gave the law, and perfect obedience to that law would lead to life. But no one could keep the law well enough to earn eternal life (Romans 7:12, 13; 8:3). In this way, the law demonstrated our need for a Savior (Galatians 3:23, 24). We all deserved to die, but God sent Jesus to die in our place, offering us life as a gift.

That plan, however, was yet to be carried out. The lawyer correctly described the offer that was in effect at that time, and Jesus agreed with him. [See question #1, page 64.]

RIGHTNESS OR RELATIONSHIP?

The legal profession is one of several about which people enjoy telling jokes. One of the reasons for this is the tendency of lawyers to complicate issues with careful definitions of terms that often confuse the person who is untrained in "legalese."

You may have heard the story about a doctor, an engineer, and a lawyer who were arguing over whose profession was the oldest. "God took one of Adam's ribs and created Eve," said the doctor. "So that makes Him a surgeon first." The engineer said, "Before that, God created the world from chaos and confusion, so He was first an engineer." "Interesting," said the lawyer smugly, "but who do you think created the chaos and confusion?"

Apparently the lawyer who questioned Jesus was trying to create confusion—or at least find a way to discredit Jesus (as a lawyer today might do to a witness testifying in court). Of course, we need those who can define certain terms carefully. At times, having such information may be crucial. However, the person who tries to define his or her relationship to God and fellow human beings legalistically is missing the point. That is what Jesus wanted the lawyer to see, both through leading him to quote the law of Moses (Luke 10:27) and telling him the parable of the good Samaritan.

Goodness, as well as eternal life, is about more than rightness; it is also about relationships—with God and others. —C. R. B.

II. Harder Question
(Luke 10:29-35)

A. "Who Is My Neighbor?" (v. 29)

29. But he, willing to justify himself, said unto Jesus, And who is my neighbor?

The law of Moses did not provide an exact definition of *neighbor*. Thus, if the lawyer's neighbors were only scribes and Pharisees who supported and helped one another, then perhaps he could claim that he loved them as himself. Then he could *justify himself*, or claim to be just according to the law he had quoted.[See question #2, page 64.]

B. Answer in a Parable (vv. 30-35)

30. And Jesus answering said, A certain man went down from Jerusalem to Jericho, and fell among thieves, which stripped him of his raiment, and wounded him, and departed, leaving him half dead.

Jesus answered this next question of the lawyer with an illustration rather than a definition. The journey *from Jerusalem to Jericho* covered approximately seventeen miles. It literally *went down* through mountainous country that provided ideal hiding places for bandits, who could ambush a traveler. Along that road *a certain man* was attacked by *thieves*. They took all he had, including the *raiment* (clothing) he was wearing. Viciously they beat him half to death, and left him naked, bleeding, and semi-conscious by the road.

31. And by chance there came down a certain priest that way; and when he saw him, he passed by on the other side.

Like many of us when confronted with someone else's trouble, the *priest* did not want to get involved. We can imagine the excuses he may have made for not stopping to help.

• The robbers might still be close at hand; he had better leave right away.
• He had no first-aid material or expertise, so what could he do?
• It looked as if the man was dead or dying, and probably beyond help at this point.
• The priest had an appointment in Jericho; there was no time to delay.
• The wounded man was none of his business anyway.

Any of these would be excuse enough for a man who did not want to get involved in the first place. [See question #3, page 64.]

32. And likewise a Levite, when he was at the place, came and looked on him, and passed by on the other side.

A *Levite* was an assistant to priests. He was more accustomed to getting his hands dirty with unpleasant menial tasks. Perhaps he would be more likely to help a man lying in his own blood. But no, he too just *looked* and went on by. He did not want to get involved either.

33. But a certain Samaritan, as he journeyed, came where he was; and when he saw him, he had compassion on him.

The Samaritans lived in an area between two Jewish regions, north of Judea and south of Galilee. They were the descendants of those people who had been displaced by Assyrian deportations in the eighth century B.C., people of mixed blood and—worse—mixed religion. There had been ill will between the Jews (Judeans) and Samaritans since the return from Babylonian captivity (see Ezra 4), and it had not cooled in Jesus' day. John 4:9 notes, "The Jews have no dealings with the Samaritans." One Samaritan village refused to let Jesus and His disciples pass through (Luke 9:51-53). A *Samaritan* would hardly be expected to help a Jew in trouble. But this Samaritan was different; unlike the Jews who had preceded him down the road, he *had compassion*. He *saw* a fellow human being in trouble, and he wanted to help.

34. And went to him, and bound up his wounds, pouring in oil and wine, and set him on his own beast, and brought him to an inn, and took care of him.

Gladly the Samaritan used whatever he had for the welfare of the man in need. *Wine* (or any alcoholic drink) is a time-honored antiseptic for emergency use. The *oil* was most likely olive oil;

it was soothing to the *wounds* that the man had sustained. We suppose the Samaritan must have torn up a portion of his own clothing to use as bandages. He probably used some of it to cover the man's nakedness.

After treating the man's injuries, this kind Samaritan placed him *on his own beast*, doubtless a donkey. Thus he would have walked beside the donkey to the nearest *inn*, where he saw that the man had a comfortable place to sleep.

35. And on the morrow when he departed, he took out two pence, and gave them to the host, and said unto him, Take care of him: and whatsoever thou spendest more, when I come again, I will repay thee.

On the morrow the Samaritan went on his way, but he did not ignore the continuing need of the wounded man. *Two pence* is literally "two denarii," which would have been two days' pay for a working man (Matthew 20:2). If the wounded man's needs required *more* than that amount, the Samaritan promised to *repay* the *host* on his return trip. [See question #4, page 64.]

III. Closing Question
(Luke 10:36, 37)

The Master Teacher was finished with His illustration. Now it must be translated into application in order to answer the question that the lawyer had raised (v. 29).

A. "Who Was the Neighbor?" (v. 36)

36. Which now of these three, thinkest thou, was neighbor unto him that fell among the thieves?

Sometimes a parable hid the truth, as we saw in the lesson last week. A hearer had to search for

"Inasmuch as ye have done it unto one of the least of these my brethren, ye have done it unto me."
Matthew 25:40

Visual for lessons 7 and 9. *Discuss how the class can be involved in such "neighborly" ministries as helping in the situations pictured here.*

the truth, or wait until it was revealed by the one who gave the parable. But in this case, the parable made the truth so plain that no one could miss it; and that too is one of the purposes of parables.

B. Correct Answer (v. 37a)

37a. And he said, He that showed mercy on him.

The lawyer gave the right answer, as any thoughtful person could have done. It was the only possible answer to the question Jesus asked. The Samaritan showed himself to be a neighbor in the basic meaning of the Hebrew word noted earlier in the Introduction. He took care of the wounded man as a shepherd takes care of sheep, providing whatever kind of care is needed.

C. Application (v. 37b)

37b. Then said Jesus unto him, Go, and do thou likewise.

Then swiftly came the application of the lesson: *Go, and do thou likewise.* Notice that the lawyer was still one step short of an answer to the question he had raised. He had asked, "Who is my neighbor?" Jesus had answered with a parable picturing a Samaritan as a neighbor, a helper, a caregiver. Who was the Samaritan's neighbor? Obviously he was the wounded man, the man who needed care.

Then Jesus told the lawyer to do as the Samaritan had done, to be a neighbor, a helper, a caregiver. Who, then, was the lawyer's neighbor? Obviously he was anyone who needed care—care that the lawyer could give, care that he would be glad to give if he really loved his neighbor as himself. [See question #5, page 64.]

AND THEN CAME THE HARD PART

At the end of 1999, as the world was gearing up for giant "Y2K" celebrations, the nation of Israel was carefully watching several groups of what were termed "millennial Christian" extremists. Late in October, Israeli police had arrested twenty foreigners—thirteen of them Americans—who were members of two Christian groups suspected of plotting violence in order to "hasten the return of Christ"!

All of the people arrested on this occasion were in Israel illegally, either with expired visas or without passports. The Israelis suspected that they might bomb the mosques on the Temple Mount or commit mass suicide as a means of fomenting trouble.

It always seems easier to do some "great thing" that will draw public attention to your cause than it is to live by the gospel day in and day out. Jesus' call to love your neighbor is rather tame stuff when your theology tells you to create chaos in hopes of hastening the Lord's return. It is actually harder to live the Christian life by patiently demonstrating the love of Christ to our neighbors, than it is to rally around a cult leader who is firing up our passions with calls to go out and create havoc in the name of the Lord!

The lawyer who prompted Jesus' parable of the good Samaritan gave the right answer to the question, "Which man was the neighbor to the victim of the thieves?" But the hard part came when Jesus said to him (and to us), "Now, *you* go and be a neighbor."   —C. R. B.

Conclusion

A. The Broadening Field

Who is my neighbor? The lawyer who stood up and questioned Jesus on this occasion was trying to "narrow the field," to designate only a few people as neighbors whom the Lord commanded him to love—perhaps only the Pharisees, or possibly only a part of the Pharisees.

Jesus turned that thinking around. An unnamed man waylaid on the Jericho road was a neighbor to be loved and helped by a passing Samaritan. That implied that the lawyer had to "broaden the field" to include all the needy of a needy world, particularly anyone whom he had the ability and opportunity to help.

How that broad field is multiplied before us today! Daily we learn of people impoverished by hurricanes and earthquakes, or of the pitiful starving children orphaned by civil war or ethnic cleansing. The vastness of the needs tends to paralyze us. We cannot help them all—but does that mean we can ignore them all?

B. Selectivity

Recently, during a single week, the mail brought me more than twenty appeals for money.

Home Daily Bible Readings

Monday, Oct. 8—Your Neighbor in Need (Deuteronomy 15:7-11)
Tuesday, Oct. 9—Sad, for He Was Rich (Luke 18:18-25)
Wednesday, Oct. 10—Follow Now; Don't Look Back (Luke 9:57-62)
Thursday, Oct. 11—Hidden From the Wise (Luke 10:17-24)
Friday, Oct. 12—Love God (Deuteronomy 6:4-9)
Saturday, Oct. 13—Love Your Neighbor (Leviticus 19:13-18)
Sunday, Oct. 14—Who Is My Neighbor? (Luke 10:25-37)

I thought every one of them came from a reputable enterprise—well managed and doing a great work for needy people. And there may be twenty more such appeals next week, and the next. If I would send a mere ten dollars to each of them, I couldn't pay my rent.

How do I choose among so many good and helpful enterprises? First, I look for enterprises that are definitely Christian, that give glory to God rather than to human beings. "Let us do good unto all men, especially unto them who are of the household of faith" (Galatians 6:10). Among the definitely Christian enterprises, I favor those involving people I know. Don't you? I favor a Christian college where some members of the faculty and staff are my long-time friends. I favor missionaries who used to be members of my home church. I favor an orphans' home and school that I visited when my niece was its school nurse. Why do I favor those enterprises? It is not just because I like the people involved in them. It is because I know those people to be loyal to the Lord, capable in their service, and unfailing in their devotion.

C. Another Kind of Choice

A multiplicity of needs confronts us. We cannot meet them all. Which one or ones shall we choose? They are so many and so urgent! The easy way is to mind our own business, to go on our way and ignore them all.

The parable in our text presents a different kind of choice. A suffering man, lying in his blood by the roadside, offered that choice to every passerby. The priest and the Levite did not want to get involved. The Samaritan did.

An injured man is trapped in his crumpled car, from which a hit-and-run driver has fled. By another road, an elderly lady stands alone, looking helplessly at her flat tire. In the mall, a terrified child is separated from his parents. A well-groomed dog, complete with license tag, follows your children home. Will you get involved?

In the brief encounter recorded in our text, Jesus twice issued the imperative *do* (vv. 28, 37). Are we listening? Are we *doing*?

D. Prayer

Dear Father, we are shamed by our failure to follow the example of Your Son, Jesus. Responding to the call of our need, He left Heaven's glory to die on the cross. Help us, we pray, to see and seize every glorious opportunity to answer the call of need and thus to serve our Savior. In His name, amen.

E. Thought to Remember

"Go, and do thou likewise."

Learning by Doing

This page contains an alternate lesson plan emphasizing learning activities.
Classes desiring such student involvement will find these suggestions helpful.

Learning Goals

After participating in this lesson, each student will be able to:

1. Describe the occasion for the parable of the good Samaritan and retell the parable.

2. Contrast the lawyer's desire to identify his neighbor with Jesus' command to *be* a neighbor.

3. Identify one person to whom he or she can be a neighbor, and state one specific act of kindness that will be done this week.

Into the Lesson

Post this statement before class begins: "God gives eternal life to those who love Him with all their heart, soul, strength, and mind!" Prepare also four signs: "Strongly Agree," "Mildly Agree," "Mildly Disagree," and "Strongly Disagree" to be placed in the four corners of the classroom, with "Strongly Agree" and "Strongly Disagree" diagonally across the room. Begin by asking the class to stand and focus their attention on the statement that you display. Say: "Quickly make a decision as to how much you agree or disagree with it. Then go to the corner of the room under the sign that best represents your opinion." After the class relocates under the signs, ask each group to discuss the reasons for its opinion. Give about two minutes. Then ask each group to express its opinion. After hearing each group, let the students return to their seats. Say: "In our lesson text today, Luke 10:25-37, Jesus stated how important love for God is to inheriting eternal life. Then He gave the well-known parable of the good Samaritan. Let's read the text and look for the setting in which this parable was given."

Into the Word

Ask a member of the class to read aloud Luke 10:25-37. Note that it is easy to miss the contextual setting of this parable. Then ask the following questions:

1. What was the setting in which Jesus gave this parable? *(A lawyer asked Jesus a question about inheriting eternal life, v. 25.)*

2. What was the lawyer trying to accomplish? *(He wanted to test Jesus' knowledge of Scripture and tradition, v. 25; he wanted to justify himself, v. 29.)*

3. What happened to the man who traveled from Jerusalem to Jericho? *(He was robbed, stripped, beaten, and left to die, v. 30.)*

4. Why would the priest and the Levite who saw the injured man not help him? *(Possible answers: They didn't want to get involved; they had no compassion; robbers might still be near; they had no first-aid experience; they didn't have time; they did not want to become "unclean.")*

5. Why did the Samaritan help the injured man? *(He had compassion for the needy, v. 33.)*

6. What did the Samaritan do for the injured man? *(He bound up his wounds, pouring oil and wine on them; put him on his donkey; took him to an inn and took care of him overnight; paid for his continued care, vv. 34, 35.)*

7. Why do you think Jesus answered the question, "Who is my neighbor?" with this parable and the command to "Go, and do thou likewise"? *(The question, "Who is my neighbor?" restricts our getting involved to those who are neighbors. It implies that to some people compassionate care would not be given. Jesus simply commands, "Be a neighbor.")*

8. According to Jesus, who is our neighbor? *(Anyone who is in need of help.)*

Into Life

Say: "The message of this parable has yet to penetrate many Christians' hearts and lives. What are situations today where Christians have 'passed by on the other side'?" *(Passing a car broken down along the highway; ignoring news of great disasters around the world; not responding to needs in the ministries of the church.)* Ask the class to turn to Matthew 22:36-40; read it. Say: "Jesus says that all the law and the prophets hang on loving God and loving your neighbor as yourself. Needs are everywhere: major catastrophes strike; houses are burned; people are homeless and hungry; mission projects need financial backing. Sending money is a worthy demonstration of being a neighbor. But we may lose the personal element of actually helping someone in need. What about the people who live near you? What are their needs? For us to ignore needs is to 'pass by on the other side.'" Ask the class to think of a specific person and a specific act of kindness for this person. Give several minutes to decide. Ask members of the class to complete a pledge card committing to be a neighbor this week in a specific way for a specific person. State: "By loving God and your neighbor as yourself, you'll demonstrate God's love anew!"

Let's Talk It Over

The questions on this page are designed to encourage review of the lesson Scriptures and to promote discussion of the lesson by the class. The answers provided are only discussion starters. Let your class talk it over from there.

1. The two great commandments in Luke 10:27 instruct us to love God wholeheartedly and to love our neighbors as ourselves. How are these Old Testament commands particularly applicable to Christians?

Of course, the keeping of them is not our means to gaining eternal life. We receive salvation from our sin and the gift of eternal life by accepting God's grace extended to us through Jesus Christ. But it can be said that because of experiencing that amazing grace, we have a greater incentive for loving God with all our heart, soul, strength, and mind. Furthermore, that love for God should lead us to the kind of obedience God expects of Christians. It should stir us to an active love for the rest of His children. We Christians have a greater incentive for lavishing on our neighbors deeds of kindness, words of encouragement, and prayers of support.

2. The lawyer wanted more to "justify himself" than to do what was right. How do people today justify themselves when they are wrong? How can we be sure we are not guilty of justifying ourselves when we are in the wrong?

The whole concept of "no absolutes" is an attempt to justify any behavior. If nothing is "wrong," then one is justified in whatever he or she wants to do. Another way of justifying oneself is to accuse the person who exposes our sin of equal or even greater sin. Somehow we think this excuses our own behavior.

Sometimes it is difficult to be objective and to accept criticism even when it is needed. Perhaps we need a trusted friend whom we can count on to be both honest and nonjudgmental. When we are criticized, we can ask that one, "Am I really guilty of that?" Our friend can advise us and help us find a solution.

3. To hear a story with a Samaritan playing the role of hero, morally superior to Jewish leaders, must have been repugnant to the Pharisees. What group or class is it hard for us to love? Why? How can we be better neighbors?

Do we grind our teeth in disgust when a pornographer makes the news for "defending the right to free speech"? Are we inflamed with anger when we watch on television as a group of gay rights advocates make fresh demands? How do we

feel about terrorists who wreak death and injury on innocent people with their guns and bombs? These are people who desperately need our prayers and, if possible, our help. Therefore, they are our neighbors. If we make up our minds to act in love toward them, our emotions are likely to follow. It is difficult to harbor hatred toward someone for whom we are fervently praying. The temptation to hate will fade if we express God's love to these people in person or through the medium of letters or cards.

4. We marvel at the Samaritan's instructions to the innkeeper. He accepted the risk that the innkeeper or the injured man might take advantage of his benevolence. What kinds of risks do we take in being "good Samaritans" today, and how should we view these risks?

How do we know when we stop to assist someone with a disabled automobile that we will not become the victim of a crime? What is the danger that, in offering aid to an injured person, we will end up being sued? These are very real possibilities today. However, we cannot shrink from helping people because we fear their taking advantage of us. Indeed, we should equip ourselves to help them. It is good to make sure that we have in our cars a set of booster cables, a tire-repair kit, and the like. It is good to learn CPR and first-aid techniques. If we have a cell phone, we can use it to summon help for a variety of needs, especially those we are not able to supply.

5. Jesus' words "Go, and do thou likewise" have powerful implications. What are some practical ways we can do "likewise"?

It is so easy to settle into a comfortable and complacent kind of Christianity. In the church we are tempted to lapse into a "caretaker ministry," basking in our fellowship and failing to make a genuine effort to reach out to our community. Jesus' charge stirs us to begin looking for people to whom we can be neighbors: shut-ins who hunger for companionship, young children who need help in staying out of trouble, illiterate persons who can be encouraged to learn, alcoholics who need support in overcoming their addiction, and the like. There are various ways in which we can demonstrate that we love our neighbors as ourselves.

Parables on Prayer

DEVOTIONAL READING: Genesis 32:22-30.

BACKGROUND SCRIPTURE: Luke 18:1-14.

PRINTED TEXT: Luke 18:1-14.

Luke 18:1-14

1 And he spake a parable unto them to this end, that men ought always to pray, and not to faint;

2 Saying, There was in a city a judge, which feared not God, neither regarded man:

3 And there was a widow in that city; and she came unto him, saying, Avenge me of mine adversary.

4 And he would not for a while: but afterward he said within himself, Though I fear not God, nor regard man;

5 Yet because this widow troubleth me, I will avenge her, lest by her continual coming she weary me.

6 And the Lord said, Hear what the unjust judge saith.

7 And shall not God avenge his own elect, which cry day and night unto him, though he bear long with them?

8 I tell you that he will avenge them speedily. Nevertheless, when the Son of man cometh, shall he find faith on the earth?

9 And he spake this parable unto certain which trusted in themselves that they were righteous, and despised others:

10 Two men went up into the temple to pray; the one a Pharisee, and the other a publican.

11 The Pharisee stood and prayed thus with himself, God, I thank thee, that I am not as other men are, extortioners, unjust, adulterers, or even as this publican.

12 I fast twice in the week, I give tithes of all that I possess.

13 And the publican, standing afar off, would not lift up so much as his eyes unto heaven, but smote upon his breast, saying, God be merciful to me a sinner.

14 I tell you, this man went down to his house justified rather than the other: for every one that exalteth himself shall be abased; and he that humbleth himself shall be exalted.

GOLDEN TEXT: He spake a parable unto them to this end, that men ought always to pray, and not to faint.—Luke 18:1.

Jesus' Ministry

Unit 2: Truth in Parables

(Lessons 6-9)

Lesson Aims

After completing this lesson, a student should be able to:

1. Summarize the two parables in today's Scripture and the lesson Jesus drew from each.

2. Tell why the attitudes of persistence and humility are so important in one's prayer life.

3. Evaluate one's own prayer life to see whether persistence and humility have their proper place, and suggest one way to improve it.

Lesson Outline

INTRODUCTION

  A. Why?

  B. Perplexed About Prayer

  C. Lesson Background

 I. PERSISTENT PRAYER (Luke 18:1-8)

  A. A Parable's Message (v. 1)

  B. A Bad Judge (v. 2)

  C. A Widow's Plea (v. 3)

  D. A Judge's Decision (vv. 4, 5)

  E. Application (vv. 6-8)

    "The World's Most Important Shortcut"

II. HUMBLE PRAYER (Luke 18:9-14)

  A. Target Audience (v. 9)

  B. Two Praying Men (v. 10)

  C. The Pharisee's Prayer (vv. 11, 12)

  D. The Publican's Prayer (v. 13)

  E. The Result (v. 14)

    No Matter How You Say It

III. CONCLUSION

  A. How We Persist Humbly

  B. Can Humility Be a Sin?

  C. Persistence in Human Relations

  D. Humility in Human Relations

  E. Prayer

  F. Thought to Remember

Introduction

A last-minute change had been made in the order of worship. In the original plan the choir was to sing immediately after the minister had offered the morning prayer, but for some reason that had been dropped. Feeling a need to alert the minister of the change, the worship leader leaned over and whispered, "After the prayer there will be no response."

Do you ever feel like, after the prayer, there is no response? Are you impatient for an answer, like Phillips Brooks—noted preacher and hymn writer of an earlier generation? A friend once found him pacing irritably in his study, so he asked him what was the trouble. "I have been praying for weeks," Brooks replied, "and nothing happened. 'The trouble' is, I am in a hurry, but God isn't."

A. Why?

Why are God's answers often so long in coming? We pray for a loved one who is suffering from some illness. We pray for healing, or we pray for release from pain—and yet our loved one finds neither healing nor release for weeks.

Sometimes it may be for the witness the suffering one has. When pain is endured patiently, it is a testimony to the sustaining power of faith and of Jesus, who is the "author and finisher of our faith" (Hebrews 12:2). It testifies to medical staff and visitors, to the saints and to the lost. In Job's case it even testified to Satan!

Sometimes it may be for the growth of the sufferer. "Count it all joy," wrote James of our trials, because "the trying of your faith worketh patience . . . that ye may be perfect and entire, wanting nothing" (James 1:2-4).

B. Perplexed About Prayer

More than one observer has remarked that God has three answers for our prayers. One is *Yes*. Another is *No*. A third is *Wait a while*. Most of us have been perplexed by a firm *No* in answer to a fervent prayer. *Wait a while* is not much less perplexing. Not until the *while* of waiting is over can we distinguish it from a *No*. In the meantime, we may wonder if our faith is deficient, for Jesus promised to grant the prayer of a believer (Mark 11:24). Or perhaps we may realize that we have prayed a selfish prayer and tried to disguise it by saying, "In Jesus' name." But the Lord is not fooled. He knows when a prayer is really in our own name. And most of us must admit that at times we do not know what to pray for. We can only trust the Holy Spirit to carry the proper request to the Father with an urgency beyond words (Romans 8:26, 27).

Today's lesson brings us two parables on prayer, and in these there is not much perplexity. In each case, Luke lets us know clearly what the parable is designed to teach. Let's learn it.

C. Lesson Background

In last week's lesson we saw Jesus teaching in and around Jerusalem during the two months between the autumn Feast of Tabernacles and the winter Feast of Dedication. Then, when the opposition of the Jewish rulers grew more determined and severe, Jesus withdrew to Perea, located "beyond Jordan," or, east of the Jordan River (John 10:39, 40). That area was not subject to the Jerusalem rulers. It belonged to the realm of Herod Antipas, king of Galilee. Jesus stayed away from Jerusalem for most of the next three months, until He returned for the springtime Feast of Passover, during which He was crucified. The two parables of our text were given during the few months Jesus spent in Perea.

I. Persistent Prayer
(Luke 18:1-8)

A. A Parable's Message (v. 1)

1. And he spake a parable unto them to this end, that men ought always to pray, and not to faint.

Most likely this *parable* was addressed primarily to Jesus' disciples, not to the Pharisees or to the larger crowd (Luke 17:22). Luke tells us at the outset what the parable is intended to teach: *men ought always to pray, and not to faint.* Here the word *faint* carries the idea of growing weary or giving up. [See question #1, page 72.]

B. A Bad Judge (v. 2)

2. Saying, There was in a city a judge, which feared not God, neither regarded man.

Having no regard for *God* or *man*, this *judge* cared nothing for either God's law or a person's rights. On what basis would such a judge render his verdict in a particular case? He would probably rule in favor of the highest bidder for his services. The bigger bribe would buy his decision. [See question #2, page 72.]

C. A Widow's Plea (v. 3)

3. And there was a widow in that city; and she came unto him, saying, Avenge me of mine adversary.

The plea of this *widow (avenge me)* was a cry for justice. We do not know the nature of her complaint against her *adversary.* Widows were a particularly helpless group in Jesus' day and were often the targets of unscrupulous men— some of them from among the religious leaders (Mark 12:38-40).

D. A Judge's Decision (vv. 4, 5)

4, 5. And he would not for a while: but afterward he said within himself, Though I fear not God, nor regard man; yet because this widow troubleth me, I will avenge her, lest by her continual coming she weary me.

This widow had no money for a bribe; thus this corrupt judge had no interest in her case. He

simply dismissed it and sent her away. But this woman would not take no for an answer; repeatedly she came back and made the same plea for justice, in spite of the judge's refusal to help her. Her *continual coming* began to irritate the judge. Finally, just to get this persistent woman "off his back," the judge decided to help her.

E. Application (vv. 6-8)

6. And the Lord said, Hear what the unjust judge saith.

Jesus wanted the disciples who were with Him (and the disciples considering this lesson today) to give some thought to the just decision of that *unjust judge*—and then to consider what is said in the next verse.

7. And shall not God avenge his own elect, which cry day and night unto him, though he bear long with them?

It may seem inappropriate for *God* to be represented by an unjust judge. But the main point of this comparison is not the similarity between God and the judge; it is the differences. The judge was bad; God is good. The judge cared nothing for truth or right or justice; God is greatly concerned about all of these. The judge cared nothing for the people who came seeking His help; God loves His people (His *elect*) with a deep and everlasting love. If repeated requests can move even a bad judge to do what is right, is it not much more certain that persistent prayer can move the good God to give what is good to those He loves?

Though he bear long with them. This seems to warn us that there may be a period of waiting before God replies to our prayers by giving us what we seek. Some versions make this a question similar in meaning to the one that precedes it. For example, the *New International Version*

Visual for
lesson 8

This poster provides a powerful contemporary illustration of the Golden Text.

reads, "Will not God bring about justice for his chosen ones, who cry out to him day and night? Will he keep putting them off?" This implies that God will *not* keep putting them off, that in time He will grant their request.

In any case, we need to remember the stated purpose of this parable. It is to teach us to keep on praying (rather than giving up) when an answer seems slow in coming (v. 1). As suggested in the Introduction to this lesson, waiting gives us time to rethink our prayer. Has our request been selfish or otherwise mistaken? If we are certain that our request is right and if the time of waiting becomes distressing, then we need to reflect upon how that distress can make us better servants of the Lord (James 1:2-4).

8. I tell you that he will avenge them speedily. Nevertheless, when the Son of man cometh, shall he find faith on the earth?

Jesus proceeded to answer the question He had just raised. *Speedily* the Lord will bring justice to His people who pray to Him night and day. Does that imply that our waiting will not be long? Consider how the latter part of the verse turns our thinking to the longest wait of all for Christians. "Surely I come quickly," said Jesus nearly two thousand years ago. And for all those years Jesus' people have been praying with John the apostle, "Even so, come, Lord Jesus" (Revelation 22:20). This shows us that *quickly* does not necessarily mean this day or this week or this year. It simply means that when Jesus does come, that event will occur suddenly—"in the twinkling of an eye" (1 Corinthians 15:52).

Remember why Jesus gave this parable. It was to teach that we "ought always to pray, and not to faint" (v. 1). The important thing is not the waiting; it is the praying. Jesus' people must keep on praying through every time of waiting, short or long, through all the weeks and years until He comes again. In addition, they must live daily in a way that keeps them prepared for His return. Jesus' question *when the Son of man cometh, shall he find faith on the earth?* expresses His concern that if people do not have enough faith and perseverance to pray continually, will they have enough to keep them spiritually alert and prepared for His return? [See question #3, page 72.]

[See question #3, page 72.]

"THE WORLD'S MOST IMPORTANT SHORTCUT"

These words have been used to describe the Panama Canal, although the history of this "shortcut" has been rather long and involved. In 1534 King Charles V of Spain ordered a survey of a possible canal route across Panama. But it was not until 1881 that a French company made the first attempt to construct a canal, only to be frustrated by bankruptcy and by the deaths of twenty thousand workers. In 1904, the United States took over the project, and by 1914 the Panama Canal was completed. Thus, a fifty-one-mile trip through the canal made the ten-thousand-mile sea voyage around South America unnecessary.

For Panama's citizens, however, patience was still in order: the canal (controlled by the United States) had cut their nation in half. Many Panamanians were restive about this state of affairs and eventually initiated a campaign to have their nation's sovereignty over the Canal Zone restored. In 1977, U.S. President Jimmy Carter signed a treaty agreeing to turn over control of the Canal to Panama on December 31, 1999. When that date finally arrived, there was great jubilation in Panama.

Regardless of what one thinks about the political, economic, or strategic wisdom of yielding control of the canal, its history is an illustration of enduring patience. This is the primary point of Jesus' parable of the unjust judge: patient supplication, anchored by a trust in God's power to work for good, is a vital part of faith in God.

Prayer may well be "the world's most important shortcut" in bringing our concerns to the Heavenly Father. We must remember, however, that in some situations it may take time to discern His hand at work.   —C. R. B.

II. Humble Prayer
(Luke 18:9-14)

A. Target Audience (v. 9)

9. And he spake this parable unto certain which trusted in themselves that they were righteous, and despised others.

Luke helped us with the first parable of our text by telling us in advance what the parable was meant to teach (v. 1). He helps us with *this parable* by telling us to whom it was directed—people who were overly proud of their own righteousness and overly contemptuous of others who did not "measure up" to their standard. From that information, we can be sure that this parable is meant to rebuke pride and teach humility in prayer.

B. Two Praying Men (v. 10)

10. Two men went up into the temple to pray; the one a Pharisee, and the other a publican.

Almost any *Pharisee* would be an example of the kind of person described in verse 9. The Pharisees were proud of knowing the law, and they were meticulous about obeying it in small matters that were often easily observed by others. Yet, as Jesus told them, they "omitted the weightier matters of the law, judgment, mercy, and faith" (Matthew 23:23). Their proud prayers

---

How to Say It

ANTIPAS. *An*-tih-pus.
HEROD. *Hair*-ud.
PEREA. Peh-*ree*-uh.
PHARISEES. *Fair*-ih-seez.

---

were intended for the ears of men rather than the mind of God. They wanted to be seen and heard and praised for their piety (Matthew 6:5).

Almost any *publican* would be an example of the kind of people whom the proud Pharisees despised. Publicans were tax collectors. They took money from their fellow Jews on behalf of the oppressive Romans, so patriotic Jews considered publicans as the vilest of sinners.

C. The Pharisee's Prayer (vv. 11, 12)

11. The Pharisee stood and prayed thus with himself, God, I thank thee, that I am not as other men are, extortioners, unjust, adulterers, or even as this publican.

The Pharisee's prayer was *with himself*, or "about himself." It was devoted mainly to bragging about how good he was, but it also showed his contempt of others. True, the prayer was spoken to *God*, but it gave Him thanks for nothing but the Pharisee's self-perceived goodness. It expressed no sense of dependence on God to supply material and spiritual needs.

12. I fast twice in the week, I give tithes of all that I possess.

This was the kind of Pharisee upon whom Jesus pronounced "woe" (Matthew 23:23). Such a man was very careful to obey the law in matters easily seen, such as fasting and giving *tithes*. The Pharisees usually fasted *twice in the week*—on Mondays and Thursdays. But there was no concern for qualities such as faith and mercy (obviously this Pharisee showed no mercy at all to the publican). He obeyed, not because he loved God, but because he loved the praise of men (Matthew 23:5-7). [See question #4, page 72.]

D. The Publican's Prayer (v. 13)

13. And the publican, standing afar off, would not lift up so much as his eyes unto heaven, but smote upon his breast, saying, God be merciful to me a sinner.

Instead of boasting about his goodness, the *publican* confessed his sin and begged for mercy. Phrase after phrase describes his sense of humility and shame before God. He stood *afar off*, perhaps at the side of the courtyard most distant from the Holy Place, because he felt unworthy to approach God's sanctuary. He bowed his head

and lowered his *eyes* because he was ashamed to show his face before God's dwelling place in *heaven*. He *smote upon his breast* with his fists—the traditional expression of deep grief. He expected his voice would somehow reach God's throne beyond the sky—but only with a humble plea, not a selfish demand. [See question #5, page 72.]

E. The Result (v. 14)

14. I tell you, this man went down to his house justified rather than the other: for every one that exalteth himself shall be abased; and he that humbleth himself shall be exalted.

The publican begged for mercy and received it. He was forgiven, which is the meaning of the word *justified*. In contrast, the Pharisee asked for no mercy and received none. He went home with the same sins he came with, and without even recognizing that he had them. His pride and arrogance were sins, but he thought they were only an objective evaluation of his goodness. No doubt he was covetous, as other Pharisees were (Luke 16:14); but he thought his greed was only a recognition of what was due to one of the best of God's people. His hatred of Jesus was a sin, but he thought it was demanded by loyalty to the ancient faith of his people. Even his hatred of sinners (such as the publican) was a sin, but he thought it was an echo of God's own hatred.

In contrast, the publican knew his sins for what they were. In agony he pleaded to be free from them, and Jesus declared him justified before God.

Jesus ended this parable with a statement that seems to contradict itself. It also challenges the thinking so prevalent in our self-centered age. *Every one that exalteth himself shall be abased; and he that humbleth himself shall be exalted.*

NO MATTER HOW YOU SAY IT

Learning to talk is one of the most difficult things anyone will ever do. The process of sorting out various sounds, the combination of those sounds into words, and the eventual organization of those words into meaningful speech is a highly complex task. The process must wait until a baby's brain and muscle control are sufficiently developed to make speech possible.

Researchers have demonstrated that deaf children who have been exposed to American Sign Language go through the same developmental process as hearing children. The hand motions mimicking those of their "signing" parents go through a "babbling" stage and finally reach meaningful speech patterns at generally the same age that hearing children reach theirs. In either case, the child's brain develops its speech capabilities according to a predictable pattern and time schedule, regardless of the language the child is learning to "speak."

The point (as it applies to this part of our lesson today) is that, both in speech and action, we reveal what is going on deep within us. In the case of children learning to speak, it is their neurological development. In the case of the Pharisee and the publican in Jesus' parable, it was their spiritual development.

What do our words and actions tell the world about how our souls are "developing"? —C. R. B.

Conclusion

Our two parables on prayer teach two different principles: persistence in prayer and humility in prayer. Are the two compatible or contradictory?

A. How We Persist Humbly

1. No matter how many times we come to our Father with some request that is dear to our heart, each time we must also present the request that is most important of all: "Not my will, but thine, be done." In doing so, we follow the example of our Savior Himself (Luke 22:42).

2. When God's answer seems to be *No*, it may be only *Wait a while*. So we must wait humbly, without resentment and without giving up, while we renew our plea as persistently as the widow in the first parable of our text renewed hers.

3. When God's answer is either *No* or *Wait a while*, we must humbly restudy our request. Perhaps we can change it to make it more in tune with our Father's will.

B. Can Humility Be a Sin?

Humility is not so admirable when it is a mask for laziness. A successful school teacher with years of experience says, "Oh no! I'm sorry. I can't teach in Sunday school. I don't know enough

about the Bible." A salesman who has set new records for his company declines a place in the Outreach and Evangelism ministry. "I wouldn't know how to persuade people to accept Christ," he says. The best cook in town doesn't want to get involved in preparing church dinners. "I'm just a family cook," she says modestly. "I don't know anything about cooking for a crowd."

C. Persistence in Human Relations

The first parable that we studied teaches us to be persistent in prayer to God. Maybe that offers some hints for human relations. Maybe you should ask that good teacher again about working in the Sunday school. Maybe you will show her what fine helps you have for teachers. When she sees how Sunday school teaching is done, maybe she will decide that it is for her after all.

Maybe you should keep after that salesman. Maybe he will go with the preacher on some calls. If you have a visiting evangelist, perhaps the salesman will go with him to help him find addresses. Maybe that salesman will decide that persuading people of their need for the Lord is no harder than selling monkey wrenches.

Maybe you should enlist that family cook for a minor role in preparing a big church dinner. When she sees what a ministry this provides, perhaps she will welcome a more involved role.

D. Humility in Human Relations

What we learn about humility in today's study can also be extended into human relations. The Pharisee of our second parable was one who despised others (vv. 9, 11) and exalted himself (v. 14). Christian teaching urges us not to think of ourselves too highly, but to have an objective opinion (Romans 12:3). We are also told, "In lowliness of mind let each esteem other better than themselves" (Philippians 2:3).

How can you esteem another better than yourself, if obviously he is not better? Instead of noting his faults and weaknesses, you can focus on his virtues and strengths. You can encourage him to do what he can do, and you can appreciate his efforts. Thus your esteem will help him become better than he is now.

E. Prayer

Forgive us, Father, if our talking with You has become less constant than Your providing of daily bread. Forgive us if we have overvalued ourselves and despised others. Help us daily to follow our Savior, who leads us in His faultless way. In His name, amen.

F. Thought to Remember

Be persistent in a humble way.

Home Daily Bible Readings

Monday, Oct. 15—Ask in Faith (James 1:2-8)
Tuesday, Oct. 16—David's Prayer to God (1 Chronicles 29:10-14)
Wednesday, Oct. 17—Pray in Secret (Matthew 6:1-8)
Thursday, Oct. 18—Pray in This Way (Matthew 6:9-14)
Friday, Oct. 19—Ask and It Will Be Given (Luke 11:9-13)
Saturday, Oct. 20—Persistence in Prayer (Luke 18:1-8)
Sunday, Oct. 21—Humility in Prayer (Luke 18:9-14)

Learning by Doing

This page contains an alternate lesson plan emphasizing learning activities.
Classes desiring such student involvement will find these suggestions helpful.

Learning Goals

After this lesson each student will be able to:

1. Summarize the two parables in today's Scripture and the lesson Jesus drew from each.

2. Tell why the attitudes of persistence and humility are so important in one's prayer life.

3. Evaluate one's own prayer life to see whether persistence and humility have their proper place, and suggest one way to improve it.

Into the Lesson

Ask the class to move into groups of three and to think about a situation in which "persistence" is illustrated. Sample ideas: a child's persistence in asking for a toy, an employee's persistence in demanding a raise, a spouse's persistence in doing a household chore, or even a pet's persistence in demanding to be taken for a walk. Ask each group of three people to select a situation and create a one- to two-minute role play that illustrates the principle. Allow approximately five minutes for the groups to develop their role plays. Then ask for volunteers to give theirs in front of the class. Encourage all groups to do so. Following the last situation, state: "From the looks of these role plays, we certainly understand and have experienced this principle of persistence. Sometimes, persistence may have got us into trouble. Other times, persistence was the key to fulfilling a dream or a task. The Bible clearly teaches the importance of this principle in our spiritual lives and, in particular, in our prayers. Open your Bibles to Luke 18, and let's read two parables Jesus told on the subject of prayer."

Into the Word

Divide the class into two groups and assign to one group the parable of the unjust judge (Luke 18:1-8) and to the second the parable of the Pharisee and the publican (Luke 18:9-14). Prior to class prepare a handout for each group listing the following questions.

Questions from Luke 18:1-8

1. What indications of the judge's character did Jesus give? *(feared not God, neither regarded man, v. 2.)*

2. How would his character influence the judge's decisions? *(The judge probably was unconcerned about justice, integrity, and fairness. Decisions may have been based upon bribery.)*

3. What did Jesus say of the widow's character? *(Concerned for justice; persistent, v. 3.)*

4. What was the judge's motivation in granting her request? *(Selfish desire to be rid of her, v. 5.)*

5. Why did Jesus present this parable? *(To teach His disciples not to give up in prayer, v. 1.)*

Questions from Luke 18:9-14

1. How would you describe the attitude of the Pharisee when he stood and prayed to God? *(Self-righteous; thankful for his own character; proud of his spiritual efforts, vv. 11, 12.)*

2. How would you describe the attitude of the publican when he stood afar off and prayed to God? *(Humble, aware of and grieved by personal sinfulness, v. 13.)*

3. How did the attitudes of these two individuals influence God's response? *(Pharisee: not justified, for he did not even know he was prideful and arrogant; publican: justified, forgiven of his sin, because God exalts the humble, v. 14.)*

4. Why did Jesus present this parable? *(To rebuke pride and to teach humility, v. 9.)*

After about five minutes, ask each group to read its questions and give its answers.

Into Life

State: "In these texts, Jesus teaches about persistence and humility when we pray." Tell your students to turn to someone beside them and discuss these questions: "Why is persistence important in one's prayer life today?" and, "Why is humility important in one's prayer life today?"

Allow several minutes for discussion; then distribute a self-evaluation sheet for each person. Prepare this sheet prior to class time with the following incomplete statements and a scale of 1 (Never) to 10 (Always) after each:

1. I practice persistence in my prayer life. . . .

2. I demonstrate humility in my prayer life. . . .

Ask the learners to reflect on their own prayer lives and to circle the number that best represents the level at which they have integrated Jesus' teaching on prayer. After a moment for reflection, say, "Jesus wants us to follow His teaching in this passage. Look at the numbers you circled for 'persistence' and 'humility.' How can Christians improve their ratings on these scales?" As answers are given, write them on the board. Ask each person to select one of these ways for implementation in his or her life; lead in a prayer of commitment.

Let's Talk It Over

The questions on this page are designed to encourage review of the lesson Scriptures and to promote discussion of the lesson by the class. The answers provided are only discussion starters. Let your class talk it over from there.

1. Why are we sometimes tempted to give up on prayer? How can we resist such a temptation?

It is a human tendency to struggle with doubts when our prayers do not seem to be receiving answers. Also, Satan is the archenemy of prayer. His influence is felt in those questions that beset us: "Why should I believe anyone is listening to me? Am I just wasting time and energy?" When we do receive that for which we have prayed, unbelievers are quick to suggest other reasons for it. All of these combine in an assault on our faith. We need to focus on the Word, which assures us that God does hear and answer prayer. Sharing our struggles and our successes with other believers will also reinforce our resolve "always to pray, and not to faint."

2. Jesus said the judge in His story "feared not God, neither regarded men." How commonly do these two traits go together? How can either or both conditions be corrected?

Our attitude toward God has a distinct bearing on our attitude toward other people. If we believe that God created us and will hold us accountable for our behavior, then we will be more likely to treat other people with respect. Conversely, John points out that if we do not love our brother whom we have seen, then we cannot love God, whom we cannot see (1 John 4:20). Since the two are related, correcting one involves correcting the other. We need to focus on loving one another as Christ has loved us. When we appreciate God's love for us, even though we are sinful and undeserving, then we can begin to love others—even those we have previously deemed "undeserving."

3. In Luke 18:8 Jesus asks whether or not He will find faith on earth at the time of His return. What can we do to be sure that He does?

We could throw up our hands in resignation and despair. It seems that we are drifting more and more into faithlessness in our society. People are largely ignorant of what the Bible teaches. They resort to prayer only when they have nowhere else to turn. They tend to mention God's name only as part of their careless oaths. Faith appears to be disappearing from human hearts. But Jesus' words are a challenge to us. When we read them, we should renew our determination that we will be faithful—that He will find faith in us when He returns (if He returns in our lifetime). We can work to cultivate faith in our children. We can be diligent about the task of evangelism at home and supporting missions abroad. Make a list of specific ministries your class can be involved in so that the "faith once delivered" can be passed on to the next generation.

4. The Pharisee's prayer was characterized by arrogance and selfishness. What are some similar prayer practices that we need to be careful to avoid?

The Pharisee's prayer did not give glory to God. Do we rush into our personal prayer agenda without giving glory to God? The Lord's Prayer (Matthew 6:9-13) shows us that we should make God's kingdom and glory matters of priority in our prayers. The Pharisee's prayer did not demonstrate a compassion toward other people. Are our prayers similarly selfish? In various places in the New Testament, we are instructed to pray for "all saints" (Ephesians 6:18), for "kings, and for all that are in authority" (1 Timothy 2:2), and for our enemies (Matthew 5:44). The Pharisee's prayer lacked any actual requests for himself. Do we ever repeat his error of telling God only how good we are and how much we have done for Him? In humility we must seek His help and guidance.

5. The publican demonstrated by his posture and physical action that he was approaching God in reverence and humility. How important in our prayers are our posture and physical actions?

It is possible to pray while standing or sitting, but sometimes kneeling or falling prostrate will help us humble ourselves before God. Jesus, while praying in the garden, adopted both of these latter postures (Matthew 26:39; Luke 22:41). If we are to follow His example, we will at times do the same. The Bible does not say anything about folding the hands in prayer, but it does speak of "lifting up holy hands" in connection with prayer (1 Timothy 2:8). If either gesture expresses a worshipfulness for us, we can legitimately use it. The closing of the eyes in prayer is also not commanded in the Bible. However, it is very useful in shutting out distractions and enhancing our concentration on God.

The Sheep and the Goats

DEVOTIONAL READING: 1 John 4:7-21.

BACKGROUND SCRIPTURE: Matthew 24, 25.

PRINTED TEXT: Matthew 25:31-46.

Matthew 25:31-46

31 When the Son of man shall come in his glory, and all the holy angels with him, then shall he sit upon the throne of his glory:

32 And before him shall be gathered all nations: and he shall separate them one from another, as a shepherd divideth his sheep from the goats:

33 And he shall set the sheep on his right hand, but the goats on the left.

34 Then shall the King say unto them on his right hand, Come, ye blessed of my Father, inherit the kingdom prepared for you from the foundation of the world:

35 For I was ahungered, and ye gave me meat: I was thirsty, and ye gave me drink: I was a stranger, and ye took me in:

36 Naked, and ye clothed me: I was sick, and ye visited me; I was in prison, and ye came unto me.

37 Then shall the righteous answer him, saying, Lord, when saw we thee ahungered, and fed thee? or thirsty, and gave thee drink?

38 When saw we thee a stranger, and took thee in? or naked, and clothed thee?

39 Or when saw we thee sick, or in prison, and came unto thee?

40 And the King shall answer and say unto them, Verily I say unto you, Inasmuch as ye have done it unto one of the least of these my brethren, ye have done it unto me.

41 Then shall he say also unto them on the left hand, Depart from me, ye cursed, into everlasting fire, prepared for the devil and his angels:

42 For I was ahungered, and ye gave me no meat: I was thirsty, and ye gave me no drink:

43 I was a stranger, and ye took me not in: naked, and ye clothed me not: sick, and in prison, and ye visited me not.

44 Then shall they also answer him, saying, Lord, when saw we thee ahungered, or athirst, or a stranger, or naked, or sick, or in prison, and did not minister unto thee?

45 Then shall he answer them, saying, Verily I say unto you, Inasmuch as ye did it not to one of the least of these, ye did it not to me.

46 And these shall go away into everlasting punishment: but the righteous into life eternal.

GOLDEN TEXT: Inasmuch as ye have done it unto one of the least of these my brethren, ye have done it unto me.—Matthew 25:40.

Jesus' Ministry
Unit 2: Truth in Parables
(Lessons 6-9)

Lesson Aims

After this lesson a student should be able to:

1. Briefly retell what our text tells about Jesus' prophecy of the final judgment.

2. Tell how this description encourages us to serve Jesus and prepare for His return.

3. Develop a project, either for the class or the church, that will seek to minister to some of the people described in the text.

Lesson Outline

INTRODUCTION
  A. Jesus Is Coming Again
  B. Lesson Background
 I. THE DAY OF JUDGMENT (Matthew 25:31-33)
  A. The Judge (v. 31)
  B. Those to Be Judged (v. 32)
  C. The Separation (v. 33)
    The Great Divide
 II. THE SHEEP (Matthew 25:34-40)
  A. The Blessing (v. 34)
  B. The Reason (vv. 35, 36)
  C. A Question (vv. 37-39)
  D. An Explanation (v. 40)
III. THE GOATS (Matthew 25:41-45)
  A. The Curse (v. 41)
  B. The Reason (vv. 42, 43)
  C. A Question (v. 44)
  D. An Explanation (v. 45)
    Sins of Omission?
IV. SUMMATION (Matthew 25:46)
CONCLUSION
  A. The Rest of the Story
  B. Salvation by Cooperation
  C. Prayer
  D. Thought to Remember

Introduction

A. Jesus Is Coming Again

Nearly ninety years ago some newspapers reported a would-be prophet's confident announcement that Jesus would return to earth in 1914. When that year had passed, the prophet conceded that he had been wrong about the event; but he still held that he was right about the date. The year 1914 saw the start of the war (World War I) that would culminate, the prophet

claimed, in the battle of Armageddon and the end of the world. Failure of that prediction did not deter other would-be prophets of the twentieth century. Different ones predicted the return of Jesus in 1927, 1948, 1972, and 1988. More cautious students of Jesus' promise to return have called attention to His words: "Of that day and hour knoweth no man, no, not the angels of heaven, but my Father only" (Matthew 24:36).

We do not know when Jesus will come again, but that must never blind us to the promise that He will.

B. Lesson Background

Today's lesson brings us to the week when Jesus died. On the first day of that week He rode into Jerusalem on a donkey, while uncounted thousands hailed Him as one coming in the name of the Lord (Matthew 21:1-9). Many in the crowd thought that Jesus was the long-expected Messiah of the Jews, but they thought of His rule only in political terms. Many were hoping He would overthrow the Romans that very week and free Israel from their oppression.

Daily Jesus taught in the temple, and the people listened eagerly to Him. The men in authority desperately wanted to stop Him, but they feared the attentive crowds (Luke 19:47, 48; 21:37, 38). They knew that if anyone tried to arrest Jesus, a riot might result (Matthew 26:3-5).

From what we can piece together concerning Jesus' last week, it appears that Tuesday was a particularly busy day of teaching for Him. It was also a day during which some of Jesus' most hostile enemies tried to trap Him with difficult questions (Luke 20:1-47). As Jesus was leaving the temple on this day, the disciples called His attention to the buildings of the temple. How impressive and beautiful they were! But Jesus replied that one day all of those buildings would be destroyed (Matthew 24:1, 2).

Later, when the disciples were alone with Jesus on the Mount of Olives, they asked Him to tell them more about that destruction, as well as His second coming and the end of the world (Matthew 24:3). In Jesus' lengthy answer (Matthew 24:4—25:46), some find it difficult to distinguish when He was covering one of these concerns and when He was addressing another. We suggest the following approach.

First, Jesus spoke about the destruction of the temple and what would lead up to it (Matthew 24:4-27). Many troubles would come (vv. 4-14). Then the followers of Jesus would see "the abomination of desolation" (v. 15; cf. Daniel 11:31; 12:11). Luke describes this "desolation" as enemy armies surrounding Jerusalem (Luke 21:20). That would be the signal for Jesus' followers to leave

Jerusalem in order to avoid the massacre that would accompany the destruction (Matthew 24:15-22). But that disturbance would not bring about Jesus' second coming (Matthew 24:23-28). He would come later—after that period of tribulation (Matthew 24:29-31; cf. Luke 21:24-28).

The destruction of the temple and of Jerusalem would occur while some people of that generation were still living (Matthew 24:32-34). (It happened in A.D. 70, about forty years after Jesus foretold it.) But only God knew (and knows) when Jesus will come again. He will come at a time when He is not expected. Therefore, His people should be ready to welcome Him at any time (Matthew 24:36-44).

Jesus then added a series of parables to emphasize preparation for His return (Matthew 24:45—25:46). Our printed text includes the last of these parables. It tells about the judgment Jesus will administer when He comes again.

I. The Day of Judgment (Matthew 25:31-33)

When Jesus comes, He will send His angels to gather His people from all parts of the earth (Matthew 24:30, 31). Those followers of Jesus who have died will be restored to life and gathered along with those who have not died (1 Thessalonians 4:16, 17). Our text for today reminds us that the people who do not belong to Jesus will be gathered as well, whether they have died or not—gathered for the great Judgment Day (John 5:28, 29). This is an appointment that all must keep (Hebrews 9:27).

A. The Judge (v. 31)

31. When the Son of man shall come in his glory, and all the holy angels with him, then shall he sit upon the throne of his glory.

Jesus' most frequently used title for Himself was *Son of man*, emphasizing His humanity. He was "made in the likeness of men" (Philippians 2:7), and He knew (and knows) all about our needs, weaknesses, and temptations. But the Son of man is also the Son of God, and God has made Him the judge of all humanity (Acts 17:31).

B. Those to Be Judged (v. 32)

32. And before him shall be gathered all nations: and he shall separate them one from another, as a shepherd divideth his sheep from the goats.

All the people of *all nations* and all times will be gathered *before* Jesus on this day. Can you imagine the countless billions of people? Yet the Judge will evaluate each one individually, separating them *one from another*—and it will not be

difficult for Him to do. A shepherd does not need a series of tests to tell a sheep from a goat; a mere glance is enough. In the same way, the all-knowing Judge recognizes instantly whether a person is His or not. The identity of an individual is apparent in what he has done or failed to do. [See question #1, page 80.]

C. The Separation (v. 33)

33. And he shall set the sheep on his right hand, but the goats on the left.

Throughout history the *right hand* of a ruler has been considered a place of honor. Jesus' own people will be placed there in recognition of what their actions have shown them to be.

THE GREAT DIVIDE

The Berlin Wall stood for twenty-eight years as a concrete symbol of the Cold War—"concrete" in more ways than one. First, it was made of steel-reinforced slabs of concrete that sliced through the heart of Berlin, Germany. It was also concrete—not abstract—as a tangible and visible symbol of the philosophical chasm that separated the free world from the Communist bloc of nations.

The West offered freedom and increasing prosperity. The East's only appeal was the drabness of a collective society where the possibility for economic success was as limited as the opportunity for political self-determination. The difference between the two sectors created a kind of "sheep and goats" scenario: on the one side, the blessings of a free society; on the other, the confining restrictions of a repressive system. When the crumbling foundations of Communism finally caused the Berlin Wall to fall on November 9, 1989, Germans on both sides of the border rejoiced at the reunification now made possible—and the world rejoiced with them.

Home Daily Bible Readings

Monday, Oct. 22—Signs of the End (Matthew 24:1-8)
Tuesday, Oct. 23—Those Who Endure Will Be Saved (Matthew 24:9-14)
Wednesday, Oct. 24—No One Knows the Hour (Matthew 24:36-44)
Thursday, Oct. 25—The Faithful Servant; the Wicked Servant (Matthew 24:45-51)
Friday, Oct. 26—Parable of the Ten Virgins (Matthew 25:1-13)
Saturday, Oct. 27—Parable of the Talents (Matthew 25:14-29)
Sunday, Oct. 28—"When Did We See You?" (Matthew 25:31-46)

While the strict separation represented by the Berlin Wall eventually ceased, the "sheep and goats" separation on Judgment Day will be eternally permanent. And it will be based, not on the caprice of political fortune, but on the decision each of us has made as to which side we have given allegiance.   —C. R. B.

II. The Sheep
(Matthew 25:34-40)

Jesus, the flawless Judge, has examined the people of "all nations," and He has separated the sheep from the goats. He now addresses the sheep, who have been placed at His right hand.

A. The Blessing (v. 34)

34. Then shall the King say unto them on his right hand, Come, ye blessed of my Father, inherit the kingdom prepared for you from the foundation of the world.

What an invitation this is! To *inherit the kingdom* is not merely to have a place in it; it is to inherit the kingship—to be a king. Thus, amid the magnificent visions of Revelation, the apostle John heard these words of praise addressed to Jesus the Lamb: "For thou wast slain, and hast redeemed us to God by thy blood out of every kindred, and tongue, and people, and nation; and hast made us unto our God kings and priests" (Revelation 5:9, 10).

If we stand with the redeemed at Jesus' *right hand*, shall we be equal to Jesus Himself? No; we shall be kings, but He will be King of kings (Revelation 17:14). "His servants shall serve him" (Revelation 22:3), but "they shall reign for ever and ever" (Revelation 22:5).

If we rule with Christ forever, who will be our subjects? Whom shall we rule? Shall we not rule ourselves and each other? Every king will be a subject, and every subject will be a king; for no one will be ruled against his will. Can you imagine yourself so well attuned to everything true and right that every desire of your heart will also be a desire of God's heart? What Heavenly harmony!

That *kingdom* eternal—that land of perfect harmony—will be neither an accident nor an afterthought in the mind of God. *From the foundation of the world* it has been *prepared* for those who will align themselves with God's Son (cf. 1 Peter 1:18-20).

B. The Reason (vv. 35, 36)

35, 36. For I was ahungered, and ye gave me meat: I was thirsty, and ye gave me drink: I was a stranger, and ye took me in: naked, and ye clothed me: I was sick, and ye visited me: I was in prison, and ye came unto me.

Visual for lessons 7 and 9. *Note how activities formerly described as neighborly are also acts of serving Jesus Himself.*

On His royal throne the Judge describes, one by one, some of the most common needs and distresses of mankind: hunger, thirst, loneliness in a strange place, lack of clothing, illness, and imprisonment. The Judge has experienced all of these situations, He says, and those people who are now at His right hand have helped Him bear the burden of them. That is the reason they are receiving the blessing described in verse 34. [See question #2, page 80.]

C. A Question (vv. 37-39)

37-39. Then shall the righteous answer him, saying, Lord, when saw we thee ahungered, and fed thee? or thirsty, and gave thee drink? When saw we thee a stranger, and took thee in? or naked, and clothed thee? Or when saw we thee sick, or in prison, and came unto thee?

Remember who these *righteous* are: they are followers of Jesus who have been gathered from all nations of the world (v. 32) and throughout all centuries of history. Very few of them have seen Jesus before; here they view Him enthroned in glory. When did they ever have the opportunity to help Him in a time of need or distress?

D. An Explanation (v. 40)

40. And the King shall answer and say unto them, Verily I say unto you, Inasmuch as ye have done it unto one of the least of these my brethren, ye have done it unto me.

Most of the righteous (v. 37) have not seen Jesus in person before His appearance on the judgment throne, but they have seen others in need. They have seen some of the righteous in distress and have helped them. Jesus calls these righteous people *my brethren*. Of course, we know that Jesus is God's "only begotten Son"

(John 3:16). But to those who believe in Him, He gives the right to become sons of God in a different way; for in a different way they too are born of God (John 1:12, 13). Therefore "he is not ashamed to call them brethren" (Hebrews 2:11). And all the help given to those "brethren" He counts as help given to Him personally.

This does not mean that we have the freedom to ignore the needs of any who are not followers of Jesus. Jesus did not do this during His earthly ministry, and neither should His people. Paul's words in Galatians 6:10 are instructive on this matter: "As we have therefore opportunity, let us do good unto all men, especially unto them who are of the household of faith." [See question #3, page 80.]

III. The Goats
(Matthew 25:41-45)

After the wonderful invitation extended to the "sheep" at His right, Jesus turns to the "goats" on His left. In light of His words recorded in Matthew 7:13, 14, we suppose that the throng on the left is much larger than the one on the right.

A. The Curse (v. 41)

41. Then shall he say also unto them on the left hand, Depart from me, ye cursed, into everlasting fire, prepared for the devil and his angels.

Notice how precisely the command to this group is the opposite of that given to the group on Jesus' right. One group is invited to come; the other is ordered to *depart*. One is called blessed; the other is called *cursed*. One is called to a kingdom; the other is sent to *everlasting fire*. Those in one group inherit a kingdom prepared for them. Those in the other have no place prepared for them; they can only share the place *prepared for the devil and his angels*. There is nowhere else to go. Notice that Hell is not a place "prepared" for human beings. God wants no one to go there (2 Peter 3:9).

B. The Reason (vv. 42, 43)

42, 43. For I was ahungered, and ye gave me no meat: I was thirsty, and ye gave me no drink: I was a stranger, and ye took me not in: naked, and ye clothed me not: sick, and in prison, and ye visited me not.

Observe that these people condemned to everlasting fire are not accused of doing anything maliciously evil: no murder, mayhem, assault, adultery, arson, or theft. They are condemned for doing nothing. They had opportunities to do good, just as the people on the right; but they chose to do nothing. The Heavenly kingdom is

prepared for doers; the "do-nothings" are left out. [See question #4, page 80.]

C. A Question (v. 44)

44. Then shall they also answer him, saying, Lord, when saw we thee ahungered, or athirst, or a stranger, or naked, or sick, or in prison, and did not minister unto thee?

Literally speaking, most of these on Jesus' left had never seen Him. In this, they were like those on the right. Seeing Him now "upon the throne of his glory" (v. 31), they could hardly believe that He had ever been a victim of poverty or imprisonment. Were they being condemned unjustly? They asked for an explanation.

D. An Explanation (v. 45)

45. Then shall he answer them, saying, Verily I say unto you, Inasmuch as ye did it not to one of the least of these, ye did it not to me.

The great majority of those at Jesus' left hand have not seen Him before that Judgment Day, but they *have* seen many of His people—those who have been born again as children of God, whom Jesus calls His brethren. They have seen some of those brethren in need and have neglected to help them. Jesus takes that neglect personally, as if He Himself were neglected. For that neglect, the people on the left are sent from the presence of Jesus into everlasting fire.

SINS OF OMISSION?

Thomas Rossi claimed that he had been a faithful husband for twenty-five years. So it came as no small shock when "out of the blue" his wife told him that she wanted a divorce. It was not until three years later that Rossi learned the reason for his wife's sudden request.

Three weeks before Denise Rossi filed for the divorce, she had won $1.3 million in the California State Lottery. She wanted to divorce Mr. Rossi to keep him from finding out about her winnings and to avoid having to share the money with him. Eventually, the truth caught up with Mrs. Rossi, and the matter was taken to court. The judge found her guilty of violating state asset disclosure laws and gave all of the money to her ex-husband!

It could be argued that Mrs. Rossi was guilty of a sin of omission—a failure to tell her husband about her money or to share it with him. However, like many (perhaps most?) sins of omission, her failure was really a sin of *commission*—a

How to Say It
ARMAGEDDON. Ar-muh-*ged*-dun.

willful decision to commit an act that she knew was wrong.

That is the reason Jesus' condemnation is so strong against those who "did it not to one of the least of these." A failure to do a good act is all too often a willful decision not to act.   —C. R. B.

IV. Summation
(Matthew 25:46)

46. And these shall go away into everlasting punishment: but the righteous into life eternal.

The invitation in verse 34 and the rejection in verse 41 are not idle words. The people placed at Jesus' right hand in the final judgment really will inherit the kingdom prepared for them from the foundation of the world. Those placed at His left really will be banished to everlasting fire prepared for the devil and his angels.

Now that our sophisticated means of communication can give us daily news of the needy around the world, we are appalled by the number of them. Unable to help all of them, we ignore all of them—but that is the way to everlasting fire. So each one of us struggles with his own decisions. Which of the needy shall I help, and how much shall I help them? Each person makes his own choice, and no two choices are alike. But let each person remember that he is choosing more than where he will spend his money. He is choosing where he will spend eternity. [See question #5, page 80.]

Conclusion

In some Bibles the words spoken by Jesus Himself are printed in red. If we would read those words only, we might conclude that we earn eternal life by what we do. Two weeks ago we considered how a lawyer cited the two all-inclusive commands as the way to eternal life, and Jesus said, "This do, and thou shalt live" (Luke 10:25-28). This week's text seems to indicate that eternal life is the reward of those who are diligent in helping the needy. But Christians know that this is not the whole story.

A. The Rest of the Story

The law did say that those who keep the law will live by it (Leviticus 18:5; Romans 10:5); however, that was not good enough, for no one kept the law well enough to earn eternal life (Romans 3:23). We get eternal life as a gift (Romans 6:23) or not at all; however, that gift is not given to everyone. God did not retract the law that sin brings death. Instead, He sent His Son to die the death that we deserved. So the gift of life is free to us, but very expensive to God and to

Jesus. Such a costly gift is offered only to those who believe in the Savior who died for the undeserving (John 3:16).

There is yet more to the rest of the story. Eternal life is not offered to all who believe in Jesus. Through the centuries, many have taught that we are saved by faith alone—but the Bible does not say that. In fact, the Bible specifically denies it (James 2:24). On the other hand, many have continued to teach that we can "win" Heaven by doing good and by doing penance to atone for our sins. The Bible does not say that either. Rather, it belittles the role of works as a means of salvation (Romans 3:20; Galatians 2:16).

B. Salvation by Cooperation

If you have been taking part in the debate about how we are saved, here is a suggestion: read the entire New Testament. Read it slowly, thoughtfully. If you read only a little while each day, it may take weeks or months to finish; but read all of it. As you read, make a list of things by which the Bible says we are saved, or by which we are justified, or by which we enter the kingdom of God. If you list more than one item, can you ever again say that you are saved by one thing *only*?

To encourage this search, here is some of what you will find:

1. We are saved by what God has done—His grace, or undeserved favor (Ephesians 2:8).

2. We are saved by what we do—namely, by putting our faith in Jesus as our Savior (Galatians 3:26), by repentance from sin (2 Corinthians 7:10), by confession of Christ (Romans 10:9), and by baptism (1 Peter 3:21).

3. We are "justified by works" (James 2:24). This means that the good things we do are done, not as a means of salvation, but because we have accepted Jesus as Lord and Savior and want to obey Him.

To summarize, God has done all He can do to provide the gift of salvation; we must do all He commands to "open" this gift.

C. Prayer

Father in Heaven, how good You are! Out of Your marvelous grace You have laid on Your own Son the death we all deserved and have given us the everlasting life we do not deserve. More than that, You have given us the privilege and joy of cooperating with You in bringing about our salvation and in furthering Your kingdom in a sinful world. Thank You, Father. In Jesus' name, amen.

D. Thought to Remember

God gives us life eternal, but not without our cooperation.

Learning by Doing

This page contains an alternate lesson plan emphasizing learning activities.
Classes desiring such student involvement will find these suggestions helpful.

Learning Goals

After participating in this lesson, each student will be able to:

1. Briefly retell what our text tells about Jesus' prophecy of the final judgment.

2. Tell how this description encourages us to serve Jesus and prepare for His return.

3. Develop a project, either for the class or the church, that will seek to minister to some of the people described in the text.

Into the Lesson

Write the words *Final Judgment* where everyone in the class can see them. Say: "When people stop to think about the final judgment, they become filled with a variety of reactions. What words, thoughts, or emotions come into your mind when you think of 'Final Judgment'?" As ideas are shared, write them on the chalkboard or an overhead transparency under the two words. *(Suggestions may include: glory, eternal, justice, punishment, fear, separation, salvation.)* State: "Some people look on the final judgment favorably, while others express fear and dread. Today's lesson from Matthew 25:31-46 presents the separation that will occur in the final judgment and encourages us to prepare for Christ's return."

Into the Word

Ask a class member to read the lesson Scripture to the class. Say: "This passage may be familiar to many. To make certain that we understand what the text tells about Jesus' prophecy of the final judgment, let's briefly retell the facts of this passage."

Write the basic facts of the passage on the chalkboard or overhead transparency. Make certain the following truths are included: 1. Jesus, the Son of man, is coming again; 2. He will sit on the throne of judgment; 3. All people will stand before Him to be judged; 4. He will divide all people into two groups; 5. The "sheep" on His right will inherit the kingdom on the basis of their compassionate service to the Christ; 6. Ministry to members of His family is accepted as ministry to Jesus (vv. 37-40); 7. The "goats" on His left will go into everlasting punishment because neglect of "the least of these" is neglect of the Lord. State: "Ministry to people's basic needs truly reflects the heart of God. So important is this practice that God accepts it as service done directly to Jesus.

Based on Jesus' description of ministry to the 'least of these,' what are these basic human needs that the righteous meet?" *(Food, water, friendship, clothing, health, and freedom.)*

Prior to class prepare a worksheet called "Contrasting Judgments." Design the worksheet with a grid pattern consisting of three columns and six rows. Use the first row to label the three columns: "Those on the Left," "Judgment Contrasts," and "Those on the Right." Down the center column, label the five rows: "Group Called," "Command Given," "Inheritance Received," "Place Prepared for," and "Ministry to the 'Least of These.'" Separate the class into small groups and give a worksheet to each person. Appoint a leader for each group and have the leaders assign specific rows to each person. After a few minutes, ask for the answers to be shared before the whole class. *(Called: Cursed/Blessed; Command: Depart/Come; Inheritance: Everlasting Fire/Kingdom; Place: Devil and His Angels/Sheep; Ministry: No/Yes.)*

Into Life

Say: "Jesus reveals here the principle that by ministering to others we minister to Him. One way we prepare for His return is to get involved in ministry to some of the 'least of these.' Let's consider how this can be applied to our class."

Prior to class prepare a second worksheet for this application activity. Make a copy for each person as well as an overhead transparency to project. Label this worksheet, "Serving Christ by Serving Others." Across the top write, "Project Development for Selected Basic Human Need." Down the left side of the page in rows write, "Who, What, When, Where, and How."

Say: "During the remainder of the class, let's develop a project that we can do as a class in preparation for Jesus' return. He wants us to be involved in ministry to the 'least of these.' Let's start by suggesting some possible projects that we could do."

Write the suggested projects on the chalkboard. Once there appears to be a general agreement about which project to develop, turn on the overhead projector and state: "Now let's develop our plan to serve Christ by serving others." Work through each category to complete the worksheet.

Conclude the class by standing together in a prayer circle, holding hands, and committing this project to the Lord.

Let's Talk It Over

The questions on this page are designed to encourage review of the lesson Scriptures and to promote discussion of the lesson by the class. The answers provided are only discussion starters. Let your class talk it over from there.

1. In verse 32 we read that the Lord will separate the righteous from the unrighteous at the judgment. How "separate" should the righteous try to be from the unrighteous now?

There are two Biblical principles that must be kept in balance. One is that of remaining separate from the world (1 Corinthians 15:33; 2 Corinthians 6:14-18; Hebrews 7:26; James 1:27; 1 John 2:15). The other is that of having an influence for good on the people of the world (Matthew 5:13-16; 1 Corinthians 7:16; Philippians 2:15). Jesus was criticized for associating with "sinners," but He continued to associate with them in order to bring them to repentance. Discuss how much a Christian can associate with unbelievers before compromising his or her witness. What are some things a believer should never do in associating— even for a good cause—with unbelievers? What are some things a believer might do, even if other Christians were uncomfortable with it—in order to reach out to the lost?

2. The hungry, thirsty, homeless, etc. in Jesus' time would have been evident everywhere. Today they are less obvious. How can we locate them and help them?

It is likely that most Christians live not far away from a prison, a children's home, a nursing home, a shelter for the homeless, or a hospital. If we are to be Jesus' sheep, following His example, we must go out of our way to visit such facilities and minister to the people in them. But many of "the least of these" are not in such places. Some of them are next door, or sitting in a pew not far from us on Sunday morning. We do not recognize them because we have not taken the time to cultivate relationships and discern their real needs. We must adopt a shepherd's heart to see those who wander like "sheep having no shepherd" (Matthew 9:36).

3. The lesson writer notes that Jesus calls the persons who were helped His "brethren" and infers that Jesus is talking of help given to the righteous. To what extent ought we to limit our help to believers? What is our responsibility to those outside the faith?

The writer also notes that we do not have "the freedom to ignore the needs of any who are not followers of Jesus" and cites Galatians 6:10: "As

we have therefore opportunity, let us do good unto all men, especially unto them who are of the household of faith." Perhaps we ought to have a program in place to be sure we care for those who are members of our own congregation. This will help them and testify to the community of our love for the "household of faith." But each individual believer ought to be quick to render aid to a neighbor or anyone else in need, regardless of whether the person is a member of the church or not. This too will be a testimony to the community and will help to win the lost.

4. The lesson writer notes that the "goats" were not necessarily the murderers, adulterers, arsonists, and the like. "They had opportunities to do good . . . but they chose to do nothing." In what situations are we tempted to "do nothing"? How can we avoid being like these "goats"?

One thing we can do is to be sure a portion of our church budget is designated for benevolence (and that it is spent on the same). That way, every time we put money into the offering basket, we are doing something to help the needy. Of course, we need to look for personal opportunities to help as well. It is easy to get busy doing "good" things, but the "better" thing is to reach out and help those who are in need.

5. There are many needs around us. Most of us get letters of appeal for help on an almost daily basis. We cannot help all who ask. How do we choose? What are some principles to keep in mind as we contemplate helping the needy?

We need to think in terms of "How *much* can I give?" rather than "How *little* can I give?" We may be tempted to give only enough to salve our consciences. But Jesus urged us toward generosity: "Give, and it shall be given unto you; good measure, pressed down, and shaken together, and running over, shall men give into your bosom" (Luke 6:38). While this statement speaks of what will be given to generous givers, it is also important that we do not become preoccupied with what we will receive as a result of our giving. Our reward may not come until eternity. It is also important that we be wise in our giving. We do an individual no good if he uses what we give to purchase alcohol or drugs, or if our giving makes him even more dependent on outside help.

Blessed Are You

DEVOTIONAL READING: **Psalm 24.**

BACKGROUND SCRIPTURE: **Matthew 5:1-16.**

PRINTED TEXT: **Matthew 5:1-16.**

Matthew 5:1-16

1 And seeing the multitudes, he went up into a mountain: and when he was set, his disciples came unto him:

2 And he opened his mouth, and taught them, saying,

3 Blessed are the poor in spirit: for theirs is the kingdom of heaven.

4 Blessed are they that mourn: for they shall be comforted.

5 Blessed are the meek: for they shall inherit the earth.

6 Blessed are they which do hunger and thirst after righteousness: for they shall be filled.

7 Blessed are the merciful: for they shall obtain mercy.

8 Blessed are the pure in heart: for they shall see God.

9 Blessed are the peacemakers: for they shall be called the children of God.

10 Blessed are they which are persecuted for righteousness' sake: for theirs is the kingdom of heaven.

11 Blessed are ye, when men shall revile you, and persecute you, and shall say all manner of evil against you falsely, for my sake.

12 Rejoice, and be exceeding glad: for great is your reward in heaven: for so persecuted they the prophets which were before you.

13 Ye are the salt of the earth: but if the salt have lost his savor, wherewith shall it be salted? it is thenceforth good for nothing, but to be cast out, and to be trodden under foot of men.

14 Ye are the light of the world. A city that is set on a hill cannot be hid.

15 Neither do men light a candle, and put it under a bushel, but on a candlestick; and it giveth light unto all that are in the house.

16 Let your light so shine before men, that they may see your good works, and glorify your Father which is in heaven.

GOLDEN TEXT: Let your light so shine before men, that they may see your good works, and glorify your Father which is in heaven.—Matthew 5:16.

Lesson Aims

After this lesson a student should be able to:

1. Tell what the primary theme of the Beatitudes is and how Jesus described the impact Christians should have in the world.

2. Tell how practicing the Beatitudes can make Christians to be "salt" and "light" in their community.

3. Choose one of the Beatitudes and seek to apply its message to his or her responsibility as salt and light.

Lesson Outline

INTRODUCTION
   A. Happiness Is . . .
   B. Lesson Background
  I. OUTDOOR SETTING (Matthew 5:1, 2)
   A. People and Place (v. 1a)
   B. Teacher and Students (vv. 1b, 2)
 II. THE BEATITUDES (Matthew 5:3-12)
   A. The Poor in Spirit (v. 3)
   B. The Mourners (v. 4)
   C. The Meek (v. 5)
   D. The Hungry (v. 6)
   E. The Merciful (v. 7)
   F. The Pure in Heart (v. 8)
   G. The Peacemakers (v. 9)
   H. The Persecuted (vv. 10-12)
       "Say It Ain't So!"
III. THE SALT (Matthew 5:13)
   A. Good Salt (v. 13a)
   B. Bad Salt (v. 13b)
       When Salt Keeps Its Savor
 IV. THE LIGHT (Matthew 5:14-16)
   A. That Others May See (vv. 14, 15)
   B. That God May Be Glorified (v. 16)
CONCLUSION
   A. How the Light Works
   B. Prayer
   C. Thought to Remember

Introduction

A. Happiness Is . . .

What makes you happy? An evening out with friends, or solitude in your easy chair after a hard day's work? Taking a journey to faraway places wild and wonderful, or coming back home? A big holiday celebration with the entire town, or a quiet evening with a good book? No matter where your happiness comes from, it's important to you!

The Greek word rendered *happy* in the *King James Version* of the New Testament is *makarios*. However, that translation is more the exception than the rule. The word *makarios* appears fifty times in the Greek New Testament and is translated *happy* only five times. In the other forty-five cases it is rendered *blessed.* Many Christian translators believe that *happiness* is not a good way to render the Greek term at all, since happiness comes from *hap,* which implies luck or chance. They affirm that the state or condition described by the term *makarios* is something more than "happiness"; it is a blessing bestowed by our Father in Heaven. It does not depend on "happenings," but on a relationship with God that sustains us regardless of what "happens."

B. Lesson Background

In September, our lessons dealt with some of Jesus' miracles. In October, they called attention to some of His parables. Now, during November, each lesson will be taken from a portion of what we call Jesus' Sermon on the Mount.

In his record of Jesus' life, Matthew does not always arrange events in chronological order. It is difficult, then, to determine exactly when Jesus gave the Sermon on the Mount. Many Bible students estimate that it was delivered during the first half of the second year of Jesus' ministry, and probably soon after He chose twelve men out of a larger group of disciples (Luke 6:12-16). He called these men *apostles,* which means "those who are sent." Jesus wanted these men to be "with him" to learn from Him; then He planned to "send them forth to preach" (Mark 3:14). The Sermon on the Mount was a part of the teaching they received, though it was given also to the larger group of disciples and to multitudes of other listeners.

I. Outdoor Setting
(Matthew 5:1, 2)

Jesus often chose wide-open spaces in which to teach because the crowds that gathered around Him were too big to be contained in the narrow streets of a town (Mark 1:45).

A. People and Place (v. 1a)

1a. And seeing the multitudes, he went up into a mountain.

Jesus *went up into a mountain* to find a good place for teaching. In today's English we would call where He went a *hill* rather than a *mountain,* for the area around the Sea of Galilee is full of hills. Probably Jesus chose a hillside that provided a natural amphitheater where the *multitudes* could both see and hear Him as He taught.

B. Teacher and Students (vv. 1b, 2)

1b. And when he was set, his disciples came unto him.

It was customary for a teacher to be seated as he taught. Here, Jesus probably sat down either on the ground or on a rock. *His disciples,* as soon as they saw the spot He had chosen, took their places in front of Him, getting as close as they could.

The word *disciples* means learners. Sometimes in the Gospels it is used of the twelve apostles; sometimes it is used of the larger group of learners. No doubt the Twelve and the larger group were both present on this occasion.

2. And he opened his mouth, and taught them, saying.

Usually I attend Sunday school with a class of about fifty members. A public-address system makes it possible for everyone to hear the teacher. Day after day Jesus *taught* uncounted thousands of people in the open air. What a magnificent voice He must have had! And His message was even more magnificent than His voice!

II. The Beatitudes
(Matthew 5:3-12)

The New Testament was originally written in Greek, and we read it in English; but for a long time Rome was considered the center of Christianity. Latin, the language of Rome, was used by Christian scholars all over Europe. Each verse of our text that begins with the word *blessed* was viewed as describing a source of blessedness or happiness. The Latin word for that is *beatitudo.* This has come over into English as *beatitude,* and so these statements of Jesus beginning with the word *blessed* are called the Beatitudes.

A. The Poor in Spirit (v. 3)

3. Blessed are the poor in spirit: for theirs is the kingdom of heaven.

One who is *poor in spirit* feels deep within himself that he is spiritually poor and needy—with a need that he cannot supply for himself. *The kingdom of heaven* belongs to those poor in spirit, because they are willing to receive it. They are willing, even eager, to be ruled by Jesus the King. They exert themselves in doing His will, and they find joy in doing it. [See question #1, page 88.]

B. The Mourners (v. 4)

4. Blessed are they that mourn: for they shall be comforted.

The publican in Jesus' parable (which we studied two weeks ago) offers a perfect example

of what this Beatitude means. He mourned over his sins; beating his breast (Luke 18:13) was the traditional expression of deep sorrow. He went home "justified," or forgiven (Luke 18:14). What blessed comfort!

C. The Meek (v. 5)

5. Blessed are the meek: for they shall inherit the earth.

Who are the *meek*? Words similar in meaning are "mild," "gentle," and "patient." Meek people prefer to avoid conflict, but that does not mean that they are weak or cowardly. Students of Greek tell us that the Greek word for *meek* was used of a horse that was trained to pull a plow or carry a rider. A meek horse does not waste his strength in conflict, as a wild horse does when he is captured. Instead, his strength is channeled toward the accomplishment of a useful purpose. Likewise, a meek person desires to use his or her energy in God-pleasing tasks rather than in combat.

In what way will the meek *inherit the earth*? Perhaps we should think of inheriting the earth as much more than just the enjoyment of material goods and wealth. There is also the sense of fulfillment and contentment that comes when one uses the resources of earth as the Creator intended them to be used. This is a blessing that those who use the earth's resources selfishly can never call their own. And when this old earth is replaced by a new one, the meek will enjoy that one even more (2 Peter 3:10-13).

D. The Hungry (v. 6)

6. Blessed are they which do hunger and thirst after righteousness: for they shall be filled.

A greater blessing than *hunger* for food is hunger *after righteousness,* or *for* righteousness.

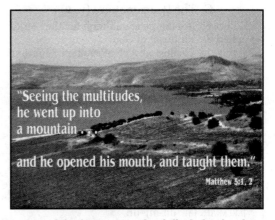

"Seeing the multitudes, he went up into a mountain...

and he opened his mouth, and taught them."

Matthew 5:1, 2

Visual for lesson 10. *This hillside by the shore of the Sea of Galilee is believed to be the site where Jesus preached the Sermon on the Mount.*

Hunger for food compels us to get some food; hunger for righteousness compels us to get some righteousness.

How do we obtain righteousness? There are two ways. One is by simply doing right. We can try to keep that up every day, but it is not enough. So God has provided a second way to obtain righteousness—a way by which our righteousness can be made complete. Speaking of this better way, Paul wrote that he desired to "be found in him, not having mine own righteousness, which is of the law, but that which is through the faith of Christ, the righteousness which is of God by faith" (Philippians 3:9). So by God's gracious forgiveness, we can be *filled* with the righteousness of Christ. But that will not take place unless we are hungry and thirsty—unless we really want to be righteous. [See question #2, page 88.]

E. The Merciful (v. 7)

7. Blessed are the merciful: for they shall obtain mercy.

Merciful people are grieved by the grief or pain of others, and they do what they can to end it. Often, when those who have been merciful are in trouble, they will *obtain mercy* from others who are aware of their kindness. Best of all, God will bless them and show mercy to them.

F. The Pure in Heart (v. 8)

8. Blessed are the pure in heart: for they shall see God.

Pure gold is solid gold all the way through; it is not mixed with anything cheaper. The *pure in heart* have hearts of solid good: their tastes, their thoughts, their desires, their motives are good. They do not value or desire anything evil. [See question #3, page 88.]

G. The Peacemakers (v. 9)

9. Blessed are the peacemakers: for they shall be called the children of God.

God is the greatest peacemaker of all. Our sins made us His enemies (Colossians 1:21); but instead of destroying us, He loved us and sent His only begotten Son to die in our place (Romans 5:8). When we believe in Jesus and obey Him,

---

How to Say It

BEATITUDES. Be-*at*-ih-tudes.
BEATITUDO (Latin). be-*at*-ih-*too*-doe (strong accent on *too*).
ELIJAH. Ee-*lye*-juh.
JEREMIAH. Jair-uh-*my*-uh.
MAKARIOS (Greek). mah-*kah*-ree-oss.
MICAIAH. My-*kay*-uh.

---

our sins are forgiven and we have peace with God (Romans 5:1). We then find a blessing in making and keeping peace with our Christian brothers and sisters and, if possible, with all men (Romans 12:18).

H. The Persecuted (vv. 10-12)

10. Blessed are they which are persecuted for righteousness' sake: for theirs is the kingdom of heaven.

Jesus' life was faultless, yet evildoers were constantly plotting to kill Him (Matthew 26:3, 4; John 5:18; 7:1). He warned His disciples that they would be *persecuted,* too (John 15:20; 16:2).

11. Blessed are ye, when men shall revile you, and persecute you, and shall say all manner of evil against you falsely, for my sake.

Here the general promise of verse 10 is applied to the disciples whom Jesus was teaching (vv. 1, 2). Is it not applicable to us as well? Notice, however, that there is no promise of blessing unless the persecution comes for Jesus' *sake*. If we suffer because we have done wrong, or because we have not been poor in spirit (v. 3) or meek (v. 5) or merciful (v. 7), then we have no blessing (cf. 1 Peter 4:15). The *evil* spoken *against* us must be false, not accurate.

12. Rejoice, and be exceeding glad: for great is your reward in heaven: for so persecuted they the prophets which were before you.

The persecution of God's people did not begin with Jesus and His disciples. God's *prophets* had been mistreated long before this. Consider such examples as Elijah (1 Kings 19:2, 13, 14), Micaiah (1 Kings 22:26, 27), and Jeremiah (Jeremiah 37:15; 38:6).

The book of Acts tells how disciples of Jesus were beaten and imprisoned (Acts 5:17, 18, 40; 8:3), killed (Acts 7:59, 60), and driven out of Jerusalem (Acts 8:1). But they were not to wail or complain. Jesus said, *Rejoice, and be exceeding glad: for great is your reward in heaven.* Acts tells of this happening as well (Acts 5:41).

"SAY IT AIN'T SO!"

Joe Jackson, who maintained a .400 batting average for the Chicago White Sox, was accused of throwing the 1919 World Series. According to baseball legend, when the charge against Jackson was made, a little boy who was a devoted fan said, "Say it ain't so, Joe."

But times have changed. Nowadays, when we hear of the antics (or even criminal activity) of professional athletes, we are supposed to look the other way if their athletic performance is noteworthy. When a "star" is suspended for illegal or questionable conduct, many fans respond, "So what? Look what a great player he is!"

Perhaps all of this would be irrelevant if sports stars were not held in such high regard by young people who see these athletes as enjoying the kind of life worth emulating. Success seems to be the only standard by which we are to measure success! But Jesus says, "Say it ain't so!" He calls us to a different standard. In the Beatitudes, He tells us that a life worth living—a happy life—is measured neither by selfish indulgence nor by disregard for how one's actions affect others, but by one's character, service to others, and the pursuit of godliness.   —C. R. B.

III. The Salt
(Matthew 5:13)

The rest of our text describes the impact Jesus' disciples are to have on the rest of the world.

A. Good Salt (v. 13a)

13a. Ye are the salt of the earth.

As commonly used, *salt* has two purposes. First, it makes foods taste better. Almost any meat or vegetable dish is bland if the cook forgets to salt it. Only a little salt is needed, but it makes a big difference. Likewise Christians may be only a minority of the world's population, but they improve the flavor of the whole.

Salt is also used to preserve foods. (Such use was much more common before there were refrigerators and freezers in homes and stores.) Seeing how much evil there is in the world, do you ever wonder why God hasn't destroyed it before now? Perhaps this old world is being preserved by the *salt of the earth*. God is giving you and me and the other Christians time to win yet more people to Christ and to eternal life (2 Peter 3:9). This brings to mind yet another application of the salt metaphor that some have suggested: just as salt makes us thirsty, Christians are meant to have such an impact that they make others thirsty for Christ.

B. Bad Salt (v. 13b)

13b. But if the salt have lost his savor, wherewith shall it be salted? it is thenceforth good for nothing, but to be cast out, and to be trodden under foot of men.

In ancient Israel, *salt* was often gathered from the shores of the Dead Sea. During the dry, hot summer, the shallow water at the edge of the Dead Sea would evaporate rapidly, leaving its salt on the beach to be picked up. This was not pure salt, of course; it was mixed with other minerals that had been suspended in the water. Pure salt is easily dissolved; so if any rain fell while the salt lay on the beach with other minerals, much of the salt was washed back into the sea.

Anyone who picked up what was left would have salt that had *lost* its *savor*, or its distinctive flavor. Such inferior salt could not improve the flavor of a piece of meat or keep it from spoiling.

What a disappointment for someone to discover that his salt had lost its savor! He would not have wanted to throw it on a field or a garden; that would make the soil less productive. Most likely he would dump it on an often *trodden* path, where nothing would grow anyway. [See question #4, page 88.]

WHEN SALT KEEPS ITS SAVOR

Chris Lapel fled from Cambodia in 1979. While in a refugee camp, he became a Christian. Later he came to America and eventually graduated from Pacific Christian College. Today Lapel ministers to the Golden West Cambodian Christian Church in Los Angeles. He also goes back to his homeland on a regular basis to tell his people about Christ.

Two small churches that Lapel started in a refugee camp have become more than a hundred churches with approximately eleven thousand members—"the closest thing [I've seen] to what is depicted in the Book of Acts," said an elder from an American church who visited the area.

During Lapel's trip back to Cambodia in 1993, he met Duch (*Dook*), the director of a Communist prison where thousands were murdered between 1974 and 1979. Lapel told Duch about Christ and Duch became a Christian. Duch has admitted his responsibility for the deaths of those thousands of prisoners. He says he is willing to face justice and wants only to "serve God by doing God's work to help people." Duch now understands that work to include preaching the gospel to others of his people.

Both Lapel and Duch are living demonstrations of what happens when Christian salt *keeps* its savor: lives are changed through the influence of people who take the words of Jesus seriously. These two men are modern-day examples of the amazing power that characterized first-century Christianity and is meant to characterize it in every century.   —C. R. B.

IV. The Light
(Matthew 5:14-16)

We cannot see the salt in our soup, but with the first spoonful we know it is there. It makes the soup taste much better. Jesus' people are like that: not flamboyant, not noisy, but quietly at work to make the world better.

Now we turn to another symbol of Jesus' people: light. Like salt, light works silently yet effectively. It comes quietly with the dawn, but its impact is far-reaching. Christians are like that too. They do not brag about their goodness, yet it cannot be hidden.

A. That Others May See (vv. 14, 15)

14. Ye are the light of the world. A city that is set on a hill cannot be hid.

On another occasion Jesus said, "I am the *light of the world*" (John 8:12). Here He describes His disciples in the same way. Could we say that Jesus is like the sun? His light is His own: it shines from His own person. His people, then, are like the moon that reflects the light of the sun; in other words, Christians shine with the light of Jesus. Just as a *city* on a hilltop can be seen for miles and just as the moon can be seen all over the world, the light of a sincere Christian is seen by all who know him.

15. Neither do men light a candle, and put it under a bushel, but on a candlestick; and it giveth light unto all that are in the house.

Some versions of the Bible more accurately read *lamp* and *lampstand* instead of *candle* and *candlestick*, for the ordinary household light in New Testament times was provided by a small lamp fueled by olive oil. Yet Jesus' words are true, whether we think of a candle, an oil-burning lamp, or an electric light bulb. The purpose of a lamp would be frustrated if we hid it *under a bushel* basket or a big salad bowl. We leave the lamp uncovered and place it where it will best fill the room with *light*.

B. That God May Be Glorified (v. 16)

16. Let your light so shine before men, that they may see your good works, and glorify your Father which is in heaven.

This instruction seems plain and straightforward, but it calls for some serious thinking. Jesus was sharply critical of people who did good "to be seen of *men*" (Matthew 23:5). He advised His people to do good secretly (Matthew 6:1-4). Now we find Him telling them to let others *see* their *good works*.

Perhaps the key to understanding this seeming contradiction is in the last phrase of our text: *glorify your Father which is in heaven*. God's people ought to be doing good, of course, but doing it in such a way that grateful people will praise God more than they praise His people. [See question #5, page 88.]

Conclusion

A. How the Light Works

Millie was a fragile widow in her nineties. She had no family except her son Ben, who had tuberculosis. The doctor said that Ben needed to live in a desert climate; it would be better for someone in his condition. So Millie fixed a bed for him in their old car and drove west.

At the edge of the desert one Saturday morning, she spent the last of her money for groceries. On a desert road that evening she ran out of gas and steered the car off the road before it stopped rolling. She slept on a cot beside the car, and in the morning she walked a mile to the church in a little town.

Millie declined invitations to lunch, explaining where her son was and what had happened to them. People took her back to her car, and others followed quickly with a hot dinner, a folding table, and some chairs. "The Lord gave us more than we needed," they said. "We think He meant it for you."

Millie said, "Praise the Lord."

There was only one vacant house in the little town, and its roof leaked badly. It was small, too, but big enough for Millie and Ben. Before sunset the men of the church covered it with a new roof, while the women cleaned the inside, got the water and electricity turned on, and stocked the refrigerator. Then someone took some gas to Millie's car and escorted her to her new house. "Nobody's using it," the owner explained. "I think God wants you to live here."

Millie said, "Praise the Lord."

Of course, Millie was grateful to the Lord's people; but she said, "Praise the Lord."

B. Prayer

Thank You, Lord. Almost daily You give us opportunities to do good. May we have eyes to see each one, strength to make use of it, and wisdom to give You the glory. In Jesus' name, amen.

C. Thought to Remember

Do good, and praise the Lord.

Learning by Doing

This page contains an alternate lesson plan emphasizing learning activities.
Classes desiring such student involvement will find these suggestions helpful.

Learning Goals

After participating in this lesson, each student will be able to:

1. Tell what the primary theme of the Beatitudes is and how Jesus described the impact Christians should have in the world.

2. Tell how practicing the Beatitudes can make Christians "salt" and "light" in their community.

3. Choose one of the Beatitudes and seek to apply its message to his or her responsibility as salt and light.

Into the Lesson

Prior to class, design an overhead transparency sheet titled, "Contrasting Perspectives of Happiness," with two columns. Label the left column "Worldly Perspectives of Happiness," and label the right column "Christian Perspectives of Happiness." When class begins, turn on the overhead projector to show this chart to the class. Say: "Today we want to contrast the worldly and the Christian perspectives of happiness. What makes people happy according to the world? Call out your ideas, and I'll write them." *(Ideas could include money, possessions, power, position, prestige, sin, selfish indulgence.)* Then ask, "Now, what do you think makes Christians happy?" *(Worship, giving, sharing, helping others, serving others, Christ, salvation.)* After ideas have been generated, say: "The worldly perspective is radically different from the Christian perspective. Open your Bibles to Matthew 5:1-16, and read what Jesus says makes us, not just happy, but blessed."

Into the Word

Ask a class member to read the lesson text to the class. Then ask, "What is the primary theme of these Beatitudes?" *(Personal qualities that make people truly happy or blessed.)* Briefly go over the meaning of these eight Beatitudes as described in the text commentary. Move the class into groups of three and distribute a handout you have prepared with the following questions:

1. How did Jesus describe the impact Christians should have in this world? *(Christians are to be salt and light.)*

2. What did Jesus mean when He said we are to be the "salt" of the earth? *(Salt cleanses, purifies, protects, and enhances flavor. We are to do the same spiritually.)*

3. Describe what Jesus meant when He said we are the "light" of the world. *(Light attracts attention, shows the path to walk, dispels darkness. We are to do the same spiritually for those who are lost.)*

4. What is the relationship between practicing these Beatitudes and Jesus' teaching His disciples to be salt and light in this world? *(These Beatitude qualities are so uncommon in this world that they become as noticeable as light in a dark room and salt on a piece of food.)*

5. What attitudes or behaviors hinder one's cultivation of these Beatitudes? *(Answers may include selfishness, pride, greed, and anger.)*

Give about ten minutes for the groups to work on these questions. Then review the questions and answers. Say: "Jesus sets before us the obligation and the responsibility of being visible witnesses for Him in a dark world. Not only does such behavior bring happiness to us, it also brings glory and praise to God (v. 16). Let's apply these principles to our lives today."

Into Life

Once again, prior to class, prepare another worksheet to give to the class members. This two-column chart should be titled, "Applying the Beatitudes to Life." Down the left column, labeled "Beatitudes," list the eight Beatitudes; label the right column "Specific Applications." Give these worksheets to the class and ask: "In what specific ways can Christians apply these Beatitudes to their responsibility of being 'light' and 'salt' in this world?"

Divide the class into four groups, and assign each group two Beatitudes. Allow ten minutes for the groups to develop some specific applications. Provide either newsprint and markers or transparency sheets and markers on which each group can write its answers. Ask each group to share its answers with the class. Say: "We have looked at ways Christians can apply these Beatitudes to their responsibility of being salt and light. Now I want you to select one Beatitude and one specific application that you especially need in your life. Meet with one other person in the room now; I'll give you a few minutes to share the Beatitude and application with one another. Then pray for each other to keep this commitment to God. This will help you feel a mutual responsibility to one another as you seek to grow in Christ."

Let's Talk It Over

The questions on this page are designed to encourage review of the lesson Scriptures and to promote discussion of the lesson by the class. The answers provided are only discussion starters. Let your class talk it over from there.

1. Jesus' commendation of "the poor in spirit" seems out of step with much popular thinking today. "Be assertive!" "Be aggressive!" "Don't let anything stand in your way!" Even Christians seem caught up in this kind of thinking. How can we encourage people to be poor in spirit?

The assertive are worried they will not get their due recognition. They work hard to succeed, and they want to be sure everyone knows it. They are like the "pagans" Jesus spoke of who "run after" the necessities of life (Matthew 6:32, *New International Version*). We need to cultivate a faith in God to provide for our needs and a confidence in the future based on God's justice. We need to help believers to make the Lord's kingdom and His righteousness their first priority.

2. How would you describe one who has a "hunger and thirst after righteousness"?

"Being good" is not good to many people! They think being good requires one to miss out on all that is "fun." Or they think that no one would want to be the friend of a truly "righteous" person. It is appropriate to point out that Jesus, as good and righteous as He was, did not lack for friends or for times of enjoyment.

One who hungers and thirsts for righteousness does not hesitate to aim for the highest level of righteousness he can reach. He longs for it as much as he does for food and drink. Like Jesus in the temple at the age of twelve, one who hungers for righteousness "must be about [his] Father's business" (Luke 2:49). Such a one will "watch and pray, that [he] enter not into temptation" (Matthew 26:41). This person will be active in ministry, involved with people, and committed to the Lord. He will be like Jesus!

3. How can we be "pure in heart" while living in a society where there is much impurity?

To be pure in heart involves pure thoughts, hopes, motives, and responses. Even if we avoid the radio, the television set, modern magazines, and the like, we are certain to be exposed to impurity. Wherever human beings gather—in the workplace, in social gatherings, at shopping areas, even in church—the way they dress and conduct themselves and speak can stir us to impure thoughts. Job had an approach to that problem that can help us. He said, "I made a covenant

with my eyes not to look lustfully at a girl" (Job 31:1, *New International Version*). What kind of similar covenant can we make? It is good to draw up a list of all the wholesome and beautiful sights on which we can focus our eyes: playful children, animals and birds, flowers and trees, great works of art, the words of the Bible, etc. We can dedicate our eyes to viewing all that is pure, and forbid their gazing upon anything that would make our thoughts impure.

4. Most Christians feel the moral state of society is in decline. How valid is the preservative figure of the "salt of the earth" metaphor for today? What implications does it have for us?

It is true that moral values are eroding, and the church must accept the fact that it has failed in this critical area. But that does not make the figure invalid; it simply shows that the salt has not been applied. And while a local congregation cannot change the whole world, it can make a difference in its own community. It will take time: the preservative value of salt is unseen and difficult to measure. So it is with our influence as Christians. Many of our words and actions seem to bring few observable results. But we never know the effect we may exert on another person in helping him to be a better husband or father, in encouraging her to be a more conscientious wife or mother, in nudging either of them along toward the decision to become a Christian. Knowing that we are like salt, working slowly and imperceptibly in this way, can encourage us in our witness for Christ during those periods where we do not appear to be accomplishing any good.

5. Contrast the behavior of those who do good deeds "to be seen of men" with those who follow Jesus' instruction to let their light shine "before men" so that they will glorify God.

The former seek only credit for doing good. They will not accept menial tasks that no one will notice. They will exaggerate their own importance in an enterprise. They will take shortcuts whenever possible so that the praise for completing a job is quicker in coming. The latter, however, take the long view. They will work behind the scenes whenever necessary—more interested in the task itself, which will glorify God, than in getting personal credit for doing it.

Jesus Fulfills the Law

DEVOTIONAL READING: Amos 5:4-15.

BACKGROUND SCRIPTURE: Matthew 5:17-48.

PRINTED TEXT: Matthew 5:17-20, 38-48.

Matthew 5:17-20, 38-48

17 Think not that I am come to destroy the law, or the prophets: I am not come to destroy, but to fulfil.

18 For verily I say unto you, Till heaven and earth pass, one jot or one tittle shall in no wise pass from the law, till all be fulfilled.

19 Whosoever therefore shall break one of these least commandments, and shall teach men so, he shall be called the least in the kingdom of heaven: but whosoever shall do and teach them, the same shall be called great in the kingdom of heaven.

20 For I say unto you, That except your righteousness shall exceed the righteousness of the scribes and Pharisees, ye shall in no case enter into the kingdom of heaven.

. . . .

38 Ye have heard that it hath been said, An eye for an eye, and a tooth for a tooth:

39 But I say unto you, That ye resist not evil: but whosoever shall smite thee on thy right cheek, turn to him the other also.

40 And if any man will sue thee at the law, and take away thy coat, let him have thy cloak also.

41 And whosoever shall compel thee to go a mile, go with him twain.

42 Give to him that asketh thee, and from him that would borrow of thee turn not thou away.

43 Ye have heard that it hath been said, Thou shalt love thy neighbor, and hate thine enemy.

44 But I say unto you, Love your enemies, bless them that curse you, do good to them that hate you, and pray for them which despitefully use you, and persecute you;

45 That ye may be the children of your Father which is in heaven: for he maketh his sun to rise on the evil and on the good, and sendeth rain on the just and on the unjust.

46 For if ye love them which love you, what reward have ye? do not even the publicans the same?

47 And if ye salute your brethren only, what do ye more than others? do not even the publicans so?

48 Be ye therefore perfect, even as your Father which is in heaven is perfect.

GOLDEN TEXT: Think not that I am come to destroy the law, or the prophets:
I am not come to destroy, but to fulfil.—Matthew 5:17.

Jesus' Ministry
Unit 3: The Sermon on the Mount
(Lessons 10-13)

Lesson Aims

After this lesson a student should be able to:

1. Tell how Jesus fulfilled the law with love and taught His disciples to do the same.

2. Compare some wrong contemporary ideas about human relationships with those of which Jesus said the people had "heard it said," but that He replaced.

3. List the names of two or three people whom he or she can love this week with *agape*, as Jesus commands us to do.

Lesson Outline

INTRODUCTION
    A. The New Testament Helps Us
    B. The Old Testament Helps Us
    C. Lesson Background
 I. JESUS AND THE LAW (Matthew 5:17-20)
    A. Fulfilling the Law (vv. 17, 18)
    B. Keeping the Law (vv. 19, 20)
II. JESUS AND HUMAN RELATIONS (Matthew 5:38-42)
    A. Nonviolence (vv. 38, 39)
    B. Generosity (vv. 40-42)
    The "Other Cheek" Approach
III. JESUS AND LOVE (Matthew 5:43-48)
    A. Well-known Saying (v. 43)
    B. Better Saying (v. 44)
    C. Follow Your Father (vv. 45-48)
    Lost in Translation
CONCLUSION
    A. Kinds of Love
    B. What Is *Agape*?
    C. Prayer
    D. Thought to Remember

Introduction

In a class of Junior boys, the teacher laid his Bible on the table. With his right hand he held the pages of the New Testament between thumb and forefinger. With his left hand he held the Old Testament pages. Then he asked, "Which of these would you rather learn and live by?"

Unanimously the boys chose the New Testament. It was smaller, so they thought it would be easier to learn and live by. The Old Testament looked three times as thick.

A. The New Testament Helps Us

There are better reasons to choose the New Testament, but there is no better choice. In the Old Testament, obedience to God and His law was linked to receiving eternal life (Leviticus 18:5; Romans 10:5). That way did not work, because no one has ever obeyed well enough (Romans 3:23). God then sent His sinless Son to suffer the death earned by sinners. Now sins can be forgiven and eternal life can be received as a gift (Romans 6:23). That offer is presented in the New Testament.

B. The Old Testament Helps Us

This does not mean that the Old Testament is no longer useful. All things recorded there, though they happened long ago, serve as "examples" for us and are recorded "for our admonition" (1 Corinthians 10:6, 11). Bad examples warn us not to repeat ancient mistakes (1 Corinthians 10:6-13). Good examples encourage us to follow them (Hebrews 11:4—12:2).

Last week we considered the first part of Jesus' Sermon on the Mount. This week we turn to the next part of it. In this section Jesus speaks of the Old Testament. He encourages us to have a high regard for it.

C. Lesson Background

Jesus had been teaching in Judea and Galilee for more than a year. Most likely many of the religious leaders in Jerusalem considered Him a lawless rebel, for He had driven from the temple those who were selling oxen, sheep, and doves to be used for sacrifices in the temple (John 2:13-21). In Galilee some Pharisees had accused Jesus and His disciples of violating the law of the Sabbath (Mark 2:23—3:6). Perhaps the accusation that Jesus was out to destroy the law of Moses was becoming more widespread.

In part of the Sermon on the Mount, Jesus contrasted some of His teachings with those of the Old Testament (Matthew 5:21-48). He prefixed those contrasts with a declaration of His respect for the Old Testament. (Note that today's printed text begins where last week's ended.)

I. Jesus and the Law (Matthew 5:17-20)

A. Fulfilling the Law (vv. 17, 18)

17. Think not that I am come to destroy the law, or the prophets: I am not come to destroy, but to fulfil.

Jesus did not intend to *destroy*, disregard, or disobey anything in God's Word. He and His disciples had not broken God's law regarding the Sabbath, as the Pharisees had charged (Mark

2:23, 24); they had ignored some mistaken interpretations of it.

The teaching of Jesus in Matthew 5:21-48 does not contradict or condemn the Old Testament law; it fulfills it. To *fulfil* is to "fill full." Let's consider four ways in which Jesus fulfilled the *law* and the *prophets*.

1. He fulfilled Old Testament laws by calling attention to their true meaning and to the need to keep the laws inwardly as well as by one's actions (Matthew 5:21-48).

2. He fulfilled the laws by obeying them fully and applying them as God intended. Driving the sellers and the money changers out of the temple is one example. [See question #1, page 96.]

3. He fulfilled Old Testament prophecies by doing what they foretold. (Compare Isaiah 53:4 with Matthew 8:16, 17; Psalm 78:2 with Matthew 13:34, 35; and Zechariah 9:9 with Matthew 21:4, 5. Many other examples could also be cited.)

4. The most significant way Jesus fulfilled the law was to complete its purpose. The law told what was right and what was wrong before God. It let people know that they were sinners, not good enough to receive eternal life (Romans 3:19, 20). It was a "schoolmaster to bring us unto Christ," by whom our sins are forgiven. When we come to Christ and are forgiven, the law is fulfilled. Its purpose is accomplished, and we are no longer under the schoolmaster (Galatians 3:24-26).

Consider one example of how to apply this principle. The law required a sinner to sacrifice an animal to atone for his sin. But the sacrifice of an animal is not enough to take away the sins of anyone. Such sacrifices were offered repeatedly until Jesus' death on the cross, through which sins really are taken away. Thus the law is fulfilled, and animal sacrifices are no longer necessary (Hebrews 10:1-18).

18. For verily I say unto you, Till heaven and earth pass, one jot or one tittle shall in no wise pass from the law, till all be fulfilled.

The *jot*, also called the *yod*, was the smallest letter in the Hebrew alphabet, just as the *i* is the smallest in the English alphabet. A *tittle* is merely a part of a letter, like the crossing of a *t* or the dotting of an *i* in English. Jesus said not even the tiniest part of the *law* would be removed *till all be fulfilled*. This happened when Jesus declared on the cross, "It is finished" (John 19:30).

B. Keeping the Law (vv. 19, 20)

19. Whosoever therefore shall break one of these least commandments, and shall teach men so, he shall be called the least in the kingdom of heaven: but whosoever shall do and teach them, the same shall be called great in the kingdom of heaven.

When Jesus said this, He had not yet died to fulfill the Old Testament law; so it was still in effect. All of God's people needed to obey it. To *break* even the *least* significant of God's *commandments* and to *teach* others to treat His law that way was unacceptable for anyone who would claim interest in *the kingdom of heaven*.

20. For I say unto you, That except your righteousness shall exceed the righteousness of the scribes and Pharisees, ye shall in no case enter into the kingdom of heaven.

The *scribes and Pharisees* claimed to be the most obedient of God's people, but they were not. They made a show of obeying in ways that could be seen and admired, but they neglected to obey in more important ways (Matthew 23:23). One could not *enter* God's *kingdom* at all unless he was more righteous than those hypocrites.

In the remainder of Matthew 5, Jesus contrasts the Old Testament law as understood and applied by the religious leaders of His day with His own teaching on a variety of subjects. In every instance, Jesus taught that sin and righteousness are found in one's thoughts and motives as well as in one's actions. To recognize this is to follow after the kind of righteousness that will "exceed" that of the scribes and Pharisees.

II. Jesus and Human Relations (Matthew 5:38-42)

One way to fulfill the law was to call attention to the need to keep God's laws inwardly as well as by one's actions. That way is demonstrated in Matthew 5:21-48. Jesus cited laws governing outward acts and then added teaching governing thoughts, feelings, and motives. He knew that if these were what they ought to be, the proper

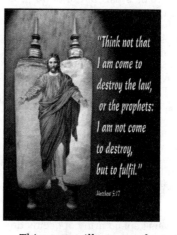

"Think not that I am come to destroy the law, or the prophets: I am not come to destroy, but to fulfil."
Matthew 5:17

Visual for lesson 11

This poster illustrates the truth that Jesus is the fulfillment of the Old Testament Scriptures.

actions would follow. The next part of our printed text focuses on a portion of Jesus' teaching that deals with person-to-person relations.

A. Nonviolence (vv. 38, 39)

38. Ye have heard that it hath been said, An eye for an eye, and a tooth for a tooth.

This had been clearly stated in the law (Exodus 21:23-25; Leviticus 24:19, 20). It established the principle of justice in the punishment of evildoers. It also served to limit acts of vengeance and thus to prevent bitter feuds from escalating into something worse. Without this law, a person who lost an eye might go so far as to seek to take the offender's life.

39. But I say unto you, That ye resist not evil: but whosoever shall smite thee on thy right cheek, turn to him the other also.

A slap on the *cheek* in Jesus' day was done to insult someone more than injure him. Some have compared it with spitting in someone's face. In such an instance, Jesus taught that the offended person should act in humility rather than seek justice or retaliation. He should even be willing to *turn . . . the other* cheek and accept an additional insult! [See question #2, page 96.]

B. Generosity (vv. 40-42)

40. And if any man will sue thee at the law, and take away thy coat, let him have thy cloak also.

Obviously this is the quickest way to settle a lawsuit—simply give the plaintiff more than he asks, but do it cheerfully, not resentfully or grudgingly. Such generosity is costly, of course—costly to the one who gives up both his *coat* (the shirt-like tunic or "inner garment" that a person usually wore) and his *cloak* (the heavier "outer garment"). That may be a part of the point Jesus was making. The generous giver gains peace, approval, and goodwill. Aren't these worth whatever price one pays?

At the same time, this verse does not mean that Christians are to be "doormats," allowing people to take advantage of them. It means that Christians are to be concerned about more than just their "rights." Such an attitude will set them apart from those who are continually demanding their rights and are quick to sue anyone who stands in their way. Jesus wants His people to be more concerned about relations with others than with personal rights.

41. And whosoever shall compel thee to go a mile, go with him twain.

In Jesus' day Israel was annexed to the Roman Empire. The Romans kept an army of occupation there to keep the peace and prevent uprisings. Jews resented the presence of these foreigners, and resented it all the more because each Roman soldier on duty was authorized to draft a civilian at will to carry his pack for a *mile*. (This *mile* was the Roman mile—about a kilometer and a half, or nine-tenths of a mile, as we measure it today.) We can imagine the angry grumbling that the soldier heard throughout that mile.

But what if a draftee would take up the pack with a cheerful smile? What if the mile was filled with friendly conversation instead of grumbling? What if the draftee would then volunteer to go another happy mile? Enmity would be swallowed up by goodwill. From this teaching of Jesus comes the familiar phrase, "going the second mile." A follower of Jesus should go above and beyond "duty" to render service.

42. Give to him that asketh thee, and from him that would borrow of thee turn not thou away.

This verse may get our attention more quickly than those before it because those who ask us for help are probably more than those who hit us in the face, file lawsuits against us, or compel us to go a mile. Since the news media keep us constantly aware of millions in desperate need, it is literally impossible for us to give meaningful help to all of them. We have to recognize at least two kinds of limitations.

First, Jesus does not want us to neglect our own families in order to help needy people (1 Timothy 5:8).

Second, Jesus does not want us to give to literally everyone who asks. [See question #3, page 96.] Years ago a friend who works downtown told me of a day when he left the office and went out for a late lunch. On the street a poorly dressed man asked him, "Can you give me some money to get a bit of lunch?"

"I'm going to lunch right now," my friend responded. "Come along and be my guest. You can have anything on the menu."

The man turned away, snarling a curse. It was easy to guess that he had eaten his lunch already. He wanted money only for cigarettes or booze or some illegal drug. Should a follower of Jesus give to him just because he asked?

Paul encouraged Christians to be among the most generous of people (Galatians 6:10). But he also instructed that if an able-bodied person would not work, then neither should he eat (2 Thessalonians 3:10).

THE "OTHER CHEEK" APPROACH

Some folks don't think much of Jesus' "other cheek" approach to interpersonal problems. Consider Sam Horrell, self-appointed "governor, mayor, sheriff, postmaster, clerk, and banker" of Sammyville (unincorporated, population about forty), located in the northeastern corner of the

How to Say It

GALILEE. *Gal*-uh-lee.
JUDEA. Joo-*dee*-uh.
PHARISEES. *Fair*-ih-seez.
YOD. yode.

state of Oregon. "No trespassing" signs abound around Sammyville, and some have the added message that "trespassers will be shot." Sam owns one hundred and fifty registered firearms and has a concealed weapon permit. No one knows how many other guns exist in Sammyville.

Sam is a devout churchgoer, but he seems to follow Teddy Roosevelt's dictum, "Speak softly and carry a big stick," more than Jesus' plea to "turn the other cheek." He is reputed to be a kind and generous man, but he has also been known to pull his guns—triggers cocked—on anyone who threatens him.

Living out Jesus' teaching on how to respond to evil has always been difficult, but that's no reason for us not to make the attempt. Jesus applies the principle to dealing with insults, fending off lawsuits (the use of which, unfortunately, is an ever-more-popular tactic, even among Christians), and responding to a simple request for help. In each case, Jesus says, "Take the initiative and be pro-active in doing good, even to those who might do otherwise to you." —C. R. B.

III. Jesus and Love (Matthew 5:43-48)

It is fitting that some teaching about love follows the teaching about generosity, for love is the motive of our generous help; and lack of love limits our willingness to be of help.

A. Well-known Saying (v. 43)

43. Ye have heard that it hath been said, Thou shalt love thy neighbor, and hate thine enemy.

Thou shalt love thy neighbor was written plainly in the law (Leviticus 19:18). In contrast, *hate thine enemy* was not in the law at all. However, at times Israel was commanded to exterminate certain enemies (Deuteronomy 7:1, 2; 20:16, 17; 1 Samuel 15:3). It is not surprising that later teachers added *hate thine enemy* to the popular teaching that was heard in the synagogues.

B. Better Saying (v. 44)

44. But I say unto you, Love your enemies, bless them that curse you, do good to them that hate you, and pray for them which despitefully use you, and persecute you.

Love your enemies. That must have surprised all who heard it! Not only did it seem contrary to popular teaching; it seemed contrary to human nature. But Jesus intended to change human nature. His way answers cursing with caring, hatred with helpfulness, persecution with prayer. [See question #4, page 96.]

C. Follow Your Father (vv. 45-48)

45. That ye may be the children of your Father which is in heaven: for he maketh his sun to rise on the evil and on the good, and sendeth rain on the just and on the unjust.

Don't say you can't love your enemies or do good to those who hate you (v. 44). *Your Father which is in heaven* provides people who are *evil* and *unjust* with both *sun* and *rain*—the same sun and rain that He gives to His *children*. Children are expected to be like their Father—to love all those He loves, to do good to all those who enjoy His goodness.

46. For if ye love them which love you, what reward have ye? do not even the publicans the same?

Of course you *love* your family and friends—the people who *love you*. So what? Those *publicans* (tax collectors), those people you think are the very worst—they also love their families and friends who love them. Are you content to be like the worst of people, or do you want to be like your Father in Heaven?

47. And if ye salute your brethren only, what do ye more than others? do not even the publicans so?

Of course you *salute*, or greet, your *brethren* with joy and affection, but that does not mark you as a Christian. If you are a child of God, you ought to be helping a wider circle of people; for your Father in Heaven is "kind unto the unthankful and to the evil" (Luke 6:35). [See question #5, page 96.]

48. Be ye therefore perfect, even as your Father which is in heaven is perfect.

Too readily we excuse our imperfections by saying, "Nobody's perfect." Yet in some ways and within human limits, we can and ought to be *perfect*, as perfect as God Himself.

The Greek New Testament has several words that are translated into English as *perfect*. The word that is used here also means "complete" or "mature." In what ways can we be as complete as our *Father which is in heaven*? We can in no way match His omnipotent power, obviously, or His unlimited knowledge and wisdom. But this text is talking about loving our enemies (v. 44). We can and ought to love all those whom God loves, and we ought to do good to them as we have opportunity (Galatians 6:10). Instead of trying to excuse our imperfections, let's try to improve our loving and helping.

LOST IN TRANSLATION

Excitement mounted among personnel at the National Aeronautics and Space Administration (NASA) as the Mars Climate Orbiter approached the "red planet" in the fall of 1999. The excitement turned to dejection, however, when the orbiter flew too close to Mars and was destroyed.

As the data were analyzed to discover what had gone wrong, the answer was found to be embarrassingly simple: the navigation team at Jet Propulsion Laboratories had used the metric system of millimeters and meters in its calculations, while the builders at Lockheed-Martin Astronautics had provided their data in the English system of feet and inches! Years of work by hundreds of people and an expenditure of $125 million dollars were lost because the data were "lost in translation" from one form of measurement to another—and no one caught the error.

Far too often, Jesus' instructions about loving our enemies have been "lost in translation" from the pages of Scripture to the pages of our lives. This isn't a matter of spoken or written languages; it's the difference between the language of godliness and the language of this world.   —C. R. B.

Conclusion

We English-speaking people are terribly unkind to that small word *love*. We load it with so many meanings that we hardly know what it means when we hear it.

The ancient Greeks were kinder. They took the many meanings we have attached to love and distributed them among at least four words, each of which describes a specific kind of love.

Home Daily Bible Readings

Monday, Nov. 5—The Law in Perspective (Galatians 3:19-29)

Tuesday, Nov. 6—Burdensome Laws Are Barriers to Faith (Luke 11:37-52)

Wednesday, Nov. 7—Hypocrisy Doesn't Work (Luke 12:1-7)

Thursday, Nov. 8—Murder, Anger, or Reconciliation (Matthew 5:21-26)

Friday, Nov. 9—Lust: Adultery in the Heart (Matthew 5:27-32)

Saturday, Nov. 10—"Swear Not at All" (Matthew 5:33-37)

Sunday, Nov. 11—To Fulfill, Not to Destroy (Matthew 5:13-20)

A. Kinds of Love

Eros (*air*-oss) refers to sexual love. That kind is proper between husband and wife, and in no other setting. In its place it ought to be strong and lasting, but it has no place in this lesson. In fact, *eros* is not found in the New Testament.

Storge (*store*-gay) is family love, especially the love of parents for children and children for parents. That word appears in the New Testament with a negative prefix, and is translated "without natural affection" (Romans 1:31; 2 Timothy 3:3).

Phileo (fih-*leh*-oh) is friendly love. The noun form is translated *friendship* in James 4:4, but the verb form of the same word appears many times and is translated *love*.

Agape (uh-*gah*-pay) is the kind of love mentioned most often in the New Testament. Its noun form appears more than a hundred times and is translated *love* or *charity*. God loves the whole world with *agape* (John 3:16), and this is the kind of love we are commanded to have for our enemies (Matthew 5:44).

B. What Is *Agape*?

Someone has defined *agape* as active, intelligent goodwill without regard for a response. It is active: it does good to the loved one (Matthew 5:44). It is intelligent: thoughtfully, it does nothing but good, and it gives the loved one what he needs rather than what he wants. It is goodwill: earnestly it desires what is best for the loved one. And it is selfless, loving not because it is loved, but whether or not it is loved in return.

Some claim that love cannot be commanded or chosen—that it is an emotion that arises unbidden, sometimes even against our will. That may be true of *eros* or *storge*, or even to some extent of *phileo*, but it certainly is not true of *agape*. Deliberately, thoughtfully, by an act of our own mind and will, we choose to love our enemies and do good to them as Jesus commands (Matthew 5:44). Thus do we demonstrate that we are children of our Father in Heaven.

"Jesus Fulfills the Law." So says the title of this lesson. As Jesus' people, we are not under the law (Romans 6:14). As Jesus' people we join Him in fulfilling the law, and we do so by living under the control of *agape* (Romans 13:8-10).

C. Prayer

Father, we thank You that Jesus has fulfilled the law, and that we are under grace. By Your grace and our effort may our love become complete. In our Master's name, amen.

D. Thought to Remember

"Love is the fulfilling of the law" (Romans 13:10).

Learning by Doing

This page contains an alternate lesson plan emphasizing learning activities.
Classes desiring such student involvement will find these suggestions helpful.

Learning Goals

After participating in this lesson, each student will be able to:

1. Tell how Jesus fulfilled the law with love and taught His disciples to do the same.

2. Compare some wrong contemporary ideas about human relationships with those of which Jesus said the people had "heard it said," but that He replaced.

3. List two or three people whom he or she can love this week with *agape*, as Jesus commands.

Into the Lesson

Prepare an overhead transparency entitled "God's Law." Under the title write the following phrase, "Ways people respond to God's law." Below that phrase provide at least nine two-inch lines with the word "it" following each line. Set the stage for this activity by saying: "Pretend that you are at your computer. You have just connected to the Internet. Using a search engine to locate specific articles, you type in the phrase, 'responding to God's law.' Soon you have a number of 'hits.' Each 'hit' has a two-word title that ends with the word *it*. Each title describes one way that people respond to God's law. The first one listed is 'Obey it.' What other titles do you see? As you mentally see them, call them out and I'll write them on the transparency." *(Titles may include "disobey it, deny it, reject it, ignore it, rebuke it, follow it, forget it, avoid it, overlook it.")*

Say: "People respond to God's law in a variety of ways. In our lesson text today, Jesus gives another response to God's law: 'fulfill it.'"

Into the Word

Have the learners open their Bibles to Matthew 5:17-20, 38-48, and ask two class members to read these two passages. State: "With someone sitting next to you, discuss the answer to this question: What did Jesus mean when He used the term *fulfil* in verse 17?" *(Possible answers: He fulfilled the law by perfectly obeying it to become the perfect sacrificial Lamb without blemish; He fulfilled the prophets by doing what the prophecies foretold [see Isaiah 53:4 and Matthew 8:16, 17 as an example]; He fulfilled the law by adding a person's thoughts and motives to the concept of obedience to the law, Matthew 5:21-37. See the comments on page 91.)* Ask the following questions:

1. What did Jesus say would not pass from the law "till all be fulfilled"? *(One jot or tittle, v. 18.)*

2. What did Jesus say determines whether a person is great in the kingdom of Heaven? *(Obedience to God's law and teaching others to do the same, v. 19.)*

3. What kind of righteousness did Jesus say was needed to enter the kingdom? *(Greater than the righteousness of the scribes and Pharisees, v. 20.)*

4. Describe the righteousness of the scribes and Pharisees. *(Diligent but hypocritical in following the law; legalistic; concerned about appearing righteous, Matthew 6:5, 16.)*

5. How could a person's righteousness exceed that of the scribes and Pharisees? *(Obedience from the heart; a recognition that salvation is undeserved and is by grace through faith.)*

6. In your own words, what is the principle of the law in verse 38? *(Treat others the way they treat you; get even; pay back equal evil for evil.)*

Into Life

State: "In verses 38-44, Jesus presents teaching that goes beyond the law in the way that we respond no matter how people treat us."

7. What is the principle underlying Jesus' teaching in verses 39-42 on how we should respond? *(Non-retaliation; generosity.)*

8. What unnatural principle does Jesus encourage us to follow when we respond to those who curse, hate, or persecute us? *(Love, v. 44.)*

9. What does Jesus say we become when we respond in the way He instructs? *(Children of our Father, v. 45.)*

10. Describe how God the Father models these principles. *(The Father treats the evil and the good, the just and the unjust, the same, v. 45.)*

State: "Loving, non-retaliatory behavior is what Jesus expects from His servants. We bless those who curse us, we do good to those who hate us, and we pray for those who persecute us. Such a response is totally unexpected and goes counter to our culture. Yet it truly reflects our Heavenly Father." Give an index card to each student in the class. Say: "Think of some people who need you to respond to them in loving non-retaliation. They may curse you, hate you, or persecute you. Write down the names of two or three. Beside each name write the specific action you will take this week to show that you love the person and that you are a child of your Father."

Let's Talk It Over

The questions on this page are designed to encourage review of the lesson Scriptures and to promote discussion of the lesson by the class. The answers provided are only discussion starters. Let your class talk it over from there.

1. Like Jesus, we should aim to fulfill the demands of the law through love. What are some practical ways we can do that?

Encourage your learners to take specific commands and suggest positive behaviors that would fulfill these. For example, the law says we should not misuse the name of the Lord. Out of love for the Lord, we should speak of God and of Christ in a constantly respectful and constructive manner. The law says we must honor our father and mother. Our love for the Lord should keep us from saying or doing anything that would reflect unfavorably on our parents. It should stir us to provide whatever care, support, and encouragement they need from us.

2. Even for a committed Christian the challenge of "turning the other cheek" is a difficult one. What are some Biblical helps we can use in meeting this challenge?

In Proverbs 15:1 we are told that "a soft answer turneth away wrath: but grievous words stir up anger." It should excite us to put this principle into practice. We may be amazed at how powerful soft words can be. Proverbs 16:32 informs us that "he that is slow to anger is better than the mighty; and he that ruleth his spirit than he that taketh a city." The world places a high value on being able to intimidate others through physical strength or intellectual superiority. But we must see that real strength lies in restraint and self-control. In the New Testament we recall the advice Paul gave in Romans 12:17-21. By going out of our way to return good for evil, we can melt the heart of our adversary, leading him to abandon his spiteful behavior toward us that now embarrasses him.

3. Jesus said, "Give to him that asketh thee." Sometimes, however, it is better *not* to give to someone. What should we do then?

Love gives us the proper perspective for resolving this dilemma. We do not refuse the one who asks because he is poorly dressed or she is rude or we are in a bad mood. But if we see that our gift would be misused on drugs or alcohol, or if it would discourage the individual from finding employment, then love dictates our withholding it. Jesus once refused the request of a man who was apparently obsessed with material things (see Luke 12:13-21). It would not have been loving for Jesus to intervene in that man's dispute with his brother. Similarly we must demur when people seek our aid in enterprises that are selfish, materialistic, or otherwise sinful. But when we see that our gift of money or assistance will positively build up the individual who is asking, then love will impel us to give as generously as possible.

4. Jesus said, "Pray for them which despitefully use you, and persecute you." How is that a very practical way of loving our enemies?

It has often been observed that it is virtually impossible to hold a grudge against someone for whom you are praying. Of course, the kind of prayer offered is important. We must not merely say, "Lord, help him see how much he has hurt me," or, "God, make her apologize to me for her hateful words." Instead, we must pray, "Help him, O Lord, with the problems and pressures that cause him to act the way he does," or, "Show her Your love, dear God, and lead her to yield up to You her hatred and bitterness." If we further pray that God will use us to communicate His love and compassion to that offending individual, such a prayer can be an even better agent for changing our heart. This prayer approach may help us fulfill Proverbs 16:7: "When a man's ways please the Lord, he maketh even his enemies to be at peace with him."

5. Some people believe that if they love and take care of their families, such love should put them in good standing with God. What did Jesus say about that viewpoint?

Jesus said that love focused only on those who love us and on those closest to us is inadequate (Matthew 5:46, 47). Love for these people, after all, involves a measure of self-interest. As Paul pointed out in Ephesians 5:28: "He that loveth his wife loveth himself." When we love husband, wife, and other family members, we have good reason to believe that such love will be returned to us. But God wants us to love the unlovable and the unloving. This kind of love is not something we develop by ourselves, and thereby earn a good standing with God. Instead, we come to God through Jesus Christ, and then this love "is shed abroad in our hearts by the Holy Ghost which is given unto us" (Romans 5:5).

Storing Treasures in Heaven

DEVOTIONAL READING: Philippians 4:4-9.

BACKGROUND SCRIPTURE: Matthew 6.

PRINTED TEXT: Matthew 6:19-34.

Matthew 6:19-34

19 Lay not up for yourselves treasures upon earth, where moth and rust doth corrupt, and where thieves break through and steal:

20 But lay up for yourselves treasures in heaven, where neither moth nor rust doth corrupt, and where thieves do not break through nor steal:

21 For where your treasure is, there will your heart be also.

22 The light of the body is the eye: if therefore thine eye be single, thy whole body shall be full of light.

23 But if thine eye be evil, thy whole body shall be full of darkness. If therefore the light that is in thee be darkness, how great is that darkness!

24 No man can serve two masters: for either he will hate the one, and love the other; or else he will hold to the one, and despise the other. Ye cannot serve God and mammon.

25 Therefore I say unto you, Take no thought for your life, what ye shall eat, or what ye shall drink; nor yet for your body, what ye shall put on. Is not the life more than meat, and the body than raiment?

26 Behold the fowls of the air: for they sow not, neither do they reap, nor gather into barns; yet your heavenly Father feedeth them. Are ye not much better than they?

27 Which of you by taking thought can add one cubit unto his stature?

28 And why take ye thought for raiment? Consider the lilies of the field, how they grow; they toil not, neither do they spin:

29 And yet I say unto you, That even Solomon in all his glory was not arrayed like one of these.

30 Wherefore, if God so clothe the grass of the field, which today is, and tomorrow is cast into the oven, shall he not much more clothe you, O ye of little faith?

31 Therefore take no thought, saying, What shall we eat? or, What shall we drink? or, Wherewithal shall we be clothed?

32 (For after all these things do the Gentiles seek:) for your heavenly Father knoweth that ye have need of all these things.

33 But seek ye first the kingdom of God, and his righteousness; and all these things shall be added unto you.

34 Take therefore no thought for the morrow: for the morrow shall take thought for the things of itself. Sufficient unto the day is the evil thereof.

GOLDEN TEXT: Seek ye first the kingdom of God, and his righteousness; and all these things shall be added unto you. Take therefore no thought for the morrow.—Matthew 6:33, 34.

Lesson Aims

After this lesson students should be able to:

1. Tell what Jesus said in this portion of the Sermon on the Mount about our treasures and our priorities.

2. Contrast Jesus' teaching about these matters with the world's perspective on material wealth.

3. Pinpoint an area of their lives where trust in God needs to replace worry, and commit that area to Him.

Lesson Outline

INTRODUCTION
  A. Many Money Problems
  B. Lesson Background
 I. CHOOSE THE BEST (Matthew 6:19-24)
  A. The Best Treasure (vv. 19-21)
  B. The Best Light (vv. 22, 23)
  C. The Best Master (v. 24)
II. TRUST THE BEST (Matthew 6:25-30)
  A. "Take No Thought" (v. 25)
  B. Consider the Birds (v. 26)
  C. Worry Is Worthless (v. 27)
  D. Consider the Flowers (vv. 28-30)
III. SUMMARY (Matthew 6:31-34)
  A. Trust God (vv. 31, 32)
  B. Put God First (v. 33)
    Forsaking All for the Kingdom
  C. Don't Worry (v. 34)
    Borrowing From Tomorrow's Troubles
CONCLUSION
  A. When to "Take *Some* Thought"
  B. Make Up Your Mind
  C. Prayer
  D. Thought to Remember

Introduction

One of the most memorable events of my childhood was our rural community's bank failure. In the language of the townspeople, the bank "went broke." Most of the farmers had recently deposited their returns from the wheat and barley harvests, and now they couldn't get a cent of their money. They had to survive the rest of the summer on the produce of their own farms. They all had chickens for eggs and cows for milk, and most had some fruits and vegetables as well.

Ultimately the farmers were able to get back most of what they had deposited in the bank. Until then there was considerable discussion of what to do with one's money if and when it became available. Put it in the other bank? That one might go broke, too. Keep it at home? You couldn't sit there all day with a shotgun to guard it. Some of the farmers devised hiding places under floors or in walls where thieves would never find their savings. But what if the house burned down?

A. Many Money Problems

Money problems have been around as long as money has. If you have no money, your problem is how to get some. If you have more than you can use immediately, your problem is how to keep it safe. A servant in one of Jesus' parables buried his money in the ground, but his master called him "wicked and slothful" (Matthew 25:25, 26). Other servants put their money to work and managed to double it. That was great, but the prospect of such a return must have involved a certain amount of risk. Today's investment counselors all warn us that there is no investment without risk, and that a big return requires a big risk.

This week's lesson brings us an exception to that rule. Just invest your treasures in Heaven. There is no risk involved, and the return is far greater than you can ever imagine.

B. Lesson Background

Today's study is the third of four lessons drawn from Jesus' Sermon on the Mount. Jesus was teaching His disciples on a hill in Galilee, and a large crowd was listening (Matthew 5:1, 2).

I. Choose the Best (Matthew 6:19-24)

Jesus' disciples must have been aware of the financial risk involved in choosing to follow Him. We are told that some of them left their jobs to become disciples of someone who had no place to lay His head (Matthew 8:20). We are also told of certain individuals who "ministered unto him of their substance," apparently meaning that they provided material assistance to Jesus and the Twelve (Luke 8:1-3).

In the portion of the Sermon on the Mount studied today, Jesus confirms that those who have chosen to follow Him have made the best choice.

A. The Best Treasure (vv. 19-21)

19. Lay not up for yourselves treasures upon earth, where moth and rust doth corrupt, and where thieves break through and steal.

Jesus' words are not a prohibition against one's efforts to provide the necessities of life for himself or his loved ones. Such work is commended in Scripture (2 Thessalonians 3:12). Jesus is warning us not to consider material wealth (the things of this *earth*) our *treasures*. Material wealth is subject to decay and corrosion. And (like the farmers who were mentioned in the Introduction to this lesson) anyone with material wealth must guard against *thieves* who are more than eager for him to "share" his wealth. It was not very hard to *break through* the walls of most houses in Jesus' day, which were made of mud bricks. [See question #1, page 104.]

20. But lay up for yourselves treasures in heaven, where neither moth nor rust doth corrupt, and where thieves do not break through nor steal.

It is hard to argue with the fact that *treasures in heaven* are eternally secure, but how can you *lay up* your treasures there? One way is to help Jesus' brethren who are in need, thereby identifying with Jesus Himself (Matthew 25:31-40). With that thought in mind, you can probably think of specific treasures that are suited to your particular circumstances.

For example, the money you send to a missionary who is holding forth the Word of life on the other side of the world or is planting a new church on the other side of your hometown—don't you know it is credited to your account beyond the skies? The sacrificial gift you give to a college that is preparing preachers of the gospel—aren't you certain that it has been deposited in your Heavenly treasure with interest beyond your imagining? And don't think that your treasure is all in money. Each precious hour you spend in unpaid Christian service will be waiting with interest when you "inherit the kingdom prepared for you from the foundation of the world" (Matthew 25:34).

There are so many ways to lay up treasures in Heaven! So choose the way that is best for you and most suited to your abilities and opportunities. Just be sure that you don't leave all your treasures on earth and end up a pauper where Heavenly treasures are concerned.

21. For where your treasure is, there will your heart be also.

Often we notice that one's *treasure* follows his *heart*. For instance, if you visit an orphans' home and really fall in love with it, some of your money will go there. But Jesus reminds us of the other side of the picture. One's *heart* follows his *treasure*. If you really aren't interested at all in what your church's favorite missionary is doing, try doubling your contribution to that mission. Of course, you won't want your money to be wasted, so you will learn all you can about the work of

the mission—and you will soon find that your heart is in that mission. Perhaps you will then double your contribution again. Or, if you have not been very interested in the local work of your church, try putting twice as much time into it. You'll be surprised to see how dear to your heart that work becomes. [See question #2, page 104.]

B. The Best Light (vv. 22, 23)

22. The light of the body is the eye: if therefore thine eye be single, thy whole body shall be full of light.

The light of the body is the eye. It is through our eyes that we become conscious of light, and with light comes a vast amount of information, understanding, and guidance. Thus does Paul use the phrase "the eyes of your understanding being enlightened" (Ephesians 1:18) to express his desire that the Ephesian Christians grow in their knowledge of the Lord.

If *therefore thine eye be single.* If your eyes (your attention and thinking) are focused only on treasure in Heaven and what produces it, *thy whole body shall be full of light*: you will be thoroughly enlightened with truth and goodness. Your motives, your thinking, your talking, and your doing will be guided in ways pleasing to the Lord. You will be laying up treasure in Heaven.

23. But if thine eye be evil, thy whole body shall be full of darkness. If therefore the light that is in thee be darkness, how great is that darkness!

On the other hand, if your attention and thinking are focused on earthly treasure without any regard for what God says is right and wrong, then you shut out the light of truth and goodness. Instead you become filled with the *darkness* of selfishness and greed. The eye is the only way you have of receiving light. If it brings you darkness instead, *how great is that darkness!*

C. The Best Master (v. 24)

24. No man can serve two masters: for either he will hate the one, and love the other; or else he will hold to the one, and despise the other. Ye cannot serve God and mammon.

It is true that a man can have two jobs with two different employers—especially if they are part-time jobs. But he cannot serve both employers with equal devotion. If both want his service at the same time, he has to make a choice. One job will be his principal one; the other will receive whatever leftover time is available.

Mammon is a word that describes treasure on earth—money and all that money can buy. It is true that most of us who serve God work for money as well. But serving God is a full-time job. Even when we are working at the job that provides

Home Daily Bible Readings

Monday, Nov. 12—Treasure of a Good Foundation (1 Timothy 6:11-17)

Tuesday, Nov. 13—Gold and Silver Don't Last (James 5:1-6)

Wednesday, Nov. 14—Be Patient (James 5:7-12)

Thursday, Nov. 15—Full Barns, Empty Soul (Luke 12:13-21)

Friday, Nov. 16—Life Is More Than Food (Luke 12:22-28)

Saturday, Nov. 17—Strive for the Kingdom (Luke 12:29-34)

Sunday, Nov. 18—"Where Your Treasure Is . . ." (Matthew 6:19-21, 25-34)

our living, God's directions are to guide every area of life. If mammon wants us to do something contrary to God's teaching, we have to make a choice. It is better to serve God and starve than to serve mammon and disobey God. [See question #3, page 104.]

II. Trust the Best
(Matthew 6:25-30)

When we choose the best Master, God, that choice relieves us of the responsibility of making some other choices that might be difficult. When God tells us plainly to do something, we do it and trust Him for the outcome. When He tells us not to do something, we refuse to do it, no matter how enticing mammon makes it seem. Either way, we trust God, and we don't worry.

A. "Take No Thought" (v. 25)

25. Therefore I say unto you, Take no thought for your life, what ye shall eat, or what ye shall drink; nor yet for your body, what ye shall put on. Is not the life more than meat, and the body than raiment?

The phrase *take no thought for your life* does not mean that we should do no planning for tomorrow's meals or fail to go to the grocery store for supplies. It simply means "don't worry."

God, the Master you have chosen, has given you *your life*. That is a greater gift than the food you eat. Don't you know that He who gives the greater gift will also give the lesser one? You know God has given you *your body*, and it is of far greater significance and value than the *raiment* (clothes) you wear. Don't you know that He who gives the body will also supply the clothing for the body? So trust God and don't worry.

This does not mean that you need not work for pay, shop for food, or cook your dinner. It means

you work, shop, and cook without being anxious, without worrying.

B. Consider the Birds (v. 26)

26. Behold the fowls of the air: for they sow not, neither do they reap, nor gather into barns; yet your heavenly Father feedeth them. Are ye not much better than they?

Perhaps some *fowls* (birds) could be seen near the hillside where Jesus and His audience were. These birds are not idle, but neither are they anxious about their daily food. They do the work they are created to do, and the *heavenly Father* provides for them. Any human being is worth *much* more than many such birds. How can anyone doubt that God will feed him if he does the work the Creator has designed him to do?

C. Worry Is Worthless (v. 27)

27. Which of you by taking thought can add one cubit unto his stature?

The basic meaning of the word translated *stature* here is "age" or "time of life." Thus, some translators think that this question refers to the length of a man's life instead of his height. The *New International Version* says, "Who of you by worrying can add a single hour to his life?" This word does sometimes refer to stature, however, both in secular Greek and elsewhere in the New Testament. And the word *cubit* is clearly a measure of distance or height, equal to about half a meter, or eighteen inches. The *American Standard Version* keeps some of the ambiguity of the original: "Which of you by being anxious can add one cubit unto the measure of his life?"

However we translate it, the question has the same answer. In fact, the dual understanding may be deliberate, for both illustrate the point Jesus is making: worry is worthless. It can neither make a man taller nor make him live longer; in fact, it may shorten his life! So why worry?

D. Consider the Flowers (vv. 28-30)

28. And why take ye thought for raiment? Consider the lilies of the field, how they grow; they toil not, neither do they spin.

In today's English we might render Jesus' words as follows: "Why worry about clothing? Look at the wildflowers that bloom every spring. They do not labor long hours, as people do, to spin wool into yarn, weave yarn into fabric, and sew fabric into garments."

29. And yet I say unto you, That even Solomon in all his glory was not arrayed like one of these.

Solomon was king of Israel at the peak of that nation's power and *glory*. Surely he wore the very best clothing that could be made at that time. Yet even he was not *arrayed* (dressed) as beautifully as one of those common wildflowers on the hillside.

30. Wherefore, if God so clothe the grass of the field, which today is, and tomorrow is cast into the oven, shall he not much more clothe you, O ye of little faith?

Don't you know that you are worth more than the wildflowers? They may be prettier than you are, but not for long. Quickly they wither, and soon they and other sun-dried plants are raked up and used as fuel to bake the bread in someone's backyard *oven*. You can see how God clothes them beautifully in spite of their short life; don't you know He will *clothe you* adequately if you faithfully do the work He designed you to do? How can you be so lacking in *faith* and trust that you worry about where your next set of clothes will come from? [See question #4, page 104.]

III. Summary
(Matthew 6:31-34)

Many people have been amused by the way one preacher described his method of constructing a sermon: "First I tell them what I'm going to tell them. Then I tell them. Then I tell them what I've told them."

Jesus did not exactly follow that procedure in the text we have before us, but He did make two points emphatic by repeating them: "Trust God" and "Don't worry."

A. Trust God (vv. 31, 32)

31. Therefore take no thought, saying, What shall we eat? or, What shall we drink? or, Wherewithal shall we be clothed?

As already noted, the phrase *take no thought* is better expressed by *don't worry* or *don't be anxious*. Jesus' counsel is particularly appropriate today, when so many worry about these items.

32. (For after all these things do the Gentiles seek:) for your heavenly Father knoweth that ye have need of all these things.

The word *Gentiles* refers to pagan peoples, idol worshipers. They know nothing of a *heavenly Father* who rules the universe and who cares for His people. They become desperate when they are hungry or when they experience hard times. Children of God do know their Father—or they ought to. They know that He lives, He rules, He knows, and He cares.

B. Put God First (v. 33)

33. But seek ye first the kingdom of God, and his righteousness; and all these things shall be added unto you.

To *seek . . . first the kingdom of God* is to seek above everything else to be ruled by Him. It means desiring to know His will and do it. When you live by God's priorities, you can be assured that He will not leave you without the food and clothing about which so many fret and worry. [See question #5, page 104.]

FORSAKING ALL FOR THE KINGDOM

H. L. Mencken called it "the greatest news story since the Resurrection." He was talking about King Edward VIII's abdication of the British throne. Edward announced that he was stepping down for the sake of "the woman he loved." The woman was Wallis Simpson, a commoner and an American, once divorced and involved in an affair with the king (although still married to her second husband). Her divorce was a major problem, since in those days it was thought scandalous for the head of the Church of England (the king) to marry such a woman. British papers kept the matter quiet as long as they could.

Edward's abdication avoided what could have been a major constitutional crisis in England. But he was willing to lose his claim to a kingdom for the sake of "the woman he loved."

In contrast, Jesus calls us to "seek *first* the kingdom of God." He challenges us to give up all other allegiances for the sake of "the God we love." While this appears to be a foolish risk in the eyes of many, we who know and serve our Heavenly Father realize that we are always in His care. The real risk—one with eternal consequences—is taken by the individual who tries to live as if he himself were king.   —C. R. B.

C. Don't Worry (v. 34)

34. Take therefore no thought for the morrow: for the morrow shall take thought for the things of itself. Sufficient unto the day is the evil thereof.

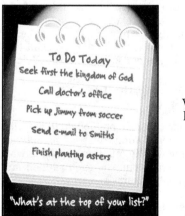

Visual for lesson 12

Use this poster to encourage your students to put the Lord's kingdom first on their priority list.

Three times in our text we have seen the words *take . . . no thought*. Like every good teacher, Jesus knew the value of repeating. He capped this section of His teaching by saying once again, "Don't worry." Don't spoil today by worrying about *the morrow*. Tomorrow will bring its own problems. Spend today dealing with today's problems, not worrying about what has not yet happened. Live one day at a time—and live it acknowledging God as the Giver of that day and of all that He allows you to enjoy that day.

BORROWING FROM TOMORROW'S TROUBLES

There was once a time when business executives could leave all their cares at the office. But now, thanks to all of our "labor-saving" devices, it is getting harder and harder to do that. Cell phones, laptop computers, and e-mail make it increasingly difficult to "disconnect."

A recent survey of five thousand executives revealed that 82 percent of them worked during their vacations. More than a fourth of them called the office on their days off, and 13 percent checked their e-mail when away from work. Cutting a vacation short because of work was admitted to by 13 percent of the executives. "If you don't stay in touch," the surveyers concluded, "you'll fall behind."

Of course, people in many occupations seldom have "days off." Farmers whose livestock need daily feeding and/or milking and stay-at-home mothers of small children are two groups of people who would love to get a day off, even if they had to "stay in touch."

Whatever our occupation, excessive involvement in our work can lead to mental burnout, poor health, disrupted family life, and decreased involvement in spirit-nurturing activities such as church attendance. Trying to get ahead of tomorrow's troubles can actually increase the trials tomorrow may bring. Our experience should tell us that Jesus was right when He said, "Take no thought for the morrow: for the morrow shall take thought for the things of itself."   —C. R. B.

Conclusion

A. When to "Take *Some* Thought"

We have noted that *take no thought* in the *King James Version* means "don't worry." Sometimes without thinking we slip into the mistake of worrying about material concerns such as food and clothing and other treasures on earth.

We ought not to worry about treasure in Heaven either, but we ought to "take *some* thought," as the word *thought* is more commonly used. Even the *King James Version* uses the word *think* in the way we usually do today. It urges us

to do some thinking about matters that are quite in harmony with laying up treasures in Heaven. Here are a few examples.

Think about good things. Fill your mind with them (Philippians 4:8). Shut out evil thoughts (1 Corinthians 13:4, 5).

Think about Jesus. Think of what a glorious Savior He is (Hebrews 3:1-3). Think how much He endured for you (Hebrews 12:3, 4).

Think about yourself. Don't be conceited, but make a fair estimate (Romans 12:3). Watch yourself lest you be tempted (Galatians 6:1).

Think about your fellow Christians. Consider ways to stir them up to love one another and to do good (Hebrews 10:24).

Think about your Christian leaders. Think about the outcome of their way of life, and imitate their faith (Hebrews 13:7).

B. Make Up Your Mind

Worry flourishes in a divided mind. Perhaps you have chosen the best Master and the best treasure; yet there is something you really need, like a new car or an extended vacation or an addition to the house. So just this once you decide to take orders from mammon. You overcharge a customer, or misrepresent your merchandise, or cheat on your income tax. It's just this once, but next year you may "really need" something else, and that will be "just this once," too. Soon mammon has you in its grip, and your worries begin to increase.

So make up your mind. Give first place to God's kingdom and His righteousness. Refuse to do anything dishonest, mean, or greedy—no matter what mammon offers. Make the old car last another year, or maybe two or three. Go camping in the nearest state park instead of taking a cruise. Put a cheaper partition in that basement bedroom instead of building an addition to the house. See if a cheaper detergent will work as well as the highly advertised one. God will bless your full allegiance, and you will stop lying awake at night with worry.

Make up your mind. God is your Master; seek to please Him day by day. Treasure in Heaven is your objective; store it up hour by hour. God's peace is a by-product of your commitment; enjoy it moment by moment (Philippians 4:7).

C. Prayer

Dear Father, gracious Father, loving Father, we do want to please You in all our thinking and talking and doing. Help us, we pray, in our efforts to do so. In Jesus' name, amen.

D. Thought to Remember

My mind is made up.

Learning by Doing

This page contains an alternate lesson plan emphasizing learning activities. Classes desiring such student involvement will find these suggestions helpful.

Learning Goals

After this lesson students will be able to:

1. Tell what Jesus said in this portion of the Sermon on the Mount about our treasures and our priorities.

2. Contrast Jesus' teaching about these matters with the world's perspective on material wealth.

3. Pinpoint an area of their lives where trust in God needs to replace worry, and commit that area to Him.

Into the Lesson

Begin by asking the class to move into groups of three. Give each group paper and pencils. Say: "This morning I'm going to ask you a question, and I'd like you to generate a list of answers. You will have about three minutes. Here is the question: 'What do people use to keep their valuables and possessions safe and secure?'" *(Possible answers: locks, security systems, alarms, computer passwords, safety deposit boxes, and safes.)* After sufficient time has been given, ask the group with the most answers to read them. Then ask if the other groups have additional answers. State: "People use many different ways to protect their valuables and possessions. Yet, security of our valuables is never guaranteed. Even very complex security systems have not always prevented the theft of valuable merchandise."

Observe that today's lesson focuses on Jesus' words about treasures and priorities. Then ask the learners to turn to Matthew 6:19-34.

Into the Word

Ask a class member to read Matthew 6:19-23 aloud to the class. Then ask these questions:

1. What happens to treasures stored on the earth? *(Moths eat the fabric; rust destroys metal; and thieves steal the treasures, v. 19.)*

2. What is the connection between a person's treasure and a person's heart? *(Your heart follows, or is directed toward, what you value, v. 21.)* State: "Jesus stated that treasures stored in Heaven are secure: they will not be eaten, will not rust, and will not be stolen by thieves."

3. What does Jesus mean by "laying up treasures in Heaven"? *(He is talking about what we value, about our priorities. Jesus illustrates this in verses 22 and 23. If we are focused upon the light of truth and that is what we value, then our whole body will be characterized by that light of truth.)*

Ask another class member to read aloud Matthew 6:24-34. Then ask these questions:

4. What contrast does Jesus make in this passage of Scripture? *(Between two life ambitions: secular and godly. The secular focus is on accumulating possessions, gaining more and more wealth. The godly focus is on serving God, seeking His kingdom, and trusting Him to provide the basics of food and clothing.)*

5. What is the point of Jesus' illustrations about birds (v. 26) and flowers (v. 28)? *(God will provide our needs, so we have no cause for worry.)*

6. What does Jesus say should be the first priority of every person? *(Seeking the kingdom of God and His righteousness, v. 33.)*

Into Life

Jesus addresses a common characteristic of people: worry. Prior to class, prepare a handout and an overhead transparency entitled, "The World of Worry." Have two columns on this handout, one column for "Non-Christians" and the other for "Christians." Ask the class to move back into the groups of three, and give this assignment: "In each of your groups, have someone write down for the respective headings the worries that concern the non-Christian and the areas of life that concern the Christian."

Give several minutes for the groups to generate answers. Then ask for the answers to be reported to the class. As answers are given, write them on an overhead transparency so the class can see the answers. *(Possible answers: money, clothes, paying bills, possessions, safety, personal appearance, health, travel safety, and broken relationships.)* Say: "As you can see, Christians and non-Christians often worry about many of the same things. But what does Jesus teach about worry?" *(Worry does not change anything, v. 27; worry indicates little faith, v. 30; worry is unnecessary, v. 32.)* Summarize: "If worry is something that Jesus does not want us to do, what does He teach we *should* do? We must seek first the kingdom of God and His righteousness and trust Him to provide those things that we need."

Note that some of us worry about many of these same items in our own lives. Tell the students, "Select one item wherein trust in God needs to replace worry. After you select it, write a prayer to God committing yourself to trust Him to take care of you."

Let's Talk It Over

The questions on this page are designed to encourage review of the lesson Scriptures and to promote discussion of the lesson by the class. The answers provided are only discussion starters. Let your class talk it over from there.

1. "Lay not up for yourselves treasures upon earth," Jesus said. Some people have taken this to mean that Christians should not have savings accounts or insurance policies. What do you think about that?

Jesus was not condemning responsible investing practices. In fact, in the parable of the talents, the wicked servant was told he ought at least to have invested his master's money in a bank (with "the exchangers") so that it could gain interest (Matthew 25:26, 27). Of course, these practices can be means of hoarding wealth, as well, and that would be "laying up treasure on earth." The thoughtful Christian, however, will use such means as savings and insurance to provide for his or her family in times of special need or to save for a special project. Wise use of these means can even increase one's ability to contribute to certain efforts that advance the kingdom of God.

2. Jesus said, "Where your treasure is, there will your heart be also." What are some means we can use to make sure our treasure and our heart are in Heaven? Specifically, what are *you* doing in this regard?

One obvious way is to invest a significant portion of our income in Heavenly enterprises. A tithe is a good starting point. However, if we are really serious about having treasure in Heaven, we will want to go beyond the tithe by giving sacrificially to missions, Bible colleges, and benevolent works. Another approach is the investment of our time in Heavenly enterprises. When we sacrifice time for worship, Bible study, and Christian service, we leave less time for worldly pursuits and focus more on Heaven. More specifically, we can lay up Heavenly treasure by winning other people to Christ. When we can envision a reunion with dozens of people we have led to the Lord, that will add greatly to our anticipation of Heaven!

3. Few people would admit that money is their master, but it surely is in many cases. What are some tests we can apply to determine if money is our master?

How much time do we spend thinking about making money or spending it? If it is constantly in our thoughts, then money may be our master. How big a role does money play in the goals we have set for the next year or two or ten or twenty? How much of our income do we spend on ourselves, how much on other persons, and how much on God's work? On occasions when we have a choice between a money-making venture and an opportunity to serve others freely, what decisions do we make? It is essential to earn money to meet our needs and the needs of those who depend on us. But can we honestly say we master our money, or is it the other way around?

4. "Behold the fowls of the air. . . . Consider the lilies of the field," Jesus said. What other illustrations from nature demonstrate God's care for us?

"The heavens declare the glory of God; and the firmament showeth his handiwork" (Psalm 19:1). The marvel of creation itself should reassure us of God's care. We often refer to the creation's testimony to the existence of God, but too often we confine this to arguments with evolutionists. The fact of creation is evidence of God's power to do what He says He will do—that is, to take care of us. Why should we worry about that when the omnipotent Creator of the universe is the one who has promised?

Encourage your students to look for specifics—such as the birds and flowers Jesus mentioned. The water cycle is one example. The rain falls to the earth, but then it is not lost. It collects in lakes and oceans, evaporates, condenses in clouds, and then falls to the earth once again—a never-ending cycle of providence.

5. What is involved in heeding Jesus' exhortation to "seek . . . first the kingdom of God"?

We should seek first the kingdom in regard to our time. Christians are called to assemble for worship on the first day of each week. That gives us the opportunity to set the tone and direction of the week by worshiping God and attuning ourselves to His will. Beginning each day with a brief period of Bible study and prayer will accomplish something similar. Seeking God's kingdom first is important in regard to our finances. The wise Christian steward sets apart God's portion of his income first and then applies the remainder to expenditures and investments. Giving to God first once again sets the tone for what we do with the rest.

Living by the Law of Love

DEVOTIONAL READING: Romans 13:8-14.

BACKGROUND SCRIPTURE: Matthew 7.

PRINTED TEXT: Matthew 7:1-5, 12-20.

Matthew 7:1-5, 12-20

1 Judge not, that ye be not judged.

2 For with what judgment ye judge, ye shall be judged: and with what measure ye mete, it shall be measured to you again.

3 And why beholdest thou the mote that is in thy brother's eye, but considerest not the beam that is in thine own eye?

4 Or how wilt thou say to thy brother, Let me pull out the mote out of thine eye; and, behold, a beam is in thine own eye?

5 Thou hypocrite, first cast out the beam out of thine own eye; and then shalt thou see clearly to cast out the mote out of thy brother's eye.

. . . .

12 Therefore all things whatsoever ye would that men should do to you, do ye even so to them: for this is the law and the prophets.

13 Enter ye in at the strait gate: for wide is the gate, and broad is the way, that leadeth to destruction, and many there be which go in thereat:

14 Because strait is the gate, and narrow is the way, which leadeth unto life, and few there be that find it.

15 Beware of false prophets, which come to you in sheep's clothing, but inwardly they are ravening wolves.

16 Ye shall know them by their fruits. Do men gather grapes of thorns, or figs of thistles?

17 Even so every good tree bringeth forth good fruit; but a corrupt tree bringeth forth evil fruit.

18 A good tree cannot bring forth evil fruit, neither can a corrupt tree bring forth good fruit.

19 Every tree that bringeth not forth good fruit is hewn down, and cast into the fire.

20 Wherefore by their fruits ye shall know them.

GOLDEN TEXT: Therefore all things whatsoever ye would that men should do to you, do ye even so to them: for this is the law and the prophets.—Matthew 7:12.

Lesson Aims

After completing this lesson, a student should be able to:

1. Tell what Jesus said about judging, not judging, and loving others in the way one wants to be loved.

2. Explain why Jesus' teaching about the narrow way and the examination of the fruits of others does not contradict living by the law of love.

3. Suggest a specific way to implement the "Golden Rule" this week, perhaps to the benefit of one he or she might be tempted to "judge" in the manner Jesus disallowed.

Lesson Outline

INTRODUCTION
    A. The Law of Love and the Golden Rule
    B. Lesson Background
  I. PROPER JUDGING (Matthew 7:1-5)
    A. Judge Not (v. 1)
    B. Judge Carefully (v. 2)
    C. Look at Yourself (vv. 3-5)
       Playing With Fire
 II. PRACTICAL GUIDANCE (Matthew 7:12-14)
    A. The Golden Rule (v. 12)
    B. The Two Ways (vv. 13, 14)
       The Dangers of the Broad Way
III. JUDGING BY RESULTS (Matthew 7:15-20)
    A. Testing Fruit (vv. 15, 16)
    B. Dependable Standards (vv. 17, 18)
    C. Unfruitful Tree's End (v. 19)
    D. Principle Reaffirmed (v. 20)
CONCLUSION
    A. Difficult Love
    B. God's Love Is Enough
    C. Prayer
    D. Thought to Remember

Introduction

"Living by the Law of Love." What a noble title for the closing lesson of this series from the life of Christ! What a ringing statement of what all of us should want to be doing! We are puzzled, then, when we read the lesson text from beginning to end, and the word *love* is not there. Have we forgotten the substance of the lesson in our search for a catchy title?

No, the title aptly states what the lesson is all about. The word *love* is not in the text, but the Golden Rule is there (v. 12). And the Golden Rule is closely related to the law of love.

A. The Law of Love and the Golden Rule

The twofold law of love appears clearly in Matthew 22:37-40: "Jesus said unto him, Thou shalt love the Lord thy God with all thy heart, and with all thy soul, and with all thy mind. This is the first and great commandment. And the second is like unto it, Thou shalt love thy neighbor as thyself. On these two commandments hang all the law and the prophets."

The Golden Rule appears in verse 12 of our text: "Therefore all things whatsoever ye would that men should do to you, do ye even so to them: for this is the law and the prophets." More often we hear the shorter paraphrase: "Do unto others as you would have them do unto you"; and that is not a bad summation. But the relation of this rule to the law of love is seen in what follows: "for this is the law and the prophets."

Thus all the law and the prophets "hang" on the twofold law of love: all the teachings of the law and the prophets are divisions and subdivisions of what is taught in that tremendous twofold law of love. And the Golden Rule "is the law and the prophets." It is the law and the prophets in action; it is their teaching applied. The Golden Rule tells briefly what you do when you are guided by the law and the prophets. So, in effect, the law of love and the Golden Rule are the same. Living by the Golden Rule is living by the law of love.

B. Lesson Background

The Sermon on the Mount is drawing to its close. Jesus has taught us how to be blessed (lesson 10). He has explained that He does not destroy the law, but fulfills it (lesson 11). He has reminded us that treasures in Heaven are vastly more precious than treasures on earth (lesson 12). He has given other important teachings, too—bright gems of truth that are not included in this short series of lessons.

Now the sermon soars to its climax in the call to live by the law of love.

I. Proper Judging (Matthew 7:1-5)

Good judgment is what we need when we choose a grocer to supply food for our table, a mechanic to repair our car, a trade to earn our living, a college to prepare us for a trade, and a husband or wife to fill life with joy. Yet our text begins with those two blunt words, "Judge not."

Does that mean we should stop trying to distinguish between good and bad, or between good and better? Of course not! Judging and choosing are necessary parts of intelligent living.

A. Judge Not (v. 1)

1. Judge not, that ye be not judged.

Often the command *Judge not* is quoted as if it were followed by a period. Faced by the most incriminating proof of his wrongdoing, someone will say, "Well, the Bible says we're not to judge." And this text is not the only one that warns against judging. "Therefore thou art inexcusable, O man, whosoever thou art that judgest: for wherein thou judgest another, thou condemnest thyself; for thou that judgest doest the same things" (Romans 2:1). (See also Romans 14:4 and James 4:12.) [See question #1, page 112.]

On the other hand, other Scriptures call us (just as clearly) to engage in judging. Look at Matthew 7:6, though it is not included in our printed text: "Give not that which is holy unto the dogs, neither cast ye your pearls before swine, lest they trample them under their feet, and turn again and rend you." No careful student thinks that this refers to literal dogs or hogs. And while there is some debate about just what Jesus meant by "that which is holy" and the "pearls," it is clear that some judgment must be made about who it is who should not receive them. This is consistent with what Jesus said, when, upon sending His disciples out to preach, He told them not to linger with hostile hearers, but to go on to another city (Matthew 10:23). The example of Paul and Barnabas also illustrates the same principle: when a Jewish audience began "contradicting and blaspheming" their efforts, they turned to the Gentiles with the holy "pearls" of the gospel (Acts 13:45-47).

Or consider verse 15 of our printed text: "Beware of false prophets." How can we do that unless we judge some so-called prophets to be false? Jesus warned against hasty judging "according to appearance," but He encouraged "righteous judgment" (John 7:24). Paul told the Corinthians to "judge" even what he himself was saying (1 Corinthians 10:15). The whole church is given the responsibility of judging unrepentant sinners, even of expelling them if they refuse to turn from their sinful ways (Matthew 18:15-17; 1 Corinthians 5).

Thus, according to Scripture, the necessity of judging is as clear as the warnings against it. Shall we conclude that the Bible contradicts itself? Certainly not. God's Word is always in harmony, but at times our understanding is faulty.

Then how should we understand *judge not* in our text? We must read the whole sentence:

Judge not, that ye be not judged. Jesus not only gives a command; He provides the reason for the command. He says that people are less likely to judge us if we do not judge them. The next verse expands on that thinking.

B. Judge Carefully (v. 2)

2. For with what judgment ye judge, ye shall be judged: and with what measure ye mete, it shall be measured to you again.

Some frequent critics seem almost gleeful in pronouncing *judgment* on others. Then they become indignant when someone points out any wrongdoing in their own lives. Jesus' counsel may be summarized as follows: if I am harsh, insensitive, and insulting in judging others, I can expect others to retaliate in the same way. And not only the one I insult will respond in kind; his friends will likely join in. If I am loud and long in my judgment of others, heaping a full *measure* of condemnation on wrongdoers, I can expect a similar measure of condemnation from others.

On the other hand, if I speak out in judgment only when absolutely necessary and if I do it with regret (more in sorrow than in anger or self-righteousness), then I can hope for an equally sympathetic judgment of my own misdeeds.

It is the "flip side," if you will, of the "Golden Rule." Do *not* do to others (judge them harshly) what you would not have them do to you (judge you thus). We are not surprised, then, when the "Golden Rule" shows up in this context (v. 12).

C. Look at Yourself (vv. 3-5)

3, 4. And why beholdest thou the mote that is in thy brother's eye, but considerest not the beam that is in thine own eye? Or how wilt thou say to thy brother, Let me pull out the mote out of thine eye; and, behold, a beam is in thine own eye?

Imagine someone concerned about a *mote* (a speck) in his *brother's eye*, while a large object (a wooden *beam*) is lodged in his *own eye*! As we try to help a Christian brother rid his life of sin, how often are we handicapped by sin in our own lives? And is our sin far more serious than his? Or perhaps it is made so by our presumption of innocence in picking at our brother's sin!

5. Thou hypocrite, first cast out the beam out of thine own eye; and then shalt thou see clearly to cast out the mote out of thy brother's eye.

We need to judge ourselves *first*. With honesty, humility, and clear thinking guided by God's Word, we can be made aware of our own sins. With the help of God's gracious forgiveness and with earnest effort on our part, we can get rid of those sins. At that point, the battle is not over; for we must guard against the sin of pride in our own goodness. If we can do that, we will be better prepared to judge our brothers with the aim of helping them get rid of their sins. Galatians 6:1 has a word about that: "Brethren, if a man be overtaken in a fault, ye which are spiritual, restore such a one in the spirit of meekness; considering thyself, lest thou also be tempted." [See question #2, page 112.]

PLAYING WITH FIRE

There seems to be no end to the production of "action" movies and television programs. These often feature special effects in which the "bad guy" gets blown to bits or the hero escapes dramatically from an exploding vehicle or building.

Pyrotechnic specialists (or "pyros" as they are called in the entertainment business) have developed to a fine science the art of fooling an audience into thinking that all the destruction they see is real. However, "pyros" recognize that they are literally "playing with fire." And on the rare occasion when something goes wrong, it can go *very* wrong. Such was the case several years ago when a special-effects explosion blew the tail rotor off a helicopter, resulting in a crash that killed an adult actor and two children.

The act of judging another requires similar caution. It is absolutely necessary for us to make judgments about the rightness or wrongness of many things; however, as Jesus clearly warns, we are playing with fire if we judge others without first judging ourselves and putting our own lives in order. Only then can we keep from getting burned when our angry spirits and stinging judgments are turned back upon us by those who see through our hypocrisy.   —C. R. B.

II. Practical Guidance (Matthew 7:12-14)

The law of Moses filled large portions of Exodus, Leviticus, Numbers, and Deuteronomy. Perhaps certain lawyers and scribes knew the laws recorded in those books, plus countless interpretations and court precedents that had been made authoritative; but no one else knew them. An ordinary farmer or merchant or carpenter did not even have the Scriptures at home, nor could he refer to them in a public library. Yet in the Sermon on the Mount (particularly in the Golden Rule), Jesus gave some simple helps for people who wanted to live according to the law and the prophets.

A. The Golden Rule (v. 12)

12. Therefore all things whatsoever ye would that men should do to you, do ye even so to them: for this is the law and the prophets.

For generations this has been known as the Golden Rule, and indeed it is more precious than

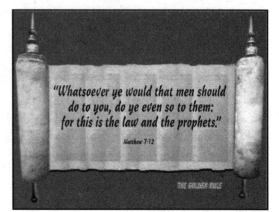

Visual for lesson 13. *The "Golden Rule," as this visual demonstrates, is a fulfillment of the law's entire code of how to treat one another.*

gold. How quickly it can be remembered! How readily it can be applied to almost anything you think of saying or doing to someone! How easily it can be passed on to children or grandchildren!

Jokesters like to have fun with the Golden Rule. One story tells of a husband who wanted a costly set of golf clubs. So, in obedience to the Golden Rule, he gave his wife such a set for Christmas, though she never played golf. A similar story tells of a wife who gave her husband a sewing machine because that was what she wanted him to give her. But Jesus' teaching is not meant to be used to further one's selfish interests; it is designed to help relationships between people be the kind that God wants them to be. [See question #3, page 112.]

B. The Two Ways (vv. 13, 14)

13. Enter ye in at the strait gate: for wide is the gate, and broad is the way, that leadeth to destruction, and many there be which go in thereat.

The word *strait* does not mean straight; it means narrow. Who wants to be like that, especially in today's society? Most of us like to go along with the crowd, to be congenial, to do what "everyone" is doing. Who wants to be labeled narrow-minded? But Jesus taught that the crowded expressway *leadeth to destruction*. If that is not where we want our lives to go, we had better not choose the *wide* road. We don't like to think that the majority is wrong more often than right, but what else can we think if we believe Jesus?

THE DANGERS OF THE BROAD WAY

During the last half of the twentieth century, many nations went on a road-building spree. In the United States, the Interstate system brought travelers new freeways and expressways of up to ten lanes in width. Europe developed a similar system of highways; perhaps the most familiar is the *autobahn* in Germany.

One of the attractions of such highways anywhere in the world is the apparent safety with which one can travel at high speed. As hills were leveled and dangerous curves straightened to construct the highways, the accident and fatality rates on these roads plummeted in spite of increasing traffic and higher velocities. Nevertheless, serious trouble still awaits the unwary. Just a couple of years ago, a crash on a German *autobahn* involved one hundred ten cars and caused one million dollars in damages. Amazingly, only two people were killed. Authorities said that fog had cut visibility to just thirty feet, and people were simply going too fast for the conditions.

These popular, broad highways almost beg drivers to travel too fast on them. The same is true of the "broad way" described by Jesus, where "fast living" can lead to destruction—with eternal consequences. Conditions on the broad way are much like those were on the German *autobahn* when the terrible crash described above occurred: too many people paying too little attention to matters involving life and death.—C. R. B.

14. Because strait is the gate, and narrow is the way, which leadeth unto life, and few there be that find it.

If *life* is our chosen destination, then we have to be content to travel with the minority. But let's not oversimplify the matter. In the choices that face us day by day, we cannot choose a position or a way just by counting the people who are in favor of it. The majority may be wrong more often than right, but it is not always wrong. In some cases, parting company with the majority

Home Daily Bible Readings

Monday, Nov. 19—Love Your Enemies (Luke 6:27-36)

Tuesday, Nov. 20—Do Not Judge (Luke 6:37-42)

Wednesday, Nov. 21—Enter Through the Strait Gate (Luke 13:22-30)

Thursday, Nov. 22—Love Fulfills the Law (Romans 13:8-14)

Friday, Nov. 23—Welcome the Weak (Romans 14:1-6)

Saturday, Nov. 24—Ask, Seek, and Knock (Matthew 7:6-11)

Sunday, Nov. 25—Who Will Enter? (Matthew 7:21-28)

might mean forsaking the truth. Therefore, day by day we must chart our course solely by God's Word, regardless of those who share the road with us. [See question #4, page 112.]

III. Judging by Results (Matthew 7:15-20)

We have been warned against judging hastily, harshly, and uncharitably, against judging by our own feelings or opinions, and against judging by majority vote. At the same time, we have learned that we must judge and make choices day by day. In the remainder of our printed text, Jesus tells us a dependable way to conduct the kind of judging that is acceptable to God.

A. Testing Fruit (vv. 15, 16)

15. Beware of false prophets, which come to you in sheep's clothing, but inwardly they are ravening wolves.

Sheep are peaceful animals. They have no claws or teeth or horns or hooves designed for battle. They depend on a shepherd for protection as well as direction. What could be more disastrous to a peaceful flock than a hungry wolf disguised as a sheep? Beware! Be alert! Don't let him fool you!

16. Ye shall know them by their fruits. Do men gather grapes of thorns, or figs of thistles?

Perhaps you don't know the difference between a fig tree and a sycamore tree—until the fruit appears. Then anyone can identify the fig tree. Perhaps you can't tell a wild grapevine from a good one until you see what grows on it. Then the good vine becomes apparent. [See question #5, page 112.]

B. Dependable Standards (vv. 17, 18)

17. Even so every good tree bringeth forth good fruit; but a corrupt tree bringeth forth evil fruit.

Here is a test that is always reliable: the nature of the *fruit* reveals the nature of the *tree*.

18. A good tree cannot bring forth evil fruit, neither can a corrupt tree bring forth good fruit.

This statement is essentially a restatement of the previous principle. A tree simply *cannot* bring forth any kind of *fruit* but its own.

C. Unfruitful Tree's End (v. 19)

19. Every tree that bringeth not forth good fruit is hewn down, and cast into the fire.

Fuel was scarce in the land where Jesus lived. A *tree* that was useless in bearing fruit still had some value in heating the oven where bread was baked. A man who does nothing *good* in this world does not even have that secondary use.

The fire where he will be cast will not benefit anyone (Matthew 25:41-46).

D. Principle Reaffirmed (v. 20)

20. Wherefore by their fruits ye shall know them.

The fruitless tree may have green leaves and even bright flowers, but the harvest season reveals that it is worthless. The fire is its destiny. Likewise, the false prophet (v. 15) or the do-nothing person (Matthew 25:42, 43) may have a handsome face and an eloquent tongue, but time will reveal his worthlessness. Judgment by one's *fruits*, or results, is an accurate judgment.

Conclusion

"Living by the Law of Love." That is the challenge in the title of this lesson. Have we wandered far from our subject in thinking so much about judging and not judging? No; for if we live by the law of love, we must constantly be judging and choosing. The wide road looks easy and inviting, but we are to judge righteously, not by appearance (John 7:24). We must look beyond the attractiveness of that easy road and judge it by its destination. It leads to destruction (Matthew 7:13). We must turn away from it and take the narrow, climbing road that leads to life (v. 14). In doing so, we will see that the law of love directs us to that same narrow way.

The law of love given through Moses directs our love in two paths: toward God and toward neighbors (Matthew 22:37-40). As expanded upon by Jesus, it prescribes a third direction—toward our enemies (Matthew 5:43-45). That compels us again to think about the nature of love. Obviously the love we give our enemies is not the kind of love that fills many fictional love stories. It is not a mutual attraction between a man and woman—a feeling that arises unbidden and sometimes becomes a consuming passion.

So what is love—the kind of love we have for God and neighbors and even for enemies? In lesson 11 we defined it as "active, intelligent goodwill." This love does not arise unbidden and dominate us against our will. We choose it because it is right. We cultivate it with difficulty, but we cultivate it persistently because it is the way of God's children.

A. Difficult Love

It is not easy to "love your enemies." It is not natural to "bless them that curse you, do good to them that hate you, and pray for them which despitefully use you, and persecute you" (Matthew 5:44). If you were coasting easily down the road that leads to destruction, you would do none of

these. But you have chosen the narrow way that leads to life. This is not a road for coasting, but a road for climbing. So keep on climbing.

How can you love your enemies? How can you speak well of those who speak evil of you? Your first battle may be with yourself—a battle for self-control. Bite your tongue to stop the curse that comes to mind when someone curses you. That scowl that would take possession of your face when someone puts you down—arrest it before it is fully formed. Replace it with a smile. Tell your enemy, "You may have a point. I know I'm not all I ought to be." Such an answer may struggle with your angry inclination at first; but if you make a habit of answering softly, you will find yourself happily turning away wrath instead of stirring up anger (Proverbs 15:1). You will learn to enjoy doing a favor for someone who does only evil to you. Can any joy on earth be more delightful than the joy of being and living like a child of your Father who is in Heaven? (Matthew 5:44, 45).

B. God's Love Is Enough

Though we may grow in love year by year, our love alone can never be enough to get us to Heaven. Even if it becomes as faultless as our Father's own (Matthew 5:48), our perfected love today cannot atone for our love's failures in the past. There is no atonement but one: Jesus' sacrifice of His life at Calvary. We cannot earn our way to Heaven, not even by perfected love and by years of doing good. Only God's love is enough. In His love He sent His Son to provide the atonement for our sins (John 3:16). For our survival we depend on His grace, His favor that we do not deserve, His forgiveness of our every sin. "For by grace are ye saved through faith; and that not of yourselves: it is the gift of God" (Ephesians 2:8). Praise the Lord!

C. Prayer

Heavenly Father, we give You thanks for the blessed privilege of living by the law of love, of growing daily in love and fruitfulness, and of serving You even in small ways. Even more we give You thanks for the greatness of Your grace by which we shall dwell forever in Your kingdom. In Jesus' name, amen.

D. Thought to Remember

"The gift of God is eternal life" (Romans 6:23).

How to Say It

BARNABAS. *Bar*-nuh-bus.
CALVARY. *Cal*-vuh-ree.
HYPOCRITE. *hip*-uh-krit.

Learning by Doing

This page contains an alternate lesson plan emphasizing learning activities. Classes desiring such student involvement will find these suggestions helpful.

Learning Goals

After this lesson each student will be able to:

1. Tell what Jesus said about judging, not judging, and loving others in the way one wants to be loved.

2. Explain why Jesus' teaching about the narrow way and the examination of the fruits of others does not contradict living by the law of love.

3. Suggest a specific way to implement the "Golden Rule" this week, perhaps to the benefit of one he or she might be tempted to "judge" in the manner Jesus disallowed.

Into the Lesson

Begin class by writing the word "hypocrite" on the chalkboard or overhead transparency. Say: "We probably know what a hypocrite is. But let's define it. Share your definition with the class." As suggested definitions are given, write them on the chalkboard or transparency. Say: "Perhaps you have known some individuals who fit this description. They give an appearance of being something they are not. They say one thing but do something else. In our text today, Jesus warns us of becoming hypocrites in the way we judge others. Later He gives us a useful alternative: 'the Golden Rule.' Turn to Matthew 7 and let's read what Jesus said."

Into the Word

Ask a volunteer to read Matthew 7:1-5, 12-20 aloud. Prior to class, prepare either a handout or a transparency with the following questions. Divide the class into groups of three. Say: "This passage provides some of Jesus' key teaching about judging, about getting along with other people, and about human nature. Answer these questions for a better view."

1. Describe the circumstances that led Jesus to call someone a hypocrite. *(Jesus rejects judging another person—even pointing out the other person's flaws—without first evaluating oneself.)*

2. What is the standard Jesus gave by which we should treat other people? *(Treat others the way we want to be treated.)*

3. Contrast the two ways Jesus described in verses 13 and 14 for each of the following: the gate, the way, the direction, and the number of people who travel. *(Gate: wide vs. strait; way: broad vs. narrow; direction: destruction vs. life; number: many vs. few.)*

4. What is the standard by which false prophets are clearly distinguished from true prophets? *(Their fruit reveals their nature.)*

5. What is the relationship between fruit and the nature of the tree? *(Good fruit comes from good trees; bad fruit comes from bad trees.)*

6. What is the relationship between the law of love in Matthew 22:37-40 and the Golden Rule in Matthew 7:12? *(Both express "the law and the prophets." Living by the law of love and living by the Golden Rule are the same.)*

7. Why does Jesus expect us to evaluate the fruits of others? *(To recognize false prophets, so that we don't find ourselves in the broad way that leads to destruction.)*

After several minutes, review the questions and answers with the class.

Into Life

Say: "Now we need to consider the principles found in our lesson text and how they may be applied. In your groups, suggest such a principle, and after several minutes, we'll discuss those principles with the class." *(Possible principles: "Self-examination precedes the correction of self and others"; "Treat others the way you want to be treated"; "Words and actions reveal character.")*

This lesson focuses specifically on living by the law of love—or the Golden Rule: "Treat others the way you want to be treated." Prior to class, prepare a life application handout called "Living Daily by the Golden Rule." This self-examination handout evaluates the extent to which the Golden Rule is practiced toward various people. List the following groups: family members, next-door neighbors, store clerks and cashiers, phone solicitors, work associates. Below each category put a scale chart that indicates the level of compliance.

Inconsistent									Consistent
1	2	3	4	5	6	7	8	9	10

Distribute copies of the handout and give the students a few minutes to rate their own practice of the Golden Rule toward the people listed. Then say: "Select the group you ranked the lowest on the handout and identify a specific person you may have treated improperly. Suggest a specific way to implement the Golden Rule this week with this person, sharing the suggestion with another class member."

Conclude the class session with a prayer that commits the class to living by the law of love.

Let's Talk It Over

The questions on this page are designed to encourage review of the lesson Scriptures and to promote discussion of the lesson by the class. The answers provided are only discussion starters. Let your class talk it over from there.

1. Many believers appear to be hypersensitive to this matter of judging. How should you respond when a brother or sister, upon a fair critique of improper behavior, quotes, "Judge not"?

Without doubt the kind of judging that Jesus condemned frequently takes place in churches. But it is clear that some believers hold a defective viewpoint in regard to judging. They do not want to be reminded about changes they should make in their attitudes and habits. They insist on being accepted just as they are, and they bristle at any suggestion that they "are not just as good as anyone else." Perhaps we could remind such a one that, in truth, we all need to grow in knowledge, holiness, and effectiveness of service. It is not a matter of judging when a fellow believer points out to us some specific area in which we need to grow. Note the lesson writer's comments on verses 1 and 2 for additional concepts in this regard.

2. Jesus' use of the term *hypocrite* in our text was hypothetical, not actually addressed to any specific person. At times, however, He did use the term to condemn hypocritical attitudes and behavior. What cautions would you suggest about people's using that term today?

Few of us would dare to imitate Jesus' bold indictment of the scribes and Pharisees as hypocrites (Matthew 23:13, 15, 23, 25, 27, 29). But on occasion we may become upset enough at the apparent inconsistency of a believer's walk that we are tempted to call him or her a hypocrite. We must ask why Jesus used the term. Was He merely venting His anger? Did He desire to embarrass and infuriate the Jewish leaders? Since Jesus uniformly acted in love, we must assume that was the case here. His harsh words were intended to break through the leaders' arrogant, hardened hearts and stir them to repentance. And if we are inclined to address anyone as "hypocrite," we must have a similar aim in view—and a reasonable hope that the person will respond in that spirit.

3. Occasionally we may hear someone say, "My religion is the Golden Rule." How should we respond to such a declaration?

Like any rule or principle for living, the Golden Rule falls short of providing eternal life and salvation from sin. No person is capable of

keeping it perfectly—selfishness is sure to intervene on occasion. We might ask this person how he intends to atone for the times he fails to live up to this standard. Then we can present Jesus, "the atoning sacrifice for our sins" (1 John 2:2, *New International Version*) and the only "name under heaven given among men, whereby we must be saved" (Acts 4:12).

4. Jesus declared that the way to life is a "narrow" one. In this age of "tolerance," the conventional wisdom is that being narrow is a thing to be shunned. How can we be "narrow" and still have a credible witness to the world?

Jesus' very message that "few there be that find [life]" is too narrow for much of the world today. Conventional wisdom is that any belief system is acceptable if "it works for you." Thus, we are bound to be viewed as too narrow by much of society no matter how graciously we try to be witnesses. However, we can be careful that our attitudes do not become self-righteous or cynical. We can demonstrate genuine love to others, even to those with whom we disagree. We can confine our disagreements to issues: we do not want to attack someone personally even if we must tear down his or her false beliefs. Jesus was not too narrow to associate with "publicans and sinners," and they did not feel put off by Him even though He called them to repentance.

5. What are some of the fruits that enable us to ascertain the genuineness of a person's faith in God? How should we respond to the absence of good spiritual fruits?

One kind of fruit that reveals the kind of persons we are is our language. Another fruit that identifies us is the way we handle money, and still another is the way we use our time. Faithful attendance in worship and regular giving to Christian causes are not guarantees of a person's commitment, but their absence certainly indicates a lack of genuine faith in God. When those fruits are missing from others' lives, we have an opportunity to apply the principles of today's lesson. We do not condemn such people. Instead, we treat them as we would want to be treated if our faithfulness should lapse. We can pray for them and work to direct them into a sincere and complete commitment to God.

Winter Quarter, 2001-2002

Light for All People
(Isaiah, Ruth, Jonah)

Special Features

Lessons

Unit 1: The Mission of God's Servant

Unit 2: The Response of God's People

Unit 3: All People May Share God's Grace

About These Lessons

The lessons of the present quarter interrupt our chronological study of Old Testament texts to remind us that God always has been interested in all people, not just the members of the Jewish race. His calling of Israel was a means of conferring blessing on all people, not just the Jews. Through the prophecies of Isaiah, through the life of Ruth, and through the experience of Jonah, that truth is clear. May we share His concern—for everyone.

Dec 2

Dec 9

Dec 16

Dec 23

Dec 30

Jan 6

Jan 13

Jan 20

Jan 27

Feb 3

Feb 10

Feb 17

Feb 24

Quarterly Quiz

The questions on this page may be used in several ways: as a pretest at the beginning of the quarter; as a review at the end of the quarter; or as a review after each lesson. The questions are based on the Scripture text of each lesson (King James Version). **The answers are on page 116.**

Lesson 1
1. The Servant said that the Lord had made His mouth like a ____ ____. (flaming fire, sharp sword, or mighty wind?) *Isaiah 49:2*
2. The Servant would become ____ for the Gentiles. (bread, water, or a light?) *Isaiah 49:6*

Lesson 2
1. Isaiah prophesied that a rod would come forth out of the stem of ____. *Isaiah 11:1*
2. Isaiah also prophesied that the ____ would eat straw like the ____. *Isaiah 11:7*

Lesson 3
1. Isaiah was told to "speak comfortably" to what city? (Jerusalem, Babylon, or Nineveh?) *Isaiah 40:2*
2. The grass withers and the flower fades. What "shall stand for ever"? *Isaiah 40:8*
3. Those who renew their strength are compared with what birds? (sparrows, doves, or eagles?) *Isaiah 40:31*

Lesson 4
1. The Child prophesied by Isaiah would be called Wonderful, ____, ____ God, ____ Father, Prince of ____. *Isaiah 9:6*
2. Upon whose throne would the promised Child sit? *Isaiah 9:7*

Lesson 5
1. Isaiah prophesied that the Servant would raise His voice and shout in the streets. T/F *Isaiah 42:2*
2. Isaiah said of the Servant, "A bruised ____ shall he not break, and the smoking ____ shall he not quench." *Isaiah 42:3*

Lesson 6
1. What group did Isaiah describe as coming to the light that God would cause to shine? (soldiers, kings, or priests?) *Isaiah 60:3*
2. In Isaiah 61 Isaiah prophesied that the Messiah would "proclaim the acceptable ____ of the Lord." (hour, day, or year?) *Isaiah 61:2*

Lesson 7
1. Isaiah extended God's offer of the sure mercies of _____. (Abraham, Moses, or David?) *Isaiah 55:3*

2. "____ ye the Lord while he may be ____, call ye upon him while he is near." *Isaiah 55:6*

Lesson 8
1. Isaiah was told to lift up his voice like what musical instrument? *Isaiah 58:1*
2. The Lord was especially concerned about the kind of ____ He had chosen. (prayer, fast, or sacrifice?) *Isaiah 58:6*
3. The Lord wanted the people to bring what group into their homes? (poor, blind, or lepers?) *Isaiah 58:7*

Lesson 9
1. Isaiah extended God's promise to create "new ____ and a new ____." *Isaiah 65:17*
2. Isaiah said that dust would be the "meat" of what animal? (lion, bear, or serpent?) *Isaiah 65:25*

Lesson 10
1. Give the names of Elimelech's two sons. *Ruth 1:2*
2. Give the names of the women whom Elimelech's two sons married. *Ruth 1:4*
3. Who said, "Whither thou goest, I will go"? *Ruth 1:16*

Lesson 11
1. Who is described as "a mighty man of wealth, of the family of Elimelech"? *Ruth 2:1*
2. At the time Boaz met Ruth in the field, he knew nothing of her background. T/F *Ruth 2:11*
3. Name the son born to Boaz and Ruth. *Ruth 4:17*

Lesson 12
1. To what city was Jonah told to go and preach? *Jonah 1:2*
2. To what city did Jonah plan to travel in order to flee from the Lord's presence? *Jonah 1:3*
3. The sailors cast lots to determine who was to blame for the storm. T/F *Jonah 1:7*

Lesson 13
1. Nineveh is described as a city of ____ days' journey. (two, three, or four?) *Jonah 3:3*
2. In how long did Jonah say Nineveh would be destroyed? *Jonah 3:4*
3. What did Jonah make for himself on the east side of Nineveh? *Jonah 4:5*

Light for the World

by David Reece

THE COMING OF JESUS, the Servant of the Lord, into our world might be likened to the appearance of a brilliant comet. However, unlike the flare of such a passing astral guest, the light of our Christ never fades.

Occasionally the arrival of a comet surprises us. It may be that the comet is traveling on such a huge orbit that it has not passed by us since records of such phenomena began to be kept. More likely, we are simply not aware of the comet's course. But when Halley's comet appeared in 1986, everyone knew it was coming. In fact, we know when this comet will reappear because we know it travels in an orbit that takes it past the earth every seventy-six years.

Like the passing of Halley's comet, the coming of Jesus and the miraculous nature of His darkness-ending ministry were no accidents. Jesus told His disciples, "All things must be fulfilled, which were written in the law of Moses, and in the prophets, and in the psalms, concerning me" (Luke 24:44). Today Christians can read both the prophecies in the Old Testament and their fulfillments as cited in the New Testament. The result will be a greater confidence in the trustworthiness of their faith.

Isaiah prophesied at the end of the eighth century and the beginning of the seventh century before Christ No other prophet had more to say about the light of the world than he. This is not to say that everything that Isaiah preached or wrote related to the ministry of our Lord. He had much to say about his own day as well. He was particularly concerned with God's displeasure with His people because of their repeated failures to live as people of the covenant should. But it is also clear that Isaiah's prophetic insight (guided by the Holy Spirit) looked beyond his own day. Isaiah looked to the inclusion of "all nations, and kindreds, and people, and tongues" (Revelation 7:9) into God's kingdom. God wants all people to come to His light! And Jesus was, is, and always will be the means by which they must do that (John 14:6).

The theme of the coming quarter is "Light for All People." The thirteen lessons will focus on God's concern for all peoples as expressed in part of the Old Testament. The first two units will be drawn from the book of Isaiah. We will see in unit one the different facets of the ministry of God's Servant. Unit two will consider various responses to the Servant and His mission. In unit three we will illustrate the "Light for All People" theme through the examples of Ruth and Jonah. It is clear that God always has wanted all people to receive the blessings and benefits of His mercy.

Unit 1: December
The Mission of God's Servant

Lesson 1: God's Servant Brings Light. God intended that Israel, through faithful obedience to Him, would demonstrate their "wisdom and . . . understanding in the sight of the nations" (Deuteronomy 4:6). However, the Old Testament is painfully honest about the many failures of Israel to be God's "servant" in this manner. Clearly another Servant was needed who would succeed in fulfilling God's purposes, and Jesus was that Servant.

Lesson 2: God's Servant Brings Peace. Here the Servant of God is described as one empowered by the Spirit of God to make judgments with righteous insight and universal fairness. The peace established by the Servant is pictured in language that portrays "natural" enemies in the animal kingdom living in harmony.

Lesson 3: God's Servant Brings Comfort. Isaiah lived through tumultuous times, including Assyria's destruction of Samaria, the capital of the northern kingdom. Although Jerusalem was spared for some 135 years, Isaiah's prophetic vision saw that her future would be the same as Samaria's. However, it was Babylon (not Assyria) that would carry out the impending destruction. To those future exiles, Isaiah wrote the words of hope and comfort found in chapter 40. But those words spoke of much more than just deliverance from captivity in Babylon. John the Baptist used them to describe his ministry of preparing for the Messiah, who would offer the ultimate comfort (Luke 3:3-6).

Lesson 4: God's Servant Brings Hope. In another prophecy, Isaiah called attention to some of the names by which this Servant would be known. This lesson, which will be taught on the Sunday before Christmas, includes Isaiah's stirring prophecy that begins, "For unto us a child is born, unto us a son is given" (Isaiah 9:6).

Lesson 5: God's Servant Brings Justice. It is a striking paradox that justice can come from One who was unjustly treated and who did not cry out for justice when He Himself was unfairly condemned. But because God's Servant follows the Lord's plan to establish justice by suffering injustice Himself, He will be the one, says the Lord, "in whom my soul delighteth" (Isaiah 42:1; cf. Matthew 3:16, 17).

Unit 2: January
The Response of God's People

Lesson 6: Hear the Good News. To be in spiritual darkness is frightening. But the focus of Isaiah's message was not just the gloom and darkness of sin. He also described the life-giving light that God has provided to dispel that darkness. Isaiah does more than point out the problem: he announces the solution! It is found only in Jesus, "the true Light, which lighteth every man that cometh into the world" (John 1:9).

Lesson 7: Seek the Lord. The pervasive darkness of sin cannot be ended by anything other than divine light. Of course, people may try to form their own light; but their efforts are no more effective than birthday candles lit in a violent windstorm. Isaiah proclaimed that deep and enduring satisfaction cannot be attained unless a person seeks the Lord.

Lesson 8: Worship in Truth. The forms of public worship do not please God unless the daily actions of faithful living accompany them. In the text to be studied for this lesson, Isaiah describes the kind of fast that is most pleasing to God. Such a fast means much more than abstaining from food; it means helping those in both physical and spiritual need.

Lesson 9: Anticipate God's New Creation. The return of a remnant to Jerusalem means, in effect, God's return to His beloved city. That return is itself prophetic of the ultimate reunion of God with His people in the "new Jerusalem" (Revelation 21:2).

Unit 3: February
All People May Share God's Grace

Lesson 10: Ruth Chooses Naomi's God. A series of tragedies, culminating in the deaths of her husband and her two sons, shattered the life of aged Naomi. But her daughter-in-law Ruth, a Moabite woman of exceptional integrity, refused to abandon Naomi to find security in Moab. In an especially moving scene, Ruth made what amounted to a "Good Confession" (Ruth 1:16, 17) and accompanied Naomi to the promised land to live as a servant of the true God.

Lesson 11: God Blesses Ruth. Ruth's exemplary devotion to Naomi and Naomi's God is especially striking when one considers that these events took place in a time when "every man did that which was right in his own eyes" (Judges 21:25). God blessed Ruth's faithfulness through His merciful and providential care. It is clear that God was the "matchmaker" who brought Boaz and Ruth to-

gether. Boaz, a God-fearing "mighty man of wealth," and Ruth, a vulnerable new resident of Bethlehem (and a Moabite at that), married and became the parents of Obed. Obed became the grandfather of David, Israel's greatest king.

Lesson 12: Jonah Rejects God's Call. When God sent Jonah to those in Nineveh who needed to be warned of His impending judgment, Jonah promptly deemed the Ninevites unworthy of such treatment. Instead of obeying, Jonah fled from God. God then sent His own special brand of discipline in the form of a large fish that swallowed Jonah. After the fish spit the contrite preacher onto the beach, he who had run *from* God began to run *with* God.

Lesson 13: God Shows Mercy to Nineveh. Jonah had received a powerful demonstration of God's grace: he had been delivered from death! Now he was ready (at least in outward obedience) to extend the Lord's grace to Nineveh. In what may be the most successful evangelistic campaign in all history, thousands of violent, unrighteous people repented and received the same amazing grace that Jonah had taken for granted.

One would think that a preacher would be elated at such results. However, as the book of Jonah concludes, Jonah is pouting from his booth east of Nineveh, where he has been awaiting the hoped-for destruction of the city. He confesses what is evident from the very beginning of the book (and what is still true today): "Thou art a gracious God, and merciful, slow to anger, and of great kindness" (Jonah 4:2).

God still wants to demonstrate that grace to those who are lost and groping in the darkness of sin. If His people fail to communicate that message, who will? May we never become so self-righteous or self-centered that we forget the "amazing grace" that has been shown to us.

Answers to Quarterly Quiz
on page 114

Lesson 1—1. sharp sword. 2. a light. **Lesson 2**—1. Jesse. 2. lion, ox. **Lesson 3**—1. Jerusalem. 2. the word of our God. 3. eagles. **Lesson 4**—1. Counselor, mighty, everlasting, Peace. 2. David. **Lesson 5**—1. false. 2. reed, flax. **Lesson 6**—1. kings. 2. year. **Lesson 7**—1. David. 2. Seek, found. **Lesson 8**—1. a trumpet. 2. fast. 3. poor. **Lesson 9**—1. heavens, earth. 2. serpent. **Lesson 10**—1. Mahlon and Chilion. 2. Orpah and Ruth. 3. Ruth. **Lesson 11**—1. Boaz. 2. false. 3. Obed. **Lesson 12**—1. Nineveh. 2. Tarshish. 3. true. **Lesson 13**—1. three. 2. forty days. 3. a booth.

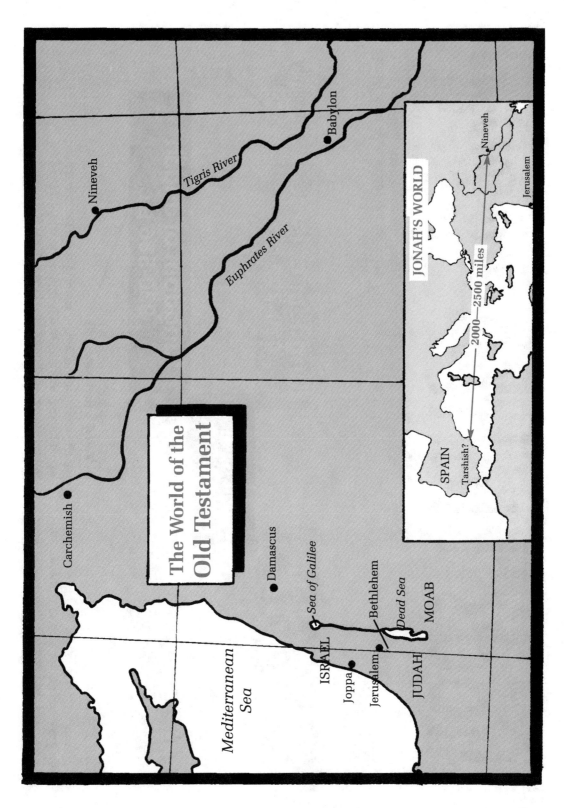

118

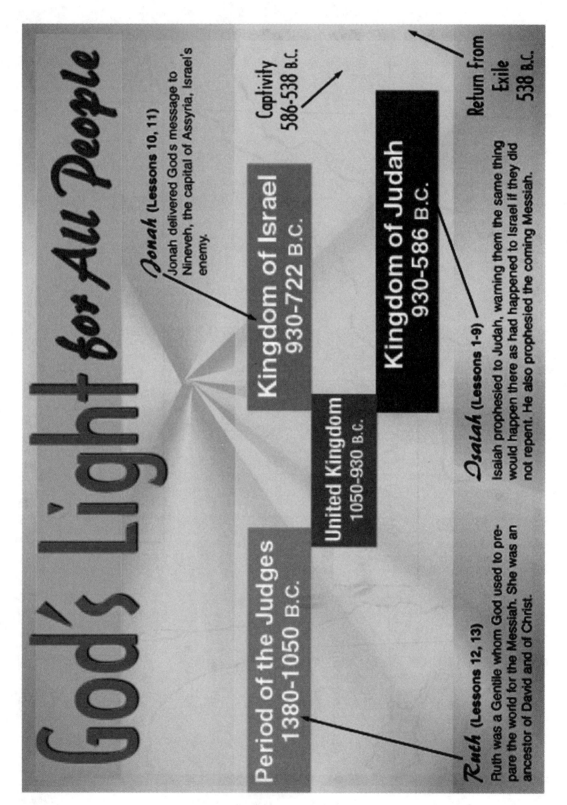

Puzzlers, Posers, and Prophecies:

Understanding the Mystery

by Ronald G. Davis

LIGHT REVEALS THAT WHICH otherwise would be hidden in darkness. God's will would have been just such a hidden matter unless He had given light. Human observation could have discovered some basic doctrines about God (see Romans 1:18-32), but His scheme of redemption had to be revealed. Only when He gave light could people know His will and way. Often that light came in small amounts, piquing interest and creating a yearning in the heart to know more.

The Christian teacher has the same purpose: giving light so that people can know, understand, believe, and practice God's will and way. We are all "stewards of the mysteries of God" (1 Corinthians 4:1). And the teacher may fulfill that purpose in the same way that God often did: as if it were a riddle to be answered, a coded message to be deciphered. God's messianic prophecies were just such puzzles—they needed that one last piece God would provide; Jesus' parables were just such enigmas—they needed His spiritual explanation and the listener's personal purity of spirit to be fully comprehended. Both had the same two requirements to be successful: adequate revelation from God and mental attention, ability, and diligence on the part of the listener or learner.

Bible lesson material that is essentially non-narrative in style may well lend itself to a variety of puzzles and word games enjoyed by many adults. The focus required and the joy of discovery and completion are learning processes the teacher of adults longs to see. In the quarter of study at hand, the lessons from the book of Isaiah—wherein God uses the cryptic language of prophecy—accommodate themselves to several word puzzles. The lessons from Ruth and Jonah, with their varied historical and geographical contexts, will do so as well.

Five Lessons, Five Words

The first five lessons highlight five elements God's Servant brings to the world: light, peace, comfort, hope, and justice. The adult teacher would be remiss if he did not emphasize those five blessings; he would be failing his task if he did not remind and reinforce the truth that all of God's servants have that same responsibility. To keep those key words before the learners, a different activity could be used each of the first five weeks. The popularity of the game show "Wheel of Fortune"™ makes a basic "fill-in-the-blank" activity a good way to start.

G_D'_ _ER_ANT _R_NG_ _ _G_T,
_EA_E, _ _ _ _ _ _RT, _ _ _ _ _E, AND
_ _ _ _T_ _ E. (Solution: *"God's servant brings light, peace, comfort, hope, and justice."*)

Follow with a simple list of the five words scrambled.

G H I L T . . . . *(light)*
A C E E P . . . . *(peace)*
C F M O O R T . . . . *(comfort)*
E H O P . . . . *(hope)*
C E I J S T U . . . . *(justice)*

Many adults will enjoy a word find puzzle.

E C I T S U J G
E P O H O D S S
E E R M V A N L
T A G O F D S I
S C E R V O A G
N E T G O D R H
S S E R V A N T

A letter substitution code is a little more challenging. In the following example, learners may quickly figure out the five words, but ask them to deduce the nature of the code. (Each letter in the original word is replaced by the letter that comes after it in the alphabet by the same number of spaces as the original letter's position in the word. That is, the first letter is replaced by the first letter after it, the second by the second letter after, etc.)

M K J L Y . . . . *(light)*
Q G D G J . . . . *(peace)*
D Q P J T X A . . . . *(comfort)*
I Q S I . . . . *(hope)*
K W V X N I L . . . . *(justice)*

Another fun code hides the words in back-to-back words (or within a word) within unrelated sentences:

1. What a delightful experience we had at the church picnic! (*light* in "de**ligh**tful")

2. We hope a century is long enough to wait. (*peace* in "ho**pe a c**entury")

3. Go to "Bible.com" for the best Bible commentary on the web. (*comfort* in Bible.**com for the**")

4. We must accept the Servant with open hearts. (*hope* in "wit**h ope**n")

5. If just I cede my property rights, will the church survive? (*justice* in "**just I ce**de")

Words and Ideas, Ideas and Words

With a series of lesson texts in which lists of attributes are predominant, the adult teacher will want to consider the variety of puzzle-type language activities that can highlight and reinforce those characteristics, whether they be desirable traits for God's servants, demeaning sins of God's people, or objective descriptors of God's leaders. Several of the texts in this series qualify.

Consider such a simple activity for lesson 1 as giving the learners a list of descriptors of Israel and asking the class to identify how each is seen in the text (Isaiah 49:1-6). Use this list (or one of your own compilation): *chosen, purposive, beloved, disappointing, prepared (i.e., gifted), glorious, strengthened, privileged, powerful.*

For a lesson such as the second, from Isaiah 11:1-9, consider doing an "A-B-C search"; that is, ask the learners to devise words for as many letters of the alphabet as possible, based in some fashion on the text, that describe the Coming One. Here are possibilities and verse references/explanations: A: all-knowing (2b); B: branch (1); C: counselor (2b); D: destroyer (4b); E: equalizer (will make things right, 4); F: fearful (3); G: girdled (5); H: human (son of Jesse); I: insightful (3b-4a); J: just (3b-4a); K: king (whole thrust of the passage emphasizing his being of the line of David); L: Lord (9); M: Messiah (2a, anointed by the Spirit); N: noble (he is of high birth and possesses outstanding characteristics—both part of most dictionary definitions of the word); O: __; P: powerful (slays with his words, 4b); Q: quick (3); R: righteous (5a); S: Spirit-filled (2a); T: transformer (see 6-8); U: unlimited (3b, not limited by human senses); V: victorious (He will be in control, see v. 9); W: well-known (9b); X: __; Y: __; Z: __. The range of responses any learning group will devise will offer much opportunity to discuss and even disagree. (And some of your students will devise words for the blank letters above!) Or as teacher you can display such a list and ask learners to identify a verse or verses that reveal the attribute.

A lesson such as number 3, from Isaiah 40 with its figurative language, lends itself to an activity called "Object Match." In this activity various objects that are designed to reflect phrases, words, and ideas from the text are displayed. Learners are called to make the matches between the objects and verses of the text. Consider this list for the verses to be studied: a quilted comforter (v. 1); a (toy) sword or gun (v. 2); a megaphone (v. 3); a cactus (v. 3); a contorted chenille wire (v. 4); sandpaper (v. 4b); tall cut grass (v. 6); wildflower—real or artificial (v. 6b); a hardcover Bible that can be stood up, (v. 8b); a newspaper (v. 9); a carpenter's rule (v. 10); a stuffed toy lamb (v. 11); a globe (v. 28); smelling salts (v. 29); an eagle image [pin or ceramic]; a pair of running shoes (v. 31). The objects could be displayed all at once, letting learners identify verses at random, or each object can be revealed at its own time, asking learners to identify a relevant verse and connection.

Thoughtworthy

The lessons from the book of Ruth are ideal study material for the one who would be godly. The book is indeed "thoughtworthy." The Spirit, by the pen of Paul, advised all to think on certain things that are in themselves of the nature of God: things that are true, honest, just, pure, lovely, of good report, virtuous, praiseworthy (Philippians 4:8). Bible texts, whether narrative or nonnarrative, are all examples—either positive or negative—of these attributes. The teacher can, by asking learners to label lessons and texts with these eight characteristics, help them to understand how the Bible helps them to think godly thoughts, even when the lessons or texts emphasize ungodly behaviors.

One way to do this is to post the verse (Philippians 4:8) with the eight attributes highlighted. Then ask the class members to examine the text for examples of any of the "thoughtworthy" characteristics. For example, in the lesson from Ruth 1, the judges existed (v. 1) to see that justice was honored; Elimelech's move of his family at a time of famine (v. 2) is certainly noble; the marriage of the sons to pagan women (v. 4) is a negative example of purity and a compromise of truth; God's revisiting Israel with the blessing of food (v. 6) is certainly praiseworthy; Naomi's prayer for her daughters-in-law to be blessed by the Lord (v. 8) is lovely indeed; and the heartfelt appeal of Ruth to accompany Naomi (vv. 16, 17) demonstrates a purity of motive seldom seen in the Scriptures or in life. Asking learners to write the eight attributes into appropriate places into a printed copy of the text, before group discussion, may be a preferable approach. If you have an "active" class, ask eight learners to sit across the front of your room; assign to each of them one of the fruits; and ask them to "pop" up whenever their attributes are referred to as the Scripture text is read. As each stands, stop and ask, "Why did you stand?" Having them hold labels can enhance learning.

"Figuring out" truth from clues and symbols is thinking at a higher level. Adults who enjoy the challenge of a daily newspaper crossword puzzle or cryptogram will find similar challenges in comparable activities in the Bible study classroom. The perceptive and committed teacher of adults will offer the challenge.

God's Servant Brings Light

December 2
Lesson 1

DEVOTIONAL READING: Isaiah 49:8-13.

BACKGROUND SCRIPTURE: Isaiah 49:1-7.

PRINTED TEXT: Isaiah 49:1-6.

Isaiah 49:1-6

1 Listen, O isles, unto me; and hearken, ye people, from far; The LORD hath called me from the womb; from the bowels of my mother hath he made mention of my name.

2 And he hath made my mouth like a sharp sword; in the shadow of his hand hath he hid me, and made me a polished shaft; in his quiver hath he hid me;

3 And said unto me, Thou art my servant, O Israel, in whom I will be glorified.

4 Then I said, I have labored in vain, I have spent my strength for nought, and in vain: yet surely my judgment is with the LORD, and my work with my God.

5 And now, saith the LORD that formed me from the womb to be his servant, to bring Jacob again to him, Though Israel be not gathered, yet shall I be glorious in the eyes of the LORD, and my God shall be my strength.

6 And he said, It is a light thing that thou shouldest be my servant to raise up the tribes of Jacob, and to restore the preserved of Israel: I will also give thee for a light to the Gentiles, that thou mayest be my salvation unto the end of the earth.

GOLDEN TEXT: I will also give thee for a light to the Gentiles, that thou mayest be my salvation unto the end of the earth.—Isaiah 49:6.

Light for All People
The Mission of God's Servant
(Lessons 1-5)

Lesson Aims

After this lesson a student should be able to:

1. Summarize the call of God's "Servant" and the scope of His mission.

2. Tell how Jesus fulfilled Isaiah's prophecy of the Servant and how the church does so today.

3. Suggest specific ways to follow the Lord's Servant in loving service today.

Lesson Outline

INTRODUCTION
   A. Golden or Yellow?
   B. Lesson Background
 I. GOD'S SERVANT DESCRIBED (Isaiah 49:1-3)
   A. His Call (v. 1)
     The Attitude of the Effective
   B. His Preparation (v. 2)
   C. His Identity (v. 3)
 II. THE SERVANT'S RESPONSE (Isaiah 49:4)
   A. Frustration (v. 4a)
   B. Assurance (v. 4b)
     Life on Purpose
III. THE SERVANT'S MISSION (Isaiah 49:5, 6)
   A. To Israel (v. 5)
   B. To the Gentiles (v. 6)
CONCLUSION
   A. Keep the Light Shining
   B. Prayer
   C. Thought to Remember

Introduction

A. Golden or Yellow?

An old adage says, "Silence is golden." Any parent of a preschooler, anyone who works in a noisy factory or operates loud machinery, or any resident who lives near an elementary school playground will surely agree. When the little ones are in bed, when the workday comes to an end, or when the children leave the playground—what a welcome relief is the ensuing silence!

There are times, however, when silence is not "golden." There are times when a person must take a stand and express the truth, for to keep silent would be taken as acceptance of falsehood. It's not easy; it takes courage. That is the reason someone has taken issue with the old saying. "Silence is not always 'golden'; sometimes it's just yellow!"

In today's text, the prophet Isaiah describes a Servant chosen and called by God to bring His light to the people of the world. The Servant expresses both His discouragement and His delight in the service of the Lord. Anyone who has faced resistance to the work of Christ appreciates the courage it takes to keep speaking up when it would be much easier to remain silent. Are we ready to speak up? Or are we yellow?

B. Lesson Background

The prophet Isaiah conducted a lengthy ministry to the nation of Judah. He served during the reigns of four kings—Uzziah, Jotham, Ahaz, and Hezekiah (Isaiah 1:1). His ministry probably covered well over fifty years.

During Isaiah's ministry the Assyrian empire, which had regained strength under Tiglath-pileser III, began moving westward with the aim of conquering new territory. Syria, Israel (the northern kingdom), and Judah (the southern kingdom) were among the lands affected by the Assyrian threat. When the kings of Syria and Israel tried to persuade King Ahaz of Judah to join them in an alliance to stand up to Assyria, he refused and instead requested help from Tiglath-pileser. The Assyrian responded by conquering Syria in 732 B.C. and Israel in 722 B.C.

Although Judah had averted the Assyrians' wrath for a short time, approximately twenty years later Judah was besieged by their forces during the reign of Hezekiah. When Hezekiah prayed earnestly to God on behalf of his people, God brought about a miraculous deliverance. The account in Isaiah 37:36, 37 (also recorded in 2 Kings 19:35, 36) reports that the angel of the Lord put to death 185,000 Assyrian soldiers.

That, however, did not end the threat of foreign domination. Isaiah predicted that another captivity would overtake Jerusalem because of her sins—a punishment that came about in 586 B.C. at the hands of the Babylonians. Isaiah also foretold the eventual return of captives through the decree of King Cyrus of Persia (Isaiah 45:1). That return took place in 538 B.C.

Isaiah 40-66 (which follows the record of events from Hezekiah's reign in chapters 36-39) moves forward in time from the threat of the Assyrian siege of Jerusalem to the destruction of Jerusalem and the Babylonian captivity over one hundred years later. Of course, Isaiah was no longer alive by then; yet these chapters describe the conditions and the fears of God's people during that time of exile. In fact, the chapters so convincingly portray the Babylonian captivity that many scholars have assumed that they must have been written by a later author—someone who had experienced firsthand the exile in Babylon.

They believe that this "someone" could not be Isaiah, since he would have died years before the Babylonian captivity of 586 B.C. However, Bible students who believe in predictive prophecy have no trouble seeing these chapters as a divinely inspired description—in advance—of the Babylonian captivity and of the promise that the Lord would one day deliver His people from their misery.

Isaiah 49, from which today's text is taken, contains the second of what are often termed the four "Servant Songs" of Isaiah. (The others are found in Isaiah 42:1-7, 50:4-9, and 52:13—53:12, though in some cases Bible students differ in exactly how many verses of a passage should be included in a "Song.")

One of the larger issues for the Bible student in the Servant Songs is the exact identity of the Servant. Is this Servant national Israel, is He a portion of national Israel, or is He an individual from within the nation, specifically the promised Messiah?

Clearly there are places in Isaiah where the "servant" language refers to the nation of Israel (Isaiah 44:21; 48:20) and others where an individual is being described (Isaiah 42:1-4; 52:13—53:12). Some students have suggested that the Servant passages be understood as a kind of pyramid. At the base of this pyramid is the nation of Israel, in the center is the righteous core of faithful servants of the Lord, and at the top is the true Servant of the Lord—Jesus the Messiah. Perhaps one could say that Isaiah's Servant Songs point to one person (Jesus) who will fulfill God's plan and serve Him in a way that the servant/nation of Israel never could because of its sins. And while some passages in the Songs may appear to describe what occurs to Israel following the captivity in Babylon, the language is such that it points to a much greater fulfillment—in Jesus and in the work of the church.

A good illustration of this fulfillment is seen in how the New Testament describes the fulfillment of one of the Servant Songs (Isaiah 42:1-7) in both personal terms (Jesus, Matthew 12:15-21) and corporate terms (the church, Acts 13:47; 26:23). In God's plan the church is now the "Israel of God" (Galatians 6:16), continuing the Servant's ministry by taking His gospel to the world.

I. God's Servant Described (Isaiah 49:1-3)

A. His Call (v. 1)

1. **Listen, O isles, unto me; and hearken, ye people, from far; The LORD hath called me from the womb; from the bowels of my mother hath he made mention of my name.**

This Servant Song begins with the Servant addressing the *isles*. The islands represent the *people, from far*, or distant heathen nations, who do not know the Lord. In Isaiah 66:19 the isles are described as "afar off, that have not heard my fame, neither have seen my glory." At the end of this verse, God declares that these "Gentiles" will hear of His glory. Other references in Isaiah that designate the islands as the subject of God's concern are 11:11; 24:14-16; 42:4, 10, 12; 51:5; and 60:9. The Servant's words in the verse before us prepare us for the description of His expanded mission in verse 6—bringing God's salvation "unto the end of the earth."

The Servant then describes Himself as being *called . . . from the womb* and *from the bowels of my mother*. This language brings to mind Jeremiah's description of his prophetic call, which included the Lord's declaration that He had ordained Jeremiah a prophet before he was born (Jeremiah 1:5). Paul considered his apostolic ministry as one designated by God "from my mother's womb" (Galatians 1:15).

The personal nature of the Servant's call is also clear from the solemn announcement of the Servant's *name*. The Lord *hath . . . made mention of my name*, the Servant says, which calls to mind a father's post-birth announcement of the name of his child. Recall that Isaiah already has predicted that a virgin would bear a son and that He would be called "Immanuel" (Isaiah 7:14). [See question #1, page 128.]

THE ATTITUDE OF THE EFFECTIVE

The earthquake that struck Los Angeles in 1994 left dozens dead and thousands homeless. One of the most impressive stories during the extensive news coverage included an interview with a lady who survived all the uncertainty and damage of

Home Daily Bible Readings

Monday, Nov. 26—God's Purpose Will Stand (Isaiah 46:8-13)
Tuesday, Nov. 27—Hear New Things (Isaiah 48:1-11)
Wednesday, Nov. 28—Draw Near and Hear (Isaiah 48:12-16)
Thursday, Nov. 29—Your God Who Teaches You (Isaiah 48:17-22)
Friday, Nov. 30—You Are Chosen (Isaiah 49:7-12)
Saturday, Dec. 1—The Lord Will Offer Comfort (Isaiah 49:13-22)
Sunday, Dec. 2—God's Servant Endures Suffering (Isaiah 50:4-9)

VISUALS FOR THESE LESSONS

The small visual pictured in each lesson (e. g., page 126) is a small reproduction of a large, full-color poster included in the *Adult Visuals* packet for the Winter Quarter. The packet is available from your supplier. Order No. 292.

the quake. She said, "We don't like this, but we won't move. We are Californians and Angelinos. We will handle anything that comes our way."

The resolve displayed by this woman was admirable. Her attitude and actions embody the words etched over the entrance to the California state capitol in Sacramento: "Give us men to match our mountains." History is shaped by people possessed with a passion, a resolve, and a purpose to conquer mountains. Their sense of identity and calling are unmistakable.

Consider other examples of resolve and purpose. At the age of seventeen, Alexander Hamilton was writing political pamphlets. At twenty-one George Washington was a colonel in the Virginia militia—and he had driven the French from the borders of Virginia. At twenty-six Napoleon conquered Italy and began a quest to rule the world. In approximately twelve years, Paul traveled over much of the Mediterranean world and saw the gospel of Christ penetrate new lands.

Effective people often describe a deep conviction that God has called them to a special task. Like the Servant of the Lord, who declared that He was "called . . . from the womb," they experience an early sense of God's call and purpose.

Are you living with a sense of God's direction and purpose? Are you His servant?   —J. A. M.

B. His Preparation (v. 2)

2. And he hath made my mouth like a sharp sword; in the shadow of his hand hath he hid me, and made me a polished shaft; in his quiver hath he hid me.

The Servant realizes that God has prepared Him with a powerful message—a message that pierces *like a sharp sword*. Isaiah 11:4 portrays the Messiah as One who will "smite the earth with the rod of his *mouth*." Elsewhere the Bible paints a picture of the Word of God as a sword, penetrating and powerful (Ephesians 6:17; Hebrews 4:12; Revelation 1:16; 2:12, 16). In the case of the Servant, God has prepared Him as any soldier in an ancient army would prepare his spear for battle. The Servant knows that He is *a polished shaft*, or arrow, in the hand of the Lord. He stands ready in His Master's *quiver* for the spiritual warfare in which He will take part.

Today Christians also have been equipped with the powerful truth of God. This truth is the weapon that Paul, in his description of the Christian's armor, called "the sword of the Spirit, which is the word of God" (Ephesians 6:17).

In addition, the Servant is aware of God's protection over Him as He carries out His ministry. The Lord hides Him *in the shadow of his hand* as if to protect him from the blazing sun of tribulation. In this way, the Servant can entrust himself to the will of the Lord and never fear.

Hostility often rises against today's servant of the Lord who seeks to bear witness of his faith. Our society continues to look for ways to ridicule the values that Christians hold dear. But believers need not fear. The God who placed the Servant in the shadow of His hand will also place soldiers of the cross under His protection and care. When Jesus commissioned His apostles to go and make disciples of all nations, He provided this assurance: "Lo, I am with you alway, even unto the end of the world" (Matthew 28:20). [See question #2, page 128.]

C. His Identity (v. 3)

3. And said unto me, Thou art my servant, O Israel, in whom I will be glorified.

Here it would seem that, since the *servant* is addressed as *Israel*, the term must represent the nation of Israel. However, *Israel* designated an individual (formerly called Jacob, Genesis 32:28) before it designated a nation. The passage thus far has focused on an individual, so it seems unwise to abandon that identity too easily. Here is a good illustration of the dynamic described on page 123, where the identity of the Servant must be understood at more than one level. The Servant's work is to bring the Lord's salvation to the end of the earth (v. 6; cf. Isaiah 66:19). That applies to Israel as well as to the Messiah. And it also applies to the church. As servants of the Servant, may we continue to carry out that grand mission!

II. The Servant's Response (Isaiah 49:4)

A. Frustration (v. 4a)

4a. Then I said, I have labored in vain, I have spent my strength for nought, and in vain.

How difficult is it to speak God's truth when people close their minds to it? The Servant knows the frustration of holding out to people the word of truth—and seeing no results except rejection. The words *in vain* and *for nought* (nothing) underscore this disappointment. Consider how Jesus wept as He agonized over Jerusalem's rejection of its only hope of deliverance (Luke 19:41-44).

The Servant's frustration stands in sharp contrast to His sense of purpose expressed earlier in verses 1-3. The Servant senses God's calling, but also knows firsthand the resistance of people to the truth. Such is the frequent experience of the servant of Christ who understands the call that he has answered, yet experiences the heartaches that trying to witness for Christ in a sinful world produce. Sometimes we may be at fault; perhaps we fail to speak the truth in love. Keep in mind, however, that we are speaking a message that asks people to surrender themselves to the Lord—and that message may not always be welcomed. In many cases the opposition may not be aimed at us as much as at the truth we proclaim. [See question #3, page 128.]

B. Assurance (v. 4b)

4b. Yet surely my judgment is with the LORD, and my work with my God.

During periods of discouragement in the Lord's work, we do well to remember that even the apostles of Christ experienced such disappointments in holding forth the light of Jesus. Often they were driven out of cities because of their message (see Acts 13:50, 51; 14:5, 6; 17:13, 14). Our confidence should remain in the One who calls us. He will see to it that our testimony for Him will not go forth in vain.

LIFE ON PURPOSE

The Servant of the Lord was frustrated, but He remained faithful. He was uncertain of His fruitfulness ("I have labored in vain"), but very sure of His reward ("Yet surely my judgment is with the Lord, and my work with my God"), because He served God's purpose.

In his book, *The Death of Ivan Ilych* (*Ill*-itch), Leo Tolstoy describes the anguish of a man who discovers on his deathbed that he has wasted his life. Ilych always had done the right things. He took the right job, married the right woman, and had the proper number of children. But he lived without passion, conviction, love, or purpose.

Dying, Ilych realizes that he has never known real happiness. He has been so busy doing what was expected—living only in the survival mode—that he never did the things he truly wanted to do, the purpose-driven things that he believed he was meant to do. It occurs to him that the entire arrangement of his life, of his family, and of all his social and professional interests has been false. He has lived for the wrong reason. He tries to defend himself and suddenly finds that there is nothing to defend. He comes to a bitter end.

Frustration is common in life, but no one has to die like Ivan Ilych. The Servant of the Lord lived free from regret because He was living His life on purpose. Are you? Determine that, even when you are frustrated, you will be faithful to the Lord. —J. A. M.

III. The Servant's Mission (Isaiah 49:5, 6)

At the moment when the Servant of the Lord needed a word of encouragement, He was reminded of the glorious task to which He had been called.

A. To Israel (v. 5)

5. And now, saith the LORD that formed me from the womb to be his servant, to bring Jacob again to him, Though Israel be not gathered, yet shall I be glorious in the eyes of the LORD, and my God shall be my strength.

The precise mission of the *Servant* is described in both this verse and the next one. Part of the Servant's task is *to bring Jacob again to him*. The name *Jacob* represents the nation of Israel. As noted under the Lesson Background, some portions of the Servant Songs appear to describe the return from Babylonian captivity, and this is one of them. The context, however, points to something far more noteworthy.

It is common in Old Testament prophecy to describe blessings of the messianic age by using Old Testament people, places, or events. The New Testament helps us to see these fulfillments. For example, the resurrection of Jesus is described as fulfilling a promise concerning "the sure mercies

---

How to Say It

AHAZ. *Ay*-haz.
ANTIOCH. *An*-tee-ock.
ASSYRIANS. Uh-*sear*-ee-uns.
BABYLON. *Bab*-uh-lun.
BABYLONIANS. Bab-uh-*low*-nee-uns.
BARNABAS. *Bar*-nuh-bus.
CYRUS. *Sigh*-russ.
HEZEKIAH. Hez-ih-*kye*-uh.
IMMANUEL. Ih-*man*-you-el.
ISAIAH. Eye-*zay*-uh.
JEREMIAH. Jair-uh-*my*-uh.
JOTHAM. *Jo*-thum.
MESSIANIC. mess-ee-*an*-ick.
PERSIA. *Per*-zhuh.
PISIDIA. Pih-*sid*-ee-uh.
SIMEON. *Sim*-ee-un.
TIGLATH-PILESER. *Tig*-lath-pih-*lee*-zer (strong accent on *lee*).
UZZIAH. Uh-*zye*-uh.

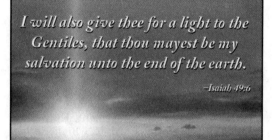

I will also give thee for a light to the Gentiles, that thou mayest be my salvation unto the end of the earth.

—Isaiah 49:6

Visual for lesson 1. *This poster illustrates the truth of today's Golden Text: Jesus is the light for "salvation unto the end of the earth."*

of David" (Acts 13:34; Isaiah 55:3). Including Gentiles in the church is said to fulfill a prophecy that the fallen tabernacle of David would be restored (Acts 15:14-17; Amos 9:11, 12). Romans 11:25-27 links turning away "ungodliness from Jacob" with a covenant that "shall take away their sins." Thus the phrase *bring Jacob again to him* can be taken to refer to the proclamation of the gospel "to the Jew first" (Romans 1:16).

The Servant then acknowledges that His ministry has not been completely successful: Israel has *not* been *gathered* to the Lord. Yet in spite of these disappointments, the Servant expresses His confidence that His mission will be blessed and used of the Lord. [See question #4, page 128.]

B. To the Gentiles (v. 6)

6. And he said, It is a light thing that thou shouldest be my servant to raise up the tribes of Jacob, and to restore the preserved of Israel: I will also give thee for a light to the Gentiles, that thou mayest be my salvation unto the end of the earth.

While the task described in verse 5 would seem significant enough, now the Servant is told that *it is a light thing* for Him to be called *to raise up the tribes of Jacob, and to restore the preserved of Israel.* The Lord has more than that in mind; the Servant's mission will extend beyond the scope of the chosen nation, reaching *the Gentiles* and extending *unto the end of the earth.* This verse should immediately call to mind Jesus' Great Commission (Acts 1:8) and the fact that His gospel "is the power of God unto salvation to every one that believeth; to the Jew first, and also to the Greek" (Romans 1:16).

The final part of this verse is alluded to in at least two places in the New Testament. The first

time occurred when Joseph and Mary took Jesus to the temple to fulfill the requirements of the law of Moses. There they were approached by a godly man named Simeon, who took the child in His arms and spoke of Him as "a light to lighten the Gentiles" (Luke 2:32). This was the same child whose birth was announced by angels to shepherds in these words: "Behold, I bring you good tidings of great joy, which shall be to *all people*" (Luke 2:10).

The second incident is recorded in the book of Acts. Acts 13 tells how Paul and Barnabas encountered opposition from the Jews when they tried to preach the gospel in Antioch of Pisidia. Paul and Barnabas responded by turning their focus to the Gentiles. They supported their actions by quoting the words of our text: "I have set thee to be a light of the Gentiles, that thou shouldest be for salvation unto the ends of the earth" (Acts 13:47).

The gospel of Jesus Christ is still intended to go worldwide. It is still the church's mission to see that that happens. After all, Jesus is "the light of the world" (John 8:12)—and so are His people (Matthew 5:14). [See question #5, page 128.]

Conclusion

A. Keep the Light Shining

The Servant of the Lord (Jesus) was sent first to the "lost sheep of the house of Israel" (Matthew 15:24). But the impact of His ministry included many "other sheep" (John 10:16). He died for the sins of the entire world so that all nations may turn from darkness to light.

Today we are the "light-bearers" who have answered the call of the gospel and whose task it is to "show forth the praises of him who hath called you out of darkness into his marvelous light" (1 Peter 2:9). Like the Servant of the Lord, we must give all of our strength to our task. Yes, there will be enemies and hardships as we labor, but these must not be allowed to stand in the way of the Lord's work. Even as the Servant took comfort in the encouragement and the protection provided by the Lord, so must we. We must continue to labor faithfully until the Servant of the Lord returns.

B. Prayer

Father, keep my light burning brightly so that the path to salvation may be seen through me. May people find Jesus, the Light of the world, through my testimony. In Jesus' name. Amen.

C. Thought to Remember

Jesus is the Light of the world; I must be a reflection of His light.

Learning by Doing

This page contains an alternate lesson plan emphasizing learning activities.
Classes desiring such student involvement will find these suggestions helpful.

Learning Goals

After participating in this lesson, each student will be able to:

1. Summarize the call of God's "Servant" and the scope of His mission.

2. Tell how Jesus fulfilled Isaiah's prophecy of the Servant and how the church does so today.

3. Suggest specific ways to follow the Lord's Servant in loving service today.

Into the Lesson

Form groups of four or five people, and give each group a piece of poster board and a marker. Ask them to draw a line down the middle of the board, creating two columns: the left to be labeled "Darkness/Evil"; the right, "Light/Good."

Ask the teams to quickly list words, phrases, and illustrations they have heard that equate good with light or darkness with evil. They may cite Scriptures, movies, books, or other sources. For example, which kind of character in a television or movie drama was more likely to have the unshaved, swarthy look? Give the groups only about three or four minutes to list these and tape the poster board to the wall.

Make the transition to Bible study by telling them the use of light and darkness as imagery for "good versus evil" is as old as Scripture and is the core of today's lesson. In today's study we can sense frustration and find help in being the light God wants us to be in this world.

Into the Word

Give a brief lecture on the background of today's text. Be sure to focus on the meaning of the word *servant* and the mission to bring light to the world. Then distribute handouts with the following questions for groups to discuss. (These questions are also included in the student book, *Adult Bible Class.*) Put this list of questions in the first of two columns on the page, using the heading "Plunging Into God's Word." Questions for column two will be listed later.

1. What is the significance of the imagery of the words *isles* and *people from far* in verse 1? What is God emphasizing in this verse?

2. Explain the following word images in verse 2: "Sharp sword," "the shadow of his hand," "a polished shaft," and "quiver." What is the main thought God and Isaiah were communicating through this verse?

3. Verses 3 and 4 are key to understanding this prophecy. Why would Israel express the frustration found in verse 4a? Give one or two illustrations from Israel's history that they could use to justify their frustration.

4. Write a three- or four-word phrase that describes the attitude of the "servant" in verse 4b, or write a slogan that summarizes verse 4.

Give the class about ten minutes. After hearing a few answers, give another brief lecture about the servant's expanded mission. Focus on the mission to become a light to the Gentiles.

Into Life

Have the small groups proceed to the column with the heading "Becoming God's Light."

1. Isaiah 49:6; Matthew 28:19, 20; and Luke 2:10, 14 have a common thread. In these passages, what message does God make clear about the scope of His offer of salvation?

2. Today's believer may echo the frustration of Isaiah 49:4a as he tries to be the light God desires. Why? What frustrations or challenges to becoming God's light would you list?

3. What lessons does verse 4b teach us about trust and perseverance?

To conclude the lesson, display another poster you have prepared before class. (Or refer the students to the student books.) This poster should have the heading: "Darkness vs. Light." Below that should be three columns divided by bold lines. Column 1 has the heading "Men Loved Darkness (John 3:19)." Column 2 has the heading "Walk in the Light (1 John 1:7)." The heading for column 3 reads, "Let Your Light Shine Before Men (Matthew 5:16)." Tell the class that sometimes it is helpful, as we struggle to be God's light in a dark world, to revisit basic concepts. Ask the students to share what these concepts mean and give illustrations of each. Emphasize in column 3 some practical ways to be God's light in a world that loves darkness. List the student's answers and illustrations.

Conclude the lesson by asking each class learner to identify a person who appears to be the best prospect with whom to share Jesus. Class members may share the names with the group, telling why these people come to mind. Ask someone in the group to pray on behalf of the group, seeking God's help in being faithful and consistent in reflecting His light.

Let's Talk It Over

The questions on this page are designed to encourage review of the lesson Scriptures and to promote discussion of the lesson by the class. The answers provided are only discussion starters. Let your class talk it over from there.

1. The lesson writer has noted that the identity of the Servant is on some levels Israel and on some levels the Messiah, and that there is also some valid application to those of us who follow Christ today, continuing His ministry. What are we doing to take the gospel to the distant "isles" and "coastlands"? What more can we do?

Is your church supporting missionaries abroad? If so, try to have some of the details—who? where? how much support? Perhaps your class could assist in the work by initiating some correspondence with a missionary for giving encouragement. What about recruiting new workers? Is your church active in encouraging young people to choose missions as a career? Does your church send people on short-term missions trips? Can your class plan to go on one together?

2. The church continues the battle suggested by the weapons imagery in verse 2, fighting against the forces of evil. Where is this battle especially being waged in our community? What can we do—individually or together—to participate in this battle?

The church is engaged in spiritual warfare with Satan's forces for human souls. Thus, the battle rages in every human heart. Whatever we can do to equip individual believers to resist temptation contributes to the battle.

There are times, however, when evil becomes much more aggressive and predatory. Pornography, strip clubs, and other facets of the illicit sex industry are wreaking havoc in some communities—is yours one of them? What can your class members do to oppose these destroyers of families? The growing popularity of gambling, particularly in state lotteries and in casinos, is also taking a toll on the spiritual health of our communities. What can be done to address this issue? What other threats need to be addressed in your community? Discuss how your class can get involved.

3. The Servant said he had "labored in vain." Have you ever felt that way about your efforts for the Lord? Why? What encouragement can you offer to one who feels similarly frustrated?

Isaiah's Servant clearly experienced the pain and frustration of preaching God's truth to those who would not listen (49:4). Nevertheless, he declares that "my judgment is with the Lord, and my work with my God." When we feel frustrated in our Christian service, we need to remember first that God requires only that we be faithful, not "successful" by human standards. Second, we need to recall that it is God, not man, who supplies the power behind the gospel (1 Corinthians 3:6). Sometimes it seems as if our work is in vain, when actually it is God working at His own pace. We may be sowing gospel seeds that God will use to produce fruit long after we are gone, perhaps even in fields far removed from us.

4. Part of the Servant's task was the spiritual restoration of Israel. What can we do to minister to members of our church who are in need of spiritual restoration?

While attending worship services is by no means the whole duty of a believer, failure to attend is often symptomatic of spiritual trouble in one's life. We need to notice when our brothers and sisters are absent from the assembly and give a call to encourage them. We can also encourage other believers to get involved in ministry, in small group Bible studies, and other activities that contribute to spiritual refreshing.

5. References to the "isles" and people "from far" (v. 1) and to the "salvation unto the end of the earth (v. 6) remind us that we, too, have a Commission to reach the whole world with the gospel. How well are we communicating the imperative of this Commission to the next generation? How can we impress on young people the need to pursue evangelism aggressively?

The first thing we need to do is to set an example. Do we share Christ with those around us? Do we talk openly of the need to win the lost, both at home and abroad? Do we give evangelism and missions priority funding in our church budget? What other good examples can your class suggest?

Then we also need to talk about it with our young people. Parents and grandparents should talk about it at home. Sunday school teachers should teach it in class. Ministers, youth ministers, and youth sponsors should talk about it as well. It needs to be a frequent topic in the church, so that the concept seems natural—not just something for the "super-spiritual" few.

God's Servant Brings Peace

December 9
Lesson 2

DEVOTIONAL READING: Isaiah 12.

BACKGROUND SCRIPTURE: Isaiah 11.

PRINTED TEXT: Isaiah 11:1-9.

Isaiah 11:1-9

1 And there shall come forth a rod out of the stem of Jesse, and a Branch shall grow out of his roots:

2 And the Spirit of the LORD shall rest upon him, the spirit of wisdom and understanding, the spirit of counsel and might, the spirit of knowledge and of the fear of the LORD;

3 And shall make him of quick understanding in the fear of the LORD: and he shall not judge after the sight of his eyes, neither reprove after the hearing of his ears:

4 But with righteousness shall he judge the poor, and reprove with equity for the meek of the earth: and he shall smite the earth with the rod of his mouth, and with the breath of his lips shall he slay the wicked.

5 And righteousness shall be the girdle of his loins, and faithfulness the girdle of his reins.

6 The wolf also shall dwell with the lamb, and the leopard shall lie down with the kid; and the calf and the young lion and the fatling together; and a little child shall lead them.

7 And the cow and the bear shall feed; their young ones shall lie down together: and the lion shall eat straw like the ox.

8 And the sucking child shall play on the hole of the asp, and the weaned child shall put his hand on the cockatrice' den.

9 They shall not hurt nor destroy in all my holy mountain: for the earth shall be full of the knowledge of the LORD, as the waters cover the sea.

GOLDEN TEXT: The wolf also shall dwell with the lamb, and the leopard shall lie down with the kid; and the calf and the young lion and the fatling together; and a little child shall lead them.—Isaiah 11:6.

Light for All People
The Mission of God's Servant
(Lessons 1-5)

Lesson Aims

After participating in this lesson, each student will be able to:

1. Describe the characteristics of the "Branch" and the unique way His ministry is pictured.

2. List some current conditions that challenge the peace and security envisioned by Isaiah.

3. Identify and pray for a person who needs Christ's peace.

Lesson Outline

INTRODUCTION
  A. Named for Peace
  B. Lesson Background
 I. THE PROMISED BRANCH (Isaiah 11:1, 2)
  A. His Humble Origins (v. 1)
  B. His Godly Character (v. 2)
II. HIS REIGN OF RIGHTEOUSNESS (Isaiah 11:3-5)
  A. Spiritual Priorities (v. 3)
    True Colors
  B. Impartial Justice (vv. 4, 5)
III. HIS KINGDOM OF PEACE (Isaiah 11:6-9)
  A. Wild Creatures Tamed (vv. 6-8)
  B. Worldwide Knowledge of God (v. 9)
    A Baby Brings Peace
CONCLUSION
  A. Paradise Regained
  B. Prayer
  C. Thought to Remember

Introduction

A. Named for Peace

Bob Shannon tells of a member of a church in Queensland, Australia, whose name is Pax Young. It is not unusual to encounter the surname Young, but one wonders how he got his unusual first name. The answer is that he was born on the very day World War I ended. The midwife who took care of his delivery asked for the privilege of naming him. She named him *Pax*, which means "peace."

While the name Pax may seem uncommon, a common name in Slavic lands is *Vladimir*. Like *Pax*, it means "peace." And sometimes one hears the name *Olivera*, which also means "peace."

But there was only person whose very *life* meant "peace." That was Jesus Christ, the Prince

of peace. Only He can give "the peace . . . which passeth all understanding" (Philippians 4:7).

The prophet Isaiah foretold a coming era of peace—during a period of great uncertainty for God's people. God grants that peace to all who trust in and obey Jesus. By knowing Him as Savior and Lord, His followers can come to know the peace of being made right with God—a peace that can sustain them during the times of uncertainty in their lives.

B. Lesson Background

The first half of the eighth century B.C. appeared quite promising for Israel (the northern kingdom) and Judah (the southern kingdom). During the reign of Jeroboam II in Israel (793-753 B.C.), a prosperity enveloped the country that reminded people of Israel's glory days. In Judah the same economic boom was felt during the reign of Uzziah (792-740 B.C.). But the outward prosperity of these times masked an inner sinfulness that eighth-century prophets such as Amos and Hosea could not overlook.

After Uzziah's death, Judah's condition began to deteriorate swiftly. While Uzziah's son, Jotham, "did that which was right in the sight of the Lord" (2 Kings 15:34), Jotham's son, Ahaz, was an extremely wicked king who engaged in many practices forbidden by God (2 Kings 16:2-4).

As noted last week, it was during Ahaz's reign that Israel and Syria joined forces to counter the rising aggression of Tiglath-pileser III of Assyria. When Judah refused to join this coalition, Syria and Israel attacked Judah in an effort to force Ahaz to join the alliance. Ahaz responded to this pressure by calling on Tiglath-pileser for assistance, in spite of Isaiah's counsel to trust in the Lord instead (Isaiah 7:3-9). The result was the Assyrian conquest of Damascus in 732 B.C. and of Samaria (capital of Israel) in 722.

It was during this crisis in Judah that some of Isaiah's most significant messianic prophecies were uttered (Isaiah 7:14; 9:1-7; and today's text in 11:1-9). Following the majestic description of a special Child in 9:1-7, the prophet returned to the crisis facing God's people. It is important to note that his prophecy of a "Branch" (11:1) is the climax to a series of messages using trees (or similar plants) to symbolize nations. For example, in 9:18 we read of his words concerning Israel's impending judgment: "For wickedness burneth as the fire: it shall devour the briers and thorns, and shall kindle in the thickets of the forest, and they shall mount up like the lifting up of smoke."

Isaiah 10 then focuses on Assyria as the instrument that God will use to administer His judgment. Assyria itself, however, is filled with a sinful pride and a "stout heart" (Isaiah 10:12) against God, which He must also judge. Note the imagery used in verse 19 to describe the outcome of this judgment: "And the rest of the trees of his forest shall be few, that a child may write them."

Chapter 10 concludes with a description of the Assyrian army's march toward Jerusalem (vv. 28-34). The Assyrians reach Jerusalem (v. 32) but go no farther because the Lord intervenes, cutting down the proud Assyrian tree. ("Lebanon" in verse 34 is probably a reference to Assyria; see Ezekiel 31:3.)

However, whereas the Assyrian tree is completely cut down, the Israelite tree, though reduced to a stump, is still alive. It indicates that God is not finished with His people. As today's text shows, He has special plans for them.

I. The Promised Branch (Isaiah 11:1, 2)

In the preceding verses, the Assyrian king is pictured reflecting on his conquests and thinking, "By the strength of my hand I have done it, and by my wisdom; for I am prudent: and I have removed the bounds of the people, and have robbed their treasures, and I have put down the inhabitants like a valiant man" (Isaiah 10:13). Isaiah now declares that another (and better) King is coming who will reign in a manner directly opposite that of the Assyrian.

A. His Humble Origins (v. 1)

1. And there shall come forth a rod out of the stem of Jesse, and a Branch shall grow out of his roots.

After Assyria overran Israel (and later Judah), the once-great nation ruled by David and Solomon was reduced to a *stem* (more accurately rendered as "stump"). A *rod* (or "shoot") would *come forth* from that *stem of Jesse*. The word *Branch* (the Hebrew term is *netzer*) is similar in meaning to *rod*. This Hebrew term is most likely the basis for Matthew's reference to the fulfillment of this passage in Jesus: "He shall be called a Nazarene" (Matthew 2:23).

Note that the state of the nation is so pitiful that it is not referred to by the name of its greatest king (David) but by the name of his father. This calls attention to the humble origins of the Branch, as well as to the fact that another "David" would be raised up by the Lord to be a righteous ruler and to provide the blessings described in the remainder of our text (cf. Ezekiel 34:23, 24). [See question #1, page 136.]

B. His Godly Character (v. 2)

2. And the Spirit of the LORD shall rest upon him, the spirit of wisdom and understanding, **the spirit of counsel and might, the spirit of knowledge and of the fear of the LORD.**

The promised Branch will also be blessed with the guidance of the *Spirit of the Lord*. Different leaders throughout the Old Testament (such as the judges) were given God's Spirit for specific tasks; however, the Spirit would *rest upon* the Branch. This indicates the continual guidance that the Spirit would provide (cf. John 3:34).

The Spirit's provisions are then listed in terms of the qualities necessary for godly leadership. Some students have found significance in the fact that there are six qualities listed, so that adding the gift of the Spirit Himself yields seven. If they are right, the symbolism implies that the Branch will be perfectly endowed by the Spirit with everything needed to carry out His mission (cf. Revelation 5:6).

II. His Reign of Righteousness (Isaiah 11:3-5)

A. Spiritual Priorities (v. 3)

3. And shall make him of quick understanding in the fear of the LORD. And he shall not judge after the sight of his eyes, neither reprove after the hearing of his ears.

The reign of this coming ruler will demonstrate all of the best in what a ruler should be. He will possess ideal royal insight to *judge*—that is, to administer justice based on a higher standard than the earthly concerns that occupy most kings. Because He is *of quick understanding in the fear of the Lord*, He will judge with a wisdom that can see into the hearts of people. Thus He will not be limited to a surface judgment based only on *the sight of his eyes* or *the hearing of his ears*. Recall that Jesus "knew all men, and needed not that any should testify of man; for he knew what was in man" (John 2:24, 25).

How to Say It

AHAZ. *Ay*-haz.
ASSYRIANS. Uh-*sear*-ee-uns.
DAMASCUS. Duh-*mass*-cus.
HOSEA. Ho-*zay*-uh.
ISAIAH. Eye-*zay*-uh.
JEROBOAM. Jair-uh-*bo*-um.
JOTHAM. *Jo*-thum.
MESSIANIC. mess-ee-*an*-ick.
NAZARENE. *Naz*-uh-reen.
NETZER (Hebrew). *net*-zer.
SAMARIA. Suh-*mare*-ee-uh.
TIGLATH-PILESER. *Tig*-lath-pih-*lee*-zer (strong accent on *lee*).
UZZIAH. Uh-*zye*-uh.

This description does not mean that true judgment ignores evidence presented to the senses. Rather, the point is that the coming Ruler will place a much higher priority on the law of God than He will on human standards that might influence His judgments in a negative manner. [See question #2, page 136.]

TRUE COLORS

As he was leaving the Disney World theme park, a man noticed an elderly couple in some distress. The wife was in a wheelchair, and the man pushing it looked exhausted. All around them, people were being rude and inconsiderate. The large crowds heading for the exit had forced them to the side, and no one would allow this couple to move through.

As the man noticed the couple's plight, he also happened to notice that the older man was wearing a Cincinnati Reds baseball cap. When he reached the exit, he played the part of a friendly traffic cop and helped the weary couple pass through the exit.

Outside, the couple expressed their thanks, and then the man asked, "Why did you do that? Why did you help?"

Their new friend replied, "For two reasons. First, because it was the right thing to do. And second, I noticed your Reds cap. I'm a Reds fan, too—and we Reds fans have to stick together!"

"Well, I have to be honest," said the man. "I'm not a Reds fans; I'm a New York Mets fan. I wore this hat only because it matches my shirt." The helpful man was still glad to have assisted the couple, but he realized anew how easy it is to be deceived. Many people don't always show their true colors. You can't always judge them by their appearance.

Isaiah's coming King would not be deceived by pretense. He Himself always displays His true colors, and His judgments are always true and just; for He sees and judges the heart. Is your heart right before Him?   —J. A. M.

B. Impartial Justice (vv. 4, 5)

4. But with righteousness shall he judge the poor, and reprove with equity for the meek of the earth: and he shall smite the earth with the rod of his mouth, and with the breath of his lips shall he slay the wicked.

Isaiah's words would have struck a responsive chord with his audience, for many rulers in his day did not treat the *poor* and the *meek* in the way described here. Previously he had voiced disapproval of the national leaders, telling them to "seek judgment, relieve the oppressed, judge the fatherless, plead for the widow" (Isaiah 1:17). Justice, then as now, was often corrupted by

being sold to the highest bidder. Under such conditions, it is usually the *poor* and the *meek* who suffer most.

In refreshing contrast, the coming messianic ruler will not permit the corruption of God's law. The wicked who oppress the poor and the meek will be smitten with *the rod of his mouth*. Earlier (Isaiah 10:5, 24) Isaiah had described Assyria as the rod of the Lord's anger, used by Him to punish Israel. But when the messianic ruler comes, He will possess this rod. He will administer true justice; all the *wicked* will be slain by *the breath of his lips*. On the Day of Judgment, the words of Jesus will seal the eternal destiny of all nations (Matthew 25:31-46). [See question #3, page 136.]

The words *poor* and *meek* call to mind Jesus' teachings in the Beatitudes about the poor in spirit and the meek (Matthew 5:3, 5). He has taught us that we are to value inner qualities that are pleasing to God instead of focusing on the outward, material concerns that occupy so many individuals' time and attention. Isaiah's words can also be taken as a challenge to Christians to treat others with impartiality (in other words, as Jesus would treat them).

5. And righteousness shall be the girdle of his loins, and faithfulness the girdle of his reins.

The phrase *girdle of his loins* is understood by considering the style of clothing worn in the ancient world. A man who was about to engage in an activity that required physical exertion and freedom of movement would gather up his loose outer garment and tuck it under his belt so his garment would not hinder him. The expression "gird the loins" thus became commonplace (1 Kings 18:46; 2 Kings 4:29) and was applied to one's spiritual preparation (1 Peter 1:13). The term *reins* is actually the word for "kidneys"; in this passage it means the same as *loins*.

Home Daily Bible Readings

Monday, Dec. 3—God's Children Have Rebelled (Isaiah 1:1-9)

Tuesday, Dec. 4—Do Justice, Not Empty Rituals (Isaiah 1:10-20)

Wednesday, Dec. 5—An Age of Peace (Isaiah 2:1-5)

Thursday, Dec. 6—Give Thanks to the Lord (Isaiah 12:1-6)

Friday, Dec. 7—Compassion for God's People (Isaiah 14:1-7)

Saturday, Dec. 8—Hope for the Remnant (Isaiah 11:1-9)

Sunday, Dec. 9—The Remnant's Second Chance (Isaiah 11:10-16)

Visual for
lesson 2

*This poster beautifully illustrates the Golden
Text for today's lesson, Isaiah 11:6.*

The words of Isaiah highlight the fact that the
Branch will be prepared for action with regard to
His pronouncements of judgment. But His actions will not be motivated by a quest for political advantage or personal gain. Instead, He will
act according to *righteousness* and *faithfulness*.
[See question #4, page 136.]

It is important to observe the parallels between the messianic rule outlined by Isaiah and
those occasions during Jesus' ministry when His
power served the purpose of healing the brokenhearted, encouraging the weak, and lifting up the
oppressed. Jesus' ministry was characterized by
the sense of impartiality described by Isaiah.

III. His Kingdom of Peace
(Isaiah 11:6-9)

The reign of the righteous messianic ruler will
usher in a period of peace that is described in the
highly poetic lines in the remainder of our
printed text.

A. Wild Creatures Tamed (vv. 6-8)

**6. The wolf also shall dwell with the lamb,
and the leopard shall lie down with the kid;
and the calf and the young lion and the fatling
together; and a little child shall lead them.**

What kind of an impact will the reign of the
Branch have? Even ferocious animals that are
normally natural enemies will live at peace with
one another, and more amazingly, with animals
that they normally hunt as prey. The *wolf* will no
longer harm the *lamb*. The *leopard* will not hunt
the *kid* (young goat) for food. The *young lion* will
not disturb the *fatling* (cattle). Peace and safety
will characterize this era—so much so that *a little child shall lead* these former rivals.

**7. And the cow and the bear shall feed; their
young ones shall lie down together: and the lion
shall eat straw like the ox.**

To emphasize further the sense of safety in
this era, Isaiah describes how fierce animals like
the *bear* and the *lion* will be tamed and will behave like domesticated cattle. The entire animal
kingdom will become an ideal world of security.

**8. And the sucking child shall play on the
hole of the asp, and the weaned child shall put
his hand on the cockatrice' den.**

Both a *sucking child* (an infant) and a *weaned
child* (approximately three years old in Bible
times) are at an especially innocent and vulnerable stage of life. They do not know when they are
in a dangerous situation, for they do not have the
experiences that teach older children what they
should avoid. Normally a parent would panic to
see his or her small child playing near the *hole* of
a deadly snake (a *cockatrice* apparently describes
some form of venomous serpent). But the new
era of peace will be blessed with such harmony
that even defenseless children will face no threat
to their safety.

B. Worldwide Knowledge of God (v. 9)

**9. They shall not hurt nor destroy in all my
holy mountain: for the earth shall be full of the
knowledge of the LORD, as the waters cover the
sea.**

This verse summarizes life in the new era of
peace just described by Isaiah. Certainly in the
prophet's own time such a world as this seemed
like an impossible dream. There appeared to be
no peace in sight—either from a national standpoint (because of the Assyrian menace) or a spiritual standpoint (because of the nation's
sinfulness, encouraged by wicked King Ahaz).

The Messiah, however, will usher in a kingdom of peace that will fulfill the longings of all
who have placed their hope in the Lord. His
kingdom will take on a character like none the
world has ever seen. The result of His righteous
reign will be the spread of *the knowledge of the
Lord* throughout the *earth.*

[See question #5, page 136.] Isaiah's language
in verses 6-9 is viewed in a literal way by some
Christians. They believe that the effects of sin on
the animal kingdom will be erased when Jesus returns, and that animals will behave in just the
way described by Isaiah. Such an interpretation
is possible, in light of Paul's description of how
"the creation waits in eager expectation for the
sons of God to be revealed" and how "the creation
itself will be liberated from its bondage to decay"
(Romans 8:19, 21, *New International Version*).

Other Bible students understand Isaiah's language to be symbolic (just as the language about

a "rod," a "stem," and a "Branch" in verse 1 must be symbolic). They see Isaiah portraying vividly and poetically the glory of the messianic kingdom by using scenes from the natural world. Very similar is the prophet's earlier description of the peace that will come when "the mountain of the Lord's house" is established as a place where all nations would go to hear the word of the Lord (Isaiah 2:2, 3). The impact of that is pictured as so dramatic that the nations will "beat their swords into plowshares, and their spears into pruning hooks" (Isaiah 2:2-4). These figures of speech are believed to paint a vivid picture of people at peace with one another because of the righteous reign of the Lord. The fact that this is pictured as occurring "in the last days" (v. 2) is considered as pointing to the messianic age as the time when Isaiah's prophecy reaches fulfillment. Christians always have lived in the "last days" (Hebrews 1:1, 2), during which those who know the Lord are to make Him known throughout the earth.

Whatever their position may be on this matter, all believers anticipate the consummation of Christ's kingdom, which will take place when He returns. They share the hope of New Testament believers regarding that glorious day. They pray, as did the apostle John toward the close of Revelation, "Come, Lord Jesus" (Revelation 22:20).

In addition, all believers can enjoy the peace of God in this present world. This is the peace described by Paul as "the peace . . . which passeth all understanding" (Philippians 4:7)—at a time when he was a prisoner in Rome! Christians today can be sustained by that same peace, no matter where they live or what their circumstances may be.

A BABY BRINGS PEACE

One of the most intriguing individuals who fought during the Civil War was Confederate General George E. Pickett. He was a flamboyant character, romantic and brave. He led the famous "Pickett's Charge" at the Battle of Gettysburg.

At Gettysburg, Pickett's army was drawn up for battle, prepared to face Ulysses S. Grant, when Pickett's first baby, a son, was born. All along the two-mile Confederate front, cheers were shouted and bonfires were built in celebration of the event. It was a beautiful sight, as the bonfires illuminated the thick darkness.

General Grant, curious to know what was happening in the Confederate Army, sent out scouts to investigate. They reported that General Pickett had a son, his first child.

General Grant replied, "Have we any kindling wood on this side of the line? Why don't we strike up a row of lights?"

Soon bonfires were blazing all along the Union line. Not a shot was fired that night; not a gun was aimed at an enemy. Bright lights and peace reigned because a baby was born. A few days later, a baby's silver service, engraved to George E. Pickett, Jr., was sent through the lines—a gift from General Grant and two other Union generals. A baby's birth produced peace—if only temporarily.

Such is the impact, and even more, of the Christmas baby—Jesus, the Prince of peace. His birth resulted in the announcement of "glory to God in the highest, and on earth *peace*" (Luke 2:14). And His peace is eternal!   —J. A. M.

Conclusion

A. Paradise Regained

To Isaiah's audience in the eighth century before Christ, the promise of peace may have given hope for a time when Assyria would be removed from power and would no longer be the enemy of God's people. In time, that did happen. However, when the "big picture" of the entire Bible is considered, Isaiah's words had a far more sweeping impact. They predicted a time in which what was lost in the Garden of Eden through sin would be regained through the reconciliation accomplished by the sinless One, Jesus.

The peace described by Isaiah can never be destroyed by anything in this world, because this peace is "not as the world giveth" (John 14:27). Isaiah's description of peace will reach its ultimate fulfillment when we are welcomed into a "new heaven and a new earth" where there will be "no more death, neither sorrow, nor crying, neither shall there be any more pain: for the former things are passed away" (Revelation 21:4).

That new creation begins the moment a person's life is changed through the gospel of Jesus Christ, because "if any man be in Christ, he is a new creature: old things are passed away; behold, all things are become new" (2 Corinthians 5:17). Thus in one sense Isaiah's words are fulfilled when we become Christians. In another sense, the best is yet to come!

B. Prayer

We anticipate with joy, O Lord, the return of Jesus and the establishment of His Heavenly kingdom. While we wait for that day, we pledge our faithfulness to the King of kings. Through Him we pray, amen.

C. Thought to Remember

"Therefore being justified by faith, we have peace with God through our Lord Jesus Christ" (Romans 5:1).

Learning by Doing

This page contains an alternate lesson plan emphasizing learning activities.
Classes desiring such student involvement will find these suggestions helpful.

Learning Goals

After participating in this lesson, each student will be able to:

1. Describe the characteristics of the "Branch" and the unique way His ministry is pictured.

2. List some current conditions that challenge the peace and security envisioned by Isaiah.

3. Identify and pray for a person who needs Christ's peace.

Into the Lesson

Write each of the letters of the word *peace* on one of five sheets of letter-sized paper. Give the five letters in random order to five students. Ask them to stand at the front and arrange themselves so that they spell out the key word to today's lesson. After they accomplish this task, tape the letters to the wall as a banner for today's lesson. State: "Peace is not usually so easily made as we have done it here. Neither in a life nor in a nation."

Brainstorm and list on a transparency or chalkboard some different definitions and applications of the word *peace*. Ask, "What are some ways people interpret and apply the word *peace?*" Ideas may include an absence of war, relationship situations, justice, and a relationship with God. State, "Today, Isaiah speaks to that need of peace as he uses beautiful imagery to describe peace."

Into the Word

Use the lesson commentary to prepare and deliver a brief lecture about the significance of the terms *rod, stem of Jesse,* and *Branch.*

Divide the class into three groups, assigning each group one of the following assignments. With its assignment, give each group a photocopy of the appropriate lesson commentary pages, a piece of poster board, and a marker.

Group #1. Read Isaiah 11:1-9. Your task is to help the class understand the "Who" of this prophecy. Answer the following questions and be ready to share your answers with the class.

1. Who is the subject of this passage, and what does Isaiah mean when he says, "the Spirit of the Lord shall rest upon him"?

2. List on a poster the character qualities of the "Branch" as cited in verses 2 and 3a. Use the commentary to locate other Scriptures that support or fulfill this prophecy.

Group #2. You will help the class understand "What" the Branch is to do. What is His mission? Read Isaiah 11:1-9 and answer these questions:

1. What mission of the Branch is emphasized in verses 3 and 4? What is His purpose?

2. Read the lesson commentary on verses 3-5 to be able to explain to the class the meaning of "shall not judge after the sight of his eyes" and "neither reprove after the hearing of his ears."

3. If the ultimate goal is peace, as described in verses 6-9, why are the previous verses loaded with harsh, violent words like *smite, slay,* and *judge*? How will these help bring peace?

Group #3. You have the privilege of exploring the "Why" of this prophecy. Read Isaiah 11:1-9 and be ready to help the class understand why the Lord was sending the "Branch."

1. Verses 6-9 portray the peaceable kingdom. List words and imagery describing this peace.

2. Read the lesson commentary and be ready to explain the significance of the imagery.

3. Is the kingdom of righteousness and peace present or future? Why? See also Luke 2:14.

Allow each group to report its findings.

Into Life

Use the visual from the introduction to reaffirm that the word *peace* has many meanings and applications. Ask the groups to apply their understanding to life today.

Group #1: Peace With God. Read Romans 5:1-11 and summarize this peace for the class. You may also comment on the impact this peace makes on the daily lives of believers.

Group #2: Peace in Church Leadership. Every church should experience a sense of peace and harmony in itself and its leadership. What are some Christlike qualities we should expect of our leaders? Isaiah 11:2, 3 and 1 Timothy 3:1-7 may be helpful.

Group #3: Peace at Home. Proverbs 17:1 highlights the importance of peace in the home. Discuss basic principles that help keep this peace.

Conclude by asking class members to recite the lines of this prayer as you read them: "Father of peace and love/ We thank You that we are no longer Your enemies/ We thank You that we are Your children through Jesus Christ/ Help us to keep peace in our church/ and in our families/ Grant peace to _____ (name of friend)/ In the name of the Prince of Peace we pray. Amen."

Let's Talk It Over

The questions on this page are designed to encourage review of the lesson Scriptures and to promote discussion of the lesson by the class. The answers provided are only discussion starters. Let your class talk it over from there.

1. The "Branch" from Jesse's "roots" is certainly the Messiah—Jesus Christ. How are the traits ascribed to Him important for leaders in His church?

Jesus used His *wisdom* and knowledge of the law to ward off Satan (Matthew 4:1-11), His *understanding* of the kingdom of Heaven to teach the people about its nature (Matthew 13), His ability to *counsel* to direct people to the Father (John 3), His *might* to cast out demons and heal the sick (Luke 4:36-41), and His *fear of the Lord* to remain obedient to His Father's will (Hebrews 5:7-9).

Similarly, the church will benefit today if its spiritual leaders exercise godly *wisdom* as they deal with congregational problems, if they use their knowledge and *understanding* of the Bible to teach people about the kingdom of Heaven, if they use spiritual insight to offer much needed godly *counsel* to those who need it, if they exercise the *power* of prayer on behalf of the sick, and if they set an example for the church by their reverent *fear of God*.

2. Isaiah said the Messiah would judge by standards other than what He saw or heard. How can we encourage believers today to value the things that cannot be seen with the eye or heard with the ear, but instead are spiritually discerned?

The lesson writer cites the Beatitudes, and that is a good place to start. The church needs to promote the values Jesus expressed in the opening of His Sermon on the Mount. Sermons and lessons should explain and apply them. Young people should be taught to memorize them. Posters could be hung on walls to illustrate them and to remind worshipers of their value.

Beyond that, we may note that Paul says "we walk by faith, not by sight" (2 Corinthians 5:7). Church leaders need to demonstrate such faith and to express openly the need to step out beyond what can be discerned with the physical senses to do what faith tells them is God's will.

3. Jesus rendered the kind of impartial justice that Isaiah predicted of the Messiah. He freely associated with sinners and outcasts because they desperately needed to find salvation (Luke 5:30-32). At the same time, Jesus openly criti- cized the powerful scribes and Pharisees for their self-righteous hypocrisy (Luke 11). How can the church demonstrate that same kind of impartiality?

James warns the church not to discriminate against the poor by giving better treatment to the wealthy. Rather than judge an individual by his wealth, the church should judge according to his faith (James 2:1-5). Likewise, Paul tells us to treat everyone alike and to associate with people of low estate (Romans 12:16). Peter also reminds us that God does not show partiality with respect to salvation, for the gospel is intended for all nations (Acts 10:34, 35). We need to be sure that our congregation is receptive to people of all social, economic, ethnic, and racial backgrounds, and not simply to those who are just like us. Ask for suggestions of practical ways to do that.

4. In verse 5 the qualities of righteousness and faithfulness are parallel. How are these two similar? How can the pursuit of one help in attaining the other?

Faithfulness is the quality of being true to a standard or ideal. If that standard or ideal is righteous, then faithfulness and righteousness are the same. Or we might view faithfulness as the motive—a desire to be true to the Lord—and righteousness as the actions that come from that motive—doing what is right.

Romans 1:17 tells us that the gospel reveals a "righteousness of [or 'from'] God." If we would be faithful to God, we will be faithful to His Word and follow this way of righteousness He has revealed.

5. Isaiah 11:6-9 gives a marvelous description of the Messiah's reign. How do we see that fulfilled even now in the church?

Isaiah assures us that the Messiah's kingdom will usher in a time of peace, harmony, and safety. Already we see the beginning of the fulfillment of these verses in the church, over which Jesus is Head. In Jesus' kingdom there is safety from sin and Satan's domination. Thus Paul declared that no power can separate us from God's love (Romans 8:35-39). When the angels proclaimed peace on earth, they spoke not of political peace, but of the spiritual peace that Jesus brought to earth (Philippians 4:7, 9).

God's Servant Brings Comfort

DEVOTIONAL READING: Isaiah 40:25-31.

BACKGROUND SCRIPTURE: Isaiah 40.

PRINTED TEXT: Isaiah 40:1-11, 28-31.

Isaiah 40:1-11, 28-31

1 Comfort ye, comfort ye my people, saith your God.

2 Speak ye comfortably to Jerusalem, and cry unto her, that her warfare is accomplished, that her iniquity is pardoned: for she hath received of the LORD's hand double for all her sins.

3 The voice of him that crieth in the wilderness, Prepare ye the way of the LORD, make straight in the desert a highway for our God.

4 Every valley shall be exalted, and every mountain and hill shall be made low: and the crooked shall be made straight, and the rough places plain:

5 And the glory of the LORD shall be revealed, and all flesh shall see it together: for the mouth of the LORD hath spoken it.

6 The voice said, Cry. And he said, What shall I cry? All flesh is grass, and all the goodliness thereof is as the flower of the field:

7 The grass withereth, the flower fadeth: because the spirit of the LORD bloweth upon it: surely the people is grass.

8 The grass withereth, the flower fadeth: but the word of our God shall stand for ever.

9 O Zion, that bringest good tidings, get thee up into the high mountain; O Jerusalem, that bringest good tidings, lift up thy voice with strength; lift it up, be not afraid; say unto the cities of Judah, Behold your God!

10 Behold, the Lord GOD will come with strong hand, and his arm shall rule for him: behold, his reward is with him, and his work before him.

11 He shall feed his flock like a shepherd: he shall gather the lambs with his arm, and carry them in his bosom, and shall gently lead those that are with young.

28 Hast thou not known? hast thou not heard, that the everlasting God, the LORD, the Creator of the ends of the earth, fainteth not, neither is weary? there is no searching of his understanding.

29 He giveth power to the faint; and to them that have no might he increaseth strength.

30 Even the youths shall faint and be weary, and the young men shall utterly fall:

31 But they that wait upon the LORD shall renew their strength; they shall mount up with wings as eagles; they shall run, and not be weary; and they shall walk, and not faint.

GOLDEN TEXT: The grass withereth, the flower fadeth: but the word of our God shall stand for ever.—Isaiah 40:8.

Light for All People
The Mission of God's Servant
(Lessons 1-5)

Lesson Aims

After participating in this lesson, each student will be able to:

1. Summarize the message of comfort given in Isaiah 40.

2. Explain how this message comforted the Israelites and comforts believers today.

3. Identify someone going through a difficult time and share God's comfort with that person.

Lesson Outline

INTRODUCTION
  A. Safe in God's Arms
  B. Lesson Background
 I. GOD'S WORDS OF COMFORT (Isaiah 40:1-5)
  A. His Pardon Offered (vv. 1, 2)
    Too Much Probing
  B. His Way Prepared (vv. 3-5)
 II. CERTAINTY OF GOD'S COMFORT (Isaiah 40:6-11)
  A. His Eternal Word (vv. 6-8)
  B. His Strong Arm (vv. 9-11)
III. GOD'S ABILITY TO COMFORT (Isaiah 40:28-31)
  A. The Strength He Has (v. 28)
  B. The Strength He Gives (vv. 29-31)
    He's Been Where You Are
CONCLUSION
  A. The God of All Comfort
  B. Prayer
  C. Thought to Remember

Introduction

A. Safe in God's Arms

Catherine Marshall, in her book *The Helper*, tells how the Holy Spirit brought her comfort in a time of emotional turmoil. Her husband, Peter (who served for several years as chaplain of the United States Senate), began to experience heart problems and had to be taken to the hospital. After the ambulance sped him away, she was left at home, feeling helpless and overwhelmed by worry. She describes in detail what followed: "My knees no sooner touched the floor than I experienced God's comfort . . . the feeling of the everlasting arms around me. . . . It was the infinite gentleness of the loving heart of God, more all-pervading than any human being's love could ever be."

All of us face discouragement or heartache at times. During such circumstances it is reassuring to know that we have a God who is both willing and able to reach out to us with everlasting arms of comfort.

The prophet Isaiah ministered at a time when God's people desperately needed a message of comfort. Today's text includes some of the words he used to convey that message. Those words have not lost their power, for the God who spoke them has not lost His.

B. Lesson Background

In lesson 1 we observed that chapters 40-66 of Isaiah have produced much debate among students and scholars. Those who believe that Isaiah was predicting the Babylonian captivity and the return home explain the detailed account as an example of a prophecy inspired by the Holy Spirit. Those who reject predictive prophecy have to invent some unknown author for these chapters, one who lived and wrote during (or not long after) the captivity and the return. Later, these students argue, the material was attached to the book of Isaiah. However, the Lord who is described in these chapters needs no assistance in speaking about things to come. That fact is emphasized several times! (See 41:21-29; 44:7, 8, 24-28; 45:20, 21; 46:8-11; 48:6, 7.)

I. God's Words of Comfort (Isaiah 40:1-5)

Isaiah 40 begins with words of comfort addressed to the exiles in Babylon. The message is one of pardon and promise.

A. His Pardon Offered (vv. 1, 2)

1. Comfort ye, comfort ye my people, saith your God.

This message begins with God's command to *comfort* His *people*, now in captivity in Babylon. The repetition of *comfort* gives added emphasis to the command. Similar double commands are found in later chapters of Isaiah (51:9, 17; 52:1, 11; 57:14; 62:10). Note the personal terms *my people* and *your God*, reflecting the covenant relationship between Israel and the Lord. [See question #1, page 144.]

2. Speak ye comfortably to Jerusalem, and cry unto her, that her warfare is accomplished, that her iniquity is pardoned: for she hath received of the LORD's hand double for all her sins.

The phrase *speak ye comfortably to Jerusalem* is literally "speak to the heart of Jerusalem." Isaiah is to let Jerusalem know *that her warfare* (meaning the hardship of her captivity) is *accomplished*, or finished.

In addition, God's message is one of pardon. The punishment that Jerusalem has received is *double for all her sins*. This does not mean that Jerusalem was punished with twice the severity she deserved. The phrase is a vivid way of saying that Jerusalem's punishment was sufficient.

Consider what is later written of the Suffering Servant, on whom the Lord will lay "the iniquity of us all" (Isaiah 53:6). Christians have the assurance that their *iniquity is pardoned* through what Jesus Christ *accomplished* at the cross. There is comfort in knowing that, although we have sinned against God and deserve condemnation, our debt has been paid. Jesus took the condemnation that should have been ours.

TOO MUCH PROBING

James A. Garfield was a remarkable man. He was a lay preacher, a classics professor, the president of Hiram College (located near Cleveland, Ohio), a general in the United States Army, and a congressman. He was so ambidextrous that he could simultaneously write in Greek with one hand and in Latin with the other!

In 1880 Garfield was elected the twentieth president of the United States. After only six months in office, he was shot in the back by a man who was angry that Garfield had not appointed him to a government position.

The president never lost consciousness. Eventually teams of doctors tried to locate the bullet, probing the wound over and over. In desperation they even asked Alexander Graham Bell to see if he could locate the bullet using an electrical device. But his efforts also failed.

Garfield lasted through July and August, but on September 9, 1881, he died. Ironically, the cause of death was not the gunshot wound. The repeated probing, by which the physicians hoped to help the president, caused a fatal blood infection.

There comes a time when too much probing of a wound is not good. That is also true in the spiritual realm. Isaiah announced to God's people that it was time to stop probing the past and move into the tomorrow of God's mercy and grace. "Comfort ye, comfort ye my people, . . . her iniquity is pardoned" was his message.

That message speaks to us today. Let's put away the past and accept the comfort of God's forgiveness. —J. A. M.

B. His Way Prepared (vv. 3-5)

Besides receiving a pardon from the Lord, Jerusalem now receives even better news. Her King is coming.

3. The voice of him that crieth in the wilderness, Prepare ye the way of the LORD, make straight in the desert a highway for our God.

At this point, the first of three voices is heard (here and verses 6 and 9). The first announces, *Prepare ye the way of the Lord*. The language of this and the next verse reflects a standard practice in the world of Isaiah. Whenever a dignitary such as a king visited a certain territory, a messenger preceded his visit by announcing that he was coming. Necessary preparations were then made, which often included repairing, or even building, roadways. Especially important in the pagan world was the construction of "processional roads" on which supposed gods would be carried to the temple sanctuaries. Many of these roads were carefully constructed with smooth pavement (using flat stones), proper drainage, and curbing.

Here, however, the Lord's people are not asked to carry or accompany Him to Jerusalem, but to prepare for His arrival. Unlike pagan idols, He does not need to be carried, but will come under His own power. If anyone does the carrying, it will be the Lord (Isaiah 46:3, 4)!

What did this command mean to those returning home from captivity in Babylon? They were not being told to initiate a massive earthmoving project. The application was primarily spiritual. The exiles should prepare their hearts, repenting of every sin, so that the way may be cleared for the Lord's arrival among His people.

In the New Testament the voice mentioned by Isaiah is linked with John the Baptist and his efforts to prepare the way for the Messiah (Luke 3:1-6; John 1:23). John declared that repentance was the pathway that prepared for the coming of the Messiah (Matthew 3:1, 8).

4. Every valley shall be exalted, and every mountain and hill shall be made low: and the crooked shall be made straight, and the rough places plain.

Building the highway on which God would travel was no small undertaking! Often great expense went into preparing a road for the arrival of a ruler. Large amounts of earth might even be transported, actually altering the topography to provide a smooth road on which to travel.

Again, the application to the situation described by Isaiah was spiritual. If God was to lead His people back home and dwell in their midst, they would need to make some changes. This is the message that John the Baptist preached, offering specific suggestions of what people could do to demonstrate their repentance (Luke 3:10-14). [See question #2, page 144.]

5. And the glory of the LORD shall be revealed, and all flesh shall see it together: for the mouth of the LORD hath spoken it.

When all of the preparations were completed, *the glory of the Lord* would be *revealed*. Judah's release from captivity, fulfilling the promise of God, would demonstrate God's ability to keep His word and to overrule earthly powers in doing so. *All flesh will see it* implies that this will be done openly and without challenge from the enemies of God and His people.

However, *all flesh* suggests a work of God that would go far beyond anything accomplished by His people's return from captivity. Ultimately, the glory of God is most fully seen in Jesus Christ. Of Jesus, John writes, "The Word was made flesh, and dwelt among us, (and we beheld his glory, the glory as of the only begotten of the Father,) full of grace and truth" (John 1:14). Paul states that God has given us "the light of the knowledge of the glory of God in the face of Jesus Christ" (2 Corinthians 4:6). This "revealing" will be completed when Jesus "shall come in his glory" (Matthew 25:31), at which time "every eye shall see him" (Revelation 1:7).

The phrase *the mouth of the Lord hath spoken it* emphasizes the certainty of this promise. Such language (or language similar to it) is used by Isaiah in other instances (see Isaiah 1:20; 9:7; 37:32; 58:14).

II. Certainty of God's Comfort (Isaiah 40:6-11)

Now the second voice urges the prophet to cry out. This message provides the assurance that God's word cannot be overruled.

A. His Eternal Word (vv. 6-8)

6. The voice said, Cry. And he said, What shall I cry? All flesh is grass, and all the goodliness thereof is as the flower of the field.

The source of the *voice* is not identified; it simply tells Isaiah to *cry* out, leaving the prophet puzzled about what to say. However, a message is provided. *All flesh is grass* is a statement of the temporary nature of human beings. A blade of *grass* or a *flower* is fragile and easily destroyed; so are human beings. By contrast, the word of the Lord is powerful and permanent (v. 8).

Goodliness describes outward beauty. From all outside appearances, both the Assyrian and Babylonian empires had seemed invincible. But these empires were part of *all flesh*, and in time they both passed from the stage of history. God is not subject to such limitations. He had promised His people that they would return home some day, and that promise would be kept.

7. The grass withereth, the flower fadeth; because the spirit of the LORD bloweth upon it: surely the people is grass.

The word for *spirit* in this verse is the same word in Hebrew for "wind," so Isaiah uses a play on words to say that as the hot wind destroys *grass*, so the *spirit of the Lord* destroys God's enemies, including those who have oppressed His people. Hebrew does not have capital letters, so it is possible that the word *spirit* should be capitalized to designate the Holy Spirit.

8. The grass withereth, the flower fadeth: but the word of our God shall stand for ever.

Peter uses this passage from Isaiah (vv. 6-8) to remind Christians that our new birth in Jesus has come about because of the "word of God, which liveth and abideth for ever," rather than by any "corruptible seed" (1 Peter 1:23-25). Whenever we need reassurance, we must remember the words of Jesus: though Heaven and earth pass away, His words will not (Mark 13:31). [See question #3, page 144.]

B. His Strong Arm (vv. 9-11)

The third voice in our text seems to be addressed to those who would return from exile to Jerusalem. It encourages them to herald the arrival of the Lord, so that all the towns and villages of Judah will hear the good news.

9. O Zion, that bringest good tidings, get thee up into the high mountain; O Jerusalem, that bringest good tidings, lift up thy voice with strength; lift it up, be not afraid; say unto the cities of Judah, Behold your God!

Once the Lord arrives in *Jerusalem* and has made His home with His people again, they are to climb to the mountaintops and shout the news. Everyone in *Judah* needs to hear it. Though Jerusalem had once sat in ruins, her people wearied with sorrow and grief, now her situation is different. This is a time to celebrate!

The announcement is to include the last phrase, *Behold your God!* These words are similar

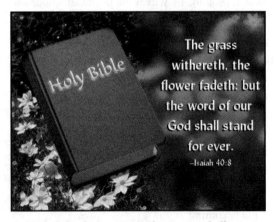

Visual for lesson 3. *Today's visual illustrates verse 8. Its message is a good reminder to have on display at any time, not just with today's lesson.*

to those of John the Baptist, who proclaimed to those from Jerusalem and the cities of Judah, "Behold the Lamb of God" (John 1:29). In a larger sense, they also apply to the truly *good tidings* to which Christians bear witness. If being released from captivity in a foreign land produces the celebration described in these verses, how much more should the release from the captivity of sin! Christians also look forward to Jesus' return, when "every eye shall see him" (Revelation 1:7).

10. Behold, the Lord GOD will come with strong hand, and his arm shall rule for him: behold, his reward is with him, and his work before him.

Remember that this promise of the Lord's coming was meant to comfort those of God's people exiled in a foreign land. The descriptions of God's *strong hand* and *arm* indicate that He has lost none of His power.

In the phrase *his work before him*, the Hebrew word for *work* can mean either work or the payment for work. Thus some versions give this phrase the same meaning as *his reward is with him*. The *New International Version* reads, "See, his reward is with him, and his recompense accompanies him." When Jesus comes again, a message similar to this one will be heard, as He announces, "Behold, I come quickly; and my reward is with me, to give every man according as his work shall be" (Revelation 22:12).

11. He shall feed his flock like a shepherd: he shall gather the lambs with his arm, and carry them in his bosom, and shall gently lead those that are with young.

While the previous verse emphasized the Lord's strength and might, this verse calls attention to the gentle manner in which He cares for His people. (Note that the same *arm* by which God rules in verse 10 now tenderly caresses His flock.) The *lambs* are those within the flock who are not very old, while *those that are with young* are the ones nursing their offspring.

The picture of God as a *shepherd* was used by other prophets to provide encouragement to the exiles in Babylon (Jeremiah 31:10; Ezekiel 34:11-16). This is how God cares today for His people as well. Christians can take genuine comfort from knowing that we are under the care of Jesus, our "good shepherd" (John 10:11). [See question #4, page 144.]

III. God's Ability to Comfort (Isaiah 40:28-31)

In the verses from Isaiah 40 that are not included in our printed text, Isaiah asks a series of rhetorical questions, intended to challenge the people to think about the greatness of the God

---

How to Say It

ASSYRIAN. Uh-*sear*-ee-un.
BABYLON. *Bab*-uh-lun.
BABYLONIAN. Bab-uh-*low*-nee-un.
ISAIAH. Eye-*zay*-uh.

---

who has promised to bless and restore His people. There is nothing (certainly no other god) with which He can be compared. In the closing verses of the chapter, the prophet concludes his questions and calls attention to the strength God provides to the discouraged and the weary.

A. The Strength He Has (v. 28)

28. Hast thou not known? hast thou not heard, that the everlasting God, the LORD, the Creator of the ends of the earth, fainteth not, neither is weary? there is no searching of his understanding.

The history of God's people was filled with examples of His mighty power at work. Certainly the events surrounding the exodus demonstrated that He *fainteth not, neither is weary*. However, during their years in exile, the people may have begun to forget or doubt what they had heard of God's power. Perhaps they had started to entertain doubts as to whether He was able to keep His promises. Yet, just as His power was demonstrated in the creation, so it will be in the "re-creation" of His people in their homeland. He will not grow tired in the middle of the project and walk away from the job. [See question #5, page 144.]

B. The Strength He Gives (vv. 29-31)

29. He giveth power to the faint; and to them that have no might he increaseth strength.

To anyone who is weakening from his struggles—whether an exile journeying homeward or a Christian today battling temptation—the Lord provides the necessary *power* and *strength*.

HE'S BEEN WHERE YOU ARE

In one of his columns for the *Chicago Tribune*, Bob Greene told the story of Doug Maurer, age fifteen, of Creve Coeur, Missouri. Doug had been feeling bad for several days. Eventually his temperature rose to 105 degrees, and he exhibited severe flu-like symptoms. Doug's mother took him to a hospital in St. Louis, where he was diagnosed with leukemia.

Upon learning the details of how his condition would be treated, including three years of chemotherapy and side effects such as baldness and bloating, Doug Maurer went into a deep depression. His aunt called to have an arrangement of flowers delivered to him. She told the clerk it was for her teenage nephew who had leukemia.

When the beautiful flowers arrived at the hospital, Doug read the card from his aunt. Then he saw a second card. It said: "Doug, I took your order at the florist's. I had leukemia when I was seven years old. I'm twenty-two years old now. Good luck. My heart goes out to you. Sincerely, Laura Bradley." After reading those words, Doug's face lit up and his spirit soared.

Doug Maurer was in a hospital filled with sophisticated medical equipment. He received treatment from expert doctors and nurses. But it was a salesclerk in a flower shop, *a woman who had been where he was*, that gave him comfort, hope, and the will to keep going.

Hear God's promise: "He giveth power to the faint; and to them that have no might he increaseth strength" (Isaiah 40:29). As Christians, we can take special comfort from these words because we know that God's Suffering Servant "was in all points tempted like as we are, yet without sin" (Hebrews 4:15). Let His encouragement cause your spirit to soar.   —J. A. M.

30. Even the youths shall faint and be weary, and the young men shall utterly fall.

Those returning to Jerusalem ranged from *young* to old, and the journey could be tiring for the young as well as for the elderly. But these words of the prophet hold a special application to today's world, in which young people are faced daily with especially severe temptations and challenges to their faith. Regardless of our age or stage of life, we need the Lord.

31. But they that wait upon the LORD shall renew their strength; they shall mount up with wings as eagles; they shall run, and not be weary; and they shall walk, and not faint.

Home Daily Bible Readings

Monday, Dec. 10—Turn to God and Be Saved (Isaiah 45:18-25)
Tuesday, Dec. 11—God Promises Better Days (Isaiah 44:1-8)
Wednesday, Dec. 12—The Folly of Idols (Isaiah 44:9-20)
Thursday, Dec. 13—God Who Redeems (Isaiah 44:21-28)
Friday, Dec. 14—Nothing Compares With God (Isaiah 40:12-17)
Saturday, Dec. 15—Human Made Idols vs. Almighty God (Isaiah 40:18-24)
Sunday, Dec. 16—Everlasting Creator God (Isaiah 40:25-31)

To *wait upon the Lord* does not imply sitting and doing nothing (like sitting in a "waiting room" today). It means trusting in Him, knowing that in His timing He will provide the direction we seek. Even while waiting for guidance during a time when God's will is not clear, we can be obedient to Him, doing what we know He wants us to do.

The Hebrew word translated *renew* is also used in Scripture to describe changing one's clothes. Thus we are encouraged to exchange our weakness for God's *strength*. *Eagles* are mentioned, most likely because of their notable strength (Psalm 103:5) and speed (2 Samuel 1:23; Jeremiah 4:13). To paraphrase Jesus' words in the Sermon on the Mount, if God thus strengthens and equips the eagles, how much more will He strengthen and equip us when we begin to grow weary and faint!

Conclusion

A. The God of All Comfort

Isaiah's words of comfort encourage Christians today to keep on serving the Lord and living for Him. When we become weary from our efforts, these words help us find renewed vigor. So does the testimony of the apostle Paul, who expressed his personal need for "the God of all comfort" (2 Corinthians 1:3). Paul told the Corinthians that God comforts individuals so "that we may be able to comfort them which are in any trouble, by the comfort wherewith we ourselves are comforted of God" (v. 4). Thus the comfort God provides His people is often provided through His people. Later in that same letter, Paul notes how God had comforted him "by the coming of Titus" (2 Corinthians 7:6).

The Lord promises to give strength and comfort to those who trust Him during the difficult stages of their walk with Him. Never forget that He often uses people to do that. If He has done that for you, why not express your gratitude to the person He used? And always be prepared for when God may use you as an instrument of comfort to someone else.

B. Prayer

O Lord, may I find in You the comfort that not only satisfies my soul, but enables me to be a source of comfort to those around me. Make me a channel of Your comfort so that others will know that You are "the God of all comfort." In Jesus' name I pray. Amen.

C. Thought to Remember

God comforts us, not just so we can be comforted, but so that someone else can be comforted through us.

Learning by Doing

This page contains an alternate lesson plan emphasizing learning activities.
Classes desiring such student involvement will find these suggestions helpful.

Learning Goals

After participating in this lesson, each student will be able to:

1. Summarize the message of comfort given in Isaiah 40.

2. Explain how this message comforted the Israelites and comforts believers today.

3. Identify someone going through a difficult time and share God's comfort with that person.

Into the Lesson

As students arrive, direct them to one of several posters you have made and placed on the wall. Each poster should have this incomplete statement on it: "Circumstances for which someone may need a word of comfort include. . . ." Ask each person to write two or three circumstances from the lives of individuals, families, or groups of people who may need encouragement. You may write an example on each poster, such as "a Sunday School class whose teacher has suddenly become unfaithful to God" or "a friend whose unmarried daughter has become pregnant."

Review the lists and circumstances. Tell the class that people define "comfort" based on their need or circumstances. Individuals, families, groups, churches, and nations need comfort at times. Today's text shows God offering compassion and comfort to a nation, but we also glimpse His love and offer of comfort to individuals.

Into the Word

Give a brief lecture about the exile of the Jews in Babylon. Emphasize their sense of despair as expressed in Psalm 137. Also highlight the wonderful sense of hope they must have experienced from Isaiah's prophecy.

Provide a photocopy of today's Scripture text and a highlighter pen for every two class members. One pair should be given a copy of the text on an overhead transparency. (This exercise is also in the student book, *Adult Bible Class*.) Ask the pairs to read the text and highlight every word or phrase of comfort and encouragement they discover. Possible answers include "her warfare is accomplished" (v. 2), "iniquity is pardoned" (v. 2), "the glory of the Lord shall be revealed" (v. 5), "the word of our God shall stand for ever" (v. 8), "be not afraid" (v. 9), "Behold your God" (v. 9), "the Lord God will come with strong hand" (v. 10), "He shall feed his flock"

(v. 11), "He shall gather the lambs . . . carry them . . . and shall gently lead" (v. 11), "the everlasting God . . . fainteth not" (v. 28), "He giveth power to the faint" (v. 29).

Give the teams about five minutes for this task. Then project the transparency that was highlighted by one of the teams. Emphasize the many words of comfort and encouragement God offered to the Jewish exiles. Explain the concepts of "making the way straight" (v. 3), "flesh as grass" (v. 6), and "wings as eagles" (v. 31).

Ask the teams to locate and circle words or phrases in this text that have a prophetic note about Jesus (concentrated in vv. 3, 5, 10, 11, and 31). Ask for volunteers to tell how these verses apply to Christ.

Into Life

Give another handout to each team. This handout should have three columns, the left column headed, "God's Comfort to Jewish Exiles." List below this heading every word or phrase included in the highlighter exercise completed in the Bible study portion of this lesson. The second column should have the heading, "A Parent Whose Child Has Died." The third column's heading will read, "A Friend Overcoming an Addiction." First, ask the teams to find two or three words or concepts from the left column that may be helpful in comforting the persons in the circumstances described in columns 2 or 3. Ask them to place a check mark (✔) under columns two or three that identify the appropriate word or concept. Second, remind them that different circumstances or crises require comforting words appropriate to that situation. Ask the teams to add other Scriptural words or teachings that may be comforting or encouraging in these two circumstances.

Finally, ask each class member to identify a friend, neighbor, or fellow Christian who may need a word of comfort or encouragement. The person may be experiencing serious illness, trying to overcome a sinful habit, struggling with a personal relationship, looking for work, grieving a death, or dealing with some other situation of stress and distress. Ask each learner to make a personal commitment to contact that person this week (by telephone, note, or personal visit). Each should identify at least one Scriptural thought to use in this personal word of comfort.

Let's Talk It Over

The questions on this page are designed to encourage review of the lesson Scriptures and to promote discussion of the lesson by the class. The answers provided are only discussion starters. Let your class talk it over from there.

1. What are some reasons God's people need comfort today? How does God meet those needs?

Just as in Biblical times, some Christians suffer from persecution because of their faith. Others suffer from disease, poverty, and other hardships. Then there are those who struggle with temptation and sin in their lives or in the lives of those they love. God never promised us lives free of all suffering. What He did promise was to provide the strength to face our hardships (Isaiah 40:29), and to reward those who faithfully endure. In Isaiah's time, God commissioned the prophets to remind the Jews that God had not forgotten them, but that He was there to help His people and pardon their sins (Isaiah 40:2). Similarly, the New Testament promises us God's strength for today (Philippians 4:10-19), and eternal life for those who are faithful to the end (2 Timothy 4:18; Revelation 21:1-7).

2. Isaiah 40:3-5 predicts the future ministry of John the Baptist (Matthew 3:3), who came to prepare the way for the Messiah. What can we do today to prepare the way for Christ's second coming?

Like John, we need to call people to repentance. Their alternative, as John warned, is to face the wrath of God in the Judgment (Matthew 3:7-12). When Jesus came the first time, it was to save the world from its sin (John 1:29; 3:16). When He comes again, it will be to bring judgment upon those who rejected Him and rewards to those who have been faithful (Matthew 25:31-46; 2 Timothy 4:7, 8). The task of the church is to reach as many people as possible before that day comes. John boldly proclaimed his message to his countrymen despite opposition that led to his death. The church needs to be just as bold in proclaiming the gospel to our generation.

3. How significant is Isaiah's statement, "All flesh is grass," to you personally? How does it help you to know that, unlike the grass, "the word of our God shall stand for ever"?

Despite all the advances of medical science, man has not been able to extend his life span more than a few years. Some of your class members may be aging, or they may have aging parents, and this truth has become more personally relevant to them. Others may have been forced into a career change by economic factors outside their control. Perhaps divorce has affected a significant number of your learners. All these factors should drive the believer to the eternal Word of God. Encourage your class members to discuss their situations and to claim security in their turbulent times by turning to the Word.

4. Isaiah 40:11 likens God to a shepherd. Identify some ways in which Jesus is a shepherd to Christians today.

First, Peter calls Jesus the "Shepherd" of our souls (1 Peter 2:25). When we were straying from God, like foolish sheep, Jesus brought us back into the fold and now keeps us there, safe from sin. Second, Jesus pointed out that a shepherd is willing to lay down his life for his sheep (John 10:11). When Jesus went to the cross, He went for our sakes, to pay the penalty for our sin. Every Christian literally owes his life to Jesus. Third, Jesus also said that the sheep know their shepherd's voice (John 10:4). Wise Christians will follow the Master's true teachings in Scripture and avoid false teachers and their destructive doctrines. Fourth, Jesus has promised to separate believers from unbelievers at the Judgment, like a shepherd separates sheep from goats (Matthew 25:32). He will be the judge of the living and the dead. Fifth, Revelation 7:17 says that the Lamb will be our Shepherd and guide us to the water of life. That is, Jesus will do everything necessary to get His followers to Heaven. If we lose our way, it is because we have not followed the Shepherd's lead.

5. What do you find most significant about Isaiah's statement that God never gets weary?

Again, your learners' own situations will lead them to find different areas of significance from others. Those whose age or health causes them to become weary easily will appreciate the stamina of God's love and providence. They will take comfort in the fact that God has the strength to empower His people to keep going until they reach their Heavenly goal (Ephesians 6:10-18). All your students should appreciate the truth that God will never give up on His people or His work. What He sets out to do, He accomplishes. When it seems as if God is no longer active, He is merely exhibiting patience (2 Peter 3:9).

God's Servant Brings Hope

DEVOTIONAL READING: Luke 2:8-20.

**BACKGROUND SCRIPTURE: Isaiah 9:1-7;
Luke 2:1-20.**

PRINTED TEXT: Isaiah 9:2-7.

Isaiah 9:2-7

2 The people that walked in darkness have seen a great light: they that dwell in the land of the shadow of death, upon them hath the light shined.

3 Thou hast multiplied the nation, and not increased the joy: they joy before thee according to the joy in harvest, and as men rejoice when they divide the spoil.

4 For thou hast broken the yoke of his burden, and the staff of his shoulder, the rod of his oppressor, as in the day of Midian.

5 For every battle of the warrior is with confused noise, and garments rolled in blood; but this shall be with burning and fuel of fire.

6 For unto us a child is born, unto us a son is given: and the government shall be upon his shoulder: and his name shall be called Wonderful, Counselor, The mighty God, The everlasting Father, The Prince of Peace.

7 Of the increase of his government and peace there shall be no end, upon the throne of David, and upon his kingdom, to order it, and to establish it with judgment and with justice from henceforth even for ever. The zeal of the LORD of hosts will perform this.

GOLDEN TEXT: For unto us a child is born, unto us a son is given: and the government shall be upon his shoulder: and his name shall be called Wonderful, Counselor, The mighty God, The everlasting Father, The Prince of Peace.—Isaiah 9:6.

Light for All People
The Mission of God's Servant
(Lessons 1-5)

Lesson Aims

After this lesson each student will be able to:
1. Cite several images Isaiah uses to tell how God's Servant, the Messiah, brings hope to His people.
2. Tell why hope was needed in Isaiah's time and remains so in ours.
3. Praise God for the hope we have in Jesus.

Lesson Outline

INTRODUCTION
   A. What We Do Matters
   B. Lesson Background
  I. HOPE AMID DARKNESS (Isaiah 9:2, 3)
   A. Light Shines (v. 2)
     A Hopeless Town
   B. Joy Is Multiplied (v. 3)
 II. HOPE BECAUSE GOD ACTS (Isaiah 9:4, 5)
   A. Deliverance Provided (v. 4)
   B. Weapons Destroyed (v. 5)
III. HOPE THROUGH A CHILD (Isaiah 9:6, 7)
   A. His Titles (v. 6)
   B. His Kingdom (v. 7)
CONCLUSION
   A. A Glorious Future
   B. Prayer
   C. Thought to Remember

Introduction

A. What We Do Matters

Today's lesson is about hope, not the kind that voices a vague wish for better times, but the kind of trust in God's plans and purposes that always has sustained His people. Such hope delivers us from the despair of thinking that nothing we do matters; in fact, it enables us to tackle even the most menial job with vigor.

Elmer Bendiner tells the story of a B-17 bomber that was flown in bombing missions over Germany during the latter days of World War II. The plane was hit several times by shells and flak, and some of the hits struck the compartment of the plane where bombs were stored. Miraculously, however, the bomber did not explode.

Later, when the plane landed, eleven unexploded twenty-millimeter shells were removed from it. The shells were dismantled, and, to the amazement of everyone, they contained no explosives! Inside one shell was a note written in the Czech language. Translated, it read, "This is all we can do for you now." A member of the Czech underground, working in a German munitions factory, had not added the explosives to at least eleven of the twenty-millimeter shells on his assembly line. Perhaps that worker often wondered whether the quiet work he had done to subvert the Nazi war effort was going to make any difference during the conflict.

How discouraging can our circumstances get? The answer: never discouraging enough to quit doing what God commands us to do. On this Sunday before Christmas, Isaiah's words challenge us to reflect on the hope we possess because Jesus came into our world. When Isaiah considered the terrible destruction that was facing God's people and the fact that few people were going to listen to his pleas (Isaiah 6:10-13), he might have concluded that nothing he said really mattered. But Isaiah's message also included a word of hope—the promise of a "great light" that would dispel the darkness of sin. That hope, which God offered to Isaiah's dark times, is the same hope that inspires our celebrations during this season of Christmas.

B. Lesson Background

The message of hope found in today's lesson text must be considered against the backdrop of the dark and discouraging conditions that were present in Judah when Isaiah spoke this message. We have noted in previous lessons that when Tiglath-pileser III came to the throne of Assyria in 745 B.C., he led in a resurgence that restored Assyria's prominence as a world power. His intentions to move westward and conquer territories there made Assyria a force with which to be reckoned. This placed immediate pressure on the kingdoms of Syria, Israel, and Judah.

Syria and Israel joined forces in an attempt to counter this threat. They tried to get King Ahaz of Judah to become part of their alliance, but he refused. So the allied forces invaded Judah to place their own king on Judah's throne and make Judah part of their alliance. Both Ahaz and the people of Judah became terrified (Isaiah 7:1, 2).

Isaiah went to Ahaz and told him not to fear the alliance, for it would not stand. He urged the king to trust God for deliverance. Judah's problems were spiritual in nature, not political (Isaiah 7:3-7). But instead of turning to God, Ahaz appealed to Assyria for help. So Isaiah warned Ahaz that the Assyrian military machine would eventually turn on Judah and leave behind extensive damage (Isaiah 7:18-25). In effect, the Lord would hide His face from His people (Isaiah 8:17).

The final verses of chapter 8 describe conditions that would exist in Judah as a consequence of the Assyrian invasion. The people would actually consult mediums and spiritists for help rather than "the law and the testimony" (vv. 19, 20). They would be engulfed in spiritual darkness, and their land would be turned into a curse. But God was not finished with them; He had other, grander plans.

Isaiah 9 begins this change in tone with the word *nevertheless*. It then refers to the troubles that afflicted the areas of Zebulun and Naphtali—two tribes located within the northernmost sector of the nation of Israel. Armies invading Israel tended to come from the north (rather than east, because of the extensive desert there). This meant that areas such as Zebulun and Naphtali would be among the first to experience any hardship that occurred. During Isaiah's time, these tribes in particular suffered during the invasion of Tiglath-pileser III (2 Kings 15:29).

Thus, perhaps the last place in Israel where one might have expected to find any reason for hope would have been the territories of Zebulun and Naphtali. Yet it is to these very people, living in "dimness" (v. 1), that Isaiah addresses his message of hope.

I. Hope Amid Darkness
(Isaiah 9:2, 3)

A. Light Shines (v. 2)

2. The people that walked in darkness have seen a great light: they that dwell in the land of the shadow of death, upon them hath the light shined.

The tense of the verbs *have seen* and *shined* normally indicate an event that already has happened. Here, however, they describe an event that is yet to take place. This is a way of emphasizing the certainty that the prophet's words will come true; he pictures a future event as if it already has occurred.

How were these afflicted regions of Zebulun and Naphtali to become so enlightened? The answer is given by Matthew, who quotes this verse from Isaiah (Matthew 4:15, 16) after recording that Jesus settled in Capernaum (which was located in the territory of Naphtali). Later Isaiah will describe a special Servant whom God will call to extend light, not only to the Jews but to the Gentile nations as well (Isaiah 42:6; 49:6). These prophecies are also fulfilled in Jesus, "the light of the world" (John 8:12) who has come "to give light to them that sit in darkness and in the shadow of death" (Luke 1:79). Wherever the darkness of sin has enslaved people, the light of the gospel can set them free. [See question #1, page 152.]

A HOPELESS TOWN

You've probably never heard of Flagstaff, Maine. That's not surprising—since it no longer exists! But once upon a time Flagstaff was a thriving New England community. It remained so until the Army Corps of Engineers erected a dam in the vicinity, and Flagstaff, Maine, was slowly but surely buried in water. The residents were forced to find new places to call home.

One resident of Flagstaff said that the most painful part of the experience of relocation was watching his hometown die. All improvements and all repairs ceased immediately. Why bother to paint a house when it is going to be flooded? Why repair a building when the whole village is going to be wiped out? Why repair potholes in streets soon to be abandoned? Why remove graffiti only fish will read?

As the weeks until the inevitable destruction passed by, the townspeople became more and more despondent. Another resident made this comment. "When there's no hope for the future, there's no power in the present." Effort diminishes, then ceases altogether when hope is absent. The Book of Proverbs declares, "Hope deferred maketh the heart sick" (Proverbs 13:12).

To people for whom oppression and suffering had become commonplace, Isaiah brought this word of hope: "The people that walked in darkness have seen a great light" (Isaiah 9:2). Only Heaven's light can dispel the darkness of a sinful world.   —J. A. M.

B. Joy Is Multiplied (v. 3)

3. Thou hast multiplied the nation, and not increased the joy: they joy before thee according to the joy in harvest, and as men rejoice when they divide the spoil.

Because of the Assyrian invasion, many of Israel's citizens had been torn from their homeland and taken captive. The promise of God, however, is that this decline in the nation's population will be dramatically reversed in the future: the *nation* will be *multiplied*. A similar promise provided hope and encouragement amid the prediction of the future Babylonian captivity (Isaiah 49:19-23; 54:1-3).

The statement *Thou hast multiplied the nation, and not increased the joy* seems to contradict itself. Why shouldn't a growing nation experience an increase in joy? Some manuscripts of Isaiah omit the word *not*, and this seems to be the preferred reading in other versions of the Bible.

The joy described by Isaiah can be linked to the joy of a *harvest*, because the multiplication of the nation is seen as a blessing from the Lord in the same way that a plentiful harvest is considered a blessing from the Lord. Likewise, the celebration can be associated with the dividing of the *spoil* of war because it implies victories in battle that have been granted by the Lord. The joy of Isaiah's prophecy is a blessing of God. [See question #2, page 152.]

Implied in these words is the truth that the hope of God's people can never be based on the changing circumstances of life. Our hope is not built on the belief that our country is strong and that no enemy can harm our land. Our hope is not built on the strength of the economy, the upward trend of the stock market, or the lower numbers of unemployment. Our hope is built on the One who is not limited by the variable winds and shifting sands of contemporary events. His enduring power gives us reason to have an enduring hope.

II. Hope Because God Acts
(Isaiah 9:4, 5)

To believe that God stands above those world and national events that often consume our attention can be a challenge. When what we see seems to be falling apart, how can we place our trust in an unseen God and His purposes? Isaiah assured his listeners that the God who acted powerfully in the past has lost none of His power.

A. Deliverance Provided (v. 4)

4. For thou hast broken the yoke of his burden, and the staff of his shoulder, the rod of his oppressor, as in the day of Midian.

The mention of the *day of Midian* brought to mind the victory that the Lord gave Israel over the Midianites during the days of Gideon (Judges

---

How to Say It

AHAZ. *Ay*-haz.
ASSYRIA. Uh-*sear*-ee-uh.
BABYLONIAN. Bab-uh-*low*-nee-un.
CAPERNAUM. Kuh-*per*-nay-um.
DAVIDIC. Duh-*vid*-ick.
GABRIEL. *Gay*-bree-ul.
GIDEON. *Gid*-ee-un.
HEZEKIAH. Hez-ih-*kye*-uh.
IMMANUEL. Ih-*man*-you-el.
ISAIAH. Eye-*zay*-uh.
MANASSEH. Muh-*nass*-uh.
MESSIANIC. mess-ee-*an*-ick.
MIDIAN. *Mid*-ee-un.
MIDIANITES. *Mid*-ee-un-ites.
NAPHTALI. *Naf*-tuh-lye.
TIGLATH-PILESER. *Tig*-lath-pih-*lee*-zer (strong accent on *lee*).
ZEBULUN. *Zeb*-you-lun.

7:19-25). In that campaign Gideon defeated the Midianites, whose soldiers were like a swarm of "grasshoppers," with camels as numerous as "the sand by the sea side" (Judges 7:12). Through the power of God, Gideon's "army" of three hundred men won the victory. This incident would have had special meaning for the tribes of Zebulun and Naphtali (mentioned in verse 1), because it occurred in the vicinity of that portion of Israel.

Again, speaking as if a future event is a fact already accomplished, Isaiah predicts that God will destroy those who are oppressing Israel and will relieve her from their oppression. The *yoke*, the *staff*, and the *rod* were all items used to control animals. Israel was reduced to such an enslaved condition during the Assyrian invasion and would have welcomed the promise of an end to such oppression.

However, the removal of the Assyrian menace could deal with only part of the reason for Israel's misery, and not the main part at that. Another menace lay at the root of Israel's woes. That was the menace of sin. Sin was the yoke, staff, and rod that was degrading the nation and leading it toward destruction (Isaiah 1:2-8). Israel never could be truly free until it was rid of this far more deadly menace.

Thus Isaiah's prediction seems to point to some event much more dramatic and comprehensive. As we shall see, it is linked with the coming of a Ruler who will reign on the throne of David in such a way that His kingdom will be everlasting (Isaiah 9:7). Isaiah's words describe a hope that speaks to the hearts of all who are weighed down by the oppression of sin. Only God can provide such a deliverance as this; it is as impossible for man to do it as it was for Gideon to conquer Midian in his own strength. [See question #3, page 152.]

B. Weapons Destroyed (v. 5)

5. For every battle of the warrior is with confused noise, and garments rolled in blood; but this shall be with burning and fuel of fire.

Continuing his message of hope, Isaiah now focuses on some of the essentials of war that will no longer be needed after the great day of the Lord's deliverance. He describes how these items will become so useless that they might as well be thrown into the *fire* to be used as *fuel*.

For every battle of the warrior is with confused noise. A better translation is, "Every boot of the warrior used in battle." Thus the soldier's boot and his *garments* that have been bloodied in battle will be discarded and burned. The picture is one of peace—but, as the next verse clearly points out, not the kind of peace that the world seeks to achieve. It is a peace that only the Lord could provide. And His primary "weapon" for bringing about this peace is to be a Child. [See question #4, page 152.]

III. Hope Through a Child (Isaiah 9:6, 7)

A. His Titles (v. 6)

6. For unto us a child is born, unto us a son is given: and the government shall be upon his shoulder: and his name shall be called Wonderful, Counselor, The mighty God, The everlasting Father, The Prince of Peace.

Here is the glorious climax of Isaiah's picture of future deliverance and joy: a *child*. The phrase *unto us a child is born* is similar to the words of the angel announcing Jesus' birth: "Unto you is born this day . . . a Saviour, which is Christ the Lord" (Luke 2:11). Not only is this Child born; He is also described as *given*. Jesus was God's greatest gift to mankind—a truth perhaps most memorably expressed in the words of John 3:16.

The government shall be upon his shoulder. The Child will be entrusted with the responsibilities of ruling. Earlier Isaiah had spoken negatively of child rulers, in the context of God's judgment upon Judah (Isaiah 3:1-5). This Child, however, is refreshingly different.

This is the second prophecy in which Isaiah has mentioned a special Child. The first was the virgin birth prophecy of Isaiah 7:14: "Behold, a virgin shall conceive, and bear a son, and shall call his name Immanuel." According to Matthew 1:23, that statement looks ahead to Jesus. It is obvious that this second Child prophecy must refer to Jesus as well.

The titles given in this verse reflect the unique characteristics that we would expect to be associated with One who entered the world in such a unique way. First, He is called *Wonderful*, implying that people will express a sense of wonder at what they see in Him. Luke 2:18 tells us that those who heard the news of Jesus' birth from the shepherds "wondered at those things which were told them." Jesus' teaching "astonished" those who heard it (Matthew 7:28).

The word *counselor* is apt for someone who will possess "the spirit of counsel" (Isaiah 11:2). Whereas most ancient kings surrounded themselves with counselors for guidance in making difficult decisions, this promised ruler will possess "all the treasures of wisdom and knowledge" (Colossians 2:3). Some understand the title Wonderful as a description of the word Counselor and render the title as "Wonderful Counselor."

In addition, He will be called *The mighty God*—a name that highlights the Child's divine character. It is interesting that immediately fol-

Visual for lesson 4

Display this poster as you begin to discuss verse 6. It is found in the Adult Visuals *packet.*

lowing the phrase "spirit of counsel" in Isaiah 11:2 come the words "and might." No earthly power will be able to withstand such might. In contrast, this ruler also will be called *The everlasting Father*. Although mighty, He will tenderly and lovingly provide for and protect the weak and unsteady (Isaiah 40:11; 42:3).

The title *Prince of Peace* is perhaps the most familiar of these accolades during the Christmas season, primarily because at Jesus' birth the Heavenly host announced peace on earth (Luke 2:14). That peace became a reality through Jesus' death on the cross, where He triumphed over "principalities and powers" (Colossians 2:15) and destroyed the devil (Hebrews 2:14, 15). There the Prince of peace paid the price of peace—His own blood (Colossians 1:20). That peace is the only true and lasting peace, for it is peace with God.

Isaiah's prophecy of a special Child gave hope to the oppressed of Israel at a time when the nation desperately needed such a message. For followers of Jesus, this same word of hope helps us to keep the challenges of life in perspective. Those who remember what life was like when they were enslaved by sin rejoice in the coming of the mighty God who has broken their chains and set them free! Those who recall moments when they despaired of life praise God that the Prince of Peace has forgiven them of every sin and given them reason to live! It is no wonder that Christians everywhere sing Christmas carols with a true spirit of joy and celebration. "Unto us a child is born"—and grew to manhood to become our Savior. [See question #5, page 152.]

B. His Kingdom (v. 7)

7. Of the increase of his government and peace there shall be no end, upon the throne of

David, and upon his kingdom, to order it, and to establish it with judgment and with justice from henceforth even for ever. The zeal of the LORD of hosts will perform this.

The line of Davidic kings certainly had its share of disappointments. Kings such as Ahaz and Manasseh (2 Kings 16:1-20; 21:1-18) darken the record of the rulers of Judah. But Isaiah looks ahead to another king who will sit *upon the throne of David*, and this king will establish a *kingdom* that will never fail. His rule will be characterized by righteousness, *justice*, and peace (cf. Isaiah 11:4-9; Jeremiah 33:15, 16). *His government and peace* will *increase* as people "out of every kindred, and tongue, and people, and nation" submit to His lordship (Revelation 5:9).

All of this leads to the conclusion that Isaiah's words do not describe a particularly great king of Judah (such as Hezekiah, for example). The magnificent description of this King and His kingdom begs the reader to look beyond these kings to the Messiah.

The mention of the *throne of David* is another signpost marking this passage as messianic. David had been promised an everlasting kingdom (2 Samuel 7:12-16). When the angel Gabriel announced to Mary that she would become the mother of the Messiah, he told her, "The Lord God shall give unto him the throne of his father David: and he shall reign over the house of Jacob for ever; and of his kingdom there shall be no end" (Luke 1:32, 33).

Today Jesus Christ has taken up a position of authority over His kingdom—the church. Paul notes that God "hath put all things under [Jesus'] feet, and gave him to be the head over all things to the church" (Ephesians 1:22). This is the kingdom that "shall never be destroyed" and that "shall stand for ever" (Daniel 2:44).

Home Daily Bible Readings

Monday, Dec. 17—A True Worship Experience (Isaiah 6:1-5)
Tuesday, Dec. 18—Isaiah Answers God's Call (Isaiah 6:6-13)
Wednesday, Dec. 19—The Lord's Special Sign (Isaiah 7:10-17)
Thursday, Dec. 20—Wounded for Our Wrongdoing (Isaiah 53:1-9)
Friday, Dec. 21—"The Lord Is With You" (Luke 1:26-38)
Saturday, Dec. 22—"My Soul Magnifies the Lord" (Luke 1:41-55)
Sunday, Dec. 23—The Birth of Jesus (Luke 2:1-7)

When Isaiah spoke these words, to think that such a dramatic turn of events could be possible for the ravaged region of Zebulun and Naphtali would have appeared to be asking the impossible. The devastating power of Assyria looked insurmountable. It would take a miracle just to get Israel back on her feet, let alone find a king who could establish the kingdom described in Isaiah 9:6, 7. How could this possibly happen?

Such a question would be echoed approximately seven centuries later in the words of a young virgin from Nazareth, who responded to the announcement from Gabriel with the question, "How shall this be?" The answer given to her was that "with God nothing shall be impossible" (Luke 1:34, 37). Isaiah's final statement in this verse served much the same purpose as the angel's answer to Mary's question. *The zeal of the Lord of hosts* is the guarantee that these events will come to pass. God's jealous love for His people and His zeal that the entire world should come to know Him mean that all He has promised He will do.

Conclusion

A. A Glorious Future

Amid the gloom of despair and death, Isaiah offered Israel the hope that comes from knowing that God has not abandoned His people. Isaiah assured them that Israel will see a glorious future because a Child will come—born to sit on David's throne and to rule a government that far transcends any political boundaries. His kingdom will be a spiritual one; He will rule, not only as a son of David, but also as the Son of God.

As we celebrate the birth of this King whom Isaiah foretold, our hearts should also be filled with the hope that we will one day see His kingdom in its fullness when He returns. Although there may be "scoffers" who question our hope, just as they did in Peter's day (2 Peter 3:3, 4), let us not be swayed by their skepticism and unbelief. In God's own time, "the zeal of the Lord of hosts will perform this."

B. Prayer

O God, who makes all things possible, thank You for the hope that we possess through Jesus Christ. During this season, we celebrate not only His birth but also His life, His death, and His resurrection. We honor Him as King of kings and Lord of lords, and we anticipate His return. In His name we pray. Amen.

C. Thought to Remember

The world cannot steal our hope, because the world did not give it to us—God did.

Learning by Doing

This page contains an alternate lesson plan emphasizing learning activities.
Classes desiring such student involvement will find these suggestions helpful.

Learning Goals

After participating in this lesson, each student will be able to:

1. Cite several images Isaiah uses to tell how God's Servant, the Messiah, brings hope to His people.

2. Tell why hope was needed in Isaiah's time and is needed today.

3. Praise God for the hope we have in Jesus.

Into the Lesson

On a poster board make a large baby announcement with the heading "It's a boy!" Do not include a name nor the parents' names on the announcement. You may include a length and a birth weight (for example, 21"; 7 lbs., 13 oz.).

Pointing to the announcement, say: "Imagine you are an invisible observer in a home that is having an open house for a newborn baby. What words to describe the baby might you hear?" Write their answers on a chalkboard or marker board. After the list is complete, point out that most of these descriptive words or adjectives deal with the baby's physical condition or appearance. None seriously describes his or her future job, career, or impact on the world. Why?

Observe that a birth announcement for Jesus would have been very different. As a matter of fact, a "we are expecting" announcement would have been very different. This could have been loaded with descriptions that told of His work, His mission, and His character. There are several announcements in the Old and New Testaments that so describe Jesus.

Ask the class to recall these characteristics. As class members call out answers, have one of the members list these on the chalkboard beside the other list of general descriptions. Suggest they remember such elements as the angels' announcement to the shepherds or the words to the "Hallelujah Chorus."

Tell the class the announcement of what was expected of the Savior's coming was more wonderful than the hearers could have imagined. The word pictures of the coming Savior were colorful, predictive, and able to give hope to these who had lost hope.

Into the Word

Mix lecture and question/answer by using the following outline:

A. Lecture on the political and spiritual circumstances at the time of Isaiah's prophecy before reading today's text.

B. Ask the following questions:

1. Why does Isaiah use the past tense in verse 2, when the event he describes has not yet happened?

2. What phrases in verses 2-4 describe wonderful changes coming for these afflicted people? What is the significance or meaning of these descriptions? *(Be sure to clarify "not increased the joy" in verse 3 and all of verse 5 for the class.)*

C. Tell the class that verses 6 and 7 could be Israel's "We're expecting" announcement. Have two poster boards available. One will be headed "What Will He Be Like?" The second will say "What Will He Do?" Ask class members to find words and phrases in verses 6 and 7 that answer each question. Ask a "scribe" to note these answers on the appropriate poster. After this is complete, review these descriptions asking, "What does this mean?" and "How will this come to pass?"

D. Remind the class of the joy this hope brought to a hopeless people.

Into Life

Ask and discuss the questions "Why do we need hope in today's world? What kind of hope do we need?" You might remind class members that one of the problems the people of Judah experienced was doubting God's faithfulness. Then they began to be unfaithful to Him and His word. What similarity is there to today's believer or our nation?

Ask groups of about three or four to work together. Tell the groups that Christmas carols are more than mere sentiment and tradition. They share messages about Christ's coming. Give each group several hymnals and ask them to look for lines that imply hope for our world. Ask them to note these lines on a piece of paper. After a few minutes, ask the groups to share those lines.

Next, ask the groups to form prayer circles. Ask each group to hold hands and give each person the chance to pray, thanking or praising God for one of the characteristics or purposes of the Savior mentioned in today's prophecy.

Post the words to the last stanza of "O Little Town of Bethlehem." Lead in singing or reciting these words and in prayer. Indeed, "the hopes and fears of all the years are met" in Christ Jesus.

Let's Talk It Over

The questions on this page are designed to encourage review of the lesson Scriptures and to promote discussion of the lesson by the class. The answers provided are only discussion starters. Let your class talk it over from there.

1. Where are some places and what are some ways in which the world walks in darkness? How can we bring light to those situations?

In areas where false religions (Islam, Hinduism, Buddhism, etc.) dominate, Christianity has a difficult time reaching the people. In Communist countries the government still hinders the preaching of the gospel. Persecution threatens Christians in South America, Africa, and Asia. In many Western nations—such as the United States—materialism and modern philosophy make people indifferent to or even hostile toward Biblical values.

Encourage students to suggest specific ways of reaching people with the gospel. Technological advances in radio, television, and the Internet open many new doors of exciting opportunity, but we dare not overlook the "low-tech" methods of talking over the fence with a neighbor. Foreign college students offer an opportunity for campus ministries to evangelize those who then can take the gospel to distant lands—lands that may be closed to "missionary" efforts. People who travel abroad for business may also have opportunities to share Christ with people of other countries.

2. How can we share in the joy of "harvest" that Isaiah describes? Consider both personal and corporate activities.

Clearly, the most important thing we can do is to get involved in the harvest—i.e., in evangelism. We can talk with our neighbors, support missionaries, take an interest in reports from the mission field, and take short-term mission trips. We can encourage our young people to consider missions or some other Christian vocation as their life's work. Our churches can give aid to those who go to Bible college to prepare for such a career. The more we commit ourselves to doing whatever we can to advance the gospel, the more joy we will experience with every soul saved and with every report of success on the mission field.

3. When have you seen God break the yoke of some oppressor and give a victory "as in the day of Midian"?

Encourage learners to tell of some victories the Lord has brought in their lives, victories over habits that enslaved them, victories over oppressive family members or coworkers who did not share their faith, or any other victory over what might have seemed a superior force (as in the day when Midian's army outnumbered Israel's more than one hundred twenty thousand to three hundred). Someone may have beaten a fierce temper; perhaps another has been delivered from drug or alcohol abuse. Maybe another was able to give a clear testimony of faith at a family reunion—with family members present who were hostile to Christianity. Use these testimonies to encourage others in the class to claim similar victories with their faith!

4. The lesson writer notes that Isaiah pictures "a peace that only the Lord could provide." Describe a time in your life when God's peace sustained you—a peace that only God could have provided.

Perhaps the most unsettling thing a person faces is the prospect of death. Diagnosis of a terminal illness in oneself or a loved one, perhaps a parent, can be a difficult truth to accept. Perhaps some of your class members have been through that and found the peace of Christ sufficient to sustain them. Others have perhaps even laid a spouse to rest, and again it was God's peace that carried them through. Perhaps another has waited patiently for a prodigal child to return—or waits even yet—and only the peace of Christ has helped them maintain their sanity. Let your learners tell their stories, and use them to encourage others who need to claim the Lord's peace.

5. What do you find most significant about each of the titles for Christ used by Isaiah in verse 6?

"Wonderful" indicates the awesome nature of His teachings and miracles (Matthew 7:28; 15:31). "Counselor" denotes His divine wisdom (Mark 1:22-27). Some interpreters believe the two terms signify a single title, meaning that the Messiah is awesome in His wisdom. "Mighty God" indicates His deity. The fact that He would also be a child means that Isaiah was predicting the incarnation—God coming to earth in the flesh. "Everlasting Father" is another term for deity. "Prince of Peace" indicates that the Messiah would be different from earthly rulers, especially in Isaiah's time, in that His reign would be one of peace, not conflict.

God's Servant Brings Justice

DEVOTIONAL READING: Isaiah 43:1-7.

BACKGROUND SCRIPTURE: Isaiah 42.

PRINTED TEXT: Isaiah 42:1-9.

Isaiah 42:1-9

1 Behold my servant, whom I uphold; mine elect, in whom my soul delighteth; I have put my Spirit upon him: he shall bring forth judgment to the Gentiles.

2 He shall not cry, nor lift up, nor cause his voice to be heard in the street.

3 A bruised reed shall he not break, and the smoking flax shall he not quench: he shall bring forth judgment unto truth.

4 He shall not fail nor be discouraged, till he have set judgment in the earth: and the isles shall wait for his law.

5 Thus saith God the LORD, he that created the heavens, and stretched them out; he that spread forth the earth, and that which cometh out of it; he that giveth breath unto the people upon it, and spirit to them that walk therein:

6 I the LORD have called thee in righteousness, and will hold thine hand, and will keep thee, and give thee for a covenant of the people, for a light of the Gentiles;

7 To open the blind eyes, to bring out the prisoners from the prison, and them that sit in darkness out of the prison house.

8 I am the LORD; that is my name: and my glory will I not give to another, neither my praise to graven images.

9 Behold, the former things are come to pass, and new things do I declare: before they spring forth I tell you of them.

GOLDEN TEXT: Behold my servant, whom I uphold; mine elect, in whom my soul delighteth; I have put my Spirit upon him: he shall bring forth judgment to the Gentiles.—Isaiah 42:1.

Light for All People
The Mission of God's Servant
(Lessons 1-5)

Lesson Aims

After this lesson each student will be able to:

1. Describe the manner by which the Lord's Servant brings justice.

2. Contrast the gentle ways of the Servant with the typical, and often unjust, ways of political rulers.

3. Consider an issue involving injustice in his or her community and suggest one specific way a Christian can address that issue in the gentle style of the "Servant."

Lesson Outline

INTRODUCTION
A. With Justice for All
B. Lesson Background
I. THE SERVANT COMMISSIONED (Isaiah 42:1)
A. Elect of God (v. 1a)
B. Empowered by God (v. 1b)
The Beaten King
II. THE SERVANT DESCRIBED (Isaiah 42:2-4)
A. Gentle Ministry (vv. 2, 3)
B. Determined Ministry (v. 4)
Tender Strength
III. THE SERVANT ASSURED (Isaiah 42:5-9)
A. God's Power (v. 5)
B. God's Purposes (vv. 6, 7)
C. God's Supremacy (vv. 8, 9)
CONCLUSION
A. A Just Kingdom
B. Prayer
C. Thought to Remember

Introduction

A. With Justice for All

A class of third-graders in Maryland was studying the American justice system. They were asked to form a "jury" and to stage a mock trial of Goldilocks, the little girl in the well-known children's story, "The Three Bears." As a result of the jury's "deliberations," Goldilocks was convicted on two breaking-and-entering charges. The jury deadlocked, however, on theft charges brought in connection with the disappearance of the bears' porridge.

Questions about justice are common in today's confused world, where many desire to live as if they were a law to themselves. Today's lesson challenges us to consider the justice established by the Servant of the Lord. We shall see that it is a different kind of justice, because the Servant of the Lord is a different kind of leader.

B. Lesson Background

In the Background to lesson 1 (pages 122, 123), we noted that Isaiah 40-66 (which follows the record of events from Hezekiah's reign in chapters 36-39) moves forward in time from the threat of the Assyrian siege of Jerusalem to the destruction of the city and to the Babylonian captivity over one hundred years later. Within that section of Isaiah are the passages usually referred to as the Servant Songs. The first of these is found in Isaiah 42, from which today's lesson is taken.

The identity of the Servant was also considered in lesson 1. There it was observed that some passages in Isaiah that mention the servant must refer to Israel. One of these is Isaiah 41:8, 9: "But thou, Israel, art my servant, Jacob whom I have chosen, the seed of Abraham my friend. Thou whom I have taken from the ends of the earth, and called thee from the chief men thereof, and said unto thee, Thou art my servant; I have chosen thee, and not cast thee away." But Israel had failed in its task because of its disobedience: "they would not walk in his ways, neither were they obedient unto his law" (Isaiah 42:24).

Clearly there was a need for another Servant of the Lord, and it is in this context that passages such as today's text must be considered. The focus of Isaiah 42:1-9 is upon an individual Servant who will "not fail" (verse 4) in carrying out the Lord's purposes. This individual emphasis is especially clear from the New Testament references to this passage. For example, Matthew 12:18-21 cites Isaiah 42:1-4 and points to its fulfillment in the ministry of Jesus. In addition Isaiah 42:6 may be the source of terminology found in Luke 2:32; Acts 13:47; and Acts 26:23 (though Isaiah 49:6 contains similar language).

Isaiah's Servant Songs are not called "songs" because they were sung, but because they present psalm-like descriptions, using poetic language and structure, of the celebration associated with the coming of the Servant of the Lord. The emphasis in Isaiah 42:1-9 is on the justice that He will promote and provide.

I. The Servant Commissioned (Isaiah 42:1)

Isaiah's prophecy in Isaiah 42:1 is linked with the last verse of the previous chapter by repeating a key word. There Isaiah describes the pagan gods in these words: "Behold, they are all vanity; their works are nothing: their molten images are wind and confusion." Israel is told to *behold* those gods, and then to *behold* God's Servant.

A. Elect of God (v. 1a)

1a. Behold my servant, whom I uphold; mine elect, in whom my soul delighteth.

The difference between the impotent idols and God's *servant* is dramatic: God upholds His Servant by His power. This stark contrast makes it clear that God is far superior and that His people should trust and obey Him.

The term *servant* often took on a royal and political connotation in the world of Isaiah (as in 2 Kings 22:12). It could describe someone in the position of a trusted envoy or representative. The word implied both the honor in holding such a title and the responsibility to obey whatever the king commanded.

It is important to remember that in the previous chapter, Isaiah had spoken of Israel as God's servant (Isaiah 41:8-10). Here in chapter 42 we see an emphasis on an individual. Thus, while we should consider Jesus to be the ultimate fulfillment of these Servant prophecies (for this is clear from the New Testament's use of them), we should also recognize the close association of the Servant with the nation of Israel. He will succeed in carrying out the Lord's purpose, in contrast to Israel's failure. Some students believe that a concept of the Messiah as the embodiment of Israel or as the epitome of Israel's mission may be the best way to explain the connection.

God also refers to the Servant as *mine elect*, in order to make clear the close, personal relationship between the two. The phrase *in whom my soul delighteth* emphasizes the Lord's approval of the Servant's efforts. These words highlight the contrast, suggested in the previous paragraph, between faithless Israel and the Servant, who was "faithful to him that appointed him" (Hebrews 3:1, 2). The phrase also foreshadows two occasions when God spoke of Jesus—at His baptism and at the transfiguration. Each time He said, "This is my beloved Son, in whom I am well pleased" (Matthew 3:17; 17:5).

B. Empowered by God (v. 1b)

1b. I have put my Spirit upon him: he shall bring forth judgment to the Gentiles.

In the Bible *judgment* implies the kind of justice or ruling associated with the wisdom of a divinely led ruler. It describes what God has "judged" to be right and true. It is this concern for righteousness and truth that lies at the heart of the Servant's ministry. That truth embraces the gospel message, which declares how all people,

including *Gentiles*, can be forgiven of past sins through the Servant's atoning death on the cross.

The word also carries the traditional sense of treating people in a fair, or just, manner. The need for such justice in our world is obvious. The corruption of justice is frequently in the news. Even when it is not, the believer may experience the corruption of justice firsthand. Those with money and influence often manipulate the system and pervert justice to their own ends. The promise of God is that His Servant will establish a justice that is pleasing to our righteous God. [See question #1, page 160.]

THE BEATEN KING

In the movie *The Last Emperor* the young child anointed as the last emperor of China lives a magical life of luxury. Among other privileges, he has a thousand servants at his command. Amazed at his surroundings, his brother asks, "What happens when you do wrong?"

"When I do wrong, someone else is punished," the young emperor replies. To demonstrate he breaks a jar, and one of the servants is immediately beaten. I would have loved a deal like that when I was growing up!

You and I, however, have a better "deal." Jesus loved us so much that He reversed the pattern described in the movie. When we servants erred, the King took the punishment. When we messed up, Jesus was beaten up.

God's justice would not allow Him to ignore our sin. But God's mercy would not allow Him to leave us hopeless and lost. So when we sinned, Jesus paid the price: He died for us. He is the Suffering Servant in whom the Father delights.

Because of His "elect," God does not treat me as I deserve to be treated. Instead, I can be treated

Visual for lesson 5

Behold my servant, whom I uphold; mine elect, in whom my soul delighteth; I have put my Spirit upon him: he shall bring forth judgment to the Gentiles.
—Isaiah 42:1

This poster illustrates the connection between verse 1 and God's declaration at Jesus' baptism.

the way Jesus deserves to be treated. That is possible only because Jesus took my punishment on Himself at the cross. Thus God can be both "just, and the justifier of him which believeth in Jesus" (Romans 3:26).

Paul describes what God has done this way: "For he hath made him to be sin for us, who knew no sin; that we might be made the righteousness of God in him" (2 Corinthians 5:21).   —J. A. M.

II. The Servant Described (Isaiah 42:2-4)

Now Isaiah begins a description of the personal qualities of the Servant who will bring about the Lord's justice.

A. Gentle Ministry (vv. 2, 3)

2. He shall not cry, nor lift up, nor cause his voice to be heard in the street.

The Servant of the Lord will be known, not for the volume of his words, but for his humble, quiet, gentle spirit. As Isaiah has earlier described Him, He will be called the Prince of peace (Isaiah 9:6). Jesus described Himself as "meek and lowly in heart" (Matthew 11:29). Such an attitude reflects the spirit of servant leadership, to which Jesus calls all who would be great in His kingdom (Mark 10:42-45).

3. A bruised reed shall he not break, and the smoking flax shall he not quench: he shall bring forth judgment unto truth.

A bruised reed is one with a cracked, perhaps partially broken, stem. It is something fragile that must be handled carefully. Here it represents someone who is weak and struggling spiritually—who has been *bruised* by sin or by difficult circumstances. *Smoking flax* describes a wick with a flame that is dimly burning. It represents those whose lives are nearly ruined; the flame of life has been almost extinguished. The Servant of the Lord will conduct His ministry in such a way that the helpless and hopeless will be saved from destruction. This will be accomplished because of the Servant's patient, compassionate manner. In contrast to the corrupt rulers of Isaiah's day, the prophet foretold a day when God's people

---

How to Say It

ASSYRIAN. Uh-*sear*-ee-un.
BABYLON. *Bab*-uh-lun.
BABYLONIAN. Bab-uh-*low*-nee-un.
CYRUS. *Sigh*-russ.
HEZEKIAH. Hez-ih-*kye*-uh.
ISAIAH. Eye-*zay*-uh.
JEREMIAH. Jair-uh-*my*-uh.

---

will be blessed with a Messiah who will *bring forth judgment* (justice) *unto truth*. This message of God's kingdom of justice should both thrill our hearts and challenge our own business practices. We should ask ourselves whether we conduct our own affairs in a way that reflects the justice of the Lord. [See question #2, page 160.]

B. Determined Ministry (v. 4)

4. He shall not fail nor be discouraged, till he have set judgment in the earth: and the isles shall wait for his law.

Here the theme of the Servant's suffering is subtly introduced. Later it will be developed more fully, and it will become especially clear in the Servant Song found in Isaiah 52:13—53:12. In spite of the pressures to *fail* or become *discouraged*, the Servant will not waver from the fulfillment of the Lord's task. Thus He is exactly like the God who has called Him, who does not faint or grow weary (Isaiah 40:28).

The repeated use of *judgment* (three times within these first four verses), indicates its prominence in the Servant's ministry. [See question #3, page 160.] Also highlighted is the impact of His ministry on *the isles*—another way of describing the Servant's desire that faraway peoples (Gentiles) hear of His *law* and be instructed by Him (cf. Isaiah 49:1). The involvement of Gentiles in God's plan is emphasized throughout Isaiah. It appears as early as Isaiah 2:2-4, where "all nations" are pictured as flowing like streams to Mount Zion in order to learn of the ways of the Lord.

TENDER STRENGTH

Isaiah describes the Servant of the Lord as one characterized by gentle strength. He will not harm the weak (Isaiah 42:3), but at the same time he is fiercely committed to fulfilling the Lord's purpose (v. 4).

An article in *National Geographic* several years ago provided a penetrating picture of gentle yet tenacious strength. After a forest fire in Yellowstone National Park, rangers began their trek up a mountain to assess the damage. One ranger found a bird literally petrified in ashes, perched upright on the ground at the base of a tree. Somewhat sickened by the eerie sight, he knocked the bird over with a stick. Immediately three tiny chicks scurried from under their dead mother's wings. The loving mother, keenly aware of impending disaster, had carried her offspring to the base of the tree and had gathered them under her wings, protecting them from smoke and fire.

This mother bird could easily have flown to safety, but she refused to abandon her babies. When the blaze arrived and the heat scorched her small body, the mother remained steadfast.

The gentle strength of her love compelled her to make the ultimate sacrifice. Because she was willing to die, those under the shelter of her wings could live.

The psalmist describes God's care in this manner: "He shall cover thee with his feathers, and under his wings shalt thou trust" (Psalm 91:4). Isaiah affirms that God's Servant will not be deterred from His purpose of bringing justice and hope to the world. Jesus did not run from the fiery wrath of God's judgment; He gave His life so that we could find shelter "under his wings."

—J. A. M.

III. The Servant Assured
(Isaiah 42:5-9)

A. God's Power (v. 5)

Isaiah declares that the Servant will be empowered by God to accomplish His mission.

5. Thus saith God the LORD, he that created the heavens, and stretched them out; he that spread forth the earth, and that which cometh out of it; he that giveth breath unto the people upon it, and spirit to them that walk therein.

The power of the One who created *the heavens* and *the earth* will be the power that undergirds the Servant's ministry. The creation of the heavens as an act in which God *stretched them out* is an image already used in Isaiah 40:22, where the prophet describes God as the One "that stretcheth out the heavens as a curtain, and spreadeth them out as a tent to dwell in." Also pictured is the creation of *the earth, and that which cometh out of it,* probably a reference to animal life (cf. Genesis 1:24).

Next, Isaiah mentions *the people* to whom God has given *breath,* most likely "the breath of life" (Genesis 2:7) that each person possesses. The term *spirit* probably means the same as *breath,* and is an example of parallelism in Hebrew poetry (the same idea in one verse or part of a verse is repeated in a slightly different form in the next verse or part of the verse).

B. God's Purposes (vv. 6, 7)

6. I the LORD have called thee in righteousness, and will hold thine hand, and will keep thee, and give thee for a covenant of the people, for a light of the Gentiles.

Here *the Lord* speaks a message of encouragement and reassurance to the Servant. (The language of this verse clearly identifies the Servant in terms of an individual rather than the nation or a group within the nation.) The Lord declares that He will *give* the Servant *for a covenant of the people.* Some students believe that *people* describes all the peoples of the world (as it does in verse 5).

The phrase would thus be parallel in meaning to *a light of the Gentiles.*

Others say that *people* refers to the Jews, and that *light of the Gentiles* points to the expanded mission of the Servant beyond the scope of the chosen people. It is interesting to note a portion of Jesus' words to Paul when He appeared to him on the road to Damascus: "delivering thee from the people, and from the Gentiles, unto whom now I send thee, to open their eyes, and to turn them from darkness to light" (Acts 26:17, 18). This would seem to favor the view that *people* describes the Jews.

If, then, the Servant is offered as a covenant for the benefit of the people of Israel, the Servant must be someone other than Israel. It is best to see the Servant as an individual—specifically, the Messiah. The concept of a new *covenant* will be spelled out in greater detail by Jeremiah (Jeremiah 31:31-34; cf. Hebrews 8:8-13).

7. To open the blind eyes, to bring out the prisoners from the prison, and them that sit in darkness out of the prison house.

The reference in Acts 26:17, 18 to opening *blind eyes* and turning individuals from *darkness* to light suggests once again an application to the ministry of Jesus and the impact of His gospel. In fact, these words are similar to those found in Isaiah 61:1 and 2, which begin another Servant Song that Jesus specifically applied to Himself. He read from those verses when He went to Nazareth and spoke in the synagogue there. After finishing His reading, He rolled up the scroll, handed it to the attendant, and said, "This day is this Scripture fulfilled in your ears" (Luke 4:20, 21).

The kind of justice that the Servant would bring is thus associated with relieving the oppression of those are who are spiritually helpless— blindly groping in the darkness of sin. At the same time, we should not ignore our responsibility as Christians to the physical needs around us or to those who are confined to *prison.* We should read Jesus' words in Matthew 25:31-46 concerning the hungry, the thirsty, the neglected, the naked, the sick, and the imprisoned. And we should give special heed when Jesus says, "Inasmuch as ye have done it unto one of the least of these my brethren, ye have done it unto me" (Matthew 25:40). [See question #4, page 160.]

C. God's Supremacy (vv. 8, 9)

8. I am the LORD; that is my name: and my glory will I not give to another, neither my praise to graven images.

This declaration of the Lord's supreme position above all gods is the foundation of the law of Moses, and specifically of the Ten Commandments (Exodus 20:1, 2). There also comes a strict warning against all forms of idolatry, or *graven images*. God is a jealous God, and He will permit no rival to be worshiped by His people. To do so would be to endorse a hoax, since the other gods are not really gods at all (an emphasis found at the conclusion of chapter 41). This verse thus summarizes the message of the first two of the Ten Commandments (Exodus 20:3, 4). [See question #5, page 160.]

These words of the Lord imply that what God does through the faithful work of His Servant contributes to the *glory* of the Lord. Paul exhibits much the same emphasis in his words to the Ephesians describing the blessings that Christians have received from God through Christ. He designates them as "spiritual blessings" and includes such items as election by God, redemption, forgiveness of sins, and the gift of the Holy Spirit (Ephesians 1:3-14). Three times within this passage Paul affirms that all of these blessings have been given by God the Father to "the praise of his glory" (vv. 6, 12, 14).

Likewise, Philippians 2:5-11 declares that Jesus' act of humbling Himself and going to the cross was followed by His exaltation so that "every knee should bow" and "every tongue should confess that Jesus Christ is Lord, *to the glory of God the Father*." Nothing that the Servant does is viewed as competition with this matchless supremacy of the Lord. Rather, His work calls attention to the Lord's supremacy.

9. Behold, the former things are come to pass, and new things do I declare: before they spring forth I tell you of them.

The former things may be a reference to earlier prophecies by Isaiah (or of the Lord's prophets in general) of events that had *come to pass*. Perhaps included here may be the rise of Cyrus and the release of the captives from Babylon (Isaiah 45:1-7).

Although from Isaiah's perspective this was yet to come, it was to take place before the glorious *new things* that would be associated with the coming of the Servant. The Lord emphasizes that all His messages concerning future events have come true. He has never had to back up and correct misstatements or predictions that have gone awry. His word can be trusted. Because of this, the Lord (through His spokesman Isaiah) can *declare* the occurrence of *new things* without any fear that they may not happen.

Isaiah's words should bring to mind the book of Revelation, which closes with a description of the eternal city built by the hands of God. The apostle John records seeing the "new Jerusalem, coming down from God out of heaven, prepared as a bride adorned for her husband" (Revelation 21:2). Then John hears the voice of God declaring, "Behold, I make all things new" (v. 5). Both Jews and Gentiles, who have become part of the covenant predicted by Isaiah, will be blessed by knowing that God's word has "come to pass"— for eternity.

Conclusion

A. A Just Kingdom

The Servant of the Lord is described in today's text as One who possesses the Lord's full support in the fulfillment of the Lord's mission and in the establishment of His truth. No one will escape the impact of the Servant's efforts. The New Testament makes it clear that the Servant thus described is Jesus Christ. Jesus' ministry fulfilled the hopes and dreams of Isaiah, who spoke the word of the Lord during especially trying circumstances in Judah.

The kingdom that Jesus established (the church) is characterized by a devotion to the righteous standards of a holy God. It will be perfected only when we join Jesus Himself in the eternal kingdom where righteousness dwells. In the meantime, we must live and labor so that the Servant's mission continues to be carried out. Like Jesus, we must seek to bring others out of darkness into light and tell prisoners how they can be set free.

B. Prayer

O Lord, may the way that Jesus has treated us affect how we treat others. Use us to make a difference in Jesus' name whenever the opportunity arises. In Jesus' name we pray, amen.

C. Thought to Remember

All Christians are servants of the Servant of the Lord. That Servant has told us, "As my Father hath sent me, even so send I you" (John 20:21).

Home Daily Bible Readings

Monday, Dec. 24—"Good News of Great Joy" (Luke 2:8-14)

Tuesday, Dec. 25—All Who Heard Were Amazed (Luke 2:15-20)

Wednesday, Dec. 26—Light for Revelation to the Gentiles (Luke 2:25-35)

Thursday, Dec. 27—Sing a New Song (Isaiah 42:10-17)

Friday, Dec. 28—Israel's Blindness (Isaiah 42:18-25)

Saturday, Dec. 29—God Has Called You by Name (Isaiah 43:1-7)

Sunday, Dec. 30—The Lord Is the Only Savior (Isaiah 43:8-15)

Learning by Doing

This page contains an alternate lesson plan emphasizing learning activities.
Classes desiring such student involvement will find these suggestions helpful.

Learning Goals

After participating in this lesson, each student will be able to:

1. Describe the manner by which the Lord's Servant brings justice.

2. Contrast the gentle ways of the Servant with the typical, and often unjust, ways of political rulers.

3. Consider an issue involving injustice in his or her community and suggest one specific way a Christian can address that issue in the gentle style of the "Servant."

Into the Lesson

Bring to class several newspaper clippings that speak of injustice or unfairness in nations around the world. The stories may focus on wartime atrocities, ethnic suppression or conflict, religious persecutions, foreign aggression, or other such evils. After you read the headline and a brief segment of each article, tape the clipping to the wall. Over the cluster of articles tape a small sign that reads "Injustice." Remind the class that many people throughout history have been forced to suffer at the hands of an unjust, ineffective government or an oppressive culture. These people have yearned for justice and compassion. God has hope for people in these circumstances, just as He offered hope for the chosen people to whom Isaiah spoke.

Into the Word

Using your lesson commentary as a resource, give a brief lecture on the background to this prophecy. Also explain and define the words *Servant* and *judgment* that are used in today's text. Read the printed text to the class.

Give groups of four or five people one of the following tasks. Also give groups 1 and 2 photocopies of the appropriate pages of the lesson commentary. (In larger classes, several groups may work on the same task.)

Group 1: Read Isaiah 42:2-4 and the attached notes from the lesson commentary. Identify and be ready to explain the colorful imageries of this passage to the class.

Group 2: Read Isaiah 42:1, 5-7 and the attached lesson commentary. Explain how these prophecies are fulfilled in Israel and in Jesus.

Group 3: Read Isaiah 42:1-9. Find every phrase or line that gives a clue to the character or nature of the Servant. List these characteristics on a piece of poster board.

Give the groups eight to ten minutes to complete their tasks. Then ask each group to report its findings.

Into Life

After group 3 reports, discuss the following questions with the entire class:

1. As you view the list by group #3, what do you see about this Servant's character and nature that is different from so many of the leaders of the world's unjust nations?

2. How does this prophecy offer hope to people suffering under suppressive national leaders today?

3. Believers may even suffer injustice or suppression in nations that are free. How may this be happening in our community?

Remind the class that the term *Servant* refers to Israel but also points to the Messiah. Then tell them that 2 Timothy 2:24 extends this image to apply to all believers. Give each of the groups a photocopy of 2 Timothy 2:14-26. Ask them to do the following:

(1) Find and highlight the verse that best expresses our mission as believers. *(It is v. 15.)*

(2) Underline every word or phrase that describes the kind of character or behavior God is wanting each of us to develop.

After the exercise, tell the class, "It is apparent God wants His workmen to have that same gentle, faithful, and persistent character that He prophesied in Isaiah." Remind the class these are qualities God wants in us even as we address injustices in our community. Ask the class, "What are some of the injustices we see in our community? What groups of people feel socially suppressed?" List answers and circumstances on a chalkboard.

Then ask, "Understanding how God wants us to work, what are some gentle and yet practical ways of fighting these injustices?" Note their suggestions next to each of the circumstances listed on the chalkboard.

Close the session by asking two volunteers to pray. One person is to thank God for the Savior, who offers hope and peace to persons experiencing injustices or oppression in their lives. The other will ask for God's help for all class members to be the servants God calls us to be, especially in matters of justice and mercy.

Let's Talk It Over

The questions on this page are designed to encourage review of the lesson Scriptures and to promote discussion of the lesson by the class. The answers provided are only discussion starters. Let your class talk it over from there.

1. What do you think is the role of the church in addressing what the lesson writer calls "corruption of justice" in society? How well are we doing in fulfilling that role? What more can or should we do?

The New Testament precedent is to work through individuals, transforming them through the power of the gospel. When significant numbers of individuals are changed, society changes. There is no record of the early church's organizing political action committees, boycotts, or even parachurch organizations to address specific needs. At the same time, the political and economic climate of the first-century church was much different from today's, so that some of these things were simply not possible then but may be very beneficial today. Look at the specific needs and opportunities around you. Compare those with the gifts your learners have. What programs or ministries are feasible in that mix?

2. The lesson writer says today's text ought to "challenge our own business practices. We should ask ourselves whether we conduct our own affairs in a way that reflects the justice of the Lord." With that in mind, what kind of business practices should we avoid? How should we conduct our business?

Obviously this means we don't want to do anything illegal. But we also want to be sure we do not take advantage of others through exaggeration or other forms of "legal" misrepresentation. If we put ourselves in the other person's position, we can imagine how we would want to be treated; then we can treat the other that way.

Perhaps some of your class members can tell of certain historic practices or practices recommended by management that they have refused to follow. Has any of them ever left a job because it required unethical behavior?

3. Suppose a friend has agreed to accompany you to church today. When he reads this text, he says, "If your God promised justice in the world, then where is it? Your God is a sham!" How would you respond?

God never promised that all injustices will be corrected in this life. What He has promised is that there will be no injustice or evil of any kind in Heaven (Revelation 21:23-27). One reason we

can believe God's promises concerning the coming judgment is that God has kept such promises in the past. When He warned Israel that her apostasy would bring judgment on the nation, He kept His word (Deuteronomy 28). Likewise, when God promised blessings upon Israel if they obeyed Him, He delivered on those promises, too. If He kept His word then, He will keep it now.

4. Some Christians believe the focus of the church should be on the Great Commission. Others think the emphasis should be on social justice for the poor and the oppressed. How can the church strike a Scriptural balance between the two views?

The New Testament church always had a proper concern for the poor as its members shared their possessions with those in need (Acts 4:34) and made provisions for the widows among them (Acts 6). The apostles also taught the believers to do good whenever possible, especially for fellow Christians (James 2:13-16; 1 John 3:17; Galatians 6:10). At the same time, the New Testament church never allowed benevolence to become more important than evangelism. Preaching the gospel was always of first importance (Acts 6:2). Today's food pantries, pro-life efforts, crisis hot lines, and the like should contribute toward the church's ministry of winning the lost. They should never compete with or replace that vital ministry.

5. God said He would not give His glory to another. What "others" compete for God's glory today? How can we be sure to glorify God alone?

The first people to hear Isaiah's words must have thought about idols in connection with these "others" with whom God would not share His glory. While we do not have idols today, we do give "religious" devotion to many things, like sports, entertainment, or making a living. While there is nothing wrong with any of these in and of themselves, when they compete with God, they become "idols." How many Christians will forsake the assembling of the saints today in order to worship at the temple known better as "the stadium," or to worship at the shrine in their living room—the television?

Hear the Good News

DEVOTIONAL READING: Isaiah 60:17-22.

BACKGROUND SCRIPTURE: Isaiah 60, 61.

PRINTED TEXT: Isaiah 60:1-3; 61:1-4, 10, 11.

Isaiah 60:1-3

1 Arise, shine; for thy light is come, and the glory of the LORD is risen upon thee.

2 For, behold, the darkness shall cover the earth, and gross darkness the people: but the LORD shall arise upon thee, and his glory shall be seen upon thee.

3 And the Gentiles shall come to thy light, and kings to the brightness of thy rising.

Isaiah 61:1-4, 10, 11

1 The Spirit of the Lord GOD is upon me; because the LORD hath anointed me to preach good tidings unto the meek; he hath sent me to bind up the brokenhearted, to proclaim liberty to the captives, and the opening of the prison to them that are bound;

2 To proclaim the acceptable year of the LORD, and the day of vengeance of our God; to comfort all that mourn;

3 To appoint unto them that mourn in Zion, to give unto them beauty for ashes, the oil of joy for mourning, the garment of praise for the spirit of heaviness; that they might be called Trees of righteousness, the planting of the LORD, that he might be glorified.

4 And they shall build the old wastes, they shall raise up the former desolations, and they shall repair the waste cities, the desolations of many generations.

. . . .

10 I will greatly rejoice in the LORD, my soul shall be joyful in my God; for he hath clothed me with the garments of salvation, he hath covered me with the robe of righteousness, as a bridegroom decketh himself with ornaments, and as a bride adorneth herself with her jewels.

11 For as the earth bringeth forth her bud, and as the garden causeth the things that are sown in it to spring forth; so the Lord GOD will cause righteousness and praise to spring forth before all the nations.

GOLDEN TEXT: Arise, shine; for thy light is come, and the glory of the LORD is risen upon thee.—Isaiah 60:1.

Light for All People
Unit 2: The Response of God's People
(Lessons 6-9)

Lesson Aims

After this lesson each student will be able to:

1. List several of the blessings that the Lord's "anointed" brings to a world plagued by darkness.

2. Tell how this description also characterizes the mission of the church in the world today.

3. Give a specific example of how an individual or the church can carry out one of the tasks described in the text.

Lesson Outline

INTRODUCTION
  A. Good News All Year
  B. The Messianic Age
  C. Lesson Background
 I. THE COMING LIGHT (Isaiah 60:1-3)
  A. Promise of Light (v. 1)
  B. Power of Light (v. 2)
  C. Product of Light (v. 3)
    Turning on the Light
 II. THE COMING LIGHT BEARER (Isaiah 61:1-4)
  A. Anointed by God (v. 1a)
  B. Bringing Good News (vv. 1b-3)
  C. Rebuilding Desolations (v. 4)
III. THE COMING JOY (Isaiah 61:10, 11)
  A. Like New Garments (v. 10)
    Wedding Wardrobes
  B. Like New Growth (v. 11)
CONCLUSION
  A. Good News for Exiles
  B. Good News for Jesus' Disciples
  C. Good News for Us
  D. Prayer
  E. Thought to Remember

Introduction

A. Good News All Year

Now that the holidays have passed, many who were caught up in the spirit of celebration and merriment find themselves back in the "daily grind" with little to make them feel cheerful. Once again the headlines seem to be dominated by all the "bad news" taking place. Occasionally these people express the desire that somehow the "spirit of Christmas"—the sense of love, joy, and goodwill that permeates the season—could last all year.

As Christians we know that such a wish can come true. The message of Christmas is about more than just a season or a spirit; it is about a Person. It is the message that God Himself put on human flesh and came to live among us. He came to make a difference—not just for a month or a day—but for all time. The "good tidings of great joy" of which the angel spoke to the shepherds (Luke 2:10) is a message that all Christians can tell to those whose lives are being spent in the gloom and darkness of sin.

Just as Isaiah brought the message of God's light and salvation to his dark times, so may we, as God's people today, bear witness faithfully to Jesus, the "light of the world."

B. The Messianic Age

Isaiah 60 and 61, from which today's texts are taken, describe the future glory that God's people will experience. Chapter 60 uses highly poetic language to prophesy that God's people, whose sins have brought the Lord's condemnation (see chapters 57-59), will become a center of attraction for peoples throughout the world. Chapter 61 describes One whom the Lord has "anointed," who will initiate an "everlasting covenant" that will spread from Israel to all nations (61:8, 9). Isaiah 62 also continues this promise of hope with a prophecy that God will be like a bridegroom to Israel. Her former shame as an adulterous wife will be replaced by God's acknowledgment that He delights in her (62:4, 5).

The relevance of this text to Christians today is seen in Jesus' appearance at the Nazareth synagogue. Having read from Isaiah 61:1 and 2, He then declared its fulfillment "this day" (Luke 4:21). Some of the verses in these chapters are quoted in the book of Revelation to describe the future glories of Heaven that await Christians. Isaiah 60:11 is quoted in Revelation 21:25, 26, and Isaiah 60:19 is cited in Revelation 21:23 and 22:5. Thus, both the ministry of Jesus and the blessings He has promised to His followers are described through the prophetic insights granted to Isaiah by God's Spirit.

The glory promised by Isaiah in these verses was therefore not for national Israel, but rather for what we might term "spiritual Israel." This includes the faithful remnant within Israel who would accept the Lord's anointed One as well as Gentiles who accepted Christ. The early Christians, at first only Jewish, were used of God to be the "light to the Gentiles" (Acts 10:34, 35, 44-48; 11:15-20). "If ye be Christ's, then are ye Abraham's seed, and heirs according to the promise" (Galatians 3:29). The church, then, consisting of both Jews and Gentiles, makes up the "household of God" (Ephesians 2:19) or the "Israel of God"

(Galatians 6:16). The church continues to spread the good news of Jesus throughout the world, and in so doing it continues the mission begun by the Lord's anointed One.

C. Lesson Background

We have noted in previous studies that Isaiah's prophetic messages touched on the threats of two world powers. The first was Assyria, who ruled the world during Isaiah's lifetime. Isaiah condemned Assyria's brutality and pride in portions of the first part of his writings (chapters 1-39; see, for example, Isaiah 10:1-19, 24-27).

But Isaiah also looked toward the distant future and saw that another power, Babylon (who was of little significance in his time), would become the real threat to Judah. His yet-to-be-born countrymen would be enslaved in that foreign empire. Beyond the heartache of captivity, however, Isaiah saw the return of God's people to their homeland.

Then he looked further into the future and saw the coming of God's Servant who would loose the chains of sin. Jesus came as that Servant; His message could be summarized by the title of today's lesson: "Hear the Good News!"

I. The Coming Light
(Isaiah 60:1-3)
A. Promise of Light (v. 1)

1. Arise, shine; for thy light is come, and the glory of the LORD is risen upon thee.

Isaiah had described the pitiful condition of God's people earlier: "Therefore is judgment far from us, neither doth justice overtake us: we wait for light, but behold obscurity; for brightness, but we walk in darkness" (Isaiah 59:9). Now the waiting is over, Isaiah declares. *Thy light is come!*

The coming of this light is connected with *the glory of the Lord*. Recall a previous lesson, in which Isaiah predicted a time when the glory of God would be "revealed" to all mankind (Isaiah 40:5). Such language finds its fulfillment in the grand event recorded in John 1:14: "The Word was made flesh, and dwelt among us, (and we beheld his glory, the glory as of the only begotten of the Father,) full of grace and truth."

B. Power of Light (v. 2)

2. For, behold, the darkness shall cover the earth, and gross darkness the people: but the LORD shall arise upon thee, and his glory shall be seen upon thee.

The picture of *darkness* covering the *earth* reminds us of the situation prior to God's creative activity in Genesis: "And the earth was without form, and void; and darkness was upon the face of the deep" (Genesis 1:2). Then God's creative

word, "Let there be light" (v. 3), shattered the darkness. Even so, the light provided by the coming of the Word made flesh has dispelled the darkness caused by sin. This is the message of the opening verses of John's Gospel (John 1:1-9) and of Paul's words in 2 Corinthians 4:6: "For God, who commanded the light to shine out of darkness, hath shined in our hearts, to give the light of the knowledge of the glory of God in the face of Jesus Christ." [See question #1, page 168.]

C. Product of Light (v. 3)

3. And the Gentiles shall come to thy light, and kings to the brightness of thy rising.

Already we have seen that the ministry of the Servant of the Lord is to have a dramatic impact on *Gentiles* (Isaiah 42:1, 6; 49:6). This passage also includes such an emphasis. While it is true that Jesus is the *light* of the world, His people are also called "the light of the world" (Matthew 5:14). God's people in every age are called "out of darkness into his marvelous light" (1 Peter 2:9) in order to let their light shine before others (Matthew 5:16). [See question #2, page 168.]

Among those turning to the light of the Lord are *kings*. In Old Testament times, kings (even those who ruled God's people) often corrupted or openly opposed the worship of the Lord, turning instead to pagan gods and practices (cf. Psalm 2:2). Isaiah predicted a radical turnaround in the attitude of kings toward the Lord. John, in his vision of the new Jerusalem, also saw evidence of this (Revelation 21:24).

TURNING ON THE LIGHT

Perhaps no inventor ever created more useful devices than Thomas Alva Edison. One that we often take for granted is the electric light bulb—

Visual for lesson 6. *Display this poster as you begin the lesson. It is a beautiful illustration of today's Golden Text.*

and it may well be the most useful of all his inventions. Edison labored tirelessly over a period of two years, trying some six thousand different fibers to find just the right filament, until he had made his light bulb. More than 120 years later, Edison's invention still brings light to the world. When Edison died, Herbert Hoover, the President of the United States at the time, asked that lights all over America be dimmed in his honor.

In contrast, Jesus is honored, not by the dimming of light, but by the turning on of light—the light that He brought to dispel the darkness caused by sin. That light still "shineth in darkness" (John 1:5), even though the times in which we live seem to grow increasingly dark. Thus we can sing such great gospel songs as "Walking in Sunlight," "The Light of the World Is Jesus," and "Stepping in the Light." Comparing Jesus to light is an illustration that people can easily understand, no matter where or when they live.

It is always dangerous to walk in the darkness—particularly in spiritual darkness. And everyone knows that we live in a dark world. We have only to read the newspaper or watch television to know that. We should rejoice that the Light of the world has given us the possibility of "stepping in the light" and of reflecting that light before others.   —R. C. S.

II. The Coming Light Bearer
(Isaiah 61:1-4)

Not long after Jesus' baptism (Matthew 3:13-17; 4:1-11), He returned to His hometown of Nazareth and announced to those gathered in the synagogue there that He had come to fulfill the words of Isaiah 61:1, 2. (See Luke 4:16-21.) Up to that point, Jesus' miracles and teachings had caused "a fame of him" to spread throughout Galilee (Luke 4:14). In Nazareth, Jesus added the witness of Scripture to His messianic credentials. He knew that Isaiah, speaking some seven hundred years earlier, had been describing Him and the beginning of the messianic age.

It is possible to see this prophecy as having two primary applications. First, it spoke a message of comfort to those who would later become captives in Babylon. Second, it was fulfilled by

---

How to Say It

ASSYRIA. Uh-*sear*-ee-uh.
BABYLON. *Bab*-uh-lun.
CHRISTOS (Greek). *Kris*-taws.
ISAIAH. Eye-*zay*-uh.
JUDEA. Joo-*dee*-uh.
MESSIANIC. mess-ee-*an*-ick.

Jesus in His messianic ministry. This fulfillment includes His ministry while He was in the flesh as well as certain elements that will not be fully realized until His second coming. That climactic event will give all Christians the ultimate "liberty" (Isaiah 61:1), when they are welcomed into Heaven. We have noted that the book of Revelation often uses imagery and vocabulary from this section of Isaiah. (Compare Isaiah 60:11 with Revelation 21:25, 26, and Isaiah 60:19 with Revelation 21:23 and 22:5.) The central theme of these levels of application is the joyous freedom (found only in the Lord) from all forms of spiritual darkness. It is a message of genuine hope!

A. Anointed by God (v. 1a)

1a. The Spirit of the Lord GOD is upon me; because the LORD hath anointed me.

To be *anointed* is to be separated, dedicated, and consecrated for a divine task. The act of anointing included pouring oil over the head of a person as he was set aside for a specific function or role. Kings were thus consecrated to office (1 Samuel 16:1, 13) as were priests (Leviticus 8:12). There is one instance of the anointing of a prophet (1 Kings 19:16). From the Hebrew word for anoint comes the word *Messiah*, which means the same as the Greek word *christos*, from which we get the word *Christ*. Whether one says "Messiah," "Christ," or "anointed One," the meaning is the same. Isaiah says that God has set aside One to carry out the tasks described in this passage. Jesus claimed to be that individual, and He supported that claim with both His words and His deeds. [See question #3, page 168.]

B. Bringing Good News (vv. 1b-3)

1b. To preach good tidings unto the meek; he hath sent me to bind up the brokenhearted, to proclaim liberty to the captives, and the opening of the prison to them that are bound.

The anointed, or chosen, One will carry out a series of tasks, beginning with preaching *good tidings unto the meek* and binding up *the brokenhearted*. This is in keeping with the kind of ministry described in last week's text from Isaiah 42: "a bruised reed shall he not break, and the smoking flax shall he not quench" (v. 3). The references to *liberty to the captives* and the *opening of the prison to them that are bound* would have given those exiled in Babylon a sense of hope for better times. But the grandeur of this entire passage (along with Jesus' declaration that He came to fulfill it) indicates something much more wonderful and inclusive than physical liberation.

2. To proclaim the acceptable year of the LORD, and the day of vengeance of our God; to comfort all that mourn.

The phrase *the acceptable year of the Lord* most likely suggests a connection with the Old Testament Year of Jubilee, described in Leviticus 25. This special year occurred every fifty years, at which time land was to be returned to the family that had originally owned it and those in bondage were to be set free. The words *proclaim liberty* (v. 1) are reminiscent of the language found in the Jubilee regulations (Leviticus 25:10). [See question #4, page 168.]

When Jesus quoted this passage in the synagogue at Nazareth and applied it to Himself, He declared His ministry to be the beginning of a new kind of Jubilee. As the New Covenant is superior to the Old, so is the new Jubilee superior to the old. The Jubilee inaugurated by Jesus accomplished goals similar to those of the old one, but on a grander scale. Jesus made it possible for all mankind to return to its original owner— namely, God Himself. He came to bring freedom from sin to those held captive in its tyranny.

In the midst of such a glowing portrayal of the future, Isaiah adds the phrase *and the day of vengeance of our God.* These words sound a somber warning to those who will not hear the good news described in the previous verse. God's justice demands that those who reject His grace must experience His justice.

3. To appoint unto them that mourn in Zion, to give unto them beauty for ashes, the oil of joy for mourning, the garment of praise for the spirit of heaviness; that they might be called Trees of righteousness, The planting of the LORD, that he might be glorified.

With poetic imagery Isaiah continues to describe the transformations that the Messiah will initiate. Those who *mourn* in repentance for their sins will see their *ashes* (a symbol of mourning) replaced with *beauty*. The term for *beauty* here actually refers to an ornamental head covering signifying joy and gladness. Similar in meaning is the phrase *the oil of joy for mourning*. The pouring of oil on someone was associated with times of celebration (Psalms 23:5; 45:7).

The expression *the garment of praise for the spirit of heaviness* calls to mind other references in Isaiah to clothing as symbolic of one's characteristics or attitudes (Isaiah 11:5; 59:16, 17). Verse 10 of our text provides another example.

Finally, Isaiah describes those who feel the impact of the ministry of the Messiah as *trees of righteousness* and as *the planting of the Lord*. Note that the speaker of verse 1 is the One who states that those who accept His "good tidings" are righteous. Although this righteousness is their own, it comes from God (cf. Isaiah 60:21). The New Testament indicates that righteousness is credited to us through faith in Jesus Christ

(Romans 3:22). It is a gift (Romans 5:17). As trees thus planted by the Lord, we are to bring forth fruit that brings glory to the Planter.

C. Rebuilding Desolations (v. 4)

4. And they shall build the old wastes, they shall raise up the former desolations, and they shall repair the waste cities, the desolations of many generations.

Here Isaiah's emphasis shifts to a consideration of the work to be done by God's "trees of righteousness." These words must have given great hope to Jewish exiles living in Babylon. But we find an even greater fulfillment when we connect them with Jesus' application of the chapter's opening words to Himself.

Acts 15:13-17 sheds light on this passage. There James was addressing the matter of including Gentiles in the church, stating that the prophets were in agreement with this action. While he quotes from Amos 9:11, 12 to support his position, that passage uses language similar to our text here, especially Acts 15:16: "After this I will return, and will build again the tabernacle of David, which is fallen down; and I will build again the ruins thereof, and I will set it up." The rebuilding of *wastes* and *desolations* is thus linked to the church's activity in expanding its outreach and bringing the gospel to others. That rebuilding still goes on—through the faithful witness of today's "trees of righteousness."

III. The Coming Joy
(Isaiah 61:10, 11)
A. Like New Garments (v. 10)

10. I will greatly rejoice in the LORD, my soul shall be joyful in my God; for he hath clothed me with the garments of salvation, he hath covered me with the robe of righteousness, as a bridegroom decketh himself with ornaments, and as a bride adorneth herself with her jewels.

Here Isaiah again utilizes poetic imagery to describe what the Lord has done for His people. To be *clothed . . . with the garments of salvation* and *covered . . . with the robe of righteousness* is His answer to our "filthy rags" (Isaiah 64:6). To have access to such a wardrobe should bring true joy to those who avail themselves of this privilege. [See question #5, page 168.]

WEDDING WARDROBES

One of the items most noticed at a wedding ceremony is the attire of those in the wedding party, particularly the bride. Many in our culture today still follow the old rule that a bride must wear "something old, something new, something borrowed, something blue." With the passing of the years, the garments considered suitable for a wedding often change; and they change in different cultures. In the Western world the bride often wears white. In Pakistan the bride wears red. And if you have attended a wedding recently, you know that there can be considerable variety in the garments of the bridegroom as well.

It is not surprising that wedding customs should be an illustration of salvation. The church is the bride of Christ (Ephesians 5:25-27; Revelation 21:2, 9). Christians are preparing for the coming "marriage supper of the Lamb" (Revelation 19:9) that will forever unite them with their Lord. We cannot be prepared for this occasion as we are: our "righteousnesses," says Isaiah, "are as filthy rags" (Isaiah 64:6). We must be clothed with "garments of salvation" and covered by the "robe of righteousness." And only God can provide that "wardrobe." There is no room for change or variety; to try to enter His presence with any other attire than what He supplies is to assure ourselves of a place in "outer darkness" (Matthew 22:11-14).   —R. C. S.

B. Like New Growth (v. 11)

11. For as the earth bringeth forth her bud, and as the garden causeth the things that are sown in it to spring forth; so the Lord GOD will cause righteousness and praise to spring forth before all the nations.

Finally, the prophet depicts the world-wide acceptance of the "good tidings" brought by the Messiah. Using the imagery of seeds *sown* in a *garden*, he describes the impact of Jesus' Great Commission (Acts 1:8)—that through the faithful efforts of the church, *all the nations* will hear and respond to the gospel. Isaiah's words continue to be fulfilled to this day as thousands of new Christians are born into the family of God.

Home Daily Bible Readings

Monday, Dec. 31—Messianic Mission (Luke 4:14-21)
Tuesday, Jan. 1—God's People Will Prosper (Isaiah 60:4-9)
Wednesday, Jan. 2—Nation's Gates Will Stay Open (Isaiah 60:10-14)
Thursday, Jan. 3—God Will Be Your Light (Isaiah 60:15-22)
Friday, Jan. 4—Anointed to Bring Good News (Isaiah 61:1-7)
Saturday, Jan. 5—Righteousness Before All Nations (Isaiah 61:8-11)
Sunday, Jan. 6—Worshipers From Afar (Matthew 2:1-12)

Conclusion

Prophecy in the Bible can be, in some respects, like looking into the heavens—first with the naked eye, then with a pair of binoculars, and finally with an extremely powerful telescope. At each level new and thrilling sights expand our knowledge and fire our imagination. In much the same way, in today's lesson three "horizons" are telescoped: the new Israel returning from exile, the messianic community (the church), and the yet-to-be realized eternal fellowship of all believers in Heaven.

A. Good News for Exiles

Isaiah delivered a message of hope. The first people to find that hope were that portion of God's people who endured the bitterness of the Babylonian captivity. Isaiah's message let them know that God had not forsaken them. God's concern was not limited by national boundaries; He cared for His people just as much when they were in Babylon as when they were in Jerusalem. But they must "seek . . . the Lord while he may be found" (Isaiah 55:6).

B. Good News for Jesus' Disciples

Like Isaiah, Jesus also spoke a message of hope and deliverance. That is what He was doing in the Nazareth synagogue when He quoted from Isaiah 61. And when the residents there rejected Him, He was not deterred; He simply spoke elsewhere (Luke 4:43, 44). But Jesus not only spoke the good news, He was and still is the good news. He is still "the way, the truth, and the life" (John 14:6).

C. Good News for Us

As Christians we are living in the messianic age, although not in the fullest form of it. What that fullest form will be, "eye hath not seen, nor ear heard, neither have entered into the heart of man, the things which God hath prepared for them that love him" (1 Corinthians 2:9; cf. Isaiah 64:4). In this life, we experience only a foretaste of what God has in store for believers. We wait expectantly for Heaven and, in the meantime, we testify of our good news to as many as we can.

D. Prayer

Father, as we learn more about Your plans for our future, we become more grateful and excited. Thank You for Jesus, our anointed One, who is preparing a place for us. Empower us to proclaim boldly His good news. In His name, amen.

E. Thought to Remember

Jesus is the Good News!

Learning by Doing

This page contains an alternate lesson plan emphasizing learning activities.
Classes desiring such student involvement will find these suggestions helpful.

Learning Goals

After participating in this lesson, each student will be able to:

1. List several of the blessings that the Lord's "anointed" brings to a world plagued by darkness.

2. Tell how this description also characterizes the mission of the church in the world today.

3. Give a specific example of how an individual or the church can carry out one of the tasks described in the text.

Into the Lesson

Early in the week ask a class member to prepare a brief report about "the Year of the Lord" (Isaiah 61:3) for Sunday's lesson. Give the student a Bible dictionary for the research.

Begin the lesson by having pairs solve the following puzzle. (Duplicate the puzzle below or refer students to the appropriate page in the student book.) Instructions should read, "The key verse of today's text is Isaiah 60:1. 'Arise, shine; for thy light is come, and the glory of the Lord is risen upon thee.' Remove the letters of that statement—in order—from the lines below. The remaining letters will reveal the key concept for today's lesson."

ARISGESOHINOEFDORTNHYLEIGW
HTISCOSMEAHNDTHAEGLSORYOF
THCELORODISRISEMNUPOENTHEE

(Answer: "Good news has come.")

After the students solve the puzzle, tell them that today's prophecy brought good news to the Israelites, brings good news to us, and promises good news for the future. Use the illustration of the naked eye/binoculars/powerful telescope from the conclusion of the lesson commentary (page 166) to illustrate this concept.

Into the Word

Give a brief lecture about the background for today's prophecy. Then read Isaiah 60:1-3. Explain that darkness probably was more significant and threatening to the ancients than to us, since we have so many sources of artificial light. To illustrate, turn out the lights and ask how we can proceed with the lesson. It's nearly impossible in some classrooms. Turn the lights back on, asking the class what the imagery of darkness implies in this text.

Give each pair of students the following chart. (Or refer the students to the appropriate page in their student book, *Adult Bible Class.*) Ask the students to read each prophecy printed and to place a check mark (✔) indicating how the prophecy would be fulfilled. Remind the class that a prophecy may have more than one fulfillment. This is an exercise that illustrates the "naked eye, binoculars, powerful telescope" concept.

The chart should have four columns. The first and largest column should be headed "Prophecy." The second should have the heading "Jews' Return From Captivity." Column 3 is "The Life of Jesus," and Column 4 is "Christ's Return." In column 1 write several prophecies from this text, such as:

"The Lord shall arise upon thee, and his glory shall be seen upon thee" (60:2).

"The Gentiles shall come to thy light, and kings to the brightness of thy rising" (60:3).

"The Lord hath anointed me to preach good tidings unto the meek" (61:1).

"He hath sent me to bind up the brokenhearted, to proclaim liberty to the captives, and the opening of the prison to them that are bound" (61:1).

"To proclaim the acceptable year of the Lord, and the day of vengeance of our God" (61:2).

"To comfort all that mourn" (61:2).

"They shall raise up the former desolations, and they shall repair the waste cities, the desolations of many generations" (61:4).

"He hath clothed me with the garments of salvation, he hath covered me with the robe of righteousness" (61:10).

After the list is completed, review each prophecy and ask how or why the groups applied it in the chart. When you get to the prophecy of "year of the Lord," ask the student who did the research to give his or her report.

Into Life

Write "Six functions of the Messiah" on the chalkboard. Ask the students to identify these functions from Isaiah 61:1-3 as you list them. Remind them that this list also gives direction for Christians and the church today. Ask, "What are ways the church or believers may carry out these tasks today?" Then ask, "In what ways is our church doing well in accomplishing these tasks? How does it need to do more? How can we help? Which of these tasks are you responsible for? How are you doing?"

Let's Talk It Over

The questions on this page are designed to encourage review of the lesson Scriptures and to promote discussion of the lesson by the class. The answers provided are only discussion starters. Let your class talk it over from there.

1. What are some different kinds of "darkness" that threaten the world today? Cite specific examples.

The lesson writer lists fear, turmoil, evil, ignorance, helplessness, selfishness, and pain. Your group may add to that list, or you may encourage them to get specific about each of these items. Take ignorance, for example. Ignorance about God or His Son because one does not know the Bible is a darkness like what Isaiah describes. Sometimes this ignorance is imposed on people, such as those who live in countries controlled by atheistic, authoritarian governments or those dominated by the proponents of a false religion. Have your learners expand on the other features in similar fashion.

2. Identify some ways the church can be a source of light in this world of darkness.

You might want to look again at the list of kinds of darkness (from the first discussion question) and talk about ways of bringing light to each situation. Ignorance, for example, can be eliminated by preaching the gospel. In addition to local preaching, the church can support missionaries who will take the light of the gospel to the ends of the earth. Additionally, the church can be a light to the world when its members demonstrate Christ-like love for one another and when they exhibit a moral lifestyle, renouncing sin and upholding Biblical standards of conduct. They can spread light at PTA meetings, in Girl Scout or Boy Scout troops, at the polls, and in many other places.

3. Jesus appropriated Isaiah 61:1 to Himself to describe His ministry (Luke 4:18). To what extent, if at all, do you think it describes the church's ministry? How can we apply this to ourselves?

Certainly preaching good tidings is important to the church, and has been since the beginning. This role must not be minimized to cater to an entertainment-saturated culture. While new methods need to be utilized, the basic concept of preaching the gospel must remain central. In fact, all these features find ultimate fulfillment in the gospel: proclaiming liberty and opening the prison both refer to a declaration of freedom from sin in Christ. Binding up the brokenhearted is a reference to the joy and hope that come to restore the heart of one who accepts the gospel. While some social and physical aspects might be applied from this passage, even as Jesus ministered to physical and social needs, our central mission, like Jesus', is to seek and to save the lost.

4. What does the connection between the Old Testament concept of the Jubilee year ("the acceptable year of the Lord") and the ministry of Christ and the church suggest to you about what the church should be and do?

The Jubilee year was a time of release and restoration (Leviticus 25). Among other things, in that year, all bondservants were to be released from their debt to return to their families. The poor who were forced to sell their land were to have the land restored to them. In the New Testament, Jesus is said to have redeemed us, or bought us back, from the curse of the Law, the debt we owed to God for our sin but were unable to pay (Galatians 3:13). In addition, the evangelistic work of the New Testament church is depicted as a restitution or restoration of all things (Acts 3:21). That is, the preaching of the gospel was to be a major part of God's program to restore the world to the way it was before man sinned.

5. Isaiah compares his relationship to God with that of a bride being adorned with jewels (61:10). Similarly, the New Testament likens the church to a bride. What practical application of that analogy can you suggest for us today?

In his letter to the Ephesians, the apostle Paul suggests several points of similarity between the church and a bride and between Christ and a bridegroom. First, he says that Christ has authority over the church, as a husband has authority over his wife (5:23). Christians need to remember that Christ, not any mere mortal, is the head of the church. His Word should be the highest authority for God's people. Second, the church is to be as pure and spotless as a bride at her wedding (5:27). Finally, Christ has promised to provide for the church as a husband does for his wife (5:29). We need to remember that we can depend on Christ to provide for all our spiritual needs. He has given us His Word and the Holy Spirit to help us live holy lives.

Seek the Lord

DEVOTIONAL READING: Psalm 85:4-9.

BACKGROUND SCRIPTURE: Isaiah 55.

PRINTED TEXT: Isaiah 55:1-9.

Isaiah 55:1-9

1 Ho, every one that thirsteth, come ye to the waters, and he that hath no money; come ye, buy, and eat; yea, come, buy wine and milk without money and without price.

2 Wherefore do ye spend money for that which is not bread? and your labor for that which satisfieth not? hearken diligently unto me, and eat ye that which is good, and let your soul delight itself in fatness.

3 Incline your ear, and come unto me: hear, and your soul shall live; and I will make an everlasting covenant with you, even the sure mercies of David.

4 Behold, I have given him for a witness to the people, a leader and commander to the people.

5 Behold, thou shalt call a nation that thou knowest not, and nations that knew not thee shall run unto thee because of the LORD thy God, and for the Holy One of Israel; for he hath glorified thee.

6 Seek ye the LORD while he may be found, call ye upon him while he is near:

7 Let the wicked forsake his way, and the unrighteous man his thoughts: and let him return unto the LORD, and he will have mercy upon him; and to our God, for he will abundantly pardon.

8 For my thoughts are not your thoughts, neither are your ways my ways, saith the LORD.

9 For as the heavens are higher than the earth, so are my ways higher than your ways, and my thoughts than your thoughts.

GOLDEN TEXT: Seek ye the LORD while he may be found, call ye upon him while he is near.—Isaiah 55:6.

Lesson Aims

After participating in this lesson, each student will be able to:

1. Summarize the invitation of Isaiah 55 and the blessings promised to those who respond.

2. Contrast those things that truly satisfy with the poor substitutes people too often crave and acquire.

3. Commit himself or herself to answering God's invitation at whatever level is needed in his or her life.

Lesson Outline

INTRODUCTION
    A. Priorities and Prosperity
    B. Lesson Background
  I. BECOMING SATISFIED (Isaiah 55:1, 2)
    A. God's Gracious Offer (v. 1)
    B. Man's Futile Efforts (v. 2)
      Thirst
  II. ENTERING A COVENANT (Isaiah 55:3-5)
    A. An Everlasting Covenant (v. 3)
    B. A Special Individual (v. 4)
    C. A Worldwide Appeal (v. 5)
III. SEEKING GOD (Isaiah 55:6-9)
    A. His Nearness (v. 6)
    B. His Demands (v. 7)
      Pardon Me
    C. His Ways (vv. 8, 9)
CONCLUSION
    A. The Everlasting Covenant
    B. The Living Water
    C. Prayer
    D. Thought to Remember

Introduction

A. Priorities and Prosperity

The boat salesman loved this customer! Every year the customer would stop by the salesman's showroom because he always wanted to buy the newest gadget or piece of equipment. These innovations intrigued the man for about a month or so; then he began to search the catalogs and to think about what his next purchase ought to be. It seemed that nothing—not the latest instruments, the biggest motor, the brightest paint, or the sleekest design—could satisfy him for very long.

If only this man could have stepped back for a moment and taken a good look at himself! His passion for boat buying reflected how unfulfilled his life had become. His zeal for new boats reflected his ambition for other new items—a new house, a new car, new sports "toys," new lawn equipment, new clothing, and eventually (and most tragic of all) a new wife. But what were his real needs? What was he really longing for? Why had his life become so empty? And why did it seem to be getting emptier in spite of his efforts to fill it with more "things"?

Rather than recognizing that their deepest needs are spiritual, many people prefer to act like hummingbirds, who flit from flower to flower to satisfy their insatiable appetites. These spiritually empty people go from boat to boat, partner to partner, in search of fulfillment. But all too quickly their infatuation with newness wears off and the excitement of novelty dissolves into dullness. Many a parent has been annoyed by a child who spent thirty-five dollars for a popular T-shirt that faded after the first wash and soon ended up in the rag box. Yet many parents act like such children; they simply do so on a larger scale.

Some people view life through a very narrow lens. They conclude that their highest priority is to experience all that this life "under the sun" has to offer—even if their experience is short-lived. Sadly, these individuals rarely discover true satisfaction and happiness. Their lives become as shallow as that of the customer in the boat showroom.

Not until we learn to look at life through the broad lens of faith will our view become clear. Only then will we set priorities that replace a feeling of frustration and futility with a genuine sense of fulfillment.

B. Lesson Background

The prophet Isaiah began his ministry to Judah in about 740 B.C.—"the year that king Uzziah died" (Isaiah 6:1). The first half of the eighth century B.C. had been extremely prosperous for both Israel and Judah. To put the situation in today's terms, the national economy was strong, housing starts were up, chariot sales were at an all-time high—in short, the gross national product was higher than at any time since David and Solomon's golden age (2 Chronicles 26:1-15).

But beneath the external affluence, Isaiah's prophetic insight saw spiritual problems in Judah that the material prosperity only disguised. Surveying the moral and spiritual landscape, he observed fragmented families, corrupt business practices, political kickbacks, and faithless religious leaders. And what Isaiah found among the wealthy citizens he saw among the rest of the population as well. All were caught up in the delusion that a person's life consists in the abundance of the things that he possesses (cf. Luke 12:15). Such thinking is quite prevalent in our materialistic age, which makes Isaiah's message as timely for us as it was for his original hearers.

I. Becoming Satisfied (Isaiah 55:1, 2)

We have noted that Isaiah 40-66 was written from the perspective of addressing Jewish captives in Babylon and comforting them with the assurance that they would one day return home. But there are portions of these chapters that extend the Lord's appeal beyond Israel to include the entire world. "Look unto me, and be ye saved, all the ends of the earth: for I am God, and there is none else," declares the prophet (Isaiah 45:22). In previous studies we have examined passages from Isaiah that indicate God's desire for the Gentiles to hear His truth and be blessed by His light (Isaiah 42:1, 6; 49:6; 60:3). That emphasis appears in today's text as well, beginning with an invitation to "every one that thirsteth."

A. God's Gracious Offer (v. 1)

1. Ho, every one that thirsteth, come ye to the waters, and he that hath no money; come ye, buy, and eat; yea, come, buy wine and milk without money and without price.

Isaiah represents the essentials of a contented life using the symbols of *waters*, *wine*, and *milk*. A similar "trinity of drinks" is used in Joel 3:18 to describe future blessings promised to Judah. Bible writers sometimes express completeness or totality by using groups of three. For example, the stranger, the fatherless, and the widow represent helpless people (Deuteronomy 14:29; Psalm 94:6; Jeremiah 7:6); sword, famine, and pestilence stand for disaster (Jeremiah 29:17; 32:24; Ezekiel 6:11); and wear sackcloth, lament, and howl are ways to express grief (Jeremiah 4:8; Joel 1:13).

Notice that Isaiah invites *every one* to obtain what he offers without paying. All who thirst for happiness, contentment, and satisfaction can have them *without money and without price*. In God's sight, poverty is not a handicap and wealth is not an advantage. All the wealth in the world cannot buy God's favor. In fact, it must be accepted as a gift or not at all.

B. Man's Futile Efforts (v. 2)

2. Wherefore do ye spend money for that which is not bread? and your labor for that which satisfieth not? hearken diligently unto me, and eat ye that which is good, and let your soul delight itself in fatness.

Given the fact that contentment in life is free, Isaiah marvels that people *labor* so hard *for that which satisfieth not*. Genuine satisfaction and fulfillment in life come not by laboring but by listening. They come only to those who *hearken diligently* to what God says. [See question #1, page 176.]

The phrase *let your soul delight itself in fatness* means to give yourself to what can really please you. Of course, in today's health-conscious culture *fatness* has lost the meaning it had for the ancient Israelites. In Hebrew thinking fatness was a synonym for festivity, joy, and prosperity (Psalm 92:13, 14; Jeremiah 31:14). These are the spiritual blessings that come when we hear and obey the Word of God and find the "bread of life" available only in Jesus (John 6:35, 68).

THIRST

We can better appreciate Isaiah's invitation to "every one that thirsteth" if we consider the land in which he lived. Palestine always has been characterized by a scarcity of water. Most of the rivers there are small and have little if any water during the summer. As a result, rain becomes particularly critical; and in the dry summers, any vegetation is dependent on the heavy dews for moisture. Irrigation is practiced where necessary. Thus Isaiah's hearers knew how dangerous—how deadly—thirst could be. Most of us, who can obtain water simply at the turn of a tap, have not experienced that.

It is said that a person can live for sixty days without food, but only six days without water. In fact, the body is sixty percent water. For that reason, thirst is a good metaphor to picture a deep spiritual longing or need. Jesus used the same language in His Sermon on the Mount: "Blessed are they which do hunger and thirst

Home Daily Bible Readings

Monday, Jan. 7—I Sought; the Lord Answered (Psalm 34:1-10)

Tuesday, Jan. 8—My Soul Thirsts for God (Psalm 63:1-8)

Wednesday, Jan. 9—Seek the Lord's Strength (Psalm 105:1-7)

Thursday, Jan. 10—The Holy One Redeems You (Isaiah 54:4-8)

Friday, Jan. 11—Heritage of the Lord's Servants (Isaiah 54:9-17)

Saturday, Jan. 12—Accept the Lord's Free Grace (Isaiah 55:1-5)

Sunday, Jan. 13—Return to the Lord (Isaiah 55:6-13)

after righteousness: for they shall be filled" (Matthew 5:6).

When you are really thirsty, only water will truly satisfy your thirst. You can drink coffee, tea, or soft drinks, but nothing quenches thirst like water. Just as the body must have water to live, so the soul must receive the kind of water offered by Isaiah in his great invitation. We are spiritual beings. We need to acknowledge our spiritual thirst—a thirst for God—and recognize that He has supplied what is needed to satisfy it. How tragic that many try to satisfy a longing for God without God's gracious provisions!—R. C. S.

II. Entering a Covenant
(Isaiah 55:3-5)

Isaiah goes on to specify the "good" that God has in store for those who will heed His voice.

A. An Everlasting Covenant (v. 3)

3. Incline your ear, and come unto me: hear, and your soul shall live; and I will make an everlasting covenant with you, even the sure mercies of David.

A *covenant* is an agreement or contract. God had made a covenant with Israel at Mount Sinai (Exodus 19:5, 6). This covenant was meant to govern the lives of God's people, though frequently it had been disregarded in the past and was largely ignored in Isaiah's time. Centuries after this covenant, God made a covenant with an individual—*David*, whom God declared to be "a man after his own heart" (1 Samuel 13:14). He promised that David's kingdom would be established forever and that David's house would rule forever (2 Samuel 7:12-29). This covenant with David was to be the basis for a "new covenant" with God's people (Jeremiah 31:31). This covenant would not be like the old one, written on stone, but would be written on the people's hearts (Jeremiah 31:33).

Other prophets called attention to the importance of this covenant with David and its *everlasting* nature. Jeremiah, who predicted the downfall of Jerusalem and then saw that sad event come to pass, nevertheless preached that God's covenant with David was as unchangeable as the laws of nature (Jeremiah 33:20-22). Ezekiel predicted the day when God's people would be established in their land with David as their king, shepherd, and prince (Ezekiel 37:24-28). It is clear from the New Testament that Jesus, the Son of David, came to fulfill the words of the prophets and to receive "the throne of his father David" (Luke 1:32). Of special note is the fact that Isaiah's words in the verse before us are quoted by Paul in Acts 13:34, where the *sure*

mercies of David are linked with the resurrection of Jesus. Christians are the beneficiaries of the everlasting covenant—the New Covenant—by which sins are forgiven and forgotten (cf. Hebrews 8:6-13). [See question #2, page 176.]

B. A Special Individual (v. 4)

4. Behold, I have given him for a witness to the people, a leader and commander to the people.

It would appear that the pronoun *him* in this verse must refer to David, mentioned in verse 3. Certainly David fulfilled the roles of *witness*, *leader*, and *commander* listed here. However, given the role of David in prophecy (see the comments under the previous verse), these words are most likely describing Jesus, the King who was to inherit David's throne. Jesus is God's witness to the world (John 18:37). As King of kings and Lord of lords (Revelation 17:14; 19:16), He is the supreme leader and commander. The prophets looked back to David and saw the future Messiah. The apostles looked back to David and declared that the Messiah had come—in Jesus.

C. A Worldwide Appeal (v. 5)

5. Behold, thou shalt call a nation that thou knowest not, and nations that knew not thee shall run unto thee, because of the LORD thy God, and for the Holy One of Israel; for he hath glorified thee.

This verse raises a question about another pronoun, *thou*, and to whom it refers. One possibility is that it describes Israel. The first Christians were Jews (Israelites), and from them the gospel went forth to other *nations*—a scene vividly depicted in Isaiah 2:2-4. But these nations would not be attracted to Israel; they would be drawn to *the Holy One of Israel*. He *glorified* Israel by sending Jesus as part of that nation and giving its people the honor of heralding the good news of salvation to other nations.

On the other hand, *thou* may refer to Jesus, who has issued a *call* to all nations to come to God through Him (Matthew 28:19, 20; John 14:6). Certainly God glorified Jesus by raising Him from the dead and giving Him a place at His right hand. Either way, the focus is on Jesus as the One through whom the nations come to know the Lord. He thus becomes, not only the Holy One of Israel, but the Holy One of all peoples.

III. Seeking God
(Isaiah 55:6-9)

The parables in Luke 15 picture two sides of what it means to seek God. The parables of the lost sheep and the lost coin (vv. 3-10) picture God seeking a sinner. The parable of the prodigal son (vv. 11-24) pictures the sinner seeking God. The lost son was not found until he said, "I will arise and go to my father." Then he took action: "he arose, and came to his father." No sinner is saved against his will; there must be a mutual seeking. The final section of our text tells us what is involved in seeking the Lord.

A. His Nearness (v. 6)

6. Seek ye the LORD while he may be found, call ye upon him while he is near.

The words *while he may be found* and *while he is near* carry with them a solemn warning. A time will come when the Lord will not be found—when it will be too late to seek Him. Such was the sad plight of the foolish virgins described in Jesus' parable (Matthew 25:11, 12). The Bible also describes instances where God "gives up" or "gives over" individuals to their sinful behavior (Romans 1:24, 26, 28). In spiritual matters, to delay or hesitate is to invite certain peril. The Scripture is clear: "Behold, now is the accepted time; behold, now is the day of salvation" (2 Corinthians 6:2). [See question #3, page 176.]

B. His Demands (v. 7)

7. Let the wicked forsake his way, and the unrighteous man his thoughts: and let him return unto the LORD, and he will have mercy upon him; and to our God, for he will abundantly pardon.

While salvation is free (v. 1), it does require repentance. The *wicked* must *forsake his way;* the one who desires God's *mercy* must sever ties with the world and its pleasures and leave his sinful lifestyle behind. Further, repentance must go deeper than mere actions and words: even sinful *thoughts* must become a thing of the past (cf. Matthew 5:28). In short, the individual must change the direction of his life and *return unto the Lord.* Then, as He did with the people of Nineveh in Jonah's day (Jonah 3:10), God *will have mercy* and *will abundantly pardon* those who give evidence of such repentance. [See question #4, page 176.]

PARDON ME

It has been said that the English language has more words than any other language on earth. (Some have estimated that there are around two million of them.) Yet, in spite of this remarkable number, many words can have more than one meaning. Such is the case with the word *pardon.* At the lower end of the scale, it means that an individual wants to be excused from some harmless discourtesy or minor infraction of the rules of decorum. After committing such an act, the

Visual for lessons 7 and 8. *Display this poster when you begin to discuss verse 6 of the text. Leave it up for next week, too.*

individual will say, "Pardon me." At the opposite end of the scale, the word means that someone is granted a reprieve from punishment for a serious crime against the laws of the state or nation.

As *pardon* is used in today's lesson (Isaiah 55:7), it is on the high end of the scale. It does not describe being excused from a harmless mistake done accidentally. It means being forgiven for serious and deliberate acts of disobedience against the laws of Heaven.

We know from experience that only a high official (the governor, the president, or the prime minister, for example) can issue a pardon. In the spiritual realm, the same is true: only God can pardon us of our sins. No one else can do it. In the situations we hear or read about, a pardon is usually issued because of some extenuating circumstances on the part of the offender. But that is not the case with spiritual pardon. It is issued solely because of grace on God's part; it is in no way linked to whether our circumstances mean that we somehow merit His forgiveness. We do not.

Augustus M. Toplady says it well in the beautiful hymn, "Rock of Ages":

> Could my zeal no respite know,
>   Could my tears forever flow,
> All for sin could not atone;
>   Thou must save, and Thou alone.
> Nothing in my hand I bring,
>   Simply to Thy cross I cling.

—R. C. S

C. His Ways (vv. 8, 9)

8, 9. For my thoughts are not your thoughts, neither are your ways my ways, saith the LORD. For as the heavens are higher than the earth, so are my ways higher than your ways, and my thoughts than your thoughts.

The word *for* should cause us to link this verse with the preceding one and to examine our thoughts and our ways. Too often they are not what God would have them to be. Like Jonah (Jonah 4), perhaps we are unmerciful and unwilling to pardon when God is. Perhaps we resemble the elder brother in Jesus' parable of the prodigal son—sour and bitter when we should be celebrating (Luke 15:25-32).

Isaiah's description of God in this passage is in line with others that we have observed previously in our study of Isaiah (40:28-31; 42:5). He is all-powerful, all-knowing, all-present, all in all. Is that the kind of God we worship and serve? Or is our view of God too limited? Have we allowed circumstances to dictate the size of our faith and to dim our vision of God's majesty and power?

On a recent preaching tour, I stayed in the home of some faithful church members. In the bedroom was a beautiful aquarium complete with ceramic castle, seaweed, colored gravel, aerator, and a happy little goldfish named Biff. Biff simply swam around his glass-encased world, totally ignorant of the greater reality beyond his experiences. He knew nothing of the music playing on the radio, nothing of the high-powered, fuel-injected pickup truck in the driveway, nothing of the angel food cake baking in the oven, nothing of the algebra that one of the boys was studying nearby. In fact, Biff knew almost nothing about anything. His experiences were limited to his own little ceramic castle, the wavy seaweed, and the bubbles from the aerator.

Humbling though it may be to us, we are, in a way, like Biff. We are in our own little world, limited by our physical experiences and unable to grasp the greater spiritual reality that lies beyond our senses. Unlike Biff, we are created in the image of God and are thus able to receive the revelation of God that He has provided. (Without God's self-revelation we could not know Him.) He has spoken to us through the witness of His creation (Romans 1:18-20) and through the greater witness of His Son (Hebrews 1:1, 2). Yet how often do we spend our days focused on and preoccupied with only our immediate surroundings. We do not see the magnitude of God. He

has shown us what can give satisfaction in life: it is a relationship with Him! To seek contentment in life apart from seeking the Lord is only an exercise in futility. [See question #5, page 176.]

Conclusion

A. The Everlasting Covenant

Isaiah extended the Lord's offer of an "everlasting covenant" (Isaiah 55:3). Today every Christian lives under this New Covenant, through which sins are forgiven and forgotten (Hebrews 8:8-12). It is in that covenant, accepted in faith, that we find our ultimate contentment. Life on earth is filled with many good things, and we know that "every good gift and every perfect gift is from above" (James 1:17), but we must never be drawn away from the eternal good that comes when we seek God.

B. The Living Water

A good example of how Isaiah's invitation is fulfilled in Jesus Christ can be found in John 4, which records Jesus' conversation at Jacob's well with a Samaritan woman. Just as Isaiah calls "Ho, every one that thirsteth, come ye to the waters," so Jesus calls, "Whosoever drinketh of the water that I shall give him shall never thirst; but the water that I shall give him shall be in him a well of water springing up into everlasting life" (John 4:14). Jesus was and is the source of that living water. The Samaritan woman was able to fill her empty soul with that water, and it remains the spiritual thirst quencher for all who thirst today. In addition, those who will dwell with the Lord in the new Jerusalem have this promise: "I will give unto him that is athirst of the fountain of the water of life freely" (Revelation 21:6).

The book of Revelation concludes with this invitation, similar to Isaiah's: "Let him that is athirst come. And whosoever will, let him take the water of life freely" (Revelation 22:17). Come and drink!

C. Prayer

Father, every time we drink deeply of Your "living water," we find honest satisfaction in life. We find a contentment and a fulfillment greater than anything the world can and offer. Thank You that Your "fountain of youth" never runs dry. May we drink deeply, and may we constantly seek to lead others to drink as well. In Jesus' name, amen.

D. Thought to Remember

No God, no peace;
Know God, know peace.

How to Say It

BABYLON. *Bab*-uh-lun.
EZEKIEL. Ee-*zeek*-yul or Ee-*zeek*-ee-yul.
ISAIAH. Eye-*zay*-uh.
JEREMIAH. Jair-uh-*my*-uh.
NINEVEH. *Nin*-uh-vuh.
SAMARITAN. Suh-*mare*-uh-tun.
UZZIAH. Uh-*zye*-uh.

Learning by Doing

This page contains an alternate lesson plan emphasizing learning activities.
Classes desiring such student involvement will find these suggestions helpful.

Learning Goals

After this lesson each student will be able to:

1. Summarize the invitation of Isaiah 55 and the blessings promised to those who respond.

2. Compare those things that truly satisfy with the substitutes people often crave and acquire.

3. Commit himself or herself to answering God's invitation at whatever level is needed in his or her life.

Into the Lesson

Before class prepare two posters. One should resemble the popular bumper sticker: "No God, no peace. Know God, know peace!"

On the second poster have the following three sentences: "I wanted one very much, so I . . ."; "I know it was too expensive, but I bought it anyway"; "I was honored to be recognized for. . . ."

Begin this lesson by asking each class member to find a partner (other than his or her own spouse). Ask each person to begin with one of the above sentences to tell his or her partner about a personal experience. Allow a few minutes; then ask volunteers to tell about their partners' experiences. Take about five minutes for these reports. Then remind the class that people always seem to be looking for satisfaction and fulfillment in life. Unfortunately, real contentment usually does not come through accumulating possessions, power, or recognition. Point to the "Know God" poster saying, "This bumper sticker gets to the heart of today's Bible lesson."

Into the Word

Use the introduction and historical background in the lesson commentary (page 170) to set the scene for this Bible study. Then choose some or all of the following activities.

Dramatization. Early in the week ask three persons to be ready to dramatize the encounter of a Samaritan woman with Jesus (John 4:1-18, 25, 26). The characters needed include a narrator, Jesus, and the woman. The team may feel free to paraphrase all or part of the text and to insert some of the problems with this encounter (such as a Jew talking to a Samaritan—and a woman, at that). After the drama, highlight the dialogue about the water that completely satisfies. Use this as an introduction to Isaiah 55:1.

Bible Paraphrase. Write the following Scripture references on a chalkboard: Isaiah 55:1, 2; Isaiah 55:3-5; Isaiah 55:6; Isaiah 55:7; Isaiah 55:8, 9. In pairs or small teams class members should write a one- or two-sentence paraphrase or interpretation of each section of Scripture. After a few minutes, allow groups to report. If you have too many groups to hear all the reports, choose a representative group for each passage. Other groups can add to each reporting group's insights.

Question Clusters. This activity may be done with the entire class or in small groups. Ask the following clusters of questions. Each cluster develops a certain theme.

Cluster #1. What teaching of Jesus does verse 1 bring to your mind? What was the circumstance or setting for Jesus' teaching? What is the application or interpretation of this teaching?

Cluster #2. Answer the question in verse 2. Why do people do this? Illustrate this foolishness. What is the lesson for Christians today?

Cluster #3. How would you interpret or apply the imperative in verse 6? What does Isaiah mean when he says "while he may be found" and "while he is near"? What does it mean to "seek the Lord"?

Cluster #4. What is the point of verses 8 and 9? What is God saying about His character? About finding satisfaction in life? About establishing life goals? How do these verses answer the question of verse 2?

Into Life

Make two columns on the chalkboard. Write over the first column "Unsatisfying Priorities." Ask the class to give practical illustrations of things people crave or pursue to find satisfaction—pursuits that do not fulfill our deepest yearnings. Write their ideas on the list. After that exercise, write "Seek the Lord—Practical Steps" over the second column. Ask learners to scan today's text, looking for clues on how to accomplish this task, and then brainstorm other practical steps to accomplish this goal.

Ask the class to share examples, good and bad, of these three Scriptures: (1) "Every one that thirsteth, come ye to the waters" (55:1). (2) "Wherefore do ye spend money for that which is not bread?" (3) "Seek ye the Lord." This exercise is in the student book, *Adult Bible Class*.

In small groups, each person who is willing is to offer a personal prayer, making a commitment to keep focused on "seeking the Lord."

Let's Talk It Over

The questions on this page are designed to encourage review of the lesson Scriptures and to promote discussion of the lesson by the class. The answers provided are only discussion starters. Let your class talk it over from there.

1. "Wherefore do ye spend . . . your labor for that which satisfieth not?" For what things does the average person today labor? Why do these things not satisfy one's true need?

Many people work hard to acquire such things as a nice home, financial security, travel, a good education, good health, and long life. None of these, by themselves, is capable of making us happy. A long life without a purpose for living is simply a meaningless existence. A nice home without a loving family is just real estate. Financial security without Christ gives no peace of mind. And every one of these things is temporal. Contentment comes not from temporal things, but from that which is eternal. Focusing on eternity gives purpose to acquiring temporal things.

2. The promise of a new "covenant" and the "sure mercies of David" must have held great appeal to the Jews who had lived in exile. How can we today make the gospel message appealing to people who are not dissatisfied with the circumstances of their lives?

We can focus on the long term. What does an unbeliever look forward to *after* death? Is there an alternative to nonexistence? We can offer the unbeliever an intellectual gamble. Can the unbeliever disprove the beliefs of Christianity? Can he prove that God does not exist or that Christ is dead? Many have come to Christ by trying to disprove Christianity! Finally, there is "Pascal's wager." The French mathematician Blaise Pascal (1623-1662) reasoned that if a person followed Christ and lived a Christian life, he would lose nothing important in this life if his belief were false, and he would gain eternal happiness if his belief were true. But if an unbeliever were right about Christianity, he would gain nothing important in this life, and if he were wrong, he would lose everything in the next. Thus, Pascal concluded, logic favors the Christian faith.

3. The lesson writer tells how important it is for the unbeliever to seek the Lord. In what sense do you think the believer also needs to submit to Isaiah's command, "Seek ye the Lord while he may be found"?

The idea is not to seek someone who is hidden. Rather, the idea is to commit oneself completely, without reservation, to following God and living for Him while there is opportunity. Solomon counseled us to remember our Creator while we are young (Ecclesiastes 12:1), because old age will harden our hearts. Jesus commanded us to "seek . . . first the kingdom of God, and his righteousness" (Matthew 6:33). That is a continual "seeking" and putting God first in our lives.

4. Do you think unbelievers today think of themselves as "wicked"? Why or why not? How can we help people see the need to apply the message of Isaiah 55:7 to themselves?

Our "tolerant" society sees almost nothing as "wicked" today—except the notion that anyone might be said to be so! But we are not likely to convince anyone with clever arguments or reasoned debate. We need to admit that we, too, are "wicked" without Christ, for "all have sinned" (Romans 3:23). We need to tell how we have forsaken our own way to accept God's way, the way of grace. As long as we speak of the "wicked" as someone other than ourselves, we will be seen as bigots. But when we appeal to unbelievers as fellow sinners, we just might get a hearing.

5. How can we relate to a God Who is infinitely greater than we are in every way?

There is no way we can know everything about God. His existence is beyond our ability to comprehend (1 Timothy 6:16; Isaiah 55:8, 9). However, God has acted in two significant ways to bridge this knowledge gap. While we cannot understand Him completely, we are able to have some understanding of Him.

First, God has revealed His will to man through His prophets and apostles (2 Peter 1:17-21). This enables us to know something about God's nature and what He expects of us. So, for example, He tells us to "be holy; for I am holy" (Leviticus 11:44). Second, God has bridged the gap through the incarnation of Christ. Jesus repeatedly said that whoever has seen Him has seen the Father (John 14:9). Because Jesus lived among men, suffered as man suffers, and was tempted as man is tempted (Hebrews 4:15), He understands what it is to be human. Likewise, we can understand more about God because He lived among men. So when we pray and wonder whether God really understands our needs, we can be sure that He does indeed.

Worship in Truth

DEVOTIONAL READING: Isaiah 58:9b-14.

BACKGROUND SCRIPTURE: Isaiah 58.

PRINTED TEXT: Isaiah 58:1-9a.

Isaiah 58:1-9a

1 Cry aloud, spare not, lift up thy voice like a trumpet, and show my people their transgression, and the house of Jacob their sins.

2 Yet they seek me daily, and delight to know my ways, as a nation that did righteousness, and forsook not the ordinance of their God: they ask of me the ordinances of justice; they take delight in approaching to God.

3 Wherefore have we fasted, say they, and thou seest not? wherefore have we afflicted our soul, and thou takest no knowledge? Behold, in the day of your fast ye find pleasure, and exact all your labors.

4 Behold, ye fast for strife and debate, and to smite with the fist of wickedness: ye shall not fast as ye do this day, to make your voice to be heard on high.

5 Is it such a fast that I have chosen? a day for a man to afflict his soul? is it to bow down his head as a bulrush, and to spread sackcloth and ashes under him? wilt thou call this a fast, and an acceptable day to the LORD?

6 Is not this the fast that I have chosen? to loose the bands of wickedness, to undo the heavy burdens, and to let the oppressed go free, and that ye break every yoke?

7 Is it not to deal thy bread to the hungry, and that thou bring the poor that are cast out to thy house? when thou seest the naked, that thou cover him; and that thou hide not thyself from thine own flesh?

8 Then shall thy light break forth as the morning, and thine health shall spring forth speedily: and thy righteousness shall go before thee; the glory of the Lord shall be thy rearward.

9a Then shalt thou call, and the Lord shall answer; thou shalt cry, and he shall say, Here I am.

**Jan
20**

GOLDEN TEXT: Is not this the fast that I have chosen? to loose the bands of wickedness, to undo the heavy burdens, and to let the oppressed go free, and that ye break every yoke?—Isaiah 58:6.

Light for All People
Unit 2: The Response of God's People
(Lessons 6-9)

Lesson Aims

After this lesson students will be able to:
1. Tell the significant points Isaiah makes about the futility of empty worship.
2. Compare the useless worship of Isaiah's day with equally futile practices of some today.
3. Identify a specific way to practice a true fast and make a commitment to do it.

Lesson Outline

INTRODUCTION
  A. Facts About Fasting
  B. Lesson Background
 I. INEFFECTIVE WORSHIP (Isaiah 58:1-5)
  A. Command to Isaiah (v. 1)
  B. Indictment of the People (v. 2)
  C. The People's Questions (v. 3a)
  D. God's Response (vv. 3b-5)
 II. TRUE WORSHIP (Isaiah 58:6, 7)
  A. Fasting as Justice (v. 6)
  B. Fasting as Compassion (v. 7)
   Helps on Helping
III. RESULTS OF TRUE WORSHIP (Isaiah 58:8, 9a)
  A. With God's People (v. 8a)
  B. With God (vv. 8b, 9a)
   When God Says No
CONCLUSION
  A. Isaiah's Words and Jesus' Teaching
  B. Isaiah, Jesus, and Us
  C. Prayer
  D. Thought to Remember

Introduction

A. Facts About Fasting

Fasting usually is defined as going without food for the purposes of (1) seeking to draw closer to God; (2) seeking God's will in a particularly important matter; or (3) showing contrition and expressing a desire to repent of particular sin or sins. Fasting is one of many acts of worship and is intended to be a deeply spiritual exercise. According to the Bible, many individuals fasted, among them Moses (Exodus 34:28), David (2 Samuel 12:22), Ezra (Ezra 10:6), Daniel (Daniel 9:3, 4), Jesus (Matthew 4:2), and the leaders of the church in Antioch including Barnabas and Saul (Acts 13:1, 2).

In the law of Moses, fasting was prescribed only on the Day of Atonement (Leviticus 16:29, 31), though the practice was not limited to that one annual event. There are many occasions in which someone fasted as a response to specific circumstances or needs.

In some cases fasting was an expression of grief (1 Samuel 31:13; 2 Samuel 1:12; Nehemiah 1:4). In other instances it reflected individual and national repentance (1 Samuel 7:6; 1 Kings 21:27; Nehemiah 9:1, 2; Jonah 3:5-8). Note that 1 Kings 21:27 mentions the fasting of wicked King Ahab, and Jonah 3:5-8 describes how even the pagan Assyrians fasted in response to Jonah's message of divine judgment.

As with all forms of worship, fasting can be reduced to a mere outward performance, intended to impress others or to try to put God in one's debt. In that sense fasting runs the same risk as giving, singing special music, attending church and Sunday school regularly, having daily devotions, offering a Communion meditation, and participating in various other religious activities. In the Sermon on the Mount, Jesus warns us not to be like the "hypocrites," who "disfigure their faces, that they may appear unto men to fast" (Matthew 6:16). True fasting is a private act of worship, springing from a heart that desires to know God more fully.

B. Lesson Background

It is clear, not only from today's text but from other references in Isaiah (1:11-17; 43:22-24) that many of God's people in the prophet's day had lost sight of the true meaning of worship. Their attitude toward fasting was only one example. To them, the practice of abstaining from food for a particular time had degenerated into nothing more than a mindless ritual. No doubt some people actually believed that their observance of the ritual impressed God, as though He needed to see evidence of their self-abasement. What a total misunderstanding (and of a staggering arrogance) they demonstrated by performing such empty actions!

The real issue of our lesson text today is not the act of fasting. Isaiah mentions fasting in order to make the point that God's people really have no heart for Him and that their forms of worship have become mere outward expressions and evidence that love has grown cold. Thus, our lesson goes to "the heart of the matter" in worship: no religious expression has any validity unless the daily life of the worshiper is characterized by godliness. For Christians, this means that we must honor God *between* Sundays as well as *on* them. Otherwise, we cannot truly honor Him on Sundays.

I. Ineffective Worship
(Isaiah 58:1-5)
A. Command to Isaiah (v. 1)

1. Cry aloud, spare not, lift up thy voice like a trumpet, and show my people their transgression, and the house of Jacob their sins.

The first item mentioned in this passage is not the people's worship; it is their *sins* against God. Isaiah is commissioned to expose these sins, for they are the reason that the people's worship has become an abomination to God. The same indictment is applicable to anyone today who would try to "play church." [See question #1, page 184.]

B. Indictment of the People (v. 2)

2. Yet they seek me daily, and delight to know my ways, as a nation that did righteousness, and forsook not the ordinance of their God: they ask of me the ordinances of justice; they take delight in approaching to God.

Using satire, Isaiah describes his countrymen as people who appear to want above all else to *know* God. If we look beneath the satire, we can get an idea of what truly characterizes a spiritual person: one who seeks God *daily*, delights to *know* His *ways*, lives by the standards of *righteousness*, asks God concerning His ideas of *justice*; and takes *delight* in coming to Him. All of this is what God's people wanted to appear to be doing; however, their lives told a different story.

C. The People's Questions (v. 3a)

3a. Wherefore have we fasted, say they, and thou seest not? wherefore have we afflicted our soul, and thou takest no knowledge?

The people of Judah *fasted* and were regular in performing many other religious duties. They professed to be concerned about instruction from the Lord. They complained that God was not taking any note of them and they wanted to know why. Their words reflect their self-centered, "me first" approach to God. They assumed that doing God's will carried with it certain benefits and rewards. Where were those benefits and rewards? What good was all this piety doing them? [See question #2, page 184.]

D. God's Response (vv. 3b-5)

Through His prophet, the Lord probed the real motivation behind the people's fasting. To these careless worshipers, the day of fasting was just like any other day—a time to make a profit, a time to serve themselves. While going through the rigors of self-imposed hunger, they intended to manipulate God and to impress Him with their "spirituality" so that He would become their servant! Instead of reporting for duty, they

were giving orders to the One in charge! But the people's daily conduct—their lack of concern for the things that mattered to God—revealed that fasting was not a genuine act of worship for them.

3b. Behold, in the day of your fast ye find pleasure, and exact all your labors.

The *day* of fasting had become a day of *pleasure* for God's people—not with the aim of pleasing God, but with the aim of pleasing their own desires. Here they are accused of dishonesty in the workplace; the phrase *exact all your labors* describes the way in which workers were unfairly treated. The *New International Version* renders this portion of the verse as follows: "Yet on the day of your fasting, you do as you please and exploit all your workers."

4. Behold, ye fast for strife and debate, and to smite with the fist of wickedness: ye shall not fast as ye do this day, to make your voice to be heard on high.

Will God hear and heed the requests of those who abuse the sacredness of fasting as these people have? If they want to *make* their *voice to be heard on high*, they must change their entire approach to fasting (and to worship in general): *ye shall not fast as ye do this day.*

5. Is it such a fast that I have chosen? a day for a man to afflict his soul? is it to bow down his head as a bulrush, and to spread sackcloth and ashes under him? wilt thou call this a fast, and an acceptable day to the LORD?

Is it such a fast that I have chosen? The implied answer is *no*. What the people were doing had no meaning as an act of genuine worship. They were merely abstaining from food. A time of fasting is meant to be a time for a person to humble himself before the Lord and examine his life in order to discard whatever he finds that is

Visual for lessons 7 and 8. *The poster you used for last week's lesson will make an excellent illustration for today's lesson also.*

displeasing to the Lord. But God's people were engaging in meaningless motions that only appeared to indicate worship. *For a man* merely *to afflict his soul . . . to bow down his head as a bulrush* was not enough. The individual made his life uncomfortable and struck a pious pose, looking like a bulrush with its "head" bowed. The presence of *sackcloth and ashes* added to the impression of sorrow and repentance. But it was all a farce! [See question #3, page 184.]

Consistency—that is what God expects from His people. One's piety should be the same every day, whether the day is a sacred day or not. It is deceptive and dangerous to hold the position that certain days or actions are "sacred," while others are to be labeled as "secular" and therefore not subject to God's authority. All of our lives should belong to the Lord and should be lived under the direction of His standards. As Paul later stated, "Whatsoever ye do in word or deed, do all in the name of the Lord Jesus, giving thanks to God and the Father by him" (Colossians 3:17).

II. True Worship
(Isaiah 58:6, 7)

Isaiah could have illustrated true worship with actions other than fasting. We are more familiar with worship activities such as singing hymns, bowing our heads in prayer, reading the Scriptures, taking the Lord's Supper, giving an offering, and listening to a sermon. When we have gathered to participate in such activities, we say that we have attended a "worship service." But is this the "service" that God seeks from His people?

Fasting is part of what we might call personal worship—as opposed to corporate worship. It goes beyond the "worship service" to engage the believer in a daily worship experience. Added to that can be prayers, Scripture reading, and meditating on the Word. But Isaiah goes even further. He challenges God's people to see that true fasting (or true worship) includes joining the struggle for justice and being actively compassionate toward those in need. Having indicted the people for their hypocritical fasting, the prophet explains the kind of "fasting" that God really desires.

A. Fasting as Justice (v. 6)

6. Is not this the fast that I have chosen? to loose the bands of wickedness, to undo the heavy burdens, and to let the oppressed go free, and that ye break every yoke?

The people of Isaiah's day thought of fasting primarily in negative terms—not eating food or engaging in other actions that were part of one's daily routine. But according to Isaiah, fasting is associated with positive, specific actions that are done to bless and encourage others. True fasting (the kind *chosen* by God and pleasing to Him) is not an end in itself; it is a means to an end, and the end is to be seen through one's actions.

The right kind of fasting will *loose the bands of wickedness*. The word translated *wickedness* carries the idea of injustice. Certainly if I have been guilty of injustice myself, I must seek to correct the wrong and make amends if possible. But I also must do what I can to correct the injustice that I see around me and that I did not personally cause. *The oppressed* could be subject to various kinds of oppression—physical, economic, social, or spiritual. Wherever such a situation is encountered, one must take action to deal with it in a way that best uses his talents and abilities.

The point is that real worship—whether the act under consideration is fasting or something else—should develop within us a sensitivity to injustice and the desire to make a difference in Jesus' name. This does not mean that we embrace a brand of "social gospel." It simply means that if we do not show the kind of love and concern for the oppressed that Jesus did, whatever acts of worship we do will be in vain. We must see people as Jesus saw them if we want people to see Jesus in us. [See question #4, page 184.]

B. Fasting as Compassion (v. 7)

7. Is it not to deal thy bread to the hungry, and that thou bring the poor that are cast out to thy house? when thou seest the naked, that thou cover him; and that thou hide not thyself from thine own flesh?

A person who truly worships God is one who also has compassion on the needy and helpless. To go through religious exercises and then display a callous attitude toward the needs of hurting people is worthless. It is sheer hypocrisy.

Home Daily Bible Readings

Monday, Jan. 14—Worship in Spirit and Truth (John 4:19-26)

Tuesday, Jan. 15—Worship With Honor (Malachi 1:6-14)

Wednesday, Jan. 16—Worship in Righteousness (Amos 5:18-24)

Thursday, Jan. 17—Heritage for Those Without Heirs (Isaiah 56:1-5)

Friday, Jan. 18—Foreigners Can Share True Sabbath (Isaiah 56:6-8)

Saturday, Jan. 19—Not Too Late to Repent (Isaiah 57:14-21)

Sunday, Jan. 20—Truly Honoring the Sabbath (Isaiah 58:9b-14)

Here four groups of people are mentioned: *the hungry, the poor, the naked,* and *thine own flesh.* The last phrase may refer to one's own family or to humanity in general. For Christians, the message is similar to what Paul teaches in Galatians 6:10: "As we have therefore opportunity, let us do good unto all men, especially unto them who are of the household of faith."

Mere sympathy for the needy is not enough. Specific action must be taken: the hungry are to be fed, the poor are to be given refuge, and the naked are to be clothed. We cannot *hide* from our responsibility to care for others. Such teaching is similar to James's challenge to show our faith by our works. Simply wishing a needy person well without addressing the need is the response of one whose faith is dead (James 2:15-17). [See question #5, page 184.]

HELPS ON HELPING

True followers of Jesus should always want to share their blessings with those who have less than they. One minister, whose church was located on a busy highway, received frequent requests for help. If those seeking help were local residents, there was usually a positive response. Often, however, the requests came from people who claimed to be "just passing through town." Such individuals would often claim to be a member of that church in another town. In fact, some would visit every congregation in town, affirming at each stop that that church was the same kind of church they belonged to back home!

Naturally, the minister became a bit selective in how he extended the church's benevolence. He developed a policy that he explained with these words: "I help everyone who comes to me and asks for assistance. Some I help by saying, 'Yes,' and some I help by saying, 'No.'"

We would be naive if we responded to every request for help without considering the kind of help an individual really needs. On the other hand, we would be very cynical if we refused to help anyone, no matter what their circumstances. We need a balanced perspective. And, while common sense may dictate that we not help someone in a particular case, we should never refuse out of selfishness or from a hard heart.   —R. C. S.

III. Results of True Worship
(Isaiah 58:8, 9a)

What happens when a people worship in truth, when they fast with pure motivation, and when their spirituality leads them to stand for righteousness and to care for the defenseless? Isaiah describes such faithful worshipers, using the metaphor of a sunrise.

Once, while hiking in the High Sierras, I began my trek early one morning before the sun had come up. Walking in the wide shadows of the surrounding peaks, I celebrated a gorgeous sunrise. Overwhelmed by the beauty and warmth of the sight, I ran ahead, moving into the shadow of another peak so I could watch the sun rise again. In fact, before the hour had passed, I watched the sun come up over the mountain seven times—an entire week's worth of astounding beauty in one morning! That magnificence is the basis for Isaiah's description of people who truly worship: they are like the exploding light of a glorious sunrise.

A. With God's People (v. 8a)

8a. Then shall thy light break forth as the morning, and thine health shall spring forth speedily.

The Hebrew poetic technique of parallelism means that the concepts of *light* and *health* are to be understood as synonyms. The person who is spiritually whole (one who worships the Lord in truth) shines brilliantly for all to see. A godly person "beams" the presence of the Lord.

B. With God (vv. 8b, 9a)

8b. And thy righteousness shall go before thee; the glory of the LORD shall be thy rearward.

When God's people worship in truth (when they engage in true fasting), God blesses them. It is not that a person should try to manipulate God by performing religious acts. Trying to finagle blessings from God is a sure sign that one is *not* spiritual. God joyfully responds to His children who honestly worship Him, and the true worshiper of the Lord is rewarded by the wonder of His presence. A sense of awe and adoration raises such a one above trivialities.

Here the promise is that *thy righteousness shall go before thee.* This *righteousness* may describe the spiritual condition of the people once they have come to understand and practice true worship. However, Jeremiah refers to One called "the Lord our Righteousness" (Jeremiah 23:6; 33:16), obviously a messianic inference. So *thy righteousness* may instead (or also) refer to the presence of the Lord going before the people. This latter explanation matches the promise in the next phrase: *the glory of the Lord shall be thy rearward* (cf. Isaiah 52:12). The word *rearward* (in many editions of the *King James Bible* this is *rereward*) means "rear guard." (See Joshua 6:13.) God's people are thus surrounded by the Lord's protective presence. This promise looks forward to the righteousness and glory of the Lord provided through the coming of Jesus (Philippians 3:9; John 1:18).

9a. Then shalt thou call, and the LORD shall answer; thou shalt cry, and he shall say, Here I am.

We have noted that the people of Isaiah's day saw fasting (as well as other acts of worship) as a means of securing God's favor. Isaiah pictured them as fasting "to make your voice to be heard on high" (v. 4). But only when God's people begin to make His priorities and concerns their priorities and concerns will they have the assurance of His answer. Isaiah had responded to the Lord's call by saying, "Here am I" (Isaiah 6:8); now the Lord responds in a similar manner to the *cry* of His people.

WHEN GOD SAYS *NO*

Some years ago in a midwestern city, a small boy set fire to a church building. When he was caught, he gave this explanation: he had prayed for something but had not received it, so he decided to get even with God!

Most of us do not react to a *no* from God that radically, but sometimes we are disappointed by the results of our prayers. We call on God, and it seems to us that He does not answer. And yet, if we would keep careful records, we would discover that most of the time we do get what we pray for. What we tend to do is forget the times our prayers were answered and focus more on the times we were disappointed by prayer.

When we receive a *no* answer to prayer, it usually is of little help to be reminded that God always answers prayer, but sometimes He says *no*. We want to know *why* God says *no*. It may even seem to us that the requests that are refused are the ones most logical for God to grant. We must recognize that we are children of God, and that no father gives a child everything he asks for.

From 1954 to 1963 one of the most popular programs on television was *Father Knows Best*. The show's subject was an earthly father, but the truth in that title can be applied to the spiritual realm. We pray best when we come to God acknowledging that our *Father Knows Best*.   —R. C. S.

Conclusion

A. Isaiah's Words and Jesus' Teaching

When one reads Jesus' words in Matthew 6:1-18, it sounds as if our Lord is preaching Isaiah's message and teaching the same lesson to His contemporaries. Read especially Jesus' penetrating words in Matthew 6:16-18 on the subject of fasting. Both He and Isaiah declare fasting (or any form of worship) to be an intensely spiritual and personal matter. Both recognize fasting as a legitimate expression of worship; and while neither commands it, each appears to assume that some

---

How to Say It

AHAB. *Ay*-hab.
ANTIOCH. *An*-tee-ock.
ASSYRIANS. Uh-*sear*-ee-uns.
BARNABAS. *Bar*-nuh-bus.
ISAIAH. Eye-*zay*-uh.

---

fasting will take place. Isaiah did not say, "Ye shall not fast," but "Ye shall not fast *as ye do this day, to make your voice to be heard on high*" (Isaiah 58:4). Jesus said "*when* ye fast," then told those who do so not to be like the hypocrites (Matthew 6:16).

B. Isaiah, Jesus, and Us

Many people today practice fasting as an expression of their deep regret for their sins, as a part of their efforts to discern the Lord's will in a particular situation, or as an aspect of their sincerity and intensity in prayer. Their intent is to elevate spiritual awareness above physical needs and to give up physical pleasures for spiritual gain. As noted above, while not specifically required of Christians, fasting still can be a legitimate and beneficial practice for Christians.

Of course, we must keep in mind that with fasting (or any act of worship), far more is involved than just the act itself. First, we must recognize that God is not impressed with any act of worship if the worshiper's heart is not participating in the act. After all, it is the heart that God sees and values (1 Samuel 16:7). Fasting, giving money, performing music, cooking, raking leaves, making hospital visits, praying, or teaching—anything done out of a self-serving motivation—is as offensive to God as were the "performances" of God's people in Isaiah's day or of the Pharisees in Jesus' day.

Second, true worship is not given to God only on Sunday morning. "Pure religion and undefiled before God" is caring for the helpless (James 1:27; Matthew 25:31-46). Shall we take Isaiah, Jesus, and James seriously? Who will perform "true worship" this week by offering relief to the hurting and the desperate?

C. Prayer

Father, thank You for today's teaching from Isaiah. Please forgive us when our fasting or any part of our worship becomes hypocritical and empty. Help us to worship in spirit and in truth and to do so through our daily living. In Jesus' name, amen.

D. Thought to Remember

True worship involves head, heart, and hands.

Learning by Doing

This page contains an alternate lesson plan emphasizing learning activities.
Classes desiring such student involvement will find these suggestions helpful.

Learning Goals

After participating in this lesson, students will be able to:

1. Tell the significant points Isaiah makes about the futility of empty worship.

2. Compare the useless worship of Isaiah's day with equally futile practices of some today.

3. Identify a specific way to practice a true fast and make a commitment to do it.

Into the Lesson

Before class begins, write these two open-ended sentences on the chalkboard or on a large poster: "When I hear of religious 'fasting,' I often think . . ." and "I have or have not tried religious fasting because. . . ." As students arrive, encourage them to think about, and be ready to complete, these two statements. Begin the session by asking some students to tell how they completed the statements.

Option: Do a brief interview of someone who has practiced fasting. Questions for the interview may include: "What is religious fasting?"; "Why do you fast?"; "How has fasting blessed you?"; and "How does fasting honor or bless the Lord?"

Make the transition to Bible study by telling the class that fasting is still a legitimate, beneficial practice for Christians. However, as we will see, fasting—as well as any other religious practice—also can become ritualistic and meaningless. Our lesson today is designed to help us keep all our worship practices vibrant and meaningful.

Into the Word

Give the following tasks or assignments to groups of three to five people. The first task should be given to only one group. The other tasks may be given to several groups. Provide written instructions for each task, as follows:

Task 1: Prepare a dramatization of "An Interview With Isaiah," based on Isaiah 58:1-9a. Examples of questions you might use include these: "Why did God ask you to speak these words about fasting to His people?" "How did the Israelites go wrong in this practice?" "What do you believe is the connection between fasting and social justice?" Use the text to come up with additional questions and answers, and be prepared to perform this dramatization for the whole class.

Task 2: Read Isaiah 58:1-9a. Then discuss the following questions:

1. What was wrong with the fasting practiced by the hearers of Isaiah's message?

2. What does God expect of those who fast? Why? *(See vv. 6, 7.)*

3. Explain the wonderful results of fasting God's way.

4. The real issue of Isaiah 58 is not really fasting. The prophet cites fasting in order to make a point; what is the point?

Task 3: The other groups in the class are reading Isaiah's preaching about how fasting had become a mere empty and ritualistic form of worship. Jesus offered similar teachings in such passages as Matthew 6:16-18 and Luke 5:33-35. Read and summarize those teachings; then explain the message these texts have for today's godly person.

Ask Group 1 to give its interview with Isaiah for the class. Then have Groups 2 and 3 report their answers.

Into Life

Encourage students to apply this Scripture to their own worship practices by asking these discussion questions:

(1) Why may fasting still be an appropriate expression of worship? How might it be practiced?

(2) God calls the empty practice of fasting a "transgression" or sin. What other forms or expressions of worship may also become empty and meaningless rituals? Why or how?

(3) What have you learned about worship as it relates to everyday life?

Write the words *Problems* and *Solutions* at the heads of two columns. Ask the class to brainstorm things that may keep corporate worship from being meaningful and personal. These may range from hurrying to church with a carload of kids to the music chosen. List those issues under the heading "Problems." Then brainstorm solutions or ways to overcome those problems.

Conclude by giving each student a personal worksheet with the heading "What should I do?" Under the heading write these questions and incomplete sentences:

1. Should I fast? How and when?

2. What social action could I do that expresses God's sense of justice?

3. I will prepare for corporate worship by. . . .

4. The area of my life that I will clean up so that my worship will bring honor to God is. . . .

Let's Talk It Over

The questions on this page are designed to encourage review of the lesson Scriptures and to promote discussion of the lesson by the class. The answers provided are only discussion starters. Let your class talk it over from there.

1. Isaiah received a strong command to "cry aloud" and "spare not" in exposing the people's sins. To whom, if anyone, does that responsibility belong today? Why?

Every teacher or preacher of the Word has a responsibility to make plain what the Bible calls sin and the deadly effects of sin. The method by which we do that, however, may be different from Isaiah's task. Paul said a spiritual person should "restore" one who was "overtaken in a fault," but "in the spirit of meekness" (Galatians 6:1). The church itself should be a voice for righteousness. And the church has a responsibility to discipline its members. Our voice to the community must always include the message of grace along with the declaration that some things are sin, and God will judge sin.

2. The lesson writer says the people of Judah "assumed that doing God's will carried with it certain benefits and rewards." What's wrong with that? How is the same error seen today?

The Lord does promise to reward the faithful. We anticipate the words, "Well done, thou good and faithful servant . . . enter thou into the joy of thy lord" (Matthew 25:21). We even expect to have blessings in this life, but we make no demands on God. We serve because He is worthy of our obedience. The "rewards" we anticipate are expected not because we have earned them, but because He has promised them. The people of Judah thought they could perform some outward rituals and then demand of God the rewards of heart-felt faith.

3. Identify some church practices that can become "meaningless motions" if not observed properly. How can the church keep these from becoming meaningless?

Anything done repetitively can become mere habit and lose its meaning. This includes singing, praying, collecting an offering, partaking of the Lord's Supper, listening to sermons, and anything else that may be a "regular" part of a "worship service." Some churches have tried to counter this by changing the "order of worship" from week to week, or even changing some of the elements of the service. This may help, but it addresses only the externals. Isaiah's solution was a change of heart, and that is the only real solution

today. Perhaps the real question, then, is "How do we change people's hearts to lead them to worship 'in spirit and in truth'?"

4. Do you think the church today would benefit from a greater emphasis on and practice of fasting? Why or why not?

The purpose of fasting is to help the believer focus on prayer and supplication to God (Joel 2:12). Jesus assumed His followers would fast when He said, "When ye fast, . . ." (Matthew 6:16-18). While no one should be forced to fast or coerced into observing the practice (Colossians 2:16-23), fasting can be a powerful means to spiritual growth. Many congregations fast and pray before important events or before important congregational decisions. Finally, there are physical limits to safe fasting, especially for persons with certain physical conditions (such as diabetes), that must be considered before one begins a fast.

5. Isaiah said the people of Judah should care for the poor, the hungry, the naked, and widows and orphans. Today, what groups of people can our church minister to in a special way?

Jesus said that we would always have the poor with us (Matthew 26:11), and that is still true, even in times of great prosperity. Churches in large metropolitan areas may have more opportunity to minister to large numbers of poor people, but economic difficulty is not confined to the city. What can your church do to help minister to the physical and spiritual needs of the poor?

Are there single parents in your congregation? Their families have special needs the church can meet. Like the widows and orphans of the first century, they often live in poverty, and the children are, statistically, more likely to fail in school and get into trouble with the law than are children of two-parent families. How can your church minister to the physical and spiritual needs of one-parent families?

Is there a prison near your church? Prison ministry is a challenging but rewarding ministry that can produce dramatically changed lives. Currently, Islam is the fastest growing religion among U.S. prison inmates. The church needs to respond to this challenge with a greater evangelistic effort. How can your church minister to the physical and spiritual needs of prison inmates?

Anticipate God's New Creation

Jan 27

DEVOTIONAL READING: Revelation 21:1-8.

BACKGROUND SCRIPTURE: Isaiah 65:17-25.

PRINTED TEXT: Isaiah 65:17-25.

Isaiah 65:17-25

17 For, behold, I create new heavens and a new earth: and the former shall not be remembered, nor come into mind.

18 But be ye glad and rejoice for ever in that which I create: for, behold, I create Jerusalem a rejoicing, and her people a joy.

19 And I will rejoice in Jerusalem, and joy in my people: and the voice of weeping shall be no more heard in her, nor the voice of crying.

20 There shall be no more thence an infant of days, nor an old man that hath not filled his days: for the child shall die an hundred years old; but the sinner being an hundred years old shall be accursed.

21 And they shall build houses, and inhabit them; and they shall plant vineyards, and eat the fruit of them.

22 They shall not build, and another inhabit; they shall not plant, and another eat: for as the days of a tree are the days of my people, and mine elect shall long enjoy the work of their hands.

23 They shall not labor in vain, nor bring forth for trouble; for they are the seed of the blessed of the LORD, and their offspring with them.

24 And it shall come to pass, that before they call, I will answer; and while they are yet speaking, I will hear.

25 The wolf and the lamb shall feed together, and the lion shall eat straw like the bullock: and dust shall be the serpent's meat. They shall not hurt nor destroy in all my holy mountain, saith the LORD.

GOLDEN TEXT: For, behold, I create new heavens and a new earth: and the former shall not be remembered, nor come into mind.
—Isaiah 65:17.

Light for All People
Unit 2: The Response of God's People
(Lessons 6-9)

Lesson Aims

After this lesson each student will be able to:

1. Recount the key points of Isaiah's description of the new heavens and earth.

2. Explain the fulfillment of this prophecy in the Jewish return from exile and in the messianic age, climaxed by the return of Christ.

3. Give thanks to God for the promise of a "new heavens and a new earth" yet to be enjoyed by God's people.

Lesson Outline

INTRODUCTION
  A. Radically New
  B. Review of Guidelines
  C. Lesson Background
 I. GOD'S PROMISE (Isaiah 65:17-19)
  A. New Heavens and Earth (v. 17)
  B. Place of Joy (v. 18)
  C. Place Without Tears (v. 19)
II. GOD'S PROVISIONS (Isaiah 65:20-25)
  A. Long Life (v. 20)
  B. Productive Labor (vv. 21-23)
    Going Home
  C. Answered Prayer (v. 24)
  D. Superior Security (v. 25)
    The Wolf and the Lamb
CONCLUSION
  A. What Might Have Been
  B. What Came to Pass
  C. Prayer
  D. Thought to Remember

Introduction

A. Radically New

Some time ago I had a student in one of my college classes who made quite an impression on me and many others. Not only was she very bright and highly motivated, but she also displayed a singular refusal to be restricted by her limitations—including the impaired mobility and speech brought on by her cerebral palsy. She was determined to live every day to its absolute fullest. It didn't surprise anyone who knew her to learn that she had even tried skydiving! From that thrilling experience, this student came to know the heavens and the earth from a radically

new perspective. She has seen them from a vantage point not appreciated by those who stay on the ground. Such acts of faith as these have transformed this student, convincing her that nothing can hold her back!

In this, our final study from Isaiah during this quarter, we see the prophet challenging God's people to let their faith go "skydiving" and to anticipate the radically new life that God has in store for His people. He wrote to encourage all future believers, both Jews and Gentiles, to view the future by faith and to seize God's promise of the new heavens and new earth.

B. Review of Guidelines

It will help us in our interpretation of this passage if we review the principles that guided our study in lesson 6 (page 164). There it was noted that Isaiah 61 may be viewed as having two levels of application or fulfillment: (1) the return of the Judean exiles from Babylonian captivity; and (2) the messianic/church age, climaxed by the eternal state of Heaven, which will be ushered in at Jesus' return.

Isaiah 65 may be interpreted in a similar manner. First, it offered hope to those who were exiles in a foreign land, far from the land that God had given to His people. Second, it describes the blessings provided through Jesus' messianic ministry, with a particular emphasis on the blessings awaiting God's people in Heaven.

In the predictions found in today's text, Isaiah employed highly poetic language. It is reminiscent of the descriptions of the Heavenly realm in the book of Revelation. When John tried to put into words what he was privileged to see, he often used the words *like* or *as* (Revelation 4:3, 7; 5:6; 6:1; 10:1; 15:2; 21:11). This is the language of someone trying to describe the indescribable. It is man's finite efforts to depict something that is infinite. Such language should whet our appetites for what the Lord has in store for all who "love his appearing" (2 Timothy 4:8).

C. Lesson Background

For some seventy years many of the people of Judah had lived in exile in Babylon. Some of them had risen to positions of power and prestige (for example, Daniel and his friends). Others (such as Ezekiel) had lived in outlying communities, where they tried to keep alive the promise of a return home. In 538 B.C. the time finally arrived for that promise to be fulfilled. Joyful anticipation grew as a remnant of Judeans headed west.

Isaiah, writing about one hundred fifty years earlier, had helped encourage those who returned to their homeland. His predictions (one of which is found in today's text) described a life of radical newness: a new heavens and earth, a new people, a new city, and a new time of unprecedented productivity and prosperity.

I. God's Promise
(Isaiah 65:17-19)

Going home to Judah after seventy years must have raised certain doubts and misgivings among the aged. Would this trip really be worth the effort? Wouldn't it be wiser to live out the rest of one's days in Babylon? On the other hand, the younger exiles had been born in Babylon and thus had no personal memories of Jerusalem. Returning to Judah did not have as much appeal to them. Thus, for both old and young, there must have been certain anxieties accompanying the kind of drastic move required in going home. However, balancing those apprehensions was the excitement of participating in a new beginning.

So it is with followers of Jesus, who see themselves as "strangers and pilgrims" (1 Peter 2:11) and are preparing to go to their real home—Heaven. Death (the process of moving to that new home) does raise certain genuine concerns, but the promise of the new heavens and earth offsets our fears and, in addition, gives us a wonderful sense of excitement and anticipation.

A. New Heavens and Earth (v. 17)

17. For, behold, I create new heavens and a new earth: and the former shall not be remembered, nor come into mind.

The people who heard these words in Isaiah's day, one hundred fifty years or so before they were to be fulfilled, must have found the prophet's message almost impossible to fathom. In the same way young, exuberant, healthy Christians may be enthusiastic about promises of Heaven, yet to them it seems a long way off. But among the elderly captives who were living as exiles in Babylon in the middle of the sixth century B.C., Isaiah's promises of a *new heavens and a new earth* would have caused intense excitement. The ability to forget their *former* bondage was a wonderful goal to anticipate!

The same anticipation of the future can capture contemporary elderly Christians who realize that they are nearing the time to "go home." The new Heaven and earth mentioned in Revelation 21 is described as a place where "the former things are passed away" (v. 4) and where "he that sat upon the throne said, Behold, I make all things new" (v. 5). Peter describes this realm as a place "wherein dwelleth righteousness" (2 Peter 3:13). There God and redeemed humanity will live in perfect, loving harmony. [See question #1, page 192.]

Note that the new heavens and earth are pictured as something that God will *create*. This highlights the fact that this activity is the work of God and God alone. The verb *create* (in the active voice) is used with only God as its subject. No human being can or will ever create in the sense that God creates. So, whether one speaks of the Jerusalem located in the land of Israel in the sixth century B.C. or the "new Jerusalem, coming down from God out of heaven" (Revelation 21:2), each is the exclusive work of God. It is He who guided history in arranging for the return of the exiled Judeans, and it is He who is guiding history to its ultimate goal of establishing the new heavens and earth.

B. Place of Joy (v. 18)

18. But be ye glad and rejoice for ever in that which I create: for, behold, I create Jerusalem a rejoicing, and her people a joy.

Jerusalem had been destroyed so completely by the Babylonians in 586 B.C. (2 Kings 25:8-10) that its rebuilding could well have been considered a new creation. There was rejoicing when the temple was completed (Ezra 6:16) and later when the city wall was finished (Nehemiah 12:27, 43).

We must also, however, think in terms of the blessings provided to God's people under the New Covenant. Hebrews 12:22 and 23 tell us that Christians have come to the "heavenly Jerusalem," which is the same as "the general assembly and church of the firstborn." So the establishment of the church fulfills this prophesy at one level. In addition, we look forward to the "new Jerusalem" described in Revelation 21. That will be a place of never-ending *joy*! [See question #2, page 192.]

Visual for lesson 9. *Have this poster on display as students arrive. It is sure to pique their interest and prepare them for Isaiah's exciting message.*

How to Say It

BABYLON. *Bab*-uh-lun.
BABYLONIAN. Bab-uh-*low*-nee-un.
CYRUS. *Sigh*-russ.
EZEKIEL. Ee-*zeek*-yul or Ee-*zeek*-ee-yul.
HAGGAI. *Hag*-eye or *Hag*-ay-eye.
ISAIAH. Eye-*zay*-uh.
JEREMIAH. Jair-uh-*my*-uh.
JUDEAN. Joo-*dee*-un.
MALACHI. *Mal*-uh-kye.
MESSIANIC. mess-ee-*an*-ick.
NEHEMIAH. Nee-huh-*my*-uh.
ZECHARIAH. Zek-uh-*rye*-uh.

C. Place Without Tears (v. 19)

19. And I will rejoice in Jerusalem, and joy in my people: and the voice of weeping shall be no more heard in her, nor the voice of crying.

The fall of *Jerusalem* in 586 B.C. signaled the finality of God's judgment on His rebellious *people*. At that time, Jeremiah wrote the book of Lamentations to express his grief over the tragedy that had befallen a sinful nation. But now the period of judgment is ending. Sorrow has turned to *joy*.

Again, these lines from Isaiah apply in a special way to the eternal new Jerusalem, where "God shall wipe away all tears from their eyes" and where there shall be "neither sorrow, nor crying" (Revelation 21:4). *Weeping* and *crying* will have no place in that land of pure joy.

II. God's Provisions
(Isaiah 65:20-25)

Isaiah now turns to more specific statements about God's new creation.

A. Long Life (v. 20)

20. There shall be no more thence an infant of days, nor an old man that hath not filled his days: for the child shall die a hundred years old; but the sinner being a hundred years old shall be accursed.

"The days of our years are threescore years and ten [seventy]," wrote Moses in Psalm 90:10. During a time of hardship (such as those in captivity in Babylon had experienced), the average life span would have been somewhat less than that. But Isaiah promised that life in God's new heavens and earth will be such that *a hundred years* will be the new standard. No person, whether an *infant* or an *old man*, will be "cheated" of a full life.

The phrase *the sinner being a hundred years old shall be accursed* is a puzzling one. It is possible that the Hebrew word translated *sinner* should be taken in its basic meaning of "missing the mark," or "failing." Thus the phrase could be saying that the individual who fails to reach a hundred will be considered as *accursed*, for he has failed to attain the age that will become the standard in God's new heavens and earth.

Applying this prophecy to any particular time is difficult. One-hundred-year life spans did not become the norm for the people of Judah after their release from Babylon. But death at any age has no place in the new heavens and earth of which John wrote. Thus, the figure must be more symbolic than literal. Perhaps its basic message is that age will not be a factor in the new order of things that God will establish. It becomes a picture, then, of the better quality of life the Jews would experience as free people in their own homeland. Under the New Covenant "eternal life" is not viewed so much in terms of quantity of years as it is in terms of a relationship with God (John 17:3). Thus, Isaiah's picture of long life portrays the eternal life that all Christians possess by virtue of their relationship with Jesus. [See question #3, page 192.]

B. Productive Labor (vv. 21-23)

21. And they shall build houses, and inhabit them; and they shall plant vineyards, and eat the fruit of them.

These words about *houses* and *vineyards* lead one to think of what the returning exiles would do when they resettled in Judah. Life is pictured as very good for them indeed. The Bible speaks of Israel's living in peace and prosperity by saying the people "dwelt safely, every man under his vine and under his fig tree" (1 Kings 4:25).

Can these words also apply to the Christian age? Probably not in the sense of literally building of *houses* and planting vineyards. Jesus told His disciples He would go to prepare a place in His Father's house for them (John 14:2). He did not say they would have to build their own houses. However, if we take the figure for a picture of security and safety, then certainly it applies. Just as living a hundred years can picture the eternal life we will enjoy in Heaven, building homes and enjoying the fruit of one's own vineyard can picture the blessing of being in Heaven.

22. They shall not build, and another inhabit; they shall not plant, and another eat: for as the days of a tree are the days of my people, and mine elect shall long enjoy the work of their hands.

The Babylonians had laid siege to Jerusalem for a year and a half before it finally fell to them (2 Kings 25:1-3). Prior to and during that time, they no doubt ravaged the land, eating what the people of Judah had planted. And when the people of the land were seized and taken captive to Babylon, others moved into whatever houses remained. Isaiah declared that in the new heavens and earth no looters or spoilers would enter and steal the wealth of the residents. God's people would *long enjoy* the prosperity that their *work* had brought them. No one would take it from them.

Isaiah adds another word picture to describe the long life of God's people in their new home: *as the days of a tree are the days of my people.* Perhaps Isaiah had in mind one of the majestic cedars of Lebanon, or a mighty oak tree. Either of these could stand for centuries, symbolizing the lengthy period of blessing and prosperity that God's people would enjoy.

GOING HOME

A group of tourists was visiting a country well known for its history of tension, war, and displaced persons. At one point, a woman ran out of a rundown shack and began speaking to them in English. "See this?" she said. "See how I live in this one room with my children? I had a lovely home in a northern city. But it was taken from me, and now I have to live here." This woman's story is similar to that of thousands upon thousands of refugees throughout the world. They built homes—now someone else lives in them.

Some time ago the newspapers carried the story of such a refugee. She had found safety in America, but she had to leave everything she owned behind—except for the key to her old house! She still had the key to a house that she had once owned but never would see again and in which someone else was living.

God gave His people in the Old Testament the promise of security in their homes as long as they were faithful to Him. Followers of Jesus have been promised a home that no one can take away from them as long as they are faithful to

Him. The Christian's sense of security is far greater than any the world can offer. It is the assurance that God is faithful to those who do not forsake Him.   —R. C. S.

23. They shall not labor in vain, nor bring forth for trouble; for they are the seed of the blessed of the LORD, and their offspring with them.

The people's *labor* was *in vain* when invaders such as the Babylonians stole the harvest. In the new heavens and earth (as mentioned in verse 22), God's people would be able to enjoy the fruit of their efforts, without fear of being plundered. This prophecy is also fulfilled in the church. Paul says, "Ye know that your labor is not in vain in the Lord" (1 Corinthians 15:58).

The phrase *bring forth* translates a Hebrew word that usually describes giving birth. *Trouble* refers to any kind of calamity or disaster. Isaiah describes God's new heavens and earth as a place where His people will not have to rear their families with the cloud of impending tribulation or affliction hanging over them. In the new heavens and earth, just the opposite is true. The future will be bright with promise and hope.

This promise concerning bearing children in hope applies to *the seed of the blessed of the Lord, and their offspring.* Surely the remnant who returned from exile considered themselves *blessed of the Lord.* Even so, this prophecy finds even greater fulfillment in the church, where the blessed are "born, not of blood, nor of the will of the flesh, nor of the will of man, but of God" (John 1:12, 13). [See question #4, page 192.]

C. Answered Prayer (v. 24)

24. And it shall come to pass, that before they call, I will answer; and while they are yet speaking, I will hear.

An essential part of all prayer is the ready, waiting presence of God to *hear* and *answer* His people. Jesus taught, "Your Father knoweth what things ye have need of, *before* ye ask him" (Matthew 6:8). Jesus promised access to the Father in His name (John 14:13; 15:16). That intimacy will be perfected in the New Jerusalem, where God Himself will dwell with His people (Revelation 21:3). [See question #5, page 192.]

D. Superior Security (v. 25)

25. The wolf and the lamb shall feed together, and the lion shall eat straw like the bullock: and dust shall be the serpent's meat. They shall not hurt nor destroy in all my holy mountain, saith the LORD.

This description is very similar to one studied in lesson 2 (Isaiah 11:6-9, pages 133 and 134).

Home Daily Bible Readings

Monday, Jan. 21—"While You Are Waiting . . ." (2 Peter 3:11-18)
Tuesday, Jan. 22—Making All Things New (Revelation 21:1-8)
Wednesday, Jan. 23—A New Spirit Within (Ezekiel 11:14-20)
Thursday, Jan. 24—Cleansed People; New Heart (Ezekiel 36:22-28)
Friday, Jan. 25—God Has Redeemed Jerusalem (Isaiah 52:7-12)
Saturday, Jan. 26—Nations Will See God's Glory (Isaiah 66:18-23)
Sunday, Jan. 27—New Heavens and New Earth (Isaiah 65:17-25)

There it was noted that some Bible students take words such as these literally. God's new heavens and earth (here called His *holy mountain*) will be free from the terrors of any creatures who would normally *hurt* or *destroy* others. Others understand Isaiah to be picturing the effects of the gospel message in bringing together people of different backgrounds, temperaments, cultures, and the like. The *mountain* of the Lord is believed to have the same meaning that it does in Isaiah 2:2-4: a place from which the Lord's Word goes forth to all the nations.

Perhaps the phrase *dust shall be the serpent's meat* means no more than the venomous snake, like the other wild animals mentioned in the passage, no longer poses a threat to human safety. But who can read this without recalling God's words to the serpent in Eden: "Upon thy belly shalt thou go, and dust shalt thou eat all the days of thy life" (Genesis 3:14)? Perhaps the real intent here is to picture the complete fulfillment of the curse of the serpent—that is, of Satan. Christ did come to "destroy the works of the devil" (1 John 3:8; Hebrews 2:14, 15), a destruction that will be completed on the Day of Judgment (Revelation 20:7-10).

THE WOLF AND THE LAMB

In children's stories, the wolf often represents danger. In the tale of "Little Red Riding Hood" it is the wolf who poses a threat to Red Riding Hood when she goes to visit Grandma. In "The Three Little Pigs" it is the wolf who wants to huff and puff and blow the pigs' houses down. The proverbial expression for hunger or poverty (dating back at least to the sixteenth century) is that "the wolf is at the door." The wolf is almost always a symbol of danger. In contrast, the lamb often symbolizes innocence.

Long before these children's tales were written, the prophet Isaiah employed similar symbolism in his striking description of the peaceful conditions to be found in God's holy mountain. Not only did he use this language in today's text, but he also included it in a previous description of life in the messianic era (Isaiah 11:1-9). For such natural enemies as the wolf and the lamb to lie down together, two changes must occur: the wolf must no longer attack, and the lamb must no longer be afraid. It is a beautifully poetic word picture of peace—the peace that God provides for His people.

The Bible has much to say about this peace. It tells us that we can be kept in God's perfect peace when our minds are fixed on Him (Isaiah 26:3). Writing from his confinement in Rome, Paul described this peace as one "which passeth all understanding" (Philippians 4:7). Jesus said that His peace is unlike that which the world offers (John 14:27). Such "peace on earth" is a foretaste of the perfect, eternal peace we shall enjoy in Heaven.   —R. C. S.

Conclusion

A. What Might Have Been

Imagine the Judean prisoners in ancient Babylon hearing King Cyrus's royal proclamation that all Judeans who want to go home to Jerusalem may do so. But this demanded a long, grueling trek of almost a thousand miles on a highway of uncertainty. Many were doubtful and fearful. Should they go, or should they cast their lot in this foreign land? And then perhaps someone recalled the words of Isaiah: "For, behold, I create new heavens and a new earth."

Isaiah's predictions may well have fired the enthusiasm of the thousands who chose to return to Judah (Ezra 2:64-67). However, their faith was apparently a shallow and short-lived one. They made it to Jerusalem but soon slipped back into a life of spiritual darkness. From the records of Ezra, Nehemiah, Haggai, Zechariah, and Malachi, it is clear that the returning exiles did not hold true to the faith. A new temple was completed some twenty-two years after the first exiles returned; but by the time of Nehemiah's governorship (almost one hundred years later), the city walls were still in deplorable ruins. Faith faltered, and the promises of God went unclaimed. To use the terminology from our opening illustration, the Judeans refused to go "skydiving."

B. What Came to Pass

Jesus initiated the fulfillment of Isaiah's prophecy. In words that call to mind the language found in today's text, 2 Corinthians 5:17 encourages each of us with the possibility of a personal re-creation: "Therefore if any man be in Christ, he is a new creature: old things are passed away; behold, all things are become new." Revelation 21 excites each of us with its description of a place where God will "make all things new" (v. 5). Every person who is a new creation in Christ is preparing to live in the place that is the new creation of God.

C. Prayer

Father, we look forward in faith to what You have prepared for Your people. We pray that You will sustain us in faith so that we may one day joyfully inherit the new heavens and new earth. In Jesus' name. Amen.

D. Thought to Remember

For the Christian, the best is yet to come!

Learning by Doing

This page contains an alternate lesson plan emphasizing learning activities.
Classes desiring such student involvement will find these suggestions helpful.

Learning Goals

After participating in this lesson, each student will be able to:

1. Recount the key points of Isaiah's description of the new heavens and earth.

2. Explain the fulfillment of this prophecy in the Jewish return from exile and in the messianic age, climaxed by the return of Christ.

3. Give thanks to God for the promise of a "new heavens and a new earth" yet to be enjoyed by God's people.

Into the Lesson

Divide the class into two large groups, giving each group a large piece of poster board. Assign one of the following activities to each group.

Group 1: Poetic and figurative language was used in both the Old and New Testaments to describe the indescribable—Heaven! Your task is to do the same. You may not use Scriptural word pictures like "streets of gold." Create your own imaginative word pictures to help people hunger for Heaven.

Group 2: Imagine a perfect city in which you would like to live. List qualities or features of these perfect earthly living conditions.

The groups will not report on their work until later in the session.

Into the Word

Using the lesson commentary for preparation, give a brief picture of the lesson background and setting for Isaiah 65:17-25. Be sure to explain the dual levels of fulfillment of this prophecy.

Activity 1: Give teams of two or more people a photocopy of today's text and two different colored highlighter pens. After they read the text, they should mark in one color all the prophecies that speak only of the new Jerusalem the Jews were anticipating. All prophecies that can be applied both to Heaven and the new Jerusalem are to be marked in the other color.

Activity 2: This activity may be done in small groups with a worksheet or as a whole class with a large visual. (It is also in the student book, *Adult Bible Class.*) The worksheet or visual should be divided into three columns. There is no heading over Column 1; the heading for Column 2 is "New Jerusalem"; the heading for Column 3 is "Heaven." List the following words or phrases in Column 1: *Anticipation, Anxieties,*

Memories Erased, A Delightful Place (v. 18), *Intimacy With God,* and *Peace/Security.*

Tell the groups or the class that they will examine each of the emotions, feelings, or hopes listed. Ask them not to work ahead of you. You will ask questions or give instructions for each of these emotions or feelings listed. Answers may be simply noted in Columns 2 and 3.

Anticipation. "What hopes may the Jews have had for new Jerusalem? What good things do Christians look forward to in Heaven?"

Anxieties. "What may have been some fears or anxieties the Jews had about returning to Jerusalem? What anxieties may Christians have about making the trip to Heaven?"

Memories Erased. (v. 17): "What do you think the exiled Jews would like to forget?" After listing answers ask, "What memories do you look forward to having erased from your mind?" Ask those willing to share specific personal examples to do so.

A Delightful Place. Allow the two large groups from the opening activity to share their thoughts. Remind them that even our wildest dreams cannot match what God has in store for us.

Intimacy With God. Use the commentary section ("What Might Have Been," page 190) to explain what happened in Jerusalem. Explain this will not happen in Heaven. Ask the students how they will experience intimacy with God in Heaven.

Peace and Security. Reread verse 25 and ask "Is this a literal or figurative prophecy? How may it be interpreted and applied to the New Jerusalem the Jews were expecting? To Heaven?"

Into Life

Remind the class that this dual prophecy was a message of hope for the Jews and for all followers of the one true God. Believers look forward to the fulfillment of the prophecy about Heaven. Second Corinthians 5:17 should be the theme for our hope: "Therefore if any man be in Christ, he is a new creature: old things are passed away; behold, all things are become new."

Give each student a large cutout of a butterfly. Explain that the butterfly has long been a symbol of new life. After the old caterpillar is transformed, a beautiful new butterfly emerges. On the butterfly cutout class members are to write a two- or three-sentence prayer expressing gratitude for God's promise of Heaven.

Let's Talk It Over

The questions on this page are designed to encourage review of the lesson Scriptures and to promote discussion of the lesson by the class. The answers provided are only discussion starters. Let your class talk it over from there.

1. When Isaiah says "the former shall not be remembered," does that mean we will not be able to remember our earthly lives when we get to Heaven? What do you think people in Heaven will remember about their lives on earth?

The promise in Isaiah need not be taken too literally. Certainly the exiles who returned to Judah did not have their memories of Babylon erased. This forgetting is like that spoken of by Jesus in John 16:21. There He said a woman who gives birth to a child "remembereth no more the anguish" of labor. This does not mean that a mother has no recall of that pain, but that she sees it in perspective and is no longer troubled by it; she gives it no thought. Our perfect understanding in Heaven will make our earthly trials not worth considering.

2. The lesson writer says the new Jerusalem "will be a place of never-ending joy." What is it about Heaven that you anticipate the most? Why is that a source of joy for you?

The Bible's descriptions of Heaven are wonderful indeed! Whether these descriptions are literal or figurative (e.g., the streets paved with gold and the walls studded with precious stones), Heaven surely will be a place of awe and wonder. But just as our surroundings are secondary to our relationships here on earth, surely such will be the case in Heaven as well. Some of your students may be widowed: for them being reunited with their spouses will come quickly to mind. Any parent who has lost a child surely will find joy in the anticipation of seeing that one again. But these also will take second place in Heaven, where earthly relationships are not as significant as they are here (Matthew 22:30). The Bible pictures the residents of Heaven as being focused on the Lamb and upon God on His throne. Surely our greatest source of joy will come from being in the presence of God!

3. In commenting on verse 20 we noted that eternal life should not be viewed "so much in terms of quantity of years as it is in terms of a relationship with God." What does that suggest to you about the nature of the Christian life *this* side of Heaven?

If the most important aspect of Heaven is our relationship with God, then a close second must be our relationship with others of God's children. These are the people with whom we will spend eternity. If we cannot get along with them in the church, how will we manage through eternity? We need to cultivate harmonious relationships with others so that we will be fitted for Heaven.

Another aspect of our relationship with God is worship. The pictures of Heaven that we see in Revelation are worship scenes. Again, we need to prepare on earth for what we will experience in Heaven. If our worship on earth is spiritless and routine, then we are not worshiping as God desires (John 4:23, 24). Heavenly worship will be exactly what God desires, so we need to begin to practice that kind of worship now!

4. If God promises that our labor is not in vain, then why doesn't all Christian work result in a successful harvest of souls?

Jesus warned us that not all evangelistic fields would be equally fruitful. In the parable of the sower (Matthew 13:3-9, 18-23) Jesus taught that some people will be more receptive to the gospel than others. We must also remember that, just as different crops mature at different speeds, different people respond to the gospel at different times. At one time, Europe provided most of the Christian missionaries to the world, while Asia was an extremely difficult mission field. Today, many countries in Europe are considered mission fields, while Christianity is flourishing in some Asian countries. As Paul said, one Christian may plant, another may water, but it is ultimately God who causes the increase (1 Corinthians 3:6).

5. What do you think would happen if we took more seriously the Bible's promises about prayer? How can we become a more praying church?

Try to get beyond generalities such as, "We could do *anything!*" to be more specific. For what are you, your class, or your church praying? What if more people were faithful in praying for those things? Try also to get specific about becoming a more praying church: suggest ideas that you can actually implement. Perhaps groups could meet for prayer before worship services. Does your church have small groups? Perhaps prayer could be a more significant part of their routine. How about an elective study on prayer?

Ruth Chooses Naomi's God

DEVOTIONAL READING: Psalm 8.

BACKGROUND SCRIPTURE: Ruth 1.

PRINTED TEXT: Ruth 1:1-8, 16-19a.

Ruth 1:1-8, 16-19a

1 Now it came to pass in the days when the judges ruled, that there was a famine in the land. And a certain man of Beth-lehem-judah went to sojourn in the country of Moab, he, and his wife, and his two sons.

2 And the name of the man was Elimelech, and the name of his wife Naomi, and the name of his two sons Mahlon and Chilion, Ephrathites of Beth-lehem-judah. And they came into the country of Moab, and continued there.

3 And Elimelech Naomi's husband died; and she was left, and her two sons.

4 And they took them wives of the women of Moab; the name of the one was Orpah, and the name of the other Ruth: and they dwelt there about ten years.

5 And Mahlon and Chilion died also both of them; and the woman was left of her two sons and her husband.

6 Then she arose with her daughters-in-law, that she might return from the country of Moab: for she had heard in the country of Moab how that the LORD had visited his people in giving them bread.

7 Wherefore she went forth out of the place where she was, and her two daughters-in-law with her; and they went on the way to return unto the land of Judah.

8 And Naomi said unto her two daughters-in-law, Go, return each to her mother's house: the LORD deal kindly with you, as ye have dealt with the dead, and with me.

. . . .

16 And Ruth said, Entreat me not to leave thee, or to return from following after thee: for whither thou goest, I will go; and where thou lodgest, I will lodge: thy people shall be my people, and thy God my God:

17 Where thou diest, will I die, and there will I be buried: the LORD do so to me, and more also, if aught but death part thee and me.

18 When she saw that she was steadfastly minded to go with her, then she left speaking unto her.

19a So they two went until they came to Bethlehem.

Feb
3

GOLDEN TEXT: Whither thou goest, I will go; and where thou lodgest, I will lodge: thy people shall be my people, and thy God my God.—Ruth 1:16.

Light for All People
Unit 3: All People May Share God's Grace
(Lessons 10-13)

Lesson Aims

After participating in this lesson, each student will be able to:

1. Tell how Ruth came to be associated with Naomi and the God of Israel.

2. Explain how the choice that Ruth made to stay with Naomi reflected great faith.

3. Suggest one or two specific ways a believer can share his or her faith with a non-Christian family member.

Lesson Outline

INTRODUCTION
  A. Uprooting One's Roots
  B. Lesson Background
  I. NAOMI'S SITUATION (Ruth 1:1-3)
    A. Famine (v. 1a)
    B. Relocation (vv. 1b, 2)
    C. Grief (v. 3)
      Take My Hand
 II. NAOMI'S SONS (Ruth 1:4, 5)
    A. Married (v. 4)
    B. Deceased (v. 5)
III. NAOMI'S RETURN (Ruth 1:6-8, 16-19a)
    A. Journey Begun (vv. 6, 7)
    B. Daughters-in-Law Dismissed (v. 8)
      The Mothers-in-Law Club
    C. Steadfast Devotion (vv. 16, 17)
    D. Companionship Accepted (vv. 18, 19a)
CONCLUSION
  A. Going Home
  B. Prayer
  C. Thought to Remember

Introduction

A. Uprooting One's Roots

In recent years many people have undertaken the challenge of putting together a family tree. In order to discover their roots, they have scoured genealogical records and other historical data. Such searches have yielded varied results: fascination, joy, frustration, disappointment—and occasionally some embarrassment.

Sometimes these investigations have revealed that someone among the ancestors made a momentous decision to uproot his family and to move to a distant location. In such cases, the final farewells to other family members must have been touching and emotional.

The lesson for today highlights two of the factors that often have motivated people to move: famine and faith. Famine will cause a person to take drastic measures to obtain food. The Great Depression in the U.S. during the 1930s resulted in some families leaving relatives and friends behind in order to seek employment in other places. Many men felt a keen responsibility to care for their families, and this motivated them to uproot their families and find a better life elsewhere.

The faith factor is illustrated by different situations described in the Bible, including Abram's departure from Ur, the exodus from Egypt by the nation of Israel, and the return of God's people from exile in Babylon. Great faith may cause an individual to do things that seem strange and unrealistic to those who prefer to stay in their "comfort zones." No doubt it took significant faith when almost fifty thousand people departed from Babylon in 538 B.C. to return to Jerusalem. Many of those who returned had never seen Jerusalem, for they were born in captivity. They made the journey because their faith compelled them to do so.

A similar motivation is seen when men and women determine to go to a mission field. With today's modes of travel, the time factor in making long trips is not as crucial. Cultural differences, however, must still be confronted. At first such differences are simply fascinating, but over a period of time that perspective can change. One person testified that only the conviction that she was doing God's will enabled her to withstand the discomforts she experienced daily.

In today's society, job transfers often compel people to move. May it be that wherever they go, they will take their faith with them!

B. Lesson Background

Two books of the Bible are designated by the names of women—Ruth and Esther. The book of Ruth will be the focus for today's and next week's lessons.

Over the last two months, our studies have come from the book of Isaiah. The events recorded in the book of Ruth took place approximately four hundred years before the time of Isaiah. Whereas Isaiah's writings provide many specific prophecies about the Messiah, the book of Ruth tells of the courageous faith of an ancestress of the Messiah (Matthew 1:5). She was also the great-grandmother of David, the second king of Israel.

The author of Ruth is not named. A Jewish tradition states that Samuel was the author, but this cannot be supported from Scripture.

I. Naomi's Situation
(Ruth 1:1-3)

A. Famine (v. 1a)

1a. Now it came to pass in the days when the judges ruled, that there was a famine in the land.

The first verse of the book of Ruth reveals several important points. At the time the book was written, the era of the *judges* was considered complete, having lasted approximately three hundred years (from about 1375-1075 B.C.). The additional judgeship of Samuel included the coronation of Saul as the first king of Israel in approximately 1050 B.C.

The generality of the statement in Ruth *(when the judges ruled)* makes it difficult to determine which judge was ruling when the *famine* occurred *in the land*—or if, perhaps, it occurred between judges. The primary function of the judges was to deliver Israel from oppressors. Perhaps this famine was not caused by climate but by oppressors who robbed the people of their grain after the harvest (cf. Judges 6:1-4). The terminology "the Lord had visited his people" (v. 6) may suggest that the Lord had raised up a new judge to deliver Israel from the raiders.

B. Relocation (vv. 1b, 2)

1b. And a certain man of Beth-lehem-judah went to sojourn in the country of Moab, he, and his wife, and his two sons.

Beth-lehem-Judah is located about six miles south of Jerusalem. (There was also a Bethlehem in northern Israel [Joshua 19:15]; thus the reference to Judah helped to clarify which Bethlehem was meant.) The word *Bethlehem* means "house of bread." It is an interesting irony that this family felt compelled to leave the "house of bread" because there was no bread!

To *sojourn* in *Moab* was no small matter. The move involved a trip of about fifty miles to an area east of the Dead Sea. It also meant that the family's land in Judah would be abandoned, at least temporarily. Besides that, the Mosaic law excluded Moabite men from the assembly of the Lord, "even to their tenth generation" (Deuteronomy 23:3-6). Since the number ten sometimes symbolizes completeness in the Bible, this may have indicated a permanent exclusion (note "for ever" in verses 3 and 6). While this may have caused some Israelites to harbor feelings of animosity toward the Moabites, it appears that this was not true of Elimelech. The presence of food in Moab may be attributed to conquest, trade, or the possibility that the famine was confined to Judah.

2. And the name of the man was Elimelech, and the name of his wife Naomi, and the name of his two sons Mahlon and Chilion, Ephrathites

of Beth-lehem-judah. And they came into the country of Moab, and continued there.

Personal names in the Bible often have great significance attached to them. *Elimelech* means "my God is king." *Naomi* means "pleasant." The significance of names is seen in Naomi's return to Judah without her husband and *two sons*. At that time she told the women of Bethlehem that they should call her *Mara* (meaning "bitter"), and not *Naomi* (Ruth 1:20). [See question #1, page 200.]

The names of the two sons are also interesting: *Mahlon* means "weak," and *Chilion* means "pining." Both names suggest physical weakness, and this trait may have been a factor in Elimelech's decision to move to a place where food was more attainable. Loving parents will do whatever they can to help their children.

The entire family is designated as *Ephrathites of Beth-lehem-judah*. *Ephrath* was a former name for Bethlehem (Genesis 35:16, 19), though it also could have designated the clan within the tribe of Judah to which this family belonged.

C. Grief (v. 3)

3. And Elimelech Naomi's husband died; and she was left, and her two sons.

Already Naomi had experienced the turmoil of being uprooted from her home, her family, and her friends. Now, in a foreign land, her *husband died*; and her sense of loss was compounded by the grief of losing a mate.

TAKE MY HAND

On one occasion Thomas A. Dorsey, who became known as the "Father of Gospel Music," was away from home leading the music for a revival in another town. His wife had stayed home because she was pregnant. While he was away,

Visual for lesson 10. *This poster will help your students place the events of the lessons of this quarter in chronological order.*

he received a telegram informing him that his wife had died.

Dorsey was so distraught at the news that he decided he would not continue in the field of gospel music. Instead, he would go into secular music. But he found he could not. One day, while still grieving deeply, he wrote a song that included these words: "Precious Lord, take my hand, Lead me on, help me stand; I am tired, I am weak, I am worn; Through the storm, through the night, Lead me on to the light, Take my hand, precious Lord, Lead me home." Dorsey's words have given hope and encouragement to many during times of grief and heartache. Mahalia Jackson sang his song at the funeral of Dr. Martin Luther King, Jr.

Faith in God is still the primary factor that sustains people during times of grief. It is what sustained Naomi during the loss of her husband and her two sons. Note that Naomi lived long before the Lord Jesus came to earth. She lived before the words of John 14:1 were spoken: "Let not your heart be troubled." She lived before the resurrection of Jesus gave a firm basis to the hope of eternal life.

Naomi did not stop believing in God when her husband and two sons died. She even had enough faith to express her frustrations about God, as Ruth 1:13, 20, 21 indicate. But she kept on believing in Him, and so must all of us.

—R. C. S.

II. Naomi's Sons
(Ruth 1:4, 5)

A. Married (v. 4)

4. And they took them wives of the women of Moab; the name of the one was Orpah, and the name of the other Ruth: and they dwelt there about ten years.

For Israelite men to marry *women of Moab* was not forbidden by the Mosaic law, but, as noted above, Moabite males were prevented from being a part of the assembly of the Lord. It is not until Ruth 4:10 that we learn that Mahlon was the son of Naomi who married *Ruth*. No mention is made of any children, so it is likely that these marriages were childless.

The statement that the family dwelled in Moab *about ten years* seems to indicate that there was no thought given to returning to Bethlehem. Apparently the sons were putting down their roots in Moab. Naomi continued to live there as well.

B. Deceased (v. 5)

5. And Mahlon and Chilion died also both of them; and the woman was left of her two sons and her husband.

How to Say It
BABYLON. *Bab*-uh-lun.
CHEMOSH. *Kee*-mosh.
CHILION. *Kil*-ee-on.
ELIMELECH. Ee-*lim*-eh-leck.
EPHRATH. *Ef*-rath.
EPHRATHITES. *Ef*-ruh-thites.
ISAIAH. Eye-*zay*-uh.
MAHLON. *Mah*-lon.
MARA. *Mah*-ruh.
MOAB. *Mo*-ab.
MOABITE. *Mo*-ub-ite.
NAOMI. Nay-*oh*-me.
ORPAH. *Or*-pah.

Naomi's burdens increased with the death of *her two sons*. A *woman* without a *husband*, son, or relative to provide for her was in desperate straits. That was especially so in ancient times, but it also can be true in today's world as well. [See question #2, page 200.]

Thus Naomi and her family had moved to Moab to better themselves; yet, tragically, the results did not fulfill their expectations. Perhaps Naomi debated with herself about the wisdom of that decision to move. Her thoughts may have started with those tragic words, "If only we had . . ." or, "If only we had not. . . ." The trials of life, however, can, in time, become a blessing and a source of rejoicing (James 1:2-4). God's plan was at work, but at this time only He knew where that plan was going. [See question #3, page 200.]

Ancient Jewish interpretations of these events suggest that the deaths of Elimelech and his sons were a punishment for their lack of faith when they decided to leave their ancestral home. But no reference whatever is made to this in the narrative, so anything that is said about such matters must be speculative. And it is dangerous to state that every tribulation is a direct result of a previous sin. Recall that this was the error that the friends of Job made as they attempted to explain his sufferings.

III. Naomi's Return
(Ruth 1:6-8, 16-19a)

A. Journey Begun (vv. 6, 7)

6. Then she arose with her daughters-in-law, that she might return from the country of Moab: for she had heard in the country of Moab how that the LORD had visited his people in giving them bread.

At some point, good news from Bethlehem reached Naomi: *the Lord had visited his people* and had ended the period of famine by *giving them bread*. The word *visit*, when used of God, highlights some specific action on His part. Sometimes it is a visitation of judgment (Exodus 20:5; Jeremiah 5:7-9); at other times, such as here, it is a visitation to bless (Exodus 4:31). This news prompted Naomi to make a courageous decision: she would go home. Of course, there was really nothing in *Moab* to make her want to stay there any longer.

7. Wherefore she went forth out of the place where she was, and her two daughters-in-law with her; and they went on the way to return unto the land of Judah.

Perhaps these three women felt such a common bond (as a result of their shared grief in losing their husbands) that they desired to stay together. [See question #4, page 200.]

B. Daughters-in-Law Dismissed (v. 8)

8. And Naomi said unto her two daughters-in-law, Go, return each to her mother's house: the LORD deal kindly with you, as ye have dealt with the dead, and with me.

Naomi was genuinely grateful to her *daughters-in-law* for exhibiting such loyalty to her, but she also knew that it would be in their best interests to marry again (v. 9). This would be more likely to occur if they remained in Moab than if they accompanied her to Judah.

Naomi's request that these younger women *return each to her mother's house* seems unusual, especially since Ruth's father was probably still alive (Ruth 2:11). We would expect a reference to the "father's house," which is where widows usually returned (Genesis 38:11; Leviticus 22:13). However, Genesis 24:28 tells how Rebekah went to "her mother's house" after speaking with Abraham's servant, who had been sent to find a wife for Isaac. Possibly Naomi knew that her daughters-in-law would find greater solace and understanding with their mothers.

A blessing was then pronounced upon Ruth and Orpah by Naomi, who expressed her appreciation for their kindness to *the dead*. By this Naomi probably referred to the respect they had shown to Naomi's husband and sons by their treatment of her. After speaking these words, Naomi probably assumed that she would continue the journey to Bethlehem alone.

THE MOTHERS-IN-LAW CLUB

It may surprise some to learn that there is such an organization as the Mothers-in-Law Club International, Inc. With headquarters on Long Island, New York, the club publishes a newsletter and holds regular meetings. It was started in 1971 with the intent "to provide aid to every

family throughout the country and the world and to dispel the hackneyed concept of the mother-in-law myth."

Certainly something needs to be said on behalf of mothers-in-law. Why are there so many negative jokes about them? Why are there so few expressions of appreciation for those who fill the role well? And why are there very few books, seminars, or discussion groups to help mothers-in-law with what can be a very difficult task?

It is obvious that Naomi filled the role of mother-in-law superbly. She was respected and loved by both her daughters-in-law. Every married person should treat his or her mother-in-law with respect. And every mother-in-law should act in such a way that she earns and deserves that respect. It is not easy to see the affection of your child transferred to someone else. It is not easy to be quiet when you think you know what your son or daughter (or son-in-law or daughter-in-law) ought to do. But it is necessary!

Every mother-in-law should see Naomi as a model and ask, "Is my attitude going to lead the one who married my child to a deep and lasting faith in God?" And everyone who has a mother-in-law should say, "This is the person who gave life to the one I love. I will treat her with the respect her position deserves." —R. C. S.

C. Steadfast Devotion (vv. 16, 17)

16. And Ruth said, Entreat me not to leave thee, or to return from following after thee: for whither thou goest, I will go; and where thou lodgest, I will lodge: thy people shall be my people, and thy God my God.

Ruth's expression of devotion is considered to be one of the most beautiful statements, not only in Scripture, but in all of literature. The first phrase, *Entreat me not to leave thee*, responded to Naomi's fourfold urging to her daughters-in-law to return to Moab (vv. 8, 11, 12, 15).

The sentiments expressed here are frequently heard at weddings. Some think they ought not to be because, in their context, the words are spoken by a daughter-in-law to her mother-in-law. However, the loyalties expressed here are certainly appropriate to marriage. There is, then, nothing inappropriate about having these words repeated by a bride or groom.

It is evident from Ruth's words that she had come to esteem her mother-in-law very highly. The jesting (but often insulting) comments that often are made about such relationships were inappropriate here. Ruth had shared grief with her mother-in-law, and she had been able to observe Naomi as she experienced the loss of her husband and two sons. It is important to remember that how the Christian handles the trials of life is noticed by others. During such trials, the value and the strength of Christian faith become especially clear.

With this commitment, Ruth was declaring her decision to leave her people and her god. The worship of Chemosh, the chief god of Moab, included child sacrifice (2 Kings 3:26, 27). Ruth, a young woman with a pagan heritage, had found the true God; and she wanted to walk in His way! To see such faith as this makes the book of Ruth a breath of fresh air in the midst of the chaotic time of the judges (Judges 17:6; 21:25). And this faith came from a Moabite—not from one of the Israelites! [See question #5, page 200.]

17. Where thou diest, will I die, and there will I be buried: the LORD do so to me, and more also, if aught but death part thee and me.

This affirmation by Ruth was not a violation of the Commandment against taking the Lord's name in vain (Exodus 20:7). Ruth was so certain that only *death* would separate her from Naomi that she called on *the Lord* to take her life if she did not keep her word!

Three little words of Ruth's statement are often overlooked: *and more also.* She not only invited death, but all the sufferings that might accompany or precede death. In some instances those sufferings can seem worse than death itself.

D. Companionship Accepted (vv. 18, 19a)

18. When she saw that she was steadfastly minded to go with her, then she left speaking unto her.

Naomi realized that Ruth's statements were not just polite expressions. For Naomi to continue to urge Ruth to return to Moab would have been disrespectful, not only to Ruth but to the Lord as well. Naomi therefore *left speaking:* she

quit trying to persuade Ruth to remain in Moab, and she surrendered to the sincere vow of her daughter-in-law.

Nothing is said about the subsequent reactions of the two women. This, however, must have been an emotional moment for both of them. It is easy to imagine tears, a joyful embrace, and a great joy that both of them were now genuine followers of the one, true, and living God! They were mother-in-law and daughter-in law, but they were also sisters in the faith!

19a. So they two went until they came to Bethlehem.

Perhaps Naomi tried to describe to Ruth what they would find when they reached *Bethlehem*—the place where Naomi had lived with Elimelech and where she had reared her two sons. The two women must have shared much as they made their fifty-mile trek together. This journey was more than a long walk. It became a journey of faith that would be recounted through the ages.

Conclusion

A. Going Home

It is usually an emotional experience to go home. Part of that emotion involves the fact that "home" never can stay the same as it was when we grew up there. Changes occur—both gradual and dramatic. Children become adults. Death removes familiar faces. Former buildings are gone, and new ones stand in their places. Yet those facts do not constitute reasons to stay away. We still look forward to going home.

The follower of Jesus Christ also anticipates "going home." He understands that he is only a temporary resident of this earth. His ultimate destination is Heaven, where he will dwell eternally with all the saints of all the ages. In many cases this will include family members and friends who have done what the lesson title suggests: they have chosen "Naomi's God." May we live in such a way that others will choose "Naomi's God," because they have seen that He is our God!

B. Prayer

Our Father, we give thanks today that we have the opportunity to choose to follow Christ. May it be that by the choices we make each day we, like Naomi of old, will be a positive influence to others. May they also desire to follow the One who said, "I am the way, the truth, and the life" (John 14:6). In the name of Christ we pray, amen.

C. Thought to Remember

"I have set before you life and death, blessing and cursing: therefore choose life, that both thou and thy seed may live" (Deuteronomy 30:19).

Home Daily Bible Readings

Monday, Jan. 28—You Were Strangers in Egypt (Deuteronomy 10:12-22)

Tuesday, Jan. 29—Tithe for Aliens, Orphans, and Widows (Deuteronomy 26:1-15)

Wednesday, Jan. 30—Act Justly; Do Not Oppress (Jeremiah 7:1-7)

Thursday, Jan. 31—Do Not Wrong Widows, Aliens (Jeremiah 22:1-9)

Friday, Feb. 1—Provide for Widows and Aliens (Deuteronomy 24:14-22)

Saturday, Feb. 2—Three Widows in Moab (Ruth 1:1-14)

Sunday, Feb. 3—Your God, My God (Ruth 1:15-22)

Learning by Doing

This page contains an alternate lesson plan emphasizing learning activities.
Classes desiring such student involvement will find these suggestions helpful.

Learning Goals

After participating in this lesson, each student will be able to:

1. Tell how Ruth came to be associated with Naomi and the God of Israel.

2. Explain how the choice that Ruth made to stay with Naomi reflected great faith.

3. Suggest one or two specific ways a believer can share his or her faith with a non-Christian family member.

Into the Lesson

Display a picture of a family tree. Ask if anyone in the class has researched his or her family history. If so, ask, "Did you find anything unusual about the religious beliefs of your ancestors?"

Next, tell the class that many families who explore the religious history of their families find someone among their ancestors who made a momentous decision to turn his or her back on family beliefs or religious indifference to accept Christian beliefs. A person may decide to accept Jesus as Savior and then become an ancestor for many generations of Christians. This kind of decision takes tremendous courage as modeled in the life of a widow pictured in today's text.

Into the Word

Activity 1: A Brief Lecture. From the commentary section of this book, use the "lesson background" and notes on verse 1 to prepare a brief lecture to introduce today's study of Ruth's adventure in faith. Write the following words on the chalkboard as you talk about each item: *Books Named for Women, Functions of Judges, Famine, Life in Moab.*

Activity 2: Outline the Story Events. In small groups or as a class, have students outline the story included in today's printed text. Subtopics are to be filled in as they happen.

Activity 3: Question and Answer. Allow the class or small groups to discuss the following questions about this text:

1. What may have been some of the crises facing the widowed Naomi when her sons died?

2. When Naomi decided to go home to Judah, she tried to send her daughters-in-law back to their childhood homes. Why? Why was Naomi pessimistic about their marriageability?

3. Ruth's commitment to Naomi is considered to be one of literature's classic statements. For Ruth, this was a monumental and courageous decision. How do you see her life changing because of this statement?

Activity 4. What's in a Name? Explain that names for people in this culture often reflected an individual's personal characteristics or circumstances at birth. Use a poster or some other visual aid to display the names from today's text and their meanings. Ask pairs of people to select two names and discuss why each may have been chosen or why it was appropriate. See the lesson commentary for ideas about the significance of each.

List the following names: *Elimelech* ("my God is king"), *Mahlon* ("weak"), *Chilion* ("pining"), *Naomi* ("my delight" or "pleasant"), *Ruth* ("a female friend"), *Mara* ("bitter"). See Ruth 1:20, 21.

Into Life

Tell the class there are tremendous lessons to be learned from the women of today's text.

From Ruth. Mention that Ruth's commitment to Naomi is a lesson in courageous decisions of faith. Ask class members to share testimonies of acquaintances or family members who have made courageous religious decisions.

From Naomi. Remind the class that Naomi provides a lesson of faith in the family. It was apparent that her faith carried a great deal of influence in Ruth's life. Discuss these questions:

1. Why do you think that some Christian families find it difficult to speak openly of their faith?

2. What are some ways to share our faith effectively with our children? With our parents or siblings? (Remind the class that there is a wonderful sense of satisfaction in seeing the family tree filled with the names of family members who follow Christ.)

Give this commitment card to class members to sign and carry. (This commitment is also in the student book, *Adult Bible Class.*)

"Like Naomi, I want my faith in Jesus Christ to be contagious to my family. To the best of my ability, I will. . . .

• Demonstrate my faith in Jesus through my speech and behavior;

• Speak gently and lovingly about God's plan and His love;

• Pray frequently for my family's relationship with the Lord."

(Signature)

Let's Talk It Over

The questions on this page are designed to encourage review of the lesson Scriptures and to promote discussion of the lesson by the class. The answers provided are only discussion starters. Let your class talk it over from there.

1. Naomi, whose name meant "pleasant," said her name should be "Mara," which means "bitter." If you were to change your name to reflect your current circumstances or the way God has dealt with you, what would you call yourself? Why?

Encourage the students to respond with the meanings of the names—they don't have to know actual Hebrew or Greek words! Also, in case Naomi's example has the class thinking of a negative change, note the example of "Joseph" in Acts, whom the apostles named "Son of Consolation" (Acts 4:36). Perhaps they would give themselves positive sounding names like "Joy" or "Faithful." Has someone come through a great trial? Perhaps he or she could be called "Tried and True" or "Grateful." Look for ways to encourage each student who shares to use his or her new situation as an occasion to glorify God.

2. What responsibility does the church have to care for widows and widowers today?

The Bible is clear that caring for widows, orphans, and other disadvantaged people is the church's responsibility. See James 1:27 and 1 Timothy 5. Specific needs may vary from time to time and situation to situation, however. Government programs, which most people assume are more generous than they really are, provide some relief that was not available in New Testament times, but that does not relieve the church of its responsibility. And there are other needs besides economic needs. Many widows need help with things like home and auto maintenance and with personal financial decisions. Especially, widows and widowers alike need lots of fellowship and spiritual encouragement, as they often must cope with loneliness and despair. They also need opportunities for service. Astute congregations can make good use of retired widows and widowers in a variety of ministry situations.

3. What kinds of trials offer the greatest challenge to your relationship to God? How can these "become a blessing and a source of rejoicing" for you?

They will vary from person to person. For some it will be a trial of pain or some other health condition. For others, the trials will come in the form of ridicule or persecution. Finally, there is the challenge of prosperity. Sometimes wealth will lull a person into trusting in his own self-sufficiency, rather than in the power of God. Allow any learners who will to be specific about the trials they face. Then others can be specific in their suggestions for help in overcoming them.

In each of these the key to making them sources of blessing or rejoicing comes in how we deal with them. Perseverance through the trial builds endurance and hope (James 1:2-4; 1 Peter 1:6, 7). And whether one finds victory in an end of the trial or through the continued grace to endure (2 Corinthians 12:9, 10), he or she will be able to rejoice and give thanks to God.

4. What experiences provide "common bonds" for people today? How can we use such connections to share the gospel with people?

Support groups abound for people who have found a common bond in some kind of experience—either positive or negative. Homeschoolers, parents or spouses of those who committed suicide, model car enthusiasts, and victims of crime are just a few. The church can make these support groups evangelistic by hosting them and providing direction. There are many potential bonds in your congregation where the connection has not yet been made. Brainstorm some interests and hobbies that might provide the basis for a small group that can help members connect with each other and to reach out to those currently outside the church who can be won to the Lord through such an activity.

5. What do some people today have to "leave behind" in order to serve God? How can we encourage them to do so?

What people leave behind will vary greatly. Some have to part with unbelieving family members. Others have left lucrative employment because the business ethics where they once worked was incompatible with their faith. Many have to walk away from former habits and amusements because these are not edifying to them in their relationship with Christ. Allow your learners to tell what they have left and what was most helpful to them in doing so. Perhaps testimonies from people about what they have given up and what they have found in Jesus might encourage some to let go of their past and give themselves to the Lord.

God Blesses Ruth

DEVOTIONAL READING: Psalm 126.

BACKGROUND SCRIPTURE: Ruth 2–4.

PRINTED TEXT: Ruth 2:1-3, 8-12; 4:13-17.

Ruth 2:1-3, 8-12

1 And Naomi had a kinsman of her husband's, a mighty man of wealth, of the family of Elimelech; and his name was Boaz.

2 And Ruth the Moabitess said unto Naomi, Let me now go to the field, and glean ears of corn after him in whose sight I shall find grace. And she said unto her, Go, my daughter.

3 And she went, and came, and gleaned in the field after the reapers: and her hap was to light on a part of the field belonging unto Boaz, who was of the kindred of Elimelech.

. . . .

8 Then said Boaz unto Ruth, Hearest thou not, my daughter? Go not to glean in another field, neither go from hence, but abide here fast by my maidens:

9 Let thine eyes be on the field that they do reap, and go thou after them: have I not charged the young men that they shall not touch thee? and when thou art athirst, go unto the vessels, and drink of that which the young men have drawn.

10 Then she fell on her face, and bowed herself to the ground, and said unto him, Why have I found grace in thine eyes, that thou shouldest take knowledge of me, seeing I am a stranger?

11 And Boaz answered and said unto her, It hath fully been showed me, all that thou hast done unto thy mother-in-law since the death of thine husband; and how thou hast left thy father and thy mother, and the land of thy nativity, and art come unto a people which thou knewest not heretofore.

12 The LORD recompense thy work, and a full reward be given thee of the LORD God of Israel, under whose wings thou art come to trust.

Ruth 4:13-17

13 So Boaz took Ruth, and she was his wife: and when he went in unto her, the LORD gave her conception, and she bare a son.

14 And the women said unto Naomi, Blessed be the LORD, which hath not left thee this day without a kinsman, that his name may be famous in Israel.

15 And he shall be unto thee a restorer of thy life, and a nourisher of thine old age: for thy daughter-in-law, which loveth thee, which is better to thee than seven sons, hath borne him.

16 And Naomi took the child, and laid it in her bosom, and became nurse unto it.

17 And the women her neighbors gave it a name, saying, There is a son born to Naomi; and they called his name Obed: he is the father of Jesse, the father of David.

GOLDEN TEXT: The LORD recompense thy work, and a full reward be given thee of the LORD God of Israel, under whose wings thou art come to trust.—Ruth 2:12

Lesson Aims

After participating in this lesson, each student will be able to:

1. Describe how God blessed Ruth through the kindness of Boaz.

2. Tell how God's providence worked with human effort to accomplish His purpose in the lives of Ruth and Naomi.

3. Keep a record this week of how God provides for him or her by working through people and circumstances.

Lesson Outline

INTRODUCTION

    A. Try a Little Kindness

    B. Lesson Background

  I. RUTH'S REQUEST (Ruth 2:1-3)

    A. Boaz Introduced (v. 1)

    B. Request Made (v. 2)

      God's Poverty Program

    C. Gleaning Begins (v. 3)

 II. RUTH'S RECOGNITION (Ruth 2:8-12)

    A. Boaz's Kindness (vv. 8, 9)

      The Worth of Work

    B. Ruth's Gratitude (v. 10)

    C. Boaz's Compliment (v. 11)

    D. Boaz's Blessing (v. 12)

III. RUTH'S REWARD (Ruth 4:13-17)

    A. Marriage and a Son (v. 13)

    B. The Women's Blessing (vv. 14, 15)

    C. Naomi's Care (v. 16)

    D. A Special Genealogy (v. 17)

CONCLUSION

    A. Channels of Blessing

    B. Prayer

    C. Thought to Remember

Introduction

A. Try a Little Kindness

It was one of those paradoxical statements—an apparent contradiction, yet the expression of something true. The person who was using it may have borrowed the statement from someone else, or perhaps it was an original analysis. The remark was this: "He's so right that he's wrong!" The person being described was always right, rigidly right, and sometimes obnoxiously right. A small amount of kindness or compassionate understanding would have gone a long way in encouraging others to see his side of an issue.

The attribute of kindness is to be a part of every Christian's life. It appears in Galatians 5:22 as the fifth aspect of the fruit of the Spirit. (In the *King James Version* it is called "gentleness," but in other places the same Greek word is often translated as "kindness"; see 2 Corinthians 6:6; Ephesians 2:7.) Some people seem to have this quality naturally, while others have to work to overcome backgrounds where kindness was the exception, not the rule.

In many respects, the church has demonstrated kindness in very tangible ways. Relief organizations are a good illustration. In recent years they have been called upon repeatedly to help during times of tragedy around the world. Such groups need financial support, and giving to meet their needs can be an opportunity for kindness that should not be overlooked. At the same time, it must be admitted that the actions of some Christians (particularly church leaders) have been so offensive as to drive people away.

In Titus 3:4, 5 Paul writes, "But after that the kindness and love of God our Saviour toward man appeared, . . . he saved us." We are the recipients of God's marvelous kindness; are we demonstrating kindness to others?

B. Lesson Background

Last week's lesson was taken from the first chapter of the book of Ruth. It followed the family of Elimelech during a time of famine, a move to a foreign land, and the deaths of Elimelech and his two sons in that land. Then the focus turned to the women who were left: Naomi and her two daughters-in-law, Ruth and Orpah. Of special significance was Ruth's decision to remain with Naomi and to follow Naomi's God (Ruth 1:16, 17).

These two women proceeded to Bethlehem, arriving in early spring just as the barley harvest was beginning (Ruth 1:22). In this second of our two studies from the book of Ruth, the happy ending of this beautiful story is considered.

I. Ruth's Request
(Ruth 2:1-3)

A. Boaz Introduced (v. 1)

1. And Naomi had a kinsman of her husband's, a mighty man of wealth, of the family of Elimelech; and his name was Boaz.

Boaz is the fourth *man* introduced in the book of Ruth. (The first three, Elimelech and his two sons, died in Moab.) The description of Boaz indicates that he was respected, wealthy, and related to *the family of Elimelech*. The word translated here as *kinsman* simply means "relative." Another Hebrew term used more frequently in the book of Ruth to describe Boaz is also translated "kinsman" or "near kinsman." In Israelite society such a person had the responsibility to care for his extended family, particularly the poor, the widows, and the orphans. In addition, he was responsible for buying back any land that had passed from the family's possession (Leviticus 25:25-28). Boaz's duty toward Naomi and Ruth will become more significant as the account unfolds.

B. Request Made (v. 2)

2. And Ruth the Moabitess said unto Naomi, Let me now go to the field, and glean ears of corn after him in whose sight I shall find grace. And she said unto her, Go, my daughter.

The Lord's economic plan for the poor in Israel did not involve giving handouts, like the modern "welfare" system in the U.S., but more like what some have dubbed "workfare." Reapers were to leave the corners of the fields unharvested, and they could not pick up any grain they had dropped. These were to be left so that the poor and the sojourner could have something to gather (Leviticus 19:9, 10; 23:22). Ruth fit both of these categories, and she apparently knew (perhaps as a result of conversations with Naomi as they traveled to Bethlehem) about this special arrangement. The reminder that Ruth was a *Moabitess* serves to emphasize her status as a stranger, and also puts Boaz in a favorable light. He showed kindness to Ruth, in spite of the fact that she was not a native Israelite. [See question #1, page 208.]

That Ruth took the initiative in going into the fields is commendable. She was willing to work in order to put food on the table for her mother-in-law and herself. Before going, however, she respectfully sought permission for what she proposed to do.

The expression *ears of corn* is used to refer to any grain, not just corn. In this case the grain was barley (Ruth 1:22), which was harvested during the months we call March and April.

GOD'S POVERTY PROGRAM

In his book, *The Tragedy of American Compassion*, author Marvin Olasky speaks of the earliest efforts to help the poor in the New World. He writes, "Human needs were answered by other human beings, not by bureaucracies." That was the case with God's plan found in Leviticus and demonstrated in today's lesson. Assisting the poor required some effort on the part of the poor and thus helped to preserve their dignity. It also required the active participation of a caring individual such as Boaz.

While designed for an agricultural society, the basic principles of God's poverty program are good for any society. No caring person should be indifferent to human suffering and human need. No person who claims to love God can close his heart to such situations (1 John 3:17). It can be difficult, however, to help the poor in a way that does not make them lifetime clients of welfare. It also can be difficult to help the poor in a way that requires their participation.

God's "poverty program" worked well during the time of Boaz and Ruth. Can we adapt that plan to today's urban, industrialized society? To do so will require a balance of compassion and wisdom. Compassion led Boaz to tell Ruth to stay in his fields. Compassion led him to tell the workers to leave a little more grain than they would have otherwise. Wisdom prevented him from sending Ruth to sit in the shade and letting others do her work.   —R. C. S.

C. Gleaning Begins (v. 3)

3. And she went, and came, and gleaned in the field after the reapers: and her hap was to light on a part of the field belonging unto Boaz, who was of the kindred of Elimelech.

The "happenings" in our lives are often under the direct control of the Lord, and certainly Ruth's *hap* falls into that category. The introduction of *Boaz* previously indicates that what was taking place was occurring within the providence of God. It was not mere chance, luck, or good fortune.

All of us would do well to reflect upon events of the past that seemed coincidental at the time, but were used of God in a special way to provide the people or the circumstances that became a pivotal part of our lives. Often some time must pass (in some cases, even years) until we become aware, like Joseph, that "God meant it unto good" (Genesis 50:20). [See question #2, page 208.]

A reminder is provided that Boaz was related to Ruth's deceased father-in-law, *Elimelech*. As noted in the comments under verse 1, this had

How to Say It
BOAZ. *Bo*-az.
ELIMELECH. Ee-*lim*-eh-leck.
MARA. *Mah*-ruh.
MOAB. *Mo*-ab.
MOABITE. *Mo*-ub-ite.
MOABITESS. *Mo*-ub-ite-ess.
MOABITISH. *Mo*-ub-ite-ish.
NAOMI. Nay-*oh*-me.
OBED. *Oh*-bed.
ORPAH. *Or*-pah.

important implications that will be developed as the account unfolds.

II. Ruth's Recognition
(Ruth 2:8-12)

A. Boaz's Kindness (vv. 8, 9)

8. Then said Boaz unto Ruth, Hearest thou not, my daughter? Go not to glean in another field, neither go from hence, but abide here fast by my maidens.

A part of God's providence or "hap" in this account is that *Boaz* came out from Bethlehem that very day to speak kindly to his reapers and to ask the Lord's blessing upon them (Ruth 2:4). While doing so, he saw *Ruth* and inquired about her identity. She was described to him as "the Moabitish damsel" (Ruth 2:6).

Boaz's kindness was then extended to this woman (a foreigner) who had come to his field to glean. He addressed her as *my daughter*, which is usually understood to mean that Boaz was older than Ruth. His kindness compelled him to give special considerations to her in order to make her situation easier: she was not to *go to another field;* she was to stay *fast* (close) to his *maidens.*

Some have suggested that the women in a harvest crew were the ones who tied the stalks of grain that the men had cut. Those who gleaned would follow the harvesting crew as it moved from field to field.

THE WORTH OF WORK

An old Greek proverb says "Work is no disgrace; the disgrace is idleness." D. W. Jerrold wrote, "The ugliest of trades have their moments of pleasure." Honest work always has been honorable. While we may call this the Protestant work ethic, the fact is that the dignity of work goes back to the creation. God is introduced to us as a God of work. He gave the first man work to do in the garden (Genesis 2:15). Jesus said, "My Father worketh hitherto, and I work" (John 5:17). Paul said that the one who would not work should not eat (2 Thessalonians 3:10). Thus Ruth did not need to feel humiliated or demeaned in any way by the work that she did gleaning grain.

A man retired after many years with the same firm. The company gave him a dinner and presented him with a plaque and a gold watch. Seated next to him was a young employee who said, "I envy you." The man who was retiring said, "Don't envy me. The greatest privilege you will ever have is to work."

Certainly Ruth was well rewarded for her willingness to work, and her reward went far beyond the harvest of the day's labor. All of us will find that work blesses us, not just in the wages we receive but in better physical and mental health. Our spiritual health will improve as well, when we seek to do our work "in the name of the Lord Jesus, giving thanks to God and the Father by him" (Colossians 3:17). —R. C. S.

9. Let thine eyes be on the field that they do reap, and go thou after them: have I not charged the young men that they shall not touch thee? and when thou art athirst, go unto the vessels, and drink of that which the young men have drawn.

Boaz expanded his gracious provisions toward Ruth. He encouraged her not to go to any other fields except those where his maidens were working. The *men* who were working would be charged not to *touch* Ruth, which meant that they should not harm her in any way. The fact that she was a foreigner and had no husband made this more likely. Boaz's final provision was that Ruth could satisfy her thirst from the containers of water that the other workers had brought with them. She would not have to be burdened with bringing her own supply of water.

Thus Boaz was practicing what his descendant, Jesus, would later advocate: the principle of going the second mile or doing more than is required (Matthew 5:41). The Mosaic law required only that the corners of the field be left unharvested and that dropped stalks of grain not be picked up by the reapers. A deed of kindness may not be the most convenient for a person to do, but it can have eternal consequences. [See question #3, page 208.]

B. Ruth's Gratitude (v. 10)

10. Then she fell on her face, and bowed herself to the ground, and said unto him, Why have I found grace in thine eyes, that thou shouldest take knowledge of me, seeing I am a stranger?

When Ruth left Naomi that morning, there was probably some uncertainty in her mind about how the events of the day would unfold. Now the kindness of Boaz overwhelmed Ruth: a place to glean, water, and the promise of safety. She responded in the manner that is still typical in that region: she *fell* to her knees and touched *her face . . . to the ground.*

Not only was Ruth moved by this unexpected kindness, but she also wanted to know *why* she was the object of this *grace,* or favor. Such treatment was not what she expected, for she was aware that she was a *stranger* in Judah.

C. Boaz's Compliment (v. 11)

11. And Boaz answered and said unto her, It hath fully been showed me, all that thou hast done unto thy mother-in-law since the death of

thine husband; and how thou hast left thy father and thy mother, and the land of thy nativity, and art come unto a people which thou knewest not heretofore.

Boaz's answer indicated that he was aware of recent events in his community. Someone had *fully* informed him concerning Ruth's decision to leave her *father*, *mother*, and *the land of* her *nativity* (birth) to become part of a *people* with whom she had had little if any prior contact. It takes a special faith and courage to leave behind the things and people that are a part of one's identity, in order to take on what amounts to a new identity. Ruth's commitment is reminiscent of that of Abram (later called Abraham), whom God told, "Get thee out of thy country, and from thy kindred, and from thy father's house, unto a land that I will show thee" (Genesis 12:1).

Visual for lesson 11

The visual for today's lesson illustrates verse 12 of the lesson text.

D. Boaz's Blessing (v. 12)

12. The LORD recompense thy work, and a full reward be given thee of the LORD God of Israel, under whose wings thou art come to trust.

Boaz then included a formal blessing that he pronounced in the name of *the Lord*—the God whom Ruth had chosen to accept as her own (Ruth 1:16). Boaz desired that Ruth would be blessed richly for all she had done. The final phrase in this verse emphasizes Ruth's decision to leave behind the god of her Moabite upbringing and to cast herself upon the Lord. Boaz used a particularly striking word picture—a young bird's taking refuge *under* the *wings* of its mother. This symbol is found in the book of Psalms (Psalms 36:7; 63:7; 91:4), and it was used by Jesus when He wept over the city of Jerusalem not long before His crucifixion (Matthew 23:37). [See question #4, page 208.]

III. Ruth's Reward
(Ruth 4:13-17)

A. Marriage and a Son (v. 13)

13. So Boaz took Ruth, and she was his wife: and when he went in unto her, the LORD gave her conception, and she bare a son.

Much transpired between the two sections of Scripture that make up our printed text. Ruth's gleaning continued through barley harvest and into wheat harvest, which occurred during our months of May and June (2:23).

Naomi then re-entered the drama as a "matchmaker." She intended to find "rest" (meaning a husband) for Ruth (3:1). She gave instructions to Ruth on how she should propose to Boaz, whom she described as "our kindred" (3:2).

Behind this plan for marriage was a command of God in the law of Moses that the brother of a man who had died childless was to marry the deceased man's widow and raise up children for him (Deuteronomy 25:5-10; Mark 12:19-23). In the case of Ruth, since there was no brother of the deceased for her to marry, it was the kinsman's duty to take over this responsibility.

Ruth did propose to Boaz, and Boaz responded in an appropriate way. He was aware that there was a "kinsman" who was more closely related than he (3:12), and that he should be given first choice concerning Ruth. (Thus Boaz is to be commended and admired for his tact and consideration in this sensitive matter.) The closer relative, however, chose not to marry Ruth (4:5, 6). Boaz was then free to purchase all that belonged to Elimelech (Naomi's late husband), which included his land and the responsibility to marry Ruth, the widow of one of Elimelech's sons.

The verse before us is very simple. Left unmentioned are the emotions that must have been experienced by Naomi, Ruth (who apparently had no children from her former marriage), and Boaz. Most important is the statement that the *conception* of Boaz and Ruth's child (a *son*) was of *the Lord*.

B. The Women's Blessing (vv. 14, 15)

14. And the women said unto Naomi, Blessed be the LORD, which hath not left thee this day without a kinsman, that his name may be famous in Israel.

Most likely the *women* of Bethlehem recalled the statement that Naomi made when she returned from Moab: she requested to be called *Mara* (meaning "bitter"), not *Naomi* (meaning "pleasant"). She added that she had left Bethlehem "full," but the Lord had brought her back "empty" (Ruth 1:20, 21). This praise to God from the women noted that He had made Naomi's life "full" again. [See question #5, page 208.]

Bible students debate the identity of the word *kinsman* in this verse. Does it refer to Boaz or to the son of Boaz and Ruth? A good case may be made for either position. The special kindnesses of Boaz highlighted in the book of Ruth seem to suggest that he is being described; on the other hand, the next verse calls attention to the son. Both Boaz and his son Obed became *famous in Israel*, and both of them are included in the ancestry of Jesus (Matthew 1:5).

15. And he shall be unto thee a restorer of thy life, and a nourisher of thine old age: for thy daughter-in-law, which loveth thee, which is better to thee than seven sons, hath borne him.

The women's pronouncements of blessing upon Naomi continued. They provided her with a confidence that the days ahead would be much brighter. Her *old age* would be a time of joy.

The person who helped make these blessings possible for Naomi was her *daughter-in-law*, Ruth, and the women praised her highly. They had observed her love for Naomi. The number *seven* is frequently used in the Bible to represent completeness. Thus the reference to *seven sons* highlights the superiority of Ruth's love for Naomi.

C. Naomi's Care (v. 16)

16. And Naomi took the child, and laid it in her bosom, and became nurse unto it.

Naomi had the privilege of caring for *the child*, who continued the line of her husband and son and thus would be considered her grandson. In this case, the word *nurse* refers to this kind of care rather than to the act of providing milk for an infant.

Home Daily Bible Readings

Monday, Feb. 4—Gleaning in the Right Field (Ruth 2:1-7)

Tuesday, Feb. 5—A Safe Place to Glean (Ruth 2:8-13)

Wednesday, Feb. 6—A Generous Kinsman (Ruth 2:14-23)

Thursday, Feb. 7—An Obedient Daughter-in-Law (Ruth 3:1-5)

Friday, Feb. 8—"You Are a Worthy Woman" (Ruth 3:6-18)

Saturday, Feb. 9—Boaz Marries Ruth, the Moabite (Ruth 4:1-12)

Sunday, Feb. 10—Ruth's Son: David's Grandfather (Ruth 4:13-22)

D. A Special Genealogy (v. 17)

17. And the women her neighbors gave it a name, saying, There is a son born to Naomi; and they called his name Obed: he is the father of Jesse, the father of David.

The women of Bethlehem named the baby and called him *Obed*. While this was unusual (the parents generally named the child), it may simply reflect the unusual circumstances behind the marriage of Boaz and Ruth. The name Obed means "servant." The reference to his being Naomi's *son* should be understood according to the word's Biblical usage, for *son* may describe any male descendant or successor. Again, it highlighted the fact that Naomi was no longer "empty."

Obed became the grandfather of *David*, Israel's second king. The mention of David indicates that the book of Ruth was written after David had become king over Israel. It also helps to give one reason why the book of Ruth was written—to give more details of the genealogy of Israel's most famous king.

Conclusion

A. Channels of Blessing

The title for this lesson is "God Blesses Ruth," and He most certainly did. While Ruth experienced many blessings, she also had many burdens. It has been observed that blessings are appreciated more if they have been preceded by trials. For example, water means much to one who is experiencing great thirst!

In addition, we must not overlook how Ruth, who was blessed so richly, became a channel of blessing to others. These "others" clearly included Naomi and Boaz; however, because of Ruth's place in the ancestry of Jesus, she also became a part of God's plan to save lost humanity through the death and resurrection of His Son.

Just as Ruth's example shone brightly amid the spiritual darkness of the days of the judges, so must we seek to shine the light of Jesus in times that are "crooked and perverse" (Philippians 2:15). True, we cannot erase all the darkness in our world, but we can, in the words of the old gospel song, "brighten the corner" where we are.

B. Prayer

Almighty God, may we become ever more resolute in living for Christ during the tough times and in exercising kindness to others who are experiencing their own tough times. In the name of Your Son, Jesus. Amen.

C. Thought to Remember

We have been blessed to bless others.

Learning by Doing

This page contains an alternate lesson plan emphasizing learning activities. Classes desiring such student involvement will find these suggestions helpful.

Learning Goals

After participating in this lesson, each student will be able to:

1. Describe how God blessed Ruth through the kindness of Boaz.

2. Tell how God's providence worked with human effort to accomplish His purpose in the lives of Ruth and Naomi.

3. Keep a record for one week of how God provides for him or her by working through people and circumstances.

Into the Lesson

As class members arrive, give each person a sheet of paper on which the word *Providence* is printed vertically. Also have these instructions written on the paper:

"Providence is defined as guidance or care that comes from God. Please complete the acrostic using words that describe God's providential care. You may work in teams if you wish." (This activity is also included in the activity page of the student book.)

After a few minutes, ask ten different class members to share one of the words they used for one of the letters. Write these responses on a master acrostic. Make the transition to Bible study by explaining that God's providential care often comes through everyday crises and circumstances of life. His care and blessings are illustrated well in the story of Ruth and Boaz.

Into the Word

Tell the class that the story of Ruth's second marriage is filled with tenderness and romance, but it is also a story of God's providence at work to bless all mankind. Write the name "Boaz" at the top of a poster and the name "Ruth" at the top of another poster. As you read Ruth 2:1-12, ask students to note clues to the character and faith of these two people. (Chapter 4 will be explored in another activity.) Appoint a "scribe" to write these characteristics on the posters while you conduct the discussion. Characteristics of Boaz might include *powerful (v. 1), wealthy (v. 1), considerate (vv. 4, 8), protective (v. 9), compassionate and kind (v. 11), and godly (vv. 4, 12).* After discovering these qualities of Boaz, mention another intriguing factor: according to Matthew 1:5, his mother was Rahab, the harlot of Jericho who helped the Israelite spies.

Characteristics of Ruth include *willing to work (v. 2), respectful (v. 2), diligent (v. 7), appreciative (v. 10), and godly (v. 12).* After discovering Ruth's qualities, explain "ears of corn," "glean," and "hap" from verses 2 and 3. Be sure to thank your "scribe" for the assistance.

Summarize the many things that happened between this portion of the text and the marriage of Ruth and Boaz. Mention Boaz's continued kindness, Naomi's matchmaking, and Ruth's unique proposal.

Next, write at the top of a blackboard or marker board "Blessings of This Marriage." Read chapter 4:13-17, asking students to note good things that happened as a result of the marriage of Boaz and Ruth. Write these blessings as students cite them. They may include *a kinsman for Naomi (v. 14), a provider for Naomi's old age (v. 15), a son, Obed (vv. 16, 17), Naomi's opportunity to care for her grandson (v. 16), and a lineage to David (v. 17)—and thus to Christ.*

Into Life

Point out that God was working through very ordinary circumstances to bring about extraordinary results. The loss of a husband for women in Ruth's culture was a traumatic event. But God used everyday cultural practices, such as gleaning grain, to accomplish a great thing in bringing Ruth and Boaz together. However, even this couple did not know God was blessing them in an even greater way than they could imagine. They did not know their great-grandson, David, would be chosen by God to become king of their nation. And they did not know the names of Ruth and Boaz would be tied to the lineage of Jesus, the Son of God. This couple fully illustrates how God may work through everyday circumstances to accomplish grand things.

Ask the class to share testimonies of how God has worked through circumstances in their own lives or in the lives of their acquaintances. While they are thinking, you might cite an illustration from your own life.

Conclude by reminding students that God often works in this way. Challenge students to keep a brief diary for at least this week, noting how God works through everyday circumstances in their lives. Conclude with prayer, telling God you will be patient as you wait for His plan to work in your lives.

Let's Talk It Over

The questions on this page are designed to encourage review of the lesson Scriptures and to promote discussion of the lesson by the class. The answers provided are only discussion starters. Let your class talk it over from there.

1. Gleaning in the fields was a way provided by the law to help the poor without humiliating them. How can the church today help its poorer members while preserving their dignity?

Sometimes the church can provide people with employment or can help them find work if they need it. Congregations should also involve the poor in ministry so that they can help others and not just receive help. Certainly, the church should teach them good financial stewardship so they can make what resources they have go farther. Perhaps the church can help provide educational loans and scholarships for needy members so they can secure better jobs, attain a better standard of living, and become better able to financially support the church's ministry. And finally, the church can teach the poor that any honest work done in faith, no matter how lowly it appears to the world, is honorable and pleasing to God (Ephesians 6:5-8; Colossians 3:22-25).

2. The lesson writer suggests we all ought to reflect on how God's providence has been at work in our lives. Tell about some apparent coincidence or chance event in your life that you now believe to have been God's providence.

Nearly every student probably could tell some story. Be careful not to endorse every event as God's *causing* things, especially bad things, to happen. James tells us that "every good gift and every perfect gift" comes from God (James 1:17). But God does *use* everything that comes to us as an opportunity to work for our good (Romans 8:28). We can trust God in His providence to protect the church from any evil that would impede the preaching of the gospel (Acts 4:25-30). God providentially "opens doors" for the church to fulfill the Great Commission (Colossians. 4:3; Acts 14:27). We can also count on God to give us spiritual protection against sin, because the Lord has pledged to always provide a way of escape from temptation (2 Peter 2:9; 1 Corinthians 10:13).

3. Boaz went the "second mile" to help and encourage a stranger, a woman of a different race and religion from his own. What does his example teach us about how Christians should treat people of other religions?

At one time it was common for people, in the name of religion, to persecute members of other faiths. In some parts of the world it still is! Most people, however, especially those in Western nations, now "tolerate" other faiths very well. Some of them hold that all religions are about the same, either equally true or equally false. The Bible, of course, does not endorse that kind of "tolerance." It does, however, teach us to live at peace with others (Romans 12:18; Hebrews 12:14) and to love our enemies (Matthew 5:43, 44). The best way to treat people who are different from us is to speak the truth in love, meeting needs when we can and always pointing them to the one and only Savior: Jesus Christ.

4. Boaz praised Ruth for trusting in God. How can we demonstrate our trust in God? How can we encourage others to do the same?

However we demonstrate our trust, we dare not "test" or "tempt" God (Matthew 4:7). Still, trusting God means we will step outside our "comfort zones" in order to do what we believe to be God's will. We may have to stand alone on some moral or theological issue. We may have to do something we have never done before. Allow your learners to tell examples of what they have done, trusting God to bless the outcome.

As for encouraging others, the best way is probably by example. Younger believers need to hear how more mature saints have stood up for their faith and been blessed by it. Even when taking a stand has resulted in persecution or martyrdom, their stories are inspiring and motivational.

5. The women gave God the credit for what some might call Naomi's "good fortune." How can we be more mindful of God's working to bless our lives in everyday events?

Perhaps the best thing we can do is to expect it. We often do not give God the credit for blessing us because we never expected Him to do so. Then, when blessing comes to our lives, we do not realize that God is the ultimate source of the blessing, even though He may use a variety of instruments and means to give those blessings to us.

One means that many have found helpful is the keeping of a spiritual notebook or prayer journal. Then we can write down our prayer requests and what we expect God to do. Alongside those notes we can record God's answers to prayer. It can be an enlightening experience!

Jonah Rejects God's Call

DEVOTIONAL READING: Psalm 40:1-8.

BACKGROUND SCRIPTURE: Jonah 1, 2; Nahum 3.

PRINTED TEXT: Jonah 1:1-7, 11-17; 2:1, 10.

Jonah 1:1-7, 11-17

1 Now the word of the LORD came unto Jonah the son of Amittai, saying,

2 Arise, go to Nineveh, that great city, and cry against it; for their wickedness is come up before me.

3 But Jonah rose up to flee unto Tarshish from the presence of the LORD, and went down to Joppa; and he found a ship going to Tarshish: so he paid the fare thereof, and went down into it, to go with them unto Tarshish from the presence of the LORD.

4 But the LORD sent out a great wind into the sea, and there was a mighty tempest in the sea, so that the ship was like to be broken.

5 Then the mariners were afraid, and cried every man unto his god, and cast forth the wares that were in the ship into the sea, to lighten it of them. But Jonah was gone down into the sides of the ship; and he lay, and was fast asleep.

6 So the shipmaster came to him, and said unto him, What meanest thou, O sleeper? arise, call upon thy God, if so be that God will think upon us, that we perish not.

7 And they said every one to his fellow, Come, and let us cast lots, that we may know for whose cause this evil is upon us. So they cast lots, and the lot fell upon Jonah.

· · · · · · · · · · · · · ·

11 Then said they unto him, What shall we do unto thee, that the sea may be calm unto us? for the sea wrought, and was tempestuous.

12 And he said unto them, Take me up, and cast me forth into the sea; so shall the sea be calm unto you: for I know that for my sake this great tempest is upon you.

13 Nevertheless the men rowed hard to bring it to the land; but they could not: for the sea wrought, and was tempestuous against them.

14 Wherefore they cried unto the LORD, and said, We beseech thee, O LORD, we beseech thee, let us not perish for this man's life, and lay not upon us innocent blood: for thou, O LORD, hast done as it pleased thee.

15 So they took up Jonah, and cast him forth into the sea: and the sea ceased from her raging.

16 Then the men feared the LORD exceedingly, and offered a sacrifice unto the LORD, and made vows.

17 Now the LORD had prepared a great fish to swallow up Jonah. And Jonah was in the belly of the fish three days and three nights.

Jonah 2:1, 10

1 Then Jonah prayed unto the LORD his God out of the fish's belly.

· · · · · · · · · · · · · ·

10 And the LORD spake unto the fish, and it vomited out Jonah upon the dry land.

GOLDEN TEXT: But Jonah rose up to flee unto Tarshish from the presence of the LORD.
—Jonah 1:3

Light for All People
Unit 3: All People May Share God's Grace
(Lessons 10-13)

Lesson Aims

After this lesson each student will be able to:

1. Tell the story of Jonah's rebellion against God's call and how he was brought to repentance.

2. Tell what factors may have made Jonah reluctant to obey God's call, and why people today are similarly reluctant.

3. Confront a situation where he or she is being challenged to carry out a task for the Lord and determine to obey Him, not run from Him.

Lesson Outline

INTRODUCTION
  A. Pride and Prejudice
  B. Lesson Background
    In the Presence of Our Enemies
 I. JONAH'S FLIGHT (Jonah 1:1-3)
  A. God's Desire (vv. 1, 2)
  B. Jonah's Defiance (v. 3)
II. THE SAILORS' FRIGHT (Jonah 1:4-7, 11-16)
  A. Dangerous Storm (v. 4)
  B. Desperate Measures (vv. 5, 6)
    Believing in Prayer
  C. Determination of Blame (v. 7)
  D. Definitive Solution (vv. 11-13)
  E. Divine Appeasement (vv. 14-16)
III. GOD'S MIGHT (Jonah 1:17; 2:1, 10)
  A. Special Fish (v. 17)
  B. Submissive Prophet (2:1)
  C. Safe Landing (v. 10)
CONCLUSION
  A. The Big Picture
  B. Prayer
  C. Thought to Remember

Introduction

A. Pride and Prejudice

"I have sinned." A theology professor once said that these are the three most difficult words for a person to say. Usually *pride* prevents one from saying them. It takes courage to tell the injured party, "I have sinned."

Marriages have been torn apart because of pride, as the husband or wife (or both) refused to admit to being guilty of certain actions or attitudes. Relationships between parents and children have remained fractured for years because of the stubborn refusal of one party or the other to say, "I was wrong." It is emotionally moving to read the accounts when such relationships have been restored to what they should be in the sight of God. Sadly, it often takes a tragedy, an illness, or a death before the people involved realize how immaturely they have acted.

Churches also have been torn apart because of struggles between personalities. Often pride is a key factor in creating and perpetuating the divisions, because no one will admit to being wrong.

Another *p* word that has caused immeasurable suffering is *prejudice*. This too has reared its ugly head among the people of God. Prejudice kept the Jewish Christians from taking any initiative to expand their outreach to the Gentiles. When Peter presented the gospel for the first time to Gentiles, he made some revolutionary admissions on that occasion: "God hath showed me that I should not call any man common or unclean. . . . Of a truth I perceive that God is no respecter of persons" (Acts 10:28, 34).

Today's study comes from the book of Jonah. It tells of a prophet who had serious problems with both pride and prejudice. The attitudes he exhibited should cause all of us to take a hard look at ourselves. Is there any of Jonah in us?

B. Lesson Background

The story of Jonah is one of the most familiar in the entire Bible. Personal information about him is found in 2 Kings 14:25. That verse tells us that Jonah's father was named Amittai (which is also mentioned in Jonah 1:1). Second, it says that Jonah's hometown was Gath-hepher, which was located about three miles northeast of Nazareth. Thus Jonah's prophetic ministry was apparently to the northern kingdom (Israel). Third, it cites a prophecy of Jonah that came to pass during the reign of Jeroboam II (who ruled Israel from 793 to 753 B.C.): the northern kingdom would expand its borders.

The specific date of God's command to Jonah to go to Nineveh (capital of Assyria) is not given in the Bible. Jonah's prophecy of the conquests of Jeroboam II probably occurred either at the end of the reign of Jeroboam's predecessor or at the beginning of Jeroboam's reign. Jonah's entire prophetic ministry would thus have included part of the first half of the eighth century before Christ. During these years, there was a power vacuum in the Near East. Assyria was weak and ineffective, and it was having difficulty with rebellions by outlying groups that they were trying to control. (That is one reason Israel was able to expand its territory as it did.)

The Assyrians had a reputation for extreme cruelty to those whom they captured. In addition, the northern kingdom had been forced to pay tribute to Assyria during the reign of Jeroboam's great-grandfather, Jehu. (This is not mentioned in the Biblical account but has been found in Assyrian records.) Jonah must have been aware of all of this, and that probably influenced how he reacted to the call to go preach there.

IN THE PRESENCE OF OUR ENEMIES

The girl was engaged to be married when her fiancé went off to fight in World War II. But he never returned, for he was killed in the Pacific theater of the war by the Japanese. So the young woman enrolled in Bible college, with plans to become a missionary. After completing her studies, she set out for her mission field. Can you guess where she went? That's right—Japan.

This woman's actions were the very opposite of Jonah's. Jesus taught us to love our enemies and pray for them. It goes without saying that we ought to try to evangelize them. Jonah could not see that the best way to treat an enemy nation is to lead that nation to the true God.

What we learn from Jonah concerning nations applies equally to individuals. Every person needs Christ, including people we do not necessarily like and people who treat us badly. The Bible is a very practical book. It never presumes that we will get through life without making enemies. What it does teach us is how to deal with them. Those lessons are seen in the experiences of Jonah, and they are reinforced in the teachings and example of both Jesus and the apostles. No nation or individual should be considered "off limits" to the good news of salvation.   —R. C. S.

I. Jonah's Flight
(Jonah 1:1-3)

A. God's Desire (vv. 1, 2)

1, 2. Now the word of the LORD came unto Jonah the son of Amittai, saying, Arise, go to Nineveh, that great city, and cry against it; for their wickedness is come up before me.

Several of God's prophets delivered messages about other lands besides Israel and Judah, but no prophet but *Jonah* was sent on a lengthy preaching ministry to a foreign land. In one instance Elisha went to Damascus, but only to tell Hazael that he would be the next king of Syria (2 Kings 8:7-15). Both Daniel and Ezekiel lived in Babylon, but they ministered primarily to God's people who were in exile. Jonah's commission is unique. (See question #1, page 216.)

The Lord describes Nineveh as *that great city*. Nineveh was great because of its influence and its size. It was located on the banks of the Tigris River, over five hundred miles from Jonah's

hometown of Gath-hepher. The reference in Jonah 4:11 to one hundred twenty thousand persons "that cannot discern between their right hand and their left hand" is considered by some as a description of small children. If so, the entire population of the city could have been as many as six hundred thousand.

Nineveh was also great in a less impressive sense: its *wickedness* was great. The phrase *is come up before me* does not imply that God had only recently become aware of conditions in Nineveh. The language implies that God is about to act to address a particular situation. Exodus 2:23 notes, just prior to the account of the call of Moses, that the cry of the Israelites in bondage in Egypt "came up unto God."

One truth seen in this account may easily be overlooked. Every nation's actions are known to God, and every nation is accountable to Him. A nation's leaders may not wish to recognize the Lord as God, but that does not eliminate their accountability to Him.

B. Jonah's Defiance (v. 3)

3. But Jonah rose up to flee unto Tarshish from the presence of the LORD, and went down to Joppa; and he found a ship going to Tarshish: so he paid the fare thereof, and went down into it, to go with them unto Tarshish from the presence of the LORD.

The location of *Tarshish* is not known for certain; it is usually believed to be the city of Tartessus, a city on the southern coast of Spain, close to two thousand miles west of Israel. It has been facetiously observed that Jonah was subscribing to the philosophy, "Go west, young man," when God had said, "Go east!" (See question #2, page 216.)

Visual for lesson 12

Display today's visual as you discuss verse 3. Note how we must choose from the same options.

Approximately two hundred years before Jonah's time, David had written a psalm that expressed the impossibility of attempting *to flee . . . from the presence of the Lord:* "Whither shall I go from thy Spirit? Or whither shall I flee from thy presence? . . . If I take the wings of the morning, and dwell in the uttermost parts of the sea; even there shall thy hand lead me, and thy right hand shall hold me" (Psalm 139:7, 9, 10). The contrast between Jonah and David is noteworthy: one wanted to escape from God; the other was grateful that he could not do so.

Jonah *went down to Joppa,* a city on the Mediterranean seacoast that was fifty to sixty miles from his hometown. He determined to board a *ship* and to leave not only Israel, but also his responsibilities to God. He *paid the fare* and was on his way.

II. The Sailors' Fright
(Jonah 1:4-7, 11-16)
A. Dangerous Storm (v. 4)

4. But the LORD sent out a great wind into the sea, and there was a mighty tempest in the sea, so that the ship was like to be broken.

The book of Jonah is unique among the twelve minor prophets in that mighty works of God take place. The first of these is the *great wind* that was *sent out* by *the Lord,* which created *a mighty tempest in the sea.* Apparently the *ship* on which Jonah traveled was a cargo vessel. Note that wares are tossed overboard in the next verse. Jonah is the only passenger (besides the crew, the "mariners," v. 5) mentioned. The raging waves crashed against the ship, and it *was like to be broken.* That is, it was in danger of breaking apart.

How to Say It

AMITTAI. Uh-*mit*-eye.
ASSYRIA. Uh-*sear*-ee-uh.
ELISHA. Ee-*lye*-shuh.
EZEKIEL. Ee-*zeek*-ee-yul or Ee-*zeek*-yul.
GATH-HEPHER. Gath-*he*-fer.
HAZAEL. *Haz*-zay-el.
JEHU. *Jay*-hew.
JEROBOAM. Jair-uh-*bo*-um.
JOPPA. *Jop*-uh.
MEDITERRANEAN. *Med*-uh-tuh-*ray*-nee-un (strong accent on *ray*).
NAZARETH. *Naz*-uh-reth.
NINEVEH. *Nin*-uh-vuh.
SYRIA. *Sear*-ee-uh.
TARSHISH. *Tar*-shish.
TARTESSUS. Tar-*tess*-us.
TIGRIS. *Tie*-griss.

B. Desperate Measures (vv. 5, 6)

5a. Then the mariners were afraid, and cried every man unto his god, and cast forth the wares that were in the ship into the sea, to lighten it of them.

Three responses of the sailors are mentioned: they were *afraid*; they prayed, each *man unto his god*; and they took action to *lighten* the *ship* so that it would not sink amid the raging waves.

That these seasoned *mariners* (sailors) responded to this storm by praying reminds us that in a crisis all rules against engaging in religious activities automatically become "null and void": suddenly prayer is permitted! When a student prays before a high school football game, there are cries of protest. But when gunfire rings out in the school hallways, many people pray, and public officials encourage it!

The genuine believer, of course, does not wait for an emergency to pray. He or she prays "without ceasing" (1 Thessalonians 5:17). (See question #3, page 216.)

BELIEVING IN PRAYER

The comic strip *Family Circus,* drawn by Bill Keane, once pictured a little girl kneeling by her bed. She is saying to her mother, "I couldn't remember the Lord's Prayer, so I said the Pledge of Allegiance." In a sense, of course, every prayer is a pledge of our allegiance to God and of our dependence upon Him for blessings both material and spiritual.

People often speak of believing in prayer, but that is not enough. We must also believe in the God who answers prayer. Pagans believe in prayer, and in times of danger almost everyone prays. (Witness the sailors on board ship with Jonah.) But merely believing in prayer can become similar to believing that there are magic words which, if you say them correctly, will cause certain things to happen. True prayer, however, is not the recitation of magic words. We are not spiritual magicians who say, "Hocus-pocus" and then witness an immediate and dramatic change. We are children who come to a loving Father, confident that He will answer our prayers if they are in accordance with His will.
—R. C. S.

5b, 6. But Jonah was gone down into the sides of the ship; and he lay, and was fast asleep. So the shipmaster came to him, and said unto him, What meanest thou, O sleeper? arise, call upon thy God, if so be that God will think upon us, that we perish not.

Jonah's ability to sleep amid such chaotic circumstances is amazing. Some have suggested the stress and weariness resulting from the journey to Joppa enabled him to sleep. Others believe his sleep was an attempt to escape from the uneasiness of his disobedience toward God.

The *shipmaster* (we would probably call him the captain) probably found Jonah while looking for items to be discarded. He awakened the sleeping prophet and, with great urgency, pleaded with him to *call upon* his *God*. The captain wanted to make certain that all the gods were being petitioned during this crisis in the hope that the prayers would somehow reach the right one. However, the one true God—the one who was responsible for the storm—was fully aware of what was taking place.

It is interesting to contrast the pagan captain's concern for all on board his ship with the callousness of God's prophet toward the people of Nineveh. It is sad, indeed, when people who do not believe in or claim to follow the Lord appear to show more kindness and consideration for others than God's people do.

C. Determination of Blame (v. 7)

7. And they said every one to his fellow, Come, and let us cast lots, that we may know for whose cause this evil is upon us. So they cast lots, and the lot fell upon Jonah.

Many peoples in the ancient Near East used casting *lots* to determine the will of their gods, including God's people. (See Joshua 14:2; Acts 1:26.) When pagan gods were involved, this practice was nothing more than blind superstition, but when it was done according to the instructions of the one true God, it was reliable. There is nothing in the Bible that suggests we today should continue this practice, however.

The exact procedure used by these sailors is not known; it may have been as simple as having one object marked, then the one considered guilty would draw the marked item. Whatever the procedure, the one true God saw to it that *the lot fell upon Jonah.*

D. Definitive Solution (vv. 11-13)

11. Then said they unto him, What shall we do unto thee, that the sea may be calm unto us? for the sea wrought, and was tempestuous.

In the verses not included in our printed text (8-10), Jonah had identified himself as a Hebrew. He stated that he feared "the Lord, the God of heaven, which hath made the sea and the dry land" (v. 9). Yet, at some point, he also had admitted to the sailors that he was trying to run away from this God (v. 10)! The sailors then made a logical assumption—that Jonah would know what should be done so that *the sea may be calm.* That *the sea wrought* means that the storm was becoming more intense.

12. And he said unto them, Take me up, and cast me forth into the sea; so shall the sea be calm unto you: for I know that for my sake this great tempest is upon you.

Jonah's offer certainly appears courageous, but his motives are open to speculation. Was he sincerely penitent for what he had done and for what his actions had caused the sailors? Did he think that he would drown as punishment for having attempted to run from God? At any rate, Jonah was very emphatic that the *sea* would become *calm* if he were thrown overboard and that it was his fault that the *tempest* had arisen.

13. Nevertheless the men rowed hard to bring it to the land; but they could not: for the sea wrought, and was tempestuous against them.

The sailors were reluctant to comply with Jonah's offer. We don't know whether they hesitated out of concern for Jonah's welfare or out of fear that causing Jonah's death would further antagonize Jonah's God. Thus they tried even harder *to bring* the ship *to the land; but they could not.* (See question #4, page 216.)

E. Divine Appeasement (vv. 14-16)

14. Wherefore they cried unto the LORD, and said, We beseech thee, O LORD, we beseech thee, let us not perish for this man's life, and lay not upon us innocent blood: for thou, O LORD, hast done as it pleased thee.

The sailors seem to have been convinced of the power of Jonah's God. They did not want to do something that would anger such a God. So they went to Him in prayer and asked for His forgiveness for what they were about to do.

15. So they took up Jonah, and cast him forth into the sea: and the sea ceased from her raging.

The situation had become desperate. The men had but two choices: they could all die in the

Home Daily Bible Readings

Monday, Feb. 11—Good News for an Ethiopian Eunuch (Acts 8:26-40)
Tuesday, Feb. 12—"What God Has Made Clean . . ." (Acts 10:1-18)
Wednesday, Feb. 13—Peter Greets Cornelius (Acts 10:19-33)
Thursday, Feb. 14—"God Shows No Partiality" (Acts 10:34-48)
Friday, Feb. 15—Jonah Flees From God's Call (Jonah 1:1-10)
Saturday, Feb. 16—Jonah Overboard; the Storm Calms (Jonah 1:11-17)
Sunday, Feb. 17—Jonah Prays From the Fish's Belly (Jonah 2:1-10)

storm, or they could *cast* Jonah *into the sea.* They chose the latter. In wonder the men beheld the hand of God at work again—this time in the calming of the sea as it *ceased from . . . raging.*

16. Then the men feared the LORD exceedingly, and offered a sacrifice unto the LORD, and made vows.

That the men *feared the Lord exceedingly* does not necessarily mean that they renounced their pagan gods. Ancient pagans believed in many gods. At the present moment, however, it was clear that the God of Jonah was supreme; for He had been in control of the events that occurred. (See question #5, page 216.)

The men expressed their reverence by what they considered to be the appropriate actions: they *offered a sacrifice* and *made vows.* We can only wonder at the contents of the vows that were made. We also wonder where the sacrifices were made. Were the sailors near land and thus able to proceed to shore, or did they offer their sacrifices on the ship? We are not told.

III. God's Might
(Jonah 1:17; 2:1, 10)
A. Special Fish (v. 17)
17. Now the LORD had prepared a great fish to swallow up Jonah. And Jonah was in the belly of the fish three days and three nights.

Again the *Lord* went to work. This time He arranged for *a great fish* to be at the right place at the right time *to swallow up Jonah.* Both the Hebrew word used here and the Greek word used in Matthew 12:40 are general terms meaning a large fish, not necessarily a whale (which many have come to associate with Jonah).

Several incidents have been documented concerning men who were swallowed by a sea creature, usually a whale, and lived through the ordeal. One involves a man named James Bartley, who was part of a whaling crew working near the Falkland Islands (east of southern Argentina). According to the account, Bartley spent a day and a night in a sperm whale, having been swallowed when the whale attacked one of the crew's small boats. The whale was caught, and Bartley was discovered the next day while the whale was being processed. He was alive, but parts of his skin were bleached white by the whale's gastric juices. Some conjecture that Jonah's appearance likewise changed as a result of his being inside the fish. They believe that this may have given added credibility to the message that Jonah would eventually preach in Nineveh.

Of course, it should be noted that even if accounts of people being swallowed by fish did not exist, this would be no reason to discredit what the Bible says. God is clearly at work throughout the book of Jonah. He could prepare a fish to do what He wanted it to do as easily as He prepared the storm and, in chapter 4, the gourd, the worm, and the hot east wind.

Jonah is one of only two minor prophets mentioned by Jesus (Matthew 12:39-41; 16:4; Luke 11:29-32; the other is Zechariah, Matthew 23:35). The Matthew 12 passage is especially significant, for in it Jesus compared Jonah's time in the fish to His time in the "heart of the earth" (the tomb), thereby predicting His resurrection.

B. Submissive Prophet (2:1)
1. Then Jonah prayed unto the LORD his God out of the fish's belly.

The contents of Jonah's prayer (vv. 2-9) indicate that Jonah was expressing gratitude for His deliverance from what appeared to be certain drowning in the sea. It is interesting that he concluded his prayer with references to sacrifice and vows (v. 9), similar to how the sailors had responded on the ship (Jonah 1:16).

C. Safe Landing (v. 10)
10. And the LORD spake unto the fish, and it vomited out Jonah upon the dry land.

The Lord responded to Jonah's prayer by initiating another special action by *the fish.* (Someone noted that a fish can stomach a backslider for only three days, and then it makes him sick!)

Conclusion
A. The Big Picture
Grasping the big picture in the book of Jonah need not involve the fish, though that is a noteworthy event. It need not involve the repentance of the people of Nineveh, even though that is also noteworthy. The big picture does include the fact that Jonah's stay inside the fish became a type of the burial of Jesus prior to His resurrection (Matthew 12:40). Jesus' resurrection is the greatest event in all of history, for by it He broke the stranglehold of sin and death on all mankind. Now those who believe and obey Him have the promise of eternal life with Him in Heaven.

B. Prayer
Lord, give us courage, so that when You give us a task to do we will not run from the task or from You. Rather, may we walk with You in accomplishing that task. Lord, please bless our ministries for You. In Jesus' name, amen.

C. Thought to Remember
Running from God always complicates our lives; obeying Him simplifies our lives.

Learning by Doing

This page contains an alternate lesson plan emphasizing learning activities.
Classes desiring such student involvement will find these suggestions helpful.

Learning Goals

After participating in this lesson, each student will be able to:

1. Tell the story of Jonah's rebellion against God's call and how he was brought to repentance.

2. Tell what factors may have made Jonah reluctant to obey God's call, and why people today are similarly reluctant.

3. Confront a situation where he or she is being challenged to carry out a task for the Lord and determine to obey Him, not run from Him.

Into the Lesson

Before class, prepare a poster with the heading: "We are not looking for members; we are looking for servants!" (This will be used later.)

Also prepare a handout with the heading "Help Wanted" and these instructions: "Read the want ads below and mark the box that would indicate your response to each." Then list several ads from the newspaper (photocopy them or scan them into your document). Include ads for laborers, nurses, truck drivers, and a variety of other jobs. Also include homemade ads for Sunday school teachers, church cleaning teams, and others. After each ad, place these choices:

❏ Would consider this job.
❏ Would consider this job with training.
❏ Would never do this job.

After the students complete the handout, ask volunteers to tell how they responded. Then ask the students to look at their "never do" list, and say, "If God called you to do this job, surely you would change your answer. Why?" Note that God does call us to service, but many of us still run from what God would have us do.

Into the Word

Prepare a lecture on the lesson background. Have a student you have contacted during the week give examples of and insights into Nineveh's reputation for extreme cruelty to prisoners of war. (Most Bible dictionaries carry helpful information under "Nineveh" or "Assyria.")

Read the printed text. Put two headings at the top of two columns on a chalkboard: "Reasons to Run" and "Reasons to Obey God's Call." Then ask the following questions.

1. Jonah 1:2 gives two clues as to why Jonah ran. What are they? *(Nineveh's wickedness; Jonah's message would be "against" it.)*

2. Why would the lesson commentator say, Jonah "had serious problems with . . . prejudice"? *(He wanted to limit God's grace to Israel.)*

3. When you consider Jonah's flight, what words would you use to describe him?

4. What are the reasons for Jonah to obey God's call? *(Mention that the result of his work will be explored next week.)*

5. Why are people today similarly reluctant to obey God's call? *(fear, lack of training, pride, etc.)*

Into Life

Display the "We are not looking for members" poster. Discuss its meaning and implications.

Read 1 Peter 4:10. Emphasize Peter's assumption that every believer has something God wants him to do. Though we may at first be as reluctant as Jonah, we must be objective and honest, not emotional nor self-deceived. Give each learner a copy of the following evaluation questions to use the next time a ministry opportunity arises. Ask the class to decide the ideal sequence in which the questions should be asked.

1. Who in our congregation is better able and more available to do this than I?

2. How would doing this task help me develop the fruit of the Spirit? How would it hinder me?

3. How would my doing this task interfere with other church tasks I am responsible for?

4. Does the Lord have something more important He wants me to do now or very soon? What?

5. Can I do this without damaging church and family relationships? If not, what negative impact do I foresee?

6. What nonessential activities in my life are consuming the time I could better use to do this task well?

7. What opportunities that I do not now have would this service provide for me to be an evangelist?

8. What specifically do I need to pray about before saying yes or no to this Christian service?

Give the students index cards and ask them to write one or two things they have been asked to do by other church members recently but have declined. Then ask them to look again at the questions and, in light of the criteria listed above, determine what they believe God wants them to be doing now for Him? Close with a quiet prayer time asking students to make a commitment to be more open to God's next call.

Let's Talk It Over

The questions on this page are designed to encourage review of the lesson Scriptures and to promote discussion of the lesson by the class. The answers provided are only discussion starters. Let your class talk it over from there.

1. God recruited Jonah as a "missionary" to a foreign land. What can the church do to recruit missionaries to serve in foreign lands today?

Many congregations sponsor short-term mission trips for their members to aid missionaries and to appreciate what mission work involves. Those who do not become missionaries often become avid supporters. Another way to recruit new missionaries is to sponsor mission fairs and faith-promise rallies in the church. Regularly invite missionaries to tell about their work and challenge your members to aspire to that high calling. A third way to recruit missionaries is to take church members to missionary conventions and conferences. Expose people as much as possible to full-time missionaries, and some of them might catch the vision. A fourth method is to provide a guest missionary for every week of Christian service camp. Make sure children learn about missions early in life.

2. Jonah resisted God's call. What are some ways Christians today try to avoid God's call to service?

Some Christians avoid service by claiming they haven't had a "call." This excuse is based on the false notion that God specifically calls each person for each job He wants done. In fact, the Bible usually issues a general call for laborers to go to the fields of service (Luke 10:2). Some claim that they are too busy with work or other responsibilities. People *make time* for the things they value most. Making time for Christian service is a matter of having proper priorities. Some beg off because they do not feel talented enough. Not every Christian has the talent to do every type of service. But God has gifted each of us with some kind of talent. Finally, there are those who use family as an excuse. While our obligations to our family should take a high priority, they should not be used to avoid ministry. The believer may have to choose between Christ and family (Luke 9:61, 62; 14:26).

3. How can we avoid using prayer only as a means of rescue in perilous situations?

We need to cultivate a regular practice of prayer. Paul instructed the Thessalonians to "pray without ceasing" (1 Thessalonians 5:17). Prayer is not a life jacket; it is a lifestyle. We need

also to broaden our prayer perspective and petition God for others (James 5:16). A Christian should regularly pray for his family, his fellow believers, his coworkers, his boss, and his country. Jesus even counseled us to pray for our enemies (Matthew 5:44). Third, we need to offer up thoughtful prayers. Jesus warned against praying with "vain repetitions" (Matthew 6:7). In other words, simply repeating the same formula every time we pray does nothing to improve our relationship to God. We need to pray sincerely, about serious prayer matters, and reverently, remembering that we are speaking to the Almighty God, Creator of Heaven and earth.

4. The sailors' vain rowing for shore illustrates the futility of doing the opposite of God's will. What are some contemporary illustrations of this principle? How can we convince people of the futility of resisting God's will?

Some of your students probably can tell how they resisted the testimony of a godly spouse or godly parents, but at some point were confronted with their need for a Savior in a way they could no longer resist. These testimonies may be some of the best tools for helping people who currently resist God to turn around. But it is not just non-Christians who resist God's will. Has your church had a hard time breaking some traditions in order to reach out to new people in your neighborhood, or to younger people with different preferences, or to people without a church background? If we believe God is "not willing that any should perish" (2 Peter 3:9), what are we doing for those who are perishing?

5. This verse tells us that the pagan sailors "feared the Lord." This reminds us of the disciples' reaction to Jesus' stilling the storm. How can we lead people today to appreciate God's awesome power and to fear the Lord?

While the sailors' fear of God probably was not a wholesale abandonment of their paganism, it was a right first step. We do not have to quiet fierce storms to lead people to such a first step today, but openly telling of how the Lord has quieted the tempests of our own hearts might help. Give God praise for His creation, for His providence, for His holiness. Do it in a positive way. Some will eventually respond.

God Shows Mercy to Nineveh

DEVOTIONAL READING: Psalm 113.

BACKGROUND SCRIPTURE: Jonah 3, 4.

PRINTED TEXT: Jonah 3:1-5, 10; 4:1-5, 11.

Jonah 3:1-5, 10; 4:1-5, 11

1 And the word of the LORD came unto Jonah the second time, saying,

2 Arise, go unto Nineveh, that great city, and preach unto it the preaching that I bid thee.

3 So Jonah arose, and went unto Nineveh, according to the word of the LORD. Now Nineveh was an exceeding great city of three days' journey.

4 And Jonah began to enter into the city a day's journey, and he cried, and said, Yet forty days, and Nineveh shall be overthrown.

5 So the people of Nineveh believed God, and proclaimed a fast, and put on sackcloth, from the greatest of them even to the least of them.

. . . .

10 And God saw their works, that they turned from their evil way; and God repented of the evil, that he had said that he would do unto them; and he did it not.

Jonah 4:1-5, 11

1 But it displeased Jonah exceedingly, and he was very angry.

2 And he prayed unto the LORD, and said, I pray thee, O LORD, was not this my saying, when I was yet in my country? Therefore I fled before unto Tarshish: for I knew that thou art a gracious God, and merciful, slow to anger, and of great kindness, and repentest thee of the evil.

3 Therefore now, O LORD, take, I beseech thee, my life from me; for it is better for me to die than to live.

4 Then said the LORD, Doest thou well to be angry?

5 So Jonah went out of the city, and sat on the east side of the city, and there made him a booth, and sat under it in the shadow, till he might see what would become of the city.

. . . .

11 And should not I spare Nineveh, that great city, wherein are more than sixscore thousand persons that cannot discern between their right hand and their left hand; and also much cattle?

GOLDEN TEXT: Thou art a gracious God, and merciful, slow to anger, and of great kindness, and repentest thee of the evil.—Jonah 4:2.

Light for All People
Unit 3: All People May Share God's Grace
(Lessons 10-13)

Lesson Aims

After this lesson each student will be able to:
1. Retell the story of Jonah's mission to Nineveh, including the people's repentance and Jonah's displeasure.
2. Contrast Jonah's anger at Nineveh's repentance with God's steadfast love for all people.
3. Suggest a specific means to demonstrate the mercy of God through some ministry of the church or in his or her relationship with another person.

Lesson Outline

INTRODUCTION
  A. Second Chances
  B. Lesson Background
 I. JONAH'S OBEDIENCE (Jonah 3:1-5, 10)
  A. The Call (vv. 1, 2)
  B. The Crusade (vv. 3, 4)
  C. The Consequences (vv. 5, 10)
    The Clothing of Repentance
II. JONAH'S OBJECTIONS (Jonah 4:1-5, 11)
  A. Jonah's Complaints (vv. 1-3)
  B. The Lord's Correction (v. 4)
    Living in Anger
  C. Jonah's Concern (v. 5)
  D. The Lord's Concern (v. 11)
CONCLUSION
  A. I Am the Light!
  B. Prayer
  C. Thought to Remember

Introduction

A. Second Chances

In the 1929 Rose Bowl game, California played Georgia Tech. One incident in that game has been related many times. During the first half, California player Roy Riegels recovered a fumble, became disoriented in the resulting confusion, and ran sixty-five yards in the wrong direction. A teammate was able to catch him and tackle him just before he reached the end zone. Later, when California attempted to punt from that spot, the kick was blocked and Georgia Tech recovered the ball for a safety (worth two points). That play turned out to be critical, since Georgia Tech won the game by a score of eight to seven.

Something else happened that day in the California locker room, which overshadowed the wrong-way run. The California coach ended his halftime comments by announcing that the players who had started the first half would also start the second half. Everyone started to leave the locker room but Riegels. He was overcome with dejection and did not want to play. But his coach proved that he had not lost faith in his player: he encouraged Riegels, and Riegels went out to play an inspired second half. He received a second chance, and he gave it his all.

God in His wisdom saw fit to record the sins of many individuals in both the Old and New Testaments. But those failures are there for a purpose; as Paul stated in Romans 15:4: "Whatsoever things were written aforetime were written for our learning, that we through patience and comfort of the Scriptures might have hope." They teach us (among other things) that failure does not mean that we are no longer useful to God. God is a God of "second chances." The study for today highlights Jonah's second chance to hear and then heed God's call to service. But note that God's requirements did not change; for Jonah to take advantage of God's second chance meant accepting God's terms. There is always hope for those willing to take that step.

Others in the Bible also illustrate this point. David was guilty of covetousness and adultery in his affair with Bathsheba. He then plotted the death of her husband in an attempt to cover up the sin. His Psalm of penitence (Psalm 51) still gives hope to those who may think that their sins have left them without hope.

Peter's three denials of Jesus followed his bold declaration that he would never do such a thing (Matthew 26:33-35). But Peter was restored to a place of useful service (John 21:15-19). He preached the first gospel sermon on the Day of Pentecost, wrote two of the epistles in the New Testament, and may have been the primary source used by Mark in the writing of his gospel.

And speaking of Mark (or John Mark)—the mention of his name brings to mind how he earned the disfavor of Paul for "bailing out" during Paul's first missionary journey (Acts 13:13). Paul therefore refused to allow John Mark to go with him on the second journey (Acts 15:36-38). But years later, when Paul was in prison in Rome, he instructed Timothy to bring Mark to him; "for he is profitable to me for the ministry" (2 Timothy 4:11).

God specializes in second chances. He was willing to forgive the entire city of Nineveh when the people turned to Him in repentance, and today He desires to forgive all who will come to Him through Jesus Christ.

B. Lesson Background

The lesson text for today begins where last week's text ended. The fish that the Lord had prepared to swallow Jonah (Jonah 1:17) vomited him on shore (2:10). We do not know how much time passed until the Lord's call came a second time to Jonah. We do know that Jonah responded quite differently when it did! However, we shall see in our study today that Jonah still harbored certain attitudes that needed to be corrected. We shall also observe God's efforts to accomplish that correction.

I. Jonah's Obedience
(Jonah 3:1-5, 10)

A. The Call (vv. 1, 2)

1, 2. And the word of the LORD came unto Jonah the second time, saying, Arise, go unto Nineveh, that great city, and preach unto it the preaching that I bid thee.

The *second* call to *Jonah* is similar to the first one (Jonah 1:1). The *word of the Lord* included no rebuke for the reluctant prophet. He was simply to *arise* and *go unto Nineveh, that great city.*

The Lord's instructions to Jonah concerning his message were slightly different on this second occasion. This time Jonah was to *preach unto it the preaching that* the Lord gave him. (Previously he was to "cry against" Nineveh, according to Jonah 1:2.) Preaching anything but the Lord's message is perilous to both the preacher and his audience. [See question #1, page 224.]

B. The Crusade (vv. 3, 4)

3. So Jonah arose, and went unto Nineveh, according to the word of the LORD. Now Nineveh was an exceeding great city of three days' journey.

This time Jonah obeyed and headed in the right direction, though apparently he still had some reservations about going, as we shall see. The trip would have been several hundred miles, depending on where Jonah was in Israel when he began. But any site on the Mediterranean coast, where the fish would have spit Jonah out, would have been hundreds of miles from Nineveh. Obviously, then, making the journey was no small undertaking. [See question #2, page 224.]

Whereas Nineveh was previously called "that great city" (1:2; 3:2), here it is described as *an exceeding great city.* Archaeological excavations have revealed that Nineveh's inner wall had a length of almost eight miles. That may not sound large to us, but it was huge by ancient standards.

The phrase *of three days' journey* must not be a reference to how long it would take Jonah to get there. A journey of hundreds of miles would

have taken many days, even weeks. Instead, the phrase is another indication of the impressive size of Nineveh itself. Usually one of the following three interpretations of the phrase is suggested: (1) it would take three days to go either across or around the city; (2) it would take Jonah three days to preach in the various neighborhoods of the city; or (3) it would take three days to travel through *Nineveh* and the towns of the surrounding area. Greater Nineveh (which would have included those towns) covered approximately sixty miles in circumference.

4. And Jonah began to enter into the city a day's journey, and he cried, and said, Yet forty days, and Nineveh shall be overthrown.

Jonah entered Nineveh *a day's journey*, which probably means that he had not been there an entire day when he began to deliver the Lord's message. In the Hebrew text, Jonah's preaching consists of only five words; in our English translation there are eight words: *Yet forty days, and Nineveh shall be overthrown.* These few words could have been sufficient to make quite an impact, but they probably represent a summary of Jonah's preaching. By themselves, they say nothing of why Nineveh would be overthrown, or by whom. The fact that the people of Nineveh "believed God" (v. 5) and repented suggests Jonah included the fact that their sin was the reason for the impending doom and that the God of Heaven would shortly execute judgment. As noted in the previous lesson, some believe that Jonah's appearance (bleached or whitened from his time inside the fish) may have enhanced the power of his message. If so, Jonah must have explained how God had turned him around and sent him to Nineveh with this message.

It is interesting to speculate about Jonah's attitude as he preached. He had not wanted to go to Nineveh, and now he was preaching where he did not want to be. Classes on preaching usually

How to Say It

AQUILA. *Ack*-wih-luh.
ASSYRIA. Uh-*sear*-ee-uh.
BABYLONIANS. Bab-uh-*low*-nee-uns.
BATHSHEBA. Bath-*she*-buh.
ELIJAH. Ee-*lye*-juh.
JEROBOAM. Jair-uh-*bo*-um.
MEDES. Meeds.
MEDITERRANEAN. *Med*-uh-tuh-*ray*-nee-un (strong accent on ray).
NAHUM. *Nay*-hum.
NINEVEH. *Nin*-uh-vuh.
PRISCILLA. Prih-*sil*-uh.
TARSHISH. *Tar*-shish.

emphasize that the message of God has warnings, but these are to be delivered so that the hearers know that both God and the preacher have a genuine love for them. Preachers often have been accused of trying to scare people into being good, but the warnings within God's message have always represented His loving concern for mankind. To what degree Jonah communicated this concern cannot be measured, but we know from the results that his preaching had an impact! The *forty days* mentioned by Jonah provided a time for the people of *Nineveh* to determine the type of response they would make to his message.

C. The Consequences (vv. 5, 10)

5. So the people of Nineveh believed God, and proclaimed a fast, and put on sackcloth, from the greatest of them even to the least of them.

To some, the most amazing event recorded in the book of Jonah is how he was swallowed by a fish. But far more amazing is what Jonah's preaching accomplished: it sparked a city-wide revival! Three responses on the part of *the people of Nineveh* are cited in this verse. They *believed God, and proclaimed a fast, and put on sackcloth*. These acts of repentance involved every citizen, *from the greatest . . . to the least*—and even the animals, as verses 7 and 8 tell us! [See question #3, page 224.]

As was stated in the Background to last week's lesson, the year that Jonah went to Nineveh is not given in the Bible. Some place this event as early as 790 B.C., in the early years of the reign of King Jeroboam II of Israel (793-753 B.C.). It probably occurred sometime during the reign of Jeroboam II, but whether early or late we cannot be certain.

Over a century later another prophet of God, Nahum, announced that Nineveh would be totally destroyed and that this time there would be no reprieve (Nahum 1:1, 2; 3:7, 18, 19). True to the prophet's word, an alliance composed mainly of the Babylonians and the Medes destroyed Nineveh completely in 612 B.C. For now, however, the people had delayed that hour of judgment.

THE CLOTHING OF REPENTANCE

Life was difficult for farm families during the Great Depression of the 1930s. Some companies that produced cattle feed put it in sacks that could be reused as dress material. Many a farm girl went to school wearing a homemade dress that had been made from feed sacks. Out of necessity, girls wore sackcloth!

Of course, the situation described in today's text is very different from that. The residents (and animals) of Nineveh wore garments made of rough, coarse material (perhaps goat's hair) as a sign of their repentance. Even the king participated in this city-wide demonstration of a willingness to turn from sin to the Lord (Jonah 3:6).

In the Sermon on the Mount, Jesus taught that certain acts of worship are best done in private. For example, those who fast should give no outward indication that they are fasting (Matthew 6:16-18). And though Jesus did not mention repentance in His sermon, it too is something that should not be done so that we receive "glory of men" (Matthew 6:2). The primary outward expression of repentance should be in the way we live, not in the way we look. We do not want men to praise us for our devotion; we want them to praise God for the changes He has made in our lives. We want to "put . . . on [or, "be clothed with"] the Lord Jesus Christ" (Romans 13:14). That is part of letting our light shine—not to draw attention to us, but to our Heavenly Father (Matthew 5:13-16).   —R. C. S.

10. And God saw their works, that they turned from their evil way; and God repented of the evil, that he had said that he would do unto them; and he did it not.

As a result of the people's repentance, God *repented of the evil* that He had promised to bring upon Nineveh; and He *did it not*. That God *repented* should not be taken to mean that God had committed a sin of which He needed to repent. *Repented* in this case simply means "changed." Because the people *turned from their evil way*, God withheld His hand of judgment. It is still true that God takes "no pleasure in the death of him that dieth" (Ezekiel 18:32). He is "not willing that any should perish, but that all should come to repentance" (2 Peter 3:9).

II. Jonah's Objections
(Jonah 4:1-5, 11)

A. Jonah's Complaints (vv. 1-3)

1. But it displeased Jonah exceedingly, and he was very angry.

Now the focus shifts from the people of Nineveh back to the interactions between Jonah and the Lord. The negative reactions of Jonah toward Nineveh's repentance were intense. The prophet was *displeased . . . exceedingly* and *very angry*, though many prophets (and preachers today) would envy such success! Jonah's experiences with the storm, the pagan sailors, and the fish had encouraged him to go to Nineveh; but he was still far from God in his attitudes. [See question #4, page 224.]

2. And he prayed unto the LORD, and said, I pray thee, O LORD, was not this my saying,

when I was yet in my country? Therefore I fled before unto Tarshish: for I knew that thou art a gracious God, and merciful, slow to anger, and of great kindness, and repentest thee of the evil.

There is one good thing that may be said about Jonah at this point: *he prayed* (though his language in this prayer differs greatly from his prayer in the sea). Certainly he knew much about the ways of God. His description of God as gracious, merciful, slow to anger, and of great kindness is similar to that found in Exodus 34:6. Jonah himself, however, did not possess these attributes—at least not toward Assyria. He had his own set of values, and they were much different. He harbored an intense dislike for the people of Assyria, apparently believing that only Israel should receive God's mercy.

3. Therefore now, O LORD, take, I beseech thee, my life from me; for it is better for me to die than to live.

In the depths of self-pity, Jonah expressed a desire for death. This was not an idle statement; it was a sincere prayer—just as sincere as his prayer in the sea. There, however, he had given thanks for the Lord's deliverance toward him personally; here he expresses scorn for that deliverance when shown toward the Assyrians. It is difficult to imagine that Jonah would view his circumstances as so depressing that death was preferred or that he would pray to that end. Yet even the Lord's servants can experience such despair; Elijah is another example (1 Kings 19:1-4).

B. The Lord's Correction (v. 4)

4. Then said the LORD, Doest thou well to be angry?

With a gentle question (again, consider the similarity to Elijah in 1 Kings 19:9), the Lord responded to the rash prayer and statement by Jonah. It is the response that a person in Jonah's situation often does not want to hear. It demands thought—reasoned thought, not merely emotional responses that center on self. One may recall God's question to angry Cain in Genesis 4:6.

LIVING IN ANGER

In Austria there is a village called Anger. It is a small place; however, if all the people whose lives are dominated by anger lived there, it would be (like Nineveh) an "exceeding great city"! Of course, the word *anger* does not have the same meaning in Austria as it does here. It is an old German word meaning *meadow*. Still, it is a sad fact that many people do live their lives in anger. By doing so they spoil life for both themselves and others.

Thus the question that God put to Jonah needs to be put to all of us. The setting may be different,

Visual for lesson 13. *Note how the descriptions of God illustrate His grace, which Jonah took for granted. Do we take it for granted?*

but the question is still valid: "Doest thou well to be angry?" (The *New International Version* reads, "Have you any right to be angry?") Sometimes, of course, the answer is "Yes." It would be strange indeed if a person never got angry. There are many injustices and cruelties in the world, to which we ought to respond with righteous indignation.

On the other hand, often the answer to God's question must be "No." Our reasons for anger can amount to nothing more than "molehills." James advised, "The wrath of man worketh not the righteousness of God" (James 1:20). We do serious spiritual damage to ourselves when we live in anger. We cannot think, speak, or act like Jesus when we are angry. And anger unchecked will feed on itself, becoming more intense and harmful in the process.

If you are living in anger, it is time to move out.
—R. C. S.

C. Jonah's Concern (v. 5)

5. So Jonah went out of the city, and sat on the east side of the city, and there made him a booth, and sat under it in the shadow, till he might see what would become of the city.

Jonah did not answer the Lord's question (at least no verbal response is recorded). He simply *went out of the city* to a vantage point *on the east side* of Nineveh. There he decided to sit and watch to *see what would become of the city*. Apparently Jonah still held to some hope that Nineveh would be destroyed. Perhaps he took God's question in verse 4 as indicating that His judgment might yet fall upon the city.

The context indicates that this occurred during the summer, so while waiting, Jonah attempted to provide himself with some relief from the heat of the sun. He *made him a booth* so he could have a shaded area in which to sit.

Verses 6-10 provide additional details concerning this encounter between the prophet and the Lord. Apparently Jonah's booth did not offer sufficient relief from the heat, so overnight the Lord "prepared a gourd," the vine of which provided the extra protection. Jonah was "exceeding glad." But the next day the Lord "prepared a worm" to attack the plant, and it died. Note that the word "prepared" was also used for the fish (Jonah 1:17), but there is a great difference in size between the fish and the worm. God is the sovereign ruler over "all creatures great and small." Without the protection of the gourd, the heat of the sun (coupled with a hot east wind that the Lord again "prepared") made Jonah miserable. Jonah again expressed that it would be "better for me to die than to live."

The confrontation between the Lord and Jonah then continued with another thoughtful question from the Lord. He asked Jonah if the prophet should really be that upset about losing a plant—upset enough to want to die. Jonah replied that he was justified to be that angry, "even unto death." The Lord knew what Jonah's reply would be, and He set him up for the real question that concludes the book. Verse 10 begins that question. There the Lord challenged Jonah to think about all the emotion that he had felt for a plant. He had not done anything to cause that plant to grow; it had arrived overnight, and it had perished in a night.

D. The Lord's Concern (v. 11)

11. And should not I spare Nineveh, that great city, wherein are more than sixscore thousand persons that cannot discern between their right hand and their left hand; and also much cattle?

Here is the lesson of the book of Jonah in the proverbial nutshell. God loves all the people of the world. Jonah was concerned about only himself. God wanted to *spare* the people of *Nineveh*, while Jonah preferred death because of losing a plant. The destruction of Nineveh did not disturb his conscience at all. [See question #5, page 224.]

The number *sixscore thousand* (one hundred twenty thousand) *persons that cannot discern between their right hand and their left hand* is usually interpreted two ways. Some believe it indicates the number of young children in Nineveh—so young that they had not yet learned the difference between right and left. If so, then the population of Nineveh was perhaps around six hundred thousand. Others think that one hundred twenty thousand was the total population of Nineveh, and that spiritually they could not discern right (the right hand) from wrong (the

left hand). In either case, the point is clear: God wanted to spare Nineveh.

The final phrase of the book is interesting: *and also much cattle* (livestock). It may reflect how such animals depend on man for receiving proper care. If the people in the city of Nineveh are destroyed, then man's protection of these animals is removed.

Conclusion

A. I Am the Light!

Over the past three months, our lessons from Isaiah, Ruth, and Jonah have provided different ways to consider the theme that God is the "Light for All People." In a time when religious pluralism is emphasized and publicized, it is often awkward and unpopular to assert that there is only one God and one way to Him. All roads do not lead to Heaven. Jesus is the one way to God: "Neither is there salvation in any other: for there is none other name under heaven given among men, whereby we must be saved" (Acts 4:12).

If this is true (and it is), then it places a great responsibility upon all followers of Jesus. It is imperative that we live as the "light of the world" (Matthew 5:14), so that others may come to Him who is the real Light of the world (John 8:12).

B. Prayer

Our Father in Heaven, lead us to develop the attitudes that we must have to defend the faith in a courageous way and to love others genuinely so that we may accomplish the task of reaching them for Your Son. We ask in His name. Amen.

C. Thought to Remember

"God is light, and in him is no darkness at all" (1 John 1:5).

Home Daily Bible Readings

Monday, Feb. 18—Gentiles to Hear the Good News (Acts 15:1-11)

Tuesday, Feb. 19—God's Wonders Among the Gentiles (Acts 15:12-21)

Wednesday, Feb. 20—No Further Burdens on Gentiles (Acts 15:22-35)

Thursday, Feb. 21—Nineveh Believes and Repents (Jonah 3:1-5)

Friday, Feb. 22—God Decides Not to Destroy Nineveh (Jonah 3:6-10)

Saturday, Feb. 23—Displeased at God's Mercy (Jonah 4:1-3)

Sunday, Feb. 24—God Concerned for People of Nineveh (Jonah 4:5-11)

Learning by Doing

This page contains an alternate lesson plan emphasizing learning activities.
Classes desiring such student involvement will find these suggestions helpful.

Learning Goals

After this lesson each student will be able to:

1. Retell the story of Jonah's mission to Nineveh, including the people's repentance and Jonah's displeasure.

2. Contrast Jonah's anger at Nineveh's repentance with God's steadfast love for all people.

3. Suggest a specific means to demonstrate the mercy of God through some ministry of the church or in his or her relationship with another person.

Into the Lesson

Use one or both of these activities to introduce today's study:

Circle Response. Seat the class in a circle or in several circles. Go around the circle (or each circle) asking each person to complete the following statement. "I believe that the toughest people to share Christ with are. . . ." To make the transition to Bible study, remind the class that God had to tell Jonah two times to take His message to a tough audience. But Jonah's experience teaches us valuable lessons about our responsibilities and about our relationship with God.

Musical Reflections. Remind the class that God's will includes sharing our faith. That commission is often reflected in songs we sing. Ask the class members to "sing out" lines of songs or song titles that encourage us to share our faith. You may wish to have a few songbooks available. List these titles and lines on a poster. In transition to Bible study remind the class it is often easier to sing and talk about this commission than it is to do it. Even Jonah found it tough to obey, but he and God teach us a valuable lesson.

Into the Word

Use the background information and notes on Jonah 3:10 (see pp. 219, 220) to prepare a brief lecture on the setting for this event and on Nineveh's future. Next, use three students to read today's printed text. Give each student a photocopy of the text with his or her part highlighted. You will need someone to read the parts of the narrator, the Lord, and Jonah. (You may broaden the reading to all of chapters 3 and 4. If so, add a fourth person to read the part of Nineveh's king.)

Arrange the class in pairs or small groups. Ask each group to write on a poster words that would describe Jonah's nature and character. (Students

may wish to reflect on last week's events for additional insights into Jonah's character.) After they have completed their lists, ask the teams or groups to circle two of Jonah's characteristics that they see as dominant in his life. Have a team member post the group's work, commenting on why the particular traits were chosen.

Make the transition to the next activity by restating Jonah's dominant traits, emphasizing that the one good thing to mention about him was that Jonah prayed. He had a close enough relationship with God that he could talk to Him freely.

Lead the class in a discussion of the following questions:

1. A huge revival took place in Nineveh. With what you know of the people there, does this surprise you? Why or why not?

2. Reread Jonah 4:1, 2. Sometimes Jonah is called "the pouting prophet." What do you think was the real reason for Jonah's pouting anger?

3. Why do you think Jonah asked the Lord to take his life?

4. How did the Lord respond to Jonah's pouting anger? What does this teach you about Him?

Into Life

Prepare and distribute a handout with a three-column chart. Label the left column "Events and Lessons," and list the following under it: "God's Mercy and Compassion," "Second Chances (3:1)," "Jonah's Nature and Character," and "Taking the Good News to Non-Jewish Nineveh." Label the middle column "Principles and Lessons Learned." Label the right column "My Responses." Ask teams or small groups to begin by completing the second column. Say, "In the second column jot a few of the reasons God would choose to include this in His Bible. What principles does He want us to learn?"

Direct: "In column 3, note what you think God is expecting from you. Be specific."

Ask students to report their answers. Focus the discussion on "Taking the Good News." Ask how the church is already doing this and for new ways to do it better. Then ask students to work alone and take a few minutes to jot a few notes about how they will respond or apply these principles to their lives. Ask them to consider adding names of people to their response. Close with a prayer for boldness in taking God's message to others.

Let's Talk It Over

The questions on this page are designed to encourage review of the lesson Scriptures and to promote discussion of the lesson by the class. The answers provided are only discussion starters. Let your class talk it over from there.

1. The lesson writer says, "Preaching anything but the Lord's message is perilous to both the preacher and his audience." How can a listener be sure the preacher is preaching what the Lord wants him to say? What should a listener do if the preacher is not preaching the truth?

Tragically, many hearers will be deceived and be led astray. Look at the many cults and the followers each has. Of course, each hearer has a responsibility to compare the speaker's message with that of the Scripture. They should follow the example of the Bereans mentioned in Acts 17:11, or of Aquila and Priscilla in Acts 18:26. Many believers are unable to do that, however. The speaker sometimes twists the Scriptures to the point that an untrained or immature believer is deceived and unable to refute the error of the false teacher. The elders of a congregation have a responsibility in such cases, as Paul charged the Ephesian elders in Acts 20:28-30.

2. Jonah did not want to go to Nineveh, but he was persuaded to do so for God. What are some things you would not do for pleasure, for money, or for anyone but God?

There are menial tasks or jobs that involve stepping outside our comfort zones that most of us would rather not do. However, if we are truly disciples of the Lord, we will do them for Him. The Twelve thought washing each other's feet was beneath them, but Jesus showed them they ought to do the job anyway (John 13). Today we may need to care for a sick and feeble elderly person, clean a dirty bathroom, show love to a rude and rebellious teenager, or take on any one of many unpleasant tasks. It may soil our hands and knees, force us to swallow our pride, or otherwise require us to do what we do not like. But if Jesus went to the cross for us, what wouldn't we do for Him?

3. When the Ninevites repented of their sins, they showed their sincerity by fasting and wearing sackcloth. What actions today would indicate a proper attitude of repentance?

One positive action is a commitment to Jesus Christ. Conversion is more than renouncing one's past sins, as important as that is. It also involves entering into a saving relationship with the Lord and beginning a new life (Romans 6:1-11). After that, a new life requires a change in one's lifestyle. Anyone serious about repentance will want to live in such a way that he will be less tempted to go back to his old life. That may mean developing new habits, participating in new pastimes, and even finding new friends. Finally, repentance involves getting to know God better. A repentant person will want to pray and study his Bible more fervently and to develop a richer relationship with the One who has forgiven his sins.

4. Jonah's heart was not in his ministry. His displeasure at the success of the Ninevite revival demonstrates that clearly! How important is a preacher's attitude to the success of his preaching? What should you do if you discover your preacher has some bad attitudes?

Paul declared that whether the gospel is preached from pure motives or from bad, the important thing is that it is being preached (Philippians 1:15-18). This applies as long as the preacher's false motives do not color the message preached. On the other hand, if a preacher becomes known for having bad attitudes like racial prejudice or greed or some other, it can seriously affect his credibility and effectiveness. At the same time, we all struggle with certain temptations and sin. If our preacher is guilty of some sin, like a bad attitude or some other, the same grace should be extended toward him as is shown to any other sinner. (See Galatians 6:1.)

5. Jonah was not the last of God's people to think more about himself than others. How can we cultivate a selfless attitude in Christians today so that they are more eager to reach out to the lost than they are to satisfy themselves?

This is a continual struggle for most of us. Our culture constantly bombards us with the message of self-indulgence. We begin to believe the marketing hype that we "deserve" to have all our wants fulfilled. We need to repeat the message over and over again that God has called us to be His agents of reaching out to the lost. In sermons, Sunday school lessons, church newsletters, and in every other media available to us we need to sound that cry. And we need to demonstrate that we have the same "others first" mentality in our own lives and example. We need to follow in the steps of Jesus.

Spring Quarter, 2002

The Power of the Gospel
(Romans, Galatians)

Special Features

Lessons

Unit 1: Justified by Faith

Unit 2: Living By Faith

Unit 3: No Other Gospel

About These Lessons

The lessons of the previous quarter showed us that, even in the Old Testament, God demonstrated His concern for all people, not just the members of the Jewish race. In the present quarter we shall see how this concern translates into a gospel of grace. Paul's letters to the Romans and the Galatians state clearly and unmistakably that God's grace is for everyone, and that only by the grace of this gospel will anyone be saved!

Mar 3

Mar 10

Mar 17

Mar 24

Mar 31

Apr 7

Apr 14

Apr 21

Apr 28

May 5

May 12

May 19

May 26

Quarterly Quiz

The questions on this page may be used in several ways: as a pretest at the beginning of the quarter; as a review at the end of the quarter; or as a review after each lesson. The questions are based on the Scripture text of each lesson (King James Version). **The answers are on page 228.**

Lesson 1
1. In addition to being a servant of Jesus Christ, Paul was also called to be an _____. *Romans 1:1*
2. Paul stated that the faith of the Roman Christians was spoken of throughout the whole world. T/F *Romans 1:8*
3. The gospel of Christ is the _____ of God unto salvation. *Romans 1:16*

Lesson 2
1. What is the reason Paul gives why the Jews are not better than the Gentiles? *Romans 3:9*
2. Paul concludes that "a man is _____ by faith without the deeds of the law." *Romans 3:28*

Lesson 3
1. What did Abraham do that was counted as righteousness? *Romans 4:3*
2. Because of his faith, Abraham is called the _____ of us all. *Romans 4:16*

Lesson 4
1. Paul tells us to glory in tribulations, since they produce _____. *Romans 5:3*
2. Where sin abounded, what abounded even more? (grace, obedience, repentance) *Romans 5:20*

Lesson 5
1. Whom did Mary suppose Jesus to be when she first spoke to Him after His resurrection? *John 20:15*
2. What does the title *Rabboni* mean? (Father, Master, Friend) *John 20:16*
3. Paul tells us to reckon ourselves _____ unto sin, but _____ unto God through Jesus Christ. *Romans 6:11*

Lesson 6
1. Who helps our infirmities and makes intercession for us? *Romans 8:26*
2. Paul wrote that all things work together for good to them that fear God. T/F *Romans 8:28*
3. Complete this verse: "If God be for us, who can ____ _____ ____?" *Romans 8:31*

Lesson 7
1. What was Paul's desire and prayer for Israel? *Romans 10:1*

2. Paul said that whosoever shall _____ upon the name of the Lord shall be _____. *Romans 10:13*

Lesson 8
1. What are we to present to God as a living sacrifice? *Romans 12:1*
2. What are we to do to those who persecute us? *Romans 12:14*
3. We are not to be overcome by evil. Instead we are to "overcome _____ with _____." *Romans 12:21*

Lesson 9
1. Paul said it's wrong to esteem one day above another. T/F *Romans 14:5, 6a*
2. We are to stop judging each other so that we don't put a _____ or an occasion to fall in our brother's way. *Romans 14:13*
3. Whom should we try to please? (ourselves, our neighbor, our enemy) *Romans 15:1, 2*

Lesson 10
1. By what means did Paul receive the gospel which he preached? (from the other apostles, by reading the Scriptures, by the revelation of Jesus Christ) *Galatians 1:11, 12*.
2. Paul said he was dead to the law so that he might live unto God. T/F *Galatians 2:19*

Lesson 11
1. As many of us as have been _____ into Christ have put on Christ. *Galatians 3:27*
2. The Spirit of God's Son in our hearts teaches us to cry to God by what name? *Galatians 4:6*

Lesson 12
1. To avoid the yoke of bondage, we are to stand fast in the _____ wherewith Christ has set us free. *Galatians 5:1*
2. All the law is fulfilled in which commandment? *Galatians 5:14*

Lesson 13
1. We will not fulfill the lust of the flesh if we _____ in the Spirit. *Galatians 5:16*
2. In what spirit should we restore a brother overtaken in a fault? *Galatians 6:1*
3. If we sow to the Spirit, what shall we reap? *Galatians 6:8*

Laws Are Not Enough

by John W. Wade

THE PAST THREE DECADES have brought an appalling increase in crime rates across the country. In response we have passed new laws with tougher penalties and built more prisons to house the growing number of convicts. Still the crime and violence persist.

If we had studied history a bit more carefully, we would have realized that laws alone are not enough to maintain a stable and healthy society. The Israelites had the best laws in the ancient world—after all, the laws had come from God. But the Mosaic code did not solve all the problems that arose in the Jewish society. The law did bring some benefits for the Jews. For one thing, the law provided some definite standards for determining whether an act was right or wrong. Any society that does not set up such standards is likely to fall into anarchy, in which each person becomes his own police force and judge over his neighbors. Further, the law was a tutor or schoolmaster to bring the people to Christ. Most important of all, the law looked to the coming of God's Messiah, who would fulfill the law perfectly.

But there were weaknesses in the law. The most glaring was that it was "weak through the flesh" (Romans 8:3). The law could identify and describe sin, but by itself it lacked the power to help overcome the sin in one's life. Further, if one broke one single commandment, he bore the guilt for the whole law. But the gospel offers the power to overcome all the weaknesses of the law. Under the law, salvation could come only through keeping all the commandments. In the gospel, however, God offered a new and better way. Salvation through the gospel was through grace by faith.

Unit 1, Justified by Faith

The **first lesson**, "God's Righteousness Revealed," provides the theological foundation for the rest of the lessons of the quarter. The key verse, Romans 1:17, affirms that the "just shall live by faith." When Martin Luther understood the meaning of this verse, he was moved to challenge the Roman Catholic Church of his day, which made salvation by works a central part of its teaching. This lesson should challenge us to examine our own thinking and practices lest we subtly succumb to the temptation to base our salvation on good works rather than on faith.

Lesson two deals with "justification." This term is more likely to be heard among theologians than among ordinary church members, but we shouldn't allow that to turn us off. In a judicial sense justification means to make or declare one just. God is our Supreme Judge, and under the terms of the law He would have to declare us guilty when we stand before Him. But because of His infinite grace, He sent His Son to die for us, and if we are by faith willing to accept that grace, we will be justified.

In **lesson three** Paul anticipates objections that Jews may raise to the gospel basis for salvation through faith. Before God ever revealed the law on Mount Sinai, Abraham was justified by his faith, not his works. Paul was able to quote Genesis 15:6 as the basis for this claim.

Lesson four deals with "reconciliation," another term used by theologians. Our sins have opened a vast chasm between us and God that we on our own can never hope to span. But God has provided a way for us to cross that gulf. He has offered His Son, who died on the cross, as a bridge over which we may cross to enjoy God's wonderful blessings.

Lesson five gives us an opportunity to study the Easter story from a little different perspective. The first part of the lesson is based on John 20, which gives the historic setting for the resurrection. The remaining portion of the lesson is based on Romans 6. In these verses Paul shows the direct relationship of baptism to our Lord's death and resurrection. The act of baptism depicts the death, burial, and resurrection of Christ. The person who is being baptized has, through his faith and confession, died to the old man of sin, who is then buried in the watery grave of baptism, only to arise again in the "newness of life."

Unit 2, Living by Faith

Romans 8, which is the Scriptural basis for **lesson six**, has been acclaimed as one of the great chapters in the entire Bible, and justifiably so. Among other things, it deals with the problem of suffering. Although we may suffer grievously in this life, yet these sufferings "are not worthy to be compared with the glory" that awaits us in the future. The lesson concludes with Paul's assurance that nothing can separate us from the love of God, an assurance that can carry us through the many trying situations that we have to face in this life.

Lesson seven urges us to "Proclaim the Gospel." Earlier in his life, Paul had been an ardent foe of

Christianity; he had pursued and persecuted Christians. Once he became a Christian, however, he was zealous to proclaim his newfound faith. His first concern was for his fellow Jews that they would also come to know the Savior, but the message of salvation is for all nations. That message must be proclaimed if all are to learn the good news of God's love. The task of sharing of the good news is not assigned just to ministers or missionaries, but is laid upon all of us. Encourage your students to think of new ways that we can share the gospel.

Therefore is a key word. Paul uses it in **lesson eight** to move from theological issues to a practical application of these issues. When one becomes a Christian, a changed life is not incidental or optional. Paul puts it very starkly: "present your bodies a living sacrifice." This kind of total commitment brings a transformation of lifestyle that keeps us from being conformed to the world.

Lesson nine continues this emphasis on living one's faith in the world. Paul addresses the problem of becoming judgmental of others who do not agree with our way of doing things. He does not suggest that we compromise the faith, but he insists that on issues that are not vital to the faith, we should learn to be tolerant of the views of others. He reminds us that ultimately we are all accountable to God and His standards.

Unit 3, No Other Gospel

The last four lessons of this quarter are based on texts taken from Paul's letter to the Galatians. The immediate occasion for Paul's writing this letter was a vital theological issue that arose when Judaizers upset the churches with their insistence that Gentiles must submit to the Mosaic law. Paul resisted this effort with some of the strongest language he used in any of his writings. If the Judaizers had prevailed, Christianity would have been reduced to just another Jewish sect and lost its appeal to the non-Jewish world.

In **lesson ten** Paul first of all established his authority to speak to this issue. He was, first of all an apostle, called by Jesus Christ and not by any human authority. He further affirmed that the gospel he preached had not been received from man but had come directly from Jesus Christ. After establishing his authority, he addressed the theological issue. He concluded by pointing out that if righteousness had come by the law, then "Christ is dead in vain."

A major emphasis of **lesson eleven** is the "Gospel of Adoption." Jewish people prided themselves on being children of Abraham, and they had come to believe that they were entitled to special blessings as a result. This led the Judaizers to insist that Gentiles be brought under the law so that they could qualify for these blessings. Paul pointed out that those who have been baptized into Christ have put on Christ, and in Christ racial and cultural differences are meaningless. All who have come into Christ have been adopted into the family of Abraham.

Freedom can be either a wonderful blessing or a serious threat. In **lesson twelve** Paul deals with this issue. Some took the position that since they were no longer under the law, they were freed from all restraints. He urges the Galatians to hold on to their freedom in Christ. At the same time, he points out that this freedom must not become an "occasion to the flesh" but should be used to benefit others. This lesson concludes with a timely admonition to avoid strife and bitterness.

Lesson thirteen closes this quarter by emphasizing the importance of life in the Spirit. Paul contrasts the "works of the flesh" with the "fruit of the Spirit." Just to read the two lists is to gain an immediate understanding of the opposite directions they lead. Realizing that no one can perfectly live up to the high standards set by the gospel, he urges brethren to assist and restore those who have been "overtaken in a fault." He concludes by reminding his readers of the law of the harvest—that we reap what we sow.

This series of lessons may stimulate your interest in the important doctrines that are at the heart of our Christian faith. As a result, you may want to study some of these issues in greater depth. We encourage you to visit your local Christian bookstore, where you will find many fine commentaries on Romans and Galatians that will help you in this study.

Answers to Quarterly Quiz on page 226

Lesson 1—1. apostle. 2. true. 3. power. **Lesson 2**—1. all are under sin. 2. justified. **Lesson 3**—1. He believed God. 2. father. **Lesson 4**—1. patience. 2. grace. **Lesson 5**— 1. the gardener. 2. Master. 3. dead, alive. **Lesson 6**—1. the Spirit. 2. false (*love* God). 3. be against us. **Lesson 7**—1. that they might be saved. 2. call, saved. **Lesson 8**— 1. our bodies. 2. bless them. 3. evil, good. **Lesson 9**—1. false (every man decides this for himself) 2. stumblingblock. 3. our neighbor. **Lesson 10**—1. by the revelation of Jesus Christ. 2. true. **Lesson 11**—1. baptized. 2. Abba, Father. **Lesson 12**—1. liberty. 2. Thou shalt love thy neighbor as thyself. **Lesson 13**—1. walk. 2. the spirit of meekness. 3. life everlasting.

229

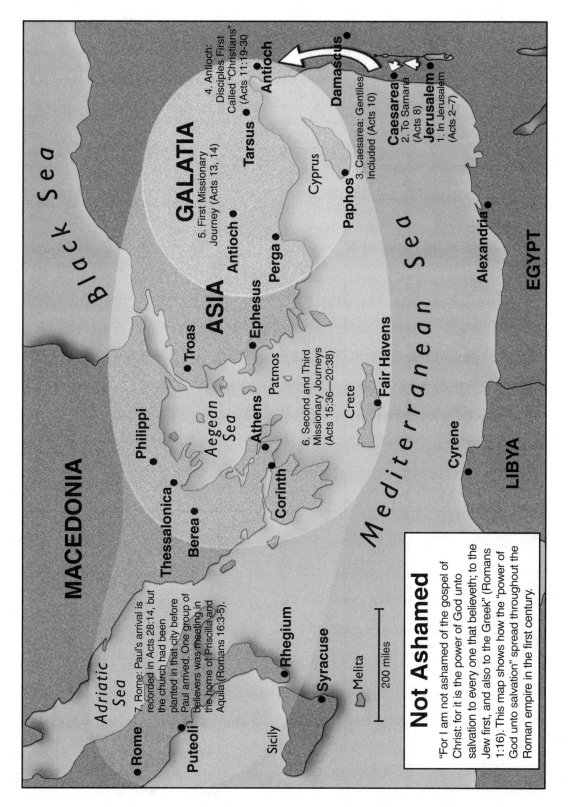

MACEDONIA

Black Sea

Adriatic Sea

• Rome

7. Rome: Paul's arrival is recorded in Acts 28:14, but the church had been planted in that city before Paul arrived. One group of believers was meeting in the home of Priscilla and Aquila (Romans 16:3-5).

• Puteoli

Sicily

• Rhegium

• Syracuse

Melita

200 miles

Philippi •

Thessalonica •

Berea •

• Troas

Aegean Sea

Corinth •

Athens •

Patmos

• Ephesus

ASIA

GALATIA

5. First Missionary Journey (Acts 13, 14)

Antioch •

Perga •

Crete

Fair Havens

6. Second and Third Missionary Journeys (Acts 15:36—20:38)

Mediterranean Sea

Cyrene •

LIBYA

4. Antioch: Disciples First Called "Christians" (Acts 11:19-30)

Tarsus •

Antioch

Cyprus

Paphos •

3. Caesarea: Gentiles Included (Acts 10)

Damascus •

Caesarea •

2. To Samaria (Acts 8)

Jerusalem •

1. In Jerusalem (Acts 2—7)

Alexandria •

EGYPT

Not Ashamed

"For I am not ashamed of the gospel of Christ: for it is the power of God unto salvation to every one that believeth; to the Jew first, and also to the Greek" (Romans 1:16). This map shows how the "power of God unto salvation" spread throughout the Roman empire in the first century.

Peter and Paul in Antioch

IN LESSON 10, in a text from Galatians 2, we encounter an event in which Paul was compelled to confront Peter publicly in Antioch. The only information we have of this event is this mention by Paul; it is not mentioned in Acts. Therefore, it is not apparent when this event occurred. Careful comparisons between Acts and Galatians, however, can yield a close approximation of when this event occurred. The chart below will assist the student in knowing how to place the event into the chronological framework of Acts.

Event	Date	Biblical Reference	Comments
Saul's Conversion	34	Acts 9:1-19	
3 Years in Arabia	34-37	Galatians 1:17, 18	Acts makes no mention of this visit to Arabia, skipping over this three-year period to tell of Paul's (Saul's) reception in Jerusalem.
First Visit to Jerusalem	37	Acts 9:26-30; Galatians 1:18-20	Acts tells of the church's reaction to Saul's conversion. Paul focuses only on his purpose in coming. The short visit of 15 days is explained in Acts: the Jews tried to kill Paul, so he was sent to Tarsus.
Second Visit to Jerusalem	46	Acts 11:25-30	This visit, to deliver famine relief (Acts 11:29, 30), is not mentioned in Paul's letter to the Galatians. It must have been very brief, and Paul apparently thought it not worth noting. The next visit, for the Jerusalem Conference, was much more significant to Paul's point in Galatians.
First Missionary Journey	47-49	Acts 13, 14	Some or all the churches in Galatia were established on this journey.
Third Visit to Jerusalem/ Jerusalem Conference	50	Acts 15; Galatians 2:1-10	Paul says he went to Jerusalem fourteen years after his first visit (Galatians 2:1). Counting both the beginning year (37) and the end gives us this date, which matches what we know of his later travels. Paul went "by revelation" (Galatians 2:2), indicating that he went, not to learn from the apostles and elders, but to demonstrate the unity that existed among God's inspired messengers. This is consistent with his message in Galatians that the gospel he preached did not come from men, but from God (Galatians 1:11, 12).
Return to Antioch	50	Acts 15:30, 35	This must be when Peter came to Antioch (Galatians 2:11).
Paul Resumes His Missionary Journeys	50	Acts 15:36	Paul wrote to the Galatians probably from Macedonia in 57 or 58.

The Drama of the Gospel
Using Drama in the Adult Classroom
by Ronald G. Davis

THE GRAND TRUTHS EXPRESSED by Paul in the epistles to the Romans and Galatians is high drama. The conflict is nothing less than good versus evil, sin versus righteousness, life versus death, law versus grace.

The "cast" finds its villain in anyone who would work on behalf of the Chief Villain, Satan. Sometimes it is the Judaizers who want to undermine and destroy Paul's work. Other times it is the Siren, Sin, that lures even the apostle.

The stage is as broad as the Roman empire, and the backdrops picture both the rural and isolated towns of Galatia and the urban sprawl and decadence of Rome itself.

The protagonist is in reality Christ himself, but Paul and the local Christians represent him in face-to-face confrontation with the Antagonist. Climax of the drama comes at the cross where the resolution of the conflict is realized and complete. Goodness, righteousness, life, grace—all are made clear and demonstrated to be victorious.

To emphasize the dramatic nature of the Bible study material, especially in Romans and Galatians, and to utilize a common interest of adults, learning activities involving drama can be good choices. To understand the human conflict of the gospel, in the first-century Roman world and in the twenty-first, dramatic approaches to teaching should prove to be worthy choices. Dramatic interviews, pantomimes, skits, and role plays offer useful techniques for studying Biblical truths.

Dramatic Interviews

A dramatic interview, a supposed face-to-face with a Biblical person or a representative of a Biblical group, lends itself to learner involvement in nonthreatening ways. The apostle Paul, a Christian named in Romans 16, a soldier who was assigned to "guard" Paul in his Roman prison later, or a Jewish legalist from Galatia—all could be worthy interviewees. Significant questions could be asked from both the Biblical text and the historical/geographical setting.

Let's interview a Jewish legalist from Galatia, "A. Lawson Lauze," as an introduction to lessons 10 through 13. Consider such questions as these:
• Mr. Lauze, what specifically is it that you are unhappy about in Paul's preaching?
• Well, Lawson, what is your strategy for contradicting the gospel of grace?

• Did you come from Jerusalem to Galatia to speak for the law? Did someone send you?
• What kind of success, brother Lauze, are you and your friends having in Galatia?
• How did the decree of the Jerusalem church (Acts 15:23-29) affect your plan, A. L.?
• When Paul's letter arrived in Galatia, how did you feel? How did you respond?
• How did the Galatian Christians respond to Paul's letter? And how did they react to you and your friends then?
• What will it take to get you to see Paul's presentation of the gospel of justification by grace?

The person to answer on behalf of Lauze needs to be recruited early and prepared for his responses. A careful reading of the whole epistle plus a study of the Judaizers' efforts to incorporate the Jewish law into the gospel will be essential. The teacher can do the interview himself, in front of the class, or he can invite the class to ask the questions he assigns or ones of their own creativity and composition. A discussion of the responses made is critical to gaining full value.

Pantomimes

Some texts lend themselves to pantomime as a way to draw the learners' attention. Pantomime, of course, implies that with a few broad strokes of wordless movement, observers can recognize what is happening. If the pantomimes are tied to a particular text, the task becomes even easier, a simple case of "matching."

The text of lesson 9, Romans 14:1-13, is a good example of such a possibility. Recruit class members to pantomime each of the following verse representations. (As you begin, you may want to do the third or fourth one yourself to show what is expected.) Tell your class to open their Bibles to the text, skim through it, and be ready to identify any verse(s) represented in a pantomime.

1. (Two players.) Both are sitting at a table filled with a variety of foodstuffs (players rub stomachs and lick lips?). One looks quickly and then picks up and eats voraciously everything there; the second looks disdainfully at him, ponders the table, and finally pinches a small morsel and sets it gingerly on his tongue (v. 2).

2. (Two players.) One player is sitting on a park bench (two folding chairs?) and idly tossing food to birds; the second one is ambling toward the

first holding a large book open in front of him and engrossed by it. The sitter sees the walker coming, picks up a large, heavy rock and places it in the walker's path. The walker arrives, stumbles, and falls—v. 3.

3. (One player.) The player goes to a calendar on the wall, puts his finger on a day, looks surprised, then falls to his knees in a prayerful attitude—vv. 5, 6.

4. (One player.) The player sits at a desk writing furiously into a book very clearly labeled "My Diary." After a brief time, he slams the book shut, stands, and lifts his eyes and the book heavenward—v. 12.

Skits

Skits are fully delineated mini-dramas, often humorous, designed to introduce a key truth to be studied or to repeat and reinforce one just immediately past. Many contemporary approaches to worship assembly use them to introduce a service's theme or a sermon's thesis. The script for a skit may be bare bones, but it is complete (in contrast to role plays to be discussed below).

Lesson 8 of this unit includes the verse "Avenge not yourselves" (Romans 12:19). Consider this skit for two players, husband and wife:

The husband sits in his easy chair holding a legal pad with a list of large-print entries. As he twiddles his pen and stares, his wife enters.

Wife: Dave, what in the world has your attention so focused?

(He turns the pad toward his wife.)

Wife: What is that a list of? It doesn't look very kind.

Husband: Kind? I don't want it to be kind. I told you what Steve did to me at work. He made me look like an idiot in front of Mr. Marsh. This is my "Get-even" list.

Wife: Oh, it's your "Even-Steven" list? (sarcastically)

Husband: Hey, I like that! Let me write that at the top.

Wife: I wasn't trying to encourage you, Dave. That doesn't sound Christian at all.

Husband: Christian? That was not my intention. Some behaviors have to be met head on—an eye for an eye, you might say.

Wife: It sounds as if you're letting your I—that's a capital one (with her index finger she draws a capital *I* in the air in front of Dave's face)—keep you from seeing what you're doing.

Husband: Well, sometimes a man has just got to stand up for himself.

Wife: (picks up a Bible, opens it, and hands it to him) Look at Romans 12:19. I guess you can make things right better than God can, huh? Wear a mask to work tomorrow; call yourself

"The Masked Avenger." Just don't call yourself a Christian.

Most classes have one or more class members who would enjoy the challenge of writing such skits on a verse or on a lesson theme.

Role Plays

Role play, sometimes called sociodrama, involves actors in a situation of conflict and undetermined resolution, designed to mimic everyday life without the consequences. The players are given initial notes as to the situation (a "jumping off" point) and brief descriptions of their individual characters, but the dialogue and direction are left to their spontaneous choices. Role play is designed to elicit discussion from the observers, so a role play can not be done incorrectly.

Consider the following role play for Lesson 1 on Romans 1:1-13, 16, 17, having to do with Paul's readiness to present the gospel in all places on every opportunity.

A mother is gathering her husband, teenage daughter, and ten-year-old son to carry a full meal to the house next door. New neighbors of Latin American heritage have moved in the day before, and she wants to bring supper for that family. The family in this role play is a faithful, church-going family. As the mother gathers her family and starts handing the food to each, she asks, "Now what do we want to talk about and not talk about?" One family member will ask, "Are we going to invite them to church?"

The teacher will need five copies of the situation: one for each player, and one for himself. As the four players meet very briefly to prepare (but not to reveal their own specific plan to each other), the teacher can describe the occasion and introduce the players.

Once the family "walks out the door, headed for the neighbor's house," the teacher can ask the class such questions as, "Did the family make the right decisions?" "Are their decisions realistic or idealistic?" "What different attitudes did you sense?" "What is there in today's text that is relevant to such a beginning relationship?"

An effective role play may well be worthy of repeating, letting new players (or the same ones) change the scenario as they go.

Theatre, as a context for presenting truth and wisdom or falsehood and folly, is as old as urbanized civilization. Manuscripts of dramas and remains of ancient theatre structures have filled the shovels of archaeologists. From the dramatic play of small children to the common adult attendance at movies, stage plays, and television, people are drawn to drama. Any way that the teacher can use that inclination will sharpen the adult learners' focus and enhance their understanding.

God's Righteousness Revealed

March 3
Lesson 1

DEVOTIONAL READING: Psalm 34:1-8.

BACKGROUND SCRIPTURE: Romans 1.

PRINTED TEXT: Romans 1:1-17.

Romans 1:1-17

1 Paul, a servant of Jesus Christ, called to be an apostle, separated unto the gospel of God,

2 (Which he had promised afore by his prophets in the holy Scriptures,)

3 Concerning his Son Jesus Christ our Lord, which was made of the seed of David according to the flesh;

4 And declared to be the Son of God with power, according to the Spirit of holiness, by the resurrection from the dead:

5 By whom we have received grace and apostleship, for obedience to the faith among all nations, for his name:

6 Among whom are ye also the called of Jesus Christ:

7 To all that be in Rome, beloved of God, called to be saints: Grace to you, and peace, from God our Father and the Lord Jesus Christ.

8 First, I thank my God through Jesus Christ for you all, that your faith is spoken of throughout the whole world.

9 For God is my witness, whom I serve with my spirit in the gospel of his Son, that without ceasing I make mention of you always in my prayers;

10 Making request, if by any means now at length I might have a prosperous journey by the will of God to come unto you.

11 For I long to see you, that I may impart unto you some spiritual gift, to the end ye may be established;

12 That is, that I may be comforted together with you by the mutual faith both of you and me.

13 Now I would not have you ignorant, brethren, that oftentimes I purposed to come unto you, (but was let hitherto,) that I might have some fruit among you also, even as among other Gentiles.

14 I am debtor both to the Greeks, and to the Barbarians; both to the wise, and to the unwise.

15 So, as much as in me is, I am ready to preach the gospel to you that are at Rome also.

16 For I am not ashamed of the gospel of Christ: for it is the power of God unto salvation to every one that believeth; to the Jew first, and also to the Greek.

17 For therein is the righteousness of God revealed from faith to faith: as it is written, The just shall live by faith.

GOLDEN TEXT: I am not ashamed of the gospel of Christ: for it is the power of God unto salvation to every one that believeth; to the Jew first, and also to the Greek. For therein is the righteousness of God revealed from faith to faith.
—Romans 1:16, 17.

The Power of the Gospel
Unit 1: Justified by Faith
(Lessons 1-5)

Lesson Aims

After this lesson each student will be able to:

1. Tell what Paul says about the substance of the gospel and his desire to visit the Christians in Rome.

2. Explain what it means for the gospel to reveal "the righteousness of God."

3. Express his or her own faith in Christ.

Lesson Outline

INTRODUCTION
  A. "The Just Shall Live by Faith"
  B. Lesson Background
 I. PAUL'S GREETING (Romans 1:1-5)
  A. His Identity (v. 1)
  B. His Message (vv. 2-4)
  C. His Credentials (v. 5)
II. PAUL'S READERS (Romans 1:6-13)
  A. Their Identity (vv. 6, 7a)
    A Community Set Apart From the World
  B. His Prayer for Them (vv. 7b-9)
  C. His Desire to Visit Them (vv. 10-13)
III. PAUL'S DEBT (Romans 1:14-17)
  A. His Debt to All (v. 14)
  B. His Readiness to Pay That Debt (v. 15)
  C. His Means of Paying That Debt (vv. 16, 17)
    Never Out of Debt
CONCLUSION
  A. We Also Are Debtors
  B. Faith in a World of Skepticism
  C. Prayer
  D. Thought to Remember

Introduction

A. "The Just Shall Live by Faith"

As a young man Martin Luther had come to believe that God was a severe judge who meted out harsh punishment to all who did not measure up to His standards of righteousness. He also had been taught that God's wrath could be turned away by doing good works. But he realized that he had no way of measuring whether he had performed enough good works to appease God's anger. So for several years, as a young monk and Bible scholar, he struggled with this soul-wrenching conflict.

As a teacher at the University of Wittenberg, he began to study the book of Romans. As he studied Romans 1:17, the truth suddenly burst upon him as a shining light. One is not saved by good works but by faith: "The just shall live by faith!" From that time on a dramatic change took place in his life, and he began to challenge many of the teachings of the Roman Catholic Church. Before long he was involved in heated controversy with the Roman Church that led to his expulsion and the beginning of the Protestant Reformation.

B. Lesson Background

The epistle to the Romans is almost universally acknowledged as the work of the apostle Paul. We are first introduced to Paul at the stoning of Stephen, when he was known as Saul (Acts 7:58). Within a short time he earned a reputation as a persecutor of Christians. After venting his rage against Christians in Jerusalem, he set out for Damascus to hunt down Christians there. But on the road to that city he was confronted by the Lord, which led to his turning to Christ, being baptized, and being called to become an apostle to the Gentiles.

Later the Holy Spirit called Barnabas and Saul to become missionaries to the Gentiles. On their first journey Saul began to go by the name Paul (Acts 13:9). Paul and Barnabas parted after this, and Paul made two other journeys accompanied by other companions. On the third of these journeys, he spent about three months at Corinth. It was here that he penned this letter in A.D. 56. The immediate occasion for his writing of the letter may have been his desire to carry on a ministry in the west with a stop in Rome on the way (Romans 15:23, 24).

While some late traditions attribute the founding of the church at Rome to Peter, there is no solid historic or Scriptural evidence to support this tradition. Among those who heard Peter at Pentecost were persons from Rome (Acts 2:10), and when they returned to Rome, it is reasonable to believe that they carried the gospel with them. Others who had been converted on Paul's missionary journeys later made their way to Rome and there found fellowship with the Christians already there. This is the reason that Paul knew so many people in the Roman church even before he had visited there.

Most scholars consider the Roman epistle to be Paul's greatest work. This letter is a profound theological thesis that deals with many aspects of the doctrine of salvation through Christ. But Paul is not just a scholar discussing theology in a remote cloistered retreat. The closing chapters of this letter deal with a number of practical issues touching on the daily lives of the saints.

I. Paul's Greeting
(Romans 1:1-5)

A. His Identity (v. 1)

1. Paul, a servant of Jesus Christ, called to be an apostle, separated unto the gospel of God.

It was a common practice for *Paul* and others of his day to introduce themselves at the beginning of a letter rather than at its close. Paul was no stranger to many persons in the Roman church. Paul had met these believers in other cities during his missionary journeys. But other Christians in the church there had never met Paul. For them, and as a reminder to his friends, Paul identifies himself as *a servant of Jesus Christ.* Literally, this word means a bond servant or slave. Paul had surrendered himself to Christ so completely that he was a slave. [See question #1, page 240.] Specifically, he had been *called to be an apostle* to the Gentiles (Romans 11:13). He was *separated* or set apart as a bearer of the good news to those who lived outside the Jewish religion (Acts 9:15).

B. His Message (vv. 2-4)

2. (Which he had promised afore by his prophets in the holy Scriptures).

For centuries Hebrew *prophets* had predicted that God would send a Messiah, an anointed One, to save His people. On Pentecost Peter boldly announced to his listeners that Jesus was that long-awaited Messiah (Acts 2:36).

3. Concerning his Son Jesus Christ our Lord, which was made of the seed of David according to the flesh.

The good news that Paul preached was about *Jesus*, the *Son* of God. The prophets had long foretold that the Messiah would be a descendant *of David.* Jesus fulfilled that requirement because He was of the seed of David *according to the flesh.*

4. And declared to be the Son of God with power, according to the Spirit of holiness, by the resurrection from the dead.

On the human side, Jesus was of the lineage of David, but according to the *Spirit of holiness,* He was *the Son of God.* This was not just an assertion on Paul's part. His deity had been confirmed *with power.* In the New Testament the word *power* often means a show of miracles. On numerous occasions Jesus gave dramatic demonstration of His deity and affirmed His claims by His miracles. And while there were others who performed miracles, only Jesus authenticated His claims by His *resurrection from the dead.*

C. His Credentials (v. 5)

5. By whom we have received grace and apostleship, for obedience to the faith among all nations, for his name.

The *apostleship* into which Paul was called was not something that he had worked for or earned in any special way. Rather, it came through *grace*, a gift from God. Paul's mission was to call *all nations*—that is, all the Gentiles. Paul recognized that Jews were to receive the gospel first (Romans 1:16), but his special ministry was to the Gentiles. Most Gentiles never had known directly about God, and as a result they were living in ignorance and disobedience. Paul's task was to lead them to faith in God and then into *obedience* to Him, to living lives of service and good works that demonstrated their obedience. Obedience is a logical consequence of faith, and any claim to faith that does not bring forth spiritual fruit is clearly a sham (James 2:17-26).

II. Paul's Readers
(Romans 1:6-13)

A. Their Identity (vv. 6, 7a)

6, 7a. Among whom are ye also the called of Jesus Christ: To all that be in Rome, beloved of God, called to be saints.

Although Paul had converted some Jews on his missionary journeys, the majority of his converts were Gentiles. It seems likely, then, that most of the Roman Christians were Gentiles. Yet Paul adds *to all that be in Rome,* thus including Jewish Christians who may have been there. All of them, Jews and Gentiles alike, were *called to be saints.* Today we often think of a saint as a person who lives on a higher spiritual plane than the rest of us. But that is not the meaning of the Greek word that is here translated "saints." Here it means persons who have been dedicated to God or set apart to His service. Thus every Christian is a saint. [See question #2, page 240.]

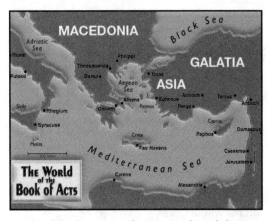

Visual for lesson 1. *The map in the* Adult Visuals *packet serves as a reminder of how the gospel spread in Paul's day.*

VISUALS FOR THESE LESSONS

The small visual pictured in each lesson (e. g., page 235) is a small reproduction of a large, full-color poster included in the *Adult Visuals* packet for the Spring Quarter. The packet is available from your supplier. Order No. 392.

A COMMUNITY SET APART FROM THE WORLD

In 1994, the new village of Vauban, Germany, was promoted as a utopia—with no need for fossil fuels to provide heat, light, or transportation. It was to be a community set apart from the "unenlightened" folks who depend on petroleum products for a luxurious standard of living. Solar power provided heat and light; narrow streets barred automobiles, which were seen as the primary symbol of the "old" way of doing things.

But compromise came soon. It turned out that many residents, who claimed not to own cars, actually did—and they were parking them illegally. So new parking lots were built on the perimeter of Vauban, where people willing to pay $17,000 for the privilege could park their cars. One of the original boosters for Vauban says that, just as in other European "auto-free" communities, "the idea always falls apart. People just can't get by without some access to a car." Vauban residents really aren't a "separated people"; they do not live in the utopia they had imagined.

Paul had once seen Judaism as the ideal faith, but Christ called him to a new way. He was separated—set apart—to be a leader in a new kind of community, one that eventually would produce a true utopia! The gospel message is that everyone can be a part of it if they are willing to commit themselves to Christ in the uncompromising obedience of faith.   —C. R. B.

B. His Prayer for Them (vv. 7b-9)

7b. Grace to you, and peace, from God our Father and the Lord Jesus Christ.

Grace and *peace* comprise a standard greeting that Paul used in several of his other letters. By using these terms, he combined a Greek greeting *(grace)* with a Jewish greeting *(peace)*, showing his ability to transcend ethnic and cultural barriers. He adds significance to the common terms, however, by declaring that grace and peace are gifts *from God our Father and the Lord Jesus Christ.*

8. First, I thank my God through Jesus Christ for you all, that your faith is spoken of throughout the whole world.

Once he completed his greeting, Paul's first thought was a word of thanks to God for them. Specifically, he was thankful for their *faith* that

had become known and talked about *throughout the whole world.* Without all the modern means of communication that we enjoy today, Paul and others had learned of their faith. This says something about how extensively people traveled throughout the Roman Empire in the first century.

In the early centuries, the church at Rome played a predominant role in the history of Christianity in western Europe, but Paul never envisioned that the ecclesiastical structure and control that the Roman church would come to demonstrate. The church's greatness in Paul's day was one of faithful example. [See question #3, page 240.]

9. For God is my witness, whom I serve with my spirit in the gospel of his Son, that without ceasing I make mention of you always in my prayers.

What a great prayer life Paul must have had! Not only did he pray for the church at Rome, but for those in Ephesus, Philippi, Colossae, and Thessalonica (Ephesians 1:16; Philippians 1:4; Colossians 1:3; 1 Thessalonians 1:2). He prayed for individuals, including Timothy and Philemon (2 Timothy 1:3; Philemon 4). To show his sincerity in praying for the Roman believers, Paul called upon *God* as his *witness.* (Note similar expressions in 2 Corinthians 1:23; Galatians 1:20; and Philippians 1:8.) Paul's example suggests that we today ought to remember in our *prayers* our brothers and sisters in Christ—both those we know and those in places we have not been.

C. His Desire to Visit Them (vv. 10-13)

10. Making request, if by any means now at length I might have a prosperous journey by the will of God to come unto you.

In verse 8 Paul offered a prayer of thanksgiving for the faith of the Romans. Here his prayer is a petition that he might be able to visit them. Apparently, he had harbored this desire for several years (Romans 15:22, 23). His prayer that *if by any means now at length* he might be able to visit Rome suggests he was even a bit frustrated that his long-standing desire had not been met. But his deep faith led him to trust *the will of God* in this matter. Eventually God did honor Paul's desire and allow him to visit Rome. But ironically he came not as a triumphant missionary but in chains as a prisoner (Acts 28:15, 16, 20).

11. For I long to see you, that I may impart unto you some spiritual gift, to the end ye may be established.

It was not Paul's desire to visit Rome as a sight-seeing tourist. He wanted to see them so that he could give *some spiritual gift* to them. The word for gift is *charisma,* which is used in the New Testament to refer to either miraculous or non-miraculous gifts. In this case it probably means the miraculous gifts, such as were bestowed by Paul on the disciples in Ephesus (Acts 19:6) and by Peter and John on the Samaritans (Acts 8:17, 18). There is no record in the New Testament of non-miraculous gifts being given by the laying on of hands; these appear to have been given directly from God.

12. That is, that I may be comforted together with you by the mutual faith both of you and me.

Even as Paul desired to bring a gift to the Romans, he also expected to be blessed himself. This is a most frequent result among those who share a *mutual faith*. When one brings a blessing to other Christians, the giver as well as the recipient is blessed.

13. Now I would not have you ignorant, brethren, that oftentimes I purposed to come unto you, (but was let hitherto,) that I might have some fruit among you also, even as among other Gentiles.

Some may have felt that he really wasn't serious in his desire to visit them. Now he assures them that he often planned to come to Rome *but was let hitherto*. That is, he was prevented from coming. We are not told what factors may have kept him from coming. He may have been so heavily involved in successful evangelistic work in other places that he could not leave and go to Rome. The Holy Spirit may have kept him from going (see Acts 16:6, 7). Nor can we rule out the possibility that Satan may have been involved in keeping Paul from visiting Rome earlier.

The *fruit* Paul expected to have may be converts that he would win to the faith or spiritual growth the Roman saints would experience as a result of his teaching. Since Paul was specially called to be God's witness to the Gentiles, it was natural that he wanted to visit a church made up predominantly of Gentile Christians. The expression *even as among other Gentiles* suggests that Paul saw the church at Rome as similar to the fields in which he had already labored, and that he expected the results to be similar.

III. Paul's Debt
(Romans 1:14-17)

A. His Debt to All (v. 14)

14. I am debtor both to the Greeks, and to the Barbarians; both to the wise, and to the unwise.

The ancient *Greeks*, like many people even today, considered themselves superior to those who were not Greeks. In a similar way, the Jews divided people into two categories—Jews and Gentiles, and considered Gentiles to be inferior. For the Greeks, anyone who did not speak Greek

was considered a barbarian. Of course, in Paul's time the Greek language was widely spoken around the Mediterranean. It is significant that Paul spoke Greek and the New Testament was written in Greek. Thus here Paul was not using *Greek* in an ethnic sense, but in a linguistic sense.

Paul's intent is to acknowledge that his debt to proclaim the gospel was to the whole human race, both Greek and barbarian. *Both to the wise, and to the unwise* is another way of saying the same thing—the debt is owed to everyone. [See question #4, page 240.]

B. His Readiness to Pay That Debt (v. 15)

15. So, as much as in me is, I am ready to preach the gospel to you that are at Rome also.

Every person who has ever lived has a debt to God as Creator. Further, every Christian has a debt to God as Savior. We cannot pay that debt, for salvation is a gift of grace. But since we are saved by grace, we have a debt to others who are yet in need of God's grace. We have an obligation to share the good news with them. Paul had a unique obligation *to preach the gospel* to all Gentiles, and in this case, to those *that are at Rome*.

C. His Means of Paying That Debt
(vv. 16, 17)

16. For I am not ashamed of the gospel of Christ: for it is the power of God unto salvation to every one that believeth; to the Jew first, and also to the Greek.

Paul had committed his life totally, every breath he breathed, to *the gospel of Christ*. He was convinced that he would never have a reason to be ashamed of this commitment. He had good reason for his confidence: the gospel *is the power of God unto salvation*. The Greek word here translated *power* is the basis for such English words as *dynamic, dynamo,* and even *dynamite*. The dynamic power of the gospel is manifested in many ways, including the blasting down of barriers between *Jew* and *Greek*, black and white, male and female (cf. Galatians 3:28). The power of the gospel to bring *salvation* has only one limitation—it comes only to those who believe.

How to Say It

BARNABAS. *Bar*-nuh-bus.
COLOSSAE. Ko-*lahss*-ee.
EPHESUS. *Ef*-uh-sus.
HABAKKUK. Huh-*back*-kuk.
PHILIPPI. Fih-*lip*-pie or *Fil*-ih-pie.
THESSALONICA. *Thess*-uh-lo-*nye*-kuh (strong accent on *nye*; *th* as in *thin*).
Wittenberg. *Wit*-ten-berg or *Vit*-ten-berg.

17. For therein is the righteousness of God revealed from faith to faith: as it is written, The just shall live by faith.

Later in the book of Romans, Paul contrasts salvation by works, as the Jews understood the law, with salvation by grace through *faith*, as the gospel presents it. Paul here adapts Habakkuk 2:4 as a basis for his position.

This *faith* that is necessary for salvation is not merely a mental action, an easy acknowledgment that one accepts the truth of a given statement. Saving faith leads one to obedience and good works—such a one *shall live* by faith. This is not to say that we may earn salvation by works, but that real faith always produces good works. As James 2:26 states: "Faith without works is dead." [See question #5, page 240.]

NEVER OUT OF DEBT

Most of us carry some debt, whether for a house, car, or other products. Eventually, we will be able to pay it off. But none will personally experience the kind of debt the Motorola Corporation incurred with their sixty-six Iridium communications satellites. The system was intended to provide worldwide wireless phone service. Instead, it put Motorola into bankruptcy, with debts of $4.4 *billion*—a debt the company could not pay.

Iridium was at the leading edge of technology when the system was conceived, but it took ten years to get the satellites into orbit. In that time improvements in ordinary cellular phones had advanced so far that the Iridium system was obsolete. So in March, 2000, the bankruptcy court gave the company permission to stop service and to let the satellites burn up in the earth's atmosphere.

Paul's debt was also great—greater, perhaps, because it was a spiritual debt. The former persecutor of the church now knew the Savior and felt compelled to try to repay his unpayable debt by telling everyone he could about the grace of God in Christ. It's a debt that every Christian owes, and we should be ready, as Paul was, to serve Christ in whatever way we are called to do so. It's a debt we never can fully repay.   —C. R. B.

Conclusion

A. We Also Are Debtors

Paul acknowledged that he was a debtor to both Greeks and barbarians to preach the gospel of salvation to them. He became a special missionary to carry the good news across the Roman Empire in the first century. This was a unique call that none of us today has received. But as Christians we are debtors to witness in whatever situation we may find ourselves. A few may be called to witness as missionaries or evangelists in cross-cultural situations. Others may be called to witness by public proclamation of the gospel as ministers and teachers. Most of us, however, will witness in less public situations in the office, the factory, or at school. Some may find their ministries in serving the sick, the poor, or the discouraged. Wherever we may be, let us never forget that we are debtors. But this debt is not an overwhelming burden that must be discharged slowly and painfully. Rather, paying this debt brings us a joy that this world cannot know.

B. Faith in a World of Skepticism

Ours is an age of skepticism and doubt. On every hand we hear of those who reject the Christian faith and sneer at believers as "weaklings." But, of course, everyone lives by a faith of some kind or other. That faith may be in one's own intellectual brilliance or physical strength, in money, or in some anti-Christian philosophy.

Since everyone lives by some kind of faith, the real issue is not faith as such but faith in what or whom. For Paul that was no problem: "The just shall live by faith." He makes it quite clear that if we are to live righteous lives before God, it must begin with a faith in Jesus Christ, who died for our sins, and who was raised from the dead to give us hope for eternal life.

C. Prayer

Gracious Father, we thank You for offering to us the forgiveness of sins and the hope for eternal life through Your Son, Jesus Christ. May we acknowledge our debt to You by seeking to serve You wherever You may call us. Through faith in Jesus Christ we pray. Amen

D. Thought to Remember

We are all debtors.

Home Daily Bible Readings

Learning by Doing

This page contains an alternate lesson plan emphasizing learning activities.
Classes desiring such student involvement will find these suggestions helpful.

Learning Goals

After participating in this lesson, each student will be able to:

1. Tell what Paul says about the substance of the gospel and about his desire to visit the Roman Christians.

2. Explain what it means for the gospel to reveal "the righteousness of God."

3. Express his or her own faith in Christ.

Into the Lesson

Purchase enough small envelopes for each member of your class (and a few extras for visitors and newcomers). Insert copies of this letter: "I am excited to be your teacher and leader for these lessons on Romans. Today we will explore Romans 1:1-17. I hope we all catch the excitement of the gospel." Sign it with your name. Use as your official title, "Teacher of the Gospel."

Have each class member write his or her own name on the outside of the envelope. After all finish, ask each one to open the envelope and read the letter. Ask the following questions: "How do you feel about mail personally addressed to you?"; "What is your first thought when you read the phrase 'excitement of the gospel'?"; "Who among your friends should receive a letter like this one?"

Into the Word

Develop a brief lecture on background and introductory material for Romans. Remind students that Paul had met many of the Roman Christians on his journeys. Incorporate Romans 1:1 into the lecture so students understand Paul's greeting and introduction.

Divide your class into groups no larger than six. If you have more than two groups, assign the following to more than one group. Give each group a large white poster board. One person in each group serves as secretary.

Direct group one to read Romans 1:1-6, 16, 17. They are to complete an acrostic of the word *gospel* with as many words, phrases, or ideas that describe the gospel in the text. Examples include: **G**od's promise, **O**bedience to the faith, **S**pirit of holiness, **P**ower of God, **E**ternal life, and **L**iving by faith. (This activity is in the student book, *Adult Bible Class.)* Tell the group to be ready to describe Paul's teaching of the gospel and his description of Jesus.

Group two will read Romans 1:7-15. They will list all the "I" messages given by Paul. For example, "I thank my God . . . for you all." This group will discuss what the desire of Paul seems to be. (This activity is in the student book.)

Call the groups together and have them present their findings to the class. Discuss any difficult points using the lesson commentary for answers. Ask the following series of questions:

1. What do we learn about Jesus in the passage? *(He is the declared Son of God. He is Lord. Grace comes through Him.)*

2. What do we learn about Paul in this passage? *(He is wholeheartedly involved in spreading the gospel. He is passionate about his message and ministry. He is eager to preach!)*

3. What is the gospel? *(The gospel is the good news that God has provided a way of salvation, for all people, through Jesus.)*

4. How does this gospel reveal "the righteousness of God"? *(Righteousness is being right with God. No human being can be right with God on his or her own merits. But God provides a way, through Jesus Christ and His righteousness, for us to be right with Him. This "good news" had to be revealed.)*

Into Life

Ask the class members to return to their small groups to discuss situations or examples of present-day individuals who are excited about sharing the gospel with others. Perhaps they will recall missionary presentations at church, a coworker's challenge, a neighbor's friendly persuasion, or a relative's concern. Encourage them to share what are the common denominators in each. Examples may include enthusiasm, perseverance, and knowledge of subject matter.

Within their small groups, have students sit in pairs. Distribute envelopes and a sheet of blank paper. Address the envelope and blank sheet to the friend he or she identified at the start of the lesson. Take these next few minutes for each to write a two-paragraph explanation of the gospel, its impact on the student's life, and the enthusiasm the student has to share this message. After a short time, ask for one or two volunteers to read the letter. (A similar activity is in the student book.)

Close the session by having the pairs pray for each other and the sharing of the gospel.

Let's Talk It Over

The questions on this page are designed to encourage review of the lesson Scriptures and to promote discussion of the lesson by the class. The answers provided are only discussion starters. Let your class talk it over from there.

1. Paul identified himself as a "servant of Jesus Christ." The concept of servitude or slavery is repugnant to most people today. How, then, can we approach servanthood to Christ in a positive manner? What makes being a "servant of Jesus Christ" a good thing?

It is important to note that servanthood to Christ involves a choice. Jesus does not force anyone into service, but invites and challenges His followers to serve. Nor does He abuse His servants, as many slave owners have done through the centuries whenever and wherever slavery has been practiced. Instead, the one who is a slave to Christ is the most free, and those who seem to be free are the most enslaved.

See Ephesians 6:5-9 for a helpful discussion of the servant-master relationship. Servanthood to Christ overshadows even the most repressive of circumstances and allows us to render heart service instead of just eye service or "I" service.

2. Do you think of yourself as a "saint"? Why or why not? What difference would it make in the church if everyone thought of himself and every other member as saints?

The common understanding of a "saint" is someone who is especially holy, more so than ordinary believers. But in Scripture we are saints by calling, not by conduct. We are saints because God has sanctified us, not because of good works we have done. Thus, we are special in God's eyes. If we could appreciate God's view of ourselves and our fellow believers, wouldn't we treat one another with greater respect? Surely we would be less likely to excuse our sins by saying, "I'm only human!" And we would be much slower to criticize one of God's saints—wouldn't we?

3. Paul said the faith of the church at Rome was "spoken of throughout the whole world." What is our church known for? Why? What would characterize a church today that was known for its faith?

Sadly, many churches today are known for negative qualities—frequent splits, dominance by a single family, or inability to keep a preacher more than a very few years. Some churches are known for their active benevolence programs. Are these also known for sharing their faith with those to whom they minister in physical ways? Some are

known for legalistic rigidity in interpreting the Scriptures. Surely these churches desire to "contend for the faith . . . once delivered" (Jude 3), but too often there seems to be more contention than faith! Some are known for their mission activities, and this is very much in line with being known for faith. Whatever else might be involved, surely a church known for its faith will be positive in outlook, open to sinners, faithful to the Word, and gracious in its conduct. A church known for its faith must practice its faith, not just talk about it.

4. What if every believer shared Paul's sense of obligation to spread the gospel? What would be the result? Why doesn't every believer feel indebted to spread the gospel? How can we cultivate such an attitude?

For most Christians the answer is that they just never have thought about it! Paul might be expected to feel such a debt because he formerly persecuted the church. But Paul was not trying to pay God back for his salvation. Rather, he saw the great need of the lost and realized that, as his salvation was only by grace, so only grace would save others. It was the desperate need of the lost that created Paul's debt.

The lost still have that desperate need. How can we be more sensitive to it? Do we feel we somehow have earned our salvation and that the lost deserve to be lost? Do we just not care about the lost? Encourage class members to think of non-Christians whom they know personally. Ask them to think of these people as whole persons—not just as "the lost." See how much we have in common with them. They are not so very different from us—they deserve to hear the gospel as much as we do. Who will tell them?

5. What do you think it means to live by faith? What attitudes and actions are characteristic of one who lives by faith?

One who lives by faith demonstrates that the one in whom he has faith has priority. Thus, such a one invests in eternal things, laying up treasure in Heaven, more than in temporal assets. He tells of his faith unashamedly. He speaks confidently of things God has promised, fully expecting them to occur. Ask your students to give specific examples, and encourage them to imitate these faithful ones.

Justified by God's Grace

DEVOTIONAL READING: Psalm 33:13-22.

BACKGROUND SCRIPTURE: Romans 3.

PRINTED TEXT: Romans 3:1-4, 9, 10, 19-31.

Romans 3:1-4, 9, 10, 19-31

1 What advantage then hath the Jew? or what profit is there of circumcision?

2 Much every way: chiefly, because that unto them were committed the oracles of God.

3 For what if some did not believe? shall their unbelief make the faith of God without effect?

4 God forbid: yea, let God be true, but every man a liar; as it is written, That thou mightest be justified in thy sayings, and mightest overcome when thou art judged.

. . . .

9 What then? are we better than they? No, in no wise: for we have before proved both Jews and Gentiles, that they are all under sin;

10 As it is written, There is none righteous, no, not one.

. . . .

19 Now we know that what things soever the law saith, it saith to them who are under the law: that every mouth may be stopped, and all the world may become guilty before God.

20 Therefore by the deeds of the law there shall no flesh be justified in his sight: for by the law is the knowledge of sin.

21 But now the righteousness of God without the law is manifested, being witnessed by the law and the prophets;

22 Even the righteousness of God which is by faith of Jesus Christ unto all and upon all them that believe; for there is no difference:

23 For all have sinned, and come short of the glory of God;

24 Being justified freely by his grace through the redemption that is in Christ Jesus:

25 Whom God hath set forth to be a propitiation through faith in his blood, to declare his righteousness for the remission of sins that are past, through the forbearance of God;

26 To declare, I say, at this time his righteousness: that he might be just, and the justifier of him which believeth in Jesus.

27 Where is boasting then? It is excluded. By what law? of works? Nay; but by the law of faith.

28 Therefore we conclude that a man is justified by faith without the deeds of the law.

29 Is he the God of the Jews only? is he not also of the Gentiles? Yes, of the Gentiles also:

30 Seeing it is one God, which shall justify the circumcision by faith, and uncircumcision through faith.

31 Do we then make void the law through faith? God forbid: yea, we establish the law.

GOLDEN TEXT: For all have sinned, and come short of the glory of God; being justified freely by his grace through the redemption that is in Christ Jesus.
—Romans 3:23, 24.

The Power of the Gospel
Unit 1: Justified by Faith
(Lessons 1-5)

Lesson Aims

After this lesson each student will be able to:

1. Contrast the way of law with justification by grace as Paul describes the difference in Romans 3.

2. Explain the importance of the doctrine of justification by grace.

3. Praise God for His grace and for the salvation that it makes available to us.

Lesson Outline

INTRODUCTION
   A. I've Been Redeemed
   B. Lesson Background
 I. ADVANTAGES OF THE JEWS (Romans 3:1-4, 9, 10)
   A. Word of God (vv. 1, 2)
   B. God's Faithfulness (vv. 3, 4)
   C. Advantaged, But Not Better (vv. 9, 10)
     Surely We're Better Than They!
II. RIGHTEOUSNESS OF GOD (Romans 3:19-26)
   A. The Function of the Law (vv. 19, 20)
   B. The Foundation of Faith (vv. 21, 22a)
   C. The Failure of All (vv. 22b, 23)
   D. The Free Gift of Grace (vv. 24-26)
     You're [Not] a Winner!
III. JUSTIFICATION (Romans 3:27-31)
   A. Nothing to Boast Of (v. 27)
   B. Not by Deeds of Law (v. 28, 29)
   C. Justified by Faith (vv. 30, 31)
Conclusion
   A. Problem of Works Salvation
   B. Prayer
   C. Thought to Remember

Introduction

A. I've Been Redeemed

Many years ago an evangelist was traveling in a railway coach. As he rode along, he sang to himself the song, "I've Been Redeemed." Another passenger sitting nearby heard him and joined in the song. When the song was finished, the evangelist asked the stranger, "Have you indeed been redeemed?"

"Yes, praise the Lord," came the reply.

"How long ago were you redeemed?"

"Nearly two thousand years ago."

"More than two thousand years ago!" echoed the evangelist in surprise.

"Yes, sir, the Lord purchased my redemption more than nineteen hundred years ago," was the reply, "but I am sorry to say that I spent years trying to earn it by good works. Only a few months ago did I finally learn that it was already mine through God's grace, if I were willing to accept it through faith."

The Scriptures do indeed tell us that we have redemption through Christ's blood if we are willing to accept it by faith. But many of us have missed the joys of that redemption because we have tried to earn it through good works.

B. Lesson Background

You may find it helpful to review the Lesson Background from last week's lesson. This will give your students a better understanding of Paul and his ministry. Having been a zealous Jewish leader who persecuted Christians because they did not keep the law, Paul (then known as Saul) was completely changed at his conversion. He became the apostle to the Gentiles, spreading the gospel of salvation in Jesus Christ. This represented a radical shift in his theology. Before, as a Jewish scholar, he held that one could be saved by meticulously observing the law. As a Christian he recognized one could be saved only by God's loving grace through faith in Jesus Christ.

Paul appreciated this concept better than most of his contemporaries. Even within the church there were some, of Jewish background, who believed law-keeping remained essential to salvation. Some of these believers stirred up no little controversy in Antioch between Paul's first and second missionary journeys. The dispute led to the "Jerusalem Conference" described in Acts 15. Whether there were similar Jewish agitators in Rome or Paul merely wanted to avoid such a situation we do not know. In any event, Paul's clearest explanation of the issue is in the letter he wrote to the Romans, and is the subject of our text today.

I. Advantages of the Jews
(Romans 3:1-4, 9, 10)

A. Word of God (vv. 1, 2)

1, 2. What advantage then hath the Jew? or what profit is there of circumcision? Much every way: chiefly, because that unto them were committed the oracles of God.

In the previous chapter Paul pointed out that God regards "circumcision . . . of the heart" over literal circumcision "in the flesh" (Romans 2:28, 29). In these verses he answers some of the objections he expects Jewish believers to raise. The most obvious question that they might raise is "What *advantage* is there in being a *Jew?*" Paul's reply is that there is *much every way*. The most important advantage is that they have been entrusted with *the oracles of God*. In the *New International Version* this is translated "the very words of God." God has revealed Himself through nature, or what is called "general revelation," which helps us know God as Creator. As helpful as this is, it is not as important as special revelation, the Scriptures. God revealed Himself and His will to prophets who wrote down their revelations in what we know as the Old Testament. This allowed the Jews to know God as a loving Heavenly Father. Of all ancient peoples, only the Jews enjoyed this great privilege. Through the Scriptures, they also knew that God intended to send them a Messiah. [See question #1, page 248.]

B. God's Faithfulness (vv. 3, 4)

3. For what if some did not believe? shall their unbelief make the faith of God without effect?

Although the Jews had the Scriptures, many of them did not accept them. At least, they did not accept them fully. Some of them might have claimed acceptance, but their behavior proved *their unbelief*. Indeed, in the past many had lived in open rebellion against God's laws. But their unfaithfulness did not invalidate God's ultimate plan for the human race any more than the unfaithfulness of many Christians cancels God's covenant of grace for Christians. The expression *the faith of God* refers to God's faithfulness, His commitment to follow through on what He promised.

4. God forbid: yea, let God be true, but every man a liar; as it is written, That thou mightest be justified in thy sayings, and mightest overcome when thou art judged.

Paul rejects the idea emphatically. The *God forbid* of the *King James Version* is more an Old English euphemism than a literal translation of the Greek, which is more like "May it never be!" God by His very nature cannot be unfaithful to His promises. It is impossible for God to lie in any way (Titus 1:2). *Let God be true*. Let everyone recognize that God is always true even if *every man* should prove to be *a liar*. The Scripture that Paul quotes is found in the Septuagint version of Psalm 51:4. The application that Paul suggests of this is that no matter how people may deny or doubt God, He will fulfill His promises.

C. Advantaged, But Not Better (vv. 9, 10)

9, 10. What then? are we better than they? No, in no wise: for we have before proved both Jews and Gentiles, that they are all under sin; as it is written, There is none righteous, no, not one.

This verse offers something of a problem. Who is the *we*? Is Paul here identifying himself with his fellow Jews or with Christians? He has previously spoken of the Jews in third person ("them,"

v. 2; "their," v. 3), so we might think the "we" refers to Christians." The following context, however, suggests that Paul has shifted his focus and that the "we" refers now to the Jews. He denies that *Jews* have any advantage over *Gentiles:* both stand *under* the condemnation of *sin*. To bolster his case, Paul paraphrases Ecclesiastes 7:20. (See also Psalm 14:1.) In the verses that follow (11-18) Paul gives more specific details about the universal sinfulness of man. It is not a pretty picture! [See question #2, page 248.]

SURELY WE'RE BETTER THAN THEY!

On Halloween night in "Christian" America nowadays, witches celebrate their paganism publicly. Really! One recent Halloween saw some two hundred of them holding a two-day pagan ritual at various memorials in Washington D.C. The purpose of the rally was to worship the "divinity" the pagans find in "trees, rocks, birds, animals, and people."

These folks come from all social classes and have varying preferences for what they should be called: Witches, Wiccans, Druids, even Radical Faeries. Most of them claim that they do not worship the devil, since "the devil is a Christian idea," as one of their spokesmen says. It is estimated that there are more than three hundred thousand pagans in America.

It's a bit hard for us Christians not to feel superior to these modern pagans, by whatever name they call themselves. After all, they have regressed to a paganism similar to that which existed two millennia ago when the church began. Doesn't our awareness of the true God make us better than they are? The apostle Paul would answer, "No, it doesn't! We are sinners just like they are. The only righteousness we have is that which Christ gives us." We are in the same position as Jewish Christians of the first century! Knowing Christ only makes us more blessed, not better, than the pagans around us.   —C. R. B.

II. Righteousness of God (Romans 3:19-26)

A. The Function of the Law (vv. 19, 20)

19. Now we know that what things soever the law saith, it saith to them who are under the law: that every mouth may be stopped, and all the world may become guilty before God.

In the previous verses Paul used several quotations from Psalms and Proverbs to show how sinful people had become, even those who had the advantages of having received God's Word. To compound their wickedness, they had denied it or attempted to blame God for their guilt. Paul faces that issue squarely in this verse.

To them who are under the law. At first glance, we might conclude that Paul is referring specifically to the Mosaic law, which would limit the application to the Jews. However, his use of other Old Testament references indicates that he has something more in mind. Many scholars believe Paul's condemnation is even more inclusive, taking in the principle of law as well as the specific law of Moses. In the first chapter of Romans, for example, Paul makes a forceful denunciation of the sinfulness of Gentiles, insisting that they knew enough about God's will to not engage in these wicked acts (Romans 1:19, 20, 32; see also Romans 2:14, 15). With the phrase *that every mouth may be stopped,* Paul seems to be depicting a court scene in which the evidence against the accused parties is so overwhelming that they have no basis for speaking in their own defense. The court plays no favorites in this judgment, for all the world is *guilty before God.*

20. Therefore by the deeds of the law there shall no flesh be justified in his sight: for by the law is the knowledge of sin.

In theory, if one could fulfill the requirements of the law perfectly, he or she could stand before the divine Judge as justified. But, of course, no one can fulfill *the deeds of the law* completely and thus earn salvation. One function of the law is to show us how sinful we are, to provide a measuring stick to evaluate our moral status. Had Paul ended his letter at this point, we would have been left in a desperately gloomy situation. Fortunately, the picture is not totally bleak. What follows offers hope. [See question #3, page 248.]

B. The Foundation of Faith (vv. 21, 22a)

21. But now the righteousness of God without the law is manifested, being witnessed by the law and the prophets.

Once he has established that human righteousness is impossible through works of the law, Paul turns to *the righteousness of God.* Even though God gave His *law* to man, He knew from the beginning that no one would be able to fulfill it perfectly. For that reason He prepared another way, a way that does not depend on the law, for man to be justified. *Now* for the first time that plan is being revealed to the world, a plan that required God's Son to bear the sins of mankind on the cross. That plan awaited the coming of Christ before it could be revealed in full, but *the law and the prophets* had testified to it. Some passages of the Old Testament give only vague hints about the nature and work of the coming Messiah while others, especially several in Isaiah, are much more explicit. Taken together, all of these witnesses provide evidence for God's plan for salvation.

22a. Even the righteousness of God which is by faith of Jesus Christ unto all and upon all them that believe.

Paul continues to show the contrast between *righteousness* through good works and righteousness through God's grace. The first method simply won't do. If we violate even one apparently insignificant part of the law, we are guilty of violating the whole law and stand condemned. By contrast, the righteousness that God now offers is *by faith.* This is not some nebulous faith in faith itself or even faith in God. It is faith in *Jesus Christ,* God's only Son. This path of salvation is open to all regardless of race or ethnic background. [See question #4, page 248.]

C. The Failure of All (vv. 22b, 23)

22b, 23. For there is no difference: for all have sinned, and come short of the glory of God.

There is no difference at the judgment seat of God between Jew and Gentile. Whatever advantages Jews may have had as custodians of the Scriptures and as ancestors of Jesus Christ, these do not really matter. *All have sinned.* The burden of sin rests crushingly on the whole human race. Some hold that this refers to the original sin of Adam, as the old New England Primer had it: "In Adam's fall, We sinned all." But Paul's statement seems more inclusive than that. It means that every person who has ever lived and reached the age of accountability has violated God's law. Some have done it knowingly and deliberately, while others may have done it in ignorance. Yet the conclusion is the same: all have sinned!

In their sinning, all *come short of the glory of God.* Scholars differ as to the precise meaning of the expression *glory of God.* Some hold that it refers to the glory that saints will share with God in eternity. Others take the view that the saints who live godly lives reflect God's glory, and thus bring glory to God in the eyes of the world. It seems more likely that it refers to the glory God Himself displays because of His holiness. Sin, which is a "falling short" of the mark, separates us from that glory.

D. The Free Gift of Grace (vv. 24-26)

24. Being justified freely by his grace through the redemption that is in Christ Jesus.

This verse sends a brilliant beam of hope into the otherwise hopelessly gloomy situation stated in verse 23: "All have sinned!" Even after sin there is hope, there is the possibility of *redemption.* The word *justified* is a legal term that describes the status of an accused person in court. When one is justified, it does not necessarily mean that he or she is innocent. Rather, it means that in the eyes of the court that one will not have

Visual for lessons 2 and 11. *This poster illustrates the universal need for salvation, "for all have sinned." Post it as you discuss verse 23.*

to pay the penalty for the crime. Christ has already paid the penalty by His death on the cross. This debt has been *freely* paid, and the only stipulation required of the condemned is that he or she accept it. That's what grace is all about. *Grace* is often defined as "unmerited favor," meaning that the recipient does not deserve it and cannot earn it. The only choice is to accept it or reject it.

"YOU'RE [NOT] A WINNER!"

Something for nothing seems to be a nearly universal human quest. Lotteries and gambling casinos in America and elsewhere prey upon people who are looking to get "lucky" and become wealthy without working for it.

A more subtle form of this fever is fed by the sweepstakes letters that come in the mail. Elderly people especially fall victim to the artfully worded "come-ons" in those letters, with the result that their savings are jeopardized. An eighty-eight-year-old man in California made two trips to Florida to claim the eleven million dollars that he mistakenly believed he had won. His sad story is like that of scores of other people—often in failing mental health—who are taken in by the get-rich-quick pitch of the sweepstakes. They believe they have put the right sticker at the right spot on the right paper and placed it in the right envelope, so the prize must be theirs!

It's much like the temptation that so many of us fall prey to. We think, "I live by the Golden Rule and the Ten Commandments (for the most part), I go to church regularly, I give my offering, I care for my family, and I do my job pretty faithfully. So, God, I guess I deserve my reward, right?" But the answer is, "No, trying to keep the law only makes you a sinner. Salvation comes only through Christ."   —C. R. B.

25. Whom God hath set forth to be a propitiation through faith in his blood, to declare his righteousness for the remission of sins that are past, through the forbearance of God.

In the Old Testament *propitiation* was associated with the mercy seat in the Holy of Holies. There each year on the day of atonement the high priest sprinkled the *blood* of the sacrificial animal on the mercy seat to atone for the people's sins. In the New Testament this term takes on a fuller meaning. Christ is not just the place where the atonement takes place, and not merely the high priest who offers the sacrifice; He is the sacrifice that makes the atonement possible.

It may seem unfair that we, the guilty, go free while Christ, the innocent, bears the penalty. But this transaction shows us that God is a just Judge who demands an accounting for all *sins*, but He is also a loving Heavenly Father, who desires that all be saved.

26. To declare, I say, at this time his righteousness: that he might be just, and the justifier of him which believeth in Jesus.

In a sense God is faced with a divine dilemma. As a holy God, He cannot tolerate sin. At the same time, He is a loving God who wants to save everyone. In the human sense, this is an impossible contradiction, but for God all things are possible. He resolved the dilemma by offering His Son as the perfect sacrifice for sin. Thus God is both *just*—exacting the fair penalty for sin—and *the justifier of him which believeth in Jesus.*

III. Justification
(Romans 3:27-31)
A. Nothing to Boast Of (v. 27)

27. Where is boasting then? It is excluded. By what law? of works? Nay; but by the law of faith.

A system that provides for salvation through the performing of good *works* leaves itself open to the danger of pride. In Jesus' day the Jews considered the Pharisees to be the most pious people among them. They kept the *law* (and their additions to the law) with meticulous dedication. This gained them the plaudits of others and fed their pride. This was the reason that they so vigorously resisted Jesus when He challenged this whole system. But if justification is an unearned gift of God's grace received by *faith*, there is no basis for pride or *boasting*. [See question #5, page 248.]

B. Not by Deeds of Law (v. 28, 29)

28. Therefore we conclude that a man is justified by faith without the deeds of the law.

This verse succinctly sums up two approaches to salvation: God's way, which is by grace through *faith*, and the human way through *deeds of the law.* It is important to note that the faith mentioned here is not simply a mental assent to a fact or a body of facts. It involves a commitment to Jesus Christ, which must result in submission to Him, or it is less than saving faith. It is worth observing that on the first occasion after the ascension that the gospel was publicly proclaimed, faith—although it is clearly implied—is not specifically mentioned. Rather, repentance and baptism are stated as necessary prerequisites for "the remission of sins" (Acts 2:38).

29. Is he the God of the Jews only? is he not also of the Gentiles? Yes, of the Gentiles also.

Through their long history the Jewish people often succumbed to the temptation to look on God as belonging exclusively to them. Although they were chosen by God for a special mission, that mission was to bring the Messiah into the world, and the Messiah would bring a blessing to the whole world (Isaiah 42:6; 49:6). Paul's rhetorical questions merely state what always had been true.

C. Justified by Faith (vv. 30, 31)

30, 31. Seeing it is one God, which shall justify the circumcision by faith, and uncircumcision through faith. Do we then make void the law through faith? God forbid: yea, we establish the law.

Both the *circumcision* (Jews) and the *uncircumcision* (Gentiles) are saved the same way— *through faith.* Some as a result might be led to believe *the law* was without value. Not so, Paul strongly affirms. Indeed, justification by faith serves to *establish the law.* It confirms that the law, though powerless to provide salvation, still has value, for it made preparation for the gospel of grace. And even in the age of grace the law serves as a guide for those who have accepted God's gift of salvation.

Conclusion

A. Problem of Works Salvation

The idea of salvation by works raises some serious practical as well as theological problems. One problem is trying to get a precise definition of just what constitutes saving works. The Jews had the law, but they soon began to define and redefine what the law meant in practical situations. For example, the law forbade working on the Sabbath, and certain things were specifically forbidden. But situations arose that were not covered. In Jesus' day the lawyers had defined walking more than about five-eighths of a mile on the Sabbath as work. They also charged Jesus with breaking the Sabbath because He performed miracles of healing on that day. In our drastically changed culture we would have to spend most of our time on nitpicky arguments trying to define the law.

Another problem that works salvation raises is trying to determine how many good works are essential. The Roman Catholic Church faced this issue prior to the Reformation in the practice of selling indulgences. It was this very issue that sent Luther on his reforming path. If, for example, one has to perform a hundred good deeds in order to be forgiven, how can he be certain that a hundred and one good deeds aren't required?

A third, and perhaps more serious, problem is that a way of salvation that is based upon good works is almost certain to lead to human pride. We take pride in the things we accomplish—the work we do, the family we rear successfully, the buildings we build, the bank accounts we accumulate. In our better moments we recognize that we were able to do these things only because God gave us the strength and intelligence necessary to do them. But still Satan is always there, tempting us to take credit for our accomplishments. The most effective temptation he can set before us is to convince us that we have earned our salvation by fulfilling the works of the law.

B. Prayer

We come to You, Father, in humble faith, recognizing that we are helpless to save ourselves by our works. Teach us to accept Your marvelous grace, and fill us with a burning desire to share Your love and Your grace with those about us.

C. Thought to Remember

Plenteous grace with thee is found,
    Grace to cover all my sin;
Let the healing streams abound;
    Make and keep me pure within.
          —Charles Wesley

Home Daily Bible Readings

Monday, Mar. 4—Grace Freely Bestowed (Ephesians 1:3-14)

Tuesday, Mar. 5—Called to Hope (Ephesians 1:15-22)

Wednesday, Mar. 6—Saved by Grace (Ephesians 2:1-10)

Thursday, Mar. 7—No Longer Strangers and Aliens (Ephesians 2:11-22)

Friday, Mar. 8—Under the Power of Sin (Romans 3:1-9)

Saturday, Mar. 9—The Law Brings Knowledge of Sin (Romans 3:10-20)

Sunday, Mar. 10—Justified by God's Grace (Romans 3:21-31)

Learning by Doing

This page contains an alternate lesson plan emphasizing learning activities. Classes desiring such student involvement will find these suggestions helpful.

Learning Goals

After participating in this lesson, each student will be able to:

1. Contrast the way of law with justification by grace as Paul describes the difference in Romans 3.

2. Explain the importance of the doctrine of justification by grace.

3. Praise God for His grace and for the salvation that it makes available to us.

Into the Lesson

"I'm really not so bad." This statement is often heard when people are confronted with a need for forgiveness of sin. Begin class by brainstorming excuses people have for not following Jesus. *(People may say, "There are other ways to God besides Jesus." "I know too many hypocrites." "All the church wants is my money!")* Continue with the following questions. Use a marker board or overhead transparency to record answers.

"What are some ways people believe one can please God?" *(Answers may include being good, obeying the commandments, going to church, and loving others.)* Next ask, "What did the Jews believe was the way to please God?" *(Answers may include obeying the commandments, being born a Jew, and knowing the words of God.)*

Paul's writing in Romans 3 presents to us the New Testament's teaching on how to please God. Some accuse God of not being fair. Paul explains in our text today that God is more than fair!

Into the Word

Secure a large piece of butcher paper four feet wide by three feet high. Write "Law vs. Grace" at the top and attach it to the wall. Read the printed text. On the left side of the paper have the class list how a person is justified by law. On the right side, how a person is justified by grace.

Once you have completed the above exercise, divide the class into at least three groups with no more than six in a group. Assign the following.

Group 1. Distribute the following questions. (Use the lesson commentary with the indicated verses for answers. Questions are included in the *Adult Bible Class* student book.)

1. What were some of the spiritual advantages the Jews enjoyed? (v. 2)

2. In what is God faithful? (vv. 3, 4)

3. How does Paul prove that all people need God's grace? (vv. 9, 10)

4. Why does the law silence every mouth? *(Because all are guilty, even the Jews, v. 19)*

5. What is the law's role? (v. 20)

6. What is the "righteousness of God without the law"? (vv. 21, 22)

Group 2. Distribute Bible dictionaries or study Bibles with dictionaries. Ask the group to prepare a short report on the meaning of the following words: *justification, redemption, propitiation,* and *atonement.* These words are critical for understanding the implications of this passage of Scripture.

Group 3. Prepare an outline based on Romans 3:21-31 of how Paul shows that we are justified by faith without the works of the law. This outline should include the following:

JUSTIFICATION BY FAITH WITHOUT THE LAW

1. All have sinned and need to be justified. (v. 23)

2. Redemption comes through Jesus. (v. 24)
   a. He is the sacrifice. (v. 25)
   b. God demonstrates His justice. (vv. 25, 26)

3. There is no room for boasting about deserving justification. (v. 27)

4. God will justify all who demonstrate faith in Jesus. (vv. 29, 30)

5. The law can now be a guide for righteous living. (v. 31)

Display this outline during their presentation.

Give each group eight to ten minutes. Each presentation should be about three minutes long.

Into Life

Say, "Paul says that we all fall short of God's glory. We are all 'guilty as charged.' We must take responsibility for our sins before God. Our text also says we cannot be made right through any action of our own. God has chosen to deal with our sin and guilt by taking on Himself the penalty and punishment due our sin. Through the sacrifice of Jesus, He freely forgives us. We can be declared 'not guilty'!

"For the next two to three minutes I want you to meditate on Romans 3:21-26, focusing on what we have said today about God's way and God's grace; then write a prayer of praise. If you need to talk about your personal salvation, please see me after class." Distribute blank cards for students to use to record their prayers.

Close this session by asking two or three students to share prayers aloud. (Ask them privately in advance.)

Let's Talk It Over

The questions on this page are designed to encourage review of the lesson Scriptures and to promote discussion of the lesson by the class. The answers provided are only discussion starters. Let your class talk it over from there.

1. Paul said the chief advantage of the Jews was that they had the Word of God. Today we have the Word of God to an extent the ancient Hebrews never would have imagined. Each person can have his or her own copy for personal study at any time and at any place. What kind of obligation or responsibility do you think that advantage places on us? How can we faithfully execute that responsibility?

The ancient Hebrews had God's Word, but copies were scarce and precious. Most of what the ordinary citizen knew had been passed down by oral teaching in the home and in the synagogue. Yet they were responsible for knowing God's will. We who have such easy access to the Word of God surely must bear a greater responsibility. We must teach our young people to read and study their Bibles, to spend time learning what it says and how it applies to their lives. The church must make Bible study a priority, both in its program and in its teaching. Explore with your class as many specific ways to encourage Bible reading, study, and memorization as the students can suggest.

2. Paul says, "There is none righteous." Contrast his message with the popular self-esteem mantra of today. How can we inject the truth of Paul's statement into our culture?

In today's relativistic culture, self-esteem has been redefined. To suggest someone—anyone—is not righteous flies in the face of relativism. Where self-esteem once meant respect for oneself as a person, it now includes acceptance of every personal behavior trait, no matter how sinful. Since relativism has eliminated any standard of right and wrong, there is no basis to judge whether an act is "sinful" or otherwise. We need to recapture the concept of self-esteem and base it on the fact of Creation (God made us) and redemption (Christ died for us). We need to separate our worth as persons, for whom Christ died, from the unworthiness of our sinful behavior.

3. The Jews depended on keeping the law to put them in good stead with God. On what do people today depend for salvation? Why?

By and large people still depend on good works for salvation, though they are not as concerned with the law as such. Comparing themselves with others, whom they consider to be "worse" than themselves, they consider they must be "okay." Unbelievers especially like to point at church members who commit highly publicized sins or even crimes and say, "If Christians can act like that, then I must be all right, too, because I would never do such a thing." We have to make clear that we all—Christians and non-Christians alike—are sinners in need of God's grace. Christians will be saved, not because they are good enough, but because they have admitted that they are not and have accepted God's gift of grace.

4. What do you find significant in the lesson writer's note that faith in God is not enough, but that faith in Jesus Christ is what will save us?

Obviously, the Jews believed in God, but they did not believe in Jesus. Today many will claim to believe in God and think that their belief will save them in the end. They refuse, however, to believe that Jesus is "the way, the truth, and the life." They want to believe that everyone who has any vague notion of a "higher power" is "going to the same place." Thus Jews, Muslims, Christians, and even those who believe in "the Force" should be treated as equals. In Paul's day, the pagans believed in many gods and even called the Christians "atheists" because they did not accept the pantheon of gods. Today's pagans call the Christians "intolerant" for not accepting the pluralism of the day. But Jesus remains the only "name . . . whereby we must be saved" (Acts 4:12).

5. Paul said the doctrine of justification by faith left no room for pride or boasting. How does pride interfere with Christian living today?

Whenever believers today act as if their salvation is a matter of their own goodness, they hinder the message of grace. Pride interferes with cooperation among Christians, as each one vies for recognition rather than putting the greatest effort into ministry. It also interferes with communicating the gospel, as it sends a mixed message. With our lips we say we are saved by God's grace, but sometimes our behavior says we are good enough on our own to be saved. Our message says there is no difference between Jew and Greek (or black and white or male and female, etc.; cf. Galatians 3:28), but our behavior sometimes says, "My kind is better than yours."

Sharing in the Promise

DEVOTIONAL READING: Psalm 32.

BACKGROUND SCRIPTURE: Romans 4.

PRINTED TEXT: Romans 4:1-5, 13-25.

Romans 4:1-5, 13-25

1 What shall we say then that Abraham our father, as pertaining to the flesh, hath found?

2 For if Abraham were justified by works, he hath whereof to glory; but not before God.

3 For what saith the Scripture? Abraham believed God, and it was counted unto him for righteousness.

4 Now to him that worketh is the reward not reckoned of grace, but of debt.

5 But to him that worketh not, but believeth on him that justifieth the ungodly, his faith is counted for righteousness.

. . . .

13 For the promise, that he should be the heir of the world, was not to Abraham, or to his seed, through the law, but through the righteousness of faith.

14 For if they which are of the law be heirs, faith is made void, and the promise made of none effect:

15 Because the law worketh wrath: for where no law is, there is no transgression.

16 Therefore it is of faith, that it might be by grace; to the end the promise might be sure to all the seed; not to that only which is of the law, but to that also which is of the faith of Abraham; who is the father of us all,

17 (As it is written, I have made thee a father of many nations,) before him whom he believed, even God, who quickeneth the dead, and calleth those things which be not as though they were:

18 Who against hope believed in hope, that he might become the father of many nations, according to that which was spoken, So shall thy seed be.

19 And being not weak in faith, he considered not his own body now dead, when he was about a hundred years old, neither yet the deadness of Sarah's womb:

20 He staggered not at the promise of God through unbelief; but was strong in faith, giving glory to God;

21 And being fully persuaded, that what he had promised, he was able also to perform.

22 And therefore it was imputed to him for righteousness.

23 Now it was not written for his sake alone, that it was imputed to him;

24 But for us also, to whom it shall be imputed, if we believe on him that raised up Jesus our Lord from the dead;

25 Who was delivered for our offenses, and was raised again for our justification.

GOLDEN TEXT: Abraham believed God, and it was counted unto him for righteousness.—Romans 4:3.

Lesson Aims

After participating in this lesson, each student will be able to:

1. Tell how Abraham and those who follow his example are considered righteous on the basis of their faith.

2. Explain the significance of Abraham's example for both Jews and Gentiles.

3. Suggest some specific means for helping people to come to know how to share in the promise of being justified by faith.

Lesson Outline

Introduction

A. When You Can't See the Bottom

One night several years ago we camped along the Green River in Utah. We noticed some people playing in the river, and since we had endured a long, hot day on the road, we donned our swimsuits and went down to the river. The river carried such a heavy load of silt that the water was opaque. I cautioned the children to stay on the bank while I tested the river for any deep places that could not be seen in the murky waters. The river proved to be quite shallow, and even after I was halfway across, the water was only waist deep. One of the girls jumped into the water to join me. "Come back," shouted Mother. "You can't see the bottom."

"I don't have to see the bottom," replied my daughter. "As long as I can see Daddy, I'll be all right."

That's what Abraham's faith was all about. He was able to walk with confidence even when he couldn't see what lay ahead because he trusted God.

B. Lesson Background

Some of the Jews who read this Roman epistle may have had some problems with Paul's teaching that one could be justified by faith. To reassure them, Paul cited the example of Abraham. Every Jew was proud to call Abraham "father" (Matthew 3:9; John 8:39). The Jews knew that both Abraham and Sarah were past the age of having children when God promised Abraham He would make of him "a great nation" (Genesis 12:2). They believed they were the heirs of that promise, that Israel was that "great nation." Paul would not argue that point, but he would not limit the promise to those who were Abraham's children by genealogy. He expanded it to those who were Abraham's children because they exhibited a faith like that of Abraham.

I. Abraham's Example
(Romans 4:1-5)

A. Introduction (vv. 1, 2)

1, 2. What shall we say then that Abraham our father, as pertaining to the flesh, hath found? For if Abraham were justified by works, he hath whereof to glory; but not before God.

As a Jew, Paul had a right to claim *Abraham* as his *father*. In so doing, he identified with his Jewish readers. Some take the phrase *as pertaining to the flesh* to refer to Abraham's relationship to all Jews. He was their physical ancestor. Others understand it to modify the verb *found*. The question that Paul is asking is how Abraham would understand the basis of his justification from a human point of view. Either interpretation is appropriate to the context here.

Some Jews may have so revered Abraham that they believed he was *justified by works*. If he had lived a sinless life, then he would have had *whereof to glory*. But the Scriptures tell us that he did not live a sinless life. For example, on two occasions he had lied about his wife, Sarah

(Genesis 12:10-20; 20:1-13). Thus on the basis of his life, he had no grounds to claim that he was justified before God. [See question #1, page 256.]

B. Believed God (v. 3)

3. For what saith the Scripture? Abraham believed God, and it was counted unto him for righteousness.

To prove that Abraham was justified by faith and not by works, Paul goes to the best authority available—*the Scripture.* Genesis 15:6 says Abraham *"believed* in the Lord; and he *counted* it to him *for righteousness."* Paul refers to this same verse in Galatians 3:6, as does James in 2:23.

C. Credited With Righteousness (vv. 4, 5)

4. Now to him that worketh is the reward not reckoned of grace, but of debt.

Paul here states an obvious fact. When a worker makes an agreement to work for wages, that person's wages are due when the assigned task is completed. The employer pays the agreed amount as wages earned, not as a gift. The parallel with salvation is obvious. If one were able to keep the law of God perfectly, that one would have earned salvation, and it would not be a gift. But since no one is able to keep the law in all its details, another way to salvation is necessary.

5. But to him that worketh not, but believeth on him that justifieth the ungodly, his faith is counted for righteousness.

Since a person cannot gain salvation by good works (all the good works of a lifetime cannot atone for one sin), God offers hope through *faith* that can justify *the ungodly.* One's faith in and of itself is not *righteousness,* but God through His grace accepts it as righteousness.

"IS THAT YOUR FINAL ANSWER?"

The most popular television program of the 1999–2000 season was *Who Wants to Be a Millionaire?* Who *hasn't* heard Regis Philbin say, "Is that your final answer?" Along with a handful of contestants who won large sums of money, the ABC Network also profited handsomely: thirty-second commercials on the program were netting ABC a half-million dollars each!

Similar offerings soon appeared on other networks, including the Fox network's appropriately named *Greed!* But *Millionaire* had staying power: in its second season it was still on four nights a week.

At first look, it may seem that Abraham was interested in a "get rich quick" scheme like *Millionaire's* participants were: come up with the right answers to a few questions and "Hey, I'm a millionaire!" But the difference is that after Abraham and Sarah tried to *work* out the promise on

their own—and brought disaster on their family in the process—their "final answer" was to believe in the promises of God and act accordingly. Ultimately, it was Abraham's faith that brought the priceless gift of righteousness. God's gift still comes through faith, not through our works, no matter how "good" we might think them to be.

—C. R. B.

II. Abraham's Promise (Romans 4:13-16)

A. Based on Faith (vv. 13-15)

13. For the promise, that he should be the heir of the world, was not to Abraham, or to his seed, through the law, but through the righteousness of faith.

A central theme of this part of the Roman epistle is the contrast between justification by performing deeds of *the law* and justification by *faith.* Here Paul illustrates the theme with the example of *Abraham.*

Paul summarizes the promise to Abraham as that of being *heir of the world.* Genesis 12:2, 3 details what this inheritance involved: God would (1) make of Abraham a great nation, (2) grant him material blessings, (3) exalt his name, and (4) use him to bless all the families of the earth.

These blessings did not come *through the law* either to Abraham or *his seed* ("offspring" in the *New International Version).* Obviously Abraham could not have been justified by the Mosaic law because he lived hundreds of years before that law was received at Sinai. Even those who still considered the Mosaic law as essential to justification had to admit that Abraham had been justified without it. Instead, all of these blessings came through the *righteousness of faith.*

Abraham believed God, and it was counted unto him for righteousness.

Visual for
lesson 3

Use this poster to illustrate verse 3. Discuss what it means to believe God as Abraham did.

And the promise was given to Abraham's seed, or offspring, during Abraham's lifetime (Genesis 17:7, 8). So they also receive the promise apart from the law. These offspring include both Abraham's physical descendants and his spiritual descendants—that is, those who believe in Jesus Christ. This is stated in verse 16 of this chapter.

14. For if they which are of the law be heirs, faith is made void, and the promise made of none effect.

If one could be justified by works of *the law,* then *faith* would have nothing to do with it. If God justified only those who kept the law, then no one would be justified, for no one has kept or does keep it. God's *promise* to Abraham, then, would not be kept. It becomes *void,* empty, meaningless.

15. Because the law worketh wrath: for where no law is, there is no transgression.

Generally speaking, the purpose of any law is to define what is right and what is wrong. *The law* also spells out the *wrath,* that is, the punishment for lawbreakers. That means everyone, for all have sinned (Romans 3:23). Abraham and others of his time could not transgress a law that did not yet exist, so they would not come under God's wrath for that reason. However, that does not mean they were safe from His wrath if they did wrong. "As many as have sinned without law shall also perish without law" (Romans 2:12). The only way of escape from wrath is Abraham's way. He believed in the Lord, and therefore the Lord credited him with righteousness even though he did not attain righteousness in his living (Genesis 15:6). [See question #2, page 256.]

THE TEACHING FUNCTION OF LAW

The clean air movement began in Donora, Pennsylvania, in October of 1948. For five days that month, a yellowish blanket of acrid smoke from the town's steel mills and zinc works literally suffocated the town. One man who lived through it recalls spraining his ankle when he stepped off a curb because the smog was so bad he couldn't see his feet! More than 40 percent of the town's citizens were made ill and twenty people were killed by the pollution. The industrial revolution had brought jobs and prosperity to millions, and (at least until 1948) the smoke belching from the factories had seemed a small price to pay for the affluence people could now enjoy.

In 1950, partly because of Donora's brush with smoggy death, President Truman convened the first national conference to face the issue of air pollution. By 1963, the first Clean Air Act was passed by Congress. That and subsequent laws have forced us to realize that we have been polluting our air, poisoning our streams, killing wildlife, and destroying the health of millions of human beings. The laws we have passed have educated us about the ethics of pollution. In similar fashion, God's law has taught us that we risk killing ourselves and others spiritually when we fail to give heed to the spiritual environment in which we live. —C. R. B.

B. Grounded in Grace (v. 16)

16. Therefore it is of faith, that it might be by grace; to the end the promise might be sure to all the seed; not to that only which is of the law, but to that also which is of the faith of Abraham; who is the father of us all.

It refers back to *"the promise"* mentioned in verse 14. *The law* could educate people and bring them to an understanding of right and wrong, but once a person had broken even one small part of the law, the law was powerless to provide a remedy. But because the promise is *of faith* and not of the law, it can become available through *grace.* As a result, it is available *to all the seed.* Grace goes beyond the scope of the law, that is, those who have tried to live according to the law. It is offered also to those who are *of the faith of Abraham.* Probably most Jews of that day believed that God's justification was offered only to the physical descendants of Abraham. Paul makes it clear that grace is offered not only to Jews but to Gentiles also, to those who have the faith of Abraham. Paul affirms this idea in Galatians 3:28, 29: "There is neither Jew nor Greek. . . . then are ye Abraham's seed, and heirs according to the promise."

III. Abraham's Faith
(Romans 4:17-22)
A. Faith in God (v. 17)

17. (As it is written, I have made thee a father of many nations,) before him whom he believed, even God, who quickeneth the dead, and calleth those things which be not as though they were.

The passage Paul quotes here is Genesis 17:5. Abraham's only child then was Ishmael, and God said the promise would not be fulfilled through him (Genesis 17:19-21). Still, Abraham *believed.*

Paul cites two reasons Abraham could believe God's promise. First, God is the one *who quickeneth the dead.* He knew God was able to give a son to Abraham and Sarah long after their normal bearing years were past (v. 18). This phrase also reminds the Christian of God's power to raise the dead—particularly, to raise Jesus from the dead. Because Jesus has been raised, we can by faith in Him be called Abraham's children.

Second, God *calleth those things which be not as though they were.* This may have reference to God's creative ability, creating from nothing everything that is. Or it may have to do with His ability to know the future and to declare what will be with the same certainty as what already is. Actually, both are involved in God's promise to make Abraham the father of many nations. When God promised it, Abraham and Sarah had no children. But God would make it possible for them to give birth to a son, Isaac, and for people of faith to be children of Abraham as well.

B. Faith With Hope (v. 18)

18. Who against hope believed in hope, that he might become the father of many nations, according to that which was spoken, So shall thy seed be.

The dictionary defines *hope* as "desire accompanied by expectation." At their advanced ages, Sarah and Abraham had no logical basis for believing that they would be the forebears *of many nations,* that their offspring would be as numerous as the stars (Genesis 15:5). And yet against all odds Abraham continued to believe. [See question #3, page 256.]

C. Strong in Faith (vv. 19, 20)

19. And being not weak in faith, he considered not his own body now dead, when he was about a hundred years old, neither yet the deadness of Sarah's womb.

In Egypt Abraham lied to the pharaoh and said that Sarah was his sister, hoping to save his life by this strategy. This certainly seems to indicate that he was *weak in faith* at a critical moment. However he may have justified this tactic, he was, in effect, taking control of the situation himself instead of trusting God to work things out.

Before we become too critical of Abraham, we need to examine our own efforts at rationalizing some of our actions and decisions. Have we ever told a little "white lie" in order to achieve some important good? Have we ever purchased an item that we wanted and then justified it as something that we needed?

The important thing to remember is that even though Abraham may have wavered in his faith occasionally, the overall judgment of the Scriptures is that he was a man of great faith (Hebrews 11:8-10). Even though he was *about a hundred years old* and *Sarah's womb* was dead, yet he never wavered in his fundamental conviction that God would fulfill His part of the covenant that He had made.

20. He staggered not at the promise of God through unbelief; but was strong in faith, giving glory to God.

The expression *he staggered not* suggests an image of a man carrying a heavy load up a long, steep trail with strong, steady strides. The reason he can make such progress is that he is *strong in*

How to Say It

ABRAHAM. Ay-bruh-ham.
ISAAC. *Eye*-zuk.
ISHMAEL. *Ish*-may-el.
UR. Er.

the *faith.* This in a way depicts the life of Abraham. When he became weary and temptations beset him, he was able to keep going because of his faith. In so doing Abraham gives all of us an example to follow. [See question #4, page 256.]

D. Fully Persuaded (vv. 21, 22)

21. And being fully persuaded, that what he had promised, he was able also to perform.

Abraham was fully persuaded that God was able to carry out His promises. His belief that the promises would be fulfilled were grounded in his faith in Almighty God. That's where faith must begin. We who come to God "must believe that he is, and that he is a rewarder of them that diligently seek him" (Hebrews 11:6).

22. And therefore it was imputed to him for righteousness.

Decisions and actions have consequences. In Abraham's case his faith had both temporal and eternal consequences. Paul closes his discussion of the results of Abraham's faith by quoting from Genesis 15:6. Abraham's faith *was imputed,* or credited, *to him for righteousness.* Abraham was not righteous in an absolute sense—without sin. Rather, God was willing to accept Abraham's faith as a substitute for absolute righteousness. As spiritual descendants of Abraham, our faith in God and in Jesus Christ serves in a similar way.

IV. Abraham's Successors: Us (Romans 4:23-25)

A. Result of Our Faith (vv. 23, 24a)

23, 24a. Now it was not written for his sake alone, that it was imputed to him; but for us also, to whom it shall be imputed.

The Jews, of course, understood God's dealings with Abraham. But they needed additional teaching from Paul to understand that God's actions with Abraham became a model for His actions under the Christian covenant. Christians who came from either Jewish or Gentile backgrounds could accept and rejoice in this.

B. Substance of Our Faith (vv. 24b, 25)

24b, 25. If we believe on him that raised up Jesus our Lord from the dead, who was delivered for our offenses, and was raised again for our justification.

In these few words Paul spells out the heart of the gospel message. Our faith is in God who raised Jesus from the dead. This is the same God who brought life to Abraham and Sarah so that they could become forebears of "a great nation." Jesus, the Son of God, was delivered for our offenses. His death on the cross purchased our redemption. Through His resurrection we can be assured that we have been justified. [See question #5, page 256.]

These basic items of faith are absolutely essential to the gospel. Without them there is no gospel.

Conclusion

A. We Couldn't Pay the Fine

Several years ago before the Iron Curtain was removed, we were traveling in East Germany. On our last day there we were headed toward the West German border, which was only an hour or so away. We stopped at a rest center and went inside to use the rest rooms. When we returned to our car, a policeman was standing there in the process of writing out a ticket. He indicated that we were parked in a no parking zone. We could not understand why we were getting a ticket when there were no signs there to indicate that it was a no parking zone, and there were other cars parked there.

The policeman then demanded that we pay the fine right there to him. I tried to explain to him that since we were leaving East Germany, we had already spent all our East German currency. He then demanded that I let him look in my billfold. In my billfold I had Austrian, West German, and American currency but no East German money. This seemed to anger him even more. I couldn't understand exactly what he was saying, but I got the impression that he was going to take us to jail.

Home Daily Bible Readings

Monday, Mar. 11—Your Descendants As the Stars (Genesis 15:1-6)
Tuesday, Mar. 12—Promise to Abraham and Descendants (Genesis 15:12-18)
Wednesday, Mar. 13—God Chose Our Ancestors (Acts 13:13-25)
Thursday, Mar. 14—Believers Set Free by Jesus (Acts 13:26-39)
Friday, Mar. 15—Continue Your Heritage (2 Timothy 3:10-17)
Saturday, Mar. 16—Abraham's Faith Reckoned as Righteousness (Romans 4:1-8)
Sunday, Mar. 17—Heirs Through Faith (Romans 4:13-25)

With the tense political situation that then existed between East Germany and the West, that was a rather grim prospect.

The policeman then called to another officer, who was obviously his superior. When he came over, I was sure we were in real trouble. He spoke with the officer for a minute, and then he demanded to see our passports and visas. After he had looked these over, he took the ticket and smiled. Pointing us toward the highway, he then waved us on.

Now that's grace! We apparently had broken the law, and although we had money, it wasn't the right kind of money, and so we couldn't pay our way out of the situation. Only through an officer's grace were we saved from a situation that could have been quite stressful.

This is rather like our situation when we stand before the Supreme Judge. We have broken His laws time and time again, and we have no way of paying our debt. But we don't have to pay our debt. It has already been paid for us by Christ's death on the cross. We are saved by grace!

B. Faith Versus Works

Theologians have long debated the place of faith and works in God's plan of salvation. Paul insists that Abraham was justified by faith. James, on the other hand, asks, "Was not Abraham our father justified by works?" (James 2:21). Then he adds, "By works a man is justified, and not by faith only" (2:24). Martin Luther was so disturbed by the writings of James that he once referred to it as a "book of straw."

But there is really no contradiction between these two writers. Paul is writing about God's involvement in justification, which is His grace.

James, on the other hand, is concerned about man's involvement. One may say he has faith, but if that faith does not lead him to act in a manner that demonstrates his faith, then that faith is dead (James 2:26). Yet the good works of a lifetime cannot wash away even one sin. That takes the blood of Christ. That's what grace is all about!

C. Prayer

We thank You, gracious Father, that through Your Word You have given us the example of Abraham as a model for us. Help us to realize that even as he was justified by his faith, even so we must seek our justification through our faith in You and Your Son, Jesus Christ. Amen.

D. Thought to Remember

By faith Abraham "looked for a city which hath foundations, whose builder and maker is God" (Hebrews 11:10).

Learning by Doing

This page contains an alternate lesson plan emphasizing learning activities.
Classes desiring such student involvement will find these suggestions helpful.

Learning Goals

After participating in this lesson, each student will be able to:

1. Tell how Abraham and those who follow his example are considered righteous on the basis of their faith.

2. Explain the significance of Abraham's example for both Jews and Gentiles.

3. Suggest some specific means for helping people to come to know how to share in the promise of being justified by faith.

Into the Lesson

Write this statement on the board: "Have it your way." Remind the class that several years ago a popular restaurant used this as an advertising slogan. Society today wants to have as many options available as possible. We want to do things our way. We want to be in control, whether we are choosing the options on a car or decorating a house. Ask your class to identify other situations where people want to "do it their way." (If your students struggle with ideas, suggest these for starters: ordering dinner at a restaurant, purchasing shoes.)

Allow two minutes for quick responses. Next, challenge the students to think of some of the ways this principle is applied to our being acceptable to God. Have them think of different religions or even specific rule-keeping. Then lead into the Bible study by saying, "As we have just discussed, one of the most important areas in which this 'have it your way' principle is lived out is in being acceptable to God. People will try many ways, each keeping the person in control of the relationship. Today we will see that God has His way of making us acceptable. That way is ancient, a principle shown true since the time of Abraham."

Into the Word

Today's study will require some background information. In order to accomplish this, divide your class into at least two groups of five or six people each. If you have a large class, make several groups and give duplicate assignments.

Group One will study Genesis 12:1-9; 15:1-7; 17:1-6; 21:1, 2. They are to prepare a brief report that will answer the following questions for each passage: Who initiated the contact/conversation? What was said? How did Abraham respond?

What were the results? Have the students report by developing narratives or by developing short skits to depict these events.

Group Two will study Romans 4 to answer the question, "What arguments are given to prove that we are saved (justified, made righteous) by faith and not by works?" Give this group a large piece of poster board and some markers. The poster is to be divided into six sections marked as follows: vv. 1-3; vv. 4-8; vv. 9-12; vv. 13-15; vv. 16, 17; vv. 18-25. In each section students are to write answers to the question based on the verses cited.

Allow ten minutes for research, then five minutes each for presentation. You may want to summarize the material for the class. The final part of this discussion of Scripture is to answer, "Why is Abraham's example important for the Jews and Gentiles?" The key to this answer is Romans 4:23-25.

Into Life

Say to the class, "It is always a tendency of humans to want to have things their own way. It may be based on likes and dislikes or upon traditions. This can be true in how we follow God and seek to be accepted by Him."

Have the groups reconvene. Point them to Romans 3 and 4. Provide markers and blank sheets of paper. After reviewing the chapters, groups are to develop a tract that will communicate how a person is justified by faith. (A similar activity is included in *Adult Bible Class.*)

As an example, you may communicate the following outline:

1. We have a problem (Romans 3:23).

2. God answers our problem with Jesus' sacrifice (Romans 3:24, 25).

3. We must respond (Romans 3:25, 26).

4. Faith has always been God's means (Romans 4:2, 3, 13).

5. We, too, come to God as Abraham did (Romans 4:23-25).

Ask one or two groups to share the message of the tract. Conduct a brief brainstorm of ways individuals can share this message with others. Examples include personal visits, acts of kindness in the community, mailings, and others.

Ask each person to consider how he or she can share the good news. Close with a prayer for strength to fulfill this challenge.

Let's Talk It Over

The questions on this page are designed to encourage review of the lesson Scriptures and to promote discussion of the lesson by the class. The answers provided are only discussion starters. Let your class talk it over from there.

1. On what grounds do some people today claim to be justified before God? How can we persuade such people that they are in need of God's grace for salvation?

Most people have the idea that works will save a person, that one has to be "good enough" by some standard. Hardly anyone will put that standard at absolute perfection, however. So most people will assume they are "just as good" as someone else, or "not as bad" as some evil character, and they figure that's okay.

Others believe that since they prayed a special prayer, repeated a special phrase, or were baptized, they are guaranteed salvation. The Bible affirms the role of such things as faith, confession, and baptism in accepting God's grace (Mark 16:16; Acts 2:38; Romans 10:10), but these are not "works." Nor do they eliminate the need to "hold fast to the profession of our faith" and to "live by faith" (Hebrews 10:23, 38).

2. The lesson writer says, "The only way of escape from wrath is Abraham's way. He believed in the Lord, and therefore the Lord credited him with righteousness." Some will ask, "But what of those who have not heard of the Lord? Is it fair that they perish?" How would you answer?

Many people assume that such people will be automatically saved, but the Bible does not affirm that. Ask your learners to suppose that "sin" is an illness, a fatal disease. The cure, however, is made from a very common herb, available to anyone who knows what to look for. What will happen to those who don't know the cure?

Sin is a fatal disease: "the wages of sin is death" (Romans 6:23). And everyone has it: "all have sinned" (Romans 3:23). The sad fact is that if sinners perish, *that* is fair; it is justice. It is up to us to deliver the good news that justice need not be served; there is grace freely available!

3. What do we mean when we say someone "hopes against hope"? How is that similar to and different from Paul's statement that Abraham "against hope believed in hope"? What lesson or lessons are there for us?

The dictionary says to "hope against hope" is to "hope without any basis for expecting a fulfillment." Such a hope is destined to disappointment,

but the Bible tells us that our hope "maketh not ashamed" (or "does not disappoint," Romans 5:5). Abraham did not hope against hope; he believed against hope. If we reorder the sentence, we can accurately express the verse this way: "In hope, Abraham believed against hope." Against all earthly basis for hope, Abraham put his hope in God, and he believed; he trusted; he had confidence. The lesson is clear: what we so often call "hope" is often little more than wishful thinking, but "hope" in the New Testament sense is a confident expectation that God will keep His promises!

4. Tell about a time when you were "weak in faith" and what you learned from the experience. Or tell of a time when you were "strong in faith." How did your faith sustain you?

You may need to tell of an event in your own life to get this discussion rolling. Or you might suggest some categories or generalized situations. Perhaps you have students who were afraid to fly, but a business trip necessitated it and they had to find the courage to do so. Did their faith play a role in that? Perhaps some have experienced tragedy, a death in the family that was especially hard to deal with. How did their faith grow? Has your church been through a major change—relocation, building program, restoration after a fire, or the like? How did each one's faith play a role in how individuals dealt with the situation?

5. Suppose some friend complained, "You Christians are always using those special 'code words' that nobody else understands! Just what do you mean by *justification*, anyway?" How would you respond?

We do need to be careful about using words that unbelievers do not understand. *Justification*, however, need not be one of these hard words. It is used in modern courtrooms and other places today in much the same sense as it is in Scripture. If a person is charged with a crime, he can be convicted, acquitted, or justified. If he is found guilty, he is convicted. If he is found not guilty, he is acquitted. But if it is determined that he committed the act but bears no legal guilt, he is justified. That is true in our case. We have sinned, but we are justified—we bear no guilt!

Reconciled by Christ's Death

DEVOTIONAL READING: **Psalm 25:1-11.**

BACKGROUND SCRIPTURE: **Romans 5.**

PRINTED TEXT: **Romans 5:1-11, 18-21.**

Romans 5:1-11, 18-21

1 Therefore being justified by faith, we have peace with God through our Lord Jesus Christ:

2 By whom also we have access by faith into this grace wherein we stand, and rejoice in hope of the glory of God.

3 And not only so, but we glory in tribulations also; knowing that tribulation worketh patience;

4 And patience, experience; and experience, hope:

5 And hope maketh not ashamed; because the love of God is shed abroad in our hearts by the Holy Ghost which is given unto us.

6 For when we were yet without strength, in due time Christ died for the ungodly.

7 For scarcely for a righteous man will one die: yet peradventure for a good man some would even dare to die.

8 But God commendeth his love toward us, in that, while we were yet sinners, Christ died for us.

9 Much more then, being now justified by his blood, we shall be saved from wrath through him.

10 For if, when we were enemies, we were reconciled to God by the death of his Son; much more, being reconciled, we shall be saved by his life.

11 And not only so, but we also joy in God through our Lord Jesus Christ, by whom we have now received the atonement.

· · · · · · · · · · · ·

18 Therefore, as by the offense of one judgment came upon all men to condemnation; even so by the righteousness of one the free gift came upon all men unto justification of life.

19 For as by one man's disobedience many were made sinners, so by the obedience of one shall many be made righteous.

20 Moreover the law entered, that the offense might abound. But where sin abounded, grace did much more abound:

21 That as sin hath reigned unto death, even so might grace reign through righteousness unto eternal life by Jesus Christ our Lord.

GOLDEN TEXT: Therefore being justified by faith, we have peace with God through our Lord Jesus Christ.—Romans 5:1.

The Power of the Gospel
Unit 1: Justified by Faith
(Lessons 1-5)

Lesson Aims

After participating in this lesson, each student will be able to:

1. Summarize Paul's description of the blessings of being justified by faith.

2. Explain what it means to be "reconciled to God by the death of His Son" and "saved by His life."

3. Seek to be a messenger of reconciliation whenever and wherever one is needed this week.

Lesson Outline

INTRODUCTION
   A. While We Were Yet Sinners
   B. Lesson Background
 I. BLESSINGS OF JUSTIFICATION (Romans 5:1-5)
   A. Peace With God (v. 1)
   B. Access Into Grace (v. 2)
   C. Endurance Through Trials (vv. 3, 4)
   D. Love of God (vv. 5-8)
    The Blessing That Comes Through Trials
 II. RESULTS OF JUSTIFICATION (Romans 5:9-11)
   A. Saved From Wrath (vv. 9, 10)
   B. Joy in God (v. 11)
    Dying for Those Who Are Evil
III. GOAL OF JUSTIFICATION (Romans 5:18-21)
   A. Imputed Righteousness (vv. 18, 19)
   B. Abundant Grace (v. 20)
   C. Reigning Grace (v. 21)
CONCLUSION
   A. Exciting Promises
   B. Joy and Peace
   C. Prayer
   D. Thought to Remember

Introduction

A. While We Were Yet Sinners

A pious English couple had only one son, but he was a fine Christian young man, the pride of their lives. When World War I began, he was called to the colors and soon found himself in the front lines in France. Within a few months his parents received the distressing news that their son had been killed in action. The only thing that softened their tragedy was the news that he had died heroically, saving the life of one of his comrades.

Some time later the man whose life had been saved returned to England on furlough, and the couple invited him to spend a few days with them. When he arrived at their home, they were shocked. He was obviously intoxicated, and his language was filled with profanities. Now the couples' agony was intensified, for it was clear that their son had given his life for a man who was crude and carnal.

For their daily devotions, the couple was reading from the book of Romans, and the next morning it so happened that they were reading from the fifth chapter. At verse 8, the husband paused. After a long silence he said quietly, "Now I begin to understand what this verse means."

B. Lesson Background

For all of us the door to the past is closed forever and we can never open it. For some of us that is a very good thing, for the past holds painful memories of mistakes we made that pulled us away from God and His will for us. For some the past holds pleasant memories, but even pleasant memories are sometimes painful because we know that we cannot bring the "good old days" back and relive them.

Just as the door to the past is closed, so also is the door to the future. None of us possesses a crystal ball that will give us the power to penetrate the darkness that shrouds the future.

Only the present is ours. Yet we dare not live just for the moment. The past has shaped us and will have an impact on how we make the decisions that will shape the future. But even the wisest and most pious of us cannot, on our own, face the future with complete assurance. An accident, an unexpected illness, the actions of a friend or an enemy, even some event in a remote part of the world may change our future dramatically.

In a world of uncertainties, two things we can know for certain. At some point days, weeks, months, or years from now, we will breathe our final breath. The other thing we can know for certain is that "while we were yet sinners, Christ died for us." Our faith in that fact can give us the assurance to face whatever the future brings us.

I. Blessings of Justification (Romans 5:1-5)

A. Peace with God (v. 1)

1. Therefore being justified by faith, we have peace with God through our Lord Jesus Christ.

Romans 4 closes with a succinct statement of the heart of the gospel message: Christ was crucified for our sins and "raised again for our justification." Here as in other places, Paul uses the word *therefore* as a transition from a theological statement to the practical applications of that statement. One thing that follows from one's justification is *peace with God*. Our sins alienate us from God. We oppose His will for us and are at war with His kingdom. As long as we continue to oppose Him, we cannot enjoy this peace. God's promise of peace is certain if we are willing to accept it. But even though we may understand this objectively in our minds, we may not always enjoy it emotionally in our hearts. We may have rebelled so long and so strongly that we find it difficult to accept His promise. Augustine (A.D. 354-430), who had long rebelled against God, observed that "our heart is not quiet until it rests" in God. If we are really to have peace, we must accept His promise both mentally and emotionally.

B. Access Into Grace (v. 2)

2. By whom also we have access by faith into this grace wherein we stand, and rejoice in hope of the glory of God.

Grace was linked with peace in the salutation of the letter (1:7) and has been mentioned three times since (3:24; 4:4, 16), the latter two drawing a clear distinction between *faith*/grace and works/law. Paul reaffirms here that faith, not works, provides the *access* to God's grace, by which we are heirs of the promise to Abraham (4:16).

As sinners, we fall short of *the glory of God* (Romans 3:23), but by grace we anticipate the time when that glory will be revealed in us (Romans 8:18). It is not surprising, then, that this grace leads the believer to *rejoice in hope!*

C. Endurance Through Trials (vv. 3, 4)

3, 4. And not only so, but we glory in tribulations also; knowing that tribulation worketh patience; and patience, experience; and experience, hope:

While God has promised us peace, He does not guarantee that our lives will be free of problems. There is a danger that when we have difficult times, our faith may waver. Paul tries to prepare his readers for the trials that may come because they are Christians. Like Peter (1 Peter 4:12, 13) and James (James 1:2), Paul wants his readers to rejoice in such trials. But the word Paul uses, *glory*, is a stronger word than *rejoice*. It is the same word that was used in Romans 4:2, where Paul says Abraham would have had cause to "glory," or "boast," if his justification were based on works.

So, while Satan uses these *tribulations* to upset and weaken our faith, Paul urges us to rejoice or even "boast" about them. They can help us to gain spiritual strength. The word *patience*, rendered "perseverance" in some translations, suggests endurance. One who has endured the fires of suffering knows that God will give him or her

the strength to survive; such a one can meet these difficulties with calm assurance.

The *New International Version* translates *experience* as "character," while the *New American Standard Bible* has "proven character." The word carries the idea of being tested, like gold that has been through the refiner's fire to burn off the impurities. In the same way, a person who has gone through the many trials of life has gained the discipline that allows the future to be viewed with hope. One who has felt the guiding hand of God through the deep shadows of life's disappointments has no apprehension about what the future may hold. Such a person knows that God will still be at his or her side. [See question #1, page 264.]

D. Love of God (vv. 5-8)

5. And hope maketh not ashamed; because the love of God is shed abroad in our hearts by the Holy Ghost which is given unto us.

Hope maketh not ashamed, or "does not disappoint us" as the *New International Version* has it. In times of testing, that hope will not leave us helpless and humiliated. The reason is that *the love of God is shed abroad in our hearts.* While this refers to God's love that has been shown toward us, it does not mean God does not love us until we express our faith and find reconciliation with Him. God's love is unconditional, as the following verses, and especially v. 8, make clear. But we do not realize the benefit of His love until we enter a relationship with Him. The father of the prodigal son loved him even when he was in the far country, but he had to return to the father before he could enjoy that love.

The Holy Spirit is the means by which God pours out His love to us. The presence of the Holy Spirit is not promised alone to a few very

Visual for lesson 4

This visual uses the image of a "peace treaty" to illustrate verse 1, "We have peace with God."

How to Say It

AUGUSTINE. *Aw*-gus-*teen* (strong accent on *Aw)* or Aw-*gus*-tin.

---

special saints, but is a gift that everyone who repents and is baptized receives (Acts 2:38, 39).

6. For when we were yet without strength, in due time Christ died for the ungodly.

In the verses that follow, Paul contrasts the human situation before Christ came with that after He came. Before Christ came, we were *without strength.* Paul is not describing our physical condition but our spiritual situation. In the first chapter of Romans Paul describes in some detail the wicked state into which the human race had fallen. The worst part of man's condition was not his evil but the fact that he was utterly helpless to do anything to save himself. Even in their efforts to worship God men "changed the glory of the uncorruptible God into an image made like to corruptible man, and to birds, and four-footed beasts, and creeping things" (Romans 1:23). God then in His infinite wisdom and mercy sent His Son to die for all sinners, *the ungodly.*

7. For scarcely for a righteous man will one die: yet peradventure for a good man some would even dare to die.

Some see in this verse a contrast between a *righteous man* and a *good man.* In this view *righteous man* describes a pious person who has a "holier-than-thou" attitude. He may be respected, but not greatly loved, and thus no one would be likely to die for him. A *good man,* on the other hand, is a moral person whose good deeds are well known and appreciated by many. As a result, people will "do anything" for him; someone might be willing even *to die* for him.

Others take the verse to present, not a contrast between two different types of persons, but two ways of saying the same thing. Either way, the idea is that it is a rare thing indeed to find a person who would be willing to die for another, and it is expected that it is some good quality in the person that would motivate one to make such a sacrifice. That contrasts sharply with Christ's sacrifice since He died for all—not just the good, righteous people but for the worst of sinners.

8. But God commendeth his love toward us, in that, while we were yet sinners, Christ died for us.

God commendeth, or demonstrates, *his love* for *us.* We might picture a person standing on the shore of a river, trying to throw a life preserver to a person who is struggling in the water to save himself. But this would not accurately portray the situation presented in this verse. Rather, the

rescuer jumps into the water to rescue the other person, who openly fights against the rescuer. As a result, the drowning person is saved, but the rescuer is drowned. [See question #2, page 264.]

THE BLESSING THAT COMES THROUGH TRIALS

Christopher de Vinck is an English teacher. Each time he introduces his class to *The Miracle Worker,* the play about the blind and deaf Helen Keller, he tells the students about his brother Oliver. Oliver lived in his parents' home for thirty-three years, blind, deaf, legs twisted, and apparently with insufficient intelligence to learn anything.

His parents had been urged to put the baby in an institution, but they said, "No, we will take him home." Rather than focus on the difficulty associated with providing the level of care Oliver required, Oliver's parents focused on their blessings. Although Oliver was profoundly disabled, he was neither hyperactive nor wild, nor did he demand constant attention. Christopher says of him, "He was the most helpless human I ever met. But we were blessed with his presence, a true presence of peace." And when the time came for Christopher to choose a wife, her reaction to his helpless brother became the litmus test by which she was judged worthy of his love.

Oliver de Vinck was the means by which a whole family and their friends learned the meaning of our text today: through trials come patience, experience, and hope in the love of God that the Spirit makes known to us.   —C. R. B.

II. Results of Justification (Romans 5:9-11)

A. Saved From Wrath (vv. 9, 10)

9. Much more then, being now justified by his blood, we shall be saved from wrath through him.

Christ died for sinners, but this was *much more* than a courageous act of love, Paul insists. Through *His blood* we are *justified.* The Scriptures tell us that "without shedding of blood is no remission" of sins (Hebrews 9:22). The Old Testament tells us of the sacrifices made in the tabernacle and temple, all of which looked forward to Jesus Christ, who was the perfect sacrifice. [See question #3, page 264.]

10. For if, when we were enemies, we were reconciled to God by the death of his Son; much more, being reconciled, we shall be saved by his life.

Justification addresses the problem of sin from a legal point of view and reconciliation from a personal point of view. In a lawsuit, a court may hand down a decision that meets the requirements of the law for justice. But there is still no reconciliation. Not until the two contestants shake hands as a sign of mutual respect can there be a reconciliation. God has extended His hand through the death of His Son. It is up to us to accept it. [See question #4, page 264.]

But even that is not the whole story. *Much more* than this great reconciliation that was effected by Jesus' death is the benefit of His resurrection and continuing *life*. By that, Paul says, *we shall be saved*. Salvation is more than a matter of having our past sins erased by Jesus' atoning death. It is a relationship with a living Lord. And if Christ was willing to die for our sins when we were sinners (and He was), how *much more* will He do for us in this living salvation relationship we now enjoy with Him!

B. Joy in God (v. 11)

11. And not only so, but we also joy in God through our Lord Jesus Christ, by whom we have now received the atonement.

The immediate and obvious response to our realization that we have been justified and reconciled is *joy in God*. This joy is not just an exciting emotion that will soon pass. It is a deep, lasting sense of security that will carry us into eternity.

We have now received the atonement. The word *atonement* is more appropriately translated as "reconciliation" in most modern versions. The word *atone* was coined by joining the words *at* and *one*. *Atonement*, then, denotes a coming together or a reconciliation of opposing persons.

DYING FOR THOSE WHO ARE EVIL

NBC TV commentator Tom Brokaw wrote *The Greatest Generation* just a couple of years ago. In it he tells of the commitment and sacrifice of a generation of Americans that grew up during the difficult days of the Great Depression and then were conscripted to fight World War II. The book has had an amazing effect. Brokaw says baby boomers who had rejected the values of their parents have told him that the book has given them "a new appreciation for the sacrifices and deprivations of their mothers and fathers." Men often tell him, "Thank you for writing. . . . I finally understand my father." One man says he read the book to his nearly blind father—a veteran of the war—and "it was the most meaningful father-son time we'd ever had." Untold thousands of that "greatest generation" died for the sake of loved ones back home and for the preservation of a homeland they would never see again.

The sacrifice these men and women made for their loved ones is not unlike the potential sacrifice Paul notes by some who might dare to die for the good. But what makes Christ's love different is that He was willing to die for every tyrant and despot, enemies and not friends—the worst in all of us! We honor those willing to die for the good; we can only be amazed at the One who died for those who are evil.   —C. R. B.

III. Goal of Justification (Romans 5:18-21)

The closing verses of today's lesson deal with some theological issues that have been debated for centuries. From verse 12 on Paul compares and contrasts the effects of Adam's sin and Christ's sacrificial death. In every point the effect of Adam's sin is answered by Christ—and "much more" (vv. 15, 17).

A. Imputed Righteousness (vv. 18, 19)

18. Therefore, as by the offense of one judgment came upon all men to condemnation; even so by the righteousness of one the free gift came upon all men unto justification of life.

This verse brings to a climax a series of contrasts between Adam and Christ. Adam's act was an *offense;* Christ's was an act of *righteousness.* Adam's act brought death; Christ's brings *life.* In one respect, however, their actions were the same—the effect of their actions *came upon all* who ever lived.

19. For as by one man's disobedience many were made sinners, so by the obedience of one shall many be made righteous.

Here Paul explains how these two actions affect everyone. First, why did judgment come upon "all men" as a result of Adam's offense? The answer is that the *many were made sinners.* (The word *many* is apparently equivalent to *all* from verse 18.) But in what sense are all *made sinners?* Everyone who comes into this world suffers consequences of Adam's sin. Just what are those consequences? As a minimum, they must include physical death (1 Corinthians 15:22a). But do they include Adam's guilt?

Further, how does "the free gift" of Christ come "upon all men unto justification of life"? Certainly it cannot mean that everyone will be saved. That would be contrary to what the Scripture says elsewhere. It does suggest that whatever consequence and guilt we inherit from Adam is erased in Christ. Death is annulled by resurrection, which happens to the righteous and the wicked alike (John 5:29). Guilt, to whatever extent is inherited from Adam, is also taken away.

Thus we are left with accountability for our own sin, and not that of Adam. And this too is answered in Christ and is available to all, for "whosoever" calls on the name of the Lord will be saved (Romans 10:13). They are *made righteous,* just as Abraham's faith "was counted unto him for righteousness" (Romans 4:3). This is the "much more" that has been running throughout Paul's argument: God's grace eliminates the effects of Adam's sin—and ours!

B. Abundant Grace (v. 20)

20. Moreover the law entered, that the offense might abound. But where sin abounded, grace did much more abound.

Law, whether it refers to the law of Moses or law in the more general sense, served at least one important function: it makes us aware of our sinfulness. As a result, our situation is exposed as hopeless. But we are not left in that desperate situation. Paul now contrasts *sin* and *grace.* No matter how desperate one's condition is as a result of sin, God's grace has provided a remedy. Just as sin is all-encompassing, so grace is just as extensive—and more powerful. Praise the Lord!

C. Reigning Grace (v. 21)

21. That as sin hath reigned unto death, even so might grace reign through righteousness unto eternal life by Jesus Christ our Lord.

The consequence of *sin* is *death*—both physical and spiritual—"for the wages of sin is death" (Romans 6:23). But the bright side of this contrast is that we have the hope of *eternal life by Jesus Christ.* [See question #5, page 264.]

Conclusion

A. Exciting Promises

At least two or three times a week we receive some exciting opportunities through the mail. We are promised a new car, a trip to Hawaii, or even a million dollars! On occasion we have been informed that we are already on the winner's list! All we have to do, we are told, is to write our name and address on a card and mail it in. Most of these are quickly disposed of without even being opened. Why? Because we know that the glowing promises are just that—promises, promises that have nothing to back them up. Yet many people have believed the promises and have been sadly disappointed when they have proven to be false. Periodically, governmental agencies take steps to curtail this kind of mail.

Yet in today's lesson we have studied promises that surpass any promises we have received through the mail. Even though we are sinners, we are promised justification. Even though we have been alienated from God, we are promised reconciliation. Even though we live under the curse of death, we are promised life.

How can we trust such promises? We can trust them because we read about them in the Scriptures. We can trust them because God sent His own Son to die for us. Why shouldn't we find these promises exciting?

B. Joy and Peace

Years ago we sang a chorus that went something like this: "I have the joy, joy, joy, joy down in my heart, down in my heart, down in my heart to stay!" Another stanza, which was always a tongue twister for me, went "I have the peace that passeth understanding down in my heart!"

Joy and peace belong together. In the first verse of today's lesson we read that we are justified by faith. All of us were sinners, facing judgment, certain of being eternally condemned, and without any way of saving ourselves—helpless and hopeless. Yet by faith we are justified. That means that even though we are sinners, we do not have to pay the penalty for our iniquities. Christ has already paid the penalty on the cross. Thus we stand justified, which someone has explained as being "just as if I'd" never sinned.

Being justified means that we can enjoy a peace that the world doesn't even begin to understand. Because of that peace we can meet the problems of life with joy that springs from the confidence that justification brings.

C. Prayer

We approach Your throne of grace with confidence, dear Father, not because of anything we have done or deserve, but because we have been justified through the death of Your Son. May our daily walk testify to the world that we have been justified and reconciled to You. In our Master's name we pray. Amen.

D. Thought to Remember

"Where sin abounded, grace did much more abound" (Romans 5:20).

Home Daily Bible Readings

Monday, Mar. 18—Happy Are Those Who Are Forgiven (Psalm 32:1-5)
Tuesday, Mar. 19—By the Grace of God (1 Corinthians 15:1-11)
Wednesday, Mar. 20—Made Alive in Christ (1 Corinthians 15:20-28)
Thursday, Mar. 21—Justified by Faith (Romans 5:1-11)
Friday, Mar. 22—Free Gift of Righteousness (Romans 5:12-17)
Saturday, Mar. 23—Your King Arrives on a Donkey (Zechariah 9:9-13)
Sunday, Mar. 24—"Hosanna in the Highest Heaven!" (Matthew 21:1-11)

Learning by Doing

This page contains an alternate lesson plan emphasizing learning activities.
Classes desiring such student involvement will find these suggestions helpful.

Learning Goals

After this lesson each student will be able to:

1. Summarize Paul's description of the blessings of being justified by faith.

2. Explain what it means to be "reconciled to God by the death of His Son" and "saved by His life."

3. Seek to be a messenger of reconciliation whenever and wherever one is needed this week.

Into the Lesson

Tell the students, "Think of all the world peace accords since you were born. We will list them here." (Refer to a marker board or poster attached to the wall.) The class might list these, among others: Yalta and Potsdam Conferences (1945, WWII); Korean Armistice (1953); Suez Canal Treaty (1956, Israel-Egypt); Paris Peace Talks (1973, Vietnam); Camp David (1978, Israel-Egypt); Oslo Agreements (1993, 1995, Israel-PLO); Dayton Peace Accords (1995, Bosnia); Wye Summit Agreement (1998, Israel-PLO).

After listing several accords, ask, "What words come to mind when you hear the word *peace?*" Allow time for responses; then ask, "Why is it difficult for the world to achieve peace?"

Today's lesson explores how a person finds peace with God. We will note what is essential for peace with God and with others.

Into the Word

Before this week's lesson, recruit a class member to read today's text. Be sure that he or she has reviewed the text, paying close attention to punctuation. If you are not using student books, you may want to copy the text for learners' use.

Say, "Justification by faith brings many blessings for the Christian. Reread the text; then circle the blessings you can find." After the class has finished its work, call for volunteers to list these on your board.

Blessings include the following: peace with God (v. 1), access into grace (v. 2), hope (v. 2), character produced in our lives (vv. 3, 4), God's love in our hearts (v. 5), being saved from God's wrath (v. 9), and life in Christ (vv. 18, 19).

Develop a short lecture to help students understand the difference between justification and reconciliation. Draw on the information given in the commentary and from your own research on vv. 9-11.

Divide the class into groups of four to six members each. If you have more than two groups, number the groups. Each group is to read v. 10. The odd-numbered groups are to brainstorm the things God had to overcome for us to be reconciled to Him while we were yet His enemies. *(These include our sin, death, and Satan's power.)* The even-numbered groups are to brainstorm what "more" God will do for us now that we are reconciled. *(These include give us real joy and give us eternal life.)*

Call the groups back together and compile your lists. Say, "As a result of Christ's death, we have been reconciled to God. Now that we are His friends, much more awaits us, as we have listed. God's work in our lives spurs us on to be messengers for Him."

Into Life

Write at the top of your board "God is. . . ." Ask students to return to their groups and reread verses 1-11. Ask each group to create two or three bumper stickers from what these verses tell about God. *(Suggestions include "God is love," "God is my friend," God is glorious," "God is the reconciler.")* Allow five minutes for this exercise.

Call the groups together, asking volunteers to share their bumper stickers. Ask, "Why is this an important image of God? How can we best communicate this truth to our neighbors and society? Where are some of the places this message needs most to be seen?"

Option. If possible, have on hand peel-and-stick labels with the letter *R.* Give one to each class member. Suggest that each student wear the label this week and be prepared to explain it to anyone who asks. The class may want to make a list of R's it could stand for: *reconciled, redeemed, rejoicing, resurrected.*

Since the group has mentioned some places where the message of reconciliation needs to be shared, close with a challenge for each to be a "reconciler" this week. Ask them to pray this prayer after you (a few words at a time). "Lord, this week help me to be Your representative. Open my eyes to see the situations where You want Your message proclaimed. Open my ears to hear the cries of those who need Your presence. Open my mouth to speak Your message. Open my arms to be an instrument of Your love. In Christ Jesus, I pray. Amen."

Let's Talk It Over

The questions on this page are designed to encourage review of the lesson Scriptures and to promote discussion of the lesson by the class. The answers provided are only discussion starters. Let your class talk it over from there.

1. How has some trial or tribulation helped to mold you into the person that you are today? How has it increased your hope?

This question can open the floor to some powerful testimonies. Perhaps some member of the class has had to resist great pressure at the workplace to stand up for her faith. Who was exerting the pressure—a client, an unscrupulous boss? How did she deal with it? What was the impact on other workers? Or perhaps another class member has had chronic health problems or a permanent disability. How has he dealt with that? Did he pray for healing? If so, how did he persevere when the answer was, or for a long time seemed to be, "No"? One thing the trials your students have faced should have done was to help them lift their focus from this world to the next, when all trials will be past!

2. It is easy to compare ourselves with those who are guilty of gross crimes and to believe that we are "not so bad." In God's eyes, however, we are all sinners, and Christ died for sinners. How can we communicate the need to accept the gift of Christ's atoning death to those sinners who see themselves as "not so bad"?

In an age that recognizes few if any absolutes, this is a difficult task. Without any moral absolutes, it is difficult to convince anyone of the reality of sin. "Right" and "wrong" become relative matters, and a person can always find someone who is worse that he or she is. To get around this, we have to admit first that we ourselves are not "good enough" for salvation. As long as the world believes that we think we somehow deserve salvation, then people of the world can make a case that they are "just as good" as we are. But when the issue is not how good one is, but whether one has Jesus, then we have made a good start.

3. A good way to remember the meaning of the word *justified* is to think of it as "just as if I'd" never sinned. Imagine living a life without any history or without any regrets. If you could make a list of those events or circumstances in your life that you would like to put behind you, what would you include?

Many class members may be reluctant to be specific about sins in their past. If there is prolonged silence at this question, be ready to suggest some categories that may be less invasive and personal for people to talk about. Perhaps some of your students will agree that they did some things in their youth that they are not proud of. Perhaps these have even compromised their ability to caution their own children against some behaviors. Or perhaps some have not been as involved in the church as they should have been. Some will admit they have not given their families the priority they should have.

None of these suggestions is specific, and so they are not as difficult to admit publicly as specific sins would be. If you have a very close-knit class, be prepared for more intimate confessions of specific wrongdoing. Do not be shocked or condemnatory, but claim the wonderful grace of Jesus for each incident revealed.

4. Paul makes it clear that Jesus, alive and living forever, is still active in our salvation. Having died to secure our reconciliation, "much more . . . we shall be saved by his life." What does this suggest to you about how to face trials? How do we use the power of Jesus' life in our lives?

When Stephen was stoned by the angry mob, he looked up and saw Jesus standing at the right hand of God (Acts 7:55). Apparently Jesus had stood and was taking an active interest in the suffering of His saint. He notices our trials as well.

When Peter was facing a severe trial, even though he did not know it yet, Jesus prayed for him that his faith would not fail (Luke 22:31, 32). Jesus is no less active in our behalf, mediating with the Father for our good.

5. When grace reigns in a person's life, what does that look like? What attitudes and actions are typical of such a one?

Jesus said, "To whom little is forgiven, the same loveth little" (Luke 7:47). One who fails to appreciate the depth of God's grace is one who, in his own mind, has been forgiven little. Grace does not reign in such a one, and neither does love. But one who rightly appreciates the wonderful grace of God is one in whom grace reigns. This one loves much and expresses that love toward others in tangible ways. This one speaks with grace (Colossians 4:6), and gives grace to those who are weak.

Made Alive in Christ

DEVOTIONAL READING: Romans 6:12-23.

BACKGROUND SCRIPTURE: John 20:1-18; Romans 6.

PRINTED TEXT: John 20:1, 11-17; Romans 6:3-11.

John 20:1, 11-17

1 The first day of the week cometh Mary Magdalene early, when it was yet dark, unto the sepulchre, and seeth the stone taken away from the sepulchre.

· · · · · · · · · · · · ·

11 But Mary stood without at the sepulchre weeping: and as she wept, she stooped down, and looked into the sepulchre,

12 And seeth two angels in white sitting, the one at the head, and the other at the feet, where the body of Jesus had lain.

13 And they say unto her, Woman, why weepest thou? She saith unto them, Because they have taken away my Lord, and I know not where they have laid him.

14 And when she had thus said, she turned herself back, and saw Jesus standing, and knew not that it was Jesus.

15 Jesus saith unto her, Woman, why weepest thou? whom seekest thou? She, supposing him to be the gardener, saith unto him, Sir, if thou have borne him hence, tell me where thou hast laid him, and I will take him away.

16 Jesus saith unto her, Mary. She turned herself, and saith unto him, Rabboni; which is to say, Master.

17 Jesus saith unto her, Touch me not; for I am not yet ascended to my Father: but go to my brethren, and say unto them, I ascend unto my Father, and your Father; and to my God, and your God.

Romans 6:3-11

3 Know ye not, that so many of us as were baptized into Jesus Christ were baptized into his death?

4 Therefore we are buried with him by baptism into death: that like as Christ was raised up from the dead by the glory of the Father, even so we also should walk in newness of life.

5 For if we have been planted together in the likeness of his death, we shall be also in the likeness of his resurrection:

6 Knowing this, that our old man is crucified with him, that the body of sin might be destroyed, that henceforth we should not serve sin.

7 For he that is dead is freed from sin.

8 Now if we be dead with Christ, we believe that we shall also live with him:

9 Knowing that Christ being raised from the dead dieth no more; death hath no more dominion over him.

10 For in that he died, he died unto sin once: but in that he liveth, he liveth unto God.

11 Likewise reckon ye also yourselves to be dead indeed unto sin, but alive unto God through Jesus Christ our Lord.

GOLDEN TEXT: We are buried with him by baptism into death: that like as Christ was raised up from the dead by the glory of the Father, even so we also should walk in newness of life.—Romans 6:4.

The Power of the Gospel
Unit 1: Justified by Faith
(Lessons 1-5)

Lesson Aims

After participating in this lesson, each student will be able to:

1. Describe the details surrounding the resurrected Christ's appearance to Mary Magdalene, and how Paul linked Christian baptism with Jesus' resurrection.

2. Explain the impact that being "raised with Christ" should have on a Christian's daily conduct.

3. Identify one behavior or attitude that needs to be put to death in order to demonstrate the "newness of life" that should characterize a believer.

Lesson Outline

INTRODUCTION
  A. He's Different
  B. Lesson Background
 I. JESUS' RESURRECTION AND MARY MAGDALENE
     (John 20:1, 11-17)
  A. Mary's Discovery (v. 1)
  B. Mary's Grief (vv. 11-13)
  C. Mary's Plea (vv. 14, 15)
  D. Mary's Master (vv. 16, 17)
II. JESUS' RESURRECTION AND CHRISTIAN BAPTISM
     (Romans 6:3-11)
  A. Buried With Christ (vv. 3, 4)
     Symbols
  B. Raised With Christ (vv. 5-7)
  C. Alive With Christ (vv. 8-11)
     Dead to Sin; Alive With Christ
CONCLUSION
  A. He Has Risen!
  B. We Have Risen!
  C. Prayer
  D. Thought to Remember

Introduction

A. He's Different

A community drama club practiced many weeks in order to present a play for their friends and family members. The play they selected required so many characters that some of the club members had to play more than one part. One young man played a character who was killed in the first act. His little nephew was in the audience when this happened, and he cried out,

"They killed Uncle Bobby! They killed Uncle Bobby!"

The young man appeared as another character in the next act. When he came on the stage, the nephew was perplexed for a moment, and he cried out once again, "Uncle Bobby's not dead! But he's different!"

Jesus used the imagery of the cross to describe His disciples' commitment to following Him (Matthew 16:24). Paul used a similar figure when he said, "I am crucified with Christ" (Galatians 2:20). Christian baptism pictures this same idea of a death for the follower of Jesus, and a new life as well. When a penitent believer is buried in Christian baptism, that one is not literally dead, but he or she rises from the water very different!

B. Lesson Background

Today's lesson deals with the Easter theme, but it is handled in a somewhat unusual way. The resurrection account is presented first. We see the resurrection through the eyes of Mary Magdalene. At least six women bear the name Mary in the New Testament, three of whom play significant roles in the Gospel accounts—Mary the mother of Jesus, Mary the sister of Martha and Lazarus, and Mary Magdalene. This designation of the latter Mary indicates she was from the town of Magdala. She is mentioned along with several other women who followed Jesus during His ministry. She must have felt a special debt to Jesus because He had healed her of evil spirits (Luke 8:2).

Mary was among the women who went to the tomb early on that first resurrection day. During the dismay and turmoil that followed the discovery that the tomb was empty, Mary returned to the tomb. Standing outside the tomb she began to weep, and as she wept the Lord appeared to her.

The second part of today's lesson deals with theological implications of the burial and resurrection of Jesus. In Romans 6 Paul points out some parallels between Christian baptism and the death, burial, and resurrection of Jesus.

I. Jesus' Resurrection and Mary Magdalene (John 20:1, 11-17)

A. Mary's Discovery (v. 1)

1. The first day of the week cometh Mary Magdalene early, when it was yet dark, unto the sepulchre, and seeth the stone taken away from the sepulchre.

Jesus was crucified on Friday and His body was hastily buried by Joseph of Arimathea and Nicodemus before the beginning of the sabbath. Then *early* on Sunday morning several women who had been followers of Jesus went to the tomb to make further preparations of His body (Luke

23:54—24:1). Apparently the work of Joseph and Nicodemus was inadequate for Jesus' final burial.

We don't know why *Mary* was the only woman mentioned by name in John's account. Perhaps it was because she plays a significant role later in this chapter. The name *Magdalene* indicates that she came from the village of Magdala, which was located south and west of Capernaum on the western shore of the Sea of Galilee. [See question #1, page 272.]

As Mary and the other women approached the tomb, their chief concern was how they were going to roll away *the stone* that sealed the mouth of the tomb (Mark 16:1-3). If Jesus' tomb was typical of those of that period, then the stone would have been massive, requiring several strong men using pry bars to move it. Imagine Mary's surprise as she approached the tomb to see that the stone already had been moved.

B. Mary's Grief (vv. 11-13)

11. But Mary stood without at the sepulchre weeping: and as she wept, she stooped down, and looked into the sepulchre.

The intervening verses tell how *Mary* left the tomb and hurried to tell Peter and John that Jesus' body was not in the tomb. They both ran to the tomb to check out her story. The other women told the rest of the apostles what they had seen, but the apostles rejected the women's story as "idle tales" (cf. Luke 24:9-11). After Peter and John had seen the empty tomb for themselves, they returned to their own home.

In the meantime, Mary, who apparently had not been able to keep up with Peter and John, returned to the tomb alone. For a time she stood outside *weeping*, confused and distraught by the events of the morning. Finally she *stooped down* and peered into the empty tomb.

12. And seeth two angels in white sitting, the one at the head, and the other at the feet, where the body of Jesus had lain.

But the tomb was no longer empty! *Two angels*, dressed *in white*, were sitting where *the body of Jesus had lain*. In that day a sepulchre usually was used for several bodies, which were placed in niches cut into the wall. The central part of the sepulchre included a stone bench on which the body was laid for preparation for final internment in one of the niches. Apparently the angels were *sitting* on this stone bench.

13. And they say unto her, Woman, why weepest thou? She saith unto them, Because they have taken away my Lord, and I know not where they have laid him.

It seems strange that Mary was not frightened when she saw the angels. Perhaps because she was too concerned and fearful over finding the tomb empty. The angels' first response was a question: *Woman, why weepest thou?*

Nothing in Mary's response suggests she expected Jesus' resurrection. *They have taken away my Lord.* It is unclear who Mary thinks *they* might be. Did Jesus' enemies steal the body? Had Jesus' friends moved the body so that His enemies could not desecrate it? Mary did not *know*.

C. Mary's Plea (vv. 14, 15)

14. And when she had thus said, she turned herself back, and saw Jesus standing, and knew not that it was Jesus.

Now *Jesus* enters the picture. When Mary *turned* away from the tomb and the angels, there stood Jesus. But why did she not recognize Him? Of course, she was not expecting to see Him; none of Jesus' followers anticipated His resurrection. Specifically, her tears may have hampered her vision, or it may be that she saw Jesus only from the corner of her eye. Later, when Jesus called her name, she "turned herself" to face Him (v. 16).

15. Jesus saith unto her, Woman, why weepest thou? whom seekest thou? She, supposing him to be the gardener, saith unto him, Sir, if thou have borne him hence, tell me where thou hast laid him, and I will take him away.

Even when *Jesus* asked two gentle questions, Mary still did not recognize Him. The word *Sir* is sometimes translated "Lord," but it was also used as a general term of respect, and all modern versions translate it as such here. Mary still does not recognize who it is who stands before her. *Supposing* that Jesus is *the gardener*, she asks where he has taken the body. Her idea apparently is to return it to the tomb. That she thinks that she would by herself be able to move the body indicates that in her emotional state she still is not thinking clearly. [See question #2, page 272.]

D. Mary's Master (vv. 16, 17)

16. Jesus saith unto her, Mary. She turned herself, and saith unto him, Rabboni; which is to say, Master.

Jesus now addresses her personally—*Mary*. This broke through the veil of her grief, and now she recognizes Him. *Rabboni* is an Aramaic word that is similar to *rabbi*, which means "teacher." It is an intensified form of *rabbi*, so it may be a more honorable title, or perhaps a more personal one. John translates the Aramaic term for non-Jewish readers, but normally we would expect the Greek word he used to be translated as "teacher" in English. The *Master* of the *King James Version* may be an attempt to differentiate *rabboni* from *rabbi*.

17. Jesus saith unto her, Touch me not; for I am not yet ascended to my Father: but go to my

brethren, and say unto them, I ascend unto my Father, and your Father; and to my God, and your God.

Jesus' words, *Touch me not,* are translated "Do not hold on to me" in the *New International Version.* The *New American Standard Bible* has "Stop clinging to Me." Jesus had an urgent mission to reach many people in a limited time. He could not afford to be delayed by Mary at this time.

Jesus no longer addresses His followers as "servants" or even "disciples," but as *brethren.* They are entering into a new relationship. On the night He was betrayed, Jesus had indicated this change in status: "Henceforth I call you not servants; for the servant knoweth not what his lord doeth: but I have called you friends" (John 15:15).

Jesus here indicates that He was preparing to return, to *ascend,* to His Father. In the limited time He had remaining on this earth, He would be preparing His followers to carry on His work after He departed.

Jesus' reference to *my Father, and your Father . . . my God, and your God* has a dual significance. First, it emphasizes the uniqueness of Jesus' relationship with His Father—no one is the Son of God in the same way Jesus is. Yet God is our Father as well. We are all "children of God" (Galatians 3:26). The same God whom Jesus called Father is our Father as well.

II. Jesus' Resurrection and Christian Baptism (Romans 6:3-11)

At first glance, one might conclude that a lesson dealing with Jesus' resurrection combined with a discussion about baptism seems a rather strange arrangement. But as we examine it more carefully, the connection seems quite appropriate. The resurrection of Christ is much more than the occasion for new clothes and a spring vacation. Its implications touch every aspect of our lives as Christians. Why then should it not be involved in the action that brings us into a

---

How to Say It

ARIMATHEA. *Air*-uh-muh-*thee*-uh
(strong accent on *thee* as in *thin*).
CAPERNAUM. Kuh-*per*-nay-um.
GALILEE. *Gal*-uh-lee.
MAGDALA. *Mag*-duh-luh.
MAGDALENE. *Mag*-duh-leen
or Mag-duh-*lee*-nee.
NICODEMUS. *Nick*-uh-*dee*-mus
(strong accent on *dee*).
RABBONI. Rab-*o*-nye.
SEPULCHRE. *sep*-ul-kur.

---

saving relationship with our Lord and marks our entrance into His church?

A. Buried With Christ (vv. 3, 4)

3. Know ye not, that so many of us as were baptized into Jesus Christ were baptized into his death?

The Jews had several observances that pictured significant events from their past. The Passover reenacted their deliverance from Egypt; the Feast of Tabernacles reenacted the wilderness wandering. The church has two such pantomimes: baptism and the Lord's Supper. In the Lord's Supper, the loaf and the cup depict Jesus' suffering and *death.* (See 1 Corinthians 11:26.) In a similar way, the burial of a penitent believer in the waters of baptism gives us a picture of Jesus' death, burial, and resurrection.

Paul here sounds like a teacher gently chiding his students to lead them to a deeper understanding. His readers who were Christians would certainly remember their own physical baptism. In the New Testament there is no such thing as an unbaptized Christian. Now Paul wants to guide them into a fuller meaning of that initiatory rite. Those who were *baptized into Jesus Christ were baptized into his death.* That is, in baptism they were able to appropriate to themselves the benefits that His death brought. Of course, these blessings are the result of God's grace. It would be foreign to Paul's teaching that we have studied thus far to suppose that baptism was some kind of a good work that purchased redemption.

4. Therefore we are buried with him by baptism into death: that like as Christ was raised up from the dead by the glory of the Father, even so we also should walk in newness of life.

This verb *buried* here is past tense and should read "were buried." It looks backward to their own baptism that had already happened. Paul uses this visual image to move on to another important point. The *death* here is not the death of Christ, but that of the believer. Of course, he is not talking about physical death. He is referring to their death to sin, an idea he introduces in verse 2, "dead to sin." Completing the visual, Paul argues that death to sin is followed by a resurrection into a *walk in newness of life,* or to "live a new life" *(New International Version).* Baptism is nothing but an empty ritual unless it is followed by a life that is so dramatically changed that it can be appropriately termed a resurrection. [See question #3, page 272.]

SYMBOLS

An automobile, at least in the United States, is much more than transportation. Very often it is a symbol—it says something significant about its owner. A Rolls-Royce, for example, tells us that its owner is very wealthy (or is trying to appear wealthy). The new electric and hybrid gasoline/ electric cars that are coming on the market may symbolize a driver's concern for pure air (or perhaps just her interest in avant-garde technology).

Other types of cars speak of their owners' personalities and/or eccentricities. For example, there are the "art cars" that appear in a Houston, Texas, parade every year. A recent parade featured a grocery cart powered by a motorcycle engine, a Volkswagen "bug" welded upside down on top of another, a Pontiac with thousands of fuzzy tennis balls hot-glued to its surfaces. Such symbols are capricious conveyors of silliness. Other symbols state profound truths: a Buick Riviera vividly pictured the evils of drunk driving with its crumpled front end covered by the huge tree it had apparently run into.

Christian baptism is more than a symbol; it is an action. But the act of being buried in the "watery grave" and lifted from it speaks eloquently about what is happening to us. It says we have accepted Christ's claim on our lives. Our baptism ushers us into a new relationship with God and empowers our lives with new purpose and direction. —C. R. B.

B. Raised With Christ (vv. 5-7)

5. For if we have been planted together in the likeness of his death, we shall be also in the likeness of his resurrection.

Planted together is translated "united with" in the *New International Version*. It can mean "planted," in the literal sense of the word, as if burial is a planting. More likely Paul is using it metaphorically, in the sense of "joining with." This does not mean that we physically die with Christ. Paul is not suggesting that we are to be nailed to a cross as Jesus was. Rather, in repentance and baptism we figuratively die to our former life of sin. Just as Christ's resurrection began a new life, so our baptismal *resurrection* is into a new life.

6. Knowing this, that our old man is crucified with him, that the body of sin might be destroyed, that henceforth we should not serve sin.

Our old man refers to the sinner's former life, unregenerate and in rebellion against God. This former way of life *is crucified*, a striking way of saying that it must be totally abandoned. The sinful thoughts, the sinful acts, the rebellion against God must all be left behind. We no longer *serve sin*, we are not bound to sin with shackles like a pitiful slave. [See question #4, page 272.]

7. For he that is dead is freed from sin.

This verse must not be taken to mean that one who has been baptized is able to live without *sin*.

Visual for lesson 5

Today's visual illustrates the link between the resurrection of Christ and Christian baptism.

This is certainly not what Paul had in mind, and such an interpretation does not square with our own observations. We know from experience that we have not been able to resist every temptation of sin in our own lives. *Freed from sin* is more accurately translated "justified from sin" in the *American Standard Version*. This conveys the idea that Christ through His death has canceled the penalty for sin, a theme that Paul has dealt with in earlier lessons.

C. Alive With Christ (vv. 8-11)

8. Now if we be dead with Christ, we believe that we shall also live with him.

Paul restates in different words the position he takes in verse 4. The words *we believe* should not be understood in the sense that this is just his personal opinion. This statement is the very heart of the gospel and a glorious affirmation of the Easter message.

9, 10. Knowing that Christ being raised from the dead dieth no more; death hath no more dominion over him. For in that he died, he died unto sin once: but in that he liveth, he liveth unto God.

Christ *died once*, but *death* could hold Him only briefly. Whatever power death held over Him has been destroyed. Once He came from the tomb alive, there was no way that death could ever again lay a claim upon him. *He liveth unto God* in the sense that He now sits at the right hand of God in the heavenly throne room.

11. Likewise reckon ye also yourselves to be dead indeed unto sin, but alive unto God through Jesus Christ our Lord.

Today's lesson text responds to the challenge that Paul raised in Romans 6:1—"Shall we continue in sin, that grace may abound?" His answer is a resounding no, "God forbid." Then in the following verses he shows how that position is false. Verse 11 sums up his argument. [See question #5, page 272.]

DEAD TO SIN; ALIVE WITH CHRIST

Wade Clark Roof is a chronicler of religious trends and a professor of religion at the University of California/Santa Barbara. In 1993 he wrote about how baby boomers were "remaking American religion," in his terms. Several years later, he visited the "boomers" again to see how their quest for spirituality was coming along.

Roof found "a grand game of religious musical chairs" going on. About 70 percent of the seekers in his first survey are now strong believers, and about the same number of strong believers in the first survey are now seekers or doubters! Perhaps Roof's most important observation is that "the real story of American religious life in this half-century is the *rise of a new sovereign self* that defines and sets limits on the very meaning of the divine." In simple terms, what that means is that people believe they can remake God in their own image.

Christian baptism proclaims a far different message: those who follow Christ are remade in *His* image. Being crucified and risen with Christ to a new way of life means that we are to be dead to this world's values and standards. Our spirituality is to be patterned after what God has revealed, not after the changing fads of human invention. —C. R. B.

Conclusion

A. He Has Risen!

As the women made their way to Jesus' tomb in the darkness of early morning, they had a

Home Daily Bible Readings

Monday, Mar. 25—Alive to God in Christ (Romans 6:1-11)
Tuesday, Mar. 26—Eternal Life in Christ (Romans 6:15-23)
Wednesday, Mar. 27—Sin Brings Death (Romans 7:7-12)
Thursday, Mar. 28—Thanks Be to God (Romans 7:14-25)
Friday, Mar. 29—Stone Removed From Tomb (John 20:1-10)
Saturday, Mar. 30—"I Have Seen the Lord" (John 20:11-18)
Sunday, Mar. 31—Jesus Came and Stood Among Them (John 20:19-23)

problem. How could they possibly move the stone that covered the entrance to the tomb? Although they were troubled by it, there were solutions to the problem. Sooner or later enough people would come to the tomb so that together they could move the stone.

When they arrived at the tomb, they had another problem. The tomb was open, solving their original problem, but Jesus' body was missing. Several possible solutions to this mystery may have occurred to them—His enemies may have stolen the body or friends may have moved the body to protect it. In any event, before long the mystery would be solved.

And solved it was! But they could not have anticipated the solution to the problems they had worried about. The tomb was open and Jesus was not in the tomb, for He had risen.

Our lives are often like this. We worry and are concerned about many problems, and we try to come up with possible solutions to them. Many, many of our worries would evaporate if only we realized that Jesus has risen and is alive today and is still working in our lives.

B. We Have Risen!

Every Christian has gone through the process of dying, dying to sin, that is, and has risen to walk in a new life. In that process, the old man has been crucified and buried in the watery grave of baptism. The old man, whether a sinner or a saint in his own eyes, has been left behind.

As new creations in Christ we no longer live in sin. That does not mean that we do not commit sins. Rather, it means that we no longer live in sinful rebellion against our Lord. It means that we will be more loving toward our friends—and our enemies, too. It means that we will be more generous, more concerned about others. It means that we will be eager to share with others the joys we know in Christ.

To live such a life is, from the human point of view, impossible. We are weak, we have problems, we become discouraged. But we don't have to fight these battles alone. We have a Savior who has risen and is with us as we strive to live as persons who have risen to a new life.

C. Prayer

Dear Father, we thank You that we do not depend upon a dead idol but can trust a risen Savior. May we look to Him each day as we strive to live a life that will be pleasing to You. In His name we pray. Amen.

D. Thought to Remember

We are alive unto God through Jesus Christ our Lord.

Learning by Doing

This page contains an alternate lesson plan emphasizing learning activities.
Classes desiring such student involvement will find these suggestions helpful.

Learning Goals

After participating in this lesson, each student will be able to:

1. Describe the details surrounding the resurrected Christ's appearance to Mary Magdalene, and how Paul linked Christian baptism with Jesus' resurrection.

2. Explain the impact that being "raised with Christ" should have on a Christian's daily conduct.

3. Identify one behavior or attitude that needs to be put to death in order to demonstrate the "newness of life" that should characterize a believer.

Into the Lesson

Wrap a large (empty) box in brown paper. Display it prominently before the class. As members are seated, ask them to guess what might be in the box. Write their guesses on the chalkboard.

Ask for a volunteer to unwrap and open the box. As the person is opening the box, ask class members for words that describe the feelings a person has when opening a plain, paper-wrapped box. Feelings could be excitement, apprehension, fear, wonder, or others.

When the box is open, it will be seen to be empty. Show the box to the class. Ask for emotions that are expressed now: disappointment, shock, disbelief, surprise, and others.

Say, "This activity reminds us that things are not always as they appear. Today we remember the empty tomb of Christ and how that event has changed history—and has changed our own lives, as well!"

Into the Word

Develop a brief outline using the introductory remarks of the commentary. Both "He's Different" and the "Lesson Background" (page 266) will give you useful information. Have two volunteers read the Scripture texts: one for John 20:1, 11-17 and one for Romans 6:3-11.

Divide the class into at least two groups of no more than six individuals. If your class is larger, give the second assignment to the extra groups.

Group One is to prepare a skit to relate the details of John 20:1-17. Encourage the group to be creative. You may need to bring props to class, such as strips of cloth and white robes. This group can use all of this passage to convey the events of that special morning.

Group Two will need pens or pencils and a handout as described below for this activity. They are to read Romans 6:3-11 and develop an interview with Paul on the resurrection significance of Christian baptism. The handout you provide will have the following interviewer's questions; the group will use the text to write Paul's answers.

Interviewer: Paul, how is the resurrection of Jesus connected to a person's being baptized? (Romans 6:3, 5)

Paul:

Interviewer: Who raised Jesus to life? Who raises us to life? How? (Romans 6:4)

Paul:

Interviewer: How are we different because we have new life? (Romans 6:6, 7)

Paul:

Interviewer: How should the Christian view sin and obedience to God? (Romans 6:7, 11)

The lesson commentary is helpful for these answers. Let the Scriptures show the students the importance of their own baptism. Paul uses baptism as a "marker" for the Christian, a point from which he or she is committed to live a different life and lifestyle.

Into Life

Say, "Because Christ has come into our lives, we are new. We no longer walk in our old ways. What are some of the behaviors or attitudes put to death by a Christian in his or her new life?"

Allow a short brainstorming session. Put the responses on the chalkboard or on a poster. Expect a variety of answers, including *jealousy, greed, lying, self-centeredness,* and many others.

Pass out small blank cards to the class members. Ask each student to choose one or more behaviors or attitudes that he or she needs to "put to death" and to write that on the card. (Students are not limited to the problem areas listed on the board. If some of them have problems with issues not listed, they should choose those. They will not have to reveal what they write.)

Ask the class to read in unison Romans 6:4-7. Then have each person write "Romans 6:4-7" over the area written on his or her card. Provide a wastebasket for each person to cast that sin away after tearing the card into pieces. Have a closing prayer and then have someone lead the class in singing the first stanza of "Amazing Grace."

Let's Talk It Over

The questions on this page are designed to encourage review of the lesson Scriptures and to promote discussion of the lesson by the class. The answers provided are only discussion starters. Let your class talk it over from there.

1. Skeptics have tried to discredit the Gospel accounts of the resurrection for years. One ploy is to allege discrepancies in the accounts. Suppose a co-worker said to you, "Look, John says Mary came to the tomb of Jesus alone, but all the other Gospels say she was in a group of women. They can't all be right, so why should I believe any of them?" How would you answer?

The simple fact of the matter is that John does not say Mary went alone to the tomb. He just says she went. He does not mention the other women, but he does not say they were not there, either. Because John is telling Mary's story, as it were, it is not important to note the presence of the other women.

Several good harmonies of the various Gospel accounts are available. A classic is J. W. McGarvey's *Fourfold Gospel*. It is now out of print, but if you can find one, you'll have a good resource. Another good one is R. C. Foster's *Life of Christ*, last published by College Press in Joplin, MO.

2. The lesson writer notes that Mary's suggestion of returning the body of Jesus to the tomb shows that she was "not thinking clearly." What does that suggest to you about what to expect from someone who is grieving the loss of a loved one? Can we expect to reason with such a one? What should be the basis of our discussion with someone in grief?

The needs of grieving people are more emotional than rational. It does little good to try to comfort someone with, "Your loved one is better off now," or, "You'll feel better in time." The statements may well be true, but what the person needs is for someone to share the pain he or she feels, or to assure the person that it is okay to feel that way. Even Jesus wept at a funeral (John 11:35)!

3. What "newness of life" have you found as a Christian? What about your life is different from before? What is better? What is the most challenging aspect of this new life?

Don't let the concept of "new" keep your long-time believers from participating in this discussion. The Christian life is ever new, new in quality even if no longer new in chronology. Let the participants mention specific ways their lives are different from what they would be outside of Christ. They might mention habits that were given up for the sake of Christ, or relationships that they have established (or repaired) because of Christ. Perhaps one of the challenges is keeping that relationship "new," not allowing themselves to get into a rut. One challenge you might want to point out if no one mentions it is the challenge to remain salt and light in the world after being a Christian for many years. New Christians often have a lot of non-Christian friends whom they can influence for the Lord. But the longer we are Christians, the fewer non-Christian associates we have.

4. Suppose someone challenged you and said, "If this 'old man of sin' as you put it has been 'crucified,' how come you still sin? Or do you think you are now perfect?" How would you respond?

John reminds us that if we think "we have no sin, we deceive ourselves" (1 John 1:8). Certainly no Christian should presume to be "perfect," or "without sin." But, as the lesson writer points out, we do not serve sin. Sin is no longer our master. We are free, even if we do occasionally slip back into our former manner of life. Our challenger should be referred to Ephesians 2:1, where Paul says the unbelievers were "dead," or to 1 Timothy 5:6, where Paul says "she that liveth in pleasure is dead while she liveth." The Bible's metaphors of being "dead" do not always imply inactivity, but destiny. The unbelievers are dead because they are destined for eternal separation from God. The Christians are dead to sin because Christ has rescued them from that end.

5. Paul says we are to reckon ourselves to be "alive unto God through Jesus." How will you do that? What kind of behavior characterizes one who is "alive unto God"?

Who has not heard the phrase "This is living"? What kind of behavior would prompt us to say that? The answer to that question may suggest what it is to which we are "alive." If we are alive to God, then "living" is something that brings God glory, not merely something that produces an adrenaline rush. Encourage students to suggest specific actions they will take that demonstrates their source of joy and feeling "alive" is not in the flesh, but in spiritual concerns, things that will matter for eternity!

Anticipate God's Glory

DEVOTIONAL READING: **Romans 8:1-11.**

BACKGROUND SCRIPTURE: **Romans 8.**

PRINTED TEXT: **Romans 8:18-28, 31b-34, 38, 39.**

Romans 8:18-28, 31b-34, 38, 39

18 For I reckon that the sufferings of this present time are not worthy to be compared with the glory which shall be revealed in us.

19 For the earnest expectation of the creature waiteth for the manifestation of the sons of God.

20 For the creature was made subject to vanity, not willingly, but by reason of him who hath subjected the same in hope;

21 Because the creature itself also shall be delivered from the bondage of corruption into the glorious liberty of the children of God.

22 For we know that the whole creation groaneth and travaileth in pain together until now.

23 And not only they, but ourselves also, which have the firstfruits of the Spirit, even we ourselves groan within ourselves, waiting for the adoption, to wit, the redemption of our body.

24 For we are saved by hope: but hope that is seen is not hope: for what a man seeth, why doth he yet hope for?

25 But if we hope for that we see not, then do we with patience wait for it.

26 Likewise the Spirit also helpeth our infirmities: for we know not what we should pray for as we ought: but the Spirit itself maketh intercession for us with groanings which cannot be uttered.

27 And he that searcheth the hearts knoweth what is the mind of the Spirit, because he maketh intercession for the saints according to the will of God.

28 And we know that all things work togeth-er for good to them that love God, to them who are the called according to his purpose.

· · · · · · · · · · · ·

31b If God be for us, who can be against us?

32 He that spared not his own Son, but delivered him up for us all, how shall he not with him also freely give us all things?

33 Who shall lay any thing to the charge of God's elect? It is God that justifieth.

34 Who is he that condemneth? It is Christ that died, yea rather, that is risen again, who is even at the right hand of God, who also maketh intercession for us.

· · · · · · · · · · · ·

38 For I am persuaded, that neither death, nor life, nor angels, nor principalities, nor powers, nor things present, nor things to come,

39 Nor height, nor depth, nor any other creature, shall be able to separate us from the love of God, which is in Christ Jesus our Lord.

GOLDEN TEXT: The sufferings of this present time are not worthy to be compared with the glory which shall be revealed in us.—Romans 8:18.

The Power of the Gospel
Unit 2: Living by Faith
(Lessons 6-9)

Lesson Aims

After participating in this lesson, students will be able to:

1. Summarize Paul's description in this text of a Christian's perspective on the future.

2. Contrast the believer's hope with conditions that might seem to challenge that hope.

3. Think of seemingly hopeless circumstances that they (or someone they know) are facing, and affirm a renewed hope that Christ is working in those situations.

Lesson Outline

INTRODUCTION
    A. Sinkers and Floats
    B. Lesson Background
 I. THE CHRISTIAN'S HOPE (Romans 8:18-28)
    A. Hope and Suffering (v. 18)
    B. Hope for Redemption (vv. 19-23)
       A "Downside" to Everything
    C. Hope and Patience (vv. 24, 25)
    D. Hope in the Holy Spirit (vv. 26-28)
       In Hope of Something Good
II. THE CHRISTIAN'S SECURITY (Romans 8:31b-34, 38, 39)
    A. God Is for Us (vv. 31b, 32)
    B. Christ Is for Us (vv. 33, 34)
    C. Nothing Can Beat Us (vv. 38, 39)
CONCLUSION
    A. Balancing the Books
    B. Prayer
    C. Thought to Remember

Introduction

A. Sinkers and Floats

A fish net, in order to be useful, must be more than just a net. For one thing, along the bottom edge of the net must be weights or sinkers to hold the net down in the water. Otherwise the bottom edge would float to the top, making the net useless. The weights are like the tribulations that come into the life of a Christian. These keep him humble and prevent him from drifting uselessly about.

A net must also have floats. These keep the net from sinking to the bottom where it would become entangled with debris, snagged, and torn. The floats correspond to Christian hope. Without hope the Christian would be dragged down by tribulations and despair. Thus both tribulations and hope are necessary for the successful and victorious Christian life.

B. Lesson Background

The eighth chapter of Romans is one of the most popular chapters in the New Testament, and for good reason. First of all, it contains some profound theological teachings. But perhaps even more important to the Romans when they received it was the hope it offered as they began to face persecutions. They had not yet felt the full impact of these persecutions as Christians in other areas had, but soon the rage of Nero would fall upon them. When that happened, they needed all the hope that was available to sustain them through those trials.

I. The Christian's Hope
(Romans 8:18-28)

A. Hope and Suffering (v. 18)

18. For I reckon that the sufferings of this present time are not worthy to be compared with the glory which shall be revealed in us.

Suffering is an inescapable fact of human existence. We see overwhelming evidence of it in our own lives and in the world around us. The fact of suffering in this life is probably the most perplexing problem that Christians have to deal with. If only the wicked suffered, there would be no problem, for we could explain it on the basis that they are getting their just deserts. But what about the suffering of the innocent, especially little babies and innocent children? Job struggled with this problem, but could find no easy intellectual answer for it. He finally was forced to accept God's actions on faith, realizing that God in His infinite wisdom operates in areas and in ways beyond human understanding.

Paul does not attempt to deal with this problem on the theological or philosophical level. His purpose in this verse is to give his readers hope that sees beyond the present suffering. The *sufferings* of the present, though they are painful and discouraging, are nothing *compared with the glory which shall be revealed*. In a feeble way, we see this in the training of an athlete, who undergoes intense agony in preparation for the contest. Long hours of practice, exhausting physical activities, and strict discipline are endured only because the athlete sees a victory in the future. But even an Olympic gold medal, bringing fame and fortune, is nothing compared with the future glory that awaits the victorious Christian. [See question #1, page 280.]

B. Hope for Redemption (vv. 19-23)

19. For the earnest expectation of the creature waiteth for the manifestation of the sons of God.

To us the word *creature* often means some strange or even hideous life form, but the translators of the *King James Version* meant no such thing in this verse. It comes from the root *create* and means something created or "creation." (The same word is translated "creation" in verse 22; the *New International Version* translates it "creation" throughout the chapter.) Some scholars believe this term is limited to animal life, while others would include all that God has created. Paul uses personification here to emphasize his point, giving to the creation feelings and aspirations of mankind. Sin has brought suffering into the human world, but sin also has had an impact on nature around us.

The earnest expectation, or anticipation, of the creation involves some kind of deliverance (v. 21). Some scholars take this to mean that the earth will not be destroyed in the event Peter describes (2 Peter 3:10-13), but merely purified. Others believe the "new heaven" and "new earth" (Revelation 21:1) will be a replacement of the current order of things, not only a recreation of the old. Whichever form the deliverance will take, it will happen in conjunction with the *manifestation of the sons of God*—when God's glory is revealed in them (v. 18).

20. For the creature was made subject to vanity, not willingly, but by reason of him who hath subjected the same in hope.

One of the purposes of the creation was to provide a place for people to dwell in harmony with God. Sin disrupted this harmony, and creation was subjected to *vanity* or futility—its purpose is not being realized. Whether we take man as the one who *subjected* the creation to futility (by his sin) or God (in response to sin), the effect is the same. But there is *hope*, as verse 21 describes.

21. Because the creature itself also shall be delivered from the bondage of corruption into the glorious liberty of the children of God.

The bondage of corruption is Paul's description of the result of sin's entering the world. Corruption, death, and decay—and all that goes with them—are the result of sin. At the resurrection, this bondage to death will end (Revelation 21:4). Of course, this *liberty* is only for the *children of God;* the wicked will endure the second death (Revelation 21:8).

22. For we know that the whole creation groaneth and travaileth in pain together until now.

Paul continues his personification of *creation*. The creation's anticipation of the resurrection is as intense and as productive as a woman's labor pains. It looks forward, not only to the end of the pain, but to a wonderful new life. In this statement Paul seems to be alluding to one of the curses that came into the world as a result of the fall (Genesis 3:16). [See question #2, page 280.]

A "DOWNSIDE" TO EVERYTHING

How do you protect a city from disaster without messing up the environment? That is a dilemma faced by the citizens of Laguna Beach, California, where winter rains and mild spring weather promote a lush growth of weeds and brush in the coastal foothills, which then turns into tinder in the dry heat of summer and fall. In 1993 this dry growth became fuel for a wildfire that consumed 14,000 acres and destroyed 440 homes. Since the fire, the city has used goats—six hundred of them—to protect the city by eating up the vegetation that would otherwise cover a two-hundred- to three-hundred-foot-wide band of earth that surrounds the city.

The benefits are the removal of potential fuel for fires and economy. The goats do the job at about one-fifth the cost of having human crews do it. The problem is that the goats will eat anything! Whether a noxious weed or an endangered species of plant, it doesn't matter. Also, in the natural process of creating "fertilizer," they deposit weed seeds indiscriminately from one canyon to another, upsetting the natural ecological balance.

It seems that even our best efforts to "subdue" the earth often end up destroying some part of it and upsetting the balance of God's creation. The same is true in the moral world. Even when we try to do what is right, there are sometimes side effects that bring hurt and pain to others. It is true as Paul says: the whole creation *does* groan in pain to this very day because of our sins.

—C. R. B.

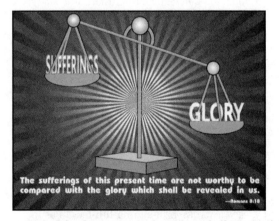

The sufferings of this present time are not worthy to be compared with the glory which shall be revealed in us.
—Romans 8:18

Visual for lesson 6. *Today's visual illustrates today's Golden Text, Romans 8:18. Display it as you begin the lesson.*

23. And not only they, but ourselves also, which have the firstfruits of the Spirit, even we ourselves groan within ourselves, waiting for the adoption, to wit, the redemption of our body.

We share in the suffering that was brought on the world as a result of Adam's sin. In the physical body, for example, we suffer many diseases and much pain. But this physical pain is nothing in comparison with the frustration and mental anguish we suffer because we are a part of the creation ruined by sin.

The idea of *firstfruits* was a prominent one in God's dealing with His people under the Old Covenant. When a crop was harvested, the first and best part of it was carefully kept and offered to God as a thank offering (Exodus 23:16-19; Leviticus 23:10). Paul uses the idea here to describe the Christian's relationship to the Holy *Spirit.* At baptism one receives the "gift of the Holy Ghost" (Acts 2:38). But this indwelling of the Holy Spirit is only a token of the blessings we shall know. In the meantime, we *groan within ourselves* as we wait for the completion or our transformation, which is *the redemption of our body.* This refers to the resurrection, when this mortal body must put on immortality (1 Corinthians 15:53). [See question #3, page 280.]

C. Hope and Patience (vv. 24, 25)

24. For we are saved by hope: but hope that is seen is not hope: for what a man seeth, why doth he yet hope for?

Since verse 18 Paul has been focusing on the believer's *hope* in salvation. We have hope of an end to suffering and revelation of glory (v. 18). Creation itself anticipates (or hopes for) that blessed event (v. 19). In fact, the creation's subjection to futility, at the time sin entered it, was done in hope of a deliverance from that futile state (vv. 20-22). We ourselves, having received the Holy Spirit as an earnest of the blessings to come, share that same longing. This verse then sums up this line of thinking: *for we are saved by hope!*

Having laid the foundation, Paul now builds on it an exhortation for patience. Obviously, what one already possesses he does not need to *hope for.* Even though we *are saved* (or have

How to Say It

INFIRMITIES. in-*fer*-muh-teez.
INTERCESSION. *in*-ter-*seh*-shun (strong accent on *seh).*
NERO. *Nee*-ro or *Nir*-oh.
PRINCIPALITIES. *prin*-suh-*pa*-luh-tees (*a* as in *at;* strong accent on *pa).*
TERTULLIAN. Tur-*tull*-yun.

been saved) we do not yet possess our final salvation. There are yet trials to be faced patiently before that glory is revealed in us (v. 18).

25. But if we hope for that we see not, then do we with patience wait for it.

Patience is not a common virtue in our "hurry up" society. Even Christians, so often caught up in this busy world, fail to work at developing patience, even though it is part of the "fruit of the Spirit" (Galatians 5:22). Paul knew that before long Christians would be facing the wrath of the Roman government, and he urged them to suffer patiently through these persecutions, relying on their *hope* to sustain them. Most of us today do not face the kind of persecutions that those in the early church faced—though in many parts of the world religious persecution remains a fact of life. Whatever level of suffering we face, we need to display patience born of hope.

D. Hope in the Holy Spirit (vv. 26-28)

26, 27. Likewise the Spirit also helpeth our infirmities: for we know not what we should pray for as we ought: but the Spirit itself maketh intercession for us with groanings which cannot be uttered. And he that searcheth the hearts knoweth what is the mind of the Spirit, because he maketh intercession for the saints according to the will of God.

The word *infirmities* means weakness or limitations. In this sin-tainted world we are weak; we are limited by the flesh. That is the reason we so earnestly yearn for the resurrection and our redemption bodies. We are so limited in the current order that we do not even know *what we should pray for as we ought.* Paul is not addressing only those situations in life that leave us without words to express our deepest desires. God has given us the Holy Spirit to make *intercession* for us before God. Note that this passage does not say the Spirit takes our groanings, as if we cannot express ourselves in words. It says the Spirit makes intercession *with groanings*—it is the Spirit who groans before God to communicate what *cannot be uttered* by humans. Of course, Jesus Christ is also our intercessor before God (Romans 8:34; 1 Timothy 2:5, 6), but the Holy Spirit is our intercessor in the special matter of prayer. [See question #4, page 280.]

28. And we know that all things work together for good to them that love God, to them who are the called according to his purpose.

Many persons quote this as one of their favorite verses, and rightly so. Properly understood, this verse offers hope for the Christian in all kinds of situations. There are some differences among several modern versions in this verse. The differences deal with the subject of the verb phrase *work together*. The *King James Version* and some modern versions have *all things* as the subject, while other versions have *God* as the subject. Either way, it is clear that God is the reason that *all things work together for good.*

God is the absolute Sovereign of the universe and nothing can occur that lies outside His will. As a part of His permissive will, He has granted humanity some freedom. We have used this freedom in many tragic ways, even defying God. Our acts of rebellion often lead to suffering. Sometimes even good people make bad decisions that lead to suffering. God could prevent this suffering, but to do so He would have to deny human freedom. Even so, God can use the most arrogant rebellion or the most tragic mistakes to achieve His ultimate purposes.

We should not understand the words *for good* to mean that the Christian is assured of material blessings or even joy and peace in all undertakings in this life. Across the centuries, Christians have suffered persecution and even martyrdom. But their suffering has led to the growth of Christianity and the preservation of the faith for modern believers. Only if we understand this verse in terms of God's ultimate purposes can we find comfort in it during our own trials. The *good* of verse 28 must be linked with the "glory" of verse 18.

IN HOPE OF SOMETHING GOOD

When smallpox was brought to the New World by Spanish explorers, it killed more than half the populations of Mexico and Haiti and killed thousands of the indigenous people of what is now the United States. Even into modern times, smallpox killed as many as 30 percent of those it affected, and survivors often were left with serious, permanent scarring. However, the process of vaccination—using a minute amount of the deadly virus to trigger the body into developing a natural immunity—led to eventual eradication of the disease. By intelligent use of a very bad organism, untold good came about. The last case of smallpox anywhere in the world was recorded in 1977, and most medical stocks of the virus and the vaccine have since been destroyed.

The two remaining known stocks of the virus—kept by the Russian and United States governments—were scheduled to be destroyed in 1999. However, this did not happen, partly in hope that the virus might someday be used to create vaccines against other, similar scourges of the human race. It may be that other, unknown good things can be developed from this deadly scourge. This is what God has promised us regarding all things in life: even in the midst of trial, God will provide *something* that is good and provides hope for His people.   —C. R. B.

II. The Christian's Security (Romans 31b-34, 38, 39)

A. God Is for Us (vv. 31b, 32)

31b. If God be for us, who can be against us?

The word *if* does not express uncertainty. This verse would be better understood if it were translated "since God is for us." Since God is indeed for us, *who can be against us?* Of course, there are many persons and forces that oppose Christianity. But this opposition cannot succeed. Paul's question may be paraphrased, "Who, with any hope of success, can be against us?" The obvious answer is, "No one!"

32. He that spared not his own Son, but delivered him up for us all, how shall he not with him also freely give us all things?

God has already shown that He will stop at nothing—not even the death of *his own Son*—to save us. We can be assured that He will continue to *give us all things* we need for continuing to walk with Him.

B. Christ Is for Us (vv. 33, 34)

33. Who shall lay any thing to the charge of God's elect? It is God that justifieth.

Verse 33 repeats the concept of verse 31 with the image of a courtroom scene. The enemies of the cross have brought charges against Christians. Of course, in some situations these charges are true. Christians have often sinned and not lived up to the high standards God has set for us. "All have sinned, and come short of the glory of God" (3:23). But our case is not hopeless; *it is God that justifieth.* Since God, the "Supreme Court," as it were, has rendered a "not guilty" verdict, what lower court can bring any charges?

34. Who is he that condemneth? It is Christ that died, yea rather, that is risen again, who is

even at the right hand of God, who also maketh intercession for us.

The eighth chapter of Romans began with the declaration, "There is therefore now no condemnation to them which are in Christ Jesus" (Romans 8:1). Here Paul reaffirms that proposition, based on the fact that God is the one who justifies and *Christ* is the One who makes *intercession for us*. We are immune from condemnation, not by our own goodness, but through Christ who *died* and *is risen again.* He now stands *at the right hand of God,* pleading our case before the Almighty Judge.

C. Nothing Can Beat Us (vv. 38, 39)

38, 39. For I am persuaded, that neither death, nor life, nor angels, nor principalities, nor powers, nor things present, nor things to come, nor height, nor depth, nor any other creature, shall be able to separate us from the love of God, which is in Christ Jesus our Lord.

I am persuaded. Paul concludes his argument with a ringing affirmation of his own faith, a faith that allowed him to face persecution and even death without flinching. He lists a variety of things that singly or together seek to *separate us from* God's *love*. Yet none of these can stand between us and *God*.

Paul invites us to share with him in that faith. It is vital that we do so! It is true that no external power or entity can separate us from God's love. But we, like the prodigal son (Luke 15), can choose to walk away from the Father and to sever our relationship with Him. (See Hebrews 10:19-39.) [See question #5, page 280.]

Conclusion

A. Balancing the Books

A devout Christian farmer lived alongside a neighbor who was an outspoken unbeliever. The Christian always attended church Sunday morning, Sunday evening, and at midweek evening service. He refused to do any unnecessary work on Sunday, while his neighbor paid no attention to Sunday or any other religious holidays, working whenever the weather was right. As a result, he was able to get his spring plowing and planting done earlier, and as a result his crops were ahead of those of his Christian neighbor. When the wheat harvest came, the unbeliever was able to get in his crop without any weather problems. The Christian, refusing to work on Sunday, lost part of his wheat crop because of rain. His soybeans and corn yielded less than the neighbor's, too, because the farmer had been late in planting them.

Later in November the two met in the local grain elevator where they were bringing their crops to sell. The unbeliever boasted of his bumper crops, and he sneered at the Christian: "Your God wasn't much help, was He? Without any help from God, I had much better crops than you did."

"Yes, you're right," admitted the Christian. "You had a better harvest than I did. But you must remember one thing: God doesn't balance the books in November."

Precisely! God balances the Lamb's book of life in eternity, not in November. But that may be a difficult truth to live with when we suffer persecution or lose out in the business world because of our trust in God.

Most of us have suffered very little for our Christian faith. In fact, in many situations we have enjoyed benefits and blessings, even material blessings, because we are Christians. But this has not always been true. In the early years of the church, Christians suffered imprisonment, exile, and even martyrdom at the hands of the pagan Roman government. And yet under these trying conditions the church continued to grow. The Christian writer Tertullian (c. A.D. 160–215) observed that "the blood of the martyrs is the seed of the church." When their blood was spilled, others sprang up to take their places.

Or think of that little band of Pilgrims who landed in Massachusetts in 1620. During that first terrible winter nearly half their number succumbed to hunger and disease. Yet they refused to give in to suffering, and those who survived gave thanks to God the following year for the meager blessings they had received. They recognized that the sufferings of the present were "not worthy to be compared with the glory" that God promised in the next life.

All of us are likely to experience suffering in this life, sometimes innocently and sometimes even because we are Christians. We can either react violently against it or we can accept it with a sense of triumph, trusting that God can use our response to it as an example for those who will come after us.

B. Prayer

We pray, merciful Father, that we may escape suffering and disappointments in our life. But when suffering does come, grant us the strength to accept it courageously. May the verses we have studied today give us the courage we need in difficult times. In our Master's name we pray. Amen.

C. Thought to Remember

"O God our help in ages past, Our hope for years to come, Our shelter from the stormy blast, And our eternal home."   —Isaac Watts

Learning by Doing

This page contains an alternate lesson plan emphasizing learning activities.
Classes desiring such student involvement will find these suggestions helpful.

Learning Goals

After this lesson students will be able to:

1. Summarize Paul's description in this text of a Christian's perspective on the future.

2. Contrast the believer's hope with conditions that might seem to challenge that hope.

3. Think of seemingly hopeless circumstances that they (or someone they know) are facing, and affirm a renewed hope that Christ is working in those situations.

Into the Lesson

Our introduction to this week's lesson will require research on your part, or you may assign this to a student who shows particular interest. Look for articles that make predictions for the future. Speaking with a public librarian, searching the Internet, or checking with a local newspaper may help accomplish this. Many of these articles appear near the beginning of each year.

Bring several of these articles to class. Ask your students to form groups of three to five and read the articles. Ask, "What do these articles have in common?" (Most will recognize that they are predictive.) Ask, "What is their view of the future?" (Most of the articles will be about a better future that the author hopes will come true.) Ask, "How believable is each?" After a few responses, ask, "Why do the answers vary?" (Reasons may include the possibility of the prediction's happening, the believability or trustworthiness of the author, and the reputation of the newspaper or magazine.)

Say, "Each of those answers is important to us in evaluating the reliability of the view of the future. Each of us can be excited or discouraged by our outlook on the future." At this point, present the "Lesson Background" section to the class.

Into the Word

Divide your class into groups of four to six students. You will need at least three groups. Otherwise, choose the activities you will use.

Give *Group One* sheets of blank 8 1/2" x 11" white paper, pencils, and colored markers. Ask them to read Romans 8:18-28 and draw a four- or five-scene "cartoon" for verses 18-21, 22-25, 26-28, 31-34, 35-39. Stick figures and elementary drawings are great! (This is in *Adult Bible Class.)*

Group Two is to paraphrase the same sections of Scripture. Each person will need blank paper and a pen or pencil. Have the students rewrite the Scripture passages in their own words and understanding, but taking care not to change Paul's original intent.

Group Three will answer the following questions concerning the text:

1. What were some of the persecutions faced by Roman Christians and others that might have been the basis for Paul's writing?

2. According to Paul, what has been the effect on the creation of mankind's sin?

3. How does the creation (as well as we ourselves) "groan" while waiting for the future?

4. When did you last feel like "groaning"?

5. What does the Spirit do for us?

6. How does verse 28 give us confidence for the future?

7. What do verses 29 and 30 say about God's work on our behalf?

8. How did God show that He is unequivocally on our side?

9. How is Jesus an intercessor?

10. How do verses 37-39 give us assurance for the future?

Allow each group to give a brief description of their projects or findings. Place the "cartoons" around the room for the class to enjoy.

Into Life

Say: "While Paul gives us strong reasons for facing and anticipating the future, many things today threaten to rob us of that anticipation. Search these newspapers and magazines for articles that threaten us. Be ready to tell the class your concerns and how Romans 8 helps you."

Distribute newspapers or magazines you have collected. (Individuals will remain in their groups.) After a few minutes, have group members do a "neighbor-nudge"; they will tell the person on their left or right why this article is threatening and how Romans 8 helps them to overcome any fear of the future. After the groups share, ask for one or two volunteers to present their case to the class.

Be ready to share a difficult situation you or someone close to you is facing. After you have shared, repeat Romans 8:31, 37-39. Have the class members turn back to the person they did the neighbor-nudge with in the preceding exercise. Now they will share a circumstance and repeat the verses. After all have shared, have a volunteer close in prayer for the class.

Let's Talk It Over

The questions on this page are designed to encourage review of the lesson Scriptures and to promote discussion of the lesson by the class. The answers provided are only discussion starters. Let your class talk it over from there.

1. How can we keep the view of victory at the forefront during suffering and difficulty, and how does our future outlook about God's goodness affect our present reaction to suffering?

In order for a Christian to visualize victory in the midst of suffering, he or she should practice visualizing victory *before* suffering arrives and *after* it leaves. The more a believer regularly focuses on God's intense love, the more bearable even intense suffering will be. Suffering often tends to draw one toward God in a renewed dependence on Him; it could be that the Christian's greatest obstacle to visualizing victory is prosperity, in which we tend to neglect our relationship to Him. Time spent in the Word and prayer, and time spent with the family of God strengthens our outlook about what God has done and is doing. In turn this will strengthen our outlook about the future. Hebrews 11 and 12 remind us of God's faithfulness, of Jesus' place in our redemption, and of the faithful "cloud of witnesses" encouraging us to press on and to visualize victory.

2. What, if any, is the connection between ecology and faith? How might the church's evangelistic efforts be affected by its views on environmental issues?

Our stewardship of God-given natural resources can't be divorced from our stewardship of God-given spiritual resources. An environmentally conscious society may lose faith in our message if they witness an attitude of indifference or disrespect toward the world that we claim God has created for us. One doesn't have to be a "tree-hugger" to reasonably care for what God has provided. A problem exists when the world shows more compassion for God's creation than the church shows toward the lost. We can find ways to promote environmental health without letting New Age ideas infiltrate our thinking.

3. How does the Christian's longing for God's adoption increase or decrease with physical and/or spiritual maturity, and what effect do physical events have on that longing?

Love for God, distress about the world's state, and physical suffering/deterioration tend to increase a Christian's faith and longing to be in Heaven with God. Fear of death, attempts to cling to this world, and attachment to relationships naturally influence us to "postpone" that longing. Paul had a balanced perspective when it came to "work still left to be done" and longing to be with God (Philippians 1:23-26). We as Christians must learn to long for complete reunion with God even when circumstances are good. A Christian must not become so heavenly minded that he or she is of no earthly good. We must remember that we are "in the world" but not "of the world." Valuing human relationships more than we value our relationship with God is a misplacement of priorities and ignores Paul's statements that our present sufferings on earth aren't worth comparing with the glory of Heaven. We must remember that we will be reunited with loved family members in Heaven, and that we will be united for the first time with new family members there. At the same time, concerning those who won't be there, God promises to wipe away every tear from our eyes.

4. When we can't adequately verbalize feelings to God, due to spiritual problems or discouragement, why should we continue to pray?

The Holy Spirit and Jesus alleviate our shortcomings by interceding to the Father for us, even during those times when we can't "find the right words." At Elijah's lowest point (1 Kings 19), when he prayed more out of his frustration than his faith, God intervened on his behalf; He will do the same for us. Paul says we do not know "what we should pray for as we ought," and he doesn't say that this is an occasional thing. So we *always* have to rely on the Spirit's intercession. No matter how eloquent our prayers sound to us or others, they still require the Spirit's help. So when we feel inadequate, we actually just better appreciate the situation that always exists, and we can rely on the Spirit then, too!

5. What impact on the church's heart for evangelism should take place when we realize that the only thing able to separate us from God is our own reluctance?

It should give us renewed conviction that God can overcome any problem, any obstacle, any resistance, in order to bridge the gap between himself and the lost, and that the church needs to be sending out renewed invitations to His wedding feast.

Proclaim the Gospel

DEVOTIONAL READING: Romans 11:1-6.

BACKGROUND SCRIPTURE: Romans 10.

PRINTED TEXT: Romans 10:1-17.

Romans 10:1-17

1 Brethren, my heart's desire and prayer to God for Israel is, that they might be saved.

2 For I bear them record that they have a zeal of God, but not according to knowledge.

3 For they, being ignorant of God's righteousness, and going about to establish their own righteousness, have not submitted themselves unto the righteousness of God.

4 For Christ is the end of the law for righteousness to every one that believeth.

5 For Moses describeth the righteousness which is of the law, That the man which doeth those things shall live by them.

6 But the righteousness which is of faith speaketh on this wise, Say not in thine heart, Who shall ascend into heaven? (that is, to bring Christ down from above:)

7 Or, Who shall descend into the deep? (that is, to bring up Christ again from the dead.)

8 But what saith it? The word is nigh thee, even in thy mouth, and in thy heart: that is, the word of faith, which we preach;

9 That if thou shalt confess with thy mouth the Lord Jesus, and shalt believe in thine heart that God hath raised him from the dead, thou shalt be saved.

10 For with the heart man believeth unto righteousness; and with the mouth confession is made unto salvation.

11 For the Scripture saith, Whosoever believeth on him shall not be ashamed.

12 For there is no difference between the Jew and the Greek: for the same Lord over all is rich unto all that call upon him.

13 For whosoever shall call upon the name of the Lord shall be saved.

14 How then shall they call on him in whom they have not believed? and how shall they believe in him of whom they have not heard? and how shall they hear without a preacher?

15 And how shall they preach, except they be sent? as it is written, How beautiful are the feet of them that preach the gospel of peace, and bring glad tidings of good things!

16 But they have not all obeyed the gospel. For Isaiah saith, Lord, who hath believed our report?

17 So then faith cometh by hearing, and hearing by the word of God.

Apr 14

GOLDEN TEXT: How shall they believe in him of whom they have not heard? and how shall they hear without a preacher? and how shall they preach, except they be sent?—Romans 10:14, 15.

The Power of the Gospel
Unit 2: Living by Faith
(Lessons 6-9)

Lesson Aims

After this lesson each student will be able to:

1. Summarize the pattern of spreading the gospel as Paul explains it in Romans 10.

2. Tell why every Christian must consider himself or herself a "herald" of the good news.

3. Become more involved with the church's or the class's efforts to take the gospel to others, both locally and globally.

Lesson Outline

INTRODUCTION
   A. The O's of Missions
   B. Lesson Background
 I. SALVATION FOR JEWS (Romans 10:1-4)
   A. Paul Desired It (v. 1)
   B. They Were Missing It (vv. 2, 3)
      Still Searching
   C. Christ Secured It (v. 4)
 II. GOD'S PLAN OF SALVATION (Romans 10:5-13)
   A. Not by Works of the Law (v. 5)
   B. Not by Mighty Deeds (vv. 6, 7)
   C. By Faith (vv. 8-11)
   D. Available to All (vv. 12, 13)
III. GOOD NEWS OF SALVATION (Romans 10:14-17)
   A. News Must Be Told (v. 14)
      Different Ways to Proclaim the Message
   B. Preachers Must Be Sent (v. 15)
   C. Message Must Be Heard (vv. 16, 17)
CONCLUSION
   A. Good News Travels Fast
   B. Prayer
   C. Thought to Remember

Introduction

A. The O's of Missions

The missionary imperative is at the heart of the Christian faith. As He closed His earthly ministry, Christ issued the Great Commission, sending His followers into the whole world with the gospel message. Paul in today's lesson text pays tribute to those who carry that message: "How beautiful are the feet of them that preach the gospel of peace." They may carry the good news across oceans to distant places in the world or across the street to their neighbors. These are the "GO" missionaries.

There are others who, for one reason or another, cannot go. We might not even think of them as missionaries at all. However, they are the "rope holders" for those who do go. Their financial and prayer support are essential to the "GO" missionaries. It would be appropriate to call them "CO" missionaries.

Unfortunately, there are some church members who are unwilling either to go as missionaries or to support missionaries. They either do not understand that those outside of Christ are lost without the gospel, or they do not understand the Great Commission. Such people might well be called "NO" missionaries. The imperative of the Great Commission demands that we move the "NO" missionaries into becoming "CO" missionaries, and that we continually challenge the "CO" missionaries into becoming "GO" missionaries.

B. Lesson Background

In Romans 9 Paul discusses God's relations with Israel. Although God had blessed the Israelites and chosen them to become a blessing to all of mankind, they had often rebelled and turned away from Him. God had endured their rebellion "with much long-suffering," but He also warned through some of the prophets that He would offer His blessings to the Gentiles, and that only a remnant of Israel would be saved. The Jews had tried to attain righteousness through works of the law, not realizing that the law was weak toward the flesh and that the law looked forward to its fulfillment in Christ. Most of the Jews had rejected Christ; thus He became a "stumblingstone and rock of offense" to them.

I. Salvation for Jews
(Romans 10:1-4)

A. Paul Desired It (v. 1)

1. Brethren, my heart's desire and prayer to God for Israel is, that they might be saved.

Brethren is generic. It does not refer exclusively to men, but to fellow Christians. Some recent translations render it "brothers and sisters." In the previous chapter Paul discussed the plight of the Jews, or *Israel*. Because they had hoped for salvation through works of the law, they had rejected the message of Christ. Those who continued to reject Christ would remain in their lost condition, but those who accepted God's grace in Jesus could yet *be saved*. Any Christian with unbelievers among his or her family has shared Paul's ardent *desire*. [See question #1, page 288.]

B. They Were Missing It (vv. 2, 3)

2. For I bear them record that they have a zeal of God, but not according to knowledge.

Paul was well qualified to testify about the *zeal* of the Jews. Only a few years before he wrote this letter he had been one of the most zealous of them. His zeal had driven him to seek out and persecute Christians in Jerusalem and even led him to journey to Damascus to seek out Christians there. While there was no question about the Jews' zeal, it was *not according to knowledge.* Their zeal for the law caused them to close their minds to the fulfillment of the law—God's offer of salvation through the Lord Jesus Christ.

One of the biggest problems of the church today is that many of its members lack zeal. They may attend church services regularly and even contribute financially to the work of the church, but they have no passion for the Lord's work. Another problem is the presence of people with misdirected zeal. Such people are adamant about music styles, time of services, or even the color of the carpeting, but they seem to ignorant of the church's first priority: winning the lost to Jesus Christ. Occasionally, however, we meet a Christian who has both knowledge and zeal. How refreshing that is!

3. For they, being ignorant of God's righteousness, and going about to establish their own righteousness, have not submitted themselves unto the righteousness of God.

God's righteousness comes by accepting His gracious offer of salvation through His Son, Jesus Christ. At the time Paul wrote, most Jews probably had not heard the gospel. But some, especially among the leaders, had heard the good news and had deliberately rejected it.

Through the long history of the church, many have substituted *their own* versions of *righteousness* for God's righteousness revealed in the Scriptures. Satan has tempted many of us to insist that our interpretation of the Scriptures represents God's true righteousness, and in our pride we try to force our views on others. The divided state of Christendom today bears painful testimony to the effectiveness of Satan's clever divisive tactic.

STILL SEARCHING

Jewish people still keep the *Seder*—the Passover feast—as a means of remembering what God did for Israel when He freed them from Egyptian slavery. Christians recognize this feast as a meal that prophetically pointed to Christ—God's "passover" for all peoples.

Religious Jews still zealously keep the feast, but strangely, so do many "secular" Jews. In a survey conducted recently in Los Angeles—which has a large Jewish population—one-fourth of those polled said that religion was of little or no significance in their lives. Two-thirds said

they were not members of any synagogue, yet they keep the *Seder!* Rabbi Lawrence Goldmark, a rabbinical leader in Southern California, says of Jews who have no place for God in their lives, "Taking God out of Passover is like taking Jesus out of Easter—what are you left with?" What they are left with is a monument to their own attempts to be righteous. One unbeliever sees Passover this way: "The importance . . . is the effort and strength of people to overcome adversity by dint of their own talents and will." How tragic to miss God's redemption because of a zeal without knowledge! The same can be said of Christians whose mistaken pride in their good works causes them to miss the point of God's grace.

—C. R. B.

C. Christ Secured It (v. 4)

4. For Christ is the end of the law for righteousness to every one that believeth.

The word here translated *end* can mean either "fulfillment" or "termination." Each seems appropriate in this case. Jesus' critics on occasion accused Him of breaking or destroying *the law*. His response was "Think not that I am come to destroy the law, or the prophets: I am not come to destroy, but to fulfil" (Matthew 5:17). The law set forth an absolute standard, which no one could live up to until Jesus came. His sinless life met every requirement of the law and thus fulfilled it.

Jesus also brought an *end* to the law. At the heart of the law was the concept that one could gain salvation by good works. But no one could live up to the requirements of the law, nor could all the elaborate sacrifices required under the law atone for one single sin. All that these sacrifices could do was to look forward to the coming of the perfect sacrifice, Jesus Christ. Thus the coming of Christ brought an end to the whole legalistic system of sacrifices for sins. Instead, our justification comes through faith in Him.

How to Say It

BABYLONIAN. Bab-ih-*low*-nee-un.
CAESAREA PHILIPPI. Sess-uh-*ree*-uh Fih-*lip*-pie or *Fil*-ih-pie.
DAMASCUS. Duh-*mass*-kus.
DISPENSATION. *dis*-pun-*say*-shun (strong accent on *say*).
JERUSALEM. Jee-*roo*-suh-lem.
JUPITER. *Joo*-puh-ter.
MAUSOLEUMS. *maw*-zuh-*lee*-umz (strong accent on *lee*).
PENTECOST. *Pent*-ih-kost.
SEDER. *Say*-der.
ZEUS. Zoose.

II. God's Plan of Salvation (Romans 10:5-13)

A. Not by Works of the Law (v. 5)

5. For Moses describeth the righteousness which is of the law, That the man which doeth those things shall live by them.

Paraphrasing Leviticus 18:5, Paul shows that one who chooses to live by *the law* must keep it perfectly. But since this is humanly impossible, the law, which served many valuable purposes, could not bring salvation from sins.

B. Not by Mighty Deeds (vv. 6, 7)

6, 7. But the righteousness which is of faith speaketh on this wise, Say not in thine heart, Who shall ascend into heaven? (that is, to bring Christ down from above:) or, Who shall descend into the deep? (that is, to bring up Christ again from the dead.)

Paul paraphrases Deuteronomy 30:11-14 and applies it to the gospel. Since the law looked to *righteousness* through works, some may have supposed that some mighty, heroic deed could accomplish what lesser deeds could not. This was not true under the law, and it certainly is not true under grace. There is an element of pride in the idea that one can somehow earn salvation. But there was no place for pride under the law, and there certainly is no place for it under grace.

C. By Faith (vv. 8-11)

8. But what saith it? The word is nigh thee, even in thy mouth, and in thy heart: that is, the word of faith, which we preach.

If salvation cannot be attained by storming the ramparts of Heaven or descending into the grave, how then may it be gained? The answer is surprisingly simple. It is as near as one's *mouth* and

---

Home Daily Bible Readings

Monday, Apr. 8—Everyone Can Be Saved (Acts 2:14-21)

Tuesday, Apr. 9—Jesus Freed From Death (Acts 2:22-36)

Wednesday, Apr. 10—The Word From the Beginning (John 1:1-5)

Thursday, Apr. 11—The Advocate to Come (John 16:4-15)

Friday, Apr. 12—Take Up the Armor of God (Ephesians 6:10-23)

Saturday, Apr. 13—The Message We Proclaim (1 John 1:1-10)

Sunday, Apr. 14—The Word Is Near You (Romans 10:5-17)

---

heart. The word of faith, when it is proclaimed by the mouth and taken into the heart, is the way of salvation. We are reminded of the experience of Elijah, who thought God would reveal Himself in a mighty wind, or an earthquake, or in fire. Instead, God spoke to him through a "still small voice" (1 Kings 19:11, 12). In the same way, God's salvation comes to us, not through some awesome experience, but through the simple preaching of the gospel. The proclamation of the good news does not depend on a few high-powered proclaimers on a few special occasions, but can be shared every day by every Christian. [See question #2, page 288.]

9, 10. That if thou shalt confess with thy mouth the Lord Jesus, and shalt believe in thine heart that God hath raised him from the dead, thou shalt be saved. For with the heart man believeth unto righteousness; and with the mouth confession is made unto salvation.

The word here translated *confess* means to agree with or to say the same thing. Of course, more than verbal agreement is involved here. The words that one uses in confessing *the Lord Jesus* must reflect the content of one's *heart* and mind.

In many congregations it is common for persons acknowledging their commitment to Christ to make a public *confession.* This is usually some version of Peter's confession at Caesarea Philippi: "Thou art the Christ, the Son of the living God" (Matthew 16:16). But the confession that Paul is talking about is much more than a one-time event. It incorporates our daily activities, our deeds confirming the profession of our mouths.

11. For the Scripture saith, Whosoever believeth on him shall not be ashamed.

Paul quotes from Isaiah 28:16, a passage he had earlier referred to in Romans 9:33. For those who are moved by secular values, being a Christian is a mark of shame. Being a Christian puts restrictions on where one will go and what one will do, say, or think. One who takes a worldly view of life will not accept such limitations. Christians, who view life from the perspective of eternity, come to a very different conclusion. When a Christian stands before the Eternal Judge, he or she shall not be *ashamed.* A Christian has Jesus' assurance that "whosoever therefore shall confess me before men, him will I confess also before my Father which is in heaven" (Matthew 10:32). The only assurance that the unbeliever has is that he will be ashamed because he has refused to accept the truth and has believed a lie instead. [See question #3, page 288.]

D. Available to All (vv. 12, 13)

12, 13. For there is no difference between the Jew and the Greek: for the same Lord over all is

rich unto all that call upon him. **For whosoever shall call upon the name of the Lord shall be saved.**

Ancient people, like many today, divided people into two categories—"us" and "them." The Jews divided the entire population into two groups: *Jew* and *Greek*. (The distinction "Jew and Gentile" means the same thing.) Paul uses the expression in that extended sense here. When Jesus sent His disciples out into the world, they were to "go . . . and teach all nations" (Matthew 28:19), to "preach the gospel to every creature" (Mark 16:15). [See question #4, page 288.]

Of course, there are differences in people—skin color, hair texture, language, customs. But in the eyes of the Lord these differences do not matter, for He is the *same Lord over all*. All have sinned and all stand in need of God's grace. This marvelous grace is available to all who *call upon the name of the Lord*. This may refer to confessing Him or it may refer to a prayer of petition.

Visual for lesson 7. *This poster illustrates missionaries in various fields. Discuss how your church is helping to send missionaries to preach.*

III. Good News of Salvation
(Romans 10:14-17)

A. News Must Be Told (v. 14)

14. How then shall they call on him in whom they have not believed? and how shall they believe in him of whom they have not heard? and how shall they hear without a preacher?

In this verse and the one that follows, Paul uses a series of rhetorical questions to show that Christians have an obligation to carry the gospel to the whole world. The fact that "whosoever shall call upon the name of the Lord shall be saved" carries a moral obligation, for it is quite obvious that no one will *call on* the name of the Lord if he or she does not *believe* in the Lord. And people cannot believe on the Lord if they have not *heard* of Him. Finally, people cannot *hear* about Christ unless a *preacher* tells them about Him.

The word translated *preacher* does not necessarily mean someone who stands behind a pulpit on Sunday morning. It refers to a herald, one who brings a message. Paul undoubtedly had in mind a flesh-and-blood messenger, whether a public speaker or a more personal messenger. Later on, the written Word became an effective messenger. Today we also rely on various electronic media to carry the message. Regardless of the method we use, we must never forget that the message is more important than the messenger.

DIFFERENT WAYS TO PROCLAIM THE MESSAGE

Hubert Eaton's name is not as well known as that of his life's work: Forest Lawn. Eaton took an uninviting, twelve-acre cemetery and turned it into a complex of five memorial parks, exceeded

as a cemetery tourist attraction only by Arlington National Cemetery.

The secret behind Eaton's success was his belief that the site of one's burial should be a beautiful place, one that speaks of resurrection and hope for eternal life. One of the most attractive features of Forest Lawn is the varied means of proclaiming the Christian message: exact reproductions of Michelangelo's marvelous statues—*David, Moses,* and *La Pietà*—are displayed in the parks, as is a stained-glass reproduction of da Vinci's painting of *The Last Supper*. Carefully staged presentations of two of the world's largest paintings depict Jesus' crucifixion and resurrection. Eaton's belief in the gospel message is readily apparent in his memorial parks.

There are no statistics on how many unbelievers have turned to Christ as a result of this method of "preaching" the good news. However, what it does say is that the gospel may be proclaimed by many different means and in even the most unlikely of places. Are we taking advantage of all our opportunities?   —C. R. B.

B. Preachers Must Be Sent (v. 15)

15. And how shall they preach, except they be sent? as it is written, How beautiful are the feet of them that preach the gospel of peace, and bring glad tidings of good things!

Our word *missionary* comes from a Latin word meaning one who is *sent*. Most persons today who are engaged in missionary activities have been sent by a congregation, some kind of parachurch organization, or a denomination. Across the centuries men and women—travelers, business persons, even prisoners—have carried the gospel to others. But even though they were not officially sent, they were, in a very real sense, sent by our Lord. The Great Commission makes every one of us a messenger.

Paul appropriately quotes from Isaiah 52:7. It is a prophecy that originally looked forward to the Israelites' return from the Babylonian captivity. The messengers were praised as the heralds of a wonderful new day. But the prophet saw beyond the return from Babylon to an even greater day. Thus, Paul applies this praise to the heralds of the good news of God's offer of salvation in Jesus Christ. [See question #5, page 288.]

C. Message Must Be Heard (vv. 16, 17)

16, 17. But they have not all obeyed the gospel. For Isaiah saith, Lord, who hath believed our report? So then faith cometh by hearing, and hearing by the word of God.

God does not impose *faith* on people by some magical process; *hearing . . . the word of God* is essential. Nor does God send the message by angels. The responsibility of spreading the word belongs to every Christian. People must hear the message to respond, and Christians must deliver the message for the lost to hear it.

Of course, not everyone who hears comes to faith. For many reasons some people reject *the gospel*. These include fear of change, social pressure, the unwillingness to give up a sinful lifestyle, personal greed, prejudices—and the list could be greatly extended. Our printed text began with Paul's noting his desire for Israel, that the Jews would cease their rejection of Christ and turn to him. But their resistance did not stop Paul from being faithful to his call to preach the gospel. And we, likewise, must be faithful to our own charge to share the good news.

Conclusion

A. Good News Travels Fast

Good news travels fast. In May of 1945, the surrender of Nazi Germany ended World War II in Europe. Within minutes this exciting good news had made its way around the world, from the battlefields in Europe to the distant outposts in the Pacific Theater. Three months later, Japan surrendered. Almost instantly the world learned this good news.

A man noticed an ominous lump on his neck, so he immediately visited his physician, who took a sample for a biopsy. When the husband and his wife returned to the physician's office a few days later, the smile on the doctor's face when he greeted them told them that the news was good. The tumor was not malignant and could be readily treated. The wife immediately got on the telephone, calling the church and all her friends with the good news.

Good news travels fast—sometimes! On the Day of Pentecost in A.D. 30, the apostle Peter stood up and preached the first gospel sermon. What glorious good news this was! Three thousand people responded to the message and were baptized. Within a few days many of these people left Jerusalem and returned to their homelands, carrying the good news with them. Churches sprang up all across the Roman Empire, and within three hundred years Christianity had become a legal religion within the Empire. Before long hundreds of missionaries carried the good news to pagan strongholds beyond the Empire. By A.D. 1000 much of Europe had become at least nominally Christianized.

About two hundred years ago Protestants in Western Europe experienced a revived interest in missions. In the past two hundred years thousands of missionaries have been sent out, carrying the gospel to Africa, Asia, and other areas, reaching into both the urban centers and the remote jungle villages. Thousands of "sent ones" still labor in mission fields around the world.

But the picture is changing. The culture of Western Europe can best be described as post-Christian. Only a small minority of the people regularly attend religious services. Europe's majestic cathedrals are but ornate mausoleums, testifying to a faith that is now dead. The good news is no longer good news there, and the United States seems headed in the same direction. Unless American Christians redouble efforts to share the good news, it may well be in another generation where Europe is today.

But the good news will not die that easily. Ironically, many of the lands that were once the recipients of missionary efforts have now become the senders of missionaries. Bearers of the good news are coming to Europe and the United States in growing numbers.

We often think of missionaries as those who go to remote and distant places to proclaim the gospel. Sometimes, however, there are ripe mission fields next door or just across the street. Let us carry the good news wherever and whenever we can, and let us spread it quickly!

B. Prayer

Gracious God, thank You for sending us Your Son. Teach us how to share the good news of His life, death, and resurrection, and give us the wisdom and courage to carry it to others as quickly as we can. In the name of our Savior we pray. Amen.

C. Thought to Remember

We would not be Christians today if there had not been missionaries yesterday.

Learning by Doing

This page contains an alternate lesson plan emphasizing learning activities. Classes desiring such student involvement will find these suggestions helpful.

Learning Goals

After participating in this lesson, each student will be able to:

1. Summarize the pattern of spreading the gospel as Paul explains it in Romans 10.

2. Tell why every Christian must consider himself or herself a "herald" of the good news.

3. Become more involved with the church's or the class's efforts to take the gospel to others, both locally and globally.

Into the Lesson

Bring into class a gift-wrapped box. Inside place a gospel tract or a New Testament to represent the sharing of the good news. Display the box prominently.

Say, "Today I am conducting an unscientific poll. How many of you would rather receive gifts than give them?" Ask those who answer yes to move to the right side (Group 1). Next say, "I assume the others of you would rather give gifts than receive them." Move them to the left side of the room (Group 2). Ask for a representative from each group to give reasons for each answer.

Ask the members of Group 1 whether any of them has ever rejected a gift. Ask whether anyone in Group 2 has ever had their gift rejected. Ask both groups, "What does rejection of a gift say to the giver?" Expect an answer that indicates the person doesn't care for the gift, has no use for it, or might even be offended by it.

Say, "The lesson today explores how the gospel was spread, how the gift was given, and how we can participate in that spreading."

Into the Word

Assign people to groups of four to six. Distribute the following outline and questions to each group. Say, "Paul seems to suggest a plan for taking the gospel to our communities. Fill in the details of this outline by answering the questions."

REACHING OTHERS FOR CHRIST

A. Show That You Care (Romans 10:1-5)
   1. How does Paul show he is not anti-Semitic?
   2. What good things does he say about the Israelites?
   3. How did the Israelites go wrong?
B. Clearly Confess Christ (Romans 10:6-13)
   1. How does Paul say we are saved?
   2. What keeps us from being ashamed?
   3. Why is this message for everyone?

C. Understand You Are Commissioned (Romans 10:14-17)
   1. With what questions does Paul challenge us to go?
   2. How does Paul show the importance of the message and the messenger?
   3. What words are used of the messenger?

After the groups have finished answering the questions, lead a brief discussion concerning difficulties encountered by those who carry the gospel, using the commentary for verses 14-17.

Into Life

Summarize by saying, "Paul is challenging the church to continue its mission of carrying the gospel. Turn to Matthew 28:18-20 to see Jesus' words." After reading these verses, remind the class that nothing has changed. Using the comments for verse 14, lead the students to see that they are "heralds" of the good news. Using the lesson writer's ideas on effective messengers, brainstorm ways we can carry the gospel.

Challenge class members to participate in carrying the word with one of the following ideas:

Option 1: Create small outlines of a pair of feet on a four-inch-by-six-inch sheet of paper or note card. Make enough for every class member. Under this pair of feet write the title, "Beautiful Feet." Across the feet write, "I will carry the good news of the gospel to _____ this week." Ask each person to think of someone with whom he or she can share the good news and to write that name in the blank. Say, "Turn to the person beside you and pray for each other to be bold." This activity is in the student book, *Adult Bible Class.*

Option 2: Contact your church's minister or missions committee. Ask for a list of missions and missionaries supported by your church. Include addresses and phone numbers or e-mail addresses. Bring envelopes, stationery, and pens. Have each person select a mission or missionary to whom he or she will write a "beautiful feet" letter. The letter should both encourage and thank the missionary for spreading the gospel.

After each has written, collect the envelopes for mailing. The class member should be asked to keep the name and make a commitment to pray for that mission or missionary for the rest of the month.

Close with prayer for the continued spreading of the gospel.

Let's Talk It Over

The questions on this page are designed to encourage review of the lesson Scriptures and to promote discussion of the lesson by the class. The answers provided are only discussion starters. Let your class talk it over from there.

1. What significance do you see in Paul's combination of "heart's desire" and "prayer" regarding his burden for the unsaved?

Paul had a special burden for the people of his homeland—the Jews. Unless we have close family members who need to accept the Lord, we probably cannot quite appreciate the depth of Paul's feelings. So he held them up in prayer. Without prayer, our efforts to win the lost can become just that—our own efforts. Petitioning God through prayer ensures that our efforts are fueled by His will and by His power.

More often our problem is the opposite. Our efforts at evangelism lack heart. We have no passion or zeal to drive us, and we have no real compassion for the lost, no real concern for their plight. Many times the lost are caught up in destructive lifestyles. Rather than feel compassion for them, we are prone to thinking they are getting just what they deserve. But we who know the grace of God ought to be driven to rescue others from what they deserve to find God's grace.

2. What are some examples of the saving power of God's Word preached by ordinary people? What responsibility do we have to join in that act of "preaching"?

The thousands converted on the Day of Pentecost (Acts 2) is one example, though some might question whether Peter and the apostles were "ordinary people" after three and a half years with Jesus. The Protestant Reformation, the Restoration Movement, and several Great Awakenings are all large-scale modern examples. But every member of our churches and Sunday school classes has received the extraordinary offer of salvation through the preaching of ordinary people and often by the invitation of humble and ordinary acquaintances. A believer doesn't have to be at the pulpit to proclaim God's Word. An invitation to a neighbor, a prayer, and support of ministerial staff are all ways that a church member can join in the church-wide act of proclaiming the gospel to the world.

3. What barriers must a Christian overcome in order to express publicly a belief in Jesus without being ashamed or embarrassed?

Christ warned us to count the cost of following Him. Fear sometimes causes a Christian to try to hide his or her faith. Pride, a willingness to "fit in," and anxiety that others look at Christians as hypocrites may cause a sense of shame. A Christian must find security in a humble gratitude to God about his or her salvation and a desire to see others receive the same in order to overcome feelings of shame or embarrassment.

4. How does an "us *vs.* them" mentality devalue the richness of the Lord's offer of salvation, and what can the church do to remove any hindrances to openly inviting and receiving all people in the name of Jesus?

Jesus' interaction with all kinds of people demonstrates that an "us *vs.* them" mentality was never meant to have a place in His church. Jesus' all-inclusiveness is one of the unique aspects of the Christian faith. At the same time, Satan tempts us toward our natural tendency of exclusiveness—even when we reject it with our words, by our actions we often gravitate toward it. Each congregation is responsible for finding and providing cross-cultural service opportunities and interaction; such opportunities will begin to tear down walls of exclusiveness.

5. How can congregations increase opportunities for people to join in the Biblical pattern of sending messengers so that others can hear the gospel and respond to God's offer of grace?

Congregations today need to recognize the need for, and shortage of, Christian missionaries and preachers. We should seek God's help in creating strategies for educating members about missions and about the call of God for ordinary people to "go." A congregation has the responsibility to send and support her members who feel the burden and desire to enlist. A large variety of media and resources about missions exists for the education of congregations, and modern transportation and communication have provided reasonably priced opportunities for short-term mission trips to most parts of the world. Having church members share the responsibility of hosting a missionary on furlough can be an eye-opening and life-changing experience. Prayer for, and study about, missions is ultimately the best combination of zeal and knowledge for church members, and often the avenue through which ordinary Christians receive a call to "go."

Live the Gospel

DEVOTIONAL READING: Romans 12:4-8.

BACKGROUND SCRIPTURE: Romans 12.

PRINTED TEXT: Romans 12:1-3, 9-21.

Romans 12:1-3, 9-21

1 I beseech you therefore, brethren, by the mercies of God, that ye present your bodies a living sacrifice, holy, acceptable unto God, which is your reasonable service.

2 And be not conformed to this world: but be ye transformed by the renewing of your mind, that ye may prove what is that good, and acceptable, and perfect will of God.

3 For I say, through the grace given unto me, to every man that is among you, not to think of himself more highly than he ought to think; but to think soberly, according as God hath dealt to every man the measure of faith.

· · · · · · · · · · · ·

9 Let love be without dissimulation. Abhor that which is evil; cleave to that which is good.

10 Be kindly affectioned one to another with brotherly love; in honor preferring one another;

11 Not slothful in business; fervent in spirit; serving the Lord;

12 Rejoicing in hope; patient in tribulation; continuing instant in prayer;

13 Distributing to the necessity of saints; given to hospitality.

14 Bless them which persecute you: bless, and curse not.

15 Rejoice with them that do rejoice, and weep with them that weep.

16 Be of the same mind one toward another. Mind not high things, but condescend to men of low estate. Be not wise in your own conceits.

17 Recompense to no man evil for evil. Provide things honest in the sight of all men.

18 If it be possible, as much as lieth in you, live peaceably with all men.

19 Dearly beloved, avenge not yourselves, but rather give place unto wrath: for it is written, Vengeance is mine; I will repay, saith the Lord.

20 Therefore if thine enemy hunger, feed him; if he thirst, give him drink: for in so doing thou shalt heap coals of fire on his head.

21 Be not overcome of evil, but overcome evil with good.

Apr 21

GOLDEN TEXT: Be not conformed to this world: but be ye transformed by the renewing of your mind, that ye may prove what is that good, and acceptable, and perfect will of God.—Romans 12:2.

The Power of the Gospel
Unit 2: Living by Faith
(Lessons 6-9)

Lesson Aims

After this lesson each student should:

1. Describe the "transformed" lifestyle Paul urges Christians to adopt.

2. Tell why it is essential that a Christian be transformed rather than conformed to the world.

3. Pinpoint an area of behavior where obedience to the Lord is lacking, and take action to be "acceptable unto God" in this area.

Lesson Outline

INTRODUCTION
  A. Metamorphosis
  B. Lesson Background
 I. GOD CALLS FOR HOLINESS (Romans 12:1-3)
  A. Living Sacrifice (v. 1)
  B. Transformed (v. 2)
    The Power to Survive and Win
  C. Humble (v. 3)
 II. GOD CALLS FOR LOVE (Romans 12:9-15)
  A. Pure (v. 9)
  B. Kind (v. 10)
  C. Industrious (v. 11)
  D. Optimistic (v. 12)
  E. Generous (vv. 13, 14)
  F. Concerned (v. 15)
III. GOD CALLS FOR PEACE (Romans 12:16-21)
  A. Seek Unity and Harmony (v. 16)
  B. Do Not Seek Revenge (vv. 17-19)
    Putting the Past to Rest
  C. Overcome Evil With Good (vv. 20, 21)
CONCLUSION
  A. 3H Religion
  B. Prayer
  C. Thought to Remember

Introduction

A. Metamorphosis

With the coming of summer we often see trees plagued with crawling caterpillars that devour the foliage. But a caterpillar does not remain a caterpillar forever. After a period of time it forms a cocoon (called a chrysalis) and remains inside for about two weeks. Then it emerges as a butterfly that bears no resemblance to its earlier form. "Metamorphosis" is the name scientists give to the changes that makes a crawling worm-like creature into a beautiful butterfly. That word comes from the Greek word that in Romans 12:2 is translated "transformed."

A line in one of our old hymns asks, "Would He devote that sacred head for such a worm as I?" Though we have crawled long in sin, we need not be worm-like creatures forever. Jesus did devote His head—His whole body—to our redemption. By His power and grace we can renew our minds, undergo a metamorphosis, and be transformed into the beautiful persons God designed us to be.

B. Lesson Background

Many Christians seem to think theology (or doctrine) and Christian living are completely separate matters. Doctrine, they believe, is discussed and debated by scholarly theologians, but it is only remotely related to what happens in local churches and in the lives of individual Christians. Scholars help perpetuate this division by writing and speaking in technical jargon that seems like a foreign language. Some non-scholars also contribute to this gap by refusing to try to understand what the theologians are talking about.

The apostle Paul was a theologian and an impressive scholar, but he certainly did not believe that doctrine and practice ought to be separated. In the earlier chapters of the Roman epistle, Paul deals with a great deal of profound theology. But in chapter 12 (the basis for today's lesson) he turns to practical applications of his doctrinal statements. *Therefore* is a key word in Paul's writings. It often signals a move from the doctrinal to the practical. That is the case in today's lesson.

As we study this lesson, it will be obvious that doctrine and practice belong together. If certain doctrines are true, then it follows that a definite attitude and a definite lifestyle should result. To separate doctrine and practice is foreign to the very nature of Christianity. We may not always agree on how the Scriptures apply to every life situation, but we must agree that the Scriptures are the standard by which we measure our lives.

I. God Calls for Holiness
(Romans 12:1-3)

Romans 12 covers several important issues for Christian living. What an impact the church would make on the world if every professing Christian took these teachings of Paul seriously. But it starts with personal surrender.

A. Living Sacrifice (v. 1)

1. I beseech you therefore, brethren, by the mercies of God, that ye present your bodies a living sacrifice, holy, acceptable unto God, which is your reasonable service.

As a divinely inspired apostle, Paul had the right to command his readers, but he chose not to do so. Instead, he makes an earnest appeal that they do as he asks because they want to, not because they have to. He reminds them of the *mercies of God.* If they stopped for a moment to consider all God had done for them, they would not hesitate to do what Paul was asking.

Paul's plea that they *present* their *bodies a living sacrifice* would have a strong impact on Jewish Christians because of the sacrificial system that was at the heart of the Mosaic law. Christians who came from pagan backgrounds also would understand this because of the many sacrifices involved in pagan worship. But unlike the sacrifices of Judaism or of the pagans, this is a living sacrifice. Those other sacrifices came to an end with the death of the animals. The Christian sacrifice is ongoing. This sacrifice is *holy* in the sense that it is set apart to God. Just as the sacrificial animals under the Mosaic law were to be without blemish, so we are to present our bodies unmarred by sin.

The concluding clause in this verse is rendered differently in different versions. Where the *King James Version* has *reasonable service,* the *New International Version* has "spiritual act of worship." The reason is that Paul chose words with double meanings: "reasonable" and "spiritual" are both valid translations of the first; "service" and "worship" both properly translate the second. The idea goes beyond that of any single translation. This response to God's mercy is reasonable: it makes sense; it is rational. It is also spiritual: it recognizes that the body is more than flesh, more than an instrument of sensual function. It is also service: it serves God and people. And it is worship: whether in a formal worship setting or in daily living, the body is used to the glory of God. [See question #1, page 296.]

B. Transformed (v. 2)

2. And be not conformed to this world: but be ye transformed by the renewing of your mind, that ye may prove what is that good, and acceptable, and perfect will of God.

The Phillips translation states this vividly: "Don't let the world around you squeeze you into its own mold." The world is not quietly inviting us to conform; it is trying to force conformity on us. In its advertising it screams a message of materialism and worldly pleasures. It passes laws that force Christians to acquiesce in its ungodly pursuits. The world is trying every way it can to force Christians to fit into its value system.

The *renewing of* the *mind* is consistent with the "reasonable" or rational aspect of the living sacrifice. Heart and mind are both important to conversion, and both remain important to Christian

living. The mind is active as one reads and studies the Scriptures, through which the Holy Spirit guides our behavior. Through the use of the mind we can evaluate and combat the pressures of the world that is trying to make us conform.

THE POWER TO SURVIVE AND WIN

Life seemed to be over for a twenty-four-year-old American athlete when, in 1996, he was struck with cancer. The cancer had spread to his lungs and brain, leaving him a 40 percent chance to live. Surgery and months of chemotherapy left him weak and nauseated.

But only three years later, in 1999, Lance Armstrong won the *Tour de France,* the most prestigious bicycle race in the world. And in 2000 he won again, decisively! The twenty-one-day race covered 2,255 miles—as great as the distance from Los Angeles to Atlanta, Georgia! Armstrong's average speed was nearly twenty-five miles per hour.

Those who saw the transformation from a beaten shell of a man into a two-time world champion just four years later spoke of Armstrong's athletic gifts, but also of his capacity to endure pain, his self-discipline, and his sense of purpose. In a bit of overstatement, a French rider said, "His mental powers are supernatural!"

This is similar to what the apostle Paul says about the means by which we may win our spiritual battles and be transformed into examples of God's goodwill: minds committed to God's noble purpose, willing to endure hardship to attain God's glorious prize. —C. R. B.

C. Humble (v. 3)

3. For I say, through the grace given unto me, to every man that is among you, not to think of himself more highly than he ought to think; but

Visual for lesson 8. *This humorous poster points out the need for Christians to be different from the mold imposed by the world.*

to think soberly, according as God hath dealt to every man the measure of faith.

Paul continues his emphasis on the mind by telling us how we are *to think*. We all experience that urge to be "number one." While we are not to think *more highly* of ourselves than we ought, we are not to think of ourselves too lowly either. *Sober* judgment neither exalts nor debases. It recognizes personal weaknesses, but it also accounts for the fact that we have been created in God's image with all the potential that involves. Keeping such a view of oneself is not easy. But Paul reassures us that God has given each of us a *measure of faith* to help us in this evaluation.

II. God Calls for Love
(Romans 12:9-15)

In verses 4-8 Paul deals with various gifts that Christians enjoy. Just as the human body has many members, each with a different function, so the church, the body of Christ, has many members with various functions.

In verse 9 Paul introduces love, which every Christian should possess. The Greeks had several words for love, each with a different meaning or connotation. The word here is *agape*, which is an active, intelligent goodwill directed toward another without consideration of a response.

A. Pure (v. 9)

9. Let love be without dissimulation. Abhor that which is evil; cleave to that which is good.

Love, like any other virtue, can be feigned—which is the concept behind the word *dissimulation*. But true love always seeks to give more than it receives. This kind of love is not based on soft, unthinking sentimentality. It is discerning, rejecting *that which is evil* and holding on to *that which is good*. This means that sometimes real love must be "tough love," refusing to tolerate evil but confronting it squarely. It means hating sin but loving the sinner. [See question #2, page 296.]

B. Kind (v. 10)

10. Be kindly affectioned one to another with brotherly love; in honor preferring one another.

In this one verse Paul uses two different words that come from the Greek word *phileo*. This is another of the Greeks' words for love, and is often applied to love among friends and family members. This normally involves mutual affection—give and take. Paul urges church members to show the same love among themselves that we expect to be shown toward members of one's own family.

The idea of *preferring one another* ahead of oneself sounds foreign to today's me-first culture.

But it is altogether consistent with the attitude Jesus displayed in the upper room (John 13). [See question #3, page 296.]

C. Industrious (v. 11)

11. Not slothful in business; fervent in spirit; serving the Lord.

Business here does not refer to one's activity in a secular occupation, but to zeal in the work of *the Lord*. Love compels us to give our best effort for the Lord's kingdom. Such spiritual fervor transforms our role on church committees from simply doing a job to truly *serving the Lord*.

D. Optimistic (v. 12)

12. Rejoicing in hope; patient in tribulation; continuing instant in prayer.

Rejoicing, even under adverse conditions, is frequently urged in the New Testament. Christians can rejoice in the midst of suffering because they take the long view of history. They know that ultimately the forces of truth will triumph. *Tribulation* is temporary; the reward is eternal. In the meantime, believers give continuous diligence to *prayer*.

E. Generous (vv. 13, 14)

13. Distributing to the necessity of saints; given to hospitality.

Most of the industrialized nations of the world are enjoying a prosperity unknown at any other time in history. Yet in the midst of this unprecedented affluence there are pockets of poverty. The admonition in this verse is to help the *saints*, or fellow Christians, who are in need. Paul expresses a similar admonition in Galatians 6:10. Yet we must not limit our charity and *hospitality* to fellow Christians. Nor should we limit it just to material things like food and clothing. Sometimes the poor need our guidance and encouragement more than they need material things.

14. Bless them which persecute you: bless, and curse not.

Love is not always "sugar and spice and everything nice." Sometimes it requires us to go contrary to human nature, to love our enemies and those who *persecute* us. Paul here reaffirms what Jesus taught in the Sermon on the Mount: "Love your enemies, bless them that curse you" (Matthew 5:44).

F. Concerned (v. 15)

15. Rejoice with them that do rejoice, and weep with them that weep.

When others *rejoice* because of some good fortune that they have received, we may find it difficult to rejoice with them because of jealousy. We may feel that we deserved the good fortune more than they did. We also sometimes have trouble weeping with those who weep because we are afraid of becoming emotionally involved. We fear that such emotional involvement will make demands on our time and resources that we are not willing to give. Our growth toward Christian maturity may be measured in how well we learn to rejoice and weep with others.

III. God Calls for Peace
(Romans 12:16-21)

Weeping with those who weep and rejoicing with those who rejoice sets the tone for harmony in our relationships.

A. Seek Unity and Humility (v. 16)

16. Be of the same mind one toward another. Mind not high things, but condescend to men of low estate. Be not wise in your own conceits.

The first part of this verse follows naturally from the previous verse. Being of the *same mind* suggests an empathy that shares with others in their rejoicing and weeping. But its application goes further. Some think being of the same mind refers to agreement in matters of doctrine. That is an important point that is dealt with in other passages, but it does not seem to be Paul's point here. Rather, he is discussing relationships. He urges believers to be concerned with one another's suffering, disappointments, and victories. He appeals for "harmony," as the *New International Version* renders it.

To *mind high things* is to take an interest in those things that make us appear superior to others. In our highly competitive society, we not only try to "keep up with the Joneses," we try to outdo them. We accumulate the status symbols that say to the world that we have the newest, the biggest, or the best.

Such a person looks down on other people, but Paul tells us to do just the opposite. To *condescend to men of low estate* is to join the lowly in their situation, to be one with them. The word condescend has a bad connotation today, usually suggesting an association with others that communicates clearly that we belong to a higher class. What Paul is saying here is that we must join with the lowly as their equal. (See James 2:1-9.) Our attention must be on others, not on our *own conceits*—our self-centered interests. [See question #4, page 296.]

B. Do Not Seek Revenge (vv. 17-19)

17. Recompense to no man evil for evil. Provide things honest in the sight of all men.

Whereas the earlier exhortations concerned relationships within the church, from here on

Paul's focus is on how to respond to unbelievers—even enemies. The Old Testament law of "an eye for an eye and a tooth for a tooth" has been transcended by Christ's higher law—when you have been wronged, don't try to get even, but love your enemy.

Paul urges the saints to think ahead and to live in such an *honest* and forthright way that their motives and actions are above reproach. In this way they will be less likely to incur anger and misunderstanding, which can lead to conflict.

18. If it be possible, as much as lieth in you, live peaceably with all men.

Paul recognizes that even those who *live* exemplary lives will not be able to avoid all conflicts. In fact, good people often incur wrath from the world because their godly lives expose the evil in the lives of sinners. It is not always *possible* to avoid conflict, but is is not necessary to incite conflict, either. We are responsible only for behaving in a proper manner ourselves; we cannot determine how others will respond. [See question #5, page 296.]

19. Dearly beloved, avenge not yourselves, but rather give place unto wrath: for it is written, Vengeance is mine; I will repay, saith the Lord.

This reaffirms what Paul stated in verse 17. There is a good reason a Christian should never seek personal revenge: *vengeance* belongs to *the Lord.* God in His own time and His own manner will reward the righteous and punish the wicked.

PUTTING THE PAST TO REST

Randolph McCoy accused Anderson "Devil Anse" Hatfield of stealing his pig. The year was 1878. McCoy's accusation was a reflection of years of ill will between the two clans over Civil War allegiances and business dealings. But this incident precipitated a series of vengeful acts. These acts of revenge comprise the essence of America's most legendary feud. Over the next dozen years a dozen Hatfields and McCoys were killed, some by ambush, some by lynching. The last to die was a Hatfield, who was hanged in 1890.

By then, most members of the two clans had had enough of violence and began to find ways

---

How to Say It

AGAPE (Greek). Uh-*gah*-pay.

CHEMOTHERAPY. *Kee*-mo-*thair*-uh-pee (strong accent on *thair*).

CHRYSALIS. *kris*-uh-liss.

METAMORPHOSIS. *met*-tuh-*mor*-fuh-suss (strong accent on *mor*).

MOSAIC. Mo-*zay*-ik.

PHILEO (Greek). fil-*leh*-oh.

to accommodate each other, if not *like* each other. But it took another century for a formal end of the feud to come. For many years, more thoughtful and decent members of both clans had found the tales of the feud to be a source of shame. They were embarrassed by the inability of their ancestors to get past the spirit of revenge and live at peace with members of the other clan.

And so, in June, 2000, the two clans gathered in Williamson, West Virginia, to visit the sites of the murders, offer prayer together, and put the past to rest.

These two clans are an excellent, yet tragic, example of what happens when we forget the teaching of today's lesson: that God's way for us is to overcome the evil of the past with the spirit of good. (And it shouldn't take us a hundred years to get around to it!)   —C. R. B.

C. Overcome Evil With Good (vv. 20, 21)

20. Therefore if thine enemy hunger, feed him; if he thirst, give him drink: for in so doing thou shalt heap coals of fire on his head.

Paul here shows us the Christian way to respond to our enemies. Give them food and *drink*—and clothing and shelter if they need it. The latter portion of this verse has been interpreted in a variety of ways. In the light of the context, it is obvious that the purpose of the *coals of fire* is not to harm one's enemy, but in some way to help him. Perhaps the idea is that returning kindness for evil will have such an impact on the enemy's conscience that he will be led to repentance and reform.

21. Be not overcome of evil, but overcome evil with good.

This verse sums up the paragraph. When we allow ourselves to seek revenge, we are playing the enemy's game. An old farmer put it this way:

"If you try to wrestle a hog in a mud hole, you are sure to get muddy yourself."

Conclusion

A. 3H Religion

The 4H organization is one hundred years old this year. It began as a "Boys and Girls Agricultural Club" meeting in the basement of the Clark County (Ohio) courthouse in January of 1902. Today it is popular all across the U.S., extending beyond the farms into the suburbs and inner cities as well. The four-leaf clover logo, with an H on each leaf, is familiar to many. The four H's stand for head, heart, hands, and health.

The name "4H" was not used, however, until 1918. In fact, the logo originally had only three leaves, for head, heart, and hands. This old logo, dating back to 1907 or 1908, could be applied to this passage in Romans, where Paul sets forth the 3H's of Christianity: HEAD—doctrines that are to be learned, HEART—changes that are to be made in attitudes, and HANDS—specific actions that should come as a result.

As Christians we apply our heads to read and study the Scriptures, the only adequate basis for our faith. God expects us to learn His Word so that we might not sin against Him (Psalm 119: 11). But more than the intellect, the head, is involved.

Our hearts (emotions, feelings, and wills) also must be involved. Unless this happens, all our Bible studies become cold, intellectual activities, unrelated to the real world in which we live.

To know the Scriptures and then to be moved by them to change our attitudes and our emotions is still not enough. We must be able to translate all of this into actions. Until our hands begin to practice what is in our heads and our hearts, our Christianity is a sham.

Paul does not suggest that following the Christian 3H's will be easy. Indeed, the application of Biblical truth to our daily lives faces formidable challenges in our times when the forces of the world are set against us. But the rewards are beyond measure. In this world we will know the peace that faithful service brings, and in the next world we are promised life eternal.

B. Prayer

Dear Lord, we thank You for the writings of the apostle Paul that spell out for us in some detail what You expect from us—to present our bodies a living sacrifice that is holy in Your sight. Guide us as we seek to become faithful servants. In our Master's name we pray. Amen.

C. Thought to Remember

Walk the talk!

Home Daily Bible Readings

Monday, Apr. 15—Be Doers of the Word (James 1:19-27)

Tuesday, Apr. 16—Love Does Not Discriminate (James 2:1-13)

Wednesday, Apr. 17—Control the Tongue (James 3:1-12)

Thursday, Apr. 18—Gentleness Born of Wisdom (James 3:13-18)

Friday, Apr. 19—Patience and Endurance (James 5:7-12)

Saturday, Apr. 20—Do Not Conform; Be Transformed (Romans 12:1-8)

Sunday, Apr. 21—Marks of Christian Living (Romans 12:9-21)

Learning by Doing

This page contains an alternate lesson plan emphasizing learning activities.
Classes desiring such student involvement will find these suggestions helpful.

Learning Goals

After participating in this lesson, each student will be able to:

1. Describe the "transformed" lifestyle Paul urges Christians to adopt.

2. Tell why it is essential that a Christian be transformed rather than conformed to the world.

3. Pinpoint an area of behavior where obedience to the Lord is lacking, and take action to be "acceptable unto God" in this area.

Into the Lesson

Place several large pieces of poster paper on the walls around the room, and have several colored markers near each poster. Say: "Several years ago there were toys called 'transformers.' Each of these toys was originally in one shape, a robot of sorts, but after you manipulated it, the robot became something else: an airplane, a tank, a helicopter, or the like. Step up to the sheets of poster paper and write what you would like to be transformed into, if it were possible."

After class members have taken a few minutes to write their choices, ask the group to give reasons for their answers. Then say, "From this activity it seems that each of us longs to be different, to be transformed. When you think of all the Christians you have met, who do you think has made the biggest transformation?"

After a short discussion say, "Today we are studying Romans 12. Paul challenges us all to be transformed. As we study, we will see ways in which Christ seeks for us to change."

Into the Word

Either during the week before class or a few minutes before you begin, recruit four readers for today. Have the Scripture read in these divisions: Romans 12:1-3, 9-13, 14-16, and 17-21. Follow the reading with a brief lecture using the Lesson Background section on page 290.

Divide your class into at least four groups of three to six. Give a copy of one of the four sections of Scripture that were read to each group. (If your class has more than twenty-four members, repeat some assignments.)

Group 1 (Romans 12:1-3) is to draw a "cartoon panel" that depicts the truth of this Scripture. To "prime the pump," you may want to challenge them to draw a picture of God's act of mercy (Jesus' sacrificial death).

Group 2 (Romans 12:9-13) is to develop a role play of an event or series of events in which the characteristics described are shown. Each of the short imperatives can lend itself to a brief scene of conflict or confrontation.

Group 3 (Romans 12:14-16) is to list the people or types of people Paul might be referring to if he were in our community today. Caution them to be careful not to insult or defame a group.

Group 4 (Romans 12:17-21) is to think of a recent news item or community happening where evil was evident. This group should agree on how a Christian should handle the situation, demonstrating the characteristics listed. Ask the group to decide how the final principle is a universal one: "Be not overcome of evil, but overcome evil with good."

Call the groups together to present their findings. Then discuss the following two questions.

1. Which characteristic are you most apt to show?

2. Which characteristic are you least likely to show?

(Items from Group 3's assignment through these group discussion questions are included in the student book, *Adult Bible Class.*)

Into Life

As you seek to bring this lesson to life, ask the groups to move back to their original places. Distribute the following questions:

1. In what areas do you think Christians are conforming to the world? Which ones are obviously negative choices? Which ones really do not matter?

2. Where do you see Christians living "transformed" lives?

3. What is the result of a transformed life?

4. Were you more "transformed" or "conformed" this week?

Say, "Often we are to live our lives playing to an audience, playing a role. We give our audience what they want. Here Paul tells us we are to live lives pleasing to God. He delineates the characteristics of godly living in Romans 12:9-21. Which characteristic or characteristics do you need to be developing? Write down the first two steps you will take this week. Tell these two steps to the person sitting beside you."

Close in prayer for each person's strength to fulfill the pledge just made.

Let's Talk It Over

The questions on this page are designed to encourage review of the lesson Scriptures and to promote discussion of the lesson by the class. The answers provided are only discussion starters. Let your class talk it over from there.

1. What is "reasonable" about offering every part of our selves wholly to God as living sacrifices? How does keeping God's mercies in view help us to see it that way?

God's mercy (or grace) is the source of our salvation. That salvation cost the Son of God His very life. Therefore, it is only reasonable that we should offer every part of ourselves as living sacrifices to Him as He has given to us. Further, His mercies toward us continue—they are "new every morning" (Lamentations 3:23). If it is already reasonable to give ourselves wholly to Christ because He gave Himself as a sacrifice on our behalf, then it is eminently reasonable to give ourselves to Him since He continues to bless us and to give us so much.

Another aspect of the reasonableness of Christianity is the rationality of making such a decision. Paul says faith comes by hearing (Romans 10:17). John said he wrote his Gospel so that people would believe (John 20:30, 31). Faith is based on evidence; it is not a blind leap. We do not have to suspend our intellect in order to have faith.

2. Paul seems to link love with righteous living in verse 9. How do transformed people ensure that their love leads to righteous living?

The bulk of Romans 12 is a virtual checklist for us to see whether our love for God is translating into righteous living—love both for our Christian family and for our enemies. Jesus is the ultimate model of unending love, and at the same time is the ultimate model for totally righteous living. While we will never be able to achieve His standard, He is our role model to whom we can look for guidance and inspiration, and to whom we can pray for help. John's first epistle clearly demonstrates to us that God's love and righteous living cannot be divorced from each other.

3. What is the difference between "people who go to the same church" and "members of the same church family"? How will that difference affect areas Paul describes, such as our intensity, our sharing of resources, our willingness to associate with everyone, and our emotional involvement in the lives of others?

The lesson writer points out the necessity of *phileo* love, "often applied to love among friends

and family members," in the church. The church must exist as a family in order to fulfill God's plan for her. The metaphors of God as our Father and Christians as brothers and sisters are more than figures of speech. We share the same flesh and blood through our communion in Jesus Christ, and we are called to be family in every way. Seeing fellow believers in our own congregation as simply "people who go to my church" reduces the church to a mere social club, an organization to which one belongs rather than a living organism of which one is a part. Paul makes it clear that the way we treat one another in the church family entails the same kinds of bonding and sharing and openness and acceptance and involvement that is experienced in the biological family.

4. How can we "condescend to men of low estate" without being "condescending," in the sense currently suggested by the term?

The prefix "con" means with, so a true understanding of Paul's command is that we go down with the lowly, we identify with them. Jesus did that with the people of low estate in His day. He touched the untouchables. He befriended the friendless. He praised the efforts of a poor widow who was all but dismissed along with her meager offering. To be condescending, in today's vernacular, is just the opposite. It makes a point of noting how much better one is than another, and then seeks to make the "lower" person feel obligated to the other for his or her favors.

5. Paul says we are to be at peace with people "if it be possible." How can we tell when it is possible and when it is not?

Sometimes we say we have done all we could do to ensure peace in a relationship when we haven't. What we mean is that we have done all we are willing to do. We need to examine ourselves and compare our motives with what Paul says. He doesn't say, "If it be convenient." He doesn't say, "If it's not too much trouble, or too embarrassing, or if it can be done without your having to eat crow." He says, "If it be possible." Following Paul's instructions here requires us to practice forgiveness, patience, and self-denial. It may also require calling on God, who does the *impossible*, to help us!

Live Unto the Lord

April 28
Lesson 9

DEVOTIONAL READING: Romans 14:14-23.

BACKGROUND SCRIPTURE: Romans 14:1—15:6.

PRINTED TEXT: Romans 14:1-13; 15:1, 2.

Romans 14:1-13

1 Him that is weak in the faith receive ye, but not to doubtful disputations.

2 For one believeth that he may eat all things: another, who is weak, eateth herbs.

3 Let not him that eateth despise him that eateth not; and let not him which eateth not judge him that eateth: for God hath received him.

4 Who art thou that judgest another man's servant? to his own master he standeth or falleth. Yea, he shall be holden up: for God is able to make him stand.

5 One man esteemeth one day above another: another esteemeth every day alike. Let every man be fully persuaded in his own mind.

6 He that regardeth the day, regardeth it unto the Lord; and he that regardeth not the day, to the Lord he doth not regard it. He that eateth, eateth to the Lord, for he giveth God thanks; and he that eateth not, to the Lord he eateth not, and giveth God thanks.

7 For none of us liveth to himself, and no man dieth to himself.

8 For whether we live, we live unto the Lord; and whether we die, we die unto the Lord: whether we live therefore, or die, we are the Lord's.

9 For to this end Christ both died, and rose, and revived, that he might be Lord both of the dead and living.

10 But why dost thou judge thy brother? or why dost thou set at nought thy brother? for we shall all stand before the judgment seat of Christ.

11 For it is written, As I live, saith the Lord, every knee shall bow to me, and every tongue shall confess to God.

12 So then every one of us shall give account of himself to God.

13 Let us not therefore judge one another any more: but judge this rather, that no man put a stumblingblock or an occasion to fall in his brother's way.

Romans 15:1, 2

1 We then that are strong ought to bear the infirmities of the weak, and not to please ourselves.

2 Let every one of us please his neighbor for his good to edification.

Apr
28

GOLDEN TEXT: Let us not therefore judge one another any more: but judge this rather, that no man put a stumblingblock or an occasion to fall in his brother's way.—Romans 14:13.

Lesson Aims

After studying this lesson, each student should:

1. Summarize what Paul says about the attitude with which a Christian should handle matters on which believers disagree.

2. Explain the significance of living unto the Lord in the context of getting along with others.

3. Suggest how a particular situation involving a disputable matter, either in the class or the church, could be handled in a way that will promote peace and will edify others.

Lesson Outline

Introduction

A. To Judge or Not to Judge

Paul's judgment against any who would preach a different gospel from the true gospel is unequivocal: "Let him be accursed" (Galatians 1:8). Yet even so forthright a statement does not justify a quick denunciation or a public proclamation of the errant preacher's guilt. Paul's co-workers, Priscilla and Aquila, took a different approach, as we can read in Acts 18.

Apollos had come to town. He knew about Jesus, to a point. But he didn't know anything beyond John's baptism (vv. 24, 25). In other words, he did not know about the death, burial, and resurrection of Jesus. He didn't know the gospel! (See 1 Corinthians 15:1-4.)

Rather than make a public spectacle, Priscilla and Aquila took the young preacher home with them. Probably over dinner they shared the gospel—they "expounded unto him the way of God more perfectly [i.e., more completely]" (v. 26). As a result, Apollos was not "accursed," but became a powerful preacher of the true gospel.

There is a time for judgment, for discernment, for careful analysis of the situation and determination of what to do in response. But that does not have to include being judgmental, condemning those with whom we have differences. We can discuss the issues in a godly manner and leave the judging to God.

B. Lesson Background

In today's lesson Paul continues his emphasis on practical Christian living based on the doctrinal teachings in Romans 1–11. In chapter 12 he laid the basis for this by setting forth our relationship to God: we are to present our bodies "a living sacrifice" to God. In chapter 13 he discussed our relationship to civil government: we are to "be subject unto the higher powers." Now he turns to relationships between Christians. We are not to deal with our brothers and sisters (or even non-Christians, for that matter) with a judgmental attitude.

I. Accept One Another
(Romans 14:1-4)

A. Receive the Weak Brother (vv. 1, 2)

1, 2. Him that is weak in the faith receive ye, but not to doubtful disputations. For one believeth that he may eat all things: another, who is weak, eateth herbs.

The expression *doubtful disputations* renders two Greek words that mean "judging" and "opinions," "disputes," or "doubts." What Paul is prohibiting here is the apparent reception of one who is *weak in the faith* for the purpose of passing judgment on his or her opinions.

At issue here is the matter of Christian liberty. From the very beginning, Christians have had to make decisions about how their Christian faith applies in their culture. Since Christians have not always come to the same conclusions about these differences, disagreements and even conflicts have followed.

The one who is *weak in the faith* takes a narrow, limited view of freedom. He or she interprets Scripture in such a way as to limit liberty. This does not pose a problem as long as these limitations are applied only to one's own life. But when the person seeks to bind others to these restrictions, conflict is likely to follow.

Paul illustrates his point with a specific example: the eating of meat. Some people today choose a vegetarian diet for health reasons, but in Paul's day the issue was religious. Some Gentile Christians had come from pagan religions that involved animal sacrifices. Much of the meat sold in the market came from these sacrifices, and eating it seemed to these people to involve them in the paganism they had just left (cf. 1 Corinthians 8). Jewish Christians, who had been taught to avoid eating meat from unclean animals or from animals not killed according to the law of Moses, often refused to eat meat also. [See question #1, page 304.]

B. Accept Those God Has Received (v. 3)

3. Let not him that eateth despise him that eateth not; and let not him which eateth not judge him that eateth: for God hath received him.

Eating meat or not eating meat was not a moral issue, but a matter of opinion. Since God accepts both groups, they are urged to accept one another. The strong, those who ate, were not to *despise*, or look down on, those who did not. Those who did not eat were not to *judge*, or condemn, those who did. [See question #2, page 304.]

C. The Master Judges His Own Servants (v. 4)

4. Who art thou that judgest another man's servant? to his own master he standeth or falleth. Yea, he shall be holden up: for God is able to make him stand.

A *master* has control over his servants, and outsiders have no right to interfere in matters between them. Since Christians are servants of God, we have no right to tell Him how He should deal with His other servants. If a "weaker brother" seems to stumble, *God* will *make him stand.*

II. Live Unto the Lord
(Romans 14:5-9)

A. Observe Days Differently (vv. 5, 6)

5. One man esteemeth one day above another: another esteemeth every day alike. Let every man be fully persuaded in his own mind.

Paul now introduces another issue that may have caused controversy within the church. Jewish Christians may have continued to observe the Sabbath and other days and feasts that they had observed under the law. Paul doesn't condemn this practice. Regardless of which position one held, the important thing was that each person *be fully persuaded in his own mind.*

6. He that regardeth the day, regardeth it unto the Lord; and he that regardeth not the day, to the Lord he doth not regard it. He that eateth, eateth to the Lord, for he giveth God thanks; and he that eateth not, to the Lord he eateth not, and giveth God thanks.

Some recognized special days to honor *the Lord.* Others honored the Lord by looking on every day as given by Him. These positions must be held as matters of opinion and personal devotion. When persons try to force their views on others in a legalistic fashion, Paul makes it clear that this is a reversion to salvation by works rather than by grace. "Let no man therefore judge you in meat, or in drink, or in respect of a holyday, or of the new moon, or of the sabbath days" (Colossians 2:16). Rather, each one should focus on the Lord, giving *thanks,* instead of focusing on differences with other believers.

WHEN YOUR NEIGHBOR HAS A DIFFERENT VIEW

How much is a scenic view worth? That's probably not something that most of us have tried to quantify. But residents of Rancho Palos Verdes have. They have paid two million dollars or more for mansions with unobstructed views of the Ocean or the Los Angeles city lights. For them a scenic view can add as much as a hundred thousand dollars to property values! Some of them bought their homes when the downhill neighbors' trees were small, but these now full-grown trees are blocking their view! Which is worth more, an unobstructed view or beautiful trees?

The matter is taken seriously enough that the municipality has passed laws that allow residents to demand that their neighbors cut their trees if the trees have impinged on their view. Heated city council meetings have resulted in numerous angry exchanges and even a heart attack for one "downhill" defender of the property values that his trees provide.

The issue that Paul discusses in today's lesson did not involve property damages or monetary values. But it did have to do with the way a person looked at life, and it had great importance in terms of the quality of life within the Christian community in Rome.

When one member of the church in Rome chose not to see a matter of personal opinion from the perspective of others, the result was a loss of Christian spirit. The spirit that Paul urges upon us goes beyond mere forbearance. We are to find positive ways to set our fellow Christians at ease even when we are convinced they are wrong on these matters of opinion.   —C. R. B.

B. Serve the Same Lord (vv. 7-9)

7, 8. For none of us liveth to himself, and no man dieth to himself. For whether we live, we live unto the Lord; and whether we die, we die unto the Lord: whether we live therefore, or die, we are the Lord's.

"No man is an Island, entire of itself," John Donne reminds us. We are by nature social creatures, and we find our greatest fulfillment in our associations with others. Because of this interrelationship, we need to learn to be tolerant of others. But Paul's statement goes beyond this. We also *live* and *die* before God. We belong to Him in this life, but our servanthood does not end at death.

9. For to this end Christ both died, and rose, and revived, that he might be Lord both of the dead and living.

One of the central themes in Paul's writings is the death and resurrection of *Christ.* Here he comes back to it again and sets it forth as a basis for building loving, trusting, and generous relationships within the church. Because He is the *Lord both of the dead and living,* He has the right to command our obedience. Part of the obedience that He demands is that we avoid making our opinions the standard by which we judge others.

III. Let God Be the Judge
(Romans 14:10-13)

A. Give an Account of Yourself (vv. 10-12)

10. But why dost thou judge thy brother? or why dost thou set at nought thy brother? for we shall all stand before the judgment seat of Christ.

Paul addresses both sides of the dispute over the eating of meat. To the weaker brother, who ate no meat, he asks, *Why dost thou judge thy brother?* By attempting to impose his rigid views on others, this weak brother was judging them, probably even accusing them of being sinners. To the stronger brother Paul asks, *Why dost thou set at nought thy brother?* Apparently the stronger believers ridiculed the views of the vegetarians, treating them as if they had no merit.

By asking these two questions, Paul reminds both parties that judging belongs to *Christ,* not to them. His words also remind us that *we shall all stand before the judgment seat of Christ.* We will all have to give an account before God. We do not dread that judgment in terms of our salvation, for we know we have an advocate, even Jesus Christ, who will plead our case before the Father. Still, it appears we will give an account for how we have treated our brothers and sisters. [See question #3, page 304.]

11. For it is written, As I live, saith the Lord, every knee shall bow to me, and every tongue shall confess to God.

Paul cites the Isaiah 45:23 as proof for his statement regarding the judgment. Bowing the *knee* is universally recognized as an act of submission. In that final scene, every person will submit to God, even those who had rejected Him in this life. In the same way *every tongue shall confess to God.* This will not be a confession of sins. It will be too late for that. It will be, rather, a recognition and acknowledgment that He is the Sovereign of the universe.

12. So then every one of us shall give account of himself to God.

These are sobering words for those who live in our times. We try to avoid personal responsibility for our mistakes and sins and blame others for our problems. But these excuses won't cut it on that final day.

B. Put No Stumblingblock
in Another's Path (v. 13)

13. Let us not therefore judge one another any more: but judge this rather, that no man put a stumblingblock or an occasion to fall in his brother's way.

To both sides in the dispute over the eating of meat Paul urges a moratorium on judging. The only way that such a moratorium will work is for both parties to observe it. Such an agreement must be based on mutual trust, respect, and love.

The latter part of the verse is directed toward the strong. They must act in such a way as to avoid putting a *stumblingblock,* or an occasion to fall, in the path of another. Our Christian liberty allows us to engage in a wide range of activities that are not of themselves sinful. Yet we must not use that liberty in such a way that it causes another person to violate his or her conscience and fall into sin. [See question #4, page 304.]

Visual for lesson 9. *Today's visual echoes Paul's admonition to stop judging one another. Display it as you discuss verse 13.*

[See question #5, page 304.]

How to Say It

AMILLENNIALISM. *ah*-muh-*len*-ee-uhl-liz-um (strong accent on *len*).

APOLLOS. Uh-*pahl*-us.

AQUILA. *Ack*-wih-luh.

CORINTHIAN. Kor-*in*-thee-un (*th* as in *thin*).

EDIFICATION. *Ed*-duh-fuh-*kay*-shun (strong accent on *kay*).

POSTMILLENNIALISM. *post*-muh-*len*-ee-uhl-liz-um (strong accent on *len*).

PREMILLENNIALISM. *pre*-muh-*len*-ee-uhl-liz-um (strong accent on *len*).

PRISCILLA. Prih-*sil*-uh.

IV. Show Concern for Others (Romans 15:1, 2)

A. Help the Weak (v. 1)

1. We then that are strong ought to bear the infirmities of the weak, and not to please ourselves.

Paul continues his discussion of the *strong* and *weak* Christians, focusing on the obligations of the strong. They are to *bear the infirmities of the weak*. The word here translated "to bear" is the same word used in Galatians 6:2—"bear ye one another's burdens." The strong not only tolerate the viewpoints of the weak; they expend themselves for the sake of these weaker believers.

SAVING THE HELPLESS

Ivers Sims, an Atlanta construction worker, was operating a 250-foot-tall cantilevered crane that towered over the work site when a fire broke out below. Soon the crane itself was on fire, and Sims was trapped high above the ground. To escape the smoke and heat, he crawled out to the concrete counterweight on the crane's horizontal arm. His only hope for rescue was from above.

As the crane swayed in the gusting wind, a forest-fire-fighting helicopter was brought in as a means of saving him. The pilot directed his craft through the smoke and turbulence caused by the flames to a spot eighty feet above Sims. Even that far above the inferno, the heat was intense. Matt Mosely, a firefighter, risked his own life by dropping by cable to the swaying crane, then strapping Sims into a harness. Both men were then lowered safely to the ground away from the fire. The rescue was in the best of the fire-fighter tradition: those with the strength, skill, and training take sometimes extraordinary risks to save the helpless who otherwise might lose their lives.

What we are asked to do in terms of coming to the aid of weaker brothers and sisters is nowhere near as exciting and attention getting as the rescue of Ivers Sims. No one is likely to be called a hero for bearing the burdens of his neighbor. However, the task is no less important, since the spiritual life of another person may be at stake. In giving aid to others who are weaker than ourselves, rather than seeking our own pleasure and convenience, we are demonstrating that we have come to a true understanding of what the gospel of Christ is about.   —C. R. B.

B. Edify One Another (v. 2)

2. Let every one of us please his neighbor for his good to edification.

Every one probably refers to the stronger Christian, thus continuing the discussion from the previous verse. In the same way, *neighbor* in this context should not be understood as including all one's neighbors but only fellow Christians. Obviously, there are some limits on how far one should go to please his fellow Christians. Paul spells out these limitations: *for his good to edification*. We are to please our neighbors only to the extent that our actions contribute to their spiritual maturity. [See question #5, page 304.]

Conclusion

A. "In All Things Love"

"In matters of faith, unity; in matters of opinion, liberty; in all things love." Some groups have taken this statement as the basis for their relationships among themselves and with others outside their group. This statement summarizes rather succinctly what Paul teaches in today's lessons. If it were understood and followed, it could well bring unity and harmony within congregations and between denominations. As noble as this statement is, however, it does pose some problems. First of all, we have to define what we mean by "faith." It must include the central facts of the gospel: Jesus Christ is the divine Son of God; He was born of a virgin, lived on earth, died for our sins, and was raised from the dead; He ascended into Heaven and someday will return. These statements do not comprise "the faith" in its entirety, but they are certainly statements that must be considered essential.

Even these statements, however, have been the center of controversy. For example, while there is agreement that the Lord will return, there is considerable disagreement about the details. Indeed, disagreements over such concepts as premillennialism, postmillennialism, and amillennialism often have been heated, dividing congregations and even whole fellowships. The list of theological issues over which people have disagreed, debated, and even fought could go on almost without end.

When we begin to deal with matters of opinion, we run into similar problems. For example, few people would want to argue that the color we paint the walls in the church nursery is a matter of faith. Yet we have seen heated debates over just such issues. All of us have been conditioned by our culture to think in different ways and to approach matters with built-in prejudices. And we all have prejudices! Separating the essential elements of faith from matters of opinion has never been an easy task. But that task is now more difficult than ever because of the intermingling of cultures from all over the world. And these cultural differences are not just national or ethnic. Some of the most serious disagreements in our churches today are intergenerational.

An objective study of church history leads one to the easy conclusion that most of the divisions and conflicts in the church have come over matters of opinion and not of faith. That's where love comes in—or needs to. In one congregation, a young woman planned for her wedding reception to take place in some of the church's Sunday school classrooms. However, a few families in the church believed that 1 Corinthians 11:22 ("What! have ye not houses to eat and to drink in?") prohibited eating in the church building. When the bride and her family learned of this, they quietly and without making an issue of it rented a nearby hall for the reception. Love won out!

Women missionaries serving in some tropical jungle areas have another problem. There the nationals expect women to wear long skirts. Of course, slacks or long trousers would make more sense, providing protection against insects and underbrush as they travel through the jungle. But because they love the people they serve and do not wish to offend them, they are willing to be guided by the sensitivities of the nationals.

Home Daily Bible Readings

Monday, Apr. 22—Act to Honor the Lord (Romans 14:1-6)

Tuesday, Apr. 23—We Are the Lord's (Romans 14:7-12)

Wednesday, Apr. 24—Do Not Cause Others to Stumble (Romans 14:13-23)

Thursday, Apr. 25—Build Up Your Neighbor (Romans 15:1-6)

Friday, Apr. 26—Gospel for Both Jews and Gentiles (Romans 15:7-13)

Saturday, Apr. 27—One Message: What Christ Accomplishes (Romans 15:14-21)

Sunday, Apr. 28—Paul's Ministry to Rome (Romans 15:22-33)

Love, however, works both ways. The weaker brother or sister has a sensitive conscience that requires him to perform certain acts or prohibits him from engaging in other activities. This in itself is not a problem. The problem arises when he or she seeks to impose these duties or restrictions on others. In this kind of a situation they need to show love toward others by carefully examining their convictions. They need to ask themselves whether their convictions are based on Scripture or on cultural preferences.

Perhaps the most troubling source of discord among churches almost everywhere deals with styles of worship. Some prefer traditional styles; others want contemporary services. By now we all recognize that there is no easy solution to these so-called "worship wars." Yet in some congregations tolerant love is winning out, and solutions are being found.

B. Judging

"Judge not, that ye be not judged," Jesus taught in the Sermon on the Mount (Matthew 7:1). Paul echoes these sentiments in today's lesson text. But we need to look more closely at what Jesus had in mind. He was condemning hypocritical, biased judgments—not all judgments. That is made evident only a few verses later when He warned against false prophets and affirmed that "by their fruits ye shall know them" (Matthew 7:15-20). Certainly a fruit inspector has to make some judgments. In the same way, Paul did not mean that Christians should never make any judgments. For instance, he insisted that the Corinthian church make some painful judgments about some of its sinful members: "Come out from among them, and be ye separate" (2 Corinthians 6:17).

Upon what basis, then, should we make judgments when we have to make them? The important thing is that we base our judgments on the Scriptures, not upon our personal feelings or biases. This is not an easy task, but it is one that we must accept if we are to have peace with our fellow Christians.

C. Prayer

Gracious God, we recognize that we live in a world that is becoming more complex with more situations in which Christians disagree among themselves. May today's lesson give us insights that help bring harmony to our discordant world.

Even as we judge others, let us never forget that each of us must stand before You in that final judgment. Through Jesus we pray. Amen.

D. Thought to Remember

"Blessed are the peacemakers: for they shall be called the children of God" (Matthew 5:9)

Learning by Doing

This page contains an alternate lesson plan emphasizing learning activities.
Classes desiring such student involvement will find these suggestions helpful.

Learning Goals

After participating in this lesson, each student will be able to:

1. Summarize what Paul says about the attitude with which a Christian should handle matters on which believers disagree.

2. Explain the significance of living unto the Lord in the context of getting along with others.

3. Suggest how a particular situation involving a disputable matter, either in the class or the church, could be handled in a way that will promote peace and will edify others.

Into the Lesson

Assign students to groups of four. Create a handout (or the appropriate page in *Adult Bible Class*) to have students answer these questions:

1. What movies should Christians never see?
2. What music should Christians not listen to?
3. What foods should Christians never eat?
4. What clothes should Christians never wear?

Collect the papers. On opposite walls of the classroom, mount two signs. Print "Agree" on one, "Disagree" on the other. Choose a few examples for each question. Read the example, then ask the individual class members to move to the sign that best represents their positions. Ask one or two members to defend each position taken.

Ask, "Who should determine such judgments?" Follow up with, "What arguments come because of such judgments?" Say, "Today's lesson is about handling controversy within the church. Paul gives us principles for getting along with others when there are disagreements."

Into the Word

Remind students of Paul's purpose in the latter part of Romans. Read the "Lesson Background" from page 298. Paul's logical teachings are to have practical applications.

Prepare a handout on which is printed Romans 14:1—15:7. Form groups of six to eight, and ask each group to read through this passage and to circle "issues" and "attitudes" cited in the text. Each group should have a reporter. After a few minutes, call the groups together for reports.

Use an overhead transparency or a marker board to list the groups' findings. *(Issues could include eating, drinking, and observing holy days. Attitudes may include accepting each other and building up each other.)*

Ask, "Why did the Roman Christians have trouble with these issues?" and "Why does Paul say it is important to reflect these attitudes?" (Romans 15:7). People should be able to see the accepting nature of the church, so that God is praised. Say, "In your group, choose what you believe is the 'key verse' of this Scripture." Focus on Romans 14:13.

Into Life

Call the class back into its original groups. Say, "Take your original list of 'nevers.' Using Romans 14 and 15, how would you help weaker Christians and stronger Christians maintain peace and unity? Be specific." Allow ten minutes for this discussion.

Option: Print the following two case studies. Distribute one to each half of the class. Discuss solutions in groups of four.

CASE ONE. The church has recently purchased a drum set to be used during worship services. Several members have expressed reservations concerning the tempo of the music, the volume of the drums, and song selections. Others believe the drums should be used more often, along with other instruments. In fact, this group would like to see more new music used. How can the opposing parties apply the teaching of Romans 14 and 15?

CASE TWO. Your church has a large fellowship hall/gymnasium. Someone has proposed that, in order to reach out to new people, you should offer exercise classes, dance lessons, and classes on self-defense so that church members can invite non-Christian friends to introduce them to your building. Several people raised objections. How do you help these two groups apply Romans 14 and 15 to your church?

Whichever option is used, call the class together and ask for groups to share their insights. Be prepared to guide students to understand the principles of Romans 14 and 15. Helpful information is contained in the commentary on Romans 15:1, 2 and in the Conclusion.

Close by asking each member to reflect on the following. "What do you do that causes someone to think less of Christ?" Follow up with "What specific steps will you take this week to bear the burdens of someone?" Allow a few minutes for each person to write several things he or she will do. Lead the class in praying Romans 15:5, 6.

Let's Talk It Over

The questions on this page are designed to encourage review of the lesson Scriptures and to promote discussion of the lesson by the class. The answers provided are only discussion starters. Let your class talk it over from there.

1. An age-old principle states: "In matters of faith, unity; in matters of opinion, liberty; in all things, love." How do we decide whether an individual practice or church practice is a matter of faith or a matter of opinion?

The Bible is naturally the place to start. Another age-old slogan popular in many churches is, "Where the Bible speaks, we speak; where the Bible is silent, we are silent." If we would not make tests of fellowship of issues not addressed by Scripture, most of the division in the church would be eliminated.

But what of matters that both sides defend with Scripture? Both sides should openly dialogue with one another to see the other side's reasoning behind their view. Those with narrower views should re-examine Scripture to determine if they have viewed a long-held tradition as Scriptural, or whether they have taken a passage out of its context to come to their own conclusions. Those with more permissive views should likewise re-examine Scripture to determine whether their accepted practices are not in line with, or in the spirit of, Scriptural truth.

2. How do we as Christians lovingly and tactfully communicate to brothers or sisters with different opinions that they are not being despised or judged because of our differences?

We should strive to communicate to such a brother or sister that we are both servants of the same Lord, that we do not need to judge one another, that we can both please the Lord (even with differing opinions or practices). There is nothing wrong with two or more Christians who "agree to disagree." In fact, such a communication often strengthens relationships that otherwise might have been damaged. We should always be sure not to fall into even the appearance of refusing to talk to someone with whom we've had a differing opinion.

3. Why do Christians on both sides of an opinion have a responsibility not to pass judgment on those with differing views?

The person with the more restricted view is in danger of labeling Christians with differing opinions as "liberals." The one with a more permissive view is in danger of labeling more restrictive Christians as "narrow-minded." When we make such judgments, we stand in danger of misinterpreting the other's motives and the other's relationship with the Lord. Paul's reasoning for asking neither side to judge has to do with the fact that we will all stand before the judgment seat one day. Jesus said, "Judge not, that ye be not judged. For with what judgment ye judge, ye shall be judged: and with what measure ye mete, it shall be measured to you again" (Matthew 7:1, 2). We should want to give the benefit of the doubt to those sincere brothers and sisters whose opinions differ from our own, with the faith that Christ on Judgment Day will give us the benefit of the doubt and honor our sincerity if some of our opinions were a little off base.

4. Of all Paul's admonitions not to judge, he finally says that we may "judge this rather, that no man put a stumblingblock or an occasion to fall in his brother's way." Why is such an issue worthy of our judgment?

If a matter of opinion is truly a matter of opinion, then it is by nature secondary in its importance. No such secondary issue would be worth the grave result of causing someone to fall or damaging someone's relationship with God. Most of us know of someone who has left the church or felt driven away from the church over some petty issue or conflict. Paul makes it clear that such a grievous exit shouldn't be the result of Christians who elevate opinions to a more prominent importance than they deserve.

5. How do we determine whether or not we are uplifting a fellow Christian "for his good to edification"?

If a Christian's time and energy are being spent dealing with pettiness and disputes within the body, we can be sure that he or she is not growing, being edified, or making an impact on the world. While Paul's point is not that we should avoid facing our differences of opinions, it is clear that we must not spend so much time and energy on them that we neglect new members of the body and those just outside of it. Ultimately, a believer with a difference in opinion will be edified by your humility if you swallow your pride and give way to the greater issues within the church. Healthy, edified members of healthy, growing churches aren't constantly fighting.

Gospel of Faith

DEVOTIONAL READING: Acts 13:26-39.

BACKGROUND SCRIPTURE: Galatians 1, 2.

PRINTED TEXT: Galatians 1:1, 2, 6-12; 2:15-21.

Galatians 1:1, 2, 6-12

1 Paul, an apostle, (not of men, neither by man, but by Jesus Christ, and God the Father, who raised him from the dead;)

2 And all the brethren which are with me, Unto the churches of Galatia.

. . . .

6 I marvel that ye are so soon removed from him that called you into the grace of Christ unto another gospel:

7 Which is not another; but there be some that trouble you, and would pervert the gospel of Christ.

8 But though we, or an angel from heaven, preach any other gospel unto you than that which we have preached unto you, let him be accursed.

9 As we said before, so say I now again, If any man preach any other gospel unto you than that ye have received, let him be accursed.

10 For do I now persuade men, or God? or do I seek to please men? for if I yet pleased men, I should not be the servant of Christ.

11 But I certify you, brethren, that the gospel which was preached of me is not after man.

12 For I neither received it of man, neither was I taught it, but by the revelation of Jesus Christ.

Galatians 2:15-21

15 We who are Jews by nature, and not sinners of the Gentiles,

16 Knowing that a man is not justified by the works of the law, but by the faith of Jesus Christ, even we have believed in Jesus Christ, that we might be justified by the faith of Christ, and not by the works of the law: for by the works of the law shall no flesh be justified.

17 But if, while we seek to be justified by Christ, we ourselves also are found sinners, is therefore Christ the minister of sin? God forbid.

18 For if I build again the things which I destroyed, I make myself a transgressor.

19 For I through the law am dead to the law, that I might live unto God.

20 I am crucified with Christ: nevertheless I live; yet not I, but Christ liveth in me: and the life which I now live in the flesh I live by the faith of the Son of God, who loved me, and gave himself for me.

21 I do not frustrate the grace of God: for if righteousness come by the law, then Christ is dead in vain.

GOLDEN TEXT: We have believed in Jesus Christ, that we might be justified by the faith of Christ, and not by the works of the law.—Galatians 2:16.

The Power of the Gospel
Unit 3: No Other Gospel
(Lessons 10-13)

Lesson Aims

After participating in this lesson, each student will be able to:

1. Relate what Paul told the Galatians about the essence and the uniqueness of the gospel.

2. Contrast the true gospel with counterfeits both ancient and modern.

3. Examine one's life for any threats of legalism, and suggest a means by which to be guided by God's grace.

Lesson Outline

INTRODUCTION
    A. Dangers of Legalism
    B. Lesson Background
 I. GOD'S MESSENGER (Galatians 1:1, 2)
    A. The Writer (v. 1)
    B. The Audience (v. 2)
 II. GOD'S MESSAGE (Galatians 1:6-12)
    A. Dangerous Counterfeit (v. 6)
       Counterfeits
    B. Troublesome False Teachers (v. 7)
    C. No Other Gospel (vv. 8, 9)
    D. No Human Origin (vv. 10-12)
III. GOD'S SALVATION (Galatians 2:15-21)
    A. Justified by Faith (vv. 15, 16)
    B. Returning to Sin? (vv. 17, 18)
    C. Crucified With Christ (vv. 19, 20)
       Law's Condemnation
    D. Accepting God's Grace (v. 21)
CONCLUSION
    A. No Other Gospel, Then or Now
    B. The Gospel of Faith
    C. Prayer
    D. Thought to Remember

Introduction

"I got my salvation the old-fashioned way: I earned it!" While few of us would ever be so bold as to say this openly, there is always the temptation to try to take matters into our own hands. Adam and Eve were impatient to share God's knowledge, so they ate the forbidden fruit. The people at Babel thought they could build their own tower to Heaven. Today, we may be tempted to think we can secure our own salvation by adding our acts of merit to the sacrifice of Christ.

Sometimes Christians, such as the believers in Galatia, turn from the gospel of faith to legalism. Legalism is the attitude of thinking we can earn salvation—and climb up the ladder of God's approval—by rigidly keeping a set of rules. Like the self-righteous Pharisee (Luke 18:11) we may even take pride in how much better we keep those rules than other people do. But the heart of the matter is this: do we trust Jesus or not? Are we saved by His blood or by our own goodness?

A. Dangers of Legalism

Even though Paul himself had planted the churches in Galatia (Acts 14), false teachers were able to come in and persuade the believers to turn back to the law for salvation. There were probably three things that made legalism so attractive to them—and us.

First, it seems so right. If rules like circumcision and Sabbath-keeping came from God, shouldn't they still be valid? Shouldn't we expect God to give His blessings on the people who keep those rules the best?

Second, it seems so innocent. What harm does it do to make just a few changes in the gospel? Perhaps we could even "help God out" by tacking on a few more requirements.

Third, it seems so easy. If I can get a surer claim on salvation by merely insisting on the rule of circumcision (or any other Old Testament law), why shouldn't I? At least with a rule like that I can know where I stand. It gives me a good feeling to have my salvation under my own control.

B. Lesson Background

The lessons of this quarter have shown that faith in Christ is the heart of the gospel. We have been justified by faith rather than works of law, and we must live by that faith. But what if the gospel of faith is changed? What if the works of law in the Old Testament are combined with the gospel of faith in the New Testament? Is it still the gospel? Will it still save?

Paul had to confront this issue in Galatia, where some had deserted the original gospel for what they thought was a new and improved version. Alarmed that they were turning away from the truth, Paul sternly warned them that there is no other gospel.

I. God's Messenger
(Galatians 1:1, 2)

Paul wrote this epistle to the Galatian churches sometime after A.D. 50, following the Jerusalem Conference of Acts 15. This makes Galatians one of Paul's earliest epistles.

A. The Writer (v. 1)

1. Paul, an apostle, (not of men, neither by man, but by Jesus Christ, and God the Father, who raised him from the dead).

Paul begins by establishing his authority as *an apostle.* He is a man chosen and sent out *by Jesus Christ* Himself. As apostles, Paul and the Twelve were given authority to be the Lord's spokesmen. The early church continued steadfastly in what they taught (Acts 2:42). In Galatia, however, Paul's authority as an apostle was being challenged. Not only were certain people rejecting Paul as an apostle, they were rejecting, by extension, the apostolic gospel as well.

Paul's stresses that his authority as an apostle comes from *God the Father.* The further note that God had *raised* Jesus *from the dead* underscores the fact that this is the same God who had accepted the sacrifice that Christ made at the cross. This was the very issue where the Galatians had lost their confidence, fearing that what Jesus did was not enough. All in all, this is a terse beginning to the letter, reflecting the seriousness of the situation in Galatia.

B. The Audience (v. 2)

2. And all the brethren which are with me, Unto the churches of Galatia.

Paul writes as a spokesman for the apostles and for *all the brethren* who knew the truth of the gospel. He does not stand alone as some kind of maverick preacher who puts his own personal spin on the gospel message.

The *churches of Galatia* were located in central Asia Minor (modern Turkey). Paul himself planted some of those churches on his first missionary journey, when he preached in Iconium, Lystra, and Derbe (Acts 13:51—14:24). While this area was located south of what was originally called Galatia, the Romans had combined both areas into a single province with that name.

II. God's Message (Galatians 1:6-12)

After the salutation of verses 1-5, Paul dives right into discussing the problem. The absence of any praise for the Galatian churches in verses 1-5 is striking when compared to the salutations of his epistles to other churches.

A. Dangerous Counterfeit (v. 6)

6. I marvel that ye are so soon removed from him that called you into the grace of Christ unto another gospel.

Rather than his customary "I give thanks for you," Paul can only offer the sarcastic *I marvel* to the churches of Galatia. It has been only a few

years since they learned about Christ, and now they are *so soon* turning away into false doctrine. They have been *called* to share in the wonderful *grace of Christ,* the undeserved favor and forgiveness of God. Now they are abandoning grace and turning to a counterfeit gospel: the gospel of legalism. [See question #1, page 312.]

COUNTERFEITS

Back in the 1990s, the United States government began redesigning its paper money, starting with the hundred-dollar bill, then the fifty-dollar and twenty-dollar bills. In May of 2000, the ten-dollar and five-dollar bills were introduced. Many people did not like the new bills, saying, "They just don't look like real money—it's more like Monopoly® money!" Even though the new bills didn't seem like the "real thing" to some, there was a very important reason for the change.

With the advent of computers, the old bills had become too easy to counterfeit. Millions of counterfeit dollars were being foisted on an unsuspecting public each year. The new bills have several features that make them more difficult to counterfeit than the old ones: a special watermark that can be seen when the bill is held up to the light, a security thread that glows a different color under ultraviolet light, more detailed portraits, and ink that changes color when viewed from different angles.

So, whether Americans like it or not, the new money will stay. In this, many of us may be in a similar position to some of the Christians in Galatia. They *liked* the old way of "working" for their salvation, and Paul's gospel of God's grace was an idea they hadn't accepted because it didn't seem like *real* religion.

However, one of the problems with the old way was that it was too easy to counterfeit. One could go through the motions of being righteous without that righteousness being the "real thing." And that raises a question for us: What counterfeit approaches to Christian faith are we confronted with? —C. R. B.

B. Troublesome False Teachers (v. 7)

7. Which is not another; but there be some that trouble you, and would pervert the gospel of Christ.

In verse 6, Paul spoke of "another gospel." Here he is quick to add that the perverted gospel that the Galatians are accepting is really *not another* gospel. The one true gospel does not come in a variety of flavors, shapes, and sizes; it cannot be altered to fit a person's own preferences.

Apparently, after Paul had left Galatia, false teachers had come in and had begun teaching that the Gentiles had to be circumcised and had

How to Say It

BABEL. *Bay*-bul.

DERBE. *Der*-be.

GALATIA. Guh-*lay*-shuh.

ICONIUM. Eye-*ko*-nee-um.

JUDAIZERS. *Joo*-duh-*ize*-ers (strong accent on *Joo).*

LYSTRA. *Liss*-truh.

PHARISEE. *Fair*-ih-see.

to keep various other Old Testament laws in order to gain God's favor. Despite the clear pronouncement of the apostles at the Jerusalem Conference (Acts 15), these men insisted that all Christians had to live like Jews. They were trying to *pervert the gospel* by combining it improperly with precepts from the Old Testament law. (The name for those who taught this way is *Judaizers.)*

C. No Other Gospel (vv. 8, 9)

8, 9. But though we, or an angel from heaven, preach any other gospel unto you than that which we have preached unto you, let him be accursed. As we said before, so say I now again, If any man preach any other gospel unto you than that ye have received, let him be accursed.

God determined what the *gospel* truth would be. He established the facts and set the terms of acceptance. No one—not even an apostle or *an angel from heaven*—has the right to overrule God.

The original gospel is the only true gospel. Whoever dares to preach a different gospel is an enemy of God. Such a person is to be recognized as *accursed* by God, which means that he or she is set aside as one whom God will destroy.

Paul repeats his warning to emphasize how serious the matter is. Whenever the gospel was preached, the Galatian believers needed to examine it to see whether it was the same as they had *received* from Paul in the beginning (cf. Revelation 22:18, 19). The original gospel is the inerrant standard. [See question #2, page 312.]

D. No Human Origin (vv. 10-12)

10. For do I now persuade men, or God? or do I seek to please men? for if I yet pleased men, I should not be the servant of Christ.

Paul may have been accused of omitting circumcision just to suit the Gentiles. His enemies could have said that he did not have the courage to make the Gentiles obey the Old Testament regulations. But Paul was not a man to fear confrontation. His bold message to the Galatians proved that he was not merely trying to *persuade* or *please men* rather than God. He knew that a servant must give an account of himself to his

own master, not to others. And Paul was *the servant of Christ.*

11. But I certify you, brethren, that the gospel which was preached of me is not after man.

Paul's gospel was the true, original gospel. He could *certify* or openly make known to them this fact. Just as his apostleship did not originate from any human source (v. 1), *the gospel* that Paul *preached* did not come from men either.

12. For I neither received it of man, neither was I taught it, but by the revelation of Jesus Christ.

When Paul said the gospel was "not after man" (v. 11), he meant it did not have a human source. When Paul says here that he did not receive the gospel *of man,* he means this divine message was not passed on to him by a human messenger. The *neither was I taught* clause that follows strengthens the fact that no human teacher brought Paul the gospel. Instead, the gospel had come directly to Paul by *revelation. Jesus Christ* Himself laid open the truth to Paul.

Paul had seen the risen Christ on the road to Damascus (Acts 9:27), where his direct revelation began (cf. Galatians 2:2). When Paul proclaimed the gospel, he was speaking for Jesus. To prove that this was so, Paul later notes that there were no occasions in his early years when he could have learned the gospel from human sources (1:13-20). [See question #3, page 312.]

III. God's Salvation (Galatians 2:15-21)

In Galatians 1:13—2:10 Paul continues his defense of his apostolic authority. Then, in 2:11-14, he notes how Peter had come to Antioch and had demonstrated acceptance of the Gentile Christians, even eating in their homes. (As a Jew he had been taught that Gentile homes and food were "unclean.") Then, when Jewish Christians from Jerusalem came to visit, Peter was suddenly afraid to be seen associating with the Gentile Christians. Paul, whose apostolic authority was second-to-none, confronted Peter with his wrongdoing.

A. Justified by Faith (vv. 15, 16)

15. We who are Jews by nature, and not sinners of the Gentiles.

Paul points out that Peter himself had ceased to keep all the Jewish laws (v. 14), even though both he and Paul were *Jews by nature.* If even natural-born Jews no longer had to keep the regulations, why should the *sinners of the Gentiles,* who had become Christians, have to keep them?

16. Knowing that a man is not justified by the works of the law, but by the faith of Jesus Christ, even we have believed in Jesus Christ,

that we might be justified by the faith of Christ, and not by the works of the law: for by the works of the law shall no flesh be justified.

This is one of the most important passages in this letter. Paul summarizes his three-fold stress to Peter that people are *not justified* (declared innocent in the sight of God) *by the works of the law.* (This is the first time in the epistle—but certainly not the last—that Paul uses the words *justified* and *law.*) [See question #4, page 312.]

The solution to the sinner's impossible predicament is not a new set of laws to keep. Paul reminded Peter that people are saved through *faith* in *Jesus Christ,* a truth that is stated three times in this verse. Paul and Peter themselves had *believed in Jesus Christ,* trusting Him and His sacrifice on the cross for their justification before God.

B. Returning to Sin? (vv. 17, 18)

17. But if, while we seek to be justified by Christ, we ourselves also are found sinners, is therefore Christ the minister of sin? God forbid.

Here Paul addresses a possible objection that might be raised: if people are saved by faith and not by keeping the law, won't this turn them loose to be worse *sinners?* And if so, wouldn't *Christ* then be to blame as the agent or *minister of sin?*

Absolutely not! To be justified by faith does not mean that we have a license to sin (cf. Romans 6:15; Jude 4). Christ does not encourage or promote sin—quite the opposite! If anyone thinks salvation by faith makes one free to sin, that person simply does not know the meaning of faith or follow the example of Christ.

It is inconceivable that Peter would have raised such an objection. Apparently, then, this is not part of what Paul said to Peter (even though many modern translations that use quotation

Visual for lesson 10

Use this poster to illustrate verse 20. Discuss what it means to be "crucified with Christ."

marks include it). Perhaps Paul is mixing his words to Peter with commentary for the sake of his Galatian readers.

18. For if I build again the things which I destroyed, I make myself a transgressor.

To make his point, Paul puts himself in the place of the Galatians. What would happen if he rejected the principle of being justified by faith and tried to *build again* his record of good works and the framework of ritual laws? These were what he *destroyed* when he became a Christian. In such a case, the very best Paul could hope to accomplish would be to prove again that he was *a transgressor,* guilty of breaking God's laws.

C. Crucified With Christ (vv. 19, 20)

19. For I through the law am dead to the law, that I might live unto God.

The *law* itself had exposed Paul as a sinner and had pronounced the sentence of death: the soul that sins will die. But once Paul was *dead to the law,* the law could do nothing more to him. When he was born again and given new life in Christ, he was free to *live unto God.*

20. I am crucified with Christ: nevertheless I live; yet not I, but Christ liveth in me: and the life which I now live in the flesh I live by the faith of the Son of God, who loved me, and gave himself for me.

Paul repeats the same point of verse 19, but with more detail. When Christ died on the cross, He carried our sins and paid our penalty. When we put our full trust and confidence in Him, we identify ourselves with Him in that death. When we are *crucified with Christ,* we not only accept his death to pay the penalty for our sins, but we also agree to die to those sins (cf. Romans 6:2).

After Christ was crucified and buried, God gave him new life. Likewise, when we die with Christ and are buried with him, we are raised to new spiritual life. We *live,* and *Christ* lives *in* us. We still *live in the flesh,* but we walk by *faith* and *live* our lives for *the Son of God, who loved* us. It is only right that we should live for Him, because He *gave himself* for us (cf. Romans 6:3, 4). [See question #5, page 312.]

LAW'S CONDEMNATION

Eighteen-year-old Daniel Altstadt was an Eagle Scout and a good student in 1975. But then he murdered his parents and sister with a hatchet. He also attacked his brother, leaving him paralyzed with a severed spinal cord. Then he set the house on fire. All of this was done apparently to collect insurance money. A jury convicted him of first-degree murder of his father and decided that he was insane by the time he killed his mother and sister and attacked his brother.

Altstadt's attorney argued that the youth had snapped under the pressure of an overbearing and demanding father, whose laws for the family included even such things as how the children were to store their socks (toe-forward) in a drawer.

Twenty-five years later, Altstadt hanged himself in his prison cell. The laws laid down by his father had made him feel like an inferior person, and the laws of the state properly condemned him for his crime. He found no grace in either set of laws and could no longer live with himself.

The laws of our heavenly Father appropriately condemn us for our sinfulness, but fortunately for all of us, there is more to the story. The same God whose laws condemn us sent His Son to pay the penalty for us. What is demanded of us is that we willingly commit a form of spiritual "suicide." We are called upon to identify with Christ in His sacrificial death for us, so that we might also experience the new life that the risen Christ can give us. Giving up or even taking our own life cannot save us, but by willingly dying *to our sins*, we receive the gift of new life in Christ, a life no one can take away. —C. R. B.

D. Accepting God's Grace (v. 21)

21. I do not frustrate the grace of God: for if righteousness come by the law, then Christ is dead in vain.

Not even the finest saints of the Old Testament were able to live sinless lives. None of them ever made a perfect score on all the tests of life. If people had been able to achieve their own perfection, if *righteousness* did indeed *come by the law*, then there would have been no need for Jesus to die on the cross for them. If people could have saved themselves, then *Christ* would have been *dead in vain*.

Home Daily Bible Readings

Monday, Apr. 29—Grace in Christ (1 John 2:1-6)
Tuesday, Apr. 30—Commandment of Love (1 John 2:7-17)
Wednesday, May 1—Living According to the Spirit (1 Corinthians 8)
Thursday, May 2—Everything for the Glory of God (1 Corinthians 10:23-31)
Friday, May 3—Commissioned Through Jesus Christ (Galatians 1:1-5)
Saturday, May 4—Gospel Is Not of Human Origin (Galatians 1:11-24)
Sunday, May 5—Salvation by Faith, Not Works (Galatians 2:15-21)

Conclusion

After Paul established churches in Galatia, certain people began to corrupt the truth of the gospel. These Judaizers wrongly taught that people couldn't become Christians without first becoming Jews. They insisted on circumcision, keeping the Sabbath, and various dietary laws. In short, they taught that the sacrifice of Jesus was inadequate and people had to add their own virtuous works to pay the price of salvation.

A. No Other Gospel, Then or Now

Just as the Judaizers came to Galatia and tried to pervert the gospel, other people through the centuries have tried to change the gospel of Jesus Christ. Sometimes they claim special visions; sometimes they claim visits from angels; sometimes they claim to be so intelligent that they no longer need the Bible to teach them God's truth.

The challenge for the church is to stand up for the truth of the gospel. Just as the Christians in the very beginning, we must continue steadfastly in the apostles' doctrine (Acts 2:42). When we hear religious teachers, we must always compare their message with the gospel preached by the apostles, the absolute and exclusive truth heard by the church in the beginning.

B. The Gospel of Faith

The true gospel is the gospel of faith. It cannot be combined with legalism. We can put our trust in Jesus or we can put our trust in our own lawkeeping, but we cannot do both at the same time. We do not commend ourselves to God by actions that prove how good we are; instead, we depend on the atoning sacrifice of Jesus. We believe that His death on the cross can take the place of our own.

The true gospel is the gospel of faith. It is not a gospel of license. People who are saved by faith must live by faith. When we come to realize what Jesus did at the cross, we acknowledge that sin is ugly and unacceptable to God. When we have our sins washed away by the precious blood of the Lamb, we are not eager to rush back to our old defilement. We do not freely continue in sin and simply charge the debt to Jesus. This would make a mockery of the price He paid to set us free.

C. Prayer

Father, thank You for saving us through the death of Jesus on the cross. Help us cling to the cross for our salvation. Show us how to let Jesus live His life in us. In His name, Amen.

D. Thought to Remember

The one true gospel is the gospel of faith.

Learning by Doing

This page contains an alternate lesson plan emphasizing learning activities.
Classes desiring such student involvement will find these suggestions helpful.

Learning Goals

After participating in this lesson, each student will be able to:

1. Relate what Paul told the Galatians about the essence and the uniqueness of the gospel.

2. Contrast the true gospel with counterfeits both ancient and modern.

3. Examine one's life for any threats of legalism, and suggest a means by which to be guided by God's grace.

Into the Lesson

Bring to class a number of monetary bills from Monopoly® or other game sets. You could also make your own five-, ten-, twenty-, and hundred-dollar bills by cutting strips of green construction paper and putting the appropriate numbers on them. Divide your class into groups of four. Ask each group to examine the money and tell you whether it is real money. (Asking the question about a counterfeit assumes that there is a "real" bill.)

Ask one or two people in each group to place a real five- or ten-dollar bill in their hand. Now ask each group to list some differences between the counterfeits and the real. *(Answers may include size, feel, color, wording.)* Next ask, "What is the effect of real as opposed to the counterfeit?" *(Possible answers include a person won't be arrested for using the real and it's worth more.)*

After several have answered, share this: "The Treasury Department trains its agents to recognize counterfeit currency by having them diligently study authentic currency. Today, as we study Galatians 1 and 2, we will look for the marks of the real gospel as Paul teaches it."

Into the Word

Your students need to understand the seriousness of Paul's concern in Galatians. Develop a short lecture from the material in the commentary Introduction (page 306).

The following activity can be done with the whole class or in groups of five or six, depending on the time. Each will need a copy of the text.

Have students put a check mark (✔) by the verses that show Paul's concern about mixing the law and the gospel. If you use groups, assign the Scripture as follows: Group 1, Galatians 1:1-12; Group 2, Galatians 1:13-24; Group 3, Galatians 2:1-14; Group 4, Galatians 2:15-21.

Say, "From the verses you have marked, we can see the characteristics Paul notes for the gospel. In your groups, list the characteristics given." On the chalkboard or on an overhead transparency make a list of the characteristics as developed by the groups. This will certainly include such attributes as *unique, revealed, true, impartial,* and *superior.* Your discussion also should include Paul's argument about how the gospel was given to Paul (by revelation, not invented or passed on to him by human agents).

Using this list and the information in the commentary, develop a brief lecture concerning the counterfeit gospel with which Paul contended. Include comments on the Judaizers and their challenge to incorporate more than God's design of the gospel.

Into Life

After your lecture, ask the class to return to their groups. Have each group list two or three counterfeits to the gospel today. *(Their answers may include the formation of cults, the desire to be good enough for God, or a list of dos and don'ts to be a Christian. See also the Conclusion in the lesson commentary, opposite page.)* Help the class to recognize that we are talking about salvation issues, not about pursuing righteousness (as we learned in the book of Romans).

On strips of paper, print Galatians 2:16. Hand a strip to each member of the class. In their groups, individuals are to indicate ways in which we are tempted to justify ourselves by law. On the back of his or her strip, each class member is to write one or two ways. *(These may include keeping the Ten Commandments, tithing, attending church, or serving as a church officer.)* Ask the learners to write the international sign for "no" (a circle with a diagonal line within the circle) over the ways they have chosen. (A similar activity is included in the student book, *Adult Bible Class.*)

Pass out index cards to each member. Have them print Galatians 2:20 on the card. If there is time in class, encourage the students to begin the process of memorizing the verse. Challenge them to keep this verse in a prominent place for the next several days so that their lives are guided by the grace of God.

Close the class by having one person in each group pray for strength to live the life of faith.

Let's Talk It Over

The questions on this page are designed to encourage review of the lesson Scriptures and to promote discussion of the lesson by the class. The answers provided are only discussion starters. Let your class talk it over from there.

1. Paul marveled that the Galatians would abandon the gospel for a code of legalism. What surprises you about people's rejection of the gospel? How can the issues in question be addressed to call people back to the truth?

Paul's surprise was that people who had found the freedom of the gospel would want to return to their old ways. Surely that is one of the surprising things your students will note as well. How can people who have testified to how much better following Christ is than their old way of life return to that old way? Too often, the issue turns out to be a coldness on the part of other Christians. The new believer is not supported in the new way of life and returns to the old out of a need for companionship. What a tragedy!

2. Paul's condemnation of any who would preach another gospel is way out of step with current views of "tolerance" and acceptance of variant viewpoints. What charges are likely to be leveled against a person or church who takes a public stand for the one true gospel today? How can we answer these charges?

Christians are labeled bigots and hatemongers for teaching that there is only one way of salvation. They are called ignorant and superstitious because of their belief in Heaven and Hell, in the deity of Christ, and in the authority of the Bible. The only way to address such issues is to behave in such a way as to put the accusers to shame (1 Peter 3:16). Of course, some of the accusers will not feel ashamed; the attacks will continue. In that case, we can only endure it in hope, looking to Jesus (Hebrews 12:1-11).

3. What is the significance for us today that Paul received the gospel he preached by revelation? How does this fact apply to situations in which churches seek to change certain doctrines to be more "contemporary" or "politically correct"?

The fact that the gospel was given by revelation is extremely significant, but not always appreciated by some believers. It indicates that we follow the Lord Himself, not simply some human interpretation of who God is. It means we have an authoritative source for our faith and practice. If the gospel—indeed, all the Bible—was given by inspiration and revelation, then we dare not change it. Councils and synods and other assemblies may meet to debate many issues, but none of them has the right to change what has been divinely given in God's Word. We may meet to discuss how to interpret or apply those teachings, but we have no authority to determine that portions of God's Word are no longer to be taught because they are not "popular" with our culture. We dare not say, "Paul saw things this way, but we understand things better now."

4. To accept the idea of being justified by faith, one must admit to being a sinner, one who needs to be justified. How might this concept, if better understood, refute the objections of those who accuse Christians of thinking they are better than other people? How can we make this point effectively?

One of the most-used excuses for not participating in church activities is that the unbeliever is "just as good as" someone in the church. Highly publicized episodes of moral impropriety by well-known Christian leaders become special opportunities to label church members as hypocritical and "no better than the rest of us."

And we can agree! We are no better than any other sinner. We know we are flawed and that we give in to temptation. Our message is not, "Be as good as we are." Our message is, "We are all sinners. Come find the solution to the sin problem—Jesus Christ—before it's too late!"

5. What are some ongoing evidences that one has been "crucified with Christ"? How is such a person different from those who have not been so united with Christ in His death?

Evidences of a Christian's crucifixion with Christ include a rejection of the old way of life (after all, it has been buried), a rejection of the kind of life that we would have embraced had we not accepted Christ, refusal to love or join in what the world enjoys (1 John 2:15-17), a willingness to sacrifice our own well-being for others (just as Jesus sacrificed Himself for us on the cross), an obedience in taking up our crosses and following Him daily, and an ongoing repentance, renewal, and transformation (Romans 12:1, 2). If we've truly been crucified with Christ and live by faith in the Son of God, everyone should be able to see the difference.

Gospel of Adoption

DEVOTIONAL READING: Galatians 4:21-31.

BACKGROUND SCRIPTURE: Galatians 3, 4.

PRINTED TEXT: Galatians 3:6-9, 23—4:7.

Galatians 3:6-9, 23-29

6 Even as Abraham believed God, and it was accounted to him for righteousness.

7 Know ye therefore that they which are of faith, the same are the children of Abraham.

8 And the Scripture, foreseeing that God would justify the heathen through faith, preached before the gospel unto Abraham, saying, In thee shall all nations be blessed.

9 So then they which be of faith are blessed with faithful Abraham.

. . . .

23 But before faith came, we were kept under the law, shut up unto the faith which should afterward be revealed.

24 Wherefore the law was our schoolmaster to bring us unto Christ, that we might be justified by faith.

25 But after that faith is come, we are no longer under a schoolmaster.

26 For ye are all the children of God by faith in Christ Jesus.

27 For as many of you as have been baptized into Christ have put on Christ.

28 There is neither Jew nor Greek, there is neither bond nor free, there is neither male nor female: for ye are all one in Christ Jesus.

29 And if ye be Christ's, then are ye Abraham's seed, and heirs according to the promise.

Galatians 4:1-7

1 Now I say, That the heir, as long as he is a child, differeth nothing from a servant, though he be lord of all;

2 But is under tutors and governors until the time appointed of the father.

3 Even so we, when we were children, were in bondage under the elements of the world:

4 But when the fulness of the time was come, God sent forth his Son, made of a woman, made under the law,

5 To redeem them that were under the law, that we might receive the adoption of sons.

6 And because ye are sons, God hath sent forth the Spirit of his Son into your hearts, crying, Abba, Father.

7 Wherefore thou art no more a servant, but a son; and if a son, then an heir of God through Christ.

GOLDEN TEXT: Ye are all the children of God by faith in Christ Jesus.
—Galatians 3:26.

The Power of the Gospel
Unit 3: No Other Gospel
(Lessons 10-13)

Lesson Aims

After participating in this lesson, each student will be able to:

1. Explain the word pictures used by Paul in this passage to describe what Jesus has done for us.

2. Relate some of the blessings and responsibilities that come with being adopted into God's family.

3. Suggest a specific way in which a Christian's life can better reflect his or her standing as an adopted child of God.

Lesson Outline

INTRODUCTION
    A. Who Will Inherit?
    B. Lesson Background
 I. BLESSED WITH ABRAHAM (Galatians 3:6-9)
    A. Example of Faith (v. 6)
    B. Following the Example (v. 7)
    C. Blessed Through Faith (vv. 8, 9)
      A Rich Legacy
 II. UNITED WITH CHRIST (Galatians 3:23-29)
    A. Brought to Christ (vv. 23-25)
    B. Joined With Christ (vv. 26, 27)
    C. Equal Heirs in Christ (vv. 28, 29)
III. ADOPTED BY GOD (Galatians 4:1-7)
    A. A Child's Situation (vv. 1, 2)
    B. A Slave's Situation (v. 3)
    C. Adoption (vv. 4, 5)
      A Touching Story of Adoption
    D. Inheritance (vv. 6, 7)
CONCLUSION
A. We Are Adopted
B. We Will Inherit
C. Prayer
D. Thought to Remember

Introduction

A. Who Will Inherit?

It is often said, "Where there's a will, there's a way." It is also often said, "Where there's a will, there are relatives!" When it is time to divide a rich estate, long-lost friends and relatives sometimes come crawling out of the woodwork. Despite what the will says, they often try to force each other out of the inheritance and claim it all for themselves.

The Judaizers in Galatia were creating trouble for the church by teaching that some of the Christians could not inherit the blessings of God. They said that if a man were not circumcised, he was not eligible to be called a child of God. Trusting Jesus, they declared, was not enough. A man had to earn the right to his heavenly inheritance!

In the eyes of the false teachers, Gentile Christians were like unwanted orphans. Unless they submitted to circumcision and lived like Jews, they were not welcome in God's family. Paul had to step in and put a stop to such nonsense. As the appointed spokesman for the Lord, Paul became like a probate court. He had the authority to declare who was and who was not a legitimately recognized heir of God.

The irony of all this is that no one—Jew or Gentile—deserves to be in God's family or can earn the right to share in the inheritance. All of us were outsiders, strangers, rebels, and enemies. But God did not reject us as unwanted orphans; He had a plan for our salvation. From the time of Adam, God was preparing to accept and bless His people. The inheritance would not come through family bloodline or personal merit—it would come through Christ.

B. Lesson Background

The lessons in this series have dealt with the power of the gospel, emphasizing the role of faith. Last week the scene shifted to Galatia, where Paul had planted churches on his first missionary journey. After he left, the truth of the gospel began to be perverted by false teachers. They minimized the value of faith in Christ. They insisted that His sacrifice on the cross was not enough to pay the price for sin; people also had to earn approval by keeping the Old Testament laws. Today's lesson goes to the heart of this issue: Who will be approved to receive the blessings of God?

I. Blessed With Abraham
(Galatians 3:6-9)

A. Example of Faith (v. 1)

1. Even as Abraham believed God, and it was accounted to him for righteousness.

In the verses leading up to this statement, Paul began a series of arguments to show that the blessings of salvation do not come by works of law. The Holy Spirit, for example, did not come upon the believers in Galatia when they kept the law, but when they believed in Christ (v. 5).

Likewise, Abraham can be put on the side of faith, rather than on the side of works of law. When Abraham was already an old man, God made him an incredible promise about future offspring and blessings. Against all reason, *Abraham believed God* and his faith *was accounted to him* as *righteousness* (Genesis 15:6). He had the kind of faith that would agree to be circumcised; it was the kind of faith that would obey the command to offer up his son Isaac. In this important historical precedent God showed that the people who would share His blessings were the people of faith, like Abraham.

B. Following the Example (v. 7)

7. Know ye therefore that they which are of faith, the same are the children of Abraham.

For nearly two thousand years the Jews had taken pride in the fact that they had descended from Abraham (cf. John 8:33, 39). Through Isaac, Jacob, and Jacob's twelve sons, the tribes of Israel had the blood of Abraham coursing through their veins. Some thought this alone made them favored by God.

The true *children of Abraham*, however, are those who *are of faith*. They are the people who believe God just as Abraham did. Even when God makes a promise that seems too good to be true, people who are like Abraham will trust what He says. When God says that the penalty for all our sins is covered by the blood of His Son, we have glad confidence that it is so. [See question #1, page 320.]

C. Blessed Through Faith (vv. 8, 9)

8. And the Scripture, foreseeing that God would justify the heathen through faith, preached before the gospel unto Abraham, saying, In thee shall all nations be blessed.

It was God's plan from the beginning to save the world *through faith*, not works. This was shown by God's statement in *the Scripture* that promised Abraham that *all nations* would *be blessed* in him. The Greek word for *nations* here is the same word rendered *heathen* just before. It refers to people groups more than political boundaries. In fact, it is the root for our English word *ethnic*. It typically refers to the Gentiles, meaning any or all non-Jewish people groups.

God's promise to Abraham was a preview, a beautiful glimpse in advance, of the good news of salvation in Christ. In effect, this simple promise *preached . . . the gospel* to Abraham long *before* it ever came to pass. As Jesus told the Jews in Jerusalem, "Abraham rejoiced to see my day" (John 8:56). [See question #2, page 320.]

9. So then they which be of faith are blessed with faithful Abraham.

There are two kinds of people who will one day stand before their final Judge. The first will try to stand on their own merit, trusting that they have done a good enough job of keeping the law

and piling up good works. The others will be the people *of faith*. They will depend on the blood of Jesus shed on the cross to pay the penalty for their sins. When they put their faith in Jesus, they are doing the same as *faithful Abraham* and will be *blessed* by God with him.

A RICH LEGACY

Osgood, Indiana, is a rather unremarkable town. Fewer than two thousand people live within its two-and-a-half square miles. Among its citizens were two apparently common people, lifelong residents of Osgood—Gilmore Reynolds and his faithful wife, Goldie. They were frugal people, investing carefully and wisely in the stock market. Little did anyone guess what a blessing to their community this couple would become.

The Reynolds had no children, so they decided to help others when they could. From time to time, the town treasurer would receive a large check from the couple, but always with the stipulation that the gift was to be strictly anonymous (even the one hundred thousand dollars given for a new town hall).

Gilmore died in 1990, and Goldie in 1998. Their whole estate—twenty-three million dollars—was left to the town of Osgood. The gift exceeded the total assessed valuation of the whole town! So now, Osgood is being blessed by the marvelous gift of Gilmore and Goldie Reynolds.

Abraham may have seemed an unremarkable person to his neighbors back in Ur of Chaldees where he had grown up. But his faithful obedience to God resulted in great blessings to him. Even more so, his faithfulness was the basis of the fulfillment of a promise God had made when He called Abraham to follow wherever God would lead. The result is a blessing for all of us:

Visual for lessons 2 and 11. *This poster illustrates the one way for anyone to be justified: "by faith." Have it on display as you begin the lesson.*

the faith of that one man (and of his wife who went with him) has become the basis for people of every nation and era to inherit the riches of the kingdom of God.   —C. R. B.

II. United With Christ (Galatians 3:23-29)
A. Brought to Christ (vv. 23-25)

23. But before faith came, we were kept under the law, shut up unto the faith which should afterward be revealed.

In the days of the Old Testament *before* God's people had *faith* in Christ, they were *kept under* guard by *the law.* They were like prisoners *shut up* until a distant day of release. Though some of them caught a glimpse of what was coming, full knowledge of God's plan and *faith* in Christ would only *be revealed* later.

24, 25. Wherefore the law was our schoolmaster to bring us unto Christ, that we might be justified by faith. But after that faith is come, we are no longer under a schoolmaster.

God had used *the law* as a *schoolmaster* for His children in Old Testament times. We should not think of this as a modern schoolteacher, for Paul's word meant a slave who was put in charge of the master's son. This slave was a male "nanny" of sorts, whose job was to watch over the child's behavior and to escort the child to and from school. This "child attendant" did not teach.

Just as the job of this schoolmaster was to take the children to the real teacher, the ultimate purpose of the law was *to bring us unto Christ.* And when the minor child comes of age, the law is *no longer* in charge (see 4:1-7 below). Once the law had fulfilled its schoolmaster role in pointing to Christ, leading people to put their *faith* in Him, its supervisory function ceased. Christians, then, whether Jewish or Gentile, are not under the law. The coming of Christ in the fullness of time (4:4) brings an end to the law's custodianship.

B. Joined With Christ (vv. 26, 27)

26. For ye are all the children of God by faith in Christ Jesus.

It was a high privilege for the Gentiles to be counted as "children of Abraham" (v. 7). Now, an even higher status is announced for them. Whether their family tree was made of Jews or Gentiles, they *all* were *the children of God* as well. God was their father, and His parenthood was not established by any human bloodline, but by their *faith in Christ Jesus.*

27. For as many of you as have been baptized into Christ have put on Christ.

At the first public preaching of the gospel after Jesus' ascension, the proclamation of the apostles was that people who believed in Jesus were to be baptized (Acts 2:38). The apostles certainly did not view having *been baptized* as a magic ritual or work of merit. Instead, baptism was the "point in time" when they *put on Christ.* This new identity in Him became more important than their own; His will replaced their will. Once they had been dressed in the filthy rags of their own unworthy deeds; now that they had put on Christ, they were clothed in the white robes of His righteousness (cf. Isaiah 61:10; Revelation 7:9).

C. Equal Heirs in Christ (v. 28, 29)

28. There is neither Jew nor Greek, there is neither bond nor free, there is neither male nor female: for ye are all one in Christ Jesus.

In the Old Testament world of the Jews, the right to inherit was not given to Gentiles, to slaves, or to women. An ancient Jewish prayer even said, "Lord, I thank thee that Thou hast not made me a Gentile, or a slave, or a woman." But things change in Christ! When sinners repent and come into the family of God through faith and baptism (v. 27), their nationality does not matter. Whether *Jew* or *Greek,* they are equally acceptable to God, who adopts them and gives them the full rights of inheritance. Similarly, neither their social standing *(bond* or *free)* nor their gender *(male* or *female)* matters. God welcomes all people at the foot of the cross and loves them all equally.

Keep in mind that God's family is not made up of "natural" children and "outsider" children. We are *all one in Christ Jesus* (cf. Romans 9:8). Whatever our color, our wealth, or our background, we all come into God's family on equal footing. Because God has welcomed us, we must welcome each other. [See question #3, page 320.]

29. And if ye be Christ's, then are ye Abraham's seed, and heirs according to the promise.

Paul now slams the door shut on the Judaizers. They tried to require circumcision (and other

---

How to Say It

ABBA. *Ab*-buh.
ABRAHAM. *Ay*-bruh-ham.
ARAMAIC. *Air*-uh-*may*-ik (strong accent on *may*).
JUDAIZERS. *Joo*-duh-ize-ers (strong accent on *Joo*).
CHALDEES. *Kal*-deez.
MEDITERRANEAN. *Med*-uh-tuh-*ray*-nee-un (strong accent on *ray*).
SYNAGOGUE. *sin*-uh-gog.
UR. Er.

legal observances) of those who wished to "join" them in being *Abraham's seed*. But those who are in Christ are part of that seed already and, by extension, *heirs* of eternal life.

III. Adopted by God
(Galatians 4:1-7)

A. A Child's Situation (vv. 1, 2)

1. Now I say, That the heir, as long as he is a child, differeth nothing from a servant, though he be lord of all;

The Gentiles in Galatia who have become Christians must not add circumcision to the gospel and thereby revert back to Judaism. The Jew of the Old Testament was like an infant in the family of God. He was potentially an *heir* but could not enjoy inheritance rights because he was not of age—he was *a child,* still under the schoolmaster (3:24). A little child may one day grow up and become *lord of all* the estate, but in the meantime he is no better than *a servant.*

2. But is under tutors and governors until the time appointed of the father.

The child who is too young and immature to handle an inheritance will be placed under the care of *tutors and governors.* Throughout his childhood he is at the bottom rung of the ladder of authority, since even the slaves in the household tell him what to do. The child will continue to be treated as a child, with no access to his inheritance, *until the time* comes which was *appointed* by his *father* for the child's coming of age.

B. A Slave's Situation (v. 3)

3. Even so we, when we were children, were in bondage under the elements of the world.

Looking back on his own Jewish ancestry, Paul described how he and his people were mere *children* in God's family. As children they could not obtain their inheritance; in fact, they were no better than slaves. They were held *in bondage* by the law, enslaved under the *elements* (elementary principles) that differed little from *dos* and *don'ts* anywhere in the pagan *world. (Elements* may also refer to the demonic bondage that enslaved the Galatian Gentiles before they heard the gospel.)

To revert to Judaism was to become both an immature child and a slave. How could anyone in the Galatian churches want this? Why would they think that was progress?

C. Adoption (vv. 4, 5)

4. But when the fulness of the time was come, God sent forth his Son, made of a woman, made under the law.

God the Father had His timetable for the master plan of salvation. In the *fulness of the time* the stage was set for the gospel. Greece had provided a common language for the Mediterranean world; Rome had provided a time of peace and a good road system. Jewish synagogues and copies of the Old Testament in Greek were already found in all the major cities. God had the world ready to hear—and spread—the gospel.

Then God *sent forth his Son* to join the human race and die for our sins. Jesus was born *of a woman* and had to live *under the law.* The Son of God became also the Son of Man. Jesus stooped down to experience all the temptations and hardships that we face. [See question #4, page 320.]

5. To redeem them that were under the law, that we might receive the adoption of sons.

Having lived a sinless life, Jesus could offer His life as a ransom *to redeem* lost sinners. He paid the price to buy out of bondage those who were still held *under the law* (Mark 10:45). Jesus' death makes it possible for each of us to *receive the adoption* into God's family. All Christians—including Gentiles, slaves, and females—are given the full inheritance rights that belong to *sons.*

If the Christians in Galatia turn back to keeping law in a futile attempt to earn God's favor, they are returning to slavery. After God has rescued them from spiritual poverty and has washed them clean in the blood of Christ, why should they be trying to sneak back to their old helpless existence? Instead, they should be grateful that God has welcomed them into His family.

A TOUCHING STORY OF ADOPTION

A wild mallard hen felt so much at home in the marina at Redondo Beach, California, that in two different years she chose the *Gypsea,* a sailboat moored there, for the site of her nest. She found a compartment on the deck that was to her liking, and there she hatched her clutch of seven eggs. When the father duck died after the ducklings were hatched, another drake adopted the family and patrolled the dock leading to the sailboat, keeping watch over his adopted family.

The owners of the Gypsea, Donald and Winifred Sudduth, also adopted the family of ducks. They accepted the inconvenience and cost of keeping the boat docked until the ducklings were mature enough to swim (or fly) away. Up to that point, the Sudduths provided food and a plastic washtub so the ducklings could eat and learn to swim.

We usually think of adoption as a relationship that exists between humans. As we have seen, it may exist between animals or between humans and animals. However, the most touching story of adoption ever told concerns God's reaching out to sinners. Although we were unworthy, God accepted the inconvenience of assuming care for any of us who is willing to become part of His family.

And yet, how insufficient a word *inconvenience* is to describe this action of adoption. This costly adoption was accomplished by Christ's willing sacrifice of His life so that all who wish may become a part of God's family. And we have full rights as heirs to all the heavenly blessings that our Father possesses!   —C. R. B.

D. Inheritance (vv. 6, 7)

6. And because ye are sons, God hath sent forth the Spirit of his Son into your hearts, crying, Abba, Father.

God has not only sent forth His Son into the world (v. 4), He has also *sent forth the Spirit of His Son* into our *hearts*. The indwelling of the Holy Spirit in us is God's down payment, or first installment, of the inheritance we will receive in Heaven (see Ephesians 1:13, 14).

The Holy Spirit in our hearts becomes our link to the Father. The Spirit helps us when we pray (see Romans 8:26), enabling us even to address God as *Abba, Father* (also Romans 8:15). The word *Abba* is Aramaic (the native language of Palestine) and was what a child called his or her father in the intimacy of the family circle.

7. Wherefore thou art no more a servant, but a son; and if a son, then an heir of God through Christ.

Paul has used two different figures of speech to illustrate what a person is like before coming to Christ. The Jews were like very young children; both Jews and Gentiles were like slaves. But in Christ a person is no longer *a servant*, but a *son* in God's family. Even more than this, the *son* is no longer a legally incompetent infant, but *an heir of God*. [See question #5, page 320.]

Conclusion

A. We Are Adopted

Adoption is a wonderful thing. Loving parents open their arms to children who are unable to fend for themselves and have nowhere else to turn, providing the love and security of family.

Some children are orphaned by war or famine. Other children need adoption because their parents cannot or will not provide for them. In our case, we were homeless by our own choice—we had chosen to abandon God. Homeless, helpless, enslaved by sin, we had no way to survive.

But God loved us in spite of ourselves. He set forth the gospel of adoption, the "good news" that Jesus has paid our debts and God has claimed us as His children. Though it is a humbling thing to realize, except for the grace of God we were unwanted and unwelcome.

God adopted us totally apart from any worth or value we could offer. We were not cuter or smarter than other orphans; we did nothing to earn His approval. He freely extended His goodwill to us at the cross. Whoever will join Him there and accept His free offer of salvation in Christ can become His child forever.

B. We Will Inherit

With adoption comes the right to inherit. Our loving Father has generously included us as heirs of eternal salvation. The promise made to Abraham also is extended to us, when we become his offspring through faith in Christ.

In Christ we already are beginning to enjoy the benefits of our inheritance. We have the load of past guilt and shame lifted from our shoulders. We are free from the fear that Satan will find us and take us back to our former squalor and deprivation. The Holy Spirit has come to reside in our hearts as God's guarantee that He will follow through with all of our inheritance.

Finally, we will inherit eternal life in Heaven. In the Father's house are many mansions, plenty of dwelling places for all of us. Like little urchins who have slept in alleys and trash bins, our eyes will be wide with wonder at the beauty of our new home. Best of all, Heaven will bring us into the very presence of God and Jesus.

C. Prayer

Abba, Father. Thank You for adopting us as Your very own children and giving us an eternal inheritance in Heaven. Help us to be grateful for everything You have done for us.

D. Thought to Remember

Because we have put on Christ, we are heirs of the promises of God.

Home Daily Bible Readings

Monday, May 6—One Body, One Bread (1 Corinthians 10:14-22)
Tuesday, May 7—All Gentiles Shall Be Blessed (Galatians 3:1-9)
Wednesday, May 8—Receive the Promise Through Faith (Galatians 3:10-14)
Thursday, May 9—Heirs According to the Promise (Galatians 3:19-29)
Friday, May 10—No Longer Slaves, But Heirs (Galatians 4:1-7)
Saturday, May 11—Do Not Turn Back (Galatians 4:8-16)
Sunday, May 12—Freedom in Christ (Galatians 4:17—5:1)

Learning by Doing

This page contains an alternate lesson plan emphasizing learning activities.
Classes desiring such student involvement will find these suggestions helpful.

Learning Goals

After participating in this lesson, each student will be able to:

1. Explain the word pictures used by Paul in this passage to describe what Jesus has done for us.

2. Relate some of the blessings and responsibilities that come with being adopted into God's family.

3. Suggest a specific way in which a Christian's life can better reflect his or her standing as an adopted child of God.

Into the Lesson

Distribute a sheet of ledger paper to each student. (A package can be bought at most office supply stores, or you can make a ledger sheet by making vertical lines on a sheet of regular ruled notebook paper.) At the top of the sheet have the person write his or her name along with the heading, "Personal Ledger Sheet." (This activity is included in the student book, *Adult Bible Class.*)

Have each person label four columns: "Items," "Expenses," "Credits," "Balance." Each person will then choose five monthly expenses to enter in the Items column, such as utilities, groceries, insurance, car expenses, and rent. The student should then enter monetary values in the next three columns for each item in such amounts that the balance is *negative.*

Have two volunteers tell their expenses and balances. After each one shares, say, "I give you a credit equal to one dollar over your expenses."

Ask the class, "What is necessary for the credit I offered to be effective?" *(Answers include the creditor's truthfulness and assets, the debtor's belief in the creditor, and the reputation of the creditor.)* Ask, "How would you feel if someone credited your account with an amount to clear your bills and debts?"

Say, "Today's study will show us how God has brought us into His family, canceling our debt, and setting us up to succeed as His child."

Into the Word

To provide background for today's text, recruit a class member to develop remarks from the Introduction to today's lesson (page 314).

Then divide the class into groups of five or six participants. Give half the groups the "Group One" assignment; the other half "Group Two." Provide a large sheet of poster paper, pencils, and markers for each group. Answering the questions will help each group understand Jesus' work on our behalf.

Group One: Read Galatians 3:1-14, and answer the following questions. Create a "before and after" poster to depict what Jesus has done for us.

1. What was the basis of the Galatians' struggle? *(Seeking God's approval by performing God's law or believing His message.)*

2. How was Abraham considered righteous? *(By believing the message of God.)*

3. What did Jesus do for us to overcome the problem of our being unable to earn our right standing with God? *(He was hung on a tree to be our sacrifice, our curse, to satisfy God's justice.)*

Group Two: Read Galatians 3:23—4:7, and answer the following questions. Create a "before and after" poster to depict what Jesus has done for us.

1. How is the law like the overseers of children? *(The child needs to be taught, directed, and cared for. The law could do that for people.)*

2. How does Paul show that all are a part of Abraham's family? *(By being joined or belonging to Christ.)*

3. According to this text, who are sons of God? *(Those who have put on Christ, who through faith have been baptized into Christ.)*

Let each group explain its poster as they repeat the answers to the questions.

Into Life

Give these instructions: "Using your ledger sheet, this time fill in several lines of what you have done to fail God's standards. For example, under 'Items' you could write 'told a lie' or 'looked lustfully at a woman (or man) or a photograph of one.' After you have written several lines, write 'paid in full—Galatians 3, 4' across the lines. This represents what Christ has done for us."

Have the class brainstorm blessings and responsibilities that are implications of being adopted into God's family, such as being called *son,* having direct access to the Father, obeying the Father, and telling others the good news.

Encourage each person to find a partner. The partners will then share what they will do this week so that their lives will reflect their adoptive status with God. They are to tell their partners, then pray silently. Close in prayer.

Let's Talk It Over

The questions on this page are designed to encourage review of the lesson Scriptures and to promote discussion of the lesson by the class. The answers provided are only discussion starters. Let your class talk it over from there.

1. Paul's remark that the Gentile Galatians could be children of Abraham was a revolutionary concept. Who do you think found it more surprising, the Jews or the Gentiles? Why?

Orthodox Jews prided themselves in having descended directly from Abraham and in the covenant that God initiated with him. Those who had become Christians knew that the Old Covenant was not sufficient for salvation. But some of them, like the Judaizers, thought it was a necessary prerequisite for grace. For them, Paul's remark was surprising. They were so devoted to the old way that they failed to see that the covenant of grace completely superseded the old way. The Gentiles may have shared their surprise. They were so used to the idea of earning favor with God (or the gods, in their old pagan way of thinking) that the idea of being saved by grace through faith must have been surprising indeed.

2. Paul said the promise to Abraham, "In thee shall all nations be blessed," was a prediction of the inclusion of Gentiles in God's plan of redemption. Why, then, do you think the Jews as a whole missed that? What significance do you think that has for us today?

While promising a blessing for all nations, the law also specifically commanded separation of the Jews from other nations. This was intended to keep the Jews from adopting pagan practices and rituals and from deserting their covenant with God. They continually violated those precepts, falling into idolatry again and again. When they finally rejected pagan idolatry, they apparently focused exclusively on the separation issue and failed to see God's ultimate plan of inclusion.

The issue is significant for us because we are Gentiles, and it is this inclusiveness that brings us into God's family. Beyond that, however, the Jews' error suggests that we, too, might not be seeing all we should see in what God wants of us. We dare not become too self-satisfied in our discipleship. We might be missing something, too!

3. What do you find most significant about the inclusive language of verse 28? How should we demonstrate this truth?

If your church is in an area where racial tension has been prevalent, then the racial equality of this verse may be the most significant. Are all races equally welcome in your church? Does it show? What would it take to open your membership to people of other races?

How about the economic equality? Does everyone in your church represent the same economic group, or are several levels represented? What are you doing to reach people of differing levels of affluence? What do you think about churches deliberately "targeting" one demographic level? Is that in harmony with what Paul says here?

Is there good gender harmony in your church? Are women as well as men free to exercise their spiritual gifts? (Remember, this verse is concerned with acceptance into the body of Christ, not specific roles of those who are in it. Still, how people are allowed to serve may say something about how "welcome" they are.)

4. Paul said Jesus was born "in the fulness of time." How does God's timing give you comfort or reassurance today? Why?

Things may have looked rather bleak for the Jews in Palestine at the time Jesus was born. Roman occupation deprived them of freedom; Pharisaic legalism burdened them with impossible demands; corruption among the Sadducees tainted their worship. And yet, everything was falling into place for the Son of God to be born!

Failed marriages, political corruption, business failings or layoffs, diminished health, and many other problems may plague your students today. Still worse, prayers may seem to bounce off the ceiling, getting no response. But God is in control. In His time, He will bring blessings and answers to the perplexing questions of our day. It may be on the other side of eternity, but the time for vindication will come!

5. What characteristics do you think should be evident in the lives of the children of God?

Paul writes that the presence of the Holy Spirit is a result of our sonship. Paul also reminds us that the Spirit and our sonship allow us to address God as "Abba, Father," the Aramaic name used within the family. This should be expressed in a confident demeanor—we know our Father has things under control. The presence of the Spirit also should be evident in the fruit of the Spirit (Galatians 5:22-25). And we should be able to tell others of the hope we have (1 Peter 3:15).

Gospel of Freedom

Devotional Reading: 1 John 2:7-17.

Background Scripture: Galatians 5:1-15.

Printed Text: Galatians 5:1-15.

Galatians 5:1-15

1 Stand fast therefore in the liberty wherewith Christ hath made us free, and be not entangled again with the yoke of bondage.

2 Behold, I Paul say unto you, that if ye be circumcised, Christ shall profit you nothing.

3 For I testify again to every man that is circumcised, that he is a debtor to do the whole law.

4 Christ is become of no effect unto you, whosoever of you are justified by the law; ye are fallen from grace.

5 For we through the Spirit wait for the hope of righteousness by faith.

6 For in Jesus Christ neither circumcision availeth any thing, nor uncircumcision; but faith which worketh by love.

7 Ye did run well; who did hinder you that ye should not obey the truth?

8 This persuasion cometh not of him that calleth you.

9 A little leaven leaveneth the whole lump.

10 I have confidence in you through the Lord, that ye will be none otherwise minded: but he that troubleth you shall bear his judgment, whosoever he be.

11 And I, brethren, if I yet preach circumcision, why do I yet suffer persecution? then is the offense of the cross ceased.

12 I would they were even cut off which trouble you.

13 For, brethren, ye have been called unto liberty; only use not liberty for an occasion to the flesh, but by love serve one another.

14 For all the law is fulfilled in one word, even in this; Thou shalt love thy neighbor as thyself.

15 But if ye bite and devour one another, take heed that ye be not consumed one of another.

GOLDEN TEXT: For, brethren, ye have been called unto liberty; only use not liberty for an occasion to the flesh, but by love serve one another.—Galatians 5:13.

The Power of the Gospel
Unit 3: No Other Gospel
(Lessons 10-13)

Lesson Aims

After this lesson each student will be able to:

1. Explain how the gospel sets us free from the bondage to, and penalty of, the law.

2. Contrast Christian liberty with license.

3. Suggest some specific way to use Christian liberty to express love to some other person in the coming week.

Lesson Outline

INTRODUCTION
   A. Three Dangers
   B. Lesson Background
 I. DON'T GO BACK (Galatians 5:1-6)
   A. Stand Fast (v. 1)
     Living Free or Returning to Bondage?
   B. Reject Circumcision (vv. 2, 3)
   C. Don't Fall From Grace (vv. 4, 5)
   D. Put Faith to Work (v. 6)
 II. DON'T BE MISLED (Galatians 5:7-12)
   A. Those Who Mislead (vv. 7-9)
     Be Careful What You Swallow
   B. Penalty for False Teachers (v. 10)
   C. Conflict With False Teachers (vv. 11, 12)
III. DON'T MISUSE FREEDOM (Galatians 5:13-15)
   A. Love Is the Reason for Freedom (v. 13)
   B. Love Fulfills the Law (v. 14)
   C. Lack of Love Destroys (v. 15)
CONCLUSION
   A. The Love of Liberty
   B. The Liberty of Love
   C. Prayer
   D. Thought to Remember

Introduction

A. Three Dangers

On January 1, 1863, Abraham Lincoln issued the Emancipation Proclamation. By this decree he set free all the slaves of the Confederacy—at least in theory.

In actual fact, little was changed. Many of the slaves were not allowed to be told about the declaration. Even when they finally heard of it, they still were not free until the outcome of the Civil War was decided. After the war when the slaves actually were set free, many did not know how to use their newfound freedom. A few even returned to their former masters. They lived in the same slave quarters and worked like slaves in the same fields.

Freedom is of little value unless a person has learned how to claim it and keep it. Our freedom from the law has been provided by Jesus Christ, but it is not a freedom we can take for granted. There are at least three dangers that could cause us to forfeit the liberty that Christ purchased with His life's blood.

Danger #1: choosing to go back. When Christians agree to add circumcision to the requirements of the gospel and to be bound by other Old Testament laws, they are choosing to go back to the Old Covenant. When they think they have to earn God's favor by keeping such rules, they do not have enough faith in what Jesus did for them at the cross. When they try to justify themselves by works of law, they fall from the grace relationship they had in Christ. When they choose not to trust Jesus for their salvation, He can do nothing for them.

Danger #2: being tricked into going back. Few Christians would knowingly choose to exchange their freedom in Christ for the chains of legalism. Many, however, have been tricked into thinking this is what God wants them to do. False teachers have persuaded them that God requires them to earn their salvation by good works, acts of penance, and blind obedience to their authority. Even though keeping all the rules may seem like a good way to earn God's approval, the gospel of freedom says "No!"

Danger #3: going back to a new slavery. A different kind of danger is the temptation to misuse the freedom of the gospel and become a slave to one's own flesh. If a person is set free from the law, but then is still trapped in his or her own sinful appetites, that person is even worse off than before!

The gospel frees us from both the condemnation of the law and the grip of sinful selfishness. Since this freedom came at a heavy price—the blood of Jesus—we should treasure it and hold on to it. The goal of our freedom is not more sinning; the goal is faith working and serving through love.

B. Lesson Background

The two preceding lessons have addressed the problem of legalism versus grace in Galatia. After Paul had planted churches in Galatia, Judaizers came in and convinced some of the Christians there that they needed to be circumcised and to keep the Old Testament laws in order to be saved. The good news of the gospel, however, is that we are saved by faith in Christ (Galatians 2:16). When we are united with Christ, God adopts us into His family and makes us heirs of salvation.

I. Don't Go Back
(Galatians 5:1-6)
A. Stand Fast (v. 1)

1. Stand fast therefore in the liberty wherewith Christ hath made us free, and be not entangled again with the yoke of bondage.

Freedom must never be taken for granted. If people do not vigilantly guard their freedom, it will soon be taken from them. Similarly, Christians must *stand fast . . . in the liberty* of the gospel of grace. *Christ* shed His blood as the ransom price for our sins; His death has *made us* forever *free* from the chains of the law.

Freedom in Christ is more than just one of the "extras" Christians enjoy. It is a precious gift and a personal responsibility. If we appreciate what it cost Jesus to purchase our freedom, we will not easily surrender it. Instead, we will stand firm and not allow ourselves to become *entangled again* in slavery to rules and rituals. We must not bow our necks again to that *yoke of bondage* (cf. Acts 15:10). [See question #1, page 328.]

LIVING FREE OR RETURNING TO BONDAGE?

Maria Jeronimo died in June of 2000. She was considered by many to be the oldest woman in the world at the time of her death. She was not recognized as such by the *Guinness Book of Records*, since the publication demands a birth certificate or other irrefutable evidence. However, church records indicated that Jeronimo was 129 years old when she died.

Jeronimo had been born a slave in Brazil and was emancipated at the age of seventeen in 1888 when that nation became the last country in the Western Hemisphere to abolish slavery. But even as a free woman, Jeronimo continued to live in the same locale as before, doing the same kind of housemaid's work as she had done before she was freed.

Freedom did not erase the memories of slavery from Maria's mind. Even in her old age, she could recall life as a slave: the rapes, the frequent sicknesses, the families torn apart. Even after her mind faded in the last months of her life, her scarred back still bore testimony to the beatings she had received from her masters more than a century earlier. In her last interview (at age 127), she said she had only one wish left: "Now, I just want to see God." Maria Jeronimo was looking forward. She had reason not to want to go back.

When it comes to the slavery of sin, we carry with us the scars of our past. Strangely, many whom Christ has emancipated find themselves going back into the yoke of bondage instead of looking forward to the blessings and rewards of freedom that God has prepared for us. —C. R. B.

B. Reject Circumcision (vv. 2, 3)

2. Behold, I Paul say unto you, that if ye be circumcised, Christ shall profit you nothing.

Paul emphasizes how important his point is by making a formal statement: *Behold, I Paul say.* In the earlier chapters of Galatians he proved his authority to speak as an apostle. The gospel he preaches is the vital message they must heed. If they continue to compel believers to *be circumcised*, they are expressing a lack of faith in Christ. If they trust the law to save them, *Christ* will not be of any value or *profit*, because they do not have confidence in Him.

Paul's warning is not addressed to everyone who has ever been circumcised (cf. 1 Corinthians 7:18). Paul will plainly say that neither circumcision nor uncircumcision matters at all (v. 6). What is at issue here is the ongoing practice of the church to require the ritual as a step to salvation. This was a key point of dispute at the "Jerusalem Council" (cf. Acts 15:5, 10).

3. For I testify again to every man that is circumcised, that he is a debtor to do the whole law.

Again Paul gives solemn testimony that one who accepts circumcision must face the enormity of the mistake he is making. If a man has put his faith in Christ but then agrees to be *circumcised*, he is returning to the Old Covenant. By accepting the badge of that covenant, he becomes *a debtor* who is obligated to keep *the whole law.*

The false promise of legalism is that, by keeping a few selected laws, one can earn "extra credit" with God. In fact, however, the moment we decide we need to add the merit of lawkeeping to the sacrifice of Christ, we are obligated to keep all the laws (James 2:10). Either we can be saved by depending on the cross of Jesus, or we can try (in vain) to save ourselves by lawkeeping.

C. Don't Fall From Grace (vv. 4, 5)

4. Christ is become of no effect unto you, whosoever of you are justified by the law; ye are fallen from grace.

Christ becomes *of no effect* for the person who does not trust Him. He cannot save people who do not put their faith in Him, nor can He save people who put their faith in Him and then take it back.

Those who trust their own ability to keep laws and do not trust the promises of God have *fallen from grace.* Such a fall does not happen by accident, nor does it result from some moral failure. It happens when a person deliberately turns away from Jesus and depends on someone or something else for salvation. Such a person has lost confidence in Christ and is outside the grace of God.

5. For we through the Spirit wait for the hope of righteousness by faith.

Christians are a people of *hope*. That hope is a confident expectation. It is not based on any merit or goodness of our own, but on the *righteousness* of Christ that is imputed to us *by* our *faith* in Him. *Through* the inner strength of God's *Spirit* (see Ephesians 3:16), we confidently *wait for* the goal of that hope: a declaration of "not guilty" on the Judgment Day. [See question #2, page 328.]

D. Put Faith to Work (v. 6)

6. For in Jesus Christ neither circumcision availeth any thing, nor uncircumcision; but faith which worketh by love.

Paul would not have anyone think his standing with God to be based on a regulation that was part of the law that was nailed to the cross (Colossians 2:14). *Circumcision* has no power to save, and neither does *uncircumcision* (cf. 1 Corinthians 7:19). What matters, rather, is a person's present relationship with Christ.

The basis of that relationship is *faith* rather than law. But we must not think that real faith is merely an opinion about who Jesus is (cf. James 2:19). Real faith is always active faith; it *worketh by*—or "is energized by"—*love*. Stated differently, "Faith without works is dead" (James 2:26).

To distinguish between works of law and works of faith is vitally important. Works of law are futile attempts to keep every one of the commandments without a single failure, and by this means attain salvation. Works of faith are the result of already having been given salvation by God's grace. When faith is real and is motivated by love, it cannot help but produce fruit.

II. Don't Be Misled
(Galatians 5:7-12)

A. Those Who Mislead (vv. 7-9)

7. Ye did run well; who did hinder you that ye should not obey the truth?

When Paul preached the gospel in Galatia on his first missionary journey, many people became Christians. Congregations were started, and soon Paul was able to appoint elders in every city (see Acts 14:23). The Galatian Christians were off to a good start and were running *well*.

Then something went wrong. Someone stepped in to *hinder* their progress in the gospel.

Someone convinced them not to *obey the truth* that is in Jesus. Now Paul challenges them to identify and expose the false teachers.

8. This persuasion cometh not of him that calleth you.

This false *persuasion*, or way of thinking, did not come from God, who calls people to accept the gospel of grace. The Galatian Christians should remember how God had called them through the preaching of Paul, and how quickly they had turned away (Galatians 1:6). Then they should ask themselves why they had allowed anyone to lead them away from the salvation of the cross and take them back to the law.

BE CAREFUL WHAT YOU SWALLOW

An article by George Rector, a food column writer, in the *Saturday Evening Post* for September 5, 1936, recommended serving green salad in a wooden bowl. The article specified that the bowl was to be unvarnished, rubbed with a clove of garlic before the salad was placed in it, and never, *never* washed. Supposedly, this practice would "cure" the wood and each successive bowl of salad would be more delicious than the previous one.

So, for decades, hosts of American cooks followed Rector's advice, not knowing that they were victims of a hoax. Sometime in the 1960s, Rector admitted that he had invented the idea to give Americans some self-esteem in the preparation of food by (supposedly) doing it in the "French way." The French were considered by many Americans of that time (and this) to be the world's experts in the culinary arts. What Rector's readers did not know was that, instead of "curing" the wood, the salad dressing soaked into the pores of the wood, and since the bowls were never washed, they became saturated with rancid oil.

When those who are reputed to be experts lead us astray, there can be serious consequences for our health, whether physical or moral and spiritual. It was the latter kind of danger the Galatians found themselves in. By listening to false teachers, they were putting their souls at risk, turning away from faith in Christ to trust in works of the law. There are still teachers who would lead us astray. The moral of the story is that we should be careful of what we swallow, whether it is salad out of a rancid bowl or ideas from a false teacher. Both can hurt us. —C. R. B.

9. A little leaven leaveneth the whole lump.

A little leaven (yeast) can be a good thing or a bad thing. In the parables of the kingdom of Heaven, Jesus used the illustration of leaven to show what great things can come from small beginnings (Matthew 13:33). But if the influence of the leaven is bad, like that of the Pharisees and Sadducees, it can cause great evil and must be avoided (Matthew 16:6). The leaven of the Judaizers in Galatia was threatening to leaven *the whole lump,* by corrupting doctrine in the entire church. [See question #3, page 328.]

B. Penalty for False Teachers (v.10)

10. I have confidence in you through the Lord, that ye will be none otherwise minded: but he that troubleth you shall bear his judgment, whosoever he be.

In spite of the attempts of the Judaizers to pervert the truth of the gospel, Paul expresses *confidence* in his converts in Galatia. He trusts them to agree with him about salvation by grace, and he is sure that they will not be *otherwise minded.*

Every false teacher who troubles the church with false doctrine will *bear his judgment* from God. It does not matter if the person is rich or powerful, *whosoever* is perverting the truth is under the curse of God (cf. Galatians 1:8, 9; Jude 12, 13). The sacred truth of the gospel of freedom must be preserved!

C. Conflict With False Teachers (vv. 11, 12)

11. And I, brethren, if I yet preach circumcision, why do I yet suffer persecution? then is the offense of the cross ceased.

Some people claimed that Paul was inconsistent in his preaching. When he was among Jews, they said, he gladly enforced *circumcision* when it suited him. But when he was among Gentiles who might balk at such a command, he would change his message. In fact, however, Paul never required anyone to be circumcised as a matter of salvation.

Comparing the cases of Timothy and Titus is insightful. On one occasion, Paul had Timothy circumcised only because it was expedient in light of his future work in evangelizing Jews (Acts 16:3). But when certain "false brothers" demanded that Titus be circumcised, as a matter of salvation, Paul refused. To have allowed it would have invalidated the message of grace (Galatians 2:3-5).

Paul shows the obvious error of the false charge: if he still preaches *circumcision,* why does he *suffer persecution* from the Jews? If Paul had preached a gospel that combined law and grace, the stumbling block or *offense of the cross* would have been removed. Jews would not object to Jesus or the gospel if it were on their own terms.

12. I would they were even cut off which trouble you.

While Paul may have meant that such people should be *cut off* from the church, it is likely that he meant something more shocking. They who *trouble* the church by insisting on a partial cutting (circumcision) might just as well castrate themselves, as did the local priests who served the pagan goddess Cybele. One cannot mix the gospel with any other form of religion, whether pagan or Jewish. Perhaps if the false teachers considered their teachings in that ugly light, they would see the error of their way. Salvation is not attained through any cutting of the flesh.

III. Don't Misuse Freedom (Galatians 5:13-15)

A. Love Is the Reason for Freedom (v. 13)

13. For, brethren, ye have been called unto liberty; only use not liberty for an occasion to the flesh, but by love serve one another.

As *brethren* in Christ (see v. 11) Christians *have been called* into *liberty.* We have been invited to enjoy freedom from the demands of the law and from the guilt of sin. But after we have accepted this liberty, Satan still does not give up. He tempts us to exploit our liberty as *an occasion to* indulge *the flesh* (cf. Jude 4). However, Christ did not give us freedom from the law so that we could be more sinful (cf. Romans 6:1, 2).

We have been given our freedom so that we can utilize liberty in love. Because we are motivated *by love,* and not because we are under compulsion by the law's demands, we can *serve one another.* [See question #4, page 328.]

B. Love Fulfills the Law (v. 14)

14. For all the law is fulfilled in one word, even in this; Thou shalt love thy neighbor as thyself.

Everything *the law* tried to compel people to do *is fulfilled* in a single statement: *Love thy*

Visual for lesson 12

The visual for today reminds us of what a great blessing our freedom in Christ really is.

neighbor just as you love yourself. When a person loves his neighbor, he does not need to be told not to kill him. Neither does he need to be warned not to steal from him, lie to him, or take his wife away from him. Love covers all the situations better than any list of laws (cf. Luke 10:25-28; Romans 13:9).

Love is a better motivator than law for doing the right action. A husband who provides for his wife only because the law requires it will not be a very good husband. Sincere love will prompt him to do many things that law would not. In the same way, Christians who know the love of God should be motivated by that love to care about the needs of others (1 John 3:17). Just as we would not ignore our own need of food, clothing, or medicine, we should have the same concern for our neighbors.

The principle of loving others "as we love ourselves" is sometimes misunderstood. It does not mean that we must first have self-love, an unhealthy preoccupation with our own needs. Neither does it mean we should admire ourselves and find ways to boost our self-esteem. What it does mean is that we should care about meeting the needs of others, just as we naturally care about meeting our own needs. [See question #5, page 328.]

C. Lack of Love Destroys (v. 15)

15. But if ye bite and devour one another, take heed that ye be not consumed one of another.

If the members of the Christian community are not motivated by love, they may begin to act out of self-interest. Their backbiting and critical spirits will make them as dangerous as wild animals, trying to *bite and devour one another*. When the law of the jungle replaces the law of love in the church, precious souls are always lost.

Home Daily Bible Readings

Monday, May 13—Lead the Life the Lord Assigns You (1 Corinthians 7:17-24)
Tuesday, May 14—Am I Not Free? (1 Corinthians 9:1-12)
Wednesday, May 15—Free, But a Slave to All (1 Corinthians 9:15-23)
Thursday, May 16—New Birth Into Living Hope (1 Peter 1:3-12)
Friday, May 17—God's Servants Are Free People (1 Peter 2:11-17)
Saturday, May 18—Free From Fear (1 Peter 3:13-22)
Sunday, May 19—You Were Called to Freedom (Galatians 5:4-15)

Conclusion

A. The Love of Liberty

On Liberty Island in New York Harbor stands the Statue of Liberty. A poem inscribed at its base says, in part, "Give me your tired, your poor, your huddled masses, yearning to breathe free." Many refugees from the chains of dictatorship or economic slavery have felt the thrill of freedom upon seeing Miss Liberty welcome them to the land of opportunity.

A more important statue of liberty stood at a place called Golgotha. It was the cross of Jesus Christ. Christ's death on that cross paid the price to set us free from the law, from the penalty of death, from the power of sin. The good news of what Jesus accomplished there is the heart of the gospel of freedom.

We show our love for Christ when we honor the freedom that He died to give us. The love of Christ and the love of liberty go hand in hand. We must stand fast in the freedom that He has secured for us and refuse to be bound by Old Testament law as our means of salvation.

B. The Liberty of Love

People love to define Christianity as a set of restrictions: "You're a Christian; you can't. . . ." In their minds, our relationship to Christ is a matter of being trapped, even enslaved, in a tangled web of "Thou shalt nots." But that isn't what Christianity really is.

Christianity is freedom. The power of love allows us to live in liberty. Because we love God and all His children, we don't need the law of Moses to keep us in line. We are merciful to our neighbors because we ourselves have received mercy; we naturally want to do the right thing. The world does not understand this freedom, and ends up enslaved.

The gospel of freedom is the Emancipation Proclamation of Jesus Christ. He died to make us holy and free. Some may not yet have heard the good news; others may not know that this war already has been won. Many seem not to know how to live in His freedom. But we are "called unto liberty," so let us "stand fast therefore in the liberty wherewith Christ hath made us free."

C. Prayer

Our Father in Heaven, thank You for sending Your Son to make us free. Teach us to honor that freedom, and help us to understand how to live as free citizens of Your kingdom. In Jesus' name. Amen.

D. Thought to Remember

Stand fast in freedom!

Learning by Doing

This page contains an alternate lesson plan emphasizing learning activities.
Classes desiring such student involvement will find these suggestions helpful.

Learning Goals

After participating in this lesson, each student will be able to:

1. Explain how the gospel sets us free from the bondage to, and penalty of, the law.

2. Contrast Christian liberty with license.

3. Suggest some specific way to use Christian liberty to express love to some other person in the coming week.

Into the Lesson

Bring a picture or model of both the Statue of Liberty and a cross. Begin class by having students identify the statue; ask if they can quote the saying engraved on its base. (This quote is in the "Conclusion" section of the commentary.) Say, "Name some of the freedoms enjoyed by United States citizens." Record these responses.

Say, "In the late 1800s and early 1900s, immigrants arriving in New York by sea could see the Statue of Liberty. What do you suppose were their first impressions?" Allow time for response, and then ask the following questions: "How would coming to the United States change their lives? What were they leaving behind? What would they lose if they went back?"

Next display the cross. Ask, "What freedoms does the cross represent?" Record these answers.

Say, "In the same way that the Statue of Liberty represents freedom in the United States, the cross represents freedom for the Christian. What feelings and thoughts do you have when you see the cross? What things have you left behind? What would you lose if you went back to your life before you became a Christian?" Say, "Today as we study Galatians 5, we will see Paul argue for us to keep on track with the gospel of grace."

Into the Word

Develop a brief lecture using the Introduction from the commentary (page 322). Students will become aware of the struggles the Galatian Christians were facing. Your lecture will focus on the three dangers Paul articulates to the Galatians.

Give the following questions to each student. (They are also listed in *Adult Bible Class.)* Divide the class into groups of four to six. Tell the groups to call for answers, beginning with the person whose birthday is closest to today and then moving to the left. The answers (from Galatians 5) are indicated with verse numbers.

1. What does Paul say happens if we slip from Christ's freedom? *(We take up a yoke of bondage, v. 1. Christ has no value for our lives, v. 2.)*

2. What is the outcome of trying to be justified by law? *(Grace is no longer the grounds for our salvation, vv. 3, 4.)*

3. How do we share in Christ's righteousness? *(By faith, v. 5)*

4. What word pictures does Paul use to describe the concerns he has for the Galatians? *(Running a race, v. 7; a lump of dough, v. 9.)*

5. What is Paul's feeling about the outcome of his teaching? *(He is confident, v. 10.)*

6. Why is Paul so concerned about the false teachers? *(These teachers are upsetting the church, causing trouble and confusion, vv. 10-12.)*

7. Paul says we are "called unto liberty." From what are we set free? *(Obedience to the law as a means of salvation, v. 3; penalty of the law, v. 4.)*

8. What should be the attitude of Christians toward each other? *(Love our neighbor as ourselves, v. 14.)*

After each group has finished, discuss the answers. Ask the group to make a list of how the cross is an offense to the Judaizers. See the commentary for verse 11 and the Conclusion (pp 325, 326).

Into Life

Show the Statue of Liberty and the cross once more. Distribute blank sheets of paper and pens or pencils. Have each member divide the paper into two equal halves. On the left side write "Statue." List responsibilities and/or guidelines for living that citizens of the United States make a part of their freedom. *(Examples may include respecting property rights, obeying laws, and paying taxes.)* On the right side of the paper write "Cross." List responsibilities or guidelines for living that Christians follow. *(Examples include serving one another in love, resisting temptation, and worshiping God.)* Ask, "Why is liberty, in both cases, not a license to behave however you wish?"

Have students turn their papers over and reread verses 6, 13-15. Each person should list one or two people to whom they can express faith through love this week. Then they should write two or three ways in which they can express that loving service. Have them turn to their neighbors and tell their examples. Each person should pray for the other.

Let's Talk It Over

The questions on this page are designed to encourage review of the lesson Scriptures and to promote discussion of the lesson by the class. The answers provided are only discussion starters. Let your class talk it over from there.

1. Suppose a guest speaker in your church said, "The idea that we are 'free' in Christ is a mistake. Paul was overreacting to Pharisaic legalism! The truth is you must follow some rules to know you are living right. Let me tell you the three rules you must follow to be a good Christian and earn salvation." In the question and answer time that followed, what would you want to say, based on today's text?

This is exactly the issue Paul was facing in the Galatian churches (and elsewhere). The idea of "earning" salvation is foreign to the gospel. The speaker should be challenged on that with several Scriptures related to salvation by grace. "Three rules"? No, Paul says you get the "whole law" if you take any of it (v. 3).

Another important issue to note here is the idea that Paul was "overreacting." The Scripture is inspired by God (2 Timothy 3:15, 16). The message of freedom in this text is not Paul's—it is God's! Alleging that Paul has made a mistake is not a viable defense for the speaker's heresy.

2. If we are waiting for "the hope of righteousness," does that mean our righteousness now does not matter? Why or why not?

In one sense our righteousness does not matter. No matter how "good" or "righteous" we are, we cannot gain salvation by that. Our own righteousness does not matter if by it we hope to secure salvation. But the righteousness that is by faith is a righteousness that must be practiced. In that sense, then, it most certainly does matter. Our faith must be active (James 2:26). That faith, not the specific works it produces, is then credited as righteousness. Living by faith in that manner gives us confidence that we will hear those words, "Well done, good and faithful servant."

3. What kinds of hindrances threaten to "leaven" the church of today and prevent her from obeying the truth of our freedom in Christ?

The view of many outside the faith (and, unfortunately, many inside it) is that Christianity is a restrictive religion that keeps us from doing what is natural, fun, or satisfying. Many ritualistic and legalistic facets of modern-day religion seem to verify that. The truth of the gospel is that Christ has freed us to fulfill our destiny as human beings and our desire to love and be loved in the context of relationship, both with God and with our fellowman. There is no one less free than someone enslaved to sin, who knows inside that his destiny is destruction. There should be no one more free than the Christian, who knows that he or she is destined for eternal life with Christ.

4. How do some people exploit Christian liberty? How can we be sure we are not guilty of doing so?

If Satan cannot trap us in an enslavement to outright sin, he will try to trap us in an enslavement to meaningless legalistic rituals. If he cannot trap us in an enslavement to rituals, he will try to use our liberation as a means to enslave us to selfish indulgence. Sadly, many give in. They exploit their liberty by treating it as a license to sin. "We are saved by grace," they say, "so it does not matter what we 'do.' God's grace will forgive us." Others are not so blatant, but they still are self indulgent. They have no concern for the lost. They demand their own way in the church. They see their faith merely as a means of pleasing themselves instead of an opportunity to serve others after the manner of Jesus Christ. Freedom was given to us, not so that we could revel in it, but so that we could release others from bondage.

5. What are some practical methods by which you can show love to your neighbors in the coming week?

As Christians, we enjoy the freedom to love and serve any whom God has placed in our paths. Is there a family in need of physical goods in our neighborhood? How can we show them the love of God? Can we offer them a ride to the grocery or to church? Can we invite them to join us for a meal and friendship?

Often those who are most downtrodden are those who will be most open to the love and healing that Christ provides. Can we participate in a ministry reaching out to those in desperate need, either at home or abroad?

Regardless of what specific acts we do, all of us should love our neighbors with prayer and fervency. We know that needs are great, but we also know that God is even greater, and that our freedom in Him will enable us to reach those He expects us to reach.

Gospel of Life by the Spirit

DEVOTIONAL READING: Colossians 3:5-17.

BACKGROUND SCRIPTURE: Galatians 5:16—6:18.

PRINTED TEXT: Galatians 5:16—6:9.

Galatians 5:16-26

16 This I say then, Walk in the Spirit, and ye shall not fulfil the lust of the flesh.

17 For the flesh lusteth against the Spirit, and the Spirit against the flesh: and these are contrary the one to the other; so that ye cannot do the things that ye would.

18 But if ye be led of the Spirit, ye are not under the law.

19 Now the works of the flesh are manifest, which are these, adultery, fornication, uncleanness, lasciviousness,

20 Idolatry, witchcraft, hatred, variance, emulations, wrath, strife, seditions, heresies,

21 Envyings, murders, drunkenness, revellings, and such like: of the which I tell you before, as I have also told you in time past, that they which do such things shall not inherit the kingdom of God.

22 But the fruit of the Spirit is love, joy, peace, long-suffering, gentleness, goodness, faith,

23 Meekness, temperance: against such there is no law.

24 And they that are Christ's have crucified the flesh with the affections and lusts.

25 If we live in the Spirit, let us also walk in the Spirit.

26 Let us not be desirous of vainglory, provoking one another, envying one another.

Galatians 6:1-9

1 Brethren, if a man be overtaken in a fault, ye which are spiritual, restore such a one in the spirit of meekness; considering thyself, lest thou also be tempted.

2 Bear ye one another's burdens, and so fulfil the law of Christ.

3 For if a man think himself to be something, when he is nothing, he deceiveth himself.

4 But let every man prove his own work, and then shall he have rejoicing in himself alone, and not in another.

5 For every man shall bear his own burden.

6 Let him that is taught in the word communicate unto him that teacheth in all good things.

7 Be not deceived; God is not mocked: for whatsoever a man soweth, that shall he also reap.

8 For he that soweth to his flesh shall of the flesh reap corruption; but he that soweth to the Spirit shall of the Spirit reap life everlasting.

9 And let us not be weary in well doing: for in due season we shall reap, if we faint not.

GOLDEN TEXT: Walk in the Spirit, and ye shall not fulfil the lust of the flesh.
—Galatians 5:16.

The Power of the Gospel
Unit 3: No Other Gospel
(Lessons 10-13)

Lesson Aims

After this lesson each student will be able to:

1. List the qualities known as the "fruit of the Spirit," and contrast them with the works of the flesh.

2. Explain how the Spirit-led life reaches out to help those who are weaker.

3. Memorize the fruit of the Spirit, and choose one area in which he needs to submit to the Spirit rather than the flesh.

Lesson Outline

INTRODUCTION
  A. This Means War!
  B. Lesson Background
 I. LUSTS OF THE FLESH (Galatians 5:16-21)
  A. What the Flesh Wants (vv. 16-18)
  B. What the Flesh Does (vv. 19-21)
II. MARKS OF THE SPIRIT (Galatians 5:22-26)
  A. Fruit of the Spirit (vv. 22, 23)
  B. Life in the Spirit (vv. 24-26)
  Distinguishing Symbols
III. SPIRITUAL LIFE (Galatians 6:1-9)
  A. Restoring the Fallen (v. 1)
  B. Bearing the Burdens (vv. 2-5)
  Doing One's Duty
  C. Sowing to the Spirit (vv. 6-8)
  D. Reaping the Reward (v. 9)
CONCLUSION
  A. Winning the War
  B. Prayer
  C. Thought to Remember

Introduction

A. This Means War!

In the history of every nation are moments of crisis that plunged its people into armed conflict. "The shot heard 'round the world" precipitated the American Revolutionary War. Events like Napoleon's escape from exile, the firing on Fort Sumter, the sinking of the *Lusitania,* the invasion of Poland, and the attack on Pearl Harbor have caused people in various nations and periods of history to cry, "This means war!"

The Conflict. Wars come and wars go, but there is one conflict with eternal consequences: the struggle of our flesh against the Spirit. The flesh has no regard for what is moral or right—it just wants what it wants. The Holy Spirit, on the other hand, directs our spirits to reject the desires of our flesh when they are wrong. The flesh and the Spirit are thus at war, even in the lives of the finest Christians.

The Soldiers. In the war of flesh versus Spirit, people can enlist on whichever side they choose. Some choose to indulge their flesh, giving in to every appetite. The carnal results of their lives eventually become obvious; they reap what they sow. Others choose to be led by the Spirit. The fruit of the Spirit in their lives becomes a ninefold thing of beauty. Sometimes, however, soldiers on the Spirit's side fall prey to the enemy. The Lord's army should not shoot its own wounded, but restore them. Working as a team, helping carry one another's burdens, the soldiers of the Spirit can win the victory.

The Victory. The winning side already has been predetermined. Even though the struggle may be hard, in due season we shall reap a rich reward if we do not give up. We who choose to walk with the Spirit will from the Spirit reap eternal life.

B. Lesson Background

This unit of four lessons from Galatians has emphasized the one true gospel—the gospel of freedom from law as a way of salvation. The verses in this final lesson were written to warn the believers in Galatia not to turn their freedom into license. Salvation by faith does not mean that Christians are free to indulge their sinful desires. The sinful works of the flesh are still wrong, even when we are saved by grace. When we are led by the Spirit, we will replace the works of the flesh with the fruit of the Spirit. Then we will be truly free.

I. Lusts of the Flesh (Galatians 5:16-21)

A. What the Flesh Wants (vv. 16-18)

16. This I say then, Walk in the Spirit, and ye shall not fulfil the lust of the flesh.

Paul already has warned the Galatians not to use their freedom as an occasion to indulge their flesh (5:13). Now, by contrast, Paul says that Christians must instead *walk in the Spirit,* meaning they are to let God's Spirit lead them in true freedom. When we follow the will of the Spirit, we will *not fulfil the lust of the flesh.* We cannot obey the Spirit and give in to every desire of the flesh at the same time. As the next verse shows, these two courses are mutually exclusive.

17. For the flesh lusteth against the Spirit, and the Spirit against the flesh: and these are contrary the one to the other; so that ye cannot do the things that ye would.

The flesh has desires that go *against* the will of *the Spirit.* While all our physical "appetites" have their necessary and appropriate ways to be satisfied, these cravings can be dangerously amoral and selfish if uncontrolled. Fleshly desires do not care if it is the wrong situation; they crave immediate fulfillment. When one's spirit tries to overrule the desires of the flesh, inner conflict begins. As Paul also wrote in Romans 7:18, 19, we *cannot* consistently *do the things* we know we should because of our stubborn flesh.

18. But if ye be led of the Spirit, ye are not under the law.

As long we try by our own power to control the lusts of our flesh, we will fail. The solution is not just to "try harder," for the demands of the law are overwhelming. The solution is to *be led of the Spirit* so we do not have to fight this battle alone. When we allow Him to do so, God's Spirit begins putting a new set of desires in us. With God's Spirit leading and empowering us, we are *not under the law.* The law could condemn us when we sinned, but it could do nothing to empower us to do any better. [See question #1, page 336.]

B. What the Flesh Does (vv. 19-21)

19. Now the works of the flesh are manifest, which are these: adultery, fornication, uncleanness, lasciviousness.

Paul now gives the Galatian believers a sample listing of the *works of the flesh,* even though such works should be *manifest.* "Manifest" does not necessarily mean that such sins were on public display, but that the source of these vices was "obvious" or "readily apparent" to the reader. They illustrate the kind of things the flesh will do when it is uncontrolled.

Adultery is a sexual union outside of the bond of marriage, by either husband or wife, while *fornication* usually refers to sexual activity by unmarried persons. It may also refer generally to all forms of sexual immorality. *Uncleanness* describes the kind of moral impurity that makes a person unfit to enter the presence of God. (The Old Testament had a large number of laws that taught this concept to the Jews.) *Lasciviousness* is total disregard for decency—in public or in private. Such sins can easily result when fleshly appetites are not restrained by the Spirit.

20. Idolatry, witchcraft, hatred, variance, emulations, wrath, strife, seditions, heresies.

Idolatry can be worshiping an idol or simply putting some part of one's own life ahead of God. (Covetousness is called idolatry in Colossians 3:5.) *Witchcraft* refers to the use of magic potions, spells, and incantations in an attempt to tap into supernatural powers. Those who practice such sorcery or "magic arts" are subject to eternal

destruction (Revelation 21:8). The modern revival of pagan practices such as Wicca that involve such activities is sobering indeed. [See question #2, page 336.]

The last seven vices in this verse could be called "social offenses." *Hatred* is the feeling of ill will and hostility toward one's enemies. *Variance* means strife or discord, a fracturing of unity within a family or group. *Emulations* are feelings of jealousy. Not all jealousy is evil—the Bible describes God Himself as jealous (Exodus 20:5). Paul also cites what he calls "godly jealousy" (2 Corinthians 11:2. *Wrath* is the explosion of temper or "fits of rage" *(New International Version).* Again, wrath or anger is not evil in and of itself. Just as there is godly jealousy, there is such a thing as righteous anger (Mark 3:5; Romans 2:8, 9).

Strife represents Paul's word for what happens when people act out of selfish ambition, pulling others down as they try to climb above them. *Seditions,* sometimes translated "divisions" (Romans 16:17), are literally "acts of standing apart." *Heresies* are acts of choosing up sides over pet doctrines. Originally this word was not about false doctrines themselves, but about choosing sides over opinions. Those who cause divisions within the church are subject to being disfellowshipped (Romans 16:17; Titus 3:10).

21. Envyings, murders, drunkenness, revelings, and such like: of the which I tell you before, as I have also told you in time past, that they which do such things shall not inherit the kingdom of God.

While jealousy may not always be bad, *envyings* are. Envy not only covets what the other person has, it would rejoice to see the other person lose it. *Murders* are the unlawful taking of human life. *Drunkenness* is the intoxicated state that comes from indulgence in alcoholic beverages.

Home Daily Bible Readings

Monday, May 20—Mystery Proclaimed by the Spirit (Ephesians 3:1-13)
Tuesday, May 21—Be Filled With God's Fullness (Ephesians 3:14-21)
Wednesday, May 22—One Body and One Spirit (Ephesians 4:1-7)
Thursday, May 23—Given the Spirit for Living (2 Corinthians 5:1-10)
Friday, May 24—Now Is the Acceptable Time (2 Corinthians 6:1-12)
Saturday, May 25—The Fruit of the Spirit (Galatians 5:16-26)
Sunday, May 26—You Reap What You Sow (Galatians 6:7-18)

Visual for
lesson 13

Display today's visual as you begin to discuss the "fruit of the Spirit" (vv. 22, 23).

Revelings are "orgies," or riotous parties featuring drinking and sexual immorality. Some translations have "carousing." As Paul has taught them *in time past,* people who do such things have no part in *the kingdom of God* (cf. 1 Corinthians 6:9, 10). This does not refer to the isolated lapse (cf. 1 John 1:9), but to willful, continuous sin.

II. Marks of the Spirit
(Galatians 5:22-26)

A. Fruit of the Spirit (vv. 22, 23)

22. But the fruit of the Spirit is love, joy, peace, long-suffering, gentleness, goodness, faith.

The *fruit of the Spirit* is the harvest of virtues that is produced in the Spirit-filled life. While these characteristics are natural products of the Spirit, we must also actively cultivate them—each one is given as a command elsewhere in Scriptures. It is not enough to put aside the destructive works of the flesh; these must be replaced by something better. [See question #3, page 336.]

Love is the primary Christian virtue. It does not count the cost or calculate the profit. Like God's own love, it is not restricted to recipients who are lovable. *Joy* is our spontaneous, happy response to life in Christ. It is not dependent on our circumstances, but triumphs over them. *Peace* is more than the absence of war; it is the sense of well-being that comes from knowing we have all we need in Christ. A rough Hebrew equivalent is the well-known *shalom.*

Long-suffering is the ability to keep from losing our tempers with people. The Bible presents God Himself as long-suffering (e.g., 1 Peter 3:20). *Gentleness,* or kindness, is the sweet disposition that wants to serve the needs of people. *Goodness* involves both correct morals and a generous heart—

it is more active than gentleness. *Faith,* as used in this context, is not so much about faith in God as it is about faithfulness in our dealings with one another and in being reliable (cf. Luke 16:10-12).

23. Meekness, temperance: against such there is no law.

The world sometimes mistakes *meekness* for weakness. The Christian, following the example of Jesus Himself, is ready to yield his or her own rights for the good of others. Meekness involves holding oneself under control (cf. Numbers 12:3; Matthew 5:5). *Temperance* is the ability of one's spirit to control one's flesh. It is not moderation in one's vices, but the kind of total self-control that is possible only when one is led by the Spirit. *Law* is designed to restrain evil, but there is no law or limitation on these virtues! When these are our pursuit, we are completely free.

B. Life in the Spirit (vv. 24-26)

24. And they that are Christ's have crucified the flesh with the affections and lusts.

Paul uses the crucifixion image in Romans 6:6 and Galatians 2:20 as well. But in those two passages, the verb is passive. Here, those who belong to Christ have themselves done something: they *have crucified the flesh.* The flesh—try as it might—no longer controls the way they live. By the strength of God's Spirit, they master the old *affections and lusts,* the uncontrolled desires that once brought guilt and shame.

25. If we live in the Spirit, let us also walk in the Spirit.

If it is true that *we live in the Spirit* and the Spirit is the source of our life, then we should *also walk in the Spirit.* If we claim to belong to God but ignore the lifestyle of the Spirit, our claim is conspicuously false (1 John 1:6). Real Christians not only "talk the talk," they also walk the walk and live the life.

26. Let us not be desirous of vainglory, provoking one another, envying one another.

Self-centered people are like proud roosters that strut around trying to intimidate their rivals. People who are always *provoking* and *envying one another* are not full of the Spirit; they are full of themselves.

DISTINGUISHING SYMBOLS

Quick: what day do you think of when you hear the word *poinsettia?* Did anyone *not* think of Christmas? It seems that we see this flower almost everywhere in December. In Mexico, where the plant is native, seventeenth-century Franciscan priests found the rangy, wild poinsettias blooming naturally in December. It was an easy decision to use poinsettias as decorations in the churches during the celebration of Christmas.

The Aztec Indians used the plant for medicinal purposes and as a source of red dye. Like other symbols of the season—such as the Christmas tree—the poinsettia has been adapted from secular usage to become a symbol of the Christmas season, as much so as wreaths, angels, and carols.

The plant is named after an American botanist Joel R. Poinsett. As American ambassador to Mexico in 1825–29, he discovered the plants there and had several sent to his home in South Carolina, where he found them to flourish as greenhouse plants. The plant has been developed over nearly a century into the variety of colors ranging from white to pink to mottled to the traditional red that we buy each Christmas. It is now a compact potted plant that graces homes, churches, and businesses throughout the world.

The virtues mentioned in our text are the distinguishing symbols of the Christian life. Just as the wild poinsettia plant has been carefully developed into a symbol of the season that speaks of the joy Christ brings, so the diligent Christian can develop these virtues into sublime "flowers" adorning the life led by the spirit.   —C. R. B.

III. Spiritual Life
(Galatians 6:1-9)

A. Restoring the Fallen (v. 1)

1. Brethren, if a man be overtaken in a fault, ye which are spiritual, restore such a one in the spirit of meekness; considering thyself, lest thou also be tempted.

Sometimes in the battle between flesh and Spirit, sincere Christians fail. When a believer is *overtaken in a fault*, found to be guilty of some specific transgression, that person is not to be cast aside as a reject. Those who are recognized as *spiritual* leaders should go and try to *restore* that person. (The word *restore* is translated "mend" in Matthew 4:21, where the fishermen were fixing their nets.) The spiritual rescue squad must do their work gently and lovingly, *in the spirit of meekness*. They must not be heavy-handed or domineering, but should watch out for their own lives, realizing that they *also* can be tempted. [See question #4, page 336.]

B. Bearing the Burdens (vv. 2-5)

2. Bear ye one another's burdens, and so fulfil the law of Christ.

Like soldiers in an army, "we are all in this thing together." We do not gloat or rejoice when we see a fellow soldier fall in battle; we realize that we are diminished by his fall. Therefore, we help each other when the going gets rough. We step in to *bear* each other's *burdens* whenever we see that the load has become heavier than a

brother or sister can carry (Romans 15:1). In this way we carry out *the law of Christ:* "Love one another, as I have loved you" (John 15:12; cf John 15:17).

3. For if a man think himself to be something, when he is nothing, he deceiveth himself.

The opening *for* ties this verse to the topic of burden-bearing. A foolish soldier, trying to be *something* great, might suppose that he or she can win the war alone. Such a soldier is always trying to bear his or her own burden and to go it alone. Actually, he is *nothing;* he simply deceives *himself*. Self-deceived, this person destroys the fabric of the community by an aloof, arrogant disdain for others.

4. But let every man prove his own work, and then shall he have rejoicing in himself alone, and not in another.

The cure for arrogance and conceit is to take an honest assessment of ourselves. We should all *prove* (test or examine) our *own work*—the tasks the Lord gives us—and not try to take personal credit for what has been accomplished by the combined teamwork of many. When we have accurately pinpointed our own small contribution, we can feel the satisfaction of a job well done and *have rejoicing* in ourselves. Then we will not be found boasting *in another* person's work, as though it were our own.

5. For every man shall bear his own burden.

There is no contradiction between verses 2 and 5. The *burden* of verse 2 comes from a word that means "very heavy," but the *burden* of verse 5 comes from a word that means "what can be carried," such as a backpack. Teamwork means that we help one another—we bear one another's burdens when those loads are too heavy to be carried alone. It also means we attend to our own assignments—*every man* should be expected to *bear his own burden.*

DOING ONE'S DUTY

Vandenberg Air Force Base on the central California coast is a rocket launch test site for the United States government. That area of America's Pacific coast is also where the U.S. Navy experienced one of its most terrible peacetime disasters.

On the afternoon of September 8, 1923, fifteen U.S. destroyers were sailing in heavy fog from San Francisco to San Diego. All of the ships had been

---

How to Say It

GALATIA. Guh-*lay*-shuh.
LASCIVIOUSNESS. luh-*sih*-vee-us-nuss.
SHALOM (Hebrew). shah-*lome*.
Wicca. *Wih*-kuh.

built just five years earlier at a cost of $1.5 million each. They were the best destroyer-class ships in the world. The commander of the squadron ordered the ships to follow his vessel, single file, at a distance of three hundred yards, and at a speed of twenty knots. Visibility was extremely limited, and the commander disagreed with the navigation signals given by Point Arguello. He thought they were many miles south and farther out to sea than their actual position. He gave the signal to turn east, and immediately his ship ran aground on the rocky shore, followed by eight of the others. Seven ships were total losses and were never even salvaged. Remarkably, only twenty-three out of eight hundred seamen lost their lives.

This tragedy may help us to understand Paul's instructions to bear each other's burdens and (just three verses later) to each bear one's own burden. The vessels letting the commander bear their navigational burden in heavy fog found themselves prey to their commander's pride. The principle of working together does not absolve any of us from the responsibility to faithfully perform our own duty. To fail in that duty may bring terrible consequences to many of those who work with us.   —C. R. B.

C. Sowing to the Spirit (vv. 6-8)

6. Let him that is taught in the word communicate unto him that teacheth in all good things.

People who are *taught in the word* have a responsibility they ought to carry (as in v. 5). Their teachers have a heavy burden (as in v. 2), being unable to support their families when they spend their lives teaching. Therefore, those who are taught should share or *communicate* what they have *in all good things.* Jesus Himself taught that the laborer is worthy of his support (Matthew 10:10); Paul said that those who preach the gospel have the right to live off their preaching (1 Corinthians 9:13-15), although he himself sometimes chose to earn his living as a tentmaker (Acts 18:3; cf. 2 Thessalonians 3:7-10).

7. Be not deceived; God is not mocked: for whatsoever a man soweth, that shall he also reap.

We must not be *deceived* about what we sow—whether it be money or anything to do with our conduct. (See 2 Corinthians 9:6.) At issue is the final outcome of the warfare between flesh and Spirit.

8. For he that soweth to his flesh shall of the flesh reap corruption; but he that soweth to the Spirit shall of the Spirit reap life everlasting.

The person who invests all personal energy into making and keeping money sows to the selfish desires of the *flesh.* Like the rich fool in Luke 12:16-20, the self-indulgent miser will lose everything when life comes to an end. Furthermore,

the person who lives life for carnal pleasure will *reap* destruction, often both now and in eternity (cf. Hosea 10:13).

But people who devote themselves to living for God are planting for eternity. Their pocketbooks and their pleasures are in the hands of God. They sow *to the Spirit.*

D. Reaping the Reward (v. 9)

9. And let us not be weary in well doing: for in due season we shall reap, if we faint not.

[See question #5, page 336.] All of us at times grow *weary in well doing.* Perhaps Paul switches to the first person *we* because he is fighting his own weariness. We try to do the right thing, but it goes unappreciated. We try to live moral lives, and the world laughs. While we struggle to make enough money to be able to contribute to the work of the Kingdom, the wicked prosper. Like the psalmist, we are envious of the foolish when we see the prosperity of the wicked (Psalm 73:3).

But there will be a day of reckoning. *In due season,* at times known only to God, *we shall reap* our harvest (cf. John 4:35). Our lives will be filled with the fruit of the Spirit. Our eternity will stretch out before us in Heaven. We cannot give up, lose heart, or tire out. The prize for the winners is too great to lose.

Conclusion

A. Winning the War

Our text has sharply drawn the battle lines in the war of the flesh against the Spirit. The battle that the Galatians faced is the same struggle we face today. With the leading of God's Spirit, we can win this war. In the process, we shall learn the meaning of true spirituality.

Wars are easily lost when combatants are unprepared. Anyone who goes into war unprepared and untrained will likely end up being a casualty. If we expect to win the war of the flesh against the Spirit, we need to have a clear idea of what we are fighting against, what we are fighting for, and how we expect to win. We are fighting against the selfish desires of our own flesh. We are fighting for a kind of life that is free in the Spirit. We expect to win because God's own Spirit is empowering us.

B. Prayer

Father, thank You for not leaving us to fight this battle alone. We praise You for giving us victory in Christ Jesus. We pray in His name. Amen.

C. Thought to Remember

If we live in the Spirit, we should walk by the Spirit.

Learning by Doing

This page contains an alternate lesson plan emphasizing learning activities.
Classes desiring such student involvement will find these suggestions helpful.

Learning Goals

After this lesson each student will be able to:

1. List the qualities known as the "fruit of the Spirit," and contrast them with the works of the flesh.

2. Explain how the Spirit-led life reaches out to help those who are weaker.

3. Memorize the fruit of the Spirit, and choose one area in which he needs to submit to the Spirit rather than the flesh.

Into the Lesson

Have chairs arranged in groups of five as students enter the room. In each group set a bowl of different kinds of fruit that you have purchased this week. (Or you could use pictures of fruit.) Supply two types of fruit for each group.

Say, "Let's suppose you are grocery shopping this week for fruit. In each group you have two types of fruit. What characteristics should you look for to know that the fruit is ripe? Take a couple of minutes to make a list." Provide paper and pencils for the groups.

Call the groups together and ask them to give their responses. Then ask, "Why is it important to know what to look for?" *(Answers may include it will taste best, you can use it to prepare certain dishes, it looks good to present to others, and you will get your money's worth.)*

Into the Word

Introduce the Bible study section by presenting a short lecture based on the Introduction section of the lesson (page 330). This lecture explains that Paul challenges the Galatians to live by the gospel of grace, but not the law of license.

You will need at least three groups for the following activity. Provide paper, pencils, Bible dictionaries, word-study books, concordances, and/or handbooks for the groups.

Group One: Read Galatians 5:19-21. Assign to each student at least two of the words used in the text to describe works of the flesh. The student is to find the definition and pertinent information on each word to report to the class.

Group Two: Read Galatians 5:22-25. Assign at least two of the words listed as the fruit of the Spirit to each. The student is to find and report the definition and pertinent information on each.

Group Three: Read Galatians 6:1-9. This group is to develop a role play of a person who had been caught in a sin and who is being restored by the church. It will be important to identify the sin as well as appropriate Scriptures to use for the restoration.

Allow ten minutes for the groups to complete the activities. Then ask Groups One and Two for reports. Group Three should be given time to demonstrate its role play.

To help with discussion, use the following open-response questions: How does the fruit of the Spirit overcome the "works of the flesh"? How does the teaching in verses 25 and 26 lead into the discussion of restoring an errant brother? What attitude should we have when restoring one who falls? What word picture does Paul use here to describe how a person's life will turn out?

Into Life

Make the transition to application by saying, "Paul is challenging the Christian to show the fruit of the Spirit in his or her life. It should be evident to those around us that we are changed, allowing the Spirit to produce good fruit in our lives. Production of the fruit is to glorify God, not self; therefore, when a Christian slips, our task is not to condemn nor act superior, but to assist the one who has fallen so that his or her life can once again glorify God."

Have class members pair up with one another. This will be a time for an old-fashioned memorization drill. Each person is to make a list of the fruit of the Spirit, then drill his or her partner on the list. This should be a five-minute exercise.

The partners are to stay together for the closing activity. Ask each person to answer the following questions:

"Which acts of the flesh are dead in your life?" "Wounded?" "Alive?" "Which fruits of the Spirit are ripe in your life?" "Which are just beginning?" "Which will you seek to develop in your life, beginning this week?"

Although the answers to these questions are difficult, encourage class members to be open. Have the pairs close in silent prayer.

As the teacher, thank the class for pursuing the study of Romans and Galatians for these last three months. Remind them of the quarter's theme, "The Power of the Gospel." That power will save them, and the Holy Spirit will help them to keep the commitment just made. Pray for the class.

Let's Talk It Over

The questions on this page are designed to encourage review of the lesson Scriptures and to promote discussion of the lesson by the class. The answers provided are only discussion starters. Let your class talk it over from there.

1. If God's Spirit empowers us to live the Christian life, why is it so hard to do sometimes?

Some people seem to think that being empowered by the Spirit should be as easy as plugging an electric cord into a socket to power up an appliance. But we are more than machines, and being empowered by the Spirit requires continuous cooperation on our parts.

Becoming a disciple involves a "once-and-for-all decision." It is a death to the old way and a resurrection to new life; it is a rebirth. But being a disciple is more than simply living in the shadow of that one decision. Each day we are confronted with options and choices. Each day—in fact, several times a day—we must decide anew to follow the Lord. If we are not diligent, we can easily make wrong choices.

2. Witchcraft is one of the works of the flesh cited by Paul. How seriously do you think people take this as a danger today? What, if any, additional precautions do you think people in general, and Christians in particular, need to take?

Most people seem to think witchcraft is no more than a game some people play, completely devoid of any power or potential to do harm. Books and television programs use it as a plot devise for intrigue or comedy. Children play games that include witches or black magic, or they dress up in witch costumes for Halloween.

Many people, including Christians, see no harm in this. As long as the person professes no real allegiance to Satan, the witch games are seen as impotent. But others observe that Satan is cunning and subtle. If he can get people to treat the subject lightly, they will dismiss it even when it poses a real threat. Then what happens when college co-eds who dressed as witches for Halloween when they were small are invited to join a coven as an alternative to a sorority?

3. Why do you think Paul called these nine qualities the fruit (singular) of the Spirit instead of fruits (plural)? What significance do you see in that for applying these things to our lives?

One reason is simply grammatical. Jesus said we are to bear fruit, not fruits, but that doesn't mean we all bear exactly the same fruit. Fruit is used collectively, like the word *produce* at the supermarket. In the produce section are many different kinds of fruits and vegetables, but it's all produce. There are different kinds of fruit in the fruit of the Spirit.

Still, if we do not observe the singular "fruit," we may miss the unity inherent in this group. These are not buffet items from which we can pick and choose. We need to cultivate *all* of these qualities in our lives. Otherwise we are not following the Spirit; we are charting our own course.

4. What is the importance of restoring fallen brothers and sisters and of bearing one another's burdens?

The only person who always completely exemplified the fruit of the Spirit was Jesus. Even those of us who are being led by the Spirit stumble occasionally, and in the church there are those who have slipped into works of the flesh or reverted to an old way of life. Paul admonishes us not to disavow them, but to restore them gently. If we don't restore those who fall, eventually there won't be anyone left!

When we work together to help the weak and restore the fallen, we demonstrate the kind of healing and growth that a healthy human body constantly experiences. The healthy body of Christ needs to experience the same kind of healing and growth. As it does, those members who have been healed and restored are stronger and able to do even more for the body and for the Head—Jesus Christ.

5. What can cause us to become "weary in well doing"? How can we find the strength to press on when fainting, or giving up, would be so much easier?

One of the biggest causes of weariness is a sense of futility. When one works hard and sees no result, it gets hard to go on. We have to remember that Jesus called us to be faithful, not "successful." Another source of weariness is a lack of appreciation. If we give our best effort and no one cares—or worse, if our efforts are disparaged—we can become angry or bitter as well as weary of the job. We have to remember that we serve the Lord, not people. He will not forget our efforts. Your students will have other ideas. Be sure to affirm them in their own service—each reason for weariness cited may reveal a growing sense of frustration in their own hearts.

Summer Quarter, 2002

Worship and Wisdom for Living

Special Features

Lessons

Unit 1: Songs for Faithful Living

Unit 2: Praise the Creator and Redeemer

Unit 3: Words for the Wise

About These Lessons

With this quarter's lessons, we transition from the doctrinally-focused studies of the spring to that of practical, "how to live" guidance. We must be careful not to separate the *doctrinal* from the *practical* too sharply, however, since the former provides the basis for the latter. Come and learn!

Jun
2

Jun
9

Jun
16

Jun
23

Jun
30

Jul
7

Jul
14

Jul
21

Jul
28

Aug
4

Aug
11

Aug
18

Aug
25

Quarterly Quiz

The questions on this page may be used in several ways: as a pretest at the beginning of the quarter; as a review at the end of the quarter; or as a review after each lesson. The questions are based on the Scripture text of each lesson (King James Version). **The answers are on page 340.**

Lesson 1

1. In Psalm 1, what object from nature does the writer use to symbolize the person who delights in God's law? (tree, flower, apple) *Psalm 1:3*
2. The judgments (laws) of the Lord are more desirable than _____ and sweeter than _____. *Psalm 19:9, 10*

Lesson 2

1. Which human need does the psalmist use to compare with his longing for God? (hunger, thirst, weariness) *Psalm 42:2*
2. When the psalmist feels "cast down" and "disquieted," what phrase does he use to encourage himself? ____ ____ ____ ____. *Psalm 42:11*

Lesson 3

1. Give two reasons why the psalmist fears no evil when he walks through the valley of the shadow of death. *Psalm 23:4*
2. What two blessings will follow the psalmist all the days of his life? *Psalm 23:6*
3. Psalm 121 states that the Lord is our sun by day and our moon by night. T/F *Psalm 121:5, 6*

Lesson 4

1. How should we help the poor and needy? *Psalm 82:4*
2. According to the psalmist, what is above the heavens? *Psalm 113:4*
3. The Lord raises the poor man out of the dust and sets him with princes. T/F *Psalm 113:7, 8*

Lesson 5

1. We should show to coming generations the praises of the Lord, His strength, and His _____ _____. *Psalm 78:4*
2. Which of the following was *not* an action to teach to the children: to set their hope in God, to keep His commandments, to live like their fathers? *Psalm 78:6-8*

Lesson 6

1. The creatures of the sea wait for the Lord to give them their meat in due season. T/F *Psalm 104:25-27*
2. What happens when the Lord looks at the earth? when He touches the hills? *Psalm 104:32*
3. How long will the psalmist sing unto the Lord? *Psalm 104:33*

Lesson 7

1. What word does the psalmist use to describe God's name? *Psalm 8:1*
2. What has God put under man's feet? *Psalm 8:6*
3. We should enter into the Lord's gates with _____ and into His courts with _____. *Psalm 100:4*

Lesson 8

1. The psalmist acknowledged his (fear, weakness, sin) to the Lord. *Psalm 32:5*
2. The wicked will have _____ _____, but the one who trusts in the Lord will be surrounded by _____. *Psalm 32:10*

Lesson 9

1. When God is merciful and blesses us, what will He do to us? *Psalm 67:1*
2. God's glory is to be declared only among His own people. T/F *Psalm 96:3*
3. We are to worship the Lord in the _____ of holiness. *Psalm 96:9*

Lesson 10

1. A man who finds (a treasure, justice, wisdom) is happy. *Proverbs 3:13*
2. The principal thing in life is to get honor and respect. T/F *Proverbs 4:7*

Lesson 11

1. Three things that God hates are a proud _____, a lying _____, and _____ that shed innocent blood. *Proverbs 6:16, 17*
2. What will our father's commandments and our mother's laws do for us while we sleep? when we awake? *Proverbs 6:20-22.*

Lesson 12

1. What will turn away wrath? *Proverbs 15:1*
2. Which is more likely to be effective: reproving a wise man or beating a fool with a hundred stripes? *Proverbs 17:10*

Lesson 13

1. What will the Lord do for the person who has pity on the poor? *Proverbs 19:17*
2. The person who takes from the poor and gives to the rich will be wealthy, but unhappy. T/F *Proverbs 22:16*

The Bible Cure

by Richard W. Baynes

THE TWENTY-FIRST CENTURY promises to be one of astounding discoveries—some might even say "miracles"—in the field of medical science. Intensive research makes the finding of cures for many of the most problematic diseases a real possibility. Already medical researchers have made significant strides toward finding treatments that may eliminate the threats of multiple sclerosis, diabetes, AIDS, and various cancers.

Everyone is interested in finding cures for all human ailments. Governments invest enormous amounts of resources attempting to improve physical comfort, longevity, and quality of life. Christians lift many prayers to God for the same ends. (In fact, if you listen to the prayer requests voiced in your Sunday school class, chances are that they will run heavily toward physical, as opposed to spiritual, concerns—probably by a ratio of fifty-to-one, or more!)

As we struggle individually and collectively with these concerns, we dare not overlook our most important source of comfort and "total person" healing: the Bible. As God's inerrant Word, this book holds the answer to life's most important questions. Though it does not claim to be a manual of medicine, the Bible is a resource for good health.

The late great preacher, Andrew Blackwood, once suggested to homiletics students a series of sermons from the Psalms that would deal with such emotional ills as worry, depression, sleeplessness, and others. Many preachers took Blackwood's advice, for even a quick read of the Psalms (described aptly as the "Old Testament Hymnbook") reveals reliable prescriptions for several common mental-health complaints. The suggested sermons were dubbed "The Bible Cure Series."

Songs for Faithful Living

Human beings are more than merely "the sum of their parts." The mental, physical, and spiritual aspects of our nature are all interconnected to the point that weakness in any one area can affect the other two. In other words, to live faithful lives spiritually can both *require* and *be the result of* our choices and well-being in the physical and mental areas. Our lessons for this unit can help us in all these areas.

Lesson 1 could be called "The Bible Cure for Indecision." The challenge of making right (i.e.,

God-honoring) choices is very real, and wrong (sinful) choices can lead to dire consequences both physically (e.g., sexually transmitted diseases) and spiritually (loss of eternal life). The instructions from Psalms 1 and 19 are true motivators in making right choices.

We might consider Psalm 42 **(Lesson 2)** to be "The Bible Cure for the Blues." Even the most mature Christian gets "down in the dumps" occasionally, and here the therapy is clear: "Hope in God." Psalms 23 and 121 **(Lesson 3)** provide "The Bible Cure for Fear." Millions have been—and continue to be—comforted by, "Yea, though I walk through the valley of the shadow of death, I will fear no evil" (Psalm 23:4). Fear can paralyze a person to the point of total inaction, something Satan surely desires!

"The Bible Cure for Cynicism" might be a good title for **Lesson 4,** drawn from Psalms 82 and 113. A person controlled by cynicism isn't much use to God's kingdom. Such a person is always thinking "What's the use in doing _____, since it will just turn out _____?" The cure begins with realizing that we must trust the Judge of all the earth to do right and ultimately to balance the inequities of this life. **Lesson 5,** based on Psalm 78, could be "The Bible Cure for Generation Gaps." The "old, old story of Jesus and His love" can be the "bridge over troubled waters" that so often separates the perspectives of youth from age.

Praise the Creator and Redeemer

The lessons in Unit 2 will remind you and your students that God not only *creates,* He also *sustains* and *redeems.* Psalm 104 **(Lesson 6)** recognizes the creative power of God as motivation enough to elicit our praises of God forever. As such, this lesson and this psalm might be called "The Bible Cure for Arrogance." The objective truth of His revealed Word, supported by the presence of creation itself, requires our humility and undergirds our rejoicing with awe.

Lesson 7 emphasizes the superiority and honor that God has given humans as we "Live as the Crown of Creation." As such, the lesson texts serve as "The Bible Cure for an Inferiority Complex." When we esteem ourselves as God esteems us, we have a proper view of ourselves in His created order, and we are more likely to love and encourage others since they, too, share this marvelous heritage.

The freedom and joy of forgiveness are the themes of **Lesson 8.** David's sweet spiritual relief as described in Psalm 32 is a classic example of an appropriate human response to God's grace and faithfulness in cleansing penitent sinners from all unrighteousness. We might call this lesson "The Bible Cure for the Guilt-Ridden." We can rejoice in the knowledge that, in Christ, our sins have been remitted, and a new heart has been created within us.

The final lesson in this unit **(Lesson 9)** invites "all people" to celebrate our great God with new songs and other expressions of worship. Worship celebrations can demonstrate that we love God with all our heart (emotions), soul (essence), mind (intellect), and strength (vigor). In bringing all of these aspects together as one, this lesson serves as "The Bible Cure for the Unfocused."

Summer Sunday school scholars may seek and find refreshment in the Psalms. Picture David playing these songs on his harp. Perhaps he sits in the coolness of a marble palace, or beneath a palm tree with a glass of lemonade nearby. Even without the lemonade, the faith and trust of "the man after God's own heart" can be sensed in these inspired lyrical poems.

In the fall, if someone asks you to tell what you did this summer, you can say, "I discovered the Bible cure for what ails me!" That is the aim of these lessons, that students (and teachers) will renew their trust in the Good Shepherd who leads them "beside the still waters."

These lessons from the Psalms speak to the needs (both actual and "felt") of Christians everywhere. We all yearn for direction, reassurance, and security. We struggle with doubts, temptations, and questions. We seek answers that will quench our spiritual thirsts and help us live lives to the full. "Bible cures" from the Psalms can provide the solutions. Bible teachers can find a wealth of material to inspire and motivate their classes in this series. These are "Psalms to Soothe the Psyche."

Words for the Wise

The third unit of lessons for this quarter is based on texts selected from Proverbs. **Lesson 10** centers on the chief topic of these sage sayings: wisdom. The thrust, simply put, is that God's wisdom "works"! And because it works, a lifestyle based on God's practical instruction will bring happiness, satisfaction, and contentment. Living without it is living beneath one's privilege.

"Run From Evil" is the title of **Lesson 11.** Underscored here are the wise principles of making and keeping lifelong commitments. Students are encouraged to reconsider instruction they may

have received from parents and/or other mentors. Such reflection can often lead them "in the paths of righteousness." In a culture where many have forgotten (or have outright rejected) the difference between right and wrong, such admonitions are critically important when we remember that eternity is at stake.

Lesson 12 dwells on an equally important ethic of a godly life: "Watch What You Say." What one does and what one says are two sides of the one coin that result in blessedness. The gift of human speech is powerful, of course, for good or evil. Wise use of communication—oral or otherwise—is a virtue enabled by divine wisdom and right choices.

The final lesson in this quarter, **Lesson 13,** gives the needed exhortation for benevolent care for the needy. This was a prime concern of our Lord (consider Matthew 25 and other relevant texts), and His followers need frequent reminders to share with those who are less fortunate than themselves. Several verses and paragraphs from Proverbs serve as the text for this lesson, evidence that this theme is a priority of the Old as well as the New Testament.

"Worship and Wisdom for Living" will prove to be a profitable and practical quarter of study for classes of adults who desire to mature in their faith by pursuing the holiness of God. Both teachers and students will be enriched by these lessons when they are conscientiously taught and learned. Give of your best to the Master!

Answers to Quarterly Quiz on page 338

Lesson 1—1. tree. 2. gold, honey. **Lesson 2**—1. thirst. 2. Hope thou in God. **Lesson 3**—1. the Lord is with him; His rod and staff comfort him. 2. goodness and mercy. 3. false (the Lord's shade protects us from the sun and the moon). **Lesson 4**—1. deliver them out of the hand of the wicked. 2. the Lord's glory. 3. true. **Lesson 5**—1. wonderful works. 2. to live like their fathers. **Lesson 6**—1. true. 2. it trembles; they smoke. 3. as long as he lives. **Lesson 7**—1. excellent. 2. all things. 3. thanksgiving, praise. **Lesson 8**—1. sin. 2. many sorrows, mercy. **Lesson 9**—1. cause His face to shine upon us. 2. false (among the heathen). 3. beauty. **Lesson 10**—1. wisdom. 2. false (get wisdom). **Lesson 11**—1. look, tongue, hands. 2. keep us; talk with us. **Lesson 12**—1. a soft answer. 2. reproving a wise man. **Lesson 13**—1. pay him back what he has given. 2. false (he will come to want).

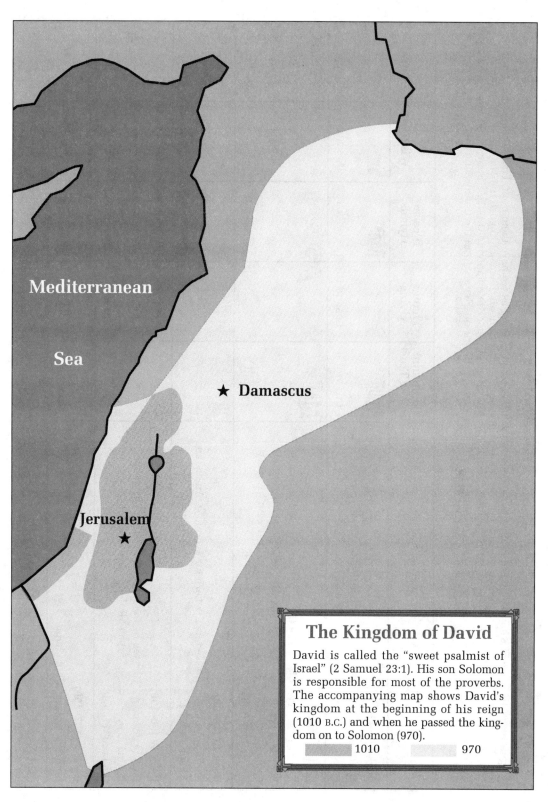

The Kingdom of David

David is called the "sweet psalmist of Israel" (2 Samuel 23:1). His son Solomon is responsible for most of the proverbs. The accompanying map shows David's kingdom at the beginning of his reign (1010 B.C.) and when he passed the kingdom on to Solomon (970).

1010   970

THE PSALMS

Beginning in the time of King David, the Psalms took about **700 years** to come together as we have them now. Traditionally, they have been divided into **five "books,"** each ending in a doxology (you can see these book divisions in all the major English translations of the Psalms).

Within these books can be found at least **five "types"** of Psalms, as this chart shows. (The notations "MANY," "Some," and "few" refer to the frequency of the five types within each of the five books.) The first nine lessons of this quarter are from the Psalms, and this chart will help you get your bearings in this very long book—the longest in the Bible!

	Complaint and/or Trust	Thanks-giving	Praise Hymns	Wisdom	Royal
Book I (1–41) *Ending doxology:* "Blessed be the Lord God of Israel from ever-lasting, and to everlasting. Amen, and Amen" (41:13).	MANY Lesson 3	Some Lesson 8	MANY Lessons 1, 7	Some Lesson 1	Some
Book II (42–72) *Ending doxology:* "Blessed be the Lord God, the God of Israel, who only doeth wondrous things. And blessed be his glorious name for ever: and let the whole earth be filled with his glory. Amen, and Amen" (72:18, 19).	MANY Lesson 2	few	Some Lesson 9	few	few
Book III (73–89) *Ending doxology:* "Blessed be the Lord for evermore. Amen, and Amen" (89:52).	Some	few	Some Lessons 4, 5	few	few
Book IV (90–106) *Ending doxology:* "Blessed be the Lord God of Israel from ever-lasting to everlasting: and let all the people say, Amen. Praise ye the Lord" (106:48).	few	few Lesson 7	MANY Lessons 6, 9	few	few
Book V (107–150) *Ending doxology:* all of chapter 150.	MANY Lesson 3	Some	MANY Lesson 4	Some	Some

The New Testament refers to the Psalms by name in Luke 20:42; 24:44 and Acts 1:20; 13:33. In Jesus' day, the Psalms were part of the "Writings" section of the Old Testament, as distinct from the "Law" and the "Prophets" (cf. Luke 24:44).

Time for Prayer

Learning in Praying

by Ronald G. Davis

PRAYER IS CERTAINLY A PART of Bible study. We honor God's Word by giving attention to it. We honor its depth and significance by asking for the wisdom of the Spirit in comprehending it and applying it.

Wise teachers of adults will use prayers and praying to enhance every aspect of the class time. Prayers can be read, heard, composed (by tongue or by pen), and sung. The Bible is full of prayers, those spoken as deeply personal responses to God's goodness and those written for the edification and the worship of God's people. Some were written to be read. Some were simply to be heard. Others were designed to be sung. All were to be heartfelt words of worship. Whether they were glad expressions of praise and thanksgiving or desperate, even frantic words of petition, all were an exclamation that God is able.

Prayer With Direction

One of the ways to make certain that prayers focus on elements of thanksgiving and petition that relate to a text and its study is to use "directed prayer." Such prayer means that the leader suggests a series of elements aloud as the praying group utters silent words to the Father.

For such a lesson as number two in this series, a study of Psalm 42, a directed prayer may offer an excellent review and reinforcement of ideas studied. Consider such prayer stimulus statements as the following (with relevant verse numbers in parentheses):

• Pray for hungering and thirsting after righteousness of which Jesus spoke (vv. 1, 2a);
• Pray for ability to make God known to those who say, "Where is thy God?" (v. 3);
• Thank God for those with whom you worship and for those who lead worship (v. 4);
• Pray for forgiveness for discouragement and depression; ask for a renewed hope (v. 5);
• Identify to God places and times when you have felt overwhelmed by life's events (vv. 6, 7);
• Address the Father as "God of my life," and ask Him to give you His song both day and night (v. 8);
• Plead for steadfastness when the enemies of God taunt and challenge you (vv. 9, 10);
• Affirm the hope that you have; tell God that you praise Him for revealing the hope we have in Him and in His Son (v. 11).

Closing such a time with oral prayer, in words and phrases from the text, is important. The following statement could be used: "O living God, we have poured out our souls to You. The help of Your presence is praiseworthy. Your lovingkindness gives health to our spirits. We thank You for the hope of Your abiding Spirit, the hope of resurrection in Your Son. Amen."

Prayer With Feet

The concept of prayer walk has an ancient origin; it is reflected in such examples as the "Stations of the Cross" prayer gardens adjoining church buildings of some religious groups. A quiet and serene pathway allowing the discipline of prayer to be practiced has found its way onto modern campgrounds and retreat properties. And it has found simplification in around-the-classroom or around-the-building-hallways manifestations. For such an experience the leader establishes a clearly defined direction of movement and posts prayer-stimulus statements (and, optionally, relevant Bible verses or other spiritual truths) at consecutive (or circular) "stations." Learners are to move from station to station, stopping to pray appropriately at each. Such an activity makes an ideal end-of-unit activity, but it can be applied to individual study occasions.

Lesson five of this unit, "Teach the Wonders of God," taken from Psalm 78, could be the base for an effective "Wonderful Works of God" prayer walk (see vv. 4, 7). A three-part walk could emphasize "Creation—Revelation—Regeneration." Consider for part 1, "Creation," such a station as one carrying the verse Genesis 1:1 and a suggestion to thank God for the very universe of which we are a part, and for its marvelous intricacy and inter-relatedness. Additional "stops" on this part could include "The Plant and Animal Creation," providing us food, clothing, and much more; "Technology," providing us comfort, ease, and breadth of experience; "Medicine," providing strength, health, and extended life; "Art and Beauty," providing us enjoyment, wonder, and an outlet for creativity. The "Revelation" part of the walk could emphasize that which the psalmist emphasizes: that God "established a testimony . . . and appointed a law" (v. 5). Using a key verse from that Psalm and an encouragement to thank God for His Word in print could lead to "stops" for thankfulness for translators and translations, publishers, and Christian booksellers.

The contemporary activity most call "prayer walking" is a similar procedure, aimed more at application of truth learned than of review and reinforcement. And prayer walking is done in a life setting rather than a classroom context. Learners are asked to consider a "path" for walking contiguous to the object(s) of the prayer; they are simply directed to pray as they walk. Lesson 10, "Embrace Wisdom," presents an excellent opportunity for a "Wisdom Walk" around a community school or college. The suggestion to walk praying that the students there will find wisdom as well as knowledge is certainly appropriate. (The praying walker could pray for each student he or she passes.) Lesson 13, "Care for the Poor," would be an ideal occasion to recommend a walk of prayer through a community of those on the lower end of the socioeconomic scale. Praying for those poor in material things to find obedient faith would be a worthy suggestion.

Prayer With Tunes

Many songs, from ancient hymns to contemporary choruses, are prayers put into verse and matched to melody. Every adult teacher needs to consider having his or her class sing—or listen to—songs related to lesson texts and themes.

Modern and classic psalters fill shelves of churches and Christian stores. Hymnals typically contain listings of "Scripture Bases for Hymns." (A class member with musical interests might relish the challenge to bring a song or songs to a study session.) Lesson 3 includes the beginning verses of Psalm 23 as text. One would be almost remiss if he did not draw attention to one of the well-known songs based on those verses: from the chorus typically sung as a round, "The Lord Is My Shepherd/I'll Follow Him Always" or the classic hymn, "The King of Love My Shepherd Is" or others. One would be equally remiss if he did not remind the class of the traditional "Old 100th": "All People That on Earth Do Dwell" when lesson 7 is studied, using the beginning of Psalm 100.

And, of course, countless songs and choruses have been written on the grand themes of this unit's study. Consider, for example, the chorus, "My Hope Is in the Lord" for lesson 2.

Prayer in a Program

The Christian discipline of keeping a prayer journal has proven to be a significant faith-building, disciple-growing practice. Though most any Bible study unit can be adapted to a worthy prayer journal—either as a class project or a personal one—this unit of study certainly lends itself to such an activity. In an inexpensive, ruled notebook, with three simple columns: Elements to be Prayed For, Date(s) of the Prayer, and Prayer Responses (with Dates), the user is ready to begin an adventure of Christian growth. Week by week in a study, the teacher and/or the class can list elements related to texts and themes. Day by day the prayers can be offered. Moment by moment the ones who pray can realize the presence and the work of God. Consider items that could be entered into the prayer journal for each lesson of this series:

Lesson 1—Pray for delight in Bible study and meditation;

Lesson 2—Thank God for hope; ask Him to remove doubt and despair;

Lesson 3—Ask God to remove fear from one's life; pray for a less materialistic approach to life;

Lesson 4—Thank God for ultimate justice; ask Him to help you see and work against injustice;

Lesson 5—Pray for the success of the church's education of children; pray for a particular family's ability to disciple their children;

Lesson 6—Petition God to remove the evil seen in your community: alcohol, drugs, greed;

Lesson 7—Seek true humility, realizing the smallness of one's self in God's scheme; ask God for greater intensity and joy in singing praise;

Lesson 8—Utter sincere thanksgiving for forgiveness; rehearse the sins that bother you most;

Lesson 9—Pray specifically for those Christians whom you know and whom the church supports in various international cultures;

Lesson 10—Thank God for those (preachers, teachers, family members) who have helped you gain wisdom in Christ; ask for more wisdom;

Lesson 11—List evils you most need strength to flee, especially lust in an immoral culture;

Lesson 12—Identify the sin of the tongue you are most prone to commit and ask the power of the Spirit to quash it;

Lesson 13—Seek a better attitude toward the poor; ask for an opportunity to assist the poor.

Listing prayer content and recording God's gracious response cannot but encourage anyone who seeks Him: "The prayer of a righteous [person] is powerful and effective" (James 5:16, *New International Version).*

Prayer Without Ceasing

Try a variety of prayer activities: directed prayer, prayer walks, a prayer list in relationship to a lesson series incorporating elements of praise and petition as a way of unifying and reinforcing the unit, a prayer journal for the unit, writing prayers (and sharing them), reading prayers of others. Prayer changes things, especially the ones who do the praying!

Follow the Way of the Righteous

DEVOTIONAL READING: Psalm 19:1-6.

BACKGROUND SCRIPTURE: Psalms 1; 19.

PRINTED TEXT: Psalms 1:1-6; 19:7-10.

Psalm 1:1-6

1 Blessed is the man that walketh not in the counsel of the ungodly, nor standeth in the way of sinners, nor sitteth in the seat of the scornful.

2 But his delight is in the law of the LORD; and in his law doth he meditate day and night.

3 And he shall be like a tree planted by the rivers of water, that bringeth forth his fruit in his season; his leaf also shall not wither; and whatsoever he doeth shall prosper.

4 The ungodly are not so: but are like the chaff which the wind driveth away.

5 Therefore the ungodly shall not stand in the judgment, nor sinners in the congregation of the righteous.

6 For the LORD knoweth the way of the righteous: but the way of the ungodly shall perish.

Psalm 19:7-10

7 The law of the LORD is perfect, converting the soul: the testimony of the LORD is sure, making wise the simple.

8 The statutes of the LORD are right, rejoicing the heart: the commandment of the LORD is pure, enlightening the eyes.

9 The fear of the LORD is clean, enduring for ever: the judgments of the LORD are true and righteous altogether.

10 More to be desired are they than gold, yea, than much fine gold: sweeter also than honey and the honeycomb.

GOLDEN TEXT: The LORD knoweth the way of the righteous: but the way of the ungodly shall perish.—Psalm 1:6.

Worship and Wisdom for Living
Unit 1: Songs for Faithful Living
(Lessons 1-5)

Lesson Aims

After this lesson, each student will be able to:
1. Tell what today's texts say about the blessings and rewards of walking in the godly way.
2. Compare the psalmist's trust in the unchanging Word of God with the relativistic "standards" of contemporary society.
3. Suggest a plan of Bible reading and meditation that a believer can follow to become better acquainted with God's law.

Lesson Outline

INTRODUCTION
  A. "Is This the Way?"
  B. Lesson Background
I. THE LORD'S PEOPLE (Psalm 1:1-6)
  A. Avoid the Sinners' Way (v. 1)
  B. Delight in God's Law (v. 2)
  C. Produce and Prosper (vv. 3-5)
  D. Enjoy God's Protection (v. 6)
    Judgment Comes
II. THE LORD'S LAW (Psalm 19:7-10)
  A. Perfect and Sure (v. 7)
  B. Right and Pure (v. 8)
  C. Clean and True (v. 9)
    Added Ingredients
  D. Rich and Sweet (v.10)
CONCLUSION
  A. Life's Map and Manual
  B. Prayer
  C. Thought to Remember

Introduction

A. "Is This the Way?"

A practical-joking preacher enjoyed pulling to the curb and asking unsuspecting pedestrians, "Can you tell me, is this the way?" The blank, puzzled look on the faces of those he joshed in this manner made him laugh as he pulled away out of earshot. This preacher was easily amused!

Jesus wasn't joshing His disciples when He announced, "I go to prepare a place for you . . . and the way ye know." Thomas objected, "Lord, we know not whither thou goest; and how can we know the way?" Jesus replied, "I am the way" (John 14:2-6). Unfortunately, too many folk are unsuccessful in finding the right way because they don't know (or haven't decided) where they are going. They aren't sure of their destination, so any road will do.

"Where am I going?" must be answered before "Is this the way?" can make any sense. Once a person has decided to go to God, then the way is clear—revealed by the Scriptures. Divinely inspired instructions detail the route to righteousness, like a TripTik® to Heaven. Today's texts are good examples.

B. Lesson Background

If you were forced to "give up" thirty-eight of the thirty-nine Old Testament books, the one book you probably would choose to keep is the Psalms. More than one commentator has declared the Psalms to be the single most important book in the Old Testament. As a window into the faith of ancient Israel, these "songs" still speak to us today since neither God nor human nature changes. And the communication to which they witness is a two-way street: not only does God speak to humanity to reveal His will, but humans also speak to God in prayer and praise.

Today we begin a nine-lesson series on the Psalms. What better place to begin than right at the beginning?

I. The Lord's People
(Psalm 1:1-6)

A. Avoid the Sinners' Way (v. 1)

1. Blessed is the man that walketh not in the counsel of the ungodly, nor standeth in the way of sinners, nor sitteth in the seat of the scornful.

The word *blessed* can mean "happy," but—as in the Beatitudes (Matthew 5:1-12)—it really means so much more. We should understand it to suggest "fulfilled," "content," or "satisfied" in one's fellowship with God. Taken together, the three verbs *walketh, standeth,* and *sitteth* serve as an example of Hebrew parallelism, a technique used frequently in Scripture. Parallelism enlists two or more slightly different words or phrases to say virtually the same thing. This parallelism also holds for the terms *ungodly, sinners,* and *scornful,* which are synonyms. Notice that the parallelism is negative, since this verse describes things that the godly are *not* to do. (A similar parallelism is found, in positive terms, in Deuteronomy 6:7.)

Avoiding *the counsel of the ungodly, the way of sinners,* and *the seat of the scornful* requires what might be called "discrimination" on the part of God's people, who must choose not to associate with certain types of people.

Discrimination is a difficult concept. Racial discrimination has blighted Western culture for centuries—and even the church has not been immune to it. Such discrimination has nothing to do with what this text is endorsing. On the other hand, to say that a person is a "discriminating" shopper is a compliment. Such a shopper will not be fooled by inferior merchandise presented as quality. True and lasting happiness in life is found by those who discriminate in the latter sense, as they learn to discern right from wrong, good from evil, throughout their lives. In this sense, discriminating people discipline themselves to become submissive and obedient to divine absolutes. They do not expose themselves any more than necessary to those who would lead them astray from those absolutes.

Those who choose not to discriminate in this way end up standing *in the way of sinners*. This means more than merely associating with nonbelievers; it implies some level of participation in wickedness. Joining *the scornful* in a mocking rejection of God's Word is ultimate folly, subjecting one's soul to terminal jeopardy. Even the way that seems right to us can lead to desperation and death (Proverbs 16:25). The happiest people on the planet are those who avoid and abstain from such evils. [See question #1, page 352.]

B. Delight in God's Law (v. 2)

2. But his delight is in the law of the LORD; and in his law doth he meditate day and night.

Delight is the personal pleasure of a godly person when reading, studying, and applying the revealed truth of God to life. That person can gladly sing, "The B-I-B-L-E, yes, that's the book for me!"

Meditating on *the law of the Lord* should indeed be a delightful experience—a real pleasure. Actually, *the law of the Lord* includes far more than the Ten Commandments and other statutes delivered through Moses. The phrase embraces all of God's revelation, all of His truth. In providing this revelation, God has given us an inerrant guidebook, a "map," for our journey. Consulting it often and following its directions grants comfort and security on the way and ultimately brings us safely to our eternal destination. [See question #2, page 352.]

C. Produce and Prosper (vv. 3-5)

3. And he shall be like a tree planted by the rivers of water, that bringeth forth his fruit in his season; his leaf also shall not wither; and whatsoever he doeth shall prosper.

Photosynthesis is the natural process by which light generates life, growth, and productivity as it acts on carbon dioxide and *water*. Water is therefore one of the three ingredients in plants necessary to keep them green and growing. In a time when the vast majority of people were involved in agriculture in some way, the illustration of the *fruit*-bearing *tree* in this verse really hit home. Spiritual productivity and prosperity are promised to those committed and faithful to God's way, God's truth, and God's life. The prophet Jeremiah repeated this promise (Jeremiah 17:7, 8) to those who trust and hope in the Lord. [See question #3, page 352.]

Meaning and hope are qualities of life for which everyone longs (cf. Ecclesiastes 3:11). Millions of people merely exist in "quiet desperation" because they are making no significant contribution to human society (or so they feel), and they possess no hope that the future will change that perception, which has become their reality.

But God is aware of all this. He knows our needs (including those slippery "felt needs"). And Scripture promises that He will supply all of our needs (Philippians 4:19). But for our part, an important obligation we have is to delight in His law; this is a key element in meeting our need to *prosper* spiritually.

4, 5. The ungodly are not so: but are like the chaff which the wind driveth away. Therefore the ungodly shall not stand in the judgment, nor sinners in the congregation of the righteous.

The ungodly are those whose attitudes and behavior do not identify them as children of God, as members of His family. In a creation sense, of course, all humans are God's children, but many do not believe that God is, nor do they trust that God rewards those who seek Him. Therefore, it is impossible for them to please Him (Hebrews 11:6).

So, sadly, millions of people are simply spiritual *chaff:* throw-away refuse, unproductive plants in the garden of God. They will not find happiness or blessedness, nor will their excuses hold up in *the judgment*. They will be held accountable for their wickedness and judged for their iniquities. Their cases will not stand up in that final "court," nor will God consider them to be included in *the congregation of the righteous*—either as assembled for worship and fellowship on earth, or in the final gathering before God in Heaven. [See question #4, page 352.]

VISUALS FOR THESE LESSONS

The small visual pictured in each lesson (e. g., page 348) is a small reproduction of a large, full-color poster included in the *Adult Visuals* packet for the Summer Quarter. The packet is available from your supplier. Order No. 492.

D. Enjoy God's Protection (v. 6)

6. For the LORD knoweth the way of the righteous: but the way of the ungodly shall perish.

For the Lord knoweth is translated in the *New International Version* as "for the Lord watches over." We can acknowledge the truth of this statement on an intellectual level, but when it comes right down to it, do we really live our lives with the continuous awareness that God is watching over us and our *way*—and that He has the power to help us on that way?

At one point in his ministry, the prophet Jeremiah affirmed God's sovereignty and that "there is nothing too hard for thee" (Jeremiah 32:17), but a bit later God repeats Jeremiah's affirmation right back to him in the form of a question (Jeremiah 32:27) as if to say, "Jeremiah, I've heard you say such-and-such about Me, but do you *really* believe it?" The "blessed" person being described in this passage does indeed believe it and live it.

JUDGMENT COMES

For Bonnie and Clyde, earthly judgment came swiftly in a hail of bullets. For Al Capone, earthly judgment moved more slowly, but he eventually went to prison and died gradually of syphilis after his release. More recently, organized crime leader John Gotti received imprisonment.

Crooks are not the only ones who are forced to face the consequences of their actions. Anyone who violates God's law will face His condemnation. "For we must all appear before the judgment seat of Christ; that every one may receive the things done in his body, according to that he hath done, whether it be good or bad" (2 Corinthians 5:10).

Fear of divine condemnation is an appropriate motive to help us live righteously. Many young people make a genuine commitment to Christ motivated by the desire to avoid Hell. Many Christians say "No" to temptation because they do not want to face God's wrath. This need not be our only motive for righteous living. But when other reasons for following the Lord's guidance fail, this one is good enough. "The Lord knoweth the way of the righteous: but the way of the ungodly shall perish" (Psalm 1:6).   —J. D. J.

II. The Lord's Law
(Psalm 19:7-10)

A. Perfect and Sure (v. 7)

7. The law of the LORD is perfect, converting the soul: the testimony of the LORD is sure, making wise the simple.

Now we turn to the results of meditating on *the law of the Lord.* Although this law is *perfect,* one cannot help but notice from the nightly news as well as many recent court cases that human law is not perfect, and that our justice system is not flawless. It can be disillusioning to see and hear the behind-the-scenes strategy sessions and plea-bargaining that go on prior to a trial.

Even so, the perfection of God's law reassures us that "the Judge of all the earth [shall] do right" (Genesis 18:25). *Converting the soul* reads "reviving the soul" in the *New International Version.* The perfection of God's revealed truth restores one's confidence in law and justice. It brings (or brings back) to one's soul convictions about sin, righteousness, and judgment (cf. John 16:8).

The Lord's *sure testimony* gives wisdom to those who are open to spiritual guidance. *Simple* does not refer to people with a low IQ (as in "simple minded"), but rather signifies something more like "inexperienced" (cf. Proverbs 1:4). Reading the Bible can be likened to digging for gems in a mine: some "gems" are very near the surface, and are easily accessible by the most inexperienced miner; other "gems" require deeper digging by the more experienced. But all "miners" can benefit from the search. "Blessed are they which do hunger and thirst after righteousness: for they shall be filled" (Matthew 5:6). Psalm 19:1-6 notes what may be learned about God through nature. As useful as such knowledge is, the knowledge gained by studying *the law of the Lord* is so much greater!

B. Right and Pure (v. 8)

8. The statutes of the LORD are right, rejoicing the heart: the commandment of the LORD is pure, enlightening the eyes.

The Hebrew parallelism noted in Psalm 1:1 is very strong here. The *law* and *testimony* of 19:7

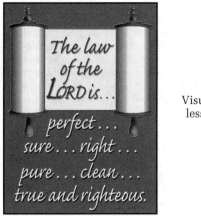

Visual for
lesson 1

Display this poster from the Adult Visuals *packet to introduce verses 7-10 of today's text.*

are synonymous with the *statutes* and *commandment.* Taken together, the picture that these four words paint is that all the words of God are important.

We must admit that human, earthly statutes do not always result in *rejoicing* of *the heart.* A speed limit of twenty-five miles per hour in a residential area may seem unusually strict if we are in a hurry, particularly if the houses are set back a good distance from the road and the yards are safely fenced. But in our "right minds," we know that such laws are needed and reasonable, particularly when we think of our own neighborhoods! How much more should the rightness of God's statutes make our hearts rejoice.

This Psalm of David also reminds us that God's laws are *enlightening.* We know that idolatry, adultery, thievery, murder, and covetousness are wrong because, quite simply, God says so. The law of God is our great teacher. The apostle Paul notes that "by the law is the knowledge of sin" (Romans 3:20).

Of particular interest here is that this enlightening comes through *the eyes.* Our eyes can be the conduit for much good as we use them to bring God's law to our awareness. But the eyes can also bring much harm to the soul if used, for example, to "read" pornography. David's most serious episode of sin began with the misuse of his eyes (2 Samuel 11:2). Perhaps as a result of this he vowed that he would "set no wicked thing before [his] eyes" (Psalm 101:3). Jesus also had some important things to say about the eyes (Matthew 5:29; 6:22, 23). [See question #5, page 352.]

C. Clean and True (v. 9)

9. The fear of the LORD is clean, enduring for ever: the judgments of the LORD are true and righteous altogether.

This verse changes the parallel structure of the previous two verses. First, we find a description of human response to God, rather than a synonym for law; *fear* in this context refers to reverential awe of God. Second, we find a reference to the excellence of God's *judgments,* as in "verdicts."

But even given this departure from the parallel structure, two interesting similarities to vv. 7, 8 present themselves. First, *fear* is closely associated with God's Word or law elsewhere in Scripture (see Exodus 9:20 and Deuteronomy 28:58). Second, the Hebrew word for *judgments* here can also be rendered as "ordinances" (as it is in the *New International Version),* thus bringing back the specific idea of His law. This word *judgments* (or ordinances) is found numerous times within Psalm 119.

How to Say It

BEATITUDE. Bee-*a*-tuh-*tood* (*a* as in bat; strong accent on *a*).
JEREMIAH. Jair-uh-*my*-uh.

Those who take seriously the Lord and His law react in a consistent, never-changing *(for ever)* way. Since divine absolutes never change, so should our reception and obedience be unchanging. The living Word, Jesus Christ, is "the same yesterday, and today, and for ever" (Hebrews 13:8), and He declared, "my words shall not pass away" (Matthew 24:35). The unchangeableness (or "immutability") of God and of His Word satisfies the human desire for sameness and security.

ADDED INGREDIENTS

For someone who does not know how to cook, adding ingredients to a recipe feels adventuresome. What would pancakes taste like with Tabasco® sauce? How would cayenne pepper affect macaroni and cheese? We can do this with food. But adding new ingredients to our faith is not wise.

When someone preaches from God's Word each Sunday, you probably do not think much about it. You assume all preachers present God's truth accurately. However, this is not the case. Many preachers add ingredients to the gospel without hesitation.

One preacher devoted his whole sermon to condemning people who let the devil into their homes. You could tell who they were, he said, because they have the devil's horns (TV antennas) on top of their houses. Another preacher changed his sermon topic when he saw a woman come to worship wearing slacks. He preached against evil, worldly women.

If the person in your church who preaches each week honestly communicates the Bible's truth, thank him. Let him know you appreciate the effort he puts into "rightly dividing the word of truth" (2 Timothy 2:15).

In addition, beware that you do not unconsciously add ingredients to the gospel yourself. It is easy, for example, to superimpose popular "steps to success" from a self-help book on our faith. What might you have added unknowingly to God's recipe for Christianity? Remember: "Too many cooks spoil the broth."   —J. D. J.

D. Rich and Sweet (v. 10)

10. More to be desired are they than gold, yea, than much fine gold: sweeter also than honey and the honeycomb.

The psalmist uses figures here that appeal to human cravings for possessions and sense experiences. It comes quite naturally for us to desire wealth and to gratify the tastebuds. Ownership and taste are two carnal drives that we can readily acknowledge. Described in this language, we are impressed by the indispensable value of the judgments (or "ordinances") of God.

These observations, of course, now challenge us about our own perceptions. Is the Bible desirable and sweet to us? The answer will be revealed in our daily Bible-reading habits. It will also be found in our outrage and action (or lack of action!) over the contemporary court battles that threaten religious expression, such as prohibiting the display of the Ten Commandments in public schools and government buildings, etc.

Jesus described God's kingdom in terms similar to the figures of speech used here to describe God's Word. He compared the kingdom to "buried treasure" and "priceless pearls," which are to be desired to the point of sacrificing all else (Matthew 13:44-46). A Christian sense of values appraises spiritual commodities as invaluable. The Holy Scriptures and the Lord's church are of inestimable eternal worth.

Conclusion

A. Life's Map and Manual

Contrary to a popular old song, life is not like a "mountain railroad"—at least in one respect. On a railroad, in the mountains or anywhere, the train follows a set of tracks in a predetermined direction. Passengers are not required to make choices regarding their route; they will simply go wherever the tracks take them. The only decision a train traveler must make is when to disembark.

Home Daily Bible Readings

Monday, May 27—Choose the Righteous Way (Psalm 1:1-6)
Tuesday, May 28—God Loves Righteousness and Justice (Psalm 33:1-5)
Wednesday, May 29—Hope in God's Steadfast Love (Psalm 33:10-22)
Thursday, May 30—The Lord Loves Righteous Deeds (Psalm 11:1-7)
Friday, May 31—God Is a Righteous Judge (Psalm 7:9-17)
Saturday, June 1—Heavens Tell of God's Glory (Psalm 19:1-6)
Sunday, June 2—The Lord's Law Is Perfect (Psalm 19:7-14)

Life, on the other hand, is packed with choices and decisions. It is more like driving a car than riding a train. We choose the road, the exits to take, the turns to make, the stops, the speed, the vehicles to pass, the yields, the merges—the number of decisions can be daunting.

Experienced auto travelers usually rely upon maps to plot their journey and upon manuals to operate their vehicles. Road signs help them find their way. Those on spiritual journeys, too, make their best progress when they consult a map and manual. Fortunately, Christians have been provided explicit directions for their spiritual journey. The Holy Bible, God's written revelation, is our guide, "a lamp unto [our] feet, a light unto [our] path" (Psalm 119:105).

God's Word will keep us on the highway to Heaven, if we read it and heed it. Although the road is narrow (Matthew 7:14), the instructions are clear. Biblical precepts and precedents show us the right way to follow into the kingdom. Choosing the right route, making the right turns, passing the wrong exits, and yielding not to temptation—the whole TripTik® is written out for us. Roadside service even is available, for God is going with us, and He will not fail or forsake us (Deuteronomy 31:6).

A mystifying trait of travelers (especially of men, so it seems) is a reluctance to ask directions. Many would rather wander for an hour to find their destination than take five minutes to ask someone how to get there. But the Word of God stresses to "Ask, and it shall be given you; seek, and ye shall find" (Matthew 7:7). Asking and seeking are necessary for finding the way to God. Asking requires humility and wisdom. It means you are admitting to being lost and not knowing the way. You are confessing helplessness: "I cannot find my way alone."

Such admissions and confessions are wise choices when one is lost. They are good for the soul, too, when you follow up by searching the Scriptures and by following Jesus, who is "the Way." God's inerrant Word is the map and manual for a successful journey into His presence.

B. Prayer

Dear Lord, thank You for clear instructions in Your Word about holy and happy living. Forgive us when we've been too proud to seek Your help and ask Your directions. Please walk beside us day by day on the Kingdom way and assist us when we stray. Rescue us when we are lost and lead us gently home. In the name of our savior Jesus Christ, amen.

C. Thought to Remember

Before all else fails, read the Book!

Learning by Doing

This page contains an alternate lesson plan emphasizing learning activities.
Classes desiring such student involvement will find these suggestions helpful.

Learning Goals

After participating in this lesson, each student will be able to:

1. Tell what today's texts say about the blessings and rewards of walking in the godly way.

2. Compare the psalmist's trust in the unchanging Word of God with the relativistic "standards" of contemporary society.

3. Suggest a plan of Bible reading and meditation that a believer can follow to become better acquainted with God's law.

Into the Lesson

OPTION: *Maze.* If you have flexible seating, a maze in your classroom can illustrate the need we have to trust in God's guidance. Ask for a volunteer to negotiate the maze of scattered chairs blindfolded. Ask for four volunteers to give guidance. Only one will give correct directions. The other three, (the ungodly, the wicked, and the scornful of Psalm 1:1) give incorrect and distracting directions. Tell the walker he or she must listen carefully to the one voice only.

Make the transition by saying, "Many voices are giving directions to us in life, but only God's words are reliable and trustworthy."

OPTION: *Trip-Ticket.* Have your class design a trip-ticket to the tree of productivity and prosperity. A trip-ticket shows a detailed map of the journey including construction sites and delays to avoid, plus scenic attractions and advice on how to get the most out of your trip.

For example, your trip-ticket might begin like this, "The journey to the tree of productivity and prosperity is a long journey through a variety of scenic country and city roads. Your travels will include many ups and downs as well as unanticipated detours. If you should get lost, do not ask for directions or counsel from the ungodly." (This activity is in the *Adult Bible Class.)*

Make the transition to the Bible study portion of the lesson by saying, "It would be impossible to give directions to a place you have never visited if you did not have an accurate road map. In life we need an accurate road map to find our way to our desired destination."

Into the Word

OPTION: *Choral Reading.* Psalms 1 and 19 both lend themselves to choral reading. Assign verses or phrases to be read by different voices. The purpose of a choral reading is to emphasize meaning and enhance enjoyment of the Psalm. For example, Psalm 1 might be assigned like this:

Blessed could be read by everyone.

Is the man, by a man.

That walketh not in the counsel of the ungodly, by a woman.

Nor standeth in the way of sinners, by a duet of two voices.

Nor sitteth in the seat of the scornful, by a trio of three voices.

But his delight, by a strong deep voice with an echoing chorus of *delight* that fades in volume.

Is in the law of the Lord, by a female voice.

And in his law doth he meditate, by a strong deep voice, with a fading echoing of *meditate.*

OPTION: *Song.* Psalms were often written to be sung. Using Psalm 1 and Psalm 19 as models for content, write a song that honors and describes the Word of God. Tell your class the song does not have to rhyme.

Select a simple, familiar melody. List ideas you want to include. Have a class member write ideas on a board or use an overhead projector. Encourage editing and rewriting. (This activity is included in the *Adult Bible Class.)*

Into Life

OPTION: *Posters or Wall Hangings.* Posters and wall hangings are popular to show what's important in one's life. Provide color markers and poster paper for your class to use in designing posters. Or provide cloth material, bubble paint, glue, and the like for class members to use in creating wall hangings to honor God's Word and show their delight in the law of God.

OPTION: *Bible Reading Plan.* Following a daily Bible-reading program is one way to make God's law one's delight. Many plans are available. A plan for reading through the Bible in a year is included in some Bibles. Standard Publishing's *Devotions* includes a daily devotional thought based on a short passage of Scripture related to this lesson series. Daily plans on a single page are available through Bible societies or Christian bookstores. Make some available to your class members and ask members to commit themselves to a daily devotional or Bible-reading plan that will make God's Word their delight and meditation. (Directions for this are included in *Adult Bible Class.)*

Let's Talk It Over

The questions on this page are designed to encourage review of the lesson Scriptures and to promote discussion of the lesson by the class. The answers provided are only discussion starters. Let your class talk it over from there.

1. If we had to produce a video illustrating the people in today's culture with whom Christians were not to walk or sit (the "ungodly . . . sinners . . . scornful"), who would be included? Did Jesus' practice of visiting and eating with sinners violate this admonition? Why or why not?

Every generation would have its own list. Twenty years ago, operators of Internet pornography sites would not have been on the list. Ask the students to make a list of people with whom it would not be good for the Christian to enter into a partnership.

Jesus associated with sinners as a means to witness to them. His goal was not just "to hang out" with them. He always called them to a higher lifestyle. He did not join the way they lived their lives. Our task is to fulfill Jesus' prayer for us that we would be "in the world . . . not of the world" (John 17:11, 14).

2. How would the average Christian's life change if he or she meditated more on Biblical themes?

"As a person thinks, so is he" is an often quoted proverb. The writer of the psalm knew that meditating on God's truth would have a profound, life-changing impact. Meditating on passages that exalt God and declare His love and mercy will lead one to become more loving—both toward God and to others. Meditating on those verses that command forgiveness of others will help us to be more forgiving. But perhaps Jesus' own example is most instructive. Being intimately familiar with God's Word (which meditating on the Word will help us to be) put Scriptural answers at His recall when the devil tempted Him.

Meditating on God's Word also has the effect of "displacing" other thoughts. It doesn't really do much good to give up habits that produce impure thoughts (such as use of pornography) unless those bad habits are *replaced* with something better. Remember the account of the unclean spirit that returned to an empty house with the result that "the last state of that man is worse than the first" (Matthew 12:45).

3. Our current generation has been dubbed the "microwave generation" because we want everything "right now." In what ways does this impatience rob Christians of learning the lessons of Psalm 1?

No matter how "convenient" life becomes, we soon adjust and want things to be even faster and better. Those of us who remember when microwave ovens first came out will recall how we marveled at the fact that we now could have a "baked" potato in three or four minutes rather than an hour and a half. But now that we're used to that speed, we wait impatiently for those few minutes to go by! If we're not careful, we will cultivate within ourselves an impatience for even more, rather than "an attitude of gratitude."

The life habits described in the psalm produce the spiritual equivalent of a strong tree that developed over several years. Its fruit-producing capacity is maximized because all the ingredients for a fruit-bearing tree have been added along the way. The process cannot be rushed (although scientists keep trying to figure out ways to speed up even these things!). Impatience will rob us of both the nutrients and the growth experience.

4. Many Christians want troublesome sinners to be dealt with in a swift fashion (blown away like chaff in a windstorm). In what ways can Christians be disappointed if God does not carry out His judgment fast enough to suit their expectations?

Once a Christian sees those who always seem to "get away with" their wickedness, disillusionment may set in. (Compare Psalm 73 to illustrate the disillusioning impact.) However, the Christian who has confidence in the final victory through Christ will be able to deal with those times when the sinners seem to be winning.

5. In what ways can the Scripture "excite the senses"?

Sometimes the eyes just want to keep reading to see what God says next. At other times, hearing the Word makes us long to hear more; this can be especially true if the speaker is a skilled orator such as Charlton Heston. Some even experience a sense of comfort when they pick up the Bible they use all the time and it has "just the right feel" about it. While these sensations by themselves will not add to our spiritual depth, they do provide encouragement and motivation to dig deeper into the treasures of the Word.

Hope in God

DEVOTIONAL READING: Psalm 43.

BACKGROUND SCRIPTURE: Psalms 42; 43.

PRINTED TEXT: Psalm 42:1-11.

Psalm 42:1-11

1 As the hart panteth after the water brooks, so panteth my soul after thee, O God.

2 My soul thirsteth for God, for the living God: when shall I come and appear before God?

3 My tears have been my meat day and night, while they continually say unto me, Where is thy God?

4 When I remember these things, I pour out my soul in me: for I had gone with the multitude, I went with them to the house of God, with the voice of joy and praise, with a multitude that kept holyday.

5 Why art thou cast down, O my soul? And why art thou disquieted in me? Hope thou in God: for I shall yet praise him for the help of his countenance.

6 O my God, my soul is cast down within me: therefore will I remember thee from the land of Jordan, and of the Hermonites, from the hill Mizar.

7 Deep calleth unto deep at the noise of thy waterspouts: all thy waves and thy billows are gone over me.

8 Yet the LORD will command his loving-kindness in the daytime, and in the night his song shall be with me, and my prayer unto the God of my life.

9 I will say unto God my rock, Why hast thou forgotten me? Why go I mourning because of the oppression of the enemy?

10 As with a sword in my bones, mine enemies reproach me; while they say daily unto me, Where is thy God?

11 Why art thou cast down, O my soul? And why art thou disquieted within me? Hope thou in God: for I shall yet praise him, who is the health of my countenance, and my God.

GOLDEN TEXT: Hope thou in God: for I shall yet praise him, who is the health of my countenance, and my God.—Psalm 42:11.

Lesson Aims

After participating in this lesson, each student will be able to:

1. Summarize the psalmist's journey from being "cast down" to finding hope in God.

2. Define "hope" in the Biblical sense.

3. Add an element of praise to personal devotional time that focuses more on God and less on personal circumstances.

Lesson Outline

Introduction

A. Hope at the End of Your Rope

Sometimes hope seems in short supply. Far from home, alone among strangers, sleepless in the night—now there's a recipe for a big batch of hopelessness! Silence, darkness, humiliation, torment—these add to the despair. Perhaps you've been there, done that.

Maybe you recall a time when you were beaten up by a bully. Perhaps you've lost your way in a big city on a dark night, and some suspicious individuals followed you too closely while your gas gauge read empty. Or maybe you lost your job and came down with the flu on the same day that your car broke down and your teenage son was arrested for hacking into the private computer files of the IRS!

We've all had those days when things just seem to pile up. You know that hopeless feeling. You're at the end of your rope. The psalmist in today's text despaired under circumstances different from those above, but the anguish is familiar. Depression sets in, and there seems to be no hope or help. When the psalmist recalls, however, that God still exists and still rewards those who seek Him, then praises and prayer witness to restored confidence, optimism, and faith.

B. Lesson Background

The book of Psalms as a whole has traditionally been divided into five sub-books. Psalm 42 before us today begins "Book Two" of that five-part subset. This passage is a poetic conversation—a conversation that is sometimes between the writer and his own soul, and at other times is with God, who does not speak except through memories, His loving presence, and songs in the night. The psalmist alternately wallows in despair, then resists it; he complains, then switches to exaltation and self-encouragement.

The author of Psalm 42 is unknown to us, although the superscription says generally that this psalm is "for [or 'of'] the sons of Korah" (in David's time they were musicians; see 1 Chronicles 6:22, 31, 32, 37). Whoever the author was, hope in God is what guided him through what John Bunyan in *Pilgrim's Progress* called the "Slough of Despond." It was the same kind of hope that kept the early Christian martyrs focused on their eternal goal despite their circumstances. And it is the kind of hope we still need today—a hope that will keep us moving toward eternity in Heaven.

I. Craving God
(Psalm 42:1-5)

A. Intense Longing (vv. 1, 2)

1. As the hart panteth after the water brooks, so panteth my soul after thee, O God.

Unquenched thirst can be painful, debilitating, and even fatal. When *the water brooks* are dry, *the hart* (that is, "deer") can die. Dehydration is the critical consequence of too little water. Most of us have seen animals as they "pant" in their search for water to slake their thirst. This is the psalmist's picture of his own search for *thee, O God.*

The image is graphic, the yearning intense. The psalmist's *soul* is drying up. The word *soul* here is not just the spiritual part of his life; it refers to his whole being. If he remains separated from the divine fellowship of worship, if he does not find satisfying communion with God soon, his entire being will die—that is clearly his conviction. He is desperately thirsty for the living water that flows from divine/human encounters; this is the type of refreshment that proceeds only from God's presence, only from the Spirit's filling, only from his God's abiding truth.

2. My soul thirsteth for God, for the living God: when shall I come and appear before God?

I remember an occasion of unforgettable thirst. It was the summer of 1962, and I was a tourist in Egypt on an overnight train trip from Cairo to Luxor. The windows had to be open due to the horrendous heat, so great clouds of dust billowed in as the train raced through the desert. As I lay in my cramped berth, my throat became so dry I thought I might choke. My tongue seemed permanently stuck to the roof of my mouth. On the wall opposite the bunk was attached a carafe of water—warm, dusty, and who-knows-how-else contaminated. Despite the risk, however, I sucked it down in a chug-a-lug frenzy as if it might save my life. I still wonder at the thirst that could cause me to do such a thing!

The writer of this Psalm sensed not a mere physical thirst like mine, but a "whole-being" thirst of great intensity. We can only speculate as to why he had been separated from venues and opportunities of worship, and from the support and encouragement of other people of faith. But we can relate to the emptiness and longing he felt when he feared he was beyond the sphere of God's presence. [See question #1, page 360.]

Remember that worship in the Old Testament era tended to be focused on the temple in Jerusalem, and separation from that place meant "no worship" (see "house of God" in v. 4 below). Even as late as Jesus' day, a Samaritan woman, when speaking to Jesus, observed that "Our fathers worshipped in this mountain; but ye say, that in Jerusalem is the place where men ought to worship" (John 4:20).

Jesus' reply to that Samaritan woman makes it clear that location no longer limits worship and certainly never precludes God's presence. A realization that God is "everywhere" allows us to quench our thirst for Him anywhere we happen to find ourselves—not just in a "church building." When the Samaritan woman had come to fill her vessel with water at Jacob's well near Sychar, Jesus offered her "living water . . . a well of water springing up into everlasting life" (John 4:10, 14). Christ promises that those who satisfy their souls with Him will never thirst again.

Today, we are privileged to look back to the reality of fulfilled prophecy in Jesus and claim this truth for ourselves. The author of today's Psalm, however, did not have this privilege. Although later in the text he will look forward in hope, his yearning could not draw upon the fulfilled

prophecy of the Messiah's coming for comfort and strength; he could see only the dire straits of his present circumstances, so he poured his heart out in song. Although today we, in contrast to the psalmist, have the clear fulfillment of the promised Messiah to look back to for assurance, sometimes our own circumstances can be so dismal that all we, too, can do is pour out our yearnings in song. In times like those, hymns such as "I Must Tell Jesus" become particularly meaningful.

In expressing his desire to *appear before God*, the psalmist is either articulating his need to worship or voicing a wish for death—it's hard to tell which. Psalm 84:7, part of a psalm also "for (or 'of') the sons of Korah," would support the worship idea in expressing the blessedness of everyone who "in Zion appeareth before God"; by association, "Zion" includes the temple, which was the focus of Israelite worship. [See question #2, page 360.]

When we *appear* before God in worship, it is a foretaste of what eternity will be like. When Jesus returns, the righteous will be in His eternal presence (1 Thessalonians 2:19; 3:13; 4:17). On the other hand, the everlasting destruction of the unrighteous means, among other things, eternal banishment from His presence (2 Thessalonians 1:9).

B. Painful Taunts (v. 3)

3. My tears have been my meat day and night, while they continually say unto me, Where is thy God?

The psalmist's perception of his separation from the presence of God causes the most profound grief (cf. Psalm 80:5). His suffering is magnified by the taunt of his enemies, *Where is thy God?* This question perhaps causes the psalmist to ask himself in turn, "Where, indeed, *is* my God?" The question "Where is . . . ?" appears as a taunt several places in Scripture, and is used by both friends and enemies of God (e.g., Psalm 79:10; Joel 2:17; 1 Corinthians 1:20; 15:55).

How to Say It

CORINTHIANS. Kor-*in*-thee-unz.
HERMONITES. *Her*-mun-ites.
JERUSALEM. Jee-*roo*-suh-lem.
JORDAN. *Jor*-dun.
KORAH. *Ko*-rah.
MIZAR. *My*-zar.
PHILIPPIANS. Fih-*lip*-ee-unz.
SAMARITAN. Suh-*mare*-uh-tun.
SYCHAR. *Sigh*-kar.
THESSALONIANS. *Thess*-uh-*lo*-nee-unz (strong accent on *lo*; *th* as in *thin*).

How many Christians today actually shed *tears* when they have to miss public worship? Unfortunately, it doesn't mean that much to many, except in countries where people are deprived of that privilege and freedom. The one whose prayer we are studying today apparently was being persecuted for his faith, or at least being restricted from practicing it. Religious harassment and persecution is a tragic reality in many areas of the world today. The global Christian community is obligated to "Remember those in prison as if you were their fellow prisoners, and those who are mistreated as if you yourselves were suffering" (Hebrews 13:3, *New International Version)*.

C. Precious Memories (v. 4)

4. When I remember these things, I pour out my soul in me: for I had gone with the multitude, I went with them to the house of God, with the voice of joy and praise, with a multitude that kept holyday.

The writer evidently has been prevented from enjoying worship and feast days in the temple as he formerly did. As already noted, the "why" is not clear. Given the taunt in verse 3, the situation likely involves some crisis where the psalmist is under the control of, or is imprisoned by, an enemy or foreign invader.

When distance, time, or other circumstances separate us from the experiences of the "good old days," our memories can still transport us to places and events that inspire and give peace. Reflecting on his worship activities and celebrations of the past—probably the *these things*—helped this poet tolerate his present troubles. In times of emotional distress and negative moods, people can encourage themselves by remembering who they are, how far they've come, and the many who have helped them on their way. Remembering good times with the church, good friends among Christians, and how our lives have been blessed by those relationships will lift our spirits and give us a more optimistic outlook.

It is possible, of course, to become nostalgic to the point of merely feeling sorry for oneself. Some church members have been known to get into trouble in this regard when the church makes changes in matters of style or methods. They sink into "pity parties" as their familiar way of doing things is left behind. But in this rapidly changing world, life will never be exactly the same as it once was. Even so, it can be better. For those who dwell negatively on the past, the apostle Paul offers help: "Forgetting those things which are behind, and reaching forth unto those things which are before, I press toward the mark for the prize of the high calling of God in Christ Jesus" (Philippians 3:13, 14).

D. Hopeful Thoughts (v. 5)

5. Why art thou cast down, O my soul? And why art thou disquieted in me? Hope thou in God: for I shall yet praise him for the help of his countenance.

Now we see the optimism and confidence of an overcomer! Having recalled pleasant memories of active worship and service in God's house, the psalmist seems to shake off his depression, question his doubts, and renew his commitment to trust and glorify God. It won't be the last time he must overcome discouragement, as we shall see in the next few verses, but for this moment, at least, he has experienced personal revival. He expresses a renewed passion for praising God. He has his head on straight, and he's ready to face the future.

Hope anticipates that God will act. When the psalmist's hope returns and God's past, present, and future *help* is acknowledged, faith comes alive. When faith is resurrected, believers long to *praise* the Lord. Then God "inhabits" (or becomes "enthroned on") the praises (Psalm 22:3), and worshipers sense His presence. So a victorious cycle of hope and help increases faith that can overcome doubt and depression.

II. Complaining to God
(Psalm 42:6-11)

A. Loneliness of Exile (vv. 6, 7)

6. O my God, my soul is cast down within me: therefore will I remember thee from the land of Jordan, and of the Hermonites, from the hill Mizar.

The *therefore* demonstrates that the depressed poet has found an effective formula for beating the blues: remember the safe places, the supportive people, and the grand worship of yesteryear. Then he (and we) can praise God for the past, if not for the present.

The locales mentioned here are in the upper Jordan Valley, north of Jerusalem. They point to the sources of the Jordan River, thus the water imagery of v. 1 returns. Unable because of circumstances to attend the ceremonies of the Hebrews in the "Holy City," he does the next best thing: he vows to *remember* God where he now finds himself. Despite his despondent state, this faithful follower will not forget his God. Such an example is instructive for our own faithfulness.

7. Deep calleth unto deep at the noise of thy waterspouts: all thy waves and thy billows are gone over me.

The poet's misery resurfaces here as the water imagery turns negative. He melodramatically describes the tragedies of his life as *all thy waves and thy billows*. The *noise* isn't comforting—

quite the opposite! Though it seems emotionally excessive, this is his perception and thus his reality. No one likes to have his problems minimized. No one should dispute the depths of the psalmist's grief. The next verse is evidence of yet another mood swing.

SECURE IN HIS STRENGTH

A framed photograph you may have seen in a Christian bookstore illustrates the reason for our hope in God. The picture shows a man standing at the back door of a lighthouse. Ten-foot waves are crashing against the structure, but the man is safe and dry in the doorway.

This Psalm pictures waves and billows of trouble washing over us (verse 7). But again and again, the author turns for strength to God. He is our Rock (verse 9).

In the photograph, as in this Psalm, the individual's sanctuary from the waves is something stronger than himself. He remains secure as long as he stays in its shelter. The Rock, the solid lighthouse, will protect him.

Unfortunately, we tend not to trust God's ability to shelter us. We often feel we must build our own addition to the protection He provides. "I trust God (plus my health insurance and IRA) to protect me." "I believe God (plus my skills and personality) will provide for me." We don't announce these heresies aloud. If we did, everyone, including ourselves, would see our faithlessness. But we continue to believe that God needs our help to get us successfully through life.

The lighthouse poster and this Psalm call us to rest in God's strength. Trust Him to handle the billows and waves. Remain in His protective shelter. This will give us another reason to praise Him.   —J. D. J.

B. God Comforts (v. 8)

8. Yet the LORD will command his lovingkindness in the daytime, and in the night his song shall be with me, and my prayer unto the God of my life.

The psalmist's emotional venting vacillates wildly: first compliance, then praise, then bad news, later good news. The psalmist is up and down like a yo-yo—a problem with many Christians today. Sometimes life experiences put us on a roller coaster of mood swings. When that happens, we may become confused about our relationship with God. "Is He true? Have I drifted? Am I connected? Is He listening when I pray? Is it wrong to have questions? Is doubting a sin? Is pretending a transgression?"

Then a surge of faith may come, and once again we confess our trust in the Lord, much as the writer does in this verse. In our heart of hearts, we know God is loving and kind. When we're honest, we are certain that His providential care surrounds us both *in the daytime* as well as *in the night*—His care is available twenty-four hours a day, seven days a week. And we feel exhilarated to acknowledge His presence and power in our prayers. He never sleeps; He never changes; great is His faithfulness.

C. Same Song, Second Verse (vv. 9-11)

9, 10. I will say unto God my rock, Why hast thou forgotten me? Why go I mourning because of the oppression of the enemy? As with a sword in my bones, mine enemies reproach me; while they say daily unto me, Where is thy God?

Not much is new here. With the same pen stroke, both blessing and cursing are scribed. Although God is addressed as *my rock*, He seems to be silent. This silence probably compels the accusatory complaints: "Why don't You do something to rescue me, Lord? Can't You see I'm unhappy? My enemies are stabbing me in the back—don't You care? And what shall I tell them when they ask *where* You are?" [See question #3, page 360.]

Most Christians can relate to that prayer. In the midst of tragedy, humans have an insatiable desire to know *why*. Both Job and Jeremiah ask similar questions (see Job 13:24 and Jeremiah 12:1). In both instances, God did indeed answer their questions, but not in the way they really wanted!

And so it might be with our own questions to Him. When we ask, we had better be prepared for (1) no answer at all (at least, not in this life), (2) a delayed answer, or (3) an answer not entirely to our liking. Remember that God is the One who is always able to see the "big picture" when we can't. Sometimes He will allow us to

Hope thou in God: for I shall yet praise him, who is the health of my countenance, and my God.
—Psalm 42:11

Visual for lesson 2

Today's visual suggests various situations that produce despair and call for hope in God.

see this "big picture" later when life turns around for us, showing us that He intended a temporary setback to result in a greater good.

When those times do come, we might end up thinking back on our complaints and accusations—frequently couched in the form of "why?" questions—with embarrassment. Unless we're careful with the questions we ask during tough times, we, like Job, might end up confessing "Surely I spoke of things I did not understand . . . therefore I despise myself and repent in dust and ashes" (Job 42:3, 6, *New International Version*). [See question #4, page 360.]

LOVED FOR LIFE

If you have been married for more than two months, you know about ups and downs in a relationship. You and your mate may love each other with all of your souls. You may be devoted with all of your hearts. However, this does not prevent you from becoming frustrated with each other and feeling estranged.

In tough times, you may wonder why your mate does not show more thoughtfulness toward you and seems uninterested in fulfilling your needs. Part of the problem is that your whole focus is on yourself. Shifting your focus can help heal the relationship.

We also get frustrated with God when we feel He is not meeting our needs. We whine in our prayers when He is (apparently) silent. A change from this self-centeredness can build a stronger relationship with God. Life is not primarily about us. "God . . . created all things by Jesus Christ: to the intent that now unto the principalities and powers in heavenly places might be known by the church the manifold wisdom of God, according to the eternal purpose which He purposed in Christ Jesus our Lord" (Ephesians 3:9-11).

Home Daily Bible Readings

Monday, June 3—Hope in Distress (Psalm 42:1-11)

Tuesday, June 4—In God I Trust (Psalm 56:1-7)

Wednesday, June 5—I Am Not Afraid (Psalm 56:8-13)

Thursday, June 6—My Hope Is From God (Psalm 62:1-12)

Friday, June 7—You Are My Hope (Psalm 71:1-8)

Saturday, June 8—I Will Hope Continually (Psalm 71:12-24)

Sunday, June 9—God: My Hope and Help (Psalm 43:1-5)

The primary purpose of our lives is to display God's wisdom. When you feel frustrated with God, when you feel your Rock has forgotten you, shift your focus. Hold on to your faith. This will honor God and help you.   —J. D. J.

11 Why art thou cast down, O my soul? And why art thou disquieted within me? Hope thou in God: for I shall yet praise him, who is the health of my countenance, and my God.

[See question #5, page 360.] This is the poet's refrain, repeated from verse 5 with only a minor change, and repeated again in Psalm 43:5. All readers are glad that the passage ends on this positive note. Of the "ups and downs" expressed, the "ups" are far more inspiring and reassuring.

When the psalmist spoke to himself, he used positive language and hopeful thoughts. With this approach, he was able to overcome doubts and fears. The same exercise will work today. "Whatever is true, whatever is noble, whatever is right, whatever is pure, whatever is lovely, whatever is admirable—if anything is excellent or praiseworthy—think about such things" (Philippians 4:8, *New International Version*).

Conclusion

A. The Substance of Things Hoped For

Faith is more than mere wishful thinking. "Things hoped for," in the context of godly faith, are certain to be received. It is a confidence that God exists, that Jesus died to save, and that Heaven is real—but it goes far beyond all of that. Faith trusts that God who has always told the truth is still telling the truth in the written Word that reveals the living Word. Belief and trust are generated by the hope born in a Christian's heart through the grace and knowledge of the Lord Jesus Christ.

Hope is substantive to faith because hope sees possibilities. Hope is visionary. Hope is a positive perception of the future. Hope is the essence of patience and prayer. Hope anticipates and predicts ultimate good because God's purposes will not be defeated. Hope always expects blessing. Hope always gives another chance.

B. Prayer

Dear Lord, thank You for the gift of hope. We praise You for Your presence and Your promises. Forgive us when we doubt Your mercy or question Your wisdom. Help us to remember Your acts of kindness and deliverance. We promise to give You glory and honor. In Jesus' name, amen.

C. Thought to Remember

When hope faces the Son, shadows fall behind.

Learning by Doing

This page contains an alternate lesson plan emphasizing learning activities.
Classes desiring such student involvement will find these suggestions helpful.

Learning Goals

After participating in this lesson, each student will be able to:

1. Summarize the Psalmist's journey from being "cast down" to finding hope in God.

2. Define "hope" in the Biblical sense.

3. Add an element of praise to his or her devotional time, during which the individual focuses more on God and less on personal circumstances.

Into the Lesson

OPTION: *Neighbor Nudge.* Ask each person to turn to the person next to him and take thirty seconds to describe (1) a place where he always feels close to God or (2) a dark hour of the soul when he experienced doubts, depression, isolation, or abandonment.

Make the transition to the Bible study by saying, "Life is filled with emotional ups and downs. Sometimes our hearts are filled with praise for God. At other times we wonder where God is and why He appears not to be concerned about our plight. Today's passage gives us a Biblical view of such fluctuations."

OPTION: *Case Study.* Ask a class member to read this case study to introduce today's lesson. (This is included in *Adult Bible Class.*)

"Wanda has come to you for help. She says, 'I've been feeling so blue lately. I thought that since the children were grown, Jack and I would have more time for each other. But between his work and mine, that hasn't happened. I must work weekends, meaning I can't attend church. I really miss the Ladies Bible Class. My devotional life is practically nonexistent. On some days I try to read my Bible and pray, but God seems so far away. Now don't preach at me—I feel bad enough already. Can you help me?'"

Read the transition statement in the activity above to lead into Bible study.

OPTION: *Picture Study.* Bring five pictures to class: (1) a picture of the interior or exterior of your church, (2) a picturesque scene of nature's splendor, (3) a picture of a mother and a baby, (4) a picture of someone playing golf or fishing, and (5) a group of people enjoying each other's company. They need to be large enough for class members to see. For a small class, full-page pictures from a magazine mounted on card stock would be appropriate. For larger classes, you

could use projected slides. Or you could make color transparencies if you have an overhead projector available. (Color pictures can be copied to transparency film at most copy service centers.) Ask a computer enthusiast for help—such a person will be delighted to share expertise!

Display the five pictures to open the session. Ask a learner to select the picture that makes him or her have hope in God and explain why.

Into the Word

OPTION: *Personalize and Paraphrase.* Provide paper and pens/pencils for class members to paraphrase today's text. In a paraphrase, class members express the ideas and emotions of the text in their own words. Most today would not describe their desire to be with God by referring to a male deer desiring water. We might say, "As a thirsty runner on a hot summer day longs for a cold drink, my heart desires you, O God."

More literal translations, such as the *King James Version* or *New American Standard Version,* work better than versions such as *The Living Bible* or *The Message,* which are already paraphrases. The process of trying to express the meaning of a verse in one's own words is a powerful study device that yields rich insights.

Ask several class members to share their paraphrases with the entire class. In larger classes, you could have people share with those seated near them.

Into Life

OPTION: *Debate.* Divide your class into two groups. Ask them to prepare to debate this proposition: "Being with people of faith is an important part of praise and worship." One side should be directed to affirm the statement, and the other side, to deny the statement.

Challenge your class members to memorize a verse that would be helpful in times of need. Both Psalm 42:1 and 42:11 are good choices. Memorizing a verse as a group can be much more fun and easier to memorize than working alone. One technique is to write the verse on a board and have the class read through it a couple of times in unison. Then erase one or two words and repeat the verse together. Continue this procedure until everything is erased and your class will be pleasantly surprised to discover they have memorized the verse.

Let's Talk It Over

The questions on this page are designed to encourage review of the lesson Scriptures and to promote discussion of the lesson by the class. The answers provided are only discussion starters. Let your class talk it over from there.

1. What words do people use today to describe their longings for God? To what extent has the New Age trend to see many things as "spiritual experiences" blinded people so that they cannot recognize that they have a deep-seated longing for God?

Suggest that students think about times when they have been tested, deserted, persecuted, or discouraged, as well as times they just wanted to be close to God. Ask them to share the phrases they would put into a psalm under those circumstances. If there is a lengthy period of silence (fifteen seconds or so), that's OK. Do not try to fill the seeming awkwardness of the silence with words (or "prompts") of your own. Give them time to think about it!

2. The lesson writer notes that the psalmist's desire to "appear before God" may express a desire to worship or a desire for death. Suppose it is the latter: what does that suggest about the need for every Christian to listen carefully to the words and intentions of other Christians?

The language here is vague, and so is ours when we express an acceptance of a tabu. Many Christians believe they are not "allowed" to be discouraged and disillusioned; so they won't admit it openly. But many circumstances in life (especially those involving financial, legal, and relationship troubles) can and do lead to disillusionment. If the disillusionment is not somehow turned around, despair and suicide can follow. Fellow Christians must "listen" with both eyes and ears to assess accurately the depth and danger of the despair. A Christian might not talk directly about suicide. Instead, he or she might say, "I wish I could just go to sleep and never wake up."

Talking openly with a depressed person about his or her suicidal thoughts—which involves mainly being a good listener and avoiding "giving advice"—tends to be comforting and helpful. That individual often reacts with "I have finally found someone who is not afraid to come into the pit with me. I can trust this person. I can be safe talking with this friend."

3. How would you counsel a struggling Christian to pray during a time of trouble? If the need gets worse, what changes would you expect to notice in the person's prayers?

Glib "advice" is not useful (and may even be harmful). Sometimes struggling people need others to pray alongside them, and you can certainly offer to do so.

As the need intensifies, one would normally expect that prayers would sound more desperate—though some believers might be afraid to voice such desperation. Compare this Psalm with the prayers of Jesus in Matthew 26:36-44; Mark 15:34; and John 17. God is the master of all languages. He has no difficulty understanding different languages as well as the emotional language (tone of voice, gestures, etc.) expressing our deep longings that cannot be put easily into words (Romans 8:26, 27). Give the desperate person permission to be honest with God!

4. The symptoms of depression usually include significant changes in sleeping and/or eating habits, indecisiveness, a negative outlook, a sense of worthlessness, and loss of interest in things that usually bring pleasure. The presence of these symptoms in the psalmist's complaint suggests that he could have been suffering from at least a mild depressive episode. In what ways could fellow Christians help someone today in this emotional state?

Christians today also suffer from episodes of depression. Fellow Christians can be helpful by not judging but listening, by encouraging the person to seek professional help if the depression lingers more than two weeks, and by consistently being a good friend. Job 2:11—31:40 gives us an example of how not to help! Conversely, God's treatment of Elijah in 1 Kings 19 shows a good way to help.

5. In this psalm, the writer's mood seems to be on a "yo-yo." Some Christian helpers prefer that the person with the problem just "get over it." What does this psalm teach us about being good people helpers?

While the chemical changes that come with clinical depression require medical treatment, consistent doses of love and spiritual support are good treatments for the kind of mild depression most of us experience from time to time. Patient reminders of God's faithfulness and of the hope we have for eternal life are valuable in this regard. "Hope thou in God" is always good advice.

Follow the Lord, Our Keeper

DEVOTIONAL READING: Psalm 80:1-3, 14-19.

BACKGROUND SCRIPTURE: Psalms 23; 80; 121.

PRINTED TEXT: Psalms 23:1-6; 121:1-8.

Psalm 23:1-6

1 The LORD is my shepherd; I shall not want.

2 He maketh me to lie down in green pastures: he leadeth me beside the still waters.

3 He restoreth my soul: he leadeth me in the paths of righteousness for his name's sake.

4 Yea, though I walk through the valley of the shadow of death, I will fear no evil: for thou art with me; thy rod and thy staff they comfort me.

5 Thou preparest a table before me in the presence of mine enemies: thou anointest my head with oil; my cup runneth over.

6 Surely goodness and mercy shall follow me all the days of my life: and I will dwell in the house of the LORD for ever.

Psalm 121:1-8

1 I will lift up mine eyes unto the hills, from whence cometh my help.

2 My help cometh from the LORD, which made heaven and earth.

3 He will not suffer thy foot to be moved: he that keepeth thee will not slumber.

4 Behold, he that keepeth Israel shall neither slumber nor sleep.

5 The LORD is thy keeper: the LORD is thy shade upon thy right hand.

6 The sun shall not smite thee by day, nor the moon by night.

7 The LORD shall preserve thee from all evil: he shall preserve thy soul.

8 The LORD shall preserve thy going out and thy coming in from this time forth, and even for evermore.

GOLDEN TEXT: I will lift up mine eyes unto the hills, from whence cometh my help. My help cometh from the LORD, which made heaven and earth.—Psalm 121:1, 2.

Worship and Wisdom for Living
Unit 1: Songs for Faithful Living
(Lessons 1-5)

Lesson Aims

After participating in this lesson, each student will be able to:

1. Compare God's care today to that of a shepherd in ancient times.

2. Contrast fear that is healthy with the kind of fear that reflects lack of faith in God.

3. Memorize portions of today's printed text for use during times when faith is in danger of being overpowered by fear.

Lesson Outline

INTRODUCTION
    A. "Who's Afraid . . . ?"
    B. Lesson Background
  I. PRAISING OUR SHEPHERD AND HOST (Psalm 23:1-6)
    A. Rest and Restoration (vv. 1-3)
      Flying Blind
    B. Protection and Provision (v. 4)
      Foxhole Reality
    C. Care Now and Care Later (vv. 5, 6)
 II. FOLLOWING OUR KEEPER (Psalm 121:1-8)
    A. Calling for Help (vv. 1, 2)
    B. Trusting the Guide (vv. 3-7)
    C. Staying the Course (v. 8)
CONCLUSION
    A. Fear and Faith
    B. Prayer
    C. Thought to Remember

Introduction

A. "Who's Afraid . . . ?"

A "Big, Bad Wolf" of life is fear. Fear wears many names: worry, anxiety, doubt, timidity, indecision, alarm, shock, terror. It isn't readily recognized when it is called names like caution, care, and discretion.

Most children grow through a stage when they are "afraid of the dark." Of course, they are actually afraid of what they imagine to be in the dark. Adults, too, often fear the imaginary. But probably 95 percent of what we worry about never happens. Worry is a form of fear. No wonder Jesus teaches us not to worry (Matthew 6:34).

But although "big, bad wolves" often exist only in our imaginations, Scripture warns us to

beware of wolves (false prophets) who come dressed "in sheep's clothing" (Matthew 7:15). And 1 Peter 5:8 cautions us against "the devil, as a roaring lion, . . . seeking whom he may devour." And ultimately, we are to "Fear him which is able to destroy both soul and body in hell" (Matthew 10:28).

So, not all fear is neurotic and faithless. Sometimes it simply amounts to a healthy respect for real danger. And, of course, fear of the Lord is proper and positive reverence for our Creator and Sustainer.

Inappropriate fears are those that emotionally paralyze us so that we become ineffectual and nonproductive, anxieties that prevent going forward in faith or that preclude bold witness. These are the fears that the apostle Paul had in mind when he wrote to Timothy, "God hath not given us the spirit of fear; but of power, and of love, and of a sound mind" (2 Timothy 1:7).

B. Lesson Background

The texts selected for this lesson are classic examples of faith-filled testimonies in song, sung by those whose adventures with God had taught them not to be afraid. They help replace fear with faith. They come from a time when life was much more difficult than it is now—physically if not spiritually. If the texts considered today inspired faith in those who lived in a time when one's health and "daily bread" were much more uncertain than they are now, how much more should these passages help us today in our own struggles!

I. Praising Our Shepherd and Host (Psalm 23:1-6)

The shepherd metaphor, so often used in Scripture, is not as meaningful to us as to the writer and earliest readers of this poem. Their pastoral lives fitted them uniquely to understand such figures and illustrations. We can, however, be humbled by the psalmist's analogies of provision, protection, and guidance based upon any meager familiarity we may have with the herding of sheep. The host imagery which then follows should intensify our humility all the more.

A. Rest and Restoration (vv. 1-3)

1. The LORD is my shepherd; I shall not want.

The needs of sheep are comparatively simple—basic sustenance and protection. Having food, water, and rest, a sheep is content. A good *shepherd*, of course, also guides, protects, and dresses the wounds of the sheep he is tending.

Our God is a shepherd to us in all those ways and more. Human needs are more complex, since we are spiritual beings as well as physical, but

God supplies all our needs "according to his riches in glory by Christ Jesus" (Philippians 4:19). [See question #1, page 368.]

2. He maketh me to lie down in green pastures: he leadeth me beside the still waters.

A shepherd's job is to find food and water for the sheep, something not always easy to do in dusty Palestine. But a good shepherd knows the best spots for pasture and water. And the water must be *still*, because sheep are afraid to drink from moving water, such as in creeks and rivers.

God knows we need food for our souls as well as for our bodies. He guides us to quiet places where spiritual sustenance is most available. As the old hymn says, "There is a place of quiet rest, near to the heart of God." Perhaps Jesus thought of this Psalm when He spoke of "living water" (John 4:10). This kind of water is that by which God quenches the thirst of our souls; it becomes in us "a spring of water welling up to eternal life" (John 4:14, *New International Version*). The deepest yearning of our hearts is completely satisfied when it is the Lord who gives us drink.

When God leads the psalmist to *lie down*, he is talking about rest. Rest—as important to good health as food and water—is for the soul as well as for the body. Surely that is the reason God created the Sabbath Day for His Old Testament people—one day out of seven when His people were to rest (Exodus 20:8-11). Spiritual renewal requires regular periods of freedom from duties, time for relaxing activities and for concentration on spiritual disciplines, such as worship and prayer. The Christian "Lord's Day" serves those same purposes.

3. He restoreth my soul: he leadeth me in the paths of righteousness for his name's sake.

The result of v. 2 is the restoration of *my soul*. Sheep need to lie down and rest as they eat, for

Home Daily Bible Readings

Monday, June 10—Restore Us, O God (Psalm 80:1-7)

Tuesday, June 11—Have Regard for Your People (Psalm 80:8-19)

Wednesday, June 12—God: Our Refuge and Strength (Psalm 46:1-11)

Thursday, June 13—God Heard My Cry (Psalm 40:1-10)

Friday, June 14—Keep Me Safe Forever (Psalm 40:11-17)

Saturday, June 15—The Lord Is My Shepherd (Psalm 23:1-6)

Sunday, June 16—The Lord Will Keep You (Psalm 121:1-8)

proper digestion and revival of energy. A good shepherd insists on it; he makes the animals lie down. This "siesta" restores their strength, providing relief from the heat and hurts of travel over desert-like terrain. David experienced this rest-and-restoration therapy in his own soul. When spiritually fatigued, God restores passion to his faith and energy to his zeal.

Sheep need a shepherd not only to provide suitable times and places for rest, but to provide guidance along *the paths*. Sheep will stray without a shepherd (cf. Mark 6:34). Without God's restoring guidance, David (and we) could not stay on the "straight and narrow" path of righteousness that leads to life.

FLYING BLIND

During the cold war, the United States Air Force's Strategic Air Command kept loaded B-52 bombers continuously "on alert," and an airborne command post flying every day, seven days per week, twenty-four hours per day.

The necessity of flying every day, in any weather, required the ability to land the airborne command post in any weather. In dense fog, Air Force flight controllers had to talk this large jet all the way down to the runway. The pilots had to listen carefully to the controllers, follow their directions exactly, and trust the controllers implicitly. Flying blind like that was not for the fainthearted.

In a very real sense, though, every person alive is flying blind. No one can see into the next year, the next week, even the next hour. People hurtle blindly into the future, hoping they can negotiate whatever obstacles or difficulties present themselves.

In Psalm 23, David assures us that the Lord, our Shepherd, is willing to serve as our air traffic controller. He will guide us in the paths of righteousness. Like a controller with a radar screen, He can see where we are headed and what lies ahead even though we cannot.

Like a pilot flying in fog, every person needs to listen carefully to this Controller, follow His directions exactly, and trust Him implicitly. Those who do this will find that the Lord will guide them to a safe landing. Those who do not will crash and burn.   —J. D. J.

B. Protection and Provision (v. 4)

4. Yea, though I walk through the valley of the shadow of death, I will fear no evil: for thou art with me; thy rod and thy staff they comfort me.

Palestinian shepherds often led their herds through dangerous spots, over steep trails bordered by sheer cliffs. Whether this refers to some particular valley or not, the implication of great risk is clear. Sometimes sheep do fall over the edges of trails and must be rescued by the shepherd with his crooked *staff*. Other times, predators attack the sheep, and the shepherd uses his *rod* (a short wooden pole, three or four feet in length) to fight them off.

We humans, too, face "valleys of *death*" in our Christian pilgrimage. Our souls often seem in jeopardy, when discouragement, doubt, or temptation threaten to devour us. The Lord, however, is with us, protecting us with His "rod" and rescuing us with His "staff." As Paul reassures us, "God is faithful, who will not suffer you to be tempted above that ye are able; but will with the temptation also make a way to escape, that ye may be able to bear it" (1 Corinthians 10:13). It is especially comforting to know, when we literally face death, that we are not alone.

FOXHOLE REALITY

A foxhole conversion can be nothing more than bargaining with God. "If You will get me out of this, Lord, I will be committed to You for the rest of my life." A promise like this is not likely to be kept. However, a face to face encounter with one's own death can change a person's sense of values. "I realized there were things more important than _____" (fill in the blank).

An encounter with death takes us to the core of our being. Amidst the darkness of this valley, David's core being felt comforted. Even at the threshold of the grave, David sensed God's reassuring presence.

A public television documentary several years ago followed two terminally ill hospital patients. Both patients' families were grief-stricken by the news that death was imminent. However, over the ensuing weeks, one family pulled together and found peace. The other family pulled apart and found nothing but pain. The first family had a living relationship with Christ; the second family did not.

You are terminal. Beyond insurance policies and a will, what are you doing to prepare yourself? David recommends you walk through this dark valley with the Lord. Then, you need fear no evil.   —J. D. J.

C. Care Now and Care Later (vv. 5, 6)

5. Thou preparest a table before me in the presence of mine enemies: thou anointest my head with oil; my cup runneth over.

David now departs from the shepherd imagery of verses 1-4. The new imagery is quite interesting: even as *enemies* threaten, the psalmist feels secure enough to anticipate a meal—a meal which has been prepared by the Lord Himself.

Since the Lord is the one preparing this meal, or *table*, He is the host of the banquet that the psalmist anticipates. Banquet imagery is found in several other passages in the Bible, including Isaiah 25:6-8; Matthew 8:11; Luke 14:15-24; 22:27; and Revelation 19:9, 17, 18. Jesus' own observance of the Passover Feast involved a table which now symbolizes the Lord's Table around which Christians gather to observe communion each Sunday (Mark 14:18; 1 Corinthians 10:21).

Also part of the banquet imagery is the anointing *with oil*. A good host at a banquet would anoint the heads of the honored guests (Luke 7:36, 46; cf. also Psalms 45:7; 92:10; 133:2). To be considered such a guest by the God of the universe and to be anointed by Him is exciting to anticipate (again, cf. Matthew 8:11; Revelation 19:9)!

The third imagery here is that of a *cup* that *runneth over*. This echoes the symbolism of care we have already seen in verses 1-4. Psalm 116:12, 13 depicts "the cup of salvation" as one of the benefits provided by the Lord (cf. 1 Corinthians 10:16). [See question #2, page 368.]

6. Surely goodness and mercy shall follow me all the days of my life: and I will dwell in the house of the LORD for ever.

David now bursts forth with personal exultation and praise. The blessings of *goodness and mercy* will be enjoyed for life's little while on earth, then in the very eternal mansions of God without end. [See question #3, page 368.]

II. Following Our Keeper (Psalm 121:1-8)

A leader can be only as successful at leading as his followers are at following. Psalm 23 praises the Lord who leads like a shepherd and draws us to His banquet, while Psalm 121 sets forth the good things that happen when we submit to God as our "keeper." What might be called "followership" is important for godly living.

A. Calling for Help (vv. 1, 2)

1. I will lift up mine eyes unto the hills, from whence cometh my help.

Israelite worshipers typically faced Jerusalem from wherever they were when they prayed. The use of the phrase *the hills* in this verse probably is a reference to the Holy City, as it is situated at high elevation on several hills surrounding Mt. Moriah, on which the temple was built (2 Chronicles 3:1). *Help* does not come literally from Jerusalem, but from God who inhabits the temple there.

2. My help cometh from the LORD, which made heaven and earth.

Old Testament worshipers often praised *the Lord* for His creation of heaven and earth (Psalms 115:15; 124:8; 134:3; 146:6; Isaiah 40:26). They got themselves into trouble, however, when they worshiped those created things rather than their Creator (2 Kings 17:16; 21:3-5; Jeremiah 19:13; Ezekiel 8:16; and others).

New Testament believers continue to worship their Creator (Romans 1:25). We have the additional blessing of having ourselves become a new creation (2 Corinthians 5:17), even as we look forward to God's final renewal of all things (Romans 8:19; Revelation 21:1). The psalmist recognized that the One who had the power to create all things originally (Genesis 1:1) is also the One who could help him in his day-to-day life. Having experienced what it means to be a "new creation" in Christ, how much more should the modern believer trust God for those day-to-day needs! [See question #4, page 368.]

B. Trusting the Guide (vv. 3-7)

3, 4. He will not suffer thy foot to be moved: he that keepeth thee will not slumber. Behold, he that keepeth Israel shall neither slumber nor sleep.

When God is allowed to guide, followers reach their destination. Their feet are not *moved*—they make no missteps. Israel learned that while traveling from Egypt to the promised land. The ancient Israelites could see the pillar of cloud that directed their paths. And further proof that God was guiding them was the pillar of fire, which became evident at night (Exodus 13:21, 22). This was visible evidence that God was not sleeping. He was guiding.

We are not consistently good followers, but God is our faithful Guide. When we react with

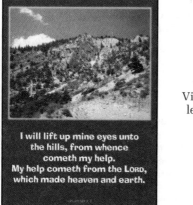

Visual for
lesson 3

I will lift up mine eyes unto
the hills, from whence
cometh my help.
My help cometh from the LORD,
which made heaven and earth.

Use this poster, which shows hills in Israel, to illustrate Psalm 121:1.

impatience as the ancient Israelites did, we are failing to trust Him and we can easily lose our way or be led astray. Yet He continues to call us, always willing to lead and provide.

5, 6. The LORD is thy keeper: the LORD is thy shade upon thy right hand. The sun shall not smite thee by day, nor the moon by night.

Keeper stresses the protective nature of God. *Shade* and *right hand* are figures of speech for protection as well. The references to *sun* and *moon* mean that God's protection is never interrupted. His companionship and guarding are constant, as He helps and leads those who call upon Him. God alone is the trustworthy guide for our lives. No matter what dangers of the day or night present themselves, God is still in control.

Human leaders had betrayed Israel for centuries. At Mt. Sinai, Aaron led them into idolatry, even as Moses was receiving the Ten Commandments on the mountaintop (Exodus 32). The judges who followed were fallible, and a minority of the numerous kings who ruled after the judges guided the people toward godliness. The nation of Israel learned the hard way that earthly leaders are not, as a whole, trustworthy. In their "right minds," at the right time, the Hebrew children confessed that they trusted only the Heavenly Father. The Lord is the one who consistently helps, guides, and protects. He alone is worthy of trust and obedience.

7. The LORD shall preserve thee from all evil: he shall preserve thy soul.

The psalmist shifts the focus from God's present protection to His future protection. But was ancient Israel indeed protected *from all evil?* Sometimes they suffered from drought and disease. They were attacked and besieged by the armies of political enemies. On a personal level, the Israelites were tempted and tried by all the usual afflictions and circumstances common to humanity. Finally, they were defeated and exiled to far-away countries. Foreigners frequently and permanently overran their homeland.

Given the witness of Scripture as a whole, the promise of this verse must be seen as conditional (e.g., 2 Chronicles 7:14). When the ancient Israelites trusted and worshiped their God only, their lives did indeed prosper both physically and spiritually. The word *soul* here is not limited to that which is spiritual, but refers to our entire life and being (see the translation in the *New International Version*).

"Why do bad things happen to good people?" is an age-old question; the reverse "Why do good things happen to bad people?" is also asked (see both in Ecclesiastes 7:15). Jesus answered these questions when He explained that "He [your Father in Heaven] maketh his sun to rise on the

How to Say It

AARON. *Air*-un.
BAAL. *Bay*-ul.
ELIJAH. Ee-*lye*-juh.
ISRAELITES. *Iz*-ray-el-ites.
JERUSALEM. Juh-*roo*-suh-lem.
JEZEBEL. *Jez*-uh-bel.
MORIAH. Mo-*rye*-uh.
MOSES. *Mo*-zes or *Mo*-zez.
SINAI. *Sigh*-nye or *Sigh*-nay-eye.

evil and on the good, and sendeth rain on the just and on the unjust" (Matthew 5:45). The laws of nature usually apply to all equally. Miracles of divine intervention sometimes happen, but God generally lets nature take its course.

Nevertheless, the righteous ultimately escape the eternal torments of Hell while the wicked do not. Christians are preserved for eternity. Considering the teaching of the Bible in its entirety, the promise of verse seven must be taken conditionally. In the New Testament era, only those who believe on Christ can claim this promise for eternity (John 3:16).

C. Staying the Course (v. 8)

8. The LORD shall preserve thy going out and thy coming in from this time forth, and even for evermore.

This is a song of the faithful. God is the eternal guardian of those who persevere in following Him. A crucial part of being faithful and persevering is remaining holy (1 Peter 1:15, 16). The pursuit of holiness must persist until one's death or the return of Christ (cf. 1 Thessalonians 5:23).

As we pursue holiness and live our lives, it is reassuring to know that God looks after us in our entire *going out* and *coming in*. Modern society seems to be increasingly "busy." Families can become so busy that they don't know whether they are "coming or going." The danger is compounded by the fact that about one in six American families moves every year, with the average American moving 11.7 times in his or her lifetime.

When considered alongside the number of automobiles owned by each family, the mobility of contemporary society is mind-boggling. Families seem to be constantly on the move. Our comings and goings can seem like organized chaos at times. But God can track all that movement and busyness and still *preserve* the faithful. Our challenge is to keep all that busyness from distracting us to the point of not having the time to pause and offer the type of prayer the psalmist just has. [See question #5, page 368.]

Conclusion

A. Fear and Faith

Franklin D. Roosevelt is remembered for having said, "The only thing we have to fear is fear itself." There are some reasons why that is true.

Fear clouds reality and produces irrational imaginations. Remember the experience of Elijah after he had killed all the prophets of Baal on Mt. Carmel? Wicked Jezebel threatened his life, and he fled in fear (1 Kings 19:3). In the wilderness, he sat beneath a juniper tree and prayed to die. He imagined that he was alone in standing for God. But God showed him that 7,000 Israelites remained faithful (1 Kings 19:18). Elijah was not killed in the desert by Jezebel, but much later was "taken up" to God in a whirlwind (2 Kings 2).

Fear can immobilize when faith is challenged. Many congregations have missed opportunities for progress and growth simply because they were afraid to venture with God. They might be afraid to change evangelistic strategies. Sometimes they fear significant changes in worship styles. Perhaps they are afraid to make commitments toward visionary goals. Whatever the case, fear often causes Christians to refuse to step through an open door. So they stand paralyzed and stagnate.

Fear inhibits trust in God. Many never speak of Christ and the church, even to friends and family, because they are afraid. They fear rejection, ridicule, and refutation. Others fail to give offerings to their church in proportion to their incomes because they are afraid they won't have enough money to maintain the lifestyle to which they've become accustomed. Fear often prevents us from obeying God.

An anonymous author noted that "Fear knocked at the door. Faith answered. No one was there." Replacing fear with faith is the key to living a life abundant with spiritual confidence, peace, optimism, and adventure.

Why not commit to memory a few of the verses considered in this lesson? A few to begin with are Psalm 23:1, 6 and Psalm 121:2, 8. Hide them in your heart and recite them whenever fear threatens to crush your faith.

B. Prayer

Dear Lord, I trust You as my Good Shepherd. Thank You for supplying all of my needs and for protecting my soul. Again today, give me and mine just what we need. And show us ways we can help the less fortunate. In Jesus' name, Amen.

C. Thought to Remember

Fear knocked at the door.
Faith answered.
No one was there.

Learning by Doing

This page contains an alternate lesson plan emphasizing learning activities. Classes desiring such student involvement will find these suggestions helpful.

Learning Goals

After participating in this lesson, each student will be able to:

1. Compare God's care and leading to that of a shepherd, and the fearless following of disciples to the security of a well-tended flock of sheep.

2. Contrast fear that is healthy with the kind of fear that reflects lack of faith in God.

3. Memorize portions of today's printed text for use during times when faith is in danger of being overpowered by fear.

Into the Lesson

OPTION: *Neighbor Nudge.* Introduce this by saying, "Everyone has had an experience like a 'valley of the shadow of death.' It might be illness, death of a loved one, a debilitating condition or disease. Turn to the person next to you and in two minutes, tell him or her your 'valley of the shadow of death' experience. Tell how you felt—your fears, concerns, and worries."

At two minutes say, "Even if you are not finished, let your partner tell you about his or her 'valley of the shadow of death' experience."

Make the transition to the Bible study by saying, "Our journey through life often includes trips through the valley of the shadow of death. How do we feel in these situations? Do circumstances of life disable us with fear? Our text today includes two passages that describe the confident response of those who trust in God when life overwhelms us with fear."

OPTION: *Brainstorming.* Help your class make a list of things people fear. Do not stop to evaluate or comment. This allows one person's response to stimulate another's thinking. If you do not have a writing board in your classroom, mount a large sheet of newsprint or poster board on the wall. As class members call out answers like, "death," "darkness," or "heights," have a recorder write down the responses.

When you have a large list of fears, ask the class to rate them according to the intensity of the fear they inspire. On a scale of 1 to 5, 1 is mild concern and 5 is fear that paralyzes and prevents action. Read the list and ask class members to respond to each source of fear by holding up the number of fingers to indicate their rating.

Ask the class to identify the difference between healthy fear and the fear that arises because of a lack of faith.

Into the Word

OPTION: *Paraphrase.* The pastoral analogy of a shepherd and his sheep that David uses is far from the experience of modern readers. Provide writing paper and pens for class members to use in paraphrasing Psalm 23. Encourage them to modernize and personalize it by using an analogy familiar to them. For example, one could use the analogy of a teacher and student or a patient and doctor. The student's Twenty-third Psalm might begin, "The Lord is my teacher. I shall not be ignorant. He makes me sit down in His classroom and pay attention. He guides me through His Biblical library. When I am mentally exhausted, He restores my mind and soul. He leads me in a course of study that results in righteousness."

OPTION: *Draw or Illustrate.* Both of these passages abound with visual images and lend themselves to illustration. Provide your class members with colored markers and paper. Have them illustrate each verse or the passage.

If you have room and flexible seating, some of your class could be seated around a table while the others are doing a discussion activity. If your classroom has pews, use lapboards to pass out for writing and drawing activities. Ask class members to explain their drawings to those seated near them.

Into Life

OPTION: *Music.* After studying Psalm 121, conclude the class by listening to Jackie Grouche Farris's rendition of "My Help." Set the mood for this activity by altering the lighting. Make a focal setting with a picture or an open Bible displayed on a table with candles and flowers. The picture might be a pastoral scene with a shepherd and sheep or maybe the Good Shepherd.

OPTION: *Memorize and Meditate.* Both of these Psalms are filled with powerful concepts beautifully stated. Memorizing and meditating on these verses is a faith-building experience. Guide your class by reading a phrase at a time and then pausing for class members to share insights. For example, "The Lord is my shepherd" may lead someone to say, "The Lord God Himself, not some man, is my shepherd." Another may respond, "*My shepherd* indicates that he has a personal interest in me and loves me." (This activity is included in *Adult Bible Class.*)

Let's Talk It Over

The questions on this page are designed to encourage review of the lesson Scriptures and to promote discussion of the lesson by the class. The answers provided are only discussion starters. Let your class talk it over from there.

1. Many citizens of the United States have grown accustomed to "looking to Capitol Hill" as a primary source of strength for solving problems both big and small. Is it easier or harder for American Christians to trust God (for short- or long-term solutions) as compared to Christians living in countries with weak or corrupt governments? Why?

A parallel discussion would ask if Christians who live in prosperous countries have an easier or harder time trusting God for their "daily bread." It is often more difficult for prosperous individuals to acknowledge that God is the source of all blessings. (See 1 Corinthians 4:7; James 1:9-11; Matthew 19:24.)

2. The metaphors (symbols) used in Psalm 23 were very powerful for people in Old Testament times. If we wanted to update the metaphors (phrases like *green pastures, quiet waters, rod, cup,* etc.) of Psalm 23 in a meaningful effort to make the message more understandable to modern people, what symbols would we use? Why?

Some Christians have grown so accustomed to their "familiarity" with songs or favorite Scripture passages that their "inspiration" comes from the "good feeling" associated with the song or passage. They may not realize that many urban non-believers do not understand the metaphors and associate them with God's loving nature.

This is a problem that continually confronts those who work at translating the Bible into the languages of the world. For example, when translating the Bible for certain tribes in northern Alaska, translators wondered what meaningful phrase they should use to convey the important truth behind the concept of "the Lamb of God" since members of that tribe had never seen a lamb. The translators decided that the best option was to use the word for "baby seal."

3. Some believers might take the phrase "goodness and mercy shall follow me" as a promise that Christians will not have any troubles "all the days of my life." What would you say to someone who expressed such a belief?

The "health and wealth," "name it and claim it," and "seed faith" approaches often leave followers disillusioned with God or questioning the genuineness of their own faith. Their initial premise is faulty, since God is not a cosmic vending machine who "dispenses" blessings once we "deposit" the right amount of faith.

Discuss how Paul's experience with a "thorn in the flesh" (2 Corinthians 12:7-10) relates to Psalm 23:6. Help students see that God's blessings are "surely" to be expected even in bad times as well as in good times—although the blessings we actually receive are not necessarily those we initially wanted or expected. (Also see 2 Corinthians 1:8; 4:7-12.)

4. In what way does the reminder that God "made heaven and earth" become helpful when trying to rely on Someone you cannot see or touch?

On the Internet you can readily find pictures of astronomical objects taken by the Hubble space telescope. These include pictures of planets and moons in our own solar system, as well as distant galaxies and nebulae. Download some of these before class and print them out (preferably on a color printer). Pass them around as a reminder that the One who is able to create such things is the same One who is the ultimate source of the promise in Psalm 23:6.

Remind your students that the God who created everything originally also has promised to *re*create everything (Revelation 21:5). This will help your students to remember the greatness of God when they face their darkest hours.

5. Picture a missionary who has been on the mission field long enough that loneliness and culture shock are taking their toll. In comparing Psalm 23 with Psalm 121, which of these two would most likely be more helpful to him or her? Why?

Do a bit of research in advance on various "types" of Psalms. Suggest to the students that they use these various types as their devotional reading for the next few weeks. Ask them to put themselves in the shoes of the different writers and imagine what had been going on in their lives that caused them to cry out to God, to praise, to focus on the present danger, etc. Remind your students that although "times change" in terms of technological advances, etc., human nature does not change. Basic hopes and fears are unchanged in six thousand years of human history.

Look to God for Justice

June 23
Lesson 4

DEVOTIONAL READING: Psalm 72:11-19.

BACKGROUND SCRIPTURE: Psalms 72; 82; 113.

PRINTED TEXT: Psalms 82:1-8; 113:5-9.

Psalm 82:1-8

1 God standeth in the congregation of the mighty; he judgeth among the gods.

2 How long will ye judge unjustly, and accept the persons of the wicked? Selah.

3 Defend the poor and fatherless: do justice to the afflicted and needy.

4 Deliver the poor and needy: rid them out of the hand of the wicked.

5 They know not, neither will they understand; they walk on in darkness: all the foundations of the earth are out of course.

6 I have said, Ye are gods; and all of you are children of the Most High.

7 But ye shall die like men, and fall like one of the princes.

8 Arise, O God, judge the earth: for thou shalt inherit all nations.

Psalm 113:5-9

5 Who is like unto the LORD our God, who dwelleth on high,

6 Who humbleth himself to behold the things that are in heaven, and in the earth!

7 He raiseth up the poor out of the dust, and lifteth the needy out of the dunghill;

8 That he may set him with princes, even with the princes of his people.

9 He maketh the barren woman to keep house, and to be a joyful mother of children. Praise ye the LORD.

GOLDEN TEXT: Arise, O God, judge the earth: for thou shalt inherit all nations.
—Psalm 82:8.

Lesson Aims

After participating in this lesson, each student will be able to:

1. Describe what today's Scriptures say about the kind of justice in which God is interested.

2. Explain how knowing that God is just provides encouragement in dealing with the seeming unfairness in a sinful world.

3. Suggest specific ways a believer or congregation can work for justice in the community.

Lesson Outline

INTRODUCTION
  A. Life Isn't Fair
  B. Lesson Background
 I. GOD CALLS FOR JUSTICE (Psalm 82:1-8)
  A. God's Supremacy Unmatched (v. 1)
  B. Bad Judges Reproved (v. 2)
  C. Human Rights Upheld (vv. 3-5)
    Welcome Home
  D. Divine Judgment Prevails (vv. 6-8)
II. GOD CHAMPIONS JUSTICE (Psalm 113:5-9)
  A. God Is Unique (vv. 5, 6)
  B. God Rights Human Wrongs (vv. 7-9)
    God Will Provide
CONCLUSION
  A. .God Is Just—and More!
  B. Prayer
  C. Thought to Remember

Introduction

A. Life Isn't Fair

Perhaps one of the most troubling realities for believers in God is the undeniable existence of inequities in human life. Why do the rich seem to get richer while the poor get poorer? Why do so many of the wicked prosper and so many of the righteous suffer? We saw this problem in our lesson last week, and we consider it again today (again, see Ecclesiastes 7:15).

So, after all we've learned in six thousand years of human history, why isn't life fairer? Why do the wheels of human justice often seem to turn so slowly at times? Why are the rights of perpetrators seemingly granted more importance than the rights of victims? Why are the wealthy, who can afford expensive lawyers, often able to elude justice and avoid prison sentences? Why do our lawmakers enact "hate crime" legislation that elevates one class of victims above another? The simple answer is that human justice is imperfect because humans themselves are imperfect. Humans make mistakes. Humans do what is "politically correct." Humans are sinners.

A more difficult question to answer is "Why does God Himself continue to allow life to be so unfair?" Theologians have debated this issue for centuries. Some propose that God, although He is good, is not powerful enough to stop injustice. Others propose that God, although He is all-powerful, is not good. Volumes have been written that struggle with this problem. Some examples are *Why Do Bad Things Happen to Good People?* by Harold S. Kushner; *When God Doesn't Make Sense,* by James C. Dobson; *Disappointment With God,* by Philip Yancey; and *Dark Threads the Weaver Needs,* by Herbert Lockyer. Although the insights in such books might help, the "answers" they propose probably will never satisfy completely the universal doubts about life's inequities—especially to the one who is suffering injustice at the moment.

Even so, there is some comfort in simply acknowledging the truth that life is not fair! John the Baptist had his life unjustly taken (Mark 6:14-29). Jesus was killed in an act of judicial murder. And Jesus warns His own disciples that, "In the world ye shall have tribulation" (John 16:33). Face it: we live in a fallen world. Realistically, we should be prepared to experience misfortune, aggravations, and grief in this "vale of tears."

Our ultimate comfort comes in the assurance that the "scales" will indeed be "balanced" by the Great Judge on the Last Day. Until that time, we rejoice that Jesus has "overcome the world" (John 16:33). God's indwelling Spirit empowers us to rise above circumstances, to tolerate suffering, to resist temptation, and to conquer despair. "Faith is the victory!"

The lesson texts for today underscore that kind of encouragement. Read and study with positive anticipation of God's presence and help.

B. Lesson Background

In the Old Testament, God is very concerned with what today we would call "social justice." In many places, He fervently stresses the importance of such justice (examples: Exodus 23:6; Deuteronomy 16:19, 20; 24:19; 27:19). In many places, He rages against its lack (examples: Isaiah 1:21; 5:7, 22, 23; 10:1, 2; 59:4; Ezekiel 22:29; Malachi 3:5). Today's lesson is about this lack.

The superscription attributes this psalm to Asaph, probably director of a guild of temple singers (1 Chronicles 6:39; 15:17; 2 Chronicles 5:12). It is both polemical (involving dispute) and imprecatory (invoking punishment upon the wicked).

I. God Calls for Justice
(Psalm 82:1-8)
A. God's Supremacy Unmatched (v. 1)
1. God standeth in the congregation of the mighty; he judgeth among the gods.

God is depicted here as the "Judge of all judges." The two clauses offer parallel ideas: first, the God who *standeth* is the same One who *judgeth;* second, *the congregation of the mighty* where He stands is an assembly of all the so-called *gods* whom the nations worship (cf. Exodus 12:12; 15:11; 18:11; and Numbers 33:4). [See question #1, page 376.]

B. Bad Judges Reproved (v. 2)
2. How long will ye judge unjustly, and accept the persons of the wicked? Selah.

Having affirmed God's supremacy over all other "gods," the psalmist adopts God's voice, bringing serious accusation against their brand of justice. These "gods" have penalized the righteous and favored *the wicked.* [See question #2, page 376.]

The meaning of *Selah* is not certain. It might be a device used in music composition comparable to our *Amen.*

C. Human Rights Upheld (vv. 3-5)
3, 4. Defend the poor and fatherless: do justice to the afflicted and needy. Deliver the poor and needy: rid them out of the hand of the wicked.

The psalmist makes God's expectations clear with four imperatives: *defend, do justice, deliver,* and *rid them out.* Again, there is a certain parallelism in thought here, with *defend* and *do justice* expressing the same idea. Similarly, *deliver* and *rid them out* are synonyms. By extension, what God expects from the "gods" (who are really no gods at all; cf. Jeremiah 2:11), He also expects of us as well.

Many Old Testament passages stress God's concern for distressed groups such as *the poor and fatherless.* Just three examples are Deuteronomy 27:19; Isaiah 1:17; and Zechariah 7:9, 10. Such passages make it clear that God desires justice for all peoples; He does not show favoritism to the "upper class" (cf. James 2:1-9). The most defenseless people are to receive protection from exploitation.

WELCOME HOME
Emma Lazarus's poem adorns the base of the Statue of Liberty. In part it reads, "Give me your tired, your poor, your huddled masses yearning to breathe free, the wretched refuse of your teeming shore. Send these, the homeless, tempest-tossed to me. I lift my lamp beside the golden door!"

The Statue of Liberty has been a welcoming sight to hundreds of thousands of immigrants. Many of these people have left homelands devastated by war. Others have fled countries ravaged by famine. Some immigrants have been chased away from their birthplace because of violent prejudice. For all of these people, the Statue of Liberty has stood as a promise of a new life.

Church buildings ought to resemble the Statue of Liberty in people's minds: a welcome home for all who feel harassed and helpless. The compassion that seeks justice for the afflicted and needy ought to shine from our churches like Liberty's torch.

You probably know Christians who genuinely open their hearts and hands to people in need. You know brothers and sisters in Christ who often practice the gift of hospitality. You may even know believers who could match the good Samaritan's active compassion.

James instructed that "Pure religion and undefiled before God and the Father is this, To visit the fatherless and widows in their affliction" (James 1:27). What can you do this week to make your church a welcome home?   —J. D. J.

5. They know not, neither will they understand; they walk on in darkness: all the foundations of the earth are out of course.

They points to the unjust "gods." Such gods—and, by extension, the nations that serve those fictitious gods—are self-condemned by what they don't *know* (cf. Isaiah 1:3) and by the *darkness* in which they *walk.* Being unenlightened, they refuse to comprehend and practice godly justice. The New Testament compares spiritual light to darkness in several places (e.g., Matthew 4:16; 6:23; 1 John 1:5-7).

The *foundations of the earth* is a figure of speech for the rule of the one true God who keeps everything in order. Left to these fake "gods," the foundations of the earth would be *out of course.* In other words, without God, darkness and chaos would result.

D. Divine Judgment Prevails (vv. 6-8)
6, 7. I have said, Ye are gods; and all of you are children of the Most High. But ye shall die like men, and fall like one of the princes.

The fate of the *gods* is now certain as the one true God sentences them to *die like men.* The mythology of one of ancient Israel's neighbors held such gods to be *children of the Most High.* In condemning these gods, the one true God is affirming that it is impossible for them to indeed be His children (cf. Psalm 89:6-8). And if the nations that serve such gods reflect the injustice of those gods, those nations are condemned as well; this is the total picture of this "courtroom scene." We should further recall that God's judgment extends both to the world we can see and to the world we can't see (Matthew 25:41; 2 Peter 2:4; Jude 6, 7; Revelation 6:12-17; 20:10, 14, 15; 21:8). Jesus draws upon Psalm 82:6 in John 10:34.

In joining together the deaths of *men* with that of *princes* in verse 7, the psalmist is using a literary technique known as "merism." In this technique a writer places two different ideas very close to each other to express completeness or totality. ("The young and the old" is an example.) So putting together *men* and *princes* here signifies "everyone." (A similar example of merism can be seen in Psalm 105:14 which places "man" and "kings" together to mean "everyone you can think of.")

8. Arise, O God, judge the earth: for thou shalt inherit all nations.

The voice of this last verse switches from God to the singers of the psalm, petitioning God for immediate judgment. God will indeed *judge the earth*, exerting justice, righteousness, and equity. But we must remember that He does so "in His own time." Though we are impatient to see retribution fall upon the wicked and reward come to the godly, the timing of final judgment remains in the realm of divine prerogative. We trust that His ultimate will shall be done, just as He has promised. Jesus Christ will ultimately rule *all nations* (Revelation 12:5).

II. God Champions Justice (Psalm 113:5-9)

A. God Is Unique (vv. 5, 6)

5. Who is like unto the LORD our God, who dwelleth on high.

The implied answer to the rhetorical question here is, "absolutely no one!" No one compares to *our God*.

But just how *on high* is our God? Despite the fact that we know that God is omnipresent (present everywhere), we generally think of His dwelling as "up," or as His "home on high." When Jesus taught us how to pray, He began,

---

How to Say It

ASAPH. *Ay*-saff.
ELKANAH. *El*-kuh-nuh or El-*kay*-nuh.
SELAH. *See*-luh.

"Our Father which art in Heaven" (Matthew 6:9). We tend to think of Heaven as being somewhere above our heads, for Christ "ascended" to the Father's right hand. Yet God is Spirit, and spirits are not subject to the same limitations as those who have physical bodies. Spirits dwell on a plane of existence that is much greater than the reality with which we are familiar on earth. The next verse brings a different perspective to the whereabouts of God.

6. Who humbleth himself to behold the things that are in heaven, and in the earth!

God is not only transcendent (existing beyond the limits of our ordinary experience) but immanent (existing nearby) as well. "He be not far from every one of us: for in him we live, and move, and have our being'" (Acts 17:27, 28).

God stoops to care for all that He has created. He is no absentee landlord. He made us, and He keeps us. It matters to Him what happens to us. He has not abandoned us; His presence protects us. [See question #3, page 376.]

B. God Rights Human Wrongs (vv. 7-9)

7. He raiseth up the poor out of the dust, and lifteth the needy out of the dunghill.

This is a quote from "Hannah's Song," found in 1 Samuel 2:8. It is a graphic picture of God rescuing His most needy children out of poverty, oppression, and social ostracism. It's a picture of the future, when "God shall wipe away all tears from their eyes; and there shall be no more death, neither sorrow, nor crying, neither shall there be any more pain: for the former things are passed away" (Revelation 21:4).

But it is also a picture of God working through His servants now, as they labor in missions and ministries around the world. Think of how God used Mother Teresa to minister to *the poor* in Calcutta. Remember David Livingstone (1813-1873), who gave himself totally to serving the physical and spiritual needs of primitive tribes in Africa.

In more recent times, God is working through dedicated missionaries in central India who remove cataracts from as many as one hundred patients per day in a small, understaffed eye clinic. The patients' children can attend a school also established by the missionaries, and hundreds of worshipers can gather in churches built in surrounding areas, too.

Pakistanis who labor seven days a week making mud bricks can now worship on Sunday evenings in mission-built churches. They can also learn to read and write in schools built and staffed by missionaries. God is rescuing them from despair.

Mission personnel in Kenya are providing food, beds, showers, schooling, and Bible lessons for scores of "street children," some not yet even in their teens, who have no homes, no jobs—no future. God is raising up His poor and needy children. He's doing it through the compassion of Christians who have been commissioned to "go into all the world." [See question #4, page 376.]

"Pure religion and undefiled before God and the Father is this, To visit the fatherless and widows in their affliction" (James 1:27). God is full of mercy, and He wants His family to reflect His grace. Jesus taught that we are the "light" and "leaven" of the world, the "salt" of the earth. All those metaphors include the idea that God wants to use us to comfort, rescue, and save the needy—not just spiritually, but physically as well. We have been not only recruited, but also empowered for this great task. We are agents of God's love, by the strength of His Spirit.

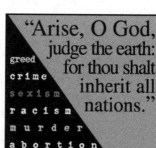

Visual for lesson 4

Use this to illustrate Psalm 82:8. Ask, "How do you think God will judge our nation for these evils?"

GOD WILL PROVIDE

Horatio Alger, Jr. told the same story in dozens of settings. Whether in *Ragged Dick, Struggling Upward,* or *Wait and Win,* Alger always urged hard work and dedication on his readers. If you followed these moral principles, you were *Bound to Rise.*

Hard work and dedication to moral principles can improve people's lives. However, everyone needs help. Joseph, in the Old Testament, rose from slave to second in command over Egypt. David rose from shepherd boy to king. Esther rose from orphan to queen. Each of these people rose because they humbled themselves, and God worked in their lives.

"[The Lord] raiseth up the poor out of the dust, and lifteth the needy out of the dunghill" (Psalm 113:7). Can you look back in your life and see where the Lord has raised you?

Our God is not a cosmic vending machine; you cannot order from Him what you want. However, God tells us whom He raises up and for whom He will provide. "Humble yourselves in the sight of the Lord, and he shall lift you up" (James 4:10). "Seek ye first the kingdom of God, and his righteousness; and all these things shall be added unto you" (Matthew 6:33).

Here is both our promise and our challenge. Humbly trust the Lord and make Him your priority. Then watch Him lift you up. —J. D. J.

8. That he may set him with princes, even with the princes of his people.

The psalmist sets forth a dramatic contrast. The poorest of the poor will one day share accommodations with the richest of the rich. God is going to balance all the inequities of the ages (cf. Luke 16:19-31). "Commoners" will sit with

royalty. Reservations of the poor and afflicted will be upgraded to "First Class"! In Heaven, life will be fair.

Jesus promised, "In my Father's house are many mansions: if it were not so, I would have told you. I go to prepare a place for you. . . . I will come again, and receive you unto myself; that where I am, there ye may be also" (John 14:2, 3). What a glorious future to anticipate (Revelation 21:1-8)!

9. He maketh the barren woman to keep house, and to be a joyful mother of children. Praise ye the LORD.

In 1 Samuel 1, Hannah, the wife of Elkanah, was unable to bear children. To be a *barren woman* was disgraceful in that place and time. Hannah wept tears of shame, and offered prayers to God "in bitterness of soul" (1 Samuel 1:10). She was so serious about her request that she promised that if God granted her petition to bear a son, she would give that son "unto the Lord all the days of his life" (1 Samuel 1:11). When Samuel was born to her and Elkanah, Hannah kept her promise. After Samuel was weaned, she delivered him to Eli, the priest at Shiloh. Samuel was dedicated to sacred service, to be mentored by Eli. The psalmist obviously had Hannah in mind as he reflected on how the Lord helps those who live, in one way or another, on the fringes of society. [See question #5, page 376.]

Conclusion

A. God Is Just—and More!

If you want some advice on what is "fair" and what isn't, just ask any seven-year-old! In fact, you usually don't even have to ask. As all parents discover, their children are quick to point out perceived differences in treatment of siblings.

But if life were perfectly fair, everyone would get exactly what he or she deserved—all the time. But considering the reality of sin, Christians should be grateful that they are *not* getting what they actually deserve, namely, eternity in Hell! "All have sinned, and come short of the glory of God" (Romans 3:23), and "the wages of sin is death" (Romans 6:23).

But to excuse sinners from the fires of Hell—which is the punishment we deserve—leaves God open to the charge of being unjust. Shouldn't sin be punished? Indeed it must, in order for God to be just. This is where the cross of Christ enters the picture. In taking our own punishment upon Himself in that agony, God "made him to be sin for us, who knew no sin; that we might be made the righteousness of God in him" (2 Corinthians 5:21). This is how God can be, at the same time, both the One who is just and the One who justifies (Romans 3:26). To be "just" means that God, in perfect "fairness," lets no sin go unpunished. To be "the One who justifies" means that true believers will receive no penalty (even though they deserve it), because Jesus already has taken that penalty upon Himself and paid it in full. This is called *grace.*

Now, in addition to fulfilling the Great Commission (Matthew 28:19, 20), God expects us to work for justice in the church and in the world (Matthew 25:35, 36; Luke 11:42; James 2:1-9). Motives are important, though, since we dare not think that we are earning God's favor by doing so (Isaiah 64:6; Ephesians 2:8, 9). Let us work for justice until He returns to judge the world in His own justice and righteousness (Acts 17:31).

Even as we look forward to that day, we probably will have to remind ourselves occasionally that although life may not seem "fair" at times, it certainly wasn't "fair" for Jesus to die at Calvary. But that's the requirement of grace: Jesus got what He did not deserve (death) so that we could get what we did not deserve (eternal life). In this respect, we should thank God for *not* being "fair"!

We also do well to remind ourselves that our own suffering is part of the human condition; it "comes with the territory" of the reality of sin. Our lives are subject to the "natural" and "scientific" laws that God ordained at creation and as a result of the fall. Germs cause infection in law-abiding citizens as well as in convicted criminals. Automobile accidents happen to both infants and drug dealers. Disease, old age, and death happen to all humans, no matter what their moral, ethical, and religious state might be. God "sendeth rain on the just and on the unjust" (Matthew 5:45).

Some trials and troubles are not directly due to our "weakness in the flesh." Many fall victim to the sin of others (e.g., murder). That doesn't seem fair—and certainly isn't fair—at all. But such human wrongs are inevitable in a fallen world. It is not God who is causing this, but our own freewill actions. All citizens of an unredeemed society may suffer temporal consequences for the rebellious and disobedient behavior of even just a few. Even so, God did promise that He will never fail nor forsake us (Joshua 1:5). He did promise that our trials never would be more than we can bear (1 Corinthians 10:13). He did promise to work all things out for our good if we keep loving Him (Romans 8:28). And He did promise to give us a "crown of life" if we are faithful unto death (Revelation 2:10).

The promise of this crown should cause us to realize that the unfair aspects and happenings of earthly life pale into insignificance when contrasted with eternal issues. "Murphy's Laws" have to do mostly with inconveniences and irritations. Think about it: what importance will common aggravations hold ten thousand years from now? As Richard Carlson's book reminds us, *Don't Sweat the Small Stuff!*

B. Prayer

Dear Lord in Heaven, we thank You for all of life's privileges and challenges, but sometimes we don't understand Your will. Show us somehow Your divine intentions and what they mean for us here and now. And help us to accept Your will, even when we don't understand it. In Jesus' name we pray, Amen.

C. Thought to Remember

Life isn't fair, but God is still just.

Home Daily Bible Readings

Monday, June 17—God of Everlasting Righteousness (Psalm 119:130-144)
Tuesday, June 18—God of Steadfast Love and Justice (Psalm 119:149-160)
Wednesday, June 19—Justice, the Foundation of God's Throne (Psalm 97:1-12)
Thursday, June 20—A Plea for God's Justice (Psalm 82:1-8)
Friday, June 21—God Helps the Poor and Needy (Psalm 113:1-9)
Saturday, June 22—Give the Ruler God's Justice (Psalm 72:1-7)
Sunday, June 23—God Delivers the Needy (Psalm 72:11-19)

Learning by Doing

This page contains an alternate lesson plan emphasizing learning activities.
Classes desiring such student involvement will find these suggestions helpful.

Learning Goals

After participating in this lesson, each student will be able to:

1. Describe what today's Scriptures say about the kind of justice in which God is interested.

2. Explain how knowing that God is good provides encouragement in dealing with the seeming unfairness in a sinful world.

3. Suggest specific ways a believer or congregation can work for justice in the community.

Into the Lesson

OPTION: *Book Review.* Our lesson writer mentions several books that deal with the issues raised in this lesson—why bad things happen to good people. Check with your church or public library or local Christian bookstore for copies of such titles. Ask one or two class members to read and review one of these books for the class.

OPTION: *Role Play.* Ask two class members to role-play a conversation between two workers riding the bus to work and discussing how unjust our legal system is, particularly in highly publicized cases. In a role play, you set the tone and establish the attitude of each character but do not provide an exact script. You might suggest some timeless issues and problems, such as, "Justice seems to favor the rich and famous," or "The little guy gets lost in the bureaucracy."

Make the transition to the Bible study by saying, "The United States' Pledge of Allegiance to the Flag ends: 'with liberty and justice for all.' Is that true? Today's lesson text looks at the issue of justice and judicial issues. As we look at today's text, maybe we can resolve or better understand the reasons for injustices in life."

Into the Word

OPTION: *Translation Study.* Bring several translations of the Old Testament to use in studying today's text. Get a sampling of the spectrum of translations. Include more literal translations, like the *King James Version*, and freer translations, like the *New English Bible*. Also have a paraphrase edition, such as *The Living Bible*.

Start the discussion of each verse by having a student read each translation.

OPTION: *Commentary Study.* Today's text lends itself well to a commentary study. In some places, it is not clear who is speaking, and a commentary is helpful in sorting out such issues

and exploring various alternatives. Bring several commentaries to class. You may want to get recommendations from your preacher.

Divide the class into groups of two to four students. Have each group read each verse and the commentary entry. Then write an explanation of the verse to share with the rest of the class.

OPTION: *Choral Reading.* Today's text is dramatic in content and voice. Assign various parts to be read dramatically. In preparation, read and discuss each verse. Decide as a class whether it should be read by a male or female or by mixed voices. Should one person, a duet, trio, or the entire class read it? Some verses might include both. For example, Psalm 113:9 could have a woman read the first phrase and another woman read the second phrase. Then the entire class could join in and say, "Praise (ye) the Lord." Or Psalm 113:5 could begin with several voices echoing, "Who?" in a questioning tone. A male voice could say, "is like the Lord," with the entire class joining in with "our God." A female voice could render the last phrase, "who dwells (dwelleth) on high." Encourage class members to exaggerate tone and voice of each part to achieve dramatic effect. What seems extreme to our own ears will be effective when heard by the group.

Into Life

OPTION: *Personal Testimony.* Probably there are people in your class or church who have great testimonies about how they have triumphed over difficulties in life. Think about people who have faced cancer, disabilities, or injustices and have been victorious through Christ. Invite one of these people to visit and speak to your class and share the testimony of how God brought him or her through the times of trouble.

Ask him to tell what the difficult experience was or is and how God brought or is bringing him through it. What has been learned in the process? Have him conclude with a verse or passage that has particularly helped him.

OPTION: *Prison/Justice Ministry.* A number of Christian organizations work in prison ministry and the justice system. Chuck Colson's Prison Fellowship is one. S. Lee Ladd's Extended Hand Ministries is another. Contact with such groups could provide helpful information to your class on a place and way to start. (Directions for this are included in *Adult Bible Class.)*

Let's Talk It Over

The questions on this page are designed to encourage review of the lesson Scriptures and to promote discussion of the lesson by the class. The answers provided are only discussion starters. Let your class talk it over from there.

1. Suppose a friend must make an appearance in court—and you have to be the judge. From today's lesson, how would you deal with the case? How would you try to imitate God?

The answer could depend on whether or not your friend is guilty. God would certainly make no mistake here, but you might!

But even if the person were guilty, God could either be harsh (and mete out the deserved punishment) or be merciful, depending on what He thinks to be best. Could you act strictly in the person's best interest—even if punishment were likely the best way for the person to learn from his or her mistake? Could you remain impartial?

Of course, we all play the "judge" at times. Use this discussion to help your learners apply these principles even without the black robes and gavels of "the bench."

2. Psalm 73 is the account of the intense spiritual struggle of an individual who could not understand why the wicked prospered and the righteous suffered at the hands of evil people. How can Psalm 73 and today's passages be an encouragement to those becoming disillusioned that the "wicked are winning"?

In trying to make sense out of a sinful world, many become disillusioned. As one observer put it, the problem is not that the world is rational or irrational, but that it seems to be *partially* rational; just when we think we have it figured out "how things work," there seems to be an exception.

Our job as Christian encouragers is to help people keep a perspective of the "big picture," the one in which God is ultimately in control of all things, all time, and all history. Job's problem was that he was not willing to accept the reality of his suffering unless he could understand "why." When the Lord responded to Job in the form of sixty-four questions, He was saying, in effect, "Look, Job, you don't understand how all these other things in creation work, but you accept them, don't you?"

3. Romans 13 implies that Christians are to honor systems of government because they have been set in motion by God to protect the good and punish evil. How does a Christian honor a system that can also be administered by very corrupt or blind leaders?

The best parallel is the church. The church is God's divine institution for taking "good news" to a dying world. We must always honor "the church." However, congregations are made up of and led by frail "sinners saved by grace." We encourage, pray for, admonish, and apply church discipline as needed because we want the best for all of the people in Christ's church. Likewise, we carefully vote for, pray for, and impeach if necessary, those who hold official positions in local and national governments (cf. Acts 5:29).

4. Suppose it becomes evident that the poor (e.g., migrant workers) in a locality are being treated unfairly or partiality is being shown in the courts or at city hall. What, if any, God-given right or duty does the Christian have to become God's "colleague" to bring about justice and fairness? Try to support your views with Scripture.

Some Christians, citing Matthew 10:27, 28, claim their only job is to preach salvation and not get involved in social justice. However, if God's people are not the "hands and feet" of God in any locality, those treated unfairly may have no representation. Still, while social justice is extremely important, Christians should never allow evangelism to become a secondary task of the church. There must be a balance.

5. Some people become cynical and say that God offers "barren promises." How can we help when a couple has prayed fervently for a child and it seems that God has not answered?

In the face of difficult situations like this, it may be good to say something like: "I do not understand exactly what God may be doing in your situation. But I do know that God loves you deeply. He proved it by providing His Son to die an undeserved death so that you and I can have life. I do not fully understand that either. I have placed my faith in the God who in the midst of unfairness made a way for me. I expect I will face unfairness as Jesus did. But I am committed to hold on to what He did for me so that eventually I can have eternal life with Him. It will be nice someday to be free from all the unfairness of this world. I share this with you hoping that your understanding of what Jesus went through can help you with what you are dealing with now."

Teach the Wonders of God

DEVOTIONAL READING: Psalm 135:1-7.

BACKGROUND SCRIPTURE: Psalm 78:1-8.

PRINTED TEXT: Psalm 78:1-8.

Psalm 78:1-8

1 Give ear, O my people, to my law: incline your ears to the words of my mouth.

2 I will open my mouth in a parable: I will utter dark sayings of old:

3 Which we have heard and known, and our fathers have told us.

4 We will not hide them from their children, showing to the generation to come the praises of the LORD, and his strength, and his wonderful works that he hath done.

5 For he established a testimony in Jacob, and appointed a law in Israel, which he com-manded our fathers, that they should make them known to their children:

6 That the generation to come might know them, even the children which should be born; who should arise and declare them to their children:

7 That they might set their hope in God, and not forget the works of God, but keep his commandments:

8 And might not be as their fathers, a stub-born and rebellious generation; a generation that set not their heart aright, and whose spirit was not steadfast with God.

GOLDEN TEXT: We will [show] to the generation to come the praises of the LORD, and his strength, and his wonderful works that he hath done.—Psalm 78:4.

Lesson Aims

After participating in this lesson, each student will be able to:

1. Tell what today's text says about the importance of teaching future generations the ways of the Lord.

2. Suggest some benefits that would come to society if God's Word were better known and followed.

3. State a specific way to help a young person know more about God.

Lesson Outline

INTRODUCTION
    A. "When I Was Your Age . . . "
    B. Lesson Background
  I. LEARNING FROM THE PAST (PSALM 78:1-3)
    A. Listen and Learn (v. 1)
    B. Parables and Proverbs (vv. 2, 3)
 II. TEACHING FOR THE FUTURE (PSALM 78:4-8)
    A. Religious Education (v. 4)
       From Generation to Generation
    B. The Law of the Lord (v. 5)
    C. The Future Faithful (vv. 6, 7)
    D. Profiting From Bad Examples (v. 8)
       Paths of Remembrance
CONCLUSION
    A. Watching The History Channel®
    B. Prayer
    C. Thought to Remember

Introduction

A. "When I Was Your Age . . . "

A grandson begs for stories about his parents, his uncles and aunts, his grandparents, and great-grandparents. He likes especially to hear humorous anecdotes of embarrassing incidents that have become family folklore. But he also listens with interest to more serious tales of historical happenings involving his ancestors' pasts that teach practical and profitable lessons.

He's only six years old, so he is still amused by his elders' reminiscences. Later, cynicism may set in, but we hope that he, and all of our grandchildren, will continue to listen with a degree of curiosity, at least, to how it was "when we were their age." Most of all, we want them to

know about the heritage of faith we pass along from generation to generation. We know the importance of lessons and sermons they will hear at the church house, but we accept the fact that our personal teaching and example will be invaluable as well.

Sharing religious traditions and explaining their meaning to children is essential to developing faith. Youngsters need to know who they are and where they came from in more than a superficial sense. "My name is Chuck, and I'm from Michigan" is not nearly enough. One's identity is wrapped up in the roots of family trees. In the religious context, it is often shaped by the influence and dynamics of several generations, as well as by contemporary environments and events.

Telling "the story" keeps faith alive. It is essential for both the storyteller and the listener. Can you honestly sing the words of A. Catherine Hankey's (1834–1911) old hymn, "I love to tell the story . . . of Jesus and His glory, of Jesus and His love"? Millions of children and adults need to hear it. Have you thought about who might need to hear it from you? Can you hear their plea?

> Tell me the story of Jesus,
> Write on my heart every word;
> Tell me the story most precious,
> Sweetest that ever was heard.
>   —Fanny J. Crosby (1820–1915)

B. Lesson Background

As we learned last week, Asaph was probably director of a guild of temple singers. His message today concerns the importance of keeping God's law alive. This psalm is a "wisdom poem," teaching that parents should instruct their children in truths of God, the foundation of their faith. The purpose of such instruction is clear: so that future generations will choose goodness over evil, and thereby be blessed rather than punished.

These final verses of this Psalm express both negatively and positively the results that come with perpetuation of the prescribed historical perspective. Future generations will not forget and rebel; they will hope in God and obey Him.

I. Learning From the Past (Psalm 78:1-3)

A. Listen and Learn (v. 1)

1. Give ear, O my people, to my law: incline your ears to the words of my mouth.

As we will see later in verse 4, the larger context here is that of communication between generations. Each generation must tell of God's *law* to the next, but that telling is only half of the communication process. The other half is hearing. The older generation must not only tell—the younger generation must also hear.

Of equal importance to the telling-hearing process is the content of the communication: that content must be *my law* and *the words of my mouth.* (Compare this with the apostle Paul's warning in 2 Timothy 4:3, 4 concerning turning one's ears away from truth and toward "fables" [or "myths" in the *New International Version*].)

The urgent message here is to parents: share the heritage of religious faith with your offspring. Tell them about how you came to believe in God; tell them what you believe and why. Explain to them the meaning of religious rites and ceremonies. Involve them in memorials and observances. Inform them of God's expectations and how one's relationship to Him is determined by one's attitude and actions. Illustrate the benefits of trust and obedience and the detriments of living in rebellion and sin. Relate both the faithfulness and the shortcomings of people from the past and emphasize the good and bad results, respectively.

In Christian families, children need to know about God and Jesus from their earliest stages of cognition. This is "home schooling" at its very best. Sunday school can be a wonderful help in this process, but it is no substitute for the "everyday school" as taught by parents and siblings. According to findings released in 1999 by Barna Research Ltd., children "between the ages of five and thirteen have a 32 percent probability of accepting Christ as their savior"; however, the rate drops to only 4 percent for those between the ages of fourteen and eighteen, and 6 percent for adults ages nineteen and up. Given these sobering figures, can we afford to neglect the teaching of children?

B. Parables and Proverbs (vv. 2, 3)

2, 3. I will open my mouth in a parable: I will utter dark sayings of old: which we have heard and known, and our fathers have told us.

Here is another example of Hebrew parallelism. *A parable* (a proverbial form of teaching) is the same as the *dark sayings.* Note the use of *parable* and *dark saying* also in Psalm 49:4 (there the *New International Version* has "proverb" and "riddle"). The writer is announcing his intention to teach, in proverbial form, the virtues of godly living and the vices of sinful living. He admits that the message is not new; in fact, he implies that his teaching possesses extra value because its source is ancient—the stories of ancestors. [See question #1, page 384.]

Parables, of course, distinguished the teaching of Jesus (Matthew 13:34). In fact, Matthew cites Psalm 78:2 as being "fulfilled" while Jesus teaches in parables (13:35). Jesus used images

and terms in those parables that usually would be understood by the general public. But although He taught in "laymen's language," many did not have "ears to hear" (Matthew 13:13-15; Acts 28:26, 27; cf. Ezekiel 20:49). [See question #2, page 384.]

The *sayings of old* also must be repeated often. And conveying understanding is easier when using vivid images and stories—in a parabolic form that the psalmist predicts. "Word pictures" are an important part of the Old Testament narratives, and these may have touched the hearts of those who had returned from Babylonian captivity as Ezra and Nehemiah read and explained the Law to them (Nehemiah 8:8). These remnant Israelites actually stood near the "water gate" from morning until noon, listening to this reading (Nehemiah 8:3)! It's hard to imagine how they endured without padded pews, but apparently they had "ears to hear."

II. Teaching for the Future (Psalm 78:4-8)

A. Religious Education (v. 4)

4. We will not hide them from their children, showing to the generation to come the praises of the LORD, and his strength, and his wonderful works that he hath done.

Israel was compelled by the urgency of the task as described in Deuteronomy 6:6-9: "And these words, which I command thee this day, shall be in thine heart: and thou shalt teach them diligently unto thy *children,* and shalt talk of them when thou sittest in thine house, and when thou walkest by the way, and when thou liest down, and when thou risest up. And thou shalt bind them for a sign upon thine hand, and they shall be as frontlets between thine eyes. And thou shalt write them upon the posts of thy house and on thy gates."

That seems a bit different from dropping the kids off at Sunday school and then going out for coffee! Not all parents take this responsibility seriously. Yet these instructions carry the weight of commands from God; notice that the psalmist characterizes his exhortation as "law" (v. 1). It is absolutely imperative that Biblical faith be passed along.

How to Say It

ASAPH. *Ay*-saff.
BELIAL. *Bee*-li-ul.
EBENEZER. *Eb*-en-*ee*-zer.
EUNICE. U-*nye*-see or *U*-nis.
ISAIAH. Eye-*zay*-uh.

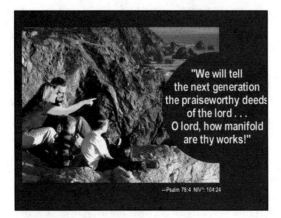

Visual for lessons 5, 6. *Display this poster as you consider verse 4. Discuss some creative ways of telling the next generation of God's works.*

Perhaps some parents are reluctant to put this plan into action because they are ill prepared or "don't know enough." Remember, however, that the teacher usually learns more than the student in the teaching process. Prepare to share Biblical faith by reviewing the material, reading, and studying the Scriptures. Pray for opportunities to tell what you remember. Most children occasionally ask hard questions; if you don't have an answer, promise you will try to find one. They probably already know you're not a genius, anyway! What they really need to know is that you are serious about your faith and the practice of your Christianity.

Remember that public schools do best when they concentrate on the basics: the "Three Rs" of Readin', 'Ritin', and 'Rithmetic. Similarly, the church will do its best when it helps parents stress to their children the three "Rs" of Repentance, Regeneration, and Righteousness. Three-dollar theological words can't be used with children, of course, but adolescents and older youth can be taught the concepts.

Important also to notice in this verse is the emphasis on positive lessons learned about God in history, as opposed to negative examples that could have been mentioned. *Praises, strength,* and *wonderful works* of the Lord are not to be hidden from the children. Hundreds of years after the Exodus, God still reminded the Israelites of that event (e.g., Isaiah 11:16; Jeremiah 7:22; Hebrews 11:22, 29). [See question #3, page 384.]

FROM GENERATION TO GENERATION

What will be your most valuable contribution to the kingdom of God? For many Christians, our best ministry will be training our children or other young people to follow the Lord.

William Farel's encouragement of John Calvin advanced and expanded the sixteenth-century Reformation. Susanna Wesley's guidance of her sons John and Charles eventually affected hundreds of thousands of lives, as John founded Methodism in the eighteenth century and Charles wrote more than nine thousand hymns and poems. Thomas Campbell's influence on his son Alexander began an entire Christian movement in the nineteenth century.

Unfortunately, the opposite can occur as well. The sons of Eli from the time of the judges provide an example: "Now the sons of Eli were sons of Belial; they knew not the Lord" (1 Samuel 2:12). Likewise, when Samuel began to age, "he made his sons judges over Israel. . . . And his sons walked not in his ways, but turned aside after lucre, and took bribes, and perverted judgment" (1 Samuel 8:1, 3).

The development of godly young adults does not happen by accident. Children must be trained to know the Lord and to follow Him from their hearts (cf. Proverbs 22:6). Timothy's grandmother Lois, his mother Eunice, and the apostle Paul all contributed to the formation of Timothy's faith and life of ministry. What can you do to guide your children, grandchildren, or young friends toward a life of service for the Lord? "These words, which I command thee this day, shall be in thine heart: And thou shalt teach them diligently unto thy children" (Deuteronomy 6:6, 7). —J. D. J.

B. The Law of the Lord (v. 5)

5. For he established a testimony in Jacob, and appointed a law in Israel, which he commanded our fathers, that they should make them known to their children.

A Cliffs Notes™ version of the Old Testament might read something like this: God chose a nation *(Israel)*, gave them a *law* (Mosaic), and insisted that each generation be informed (Deuteronomy 6:6-9). That's an oversimplification, of course, but it does pretty well summarize the thrust of Asaph's message. *Jacob* stands for all the tribes of Israel—the law was for everyone.

Christians live under the New Covenant, of course, and not under this old law appointed for Israel. But Paul tells us the Old Testament provides instruction for New Testament disciples (1 Corinthians 10:11). It thus remains incumbent upon all readers to share and model the faith of their spiritual *fathers*. Discipling future generations is not optional—it is God's will. [See question #4, page 384.]

C. The Future Faithful (vv. 6, 7)

6. That the generation to come might know them, even the children which should be born;

who should arise and declare them to their children.

Faith often seems not to survive beyond the third generation. But if the instructions of this passage are carried out, many fewer descendants will be lost. Consider young Timothy, whose mother Eunice and grandmother Lois passed along their faith to him. They told "the story" to Timothy, the apostle Paul confirmed it, and then commissioned the young preacher to instruct others who will subsequently teach still others (2 Timothy 1:5; 2:2). The evangelistic implications multiply like compounding interest. Frank C. Laubach (1884–1970) fought illiteracy with his "each one teach one" technique. Think how soon all the world could hear the good news if each Christian taught just one more. What if each one taught three?! [See question #5, page 384.]

7. That they might set their hope in God, and not forget the works of God, but keep his commandments.

Here's the purpose and motivation for telling the story of God's love and law: that future generations might, in the words of John H. Sammis (1846–1919), "trust and obey, for there's no other way to be happy in Jesus."

Some have been known to bring the charge of "manipulation" against Christian parents, accusing them of "indoctrinating" their children in the sense of "brainwashing" them. But instructing children in the faith is not any more about manipulation than is instructing children about good nutrition and personal hygiene. Nor is such instruction merely to earn bragging rights for successful parenting. One does not pass the faith along so that conversations at family reunions will be less controversial.

Rather, we educate our descendants about God, His Word, and His church so that the generations to follow will have the privilege of knowing their Maker not only as Creator, but also as Lord and Savior. The abundance of their lives and their eternal destinies are at stake. Breaking the chain of discipling not only will jeopardize your own faith, but will very likely leave your kin with no witness, no testimony to God's grace. Such unfaithfulness has eternal consequences.

Making God's law and *works* known is a continuing process. It is not enough that children are taught once. They must be reminded again and again. (You don't tell them only once to clean their rooms, do you?) They will put *their hope in God* if they do *not forget* His works (Exodus 10:2; 12:26, 27; 13:8; cf. Deuteronomy 6:20-25). And they will not forget if we are faithful and persistent in telling "the story of unseen things above, of Jesus and His glory, of Jesus and

His love. . . . The old, old story that I have loved so long."

D. Profiting From Bad Examples (v. 8)

8. And might not be as their fathers, a stubborn and rebellious generation; a generation that set not their heart aright, and whose spirit was not steadfast with God.

Do you suppose that any of the ancient Israelites ever told a child, "Don't do as I do; do as I say!"? It is possible, even for parents who are careful to speak of religious values to children, to be far less faithful in their walk than in their talk. Probably the majority of Israelites were regular attendees at feast days, ceremonies, and formalities of their religion. But as this verse makes plain, the Israelites' fore*fathers* were *stubborn*, *rebellious*, and inconsistent in performing the will of God; their *heart* and *spirit* was not in tune with God's (again we see Hebrew parallelism, with *heart* and *spirit* meaning just about the same thing). Though He wanted to abide in them, they were not abiding in Him. More than a dozen times in the Old Testament God calls the Israelites "stiff-necked" (e.g., 2 Chronicles 30:8).

Being *not steadfast* is virtually the same as being unfaithful. Apparently, their relationship to the Lord was only nominal. They went through some of the motions, but rebellious lifestyles betrayed their pretense. "This people draw near me with their mouth, and with their lips do honor me, but have removed their heart far from me" (Isaiah 29:13). Most Christians know, of course, that actions speak much louder than words. Our families see us when we aren't surrounded by church members. They observe our language and behavior in casual and careless moments, in stressful situations, and even when we think no one is paying attention. It becomes a question of "Will the real Christian please stand up?"

Asaph, like the prophet Isaiah, had the right message, but it likely was too late by itself to correct the rebellion of the "church of tomorrow." More stern measures would be needed—these would come in 586 B.C. in the form of the Babylonian exile.

PATHS OF REMEMBRANCE

How can we keep from becoming a generation whose stubborn hearts are not right? The New Testament counsels, "Therefore we ought to give the more earnest heed to the things which we have heard, lest at any time we should let them slip" (Hebrews 2:1).

God constructed the human brain to form "paths of remembrance." A computer will take approximately the same amount of time to bring up information stored in its memory or disk drive no matter how much or how little you use that information. The human brain, however, gets faster and better with use. Remembering how to tie your shoes took you a long time as a young child. Now, you can do it accurately and quickly without thinking.

The same holds true in the practice of your faith. The more you humble yourself before the Lord, the less likely it is that you will become stubborn. The more you implant God's word in your mind and heart, the less likely you are to drift away from it. The more you recognize and repent of daily self-centeredness and sin, the less likely it is that your heart will not be right.

Every day you have an opportunity to review some of God's works: the Exodus, David and Goliath, Daniel in the lion's den, etc. Every week you have an opportunity to commune with God, remembering the cross. Every hour you can set your hope on God and obey Him. Build "paths of remembrance" into your brain to help you remain steadfast.   —J. D. J.

Conclusion

A. Watching the History Channel®

Occasionally, television executives come up with some programming that has more than a sound bite of "redeeming social value." The History Channel® is a positive example. That is, it can be helpful if viewers are perceptive in discerning the lessons to be learned from history and are conscientious in applying those lessons in order to influence today and tomorrow for good. The serious study of the past can be socially redemptive in the future.

Cases in point: reviewing the atrocities of the World War II "Holocaust" and the more recent

Balkan "ethnic cleansings" that were inflicted upon certain peoples can inspire determination that madmen never will be allowed to perpetrate such war crimes again. Seeing and hearing graphic reports of the Hiroshima bombing can, and should, weld the resolve of world powers against all future use of atomic and nuclear power to destroy. Documentaries of race riots, campus demonstrations, and cult-hostage situations might so sicken citizens that future episodes of civil disobedience will be precluded.

Are such results too much to hope for? God's messenger who wrote this lesson text was convinced that untarnished and unvarnished truth from the past would change the future for good.

Reviewing the sad results of ancient Israel's centuries-long rebellion against God's law should have influenced future descendants to trust and obey. What a travesty that God's law had to be periodically "rediscovered" (e.g., 2 Kings 23:2)! Knowing God's commandments and His history of blessing the faithful can inspire faithfulness among contemporary believers. Biblical history teaches the basic underlying lesson: righteousness works, corruption fails; morality wins, wickedness loses. These lessons need to be shared with all who come behind us. Our followers can avoid pitfalls, resist temptation, and "work out [their] own salvation" (Philippians 2:12).

When Joshua led the Israelite nation into their Promised Land, God instructed him to leave a memorial "unto the children of Israel for ever" (Joshua 4:7) at the Jordan River. Later, Samuel erected an "Ebenezer" (or "stone of help") to remind the Israelites of the Lord's help (1 Samuel 7:12). Jesus instituted the Lord's Supper as an enduring reminder of His sacrifice (1 Corinthians 11:23-26). Will you be ready with answers when your children or grandchildren ask, "What is the meaning of baptism? . . . of this cup and bread? . . . of this nativity scene?" Be ready for the time when they ask. Better yet, tell them even before they ask.

B. Prayer

Dear God, thank You for inspiring and preserving the written Word, which tells the experiences of Your people in history. Help us to learn and share the lessons revealed there, to keep us from making big mistakes. "Lead us not into temptation, and deliver us from evil." Give us whatever we need to tell Your story at every opportunity, and let us recognize those opportunities as they arise. In Jesus' name we pray, Amen.

C. Thought to Remember

Continue to tell the old, old story.

Home Daily Bible Readings

Monday, June 24—Proclaim to All Generations (Psalm 89:1-7)
Tuesday, June 25—God Rules Heavens and Earth (Psalm 89:8-18)
Wednesday, June 26—From Everlasting to Everlasting (Psalm 90:1-6)
Thursday, June 27—God's Name Endures for Generations (Psalm 102:12-22)
Friday, June 28—Remember God's Wonders of Old (Psalm 77:11-20)
Saturday, June 29—Teach Generation to Generation (Psalm 78:1-8)
Sunday, June 30—The Lord Above All Other Gods (Psalm 135:1-7)

Learning by Doing

This page contains an alternate lesson plan emphasizing learning activities.
Classes desiring such student involvement will find these suggestions helpful.

Learning Goals

After participating in this lesson, each student will be able to:

1. Tell what today's text says about the importance of teaching future generations the ways of the Lord.

2. Suggest some benefits that would come to society if God's Word were better known and followed.

3. State a specific way to help a young person know more about God.

Into the Lesson

OPTION: *Listening Game.* Today's text begins with an admonition to listen carefully. To prepare for the lesson, have your class play the party game of "gossip," in which each person listens to a complex statement whispered to him or her and then whispers it to the next person as accurately as possible. Read this statement to the first person to start the game, "On June 23, 2002, we studied justice from Psalms 82 and 113. Today, June 30, 2002, we look at Psalm 78." Write the sentence on a poster or overhead transparency so that, at the end, you can show the class how well they listened.

Make the transition to Bible study by saying, "This party game shows how poor our listening skills usually are. Maybe that is why today's text begins with a call to listen carefully. Listening attentively is a foundational step for accurately passing on detailed information to others."

OPTION: *Hymn Study.* Provide copies of hymn books for each class member. Have them study the stanzas of hymns that capture the command of today's lesson, like "Tell Me the Old, Old Story" or "Wonderful Words of Life." Begin the class by singing selected stanzas. Recruit a class member to lead the singing and a musician to accompany. Make the transition to the lesson by saying, "These hymns capture the command of today's lesson. Every generation is charged with the responsibility to pass faith on to the next generation. As we study Psalm 78:1-8, look for ideas included in these hymns." (This activity is included in *Adult Bible Class.)*

Into the Word

OPTION: *Illustrate the Passage.* Provide paper and pencils for your class members to illustrate the first eight verses of Psalm 78. The process of trying to present the truth of each verse in visual form will help your class understand the passage. It might be helpful to copy the text in the left column of a page, leaving the right side for the artwork.

OPTION: *Discussion Questions.* Copy the following questions for use with your class. Give two questions to each of four groups. Allow four to six minutes and then reassemble for answers to be shared. (This activity is included in *Adult Bible Class.)*

Why does faith have to be verbalized to be passed on?

What parables have helped to form your faith?

Describe the special place that fathers have in the transmission of faith.

Why would any parent hide the things God had done?

How many generations are mentioned in this passage?

What causes children to trust God?

What effect do stubborn and rebellious parents have on children?

What benefits would come to society if God's Word were better known and followed?

Into Life

OPTION: *Brainstorm.* Have your class brainstorm for ways they can pass along their personal faith to children and grandchildren. Don't stop to evaluate ideas. Just write them as fast as possible and let class members feed on each other's ideas and creativity. Write the list large enough that everyone in the class can see it. When you have finished your list, have class members vote on the three best ideas. Suggest that each member select one of the ways and commit to implementing it.

OPTION: *Testimony.* Most churches have some people who are second, third, or fourth (or more) generation believers. Ask one of these people to visit your class and share a testimony of how this was accomplished and the blessing it has been to the family. Make sure you carefully explain the purpose of the testimony—to inspire and encourage your class members to tell diligently the next generation the praiseworthy deeds of God. Review Psalm 78 with your guest speaker to help her or him focus on this lesson's key truth and indicate how long you have allowed in your lesson plan for him or her to speak.

Let's Talk It Over

The questions on this page are designed to encourage review of the lesson Scriptures and to promote discussion of the lesson by the class. The answers provided are only discussion starters. Let your class talk it over from there.

1. Why is the use of parables such an effective method of teaching? How can children (and adults) be made more curious about God's truth through the use of parables and puzzles?

Word pictures capture the imagination (e.g., 2 Samuel 12:1-14). Rather than simply being told "what to believe," parables and puzzles make us think for ourselves. They make us look for connections and seek answers to "why is this true?" They remind us quickly of both the question and the point. They are often easier to share with others. They can be put to music. They are memorable. Is it any wonder that Jesus taught in parables?

2. Occasionally one hears a cry that the educational systems need to provide more math and science majors to meet the demands of a highly technical society. But if it is true that "those who neglect the lessons of history are doomed to repeat them," should not modern culture also put a high priority on history majors to learn and teach correctly the lessons from the past?

A high-school senior expressed interest in majoring in history in college. His father quickly cautioned him about choosing this path by observing that "the only use for a degree in history is to teach history." A professor who teaches church history at a Bible college occasionally hears the following line in student-led prayers before class begins: " . . . and dear Lord, please help us to see some relevance in all this stuff."

Before we can effectively teach history, we must first convince people of the importance of *studying* history! God knows how quickly humans forget, and we see Him reminding His people over and over of their history in the pages of the Old Testament. (Go through a concordance and count how many times the phrase "out of Egypt" is used!) The stories of Israel and Judah recount the many times God had to "jog their memories." Modern culture's craving for materialism and sensationalism is the result of forgetting God and substituting an insatiable desire for self-gratification. This is always a path to destruction.

3. In a sincere effort to help their children escape the entrapment of evil, many parents teach their children repeatedly the rules about right and wrong, but do not introduce them to the God whose very nature defines what is right and wrong. Does this explain why children often are not motivated to keep "arbitrarily established" adult rules? Why or why not?

God's holiness is the "why" behind our obedience (cf. 1 Peter 1:15, 16). His holy nature is the reason why lying, for example, is wrong. Without knowing why a rule is important, children have no reason to honor the rule in the long run. Instead, they will try to find a way to disobey and not get caught. A rule that stands alone tends not to be honored because it has no lasting value in and of itself. (But remember that giving a child a *reason* is not the same as *reasoning with* the child—who may just want to argue!)

4. Old Testament parents could readily share their faith in what God had done and was doing. They learned this through the family because they had a "testimony in Jacob." They could share on a moment's notice "this is how God has influenced my family and my faith." How can a church help parents and church members develop their own natural "testimony in Jesus"?

Too often Christians think a "testimony" has to be elaborate and very moving. A testimony is usually a three-minute summary of "who God is to me and how He has changed my life." A class is a great place for Christians to help each other find interesting ways to raise a listener's curiosity about what God has done in a Christian's life.

5. Christian parents receive little instruction on the most effective ways to teach about God and His truths. What can the church do to help parents upgrade their skills in this area?

Parents do not come "programmed" with directions on how to do everything. Parents tend to imitate their own parents' teaching style (for good or for ill!). New parents do not usually consider the fact that their parents also were novices when they undertook the parenting role. Churches will be stronger when they develop programs to help parents learn a variety of effective teaching methods. Children go through several "developmental stages" as they grow, and the appropriate teaching techniques are different in each stage. The church needs to plan events and ministries that help parents understand each stage.

Worship the Creator and Sustainer

DEVOTIONAL READING: Psalm 65.

BACKGROUND SCRIPTURE: Psalms 65; 104.

PRINTED TEXT: Psalm 104:24-35.

Psalm 104:24-35

24 O LORD, how manifold are thy works! In wisdom hast thou made them all: the earth is full of thy riches.

25 So is this great and wide sea, wherein are things creeping innumerable, both small and great beasts.

26 There go the ships: there is that leviathan, whom thou hast made to play therein.

27 These wait all upon thee; that thou mayest give them their meat in due season.

28 That thou givest them they gather: thou openest thine hand, they are filled with good.

29 Thou hidest thy face, they are troubled: thou takest away their breath, they die, and return to their dust.

30 Thou sendest forth thy spirit, they are created: and thou renewest the face of the earth.

31 The glory of the LORD shall endure for ever: the LORD shall rejoice in his works.

32 He looketh on the earth, and it trembleth: he toucheth the hills, and they smoke.

33 I will sing unto the LORD as long as I live: I will sing praise to my God while I have my being.

34 My meditation of him shall be sweet: I will be glad in the LORD.

35 Let the sinners be consumed out of the earth, and let the wicked be no more. Bless thou the LORD, O my soul. Praise ye the LORD.

GOLDEN TEXT: O LORD, how manifold are thy works! In wisdom hast thou made them all: the earth is full of thy riches.—Psalm 104:24.

Worship and Wisdom for Living
Unit 2: Praise the Creator and Redeemer
(Lessons 6-9)

Lesson Aims

After participating in this lesson, each student will be able to:

1. List some of the ways God is glorified in His creation.

2. Tell how the psalmist says we should relate to God's creation and to Him.

3. Praise God for His role as Creator and Sustainer of the universe.

Lesson Outline

INTRODUCTION
    A. God's Relationship to the Natural World
    B. Lesson Background
  I. GOD CARES FOR HIS CREATION (Psalm 104: 24-30)
    A. The Wisdom of God (v. 24)
    B. The Creatures of the Sea (vv. 25, 26)
      Mayberry Sea Monster
    C. The Ongoing Provision of God (vv. 27-30)
      Cycles of Life
  II. GOD'S GLORY ENDURES FOREVER (Psalm 104: 31, 32)
    A. God Rejoices in the Glory of His Creation (v. 31)
    B. God Continues to Reveal Himself (v. 32)
  III. PRAISE FOR THE CREATOR (Psalm 104:33-35)
    A. Praise Expressed in Singing (v. 33)
    B. Praise Expressed in Meditation (v. 34)
    C. Praise Expressed in a Desire for Harmony (v. 35)
CONCLUSION
    A. Truths for Worship
    B. Prayer
    C. Thought to Remember

Introduction

A. God's Relationship to the Natural World

Devout people from many religions gather weekly (and sometimes daily) all over the world to worship God as they understand Him. But their concepts of God are all different and often contradictory! Does God care? Jesus seems to think so when He declares that "the true worshippers shall worship the Father in spirit and in truth" (John 4:23). The passage we consider today offers us truth that is important for our worship of Him. To worship God in truth surely includes a proper understanding of His relationship to us and our world.

B. Lesson Background

With this week's lesson, we begin a new unit of study focusing on humanity's praise of the Creator and Redeemer. We will study what several Psalms teach us about worshiping the Creator of life, about living as the crown of God's creation, about finding joy in forgiveness, and about all people praising God.

Psalm 104, for today's lesson, is a magnificent psalm of praise. Although we can't be sure, the historical setting probably involved the psalmist's own worship at the temple in Jerusalem. The psalmist reminds us here that God not only *creates*, but also actively *sustains* His creation. These truths should be part of our own worship.

I. God Cares for His Creation (Psalm 104:24-30)

A key feature that sets this subsection apart from verses 31-35 to follow is its *direct address* to God. The psalmist talks to God directly, and we can, too!

A The Wisdom of God (v. 24)

24. O LORD, how manifold are thy works! In wisdom hast thou made them all: the earth is full of thy riches.

God's wisdom made possible all life and the forces of nature of which we know—and those we are yet to discover! The ancient Greeks knew only of four "elements": earth, air, fire, and water. Modern chemistry's "periodic table of the elements," however, contains over one hundred entries, with more presumably to come. In light of these impressive discoveries, humans often think themselves to be wise. But if humanity—which has yet to cure many diseases—is wise, then how much wiser must be the One who created all the intricacies of the universe in the first place!

On the timetable of human history, we have only recently begun to explore the wonders of outer space and the complexities of the life forms found in the depths of the oceans. God's wisdom in creating the universe is beyond our ability to comprehend fully. We look around and continually find new things to astonish and confound us. How sadly ironic to see humans congratulate themselves for their intellect in these matters, and yet ignore their Creator whose wisdom makes their own possible. [See question #1, page 392.]

B. The Creatures of the Sea (vv. 25, 26)

25. So is this great and wide sea, wherein are things creeping innumerable, both small and great beasts.

The psalmist has a sincere appreciation for the Mediterranean Sea, which stretches to the horizon. Although this is indeed an immense body of water, it hardly compares in size with the Atlantic or Pacific Oceans. Imagine how overwhelmed the psalmist might have been to have known of those immensely larger bodies of water!

The psalmist stands in awe of the varieties of life the sea. But again, the psalmist's knowledge is limited compared with what we know today. In ancient times, there was no way to dive very deeply into any body of water. One could go down only as far as a single breath would allow. Our modern deep-sea research capabilities and discoveries would astound anyone living just two hundred years ago. In fact, they continue to astound even modern science, as new life forms are continually discovered and cataloged. Our increasingly sophisticated instruments of magnification make their contributions as well. Should not our greater knowledge lead to proportionately greater awe of the Creator? [See question #2, page 392.]

26. There go the ships: there is that leviathan, whom thou hast made to play therein.

The sea provides not only a habitat for God's creatures, but also a means of passage for human commerce. Both are sources of wonder and awe to the psalmist, especially since the ancient Jew was a landlubber for whom the sea held terror.

Of special interest here is the mention of *that leviathan*. This creature is also noted in Job 41:1; Psalm 74:14; and Isaiah 27:1, although no one really knows what a leviathan is (or was). From the psalmist's perspective, it may simply refer to a large marine creature, such as a whale. The psalmist's point is that it was God and no other who created this beast and gave it vast bodies of water to *play therein*. We are thus impressed again by God's creative power and His desire to provide for His creation.

MAYBERRY SEA MONSTER

Andy Griffith's TV neighbors (especially Barney Fife) were terrorized by sightings of what appeared to be a huge water dinosaur in a local lake. Barney's antics, as usual, were hysterical as he "fished" for the monster using whole chickens for bait. The episode concluded with the discovery that the lake creature was merely a fake—carved from wood and used by the owner of a resort restaurant to create publicity for his business.

Human nature is fascinated by "believe it or not" reports of new and unusual discoveries. The mystery of unknown elements of creation is intriguing. Perhaps the psalmist actually had never seen "leviathan," but reports of large sea creatures surely had drifted inland. Since he already believed in a God great enough to create such beings, his mind was open to new evidence.

Barney Fife was hardly a credible witness, but the God-breathed testimony of Holy Scripture is reliable. Even centuries ago, the Spirit convinced believers of the limitless power of God to create mighty whales as well as aquatic microbes (and everything in between). "Is any thing too hard for the Lord?" (Genesis 18:14). —R. W. B.

C. The Ongoing Provision of God (vv. 27-30)

27. These wait all upon thee; that thou mayest give them their meat in due season.

The psalmist depicts the creatures of the sea as almost helpless. They wait on God to feed them and take care of them. While we might not think of God in terms of personally arranging every daily feeding schedule for the animals and fish, there is a sense in which He is very much in control of these processes. God placed within these creatures instincts that drive them to certain places at certain times. For some, those instincts will lead them to find food. For others, those instincts lead them to *be* food. (Most know this as the food chain.) God can personally direct and override these instincts anytime He wishes, as He did in the case of the giant fish that swallowed Jonah.

Some may ask, "But how is God caring for some creatures when He provides them to be food for others?" This concern arises because humans tend to look at members of the animal kingdom in terms of a hierarchy of "values."

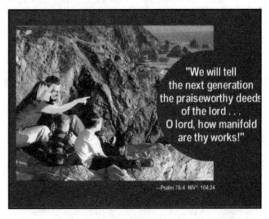

"We will tell the next generation the praiseworthy deeds of the lord . . . O lord, how manifold are thy works!"

—Psalm 78:4 NIV; 104:24

Visual for lessons 5, 6. *Display again the poster from last week.* Discuss some of the "manifold works" of God your students have admired.

Cute, furry animals seem to draw our compassion, while insects are swatted!

But in God's plan insects can be food for some animals (such as bats) just as certain mammals and fish can be food for others (such as seal pups for killer whales). On certain occasions when humans have removed predators from an environment, the result has been overpopulation and starvation of the prey remaining. God has worked out the various orders of creation according to His own priorities and values, not ours.

28. That thou givest them they gather: thou openest thine hand, they are filled with good.

The hunting instincts in sea (and other) creatures are innate—God made them that way. Some varieties of whales exhale underwater, and their food is trapped in the bubbles that float to the surface. The whales then surface and eat. God provides the food and the whales gather it in.

Humanistic scientists see this as the result of evolutionary processes at work. But these folks are never able to explain all the in-between steps that would have to occur for the whale to reach this final point in its "evolution." The psalmist, on the other hand, chooses to recognize God's care for His creation, and marvel at the fact.

29. Thou hidest thy face, they are troubled: thou takest away their breath, they die, and return to their dust.

Every creature is dependent on God. Their (and our) continued existence is due to forces of nature that God has put in place and continues to control. Suppose God were to withdraw the moon and other forces that control the ocean tides and currents. How many life forms would perish as a result? These forces of nature, created and continually sustained by God, demonstrate His presence. And when God withdraws His presence, either personally or through the forces of nature He controls, creatures suffer or die. This includes humans. "Thou didst hide thy face, and I was troubled" (Psalm 30:7).

When reading this passage, the Christian also recalls the spiritual renewal that is available only in Jesus. "Therefore if any man be in Christ, he is a new creature: old things are passed away; behold, all things are become new" (2 Corinthians 5:17). [See question #3, page 392.]

30. Thou sendest forth thy spirit, they are created: and thou renewest the face of the earth.

Without God there is no life. In noting the role of God's Spirit in creating sea creatures, the psalmist is perhaps recalling Genesis 1:2: "And the Spirit of God moved upon the face of the waters." But alongside the fact of creation the psalmist adds another idea: renewal. Renewal can be thought of as God "recreating" things.

Interestingly, the Old Testament places these "create" and "renew" ideas alongside each other in several other places as well. One example is Psalm 51:10 which says, "Create in me a clean heart, O God; and renew a right spirit within me." As new creations themselves, Christians look forward to the day when the old creation is renewed (Revelation 21:4, 5).

CYCLES OF LIFE

A few years ago, some criticized the popular film *The Lion King* for alleged New Age overtones. (For example, did Elton John's song "The Circle of Life" teach reincarnation?) Other movie fans preferred simply to enjoy the fable and music without analyzing the message.

There are, of course, cycles to life. Both flora and fauna demonstrate the fact. Grass, leaves, and flowers "die" in the fall and "come alive" again in the spring. Many animals and humans die each year, and many more are born. "The wind returneth again according to his circuits. All the rivers run into the sea; yet the sea is not full: unto the place from whence the rivers come, thither they return again" (Ecclesiastes 1:6, 7). And "to every thing there is a season" (Ecclesiastes 3:1).

"What goes around comes around," the saying goes. It seems clear, yet mysterious. There is evident design in the universe, and God is the awesome architect. The cycles and passages of life are part of His grand plan. All that man has discovered, God invented. It is He who enhances our existence with His wise and gracious gifts of natural law. It is He who maintains order and sustains life in His creation. It is He who has made us, and He who gives "life to the full."

—R. W. B.

II. God's Glory Endures Forever (Psalm 104:31, 32)

The psalmist now shifts away from addressing God directly. The focus moves from creation and sustenance to glory and power.

A. God Rejoices in the Glory of His Creation (v. 31)

31. The glory of the LORD shall endure for ever: the LORD shall rejoice in his works.

Humanistic thinkers have sought to have God declared dead or irrelevant. They have failed. There are more Christians in the world today than ever before. Human reason or decision cannot diminish the glory of God.

An interesting exercise is to look at some of these attempts and see how they have failed. Some thought, for example, that the space program would eliminate the need to rely on God, as humans on their own would eventually be able to unlock the mysteries of the universe and explain everything in humanistic ways.

Instead, the opposite has happened. Every answer gained seems to spawn two more questions. The intricacies of the universe defy humanistic explanations that exclude the concept of creation (otherwise known as "intelligent design"). Take some time and look at the breathtaking images that have come back from the Hubble space telescope. (You can find these easily on the Internet.) "The heavens declare the glory of God" (Psalm 19:1). [See question #4, page 392.]

B. God Continues to Reveal Himself (v. 32)

32. He looketh on the earth, and it trembleth: he toucheth the hills, and they smoke.

God continues to offer us evidence of His existence through earthquakes and other forces of nature. Human beings, who often consider themselves to be too intelligent and sophisticated to believe in supernatural forces, have "produced" some mighty powers of their own, such as nuclear energy. These efforts, of course, are nothing more than the harnessing of forces that God Himself already has created.

Even given our efforts to harness such forces, the results pale in comparison to the energy and force produced naturally by an earthquake or a volcano. The eruption of Mount Saint Helens in 1980, for example, released energy equivalent to five hundred atomic bombs of the type dropped on Hiroshima. A single solar flare (of which the psalmist knew nothing!) releases energy equivalent to millions of one-hundred-megaton hydrogen bombs. A discovery such as this should lead to even greater awe of the Creator than the psalmist demonstrated.

III. Praise for the Creator (Psalm 104:33-35)

In our final subsection, we find the psalmist singing, meditating, and expressing a specific desire. The psalmist seems to be overcome with emotion.

A. Praise Expressed in Singing (v. 33)

33. I will sing unto the LORD as long as I live: I will sing praise to my God while I have my being.

When we consider the wonders of God, the proper reaction is to break forth in praise, which will often take the form of singing. (The word *psalm* itself can be used to designate song or instrumental music.) The psalmist expresses a lifelong commitment to sing praises to God.

Sadly, some people never sing to God. In church, this may be due at times to embarrassment at having an untrained singing voice. (In such cases, the local church could offer encouragement and even basic voice training where appropriate.) At other times, stubbornness may be the reason. In this case, the words of the old hymn "We're Marching to Zion" might come to mind: "Let those refuse to sing Who never knew our God." Although it is up to God to judge motives in such cases, one cannot help but wonder about those who are able to sing but refuse to do so. [See question #5, page 392.]

The psalmist's expressive style conveys a very personal relationship with God, calling Him *my God*. That small possessive adjective "my" speaks volumes! The psalmist does not feel that God is distant or unapproachable. The God who created the universe and set in motion all the processes and forces we know and experience is also a very personal God. He is personally interested in each of us. The psalmist recognizes that fact and responds to it. Notice that the psalmist's commitment to lifelong praise-through-song is not an "as long as everything is going well" commitment.

B. Praise Expressed in Meditation (v. 34)

34. My meditation of him shall be sweet: I will be glad in the LORD.

The psalmist is committed to *meditation* as well as praise-through-song. When Joshua took the mantle of leadership following the death of Moses, the Lord told him to meditate on His word (Joshua 1:8). The Psalms themselves open by noting the importance of meditation (Psalm 1:2). There are many other references in the Psalms on the importance of meditating on God, His Word, and His works (see Psalm 19:14; 63:6; 77:12; 119:97, 99; and 143:5).

Meditating on the Scriptures seems to be a "lost art." Most people think they are just too busy. In a fast food, instant gratification culture, we have become unaccustomed to meditating, pondering, or thinking for extended periods of time. Many seem to have a need to hear the drone of a TV in the background at all times—even "muting" the sound during commercials is unknown in most households! The excesses of the Information Age and an entertainment-oriented culture tempt people away from private time with God. When one becomes used to thinking in "sound bites," meditation becomes "too much work." Undoubtedly, much of our unhappiness

---

How to Say It

LEVIATHAN. luh-*vye*-uh-thun.

can be traced to a lack of time or effort in meditating on the Word of God.

The psalmist, however, finds meditation to be *sweet*. This unique time to reflect on God—perhaps in solitude, perhaps during worship with others—makes the psalmist *glad in the Lord*. We might discover the psalmist's joy for ourselves if we minimized the time we spend pursuing entertainment in order to create more time to meditate upon God and His Word.

C. Praise Expressed in a Desire for Harmony (v. 35)

35. Let the sinners be consumed out of the earth, and let the wicked be no more. Bless thou the LORD, O my soul. Praise ye the LORD.

Suddenly, a "negative wish" presents itself. The desire expressed here, at first glance, seems to shatter the sweet gentleness of this psalm. How can the one who offered unrestrained praise to God express, in the same breath, such animosity toward humanity, the crown of God's creation?

In expressing a desire for the destruction of sinners, the psalmist longs for God's creation to be restored to its original, sinless purity. The apostle Paul notes that all of creation has been in disharmony since sin entered the world (Romans 8:22). The psalmist's desire for the removal of sinners reflects what God had already done once in the flood (Genesis 6–8) and promises to do again on the last day (Revelation 20).

But why has God waited so long to bring about this renewed harmony? Why does He continue to permit humanity to go on sinning and spoiling His creation? The answer is that God is waiting for people to answer the call of the gospel. God "is long-suffering to us-ward, not willing that any should perish, but that all should come to repentance" (2 Peter 3:9). Even

so, "the day of the Lord will come" (2 Peter 3:10). In His time, God will answer the prayer of the psalmist. God's patience and the promised restoration of His creation should cause all that know Him to say *Praise ye the Lord* (untranslated, "Hallelujah").

Conclusion

A. Truths for Worship

Many today do not believe in creation, preferring instead to suppose that life "evolved" through random chance and "natural selection." Others, who might accept the concept of creation and believe in the existence of a Creator, deny that that Creator continually cares for His creation and intervenes on its behalf. The latter is part of a philosophy known as "Deism"; several of America's founding fathers, including Thomas Jefferson and Benjamin Franklin, were influenced by this belief system.

A persistent viewpoint in ancient and Eastern religions is that "god" is not distinct from creation, but is actually part of it. This philosophy has been called "pantheism" (literally, "everything is god"), but more foundational is an idea known as "pagan monism." Under this philosophy, we are ultimately not to see "boundary lines" between anything. Thus, we are "god" and "god" is us—there is to be no distinction or dividing line. This philosophy is supposed to apply to other aspects within creation. For example, we are told to see no difference between humans and animals, or even between the sexes themselves (cf. Genesis 1:27; Deuteronomy 22:5).

But in a few short lines, the psalmist challenges all of these lies. As we noted in the Introduction, centuries after the Psalms were written Jesus would contend for the importance of truth-in-worship (John 4:23). The truths of Psalm 104 deserve to be engraved on our hearts as we worship. The rightness of the psalmist's attitude rings clearly down through the centuries. It is an attitude that should (and could) be ours as well.

B. Prayer

Eternal Heavenly Father, thank You for creating us. Thank You for making us in Your image. Thank You for sustaining our lives, keeping us alive by the forces You have put in place and by Your personal care for us. Thank You for sustaining all of creation for Your glory. Help us express our appreciation to You by living for You every moment of every day. In Jesus' name, amen.

C. Thought to Remember

God is entitled to our praise because He made us and sustains us.

Home Daily Bible Readings

Monday, July 1—Creator With Steadfast Love (Psalm 136:1-9)

Tuesday, July 2—Sustainer of Land and People (Psalm 147:1-11)

Wednesday, July 3—Mortals Sustained by Eternal God (Psalm 103:15-22)

Thursday, July 4—God Has Established the World (Psalm 93:1-5)

Friday, July 5—God Set the Earth's Foundations (Psalm 104:1-9)

Saturday, July 6—Sustainer of Life (Psalm 104:10-23)

Sunday, July 7—God Creates and Sustains (Psalm 65:1-13)

Learning by Doing

This page contains an alternate lesson plan emphasizing learning activities.
Classes desiring such student involvement will find these suggestions helpful.

Learning Goals

After participating in this lesson, each student will be able to:

1. List some of the ways God is glorified in His creation.

2. Tell how the psalmist says we should relate to God's creation and to Him.

3. Praise God for His role as Creator and Sustainer of the universe.

Into the Lesson

CHOICE: *Creation Collage.* The psalmist looked at the created world and broke out in praise to God, the Creator. Bring a stack of old magazines with colorful photographs of the beauty of the world. Ask your class to tear or cut out pictures that show the glory of God through His creation. Provide large sheets of newsprint or poster board on which these pictures can be glued or taped. This can be set up ahead of time and can begin when the first person walks in.

Make the transition to Bible study by saying, "We have looked for pictures that show the glory of God in His creation. Our study today is from Psalm 104; the psalmist looks at the creatures of the sea and breaks forth in praise to the Creator. Let's read of what we have done with pictures."

CHOICE: *Hymn Study.* Provide a hymnbook for each person in your class. If you are not a good song leader, ask for help. Explain what your goals are for the activity. Select some hymns that focus on creation and the glory it brings to the Creator, such as, "How Great Thou Art," and "For the Beauty of the Earth." Begin by having members turn to these hymns and analyze what the creation tells us about the Creator. Sing the stanzas especially appropriate for today's lesson: stanza 1 of "For the Beauty of the Earth," stanzas 1 and 2 of "How Great Thou Art." (This activity is in *Adult Bible Class.)*

Into the Word

CHOICE: *Research.* Assign a class member to research the leviathan the psalmist mentions in Psalm 104:26. (See also Job 41:1, Psalm 74:14, and Isaiah 27:1.) A little work in commentaries or the Internet will yield interesting results. (This activity is in *Adult Bible Class.)*

CHOICE: *Outline.* Provide class members with pens and paper for outlining the passage. This is a good Bible study activity because readers have to examine the text carefully to find basic ideas and how the theme is developed. Have your class work in groups of three or four. After they have completed the outline, have them share their outline with the class. You might show them the lesson writer's outline on page 386.

Into Life

CHOICE: *Poetry Writing.* Haiku is a type of Japanese poetry consisting of three lines of five, seven, and five syllables respectively. The topic is usually a subject from the natural world. Haiku has no rhyme or meter requirements. Here is an example.

> The sea at springtime.
> All day it rises and falls,
> Yes, rises and falls.

Show and read this one to your class, and then encourage them to write a haiku based on ideas from Psalm 104:24-35. You can lead your class in writing a haiku one line at a time. Ask your class to give you a five-syllable phrase on the topic of "the sea." For example, they might suggest, "The Lord made the sea." Then ask for a seven-syllable line. Conclude by asking for another five-syllable line. Write their suggestions on a poster, chalkboard, or transparency. Edit as necessary.

Your class is doing what the psalmist did—looking at nature and writing poetry to praise the Creator! (Directions for this activity are included in *Adult Bible Class.)*

CHOICE: *Write a Song.* Psalm 104:33 shows that singing praise to God is the proper response after pondering the wonder of His Creation. Lead your class to write a song of praise based on this passage. Use a familiar melody, maybe one from the songs suggested in the hymn study that introduced this lesson. Then use ideas from the text and adjust the wording to fit the meter of the melody. For example, using the melody from "How Great Thou Art!" one could write the following verse based on Psalm 104:20-35.

> O Lord, my God.
> Your works, they are unnumbered.
> In wisdom You have made them one and
> all.
> There is the sea, it is so vast and spacious;
> Teeming with life, with creatures large and
> small.

(The directions for this activity are included in *Adult Bible Class.)*

Let's Talk It Over

The questions on this page are designed to encourage review of the lesson Scriptures and to promote discussion of the lesson by the class. The answers provided are only discussion starters. Let your class talk it over from there.

1. While there is a growing commitment to valuing and protecting our natural environment today, there seems to be a diminishing recognition that it is all the product of God's wisdom and work. Why do you think this is the case?

It is a strange contradiction that seems to have its roots in man's inclination to worship the created rather than the Creator. It is identified in Romans 1:21-25. Unfortunately, the more we learn about the remarkable characteristics of the natural world in which we live, the more some people seem to want to deify it. That is, they view our environment and the creatures in it as having inherent worth, rather than purposeful value in the wisdom of God.

As Christians, we must always seek to understand the Creator's divine intention in all things. (Compare Genesis 1:11, 12, 28-30.)

2. The more we learn about God's creation, the more we realize that all living things, including "both small and great beasts," have their place in the scheme of things. In a day when size, speed, volume, and the like seem to be the measure of worth, how can we learn to appreciate and value "both small and great"?

Perhaps it begins with acknowledging that God "made them all," and in His wisdom all creation is purposeful. Quantitative value is not always the determinant of true value. "Micro" may have more use than "macro." A whisper may contain more wisdom than a shout. Seeds may hold more potential than a tree (Matthew 13:31). A little child may exhibit more Christlikeness than a grown man or woman (Matthew 18:1-4).

Furthermore, we might begin to thank God more regularly for the not-so-simple and not-so-ordinary things we take for granted each day (Psalm 104:10-23). We might also seek to enrich the lives of the most dependent in society, both animal and human. A society that ceases to value the life of dependent, innocent human beings ceases to have value itself!

3. Verses 27-29 suggest that there is interdependency in the universe that is part of God's creative intention. What are some of the evidences of this life-sustaining interdependency?

Life as we know it on our planet would be impossible without a balance of giving and receiving.

Encourage the class to identify examples of the interdependency we have with plant life. We depend on the oxygen that plants produce, and they depend on the carbon dioxide that we produce. Neither can survive without the other.

Another example is found in Newton's Third Law of Motion, which says, "For every action, there is an equal and opposite reaction." If this law did not function, then we would experience random, unpredictable motion, and the result would be a physical world in chaos.

How can this same principle of interdependency apply in our relationships with each other? (See Psalm 104:28 and 2 Corinthians 8:14.)

4. It seems incredible that some continue to insist that our solar system is a fortuitous cosmic consequence. In what ways does our world bring glory to God as Designer and Creator?

One way is through the reliable, dependable, functional laws that He has put in place to govern this system (see Newton's Third Law above). The more we learn about these laws, the more they reveal the wisdom of God in creation.

Another way is through the unity and harmony we discover in nature. Wernher von Braun once observed, "Nothing disappears without a trace." There is a sustaining quality about matter that suggests a Grand Designer with purposeful intent. The Creator looked upon what He had made, and "it was very good" (Genesis 1:31), and he continues to look upon it and "rejoice in his works" (Psalm 104:31).

5. Isaiah tells us that all of nature bursts forth in song and praise to the Lord (Isaiah 55:12). Why then, if all these created things seem to honor their Creator, is it so difficult for us, the crown of God's creation, to burst forth in spontaneous expressions of praise and adoration (vv. 33, 34)?

Could it be that we are forgetting that God could choose, at any moment, to withdraw His creating and sustaining Spirit from us, meaning that we would cease to exist? We have no life apart from Him, but many continue to assume that they are self-sufficient.

Ingratitude is the enemy of praise. Rejoicing in the gifts of God flows only from a grateful heart.

Live as the Crown of Creation

DEVOTIONAL READING: Psalm 144:3-9.

BACKGROUND SCRIPTURE: Psalms 8; 100.

PRINTED TEXT: Psalm 8:1-9; 100:1-5.

Psalm 8:1-9

1 O LORD our Lord, how excellent is thy name in all the earth! who hast set thy glory above the heavens.

2 Out of the mouth of babes and sucklings hast thou ordained strength because of thine enemies, that thou mightest still the enemy and the avenger.

3 When I consider thy heavens, the work of thy fingers, the moon and the stars, which thou hast ordained;

4 What is man, that thou art mindful of him? and the son of man, that thou visitest him?

5 For thou hast made him a little lower than the angels, and hast crowned him with glory and honor.

6 Thou madest him to have dominion over the works of thy hands; thou hast put all things under his feet:

7 All sheep and oxen, yea, and the beasts of the field;

8 The fowl of the air, and the fish of the sea, and whatsoever passeth through the paths of the seas.

9 O LORD our Lord, how excellent is thy name in all the earth!

Psalm 100:1-5

1 Make a joyful noise unto the LORD, all ye lands.

2 Serve the LORD with gladness: come before his presence with singing.

3 Know ye that the LORD he is God: it is he that hath made us, and not we ourselves; we are his people, and the sheep of his pasture.

4 Enter into his gates with thanksgiving, and into his courts with praise: be thankful unto him, and bless his name.

5 For the LORD is good; his mercy is everlasting; and his truth endureth to all generations.

GOLDEN TEXT: What is man, that thou art mindful of him? and the son of man, that thou visitest him?—Psalm 8:4.

Worship and Wisdom for Living
Unit 2: Praise the Creator and Redeemer
(Lessons 6-9)

Lesson Aims

After this lesson each student will be able to:
1. Summarize God's position with regard to creation, His work in creation, and our place in that creation.
2. Understand his or her obligation to praise the Creator.
3. Praise God from a prepared heart for His goodness, mercy, and truthfulness as Creator.

Lesson Outline

INTRODUCTION
    A. "A Short, Exquisite Lyric"
    B. Lesson Background
 I. THE MAJESTY OF GOD (Psalm 8:1-3)
    A. God's Excellent Name (v. 1a)
    B. God's Revealed Glory (v. 1b)
    C. Unsolicited Praise for God (v. 2)
    D. Visible Testimony About God (v. 3)
 II. THE POSITION OF HUMANITY (Psalm 8:4-9)
    A. A Humble Question (v. 4)
    B. A Confident Answer (v. 5)
    C. A Careful Description (vv. 6-8)
      Whales or Souls?
    D. A Potent Reminder (v. 9)
III. THE PRAISE WE OFFER GOD (Psalm 100:1-5)
    A. Joyful and Glad (vv. 1, 2)
    B. Humble and Meek (v. 3)
    C. Prepared and Reasoned (vv. 4, 5)
      Worship Wars
CONCLUSION
    A. "Unbridled Enthusiasm"?
    B. Prayer
    C. Thought to Remember

Introduction

A. "A Short, Exquisite Lyric"

C. S. Lewis (1898–1963) possessed one of the sharpest intellects of the twentieth century. Chair of Medieval and Renaissance Literature at Cambridge, he was a prolific writer of science fiction, fantasy, poetry, and prose. His works have been hailed as some of the finest literary products of all time. C. S. Lewis was an intellectual giant who found no satisfaction in the atheistic philosophies of his time. C. S. Lewis became a Christian.

Among Lewis's many works is a book entitled *Reflections on the Psalms*. In it he refers to Psalm 8 as a "short, exquisite lyric." As Lewis came to appreciate this psalm's depth of insight into the natures of God and mankind, so may we as well. Our own appreciation of Psalm 8 will then help us meet the challenge of Psalm 100 to "make a joyful noise unto the Lord." Today, it's "all about praise" as we explore Psalms 8 and 100. To offer praise to our Creator: what could be more basic?

B. Lesson Background

King David, who lived about a thousand years before Christ, wrote Psalm 8. We are not entirely sure of its historical context; its address "to the chief musician" is tantalizingly brief.

One conjecture is that this psalm came to David while he was still a shepherd, and he wrote it down later for his musician after becoming king. Lying on his back under the open sky with his flock of sheep, the young David may have marveled at the arrangement of stars splashed upon the ebony canvas of the heavens above. He may have pondered his own apparent insignificance within the vastness of creation. Such thoughts may have inspired him to write the psalm.

The author of Psalm 100, on the other hand, is unknown. The author may have composed it for the specific purpose of leading people to worship. This possibility certainly suits its title: "A Call to Praise the Lord." Perhaps you will recognize it as a call to worship or as part of a praise chorus that has been used in your own church on occasion.

I. The Majesty of God (Psalm 8:1-3)

Praise that is acceptable to God has its foundation in understanding His position with regard to our own. David is about to teach us what he knows in this regard.

A. God's Excellent Name (v. 1a)

1a. O LORD our Lord, how excellent is thy name in all the earth!
Psalm 8 begins with a celebration of God's *name*. Notice the appearance of *Lord* twice. The first (seen with small, upper case letters as "LORD") is literally "Yahweh," a name so holy that the Israelites stopped using it, fearing that they would accidentally commit some blasphemy. The second word translated as *Lord* is literally "Adonai," which means something like "governor" or "ruler." So translated in terms of how the original reader would have understood it, the meaning is something like "O Yahweh, our governor."

In this brief phrase, then, David has addressed God by a very holy name (which he calls "excellent" in the phrase to follow), and has recognized one of God's most important functions. By implication, David is humbling himself as one who is to *be* governed.

B. God's Revealed Glory (v. 1b)

1b. Who hast set thy glory above the heavens.
This half-verse can be understood in two ways. First, there is a sense in which God's glory is revealed through that which we view around us. Although David's view of the *heavens* was not as complete as ours, he beheld God's *glory* nonetheless. As David looked into the night sky without the aid of a telescope, could he have had any inkling of the distance to those stars? Could he have imagined the size of a star, or even what a star actually was? To him, a star was a mysterious twinkling point of light in a dark sky. Yet even with that limited perception, David recognized the glory of God in creating such wonders.

A second way of understanding this half-verse focuses on the word *above*. To those who lived in the ancient world, what was visible in the night sky may have been merely a "preview" of what was above even that. The ancient mind may have sensed that there was a greater realm of glory known to God, but invisible to mankind. In either sense, God's creative power, even if incompletely revealed, compels us to recognize His glory.

C. Unsolicited Praise for God (v. 2)

2. Out of the mouth of babes and sucklings hast thou ordained strength because of thine enemies, that thou mightest still the enemy and the avenger.
Persuasive testimony comes from unlikely sources! At Jesus' triumphal entry into Jerusalem, children greet Him with shouts of "Hosanna to the Son of David" (Matthew 21:15). This acclamation irritated the chief priests and scribes. When they complained to Jesus about what the children were proclaiming, He quoted the first half of Psalm 8:2 to them (Matthew 21:16). Upon hearing this response, these "experts" in the law could hardly miss the unspoken jab from the second half of Psalm 8:2: Jesus was implying that they themselves were the enemies of God.

Earlier Jesus had taught that those who would come to Him needed to do so in the manner of a child approaching someone he or she instinctively knew to be superior (Matthew 18:1-4). That admonition calls for self-humility. [See question #1, page 400.]

D. Visible Testimony About God (v. 3)

3. When I consider thy heavens, the work of thy fingers, the moon and the stars, which thou hast ordained.
David's mind turns again to the testimony of God he has witnessed in the night sky. Its splendor should remind the reader of its Source. Unfortunately, the Israelite people got themselves into serious trouble at this very point. Early in their history, just before entering the promised land, Moses had warned them specifically not to bow down in worship of the created heavenly bodies (Deuteronomy 4:19). Yet some eight hundred years later, they will find themselves cast into exile because of doing just that (cf. Jeremiah 7:18; 8:2; 44:17-30; Ezekiel 8:16; Acts 7:42, 43). How ironic that such a majestic part of creation should have led God's people closer to Him, but instead they allowed it to have the opposite effect! [See question #2, page 400.]

II. The Position of Humanity (Psalm 8:4-9)

Verse 3, just considered, serves as a lead-in to verse 4. It is the magnificence of the night sky (v. 3) that leads David to contemplate his own apparent insignificance (v. 4).

A. A Humble Question (v. 4)

4. What is man, that thou art mindful of him? and the son of man, that thou visitest him?
Many Bible scholars believe that this verse may have two "layers" of interpretation: David, in speaking of *man* in the strictly human sense, may at the same time be speaking prophetically of the Messiah who is to come. Note the phrase *son of man*, which Jesus will later use to describe

Visual for lesson 7

What is man that you are mindful of him, the son of man that you care for him?

Use this poster to illustrate God's care for all people of every race.

Himself in the gospels (cf. also Daniel 7:13). On the other hand, this phrase is also used extensively in the book of Ezekiel to refer to that prophet's frailty and mortality.

The writer of Hebrews quotes from this section of Psalm 8 in a context which many commentators and translators believe applies to Jesus. Others think, however, that Psalm 8:4-6 as used in Hebrews 2:6-8 applies to mortals instead—so we see the two "layers" of interpretation in the New Testament as well. For deeper study, compare the translation of the *King James Version* with that of the *New Revised Standard Version* at this point. [See question #3, page 400.]

B. A Confident Answer (v. 5)

5. For thou hast made him a little lower than the angels, and hast crowned him with glory and honor.

If David's question in verse 4 was full of humility, then his answer in verse 5 is full of confidence. God created us to be a little lower than angelic beings for a time. Remember that the Bible describes only humans as being created in God's image (Genesis 1:26, 27). Ultimately, we will sit in judgment on angels (1 Corinthians 6:3).

The second part of verse 5 also speaks to humanity's place in God's created order, surely an important issue if we are to have a Biblical view of mankind. To be *crowned with glory and honor* reflects the result of being created in the image of God (again, Genesis 1:26, 27). Our greatest attribute was not attained by our own effort; it was a gift from the Creator.

C. A Careful Description (vv. 6-8)

6. Thou madest him to have dominion over the works of thy hands; thou hast put all things under his feet.

Again, is this referring to humans only, or to humans as well as the coming Messiah in two "layers" of meaning? Assuming that it refers "at least" to humans, this verse reveals great privilege and great responsibility. God set the world and the forces of nature in place, then He put us in charge of His creation (Genesis 1:26).

However, the entrance of sin into the world upset this ideal plan of God. Now humans must struggle constantly with nature to earn a living (cf. Genesis 3:17-19). We look forward to the day when the ideal of Psalm 8:6 and Genesis 1:26 will be restored (see Revelation 21:4, 5). While we wait expectantly for that day, we should note that Psalm 8:6 has implications for ecology and stewardship of current resources.

7. All sheep and oxen, yea, and the beasts of the field.

David gives a more detailed description of mankind's responsibility. Interestingly, the first animals he mentions are *sheep*. Perhaps David still had the heart of a shepherd.

Some contemporary movements have sought to make animals equal to human beings in value. This is not Biblical. Animals were not created in God's image. They do not possess an eternal spirit, as humans do.

8. The fowl of the air, and the fish of the sea, and whatsoever passeth the paths of the sea.

The description moves from land-bound creatures to those of the *air* and water. The picture is now complete: humanity's dominion is (or, ideally, should be) extended to all earthly creatures. This dominion, of course, is not a license for abuse or cruelty.

Christians should have a proper perspective concerning their ideal position in God's created order. Particularly questionable is the theory of evolution, which places us in a position of being no more than the most highly developed member of the animal kingdom. As wonderful as it might be to think of one's self solely as the top of that heap, such a "status" cannot compare with the Biblical fact of being created in the very image of God. Humankind is the crowning achievement of creation precisely because we alone are created in God's image.

WHALES OR SOULS?

Bumper stickers can be thought provoking. One admonished, "Forget whales; save souls!" Obviously, the owner was making a statement about the sometimes twisted priorities of ecologists. The extinction of whales is a legitimate concern, and humans who prey upon them for greed or sport should be restricted and restrained by law. But inordinate expenditures of money, time, and effort to "save" mere mammals of the sea must be viewed as excessive when contrasted with the usually meager investments made for world evangelism.

It's a matter of perspective. Christians consider human life to be of greater value than animal life. Despite his shortcomings, Captain Ahab is worth more than Moby Dick. Mankind is superior to the animals, for we alone are made in God's image.

Godly people should pursue a balanced viewpoint on environmental issues. Clean air and water, preservation of natural resources, and protection of threatened species—all of these causes are worthy to a degree. Our primary concern, however, must be the welfare and eternal destiny of *Homo sapiens*. Saving whales may be a *good* thing, but saving souls is the *best* thing.

—R. W. B.

D. A Potent Reminder (v. 9)

9. O LORD our Lord, how excellent is thy name in all the earth!

David repeats the phrase with which he opens the Psalm. These two identical phrases thus form "bookends" that reinforce a straightforward theme: God is so wonderful that the excellence of His *name* extends to the entire *earth!* The second use of David's exclamation becomes more profound than the first, though, when we think of all he has had to say in verses 2-8. While we're thinking about the excellence of God's name, we should note God's concern that His name not be used carelessly or disrespectfully (Exodus 20:7).

III. The Praise We Offer God (Psalm 100:1-5)

Psalm 8 humbles us. As such, it prepares us to offer the praise encouraged by Psalm 100.

A. Joyful and Glad (vv. 1, 2)

1. Make a joyful noise unto the LORD, all ye lands.

God calls *all* people to praise Him. This praise should come from our lips naturally; it should not be coerced. We will see why when we consider verse 3 below.

Interestingly, this praise is to come from *all ye lands,* not just Israel. (Psalms 98:4 and 117:1 give similar instructions.) But in many lands God—the true God—is not known. In some lands He is known only partially, for in those lands the Son is not recognized as one with the Father (John 10:30). How shall these lands praise Him? The answer is in Romans 10:14.

2. Serve the LORD with gladness: come before his presence with singing.

Serving with gladness does not mean serving with a giddy silliness, which is devoid of reason and propriety. It means, rather, that we willingly and wholeheartedly offer ourselves to God, without reluctance or hesitation. There is no "I wish I didn't have to do this" in the psalmist's heart.

Remember, to *serve the Lord with gladness* and to enter into *His presence with singing* for worship are privileges the Creator has granted, not a monotonous obligation. Do we view worship as a

---

How to Say It

ADONAI (HEBREW). Ad-owe-*nye.*
AGRIPPA. Uh-*grip*-puh.
BABEL. *Bay*-bul.
EZEKIEL. Ee-*zeek*-ee-ul or Ee-*zeek*-yul.
HEROD. *Hair*-ud.

---

privilege, or are we mainly just "going through the motions" while we think of where we're going to eat lunch after church is over? [See question #4, page 400.]

B. Humble and Meek (v. 3)

3. Know ye that the LORD he is God: it is he that hath made us, and not we ourselves; we are his people, and the sheep of his pasture.

The people who came to worship were to do so in the proper spirit: the spirit of humility and meekness. That spirit comes when we recognize who *God* is and who we are. God is the Creator and *we ourselves* are *not!*

That may sound a bit "obvious." But it must not be obvious to everyone since the Bible offers several examples of people who get themselves into trouble when they try to elevate themselves to positions that belong only to Him. Eve accepted Satan's temptation to eat the forbidden fruit upon hearing his promise that "ye shall be as gods" (Genesis 3:5). Herod Agrippa I allowed others to see him as a "god" and paid the price (Acts 12:22, 23). The tower of Babel was an attempt by humans to become more than they ought (Genesis 11:1-9); modern science has the potential of leading us down a similar path unless we exercise care. We avoid these dangers when in humility we recognize that God is the Creator and we are not. This includes recognizing that we have many limitations, we are guilty of past sin, and we will continually be plagued by sin throughout this life.

A proper understanding of the natures of God and mankind is fundamental to our worship of God. It also is necessary for us to understand our proper role in serving God and to appreciate God's desire to have a relationship with us. And along with that understanding is the recognition that the *pasture*—the place in which we have our existence—is also His, and He has put us in it.

C. Prepared and Reasoned (vv. 4, 5)

4. Enter into his gates with thanksgiving, and into his courts with praise: be thankful unto him, and bless his name.

This verse recalls the layout of ancient Jerusalem and its temple. The city itself was walled on all sides for protection, and entrance was only through a limited number of *gates.* Within those walls was the temple, the focal point of ancient Israel's worship after its construction by Solomon. The temple consisted of, among other things, a series of *courts.* People would gather for worship in these courts. (Access to some courts was restricted, based on a person's status.) Even nearly ten centuries after its initial construction, the rebuilt temple of

Jesus' day still served as the focus of Israelite worship (see Mark 13:1; John 2:13-17; and 4:20).

Note that the psalmist challenges the reader to enter the gates and courts *with*—meaning "already having"—a spirit of *praise* and thankfulness. In other words, the psalmist's challenge is for the reader to "be prepared" to bless God's name when arriving at the place for worship.

This wasn't necessarily easy, as the psalmist's world was full of pressures that would distract from being prepared for worship. Trips to Jerusalem could be time-consuming and dangerous. Bringing an animal to sacrifice each time could be an expensive proposition. Leaving part of the family behind to watch the farm was something to think about. Even so, the psalmist desires the reader to be *ready* to worship. After all, if a person arrives at the place of worship having a negative spirit because he or she is dwelling on all the time and trouble it took to get there, then what would be the point of even coming? [See question #5, page 400.]

WORSHIP WARS

Volumes already have been written concerning the ongoing conflicts in the church at large (and in nearly every local congregation) over the subjective issue of worship styles. It mostly boils down to disagreements as to personal preferences—nothing as important as "thus saith the Lord." The breaches in Christianity, however, seem to have dichotomized disciples into the younger contemporary camp and the older traditional camp. Can these diversities be reconciled without splitting churches?

Some feel that the senior saints (supposedly more mature) should forfeit their hymns and formality in the interest of unity and outreach. Others are adamant that the "Boomers and X'ers"

Home Daily Bible Readings

Monday, July 8—Sing of God's Abundant Goodness (Psalm 145:1-7)
Tuesday, July 9—All God's Works Give Thanks (Psalm 145:8-13)
Wednesday, July 10—The Lord Watches Over All (Psalm 145:14-21)
Thursday, July 11—Everything That Breathes Give Praise (Psalm 150)
Friday, July 12—Praise God, All Creation (Psalm 148:1-6)
Saturday, July 13—Thanks for God's Wondrous Deeds (Psalm 75)
Sunday, July 14—Worship God Who Made Us (Psalm 100)

should put aside their secular and sensational proclivities and give sober, objective praise to God with optimum decency and order.

Will these "worship wars" ever end? Some congregations have achieved at least temporary armistice by bending and blending their style of worship to please most folks in both camps. Other local bodies offer different styles at different hours (even different days) to give appeasing options to opposing groups.

Some sort of compromise seems to be necessary. Whatever it takes, we must keep "the main thing" (honoring God) "the main thing."

—R. W. B.

5. For the LORD is good; his mercy is everlasting; and his truth endureth to all generations.

The psalmist closes by setting forth three reasons why we are to worship with thanksgiving. Imagine what it would be like to worship a fickle god: sometimes he is *good*, sometimes he is not; his *mercy* runs hot and cold, depending on his whim; his truthfulness cannot always be counted on. Such were the "gods" of the surrounding peoples in the psalmist's day. But the God we serve, who promises to take the true believers home for all eternity (John 14:1-4), is not that way. He is the perfect "promise keeper"!

Conclusion

A. "Unbridled Enthusiasm"?

We all have seen the unbridled enthusiasm of fans at sporting events. Sadly, enthusiasm to praise our Creator is often absent from our worship services. Although it is right that we do things "decently and in order" (1 Corinthians 14:40), that need not translate into that which is lifeless and dreary. Will your praise be enthusiastic this week?

We also see that offering praise that really "means something"—both to God and to us—is more complicated than we may have first thought. We are also now more aware of where Satan's points of attack may come as he tries to distract us from meaningful praise. Advance preparation for worship should be a key.

B. Prayer

Father, thank You for creating us in Your image. Make us so aware of who You are that we cannot contain our joy. May our worship and service bring You joy, and may You rejoice in Your creation. Remind us that our worship must be meaningful to You. In Jesus' name, amen.

C. Thought to Remember

Live as the crown of God's creation!

Learning by Doing

This page contains an alternate lesson plan emphasizing learning activities.
Classes desiring such student involvement will find these suggestions helpful.

Learning Goals

After participating in this lesson, each student will be able to:

1. List some of the ways God is glorified in His creation.

2. Tell how the psalmist says we should relate to God's creation and to Him.

3. Praise God for His role as Creator and Sustainer of the universe.

Into the Lesson

CHOICE: *Singing*. Begin your class today by having members sing Psalm 8. Michael W. Smith has written a version widely recognized. Include the enthusiastic clapping! Play a tape or CD and have the class sing along.

CHOICE: *Debate*. Have your class prepare a debate on the nature of God and the nature of man. On one side, the universe could be described as formed by chance and natural elements. The other side would contend that God created the universe. In regard to man, one side would declare that man is created in the image of God and thereby endowed with dignity and honor. The opposing side could take either of two extremes: they could portray man as the accidental result of meaningless evolution and therefore an inconsequential blob of protoplasm, or they could pursue the opinion that man is god-like among the products of evolution and his decisions are all that there is.

Into the Word

CHOICE: *Discussion Questions*. Lead your class in a discussion by asking the following questions:

What is God's name that is so excellent? (8:1)

How does the praise of babies silence enemies? (8:2)

What do the heavens tell us about God's power? (8:3)

Why is God concerned about mankind? (8:4)

What difference does it make if it is "God" instead of "angels"? (8:5)

What is an appropriate view of creation, since God has given us "dominion" over it? (8:6-8)

What do these verses suggest in regard to testing products on animals prior to human use? (8:6-8)

Why is our worship not more typified by "joyful noise"? (100:1)

What songs help you to connect gladness and singing? (100:2)

What does 100:3 say about the so-called "self-made man"?

How are thanksgiving, praise, and blessing connected? (100:4)

Why are God's mercy and truth described as eternal? (100:5)

CHOICE: *Illustration*. Ask class members to illustrate each verse, or suggest that they attempt a drawing that would capture the essence of the chapter. The images in both chapters are graphic and visual. For example, Psalm 8:1 could show "I AM" written in billowy, glowing clouds shining with the glory of God. Verse 2 might show children at Jesus' triumphal entry praising God with palm fronds and shouting "Hosanna!"

Provide unlined paper and pencils or markers for each class member. Or you might want to do a mural: tape white table-cover paper to a wall, and write or draw on it with colored markers.

Into Life

CHOICE: *Write a Prayer*. The content of Psalm 8:1, 2 should move the reader to prayerful response. Ask your class members to write a prayer in response to each verse. Read each verse and then discuss its application in daily life. Express that concept in a personalized prayer. For example, these two verses could inspire these words, "My Lord, Your name and character are majestic and glorious above all things You have made. With childlike adoration I offer you the praise of my lips. May my praise silence your enemies who refuse to honor Your name."

(The directions for this activity are included in *Adult Bible Class*.)

CHOICE: *Responsive Reading*. Have your class members create a responsive reading based on these two familiar chapters. One technique is to have a refrain that is repeated after each verse, like "His love endures for ever" in Psalm 136.

The most obvious refrain for Psalm 8 is the first verse, used as a refrain at the end of the chapter. Have a leader read the chapter with the class repeating verse one after each verse.

For Psalm 100, the phrase, "For the Lord is good" from verse 5, expresses a central truth of the chapter.

(The directions for this activity are included in *Adult Bible Class*.)

Let's Talk It Over

The questions on this page are designed to encourage review of the lesson Scriptures and to promote discussion of the lesson by the class. The answers provided are only discussion starters. Let your class talk it over from there.

1. Children seem to have no difficulty at all acknowledging the majesty and glory of God. Why is it that we are often so reluctant to express such spontaneous adoration of Him?

Perhaps it is because we believe we must subject every expression of faith to the test of our intelligence and rationality. When Jesus was healing in the temple, the "scribes saw the wonderful things that he did" (Matthew 21:15). However, instead of praising God, they were indignant because the children were expressing praise. Jesus quoted this verse from Psalm 8 as a reminder that the humility of a child often opens their minds to truth that intellectual pride in an adult may blot out.

2. The phrase *When I consider thy heavens* seems to be the agenda of modern man. We are intrigued by what is still beyond us, and we want to know more. How can we balance this interest in the world beyond with an appropriate concern for the world around and within?

Perhaps the most important element needed is the recognition that it is all God's world, and we are God's children by creation. Once we lose sight of the fact that God is the One who holds it all together (Colossians 1:17), and it is His will and purpose that will ultimately prevail, then we begin to construct a universe with ourselves at the center. This self-centeredness inevitably results in self-destruction. When David considered God's heavens, he did so with humility, yet realizing his own significance. So must we.

3. Psalm 8 deals with two closely related questions: who is God? and who are we in God's creation? How would you answer these questions?

The heavens stand as a silent witness to the wisdom and majesty of God. But as impressed as we are with their vastness and glory, they cannot begin to match the glory of their Creator.

When we face the inevitable question of our own significance, we are often ambivalent. What is our place and purpose? One answer is the answer of the humanist. As an intelligent, rational being, man is an animal of the highest order, but still only an animal. He has no significance or purpose beyond this physical existence. Bertrand Russell expressed this view when he said, "Brief and powerless is man's life."

A more accurate answer is that we have a unique relationship to God by virtue of creation (Genesis 1:26, 27). In this relationship, we are to be the instruments through whom God accomplishes His purposes in the world. What grand significance our lives have when we accept who we are in God's plan!

4. Psalm 100 invites us to "come before" the Lord, and to do so with "gladness" and "singing." In what sense is this a part of our worship?

For the ancient Hebrew, the command to "come before his presence" might have called them to enter the temple with a personal sense of God's presence in the Holy Place. Often they would come from distant places and upon arrival at the outer gate, they were met by an official who had them turn their backs on the temple, face the distant nations from which they came and repeat these words (vv. 1, 2) followed by shouting "Know that the Lord is God." Then facing each other, they would declare, "It is he who made us, and we are his."

It might be appropriate for us to pause for a moment as we enter to worship our Lord and remind ourselves that we are "a chosen generation, a royal priesthood, a holy nation" (1 Peter 2:9). Then we might have a sense of awe when coming into His presence rather than having a sense of coming to a performance.

5. How can this Psalm help us to understand what constitutes true worship and to express it appropriately?

It identifies some of the most significant elements and attitudes of true worship—joy, gladness, humility, thanksgiving, praise, and adoration. Each of these should be manifest in some way during our worship.

We fail to worship adequately when we have an inadequate view of God. The psalmist reminds us who He is. He is God, the One who made us (v. 3). He is good, loving, and faithful (v. 5). We acknowledge this in true worship.

We may also fail to worship appropriately when we have an inappropriate view of ourselves. The psalmist says, "We are his people." Pride has no place in worship. We are not self-made. Humility, confession, and thanksgiving are the appropriate attitudes we must bring to worship.

Find Joy in Forgiveness

DEVOTIONAL READING: **Psalm 51:1-12.**

BACKGROUND SCRIPTURE: **Psalms 32; 51.**

PRINTED TEXT: **Psalm 32:1-11.**

Psalm 32:1-11

1 Blessed is he whose transgression is forgiven, whose sin is covered.

2 Blessed is the man unto whom the LORD imputeth not iniquity, and in whose spirit there is no guile.

3 When I kept silence, my bones waxed old through my roaring all the day long.

4 For day and night thy hand was heavy upon me: my moisture is turned into the drought of summer. Selah.

5 I acknowledged my sin unto thee, and mine iniquity have I not hid. I said, I will confess my transgressions unto the LORD; and thou forgavest the iniquity of my sin. Selah.

6 For this shall every one that is godly pray unto thee in a time when thou mayest be found: surely in the floods of great waters they shall not come nigh unto him.

7 Thou art my hiding place; thou shalt preserve me from trouble; thou shalt compass me about with songs of deliverance. Selah.

8 I will instruct thee and teach thee in the way which thou shalt go: I will guide thee with mine eye.

9 Be ye not as the horse, or as the mule, which have no understanding: whose mouth must be held in with bit and bridle, lest they come near unto thee.

10 Many sorrows shall be to the wicked: but he that trusteth in the LORD, mercy shall compass him about.

11 Be glad in the LORD, and rejoice, ye righteous: and shout for joy, all ye that are upright in heart.

GOLDEN TEXT: Blessed is he whose transgression is forgiven, whose sin is covered.
—Psalm 32:1.

Worship and Wisdom for Living
Unit 2: Praise the Creator and Redeemer
(Lessons 6-9)

Lesson Aims

After this lesson, each student will be able to:

1. Summarize what David says in Psalm 32 about the blessing of confessing sin, experiencing God's forgiveness, and seeking God's counsel.

2. Contrast the condition of one who is forgiven with the miserable state of the one who tries to hide his or her sin.

3. Specify someone who needs to hear the message of forgiveness, and tell that person what God has done in Jesus.

Lesson Outline

INTRODUCTION
    A. Augustine's Favorite Psalm
    B. Lesson Background
  I. THE ONE WHO IS BLESSED (Psalm 32:1, 2)
    A. Sins Forgiven and Covered (v. 1)
    B. "This Won't Count Against You" (v. 2)
 II. THE ONE WHO IS MISERABLE (Psalm 32:3, 4)
    A. The Power of Unconfessed Sin (v. 3)
    B. The Power of Conscience (v. 4)
III. THE ONE WHOSE BURDENS ARE LIFTED (Psalm 32:5)
    A. Man Confesses (v. 5a)
    B. God Forgives (v. 5b)
    Can You Say, "I'm Sorry"?
IV. THE ONE WHO TRUSTS IN THE LORD (Psalm 32:6-11)
    A. Finds a Hiding Place (vv. 6, 7)
    B. Learns From the Lord (vv. 8, 9)
    C. Is Surrounded by Love (v. 10)
    D. Is Filled with Praise (v. 11)
    Happy Are the Forgiven
CONCLUSION
    A. Lifesaving News
    B. Prayer
    C. Thought to Remember

Introduction

A. Augustine's Favorite Psalm

Augustine of Hippo (A.D. 354–430) is one of the most well-known figures in church history. After spending the early years of his life as a reprobate, he turned to Christ and found the joy of new life in Him. Psalm 32 is said to have been Augustine's favorite Psalm. Perhaps he felt a kinship with David, whose sins had been so egregious. Perhaps he was simply delighted with the testimony of one whose life in many ways mirrored his own.

Augustine supposedly had Psalm 32 inscribed on the wall beside his bed as he approached his death. He apparently wanted to remember the greatness and wonder of a God who is full of compassion for sinners.

B. Lesson Background

Psalm 32 is one of the seven "penitential Psalms" (the other six are Psalms 6, 38, 51, 102, 130, and 143). This Psalm comes alive when read in light of the second of those other six, namely Psalm 51. There we find David's hymn of repentance over the Bathsheba incident (cf. 2 Samuel 11). David's anguish is almost palpable as you read that psalm. You feel that his sorrow for his sin has brought him to the point of physical pain. In Psalm 32 we find David's instruction about forgiveness. He learned a powerful lesson about the horror of guilt and the joy of forgiveness. In Psalm 51:13, he promised God that he would help change other people's lives by instructing them about His forgiveness. He fulfilled that promise as he penned the words of Psalm 32.

I. The One Who Is Blessed (Psalm 32:1, 2)

A. Sins Forgiven and Covered (v. 1)

1. Blessed is he whose transgression is forgiven, whose sin is covered.

Psalm 1 begins with these words: "Blessed is the man that walketh not in the counsel of the ungodly, nor standeth in the way of sinners, nor sitteth in the seat of the scornful." How many of us can take honest inventory of our lives and feel *blessed* because we have lived out the instruction of that verse? Most of us would readily admit that we have fallen far short of those ideals. The opening verse of Psalm 32 brings the promise of blessing to the person who has completely failed to measure up to the precepts of Psalm 1. As one who himself had experienced forgiveness from grievous sin, the depth of David's joyous proclamation must not be understated. It is a blessing to know that our sins are *forgiven!* The blessing of God is not withheld from us because we fail in our human attempts to live up to His standards.

God forgives our *transgression.* The Hebrew word carries the idea of disloyalty or rebellion. Although we sin against people and hurt others by our sin, we must remember that sin is ultimately rebellion against God's ideal for our lives and is thus an affront to Him. [See question #1, page 408.]

The Hebrew word for *sin* here includes the idea of missing God's will. Although we will never reach the goal of godly perfection in this life in following His will, this does not excuse us from trying (cf. Matthew 5:48). The joyous news that David proclaimed was that God forgives us even when we miss or rebel against His will.

The thought behind the word *forgiveness* is to have something "lifted off," "removed," or "carried away." David used a potent word picture in Psalm 103:12: "As far as the east is from the west, so far hath he [God] removed our transgressions from us." God did not simply set our sin aside. He moved it so far away that it is out of our sight and His.

In helping us to understand God's forgiveness, David also rejoices that our sins have been *covered.* When something is covered, it is not visible. We do not notice it. We can be right next to something covered and not know it is there. That is how God deals with our sin. He covers it.

B. "This Won't Count Against You" (v. 2)

2. Blessed is the man unto whom the LORD imputeth not iniquity, and in whose spirit there is no guile.

Taken with verse 1, this verse again demonstrates the Hebrew parallelism that we've seen in other places in the Psalms. The three different Hebrew words translated in verses 1 and 2 as *transgression, sin,* and *iniquity* are all synonyms for *sin.* Likewise, the Hebrew verbs for *forgive, covered,* and *imputeth not* are synonyms. *Imputeth not* is an accounting term; it suggests God will not place our sins against our "account." The apostle Paul quotes these verses in Romans 4:7, 8. He, too, felt the wonder of God's mercy in not counting his sin against him. Paul had been a

Visual for lesson 8. *Display this poster as you begin. Ask, "Do you think Christians appreciate the blessing of forgiveness? Why or why not?"*

murderous persecutor of Christians. After his experiences on the road to, and in the city of, Damascus, he found the joy of not having his sins counted against him.

When we know that our sins do not count against us, we can live without *guile* (or "deceit," *New International Version*). We can be honest about ourselves, just as David was. We do not have to try to fool anyone by pretending to be someone we're not. People do not like phonies, nor does God (cf. Matthew 23). The person who has been forgiven does not have to be a phony anymore. [See question #2, page 408.]

II. The One Who is Miserable (Psalm 32:3, 4)

A. The Power of Unconfessed Sin (v. 3)

3. When I kept silence, my bones waxed old through my roaring all the day long.

Sin that is unconfessed and unforgiven ravages the body and the spirit. This verse may refer to David's feelings between the time of his adultery with Bathsheba and his arranging for Uriah's death, and the time of his confrontation by Nathan and subsequent confession of sin.

Medical science has confirmed the harm done to the body by unresolved issues. Guilt leads to stress and depression. Guilt can result in a person taking his or her own life. Although we are bombarded with worldly ways to relieve stress and rid ourselves of guilt, we, like David, know that the only true resolution to the problem of guilt is to find forgiveness. Only then will one find relief from the daylong *roaring* (or "groaning," *New International Version*).

B. The Power of Conscience (v. 4)

4. For day and night thy hand was heavy upon me: my moisture is turned into the drought of summer. Selah.

The part of the Mediterranean world in which David lived had two seasons: a wet (rainy) season and a dry season. As the unconfessed sin of verse 3 takes its toll, to David it is like moving from that wet season to the *drought of summer.* [See question #3, page 408.]

God gave us a great gift in the form of our conscience. While some may be ignorant of certain specific laws, all people share an instinctive knowledge of right and wrong (cf. Romans 2:14-15). That is part of being created in God's image. We dare not ignore that instinct! To do so is to sap oneself of spiritual strength, to have God turn our productive moisture into a dreary, lifeless dryness (cf. Ezekiel 37:1, 2).

Paul wrote of the abandonment of conscience in Romans 1:18-32. He warns against disregarding both conscience and instinctive knowledge of God. He describes those who have disregarded God's desires in truly horrifying terms.

The use of *Selah* is interesting. While it is found in many places in the Old Testament, no one really knows what it means. Here it appears to draw special attention to what had just been written. It seems to say to the reader, "Stop and take special notice of this!" Today we might bold-face and italicize the passage. In Hebrew, the ancients may have used the word *Selah* to highlight the importance of what had been written.

III. The One Whose Burdens Are Lifted (Psalm 32:5)

A. Man Confesses (v. 5a)

5a. I acknowledged my sin unto thee, and mine iniquity have I not hid. I said, I will confess my transgressions unto the LORD.

The same three Hebrew words for *iniquity*, *transgression*, and *sin* in verses 1 and 2 occur here again in verse 5. Alongside these we now see three parallel verbs translated *acknowledged*, *not hid*, and *confess*. Unquestionably David did not want anyone to share his misery. If you know a cure for a dread disease, you share it with others. David certainly knew the cure for guilt, and he was eager to share it with all who suffered from the anxiety that guilt produces.

A dramatic turning point in David's life came when Nathan confronted him with his *sin* (2 Samuel 12:1-14). David could have reacted in several ways. He could have denied the charge brought by Nathan. He could have threatened Nathan or had him put to death. He could have waffled and minimized his sin as his predecessor King Saul was known to have done (1 Samuel 15: 20, 21, 24). He could have been so ashamed that he committed suicide. But by God's grace, none of those things occurred.

Whether this half-verse refers to the Bathsheba incident or not, David was one who admitted his guilt and confessed his sin to the Lord. Perhaps this is the reason the Lord could foresee that David would be "a man after his own heart" (1 Samuel 13:14; cf. 1 Kings 15:3, 5). Sin must be confessed before God can deal with us.

The apostle John wrote to Christians that, "If we *confess* our sins, he is faithful and just to forgive us our sins, and to cleanse us from all unrighteousness" (1 John 1:9). While it is very tempting to focus entirely on God's forgiveness in this verse, one must remember the conditional phrase "if we confess" at the beginning of the verse. While God's grace is the source of forgiveness, confession is seen here as an activating agent of that grace. [See question #4, page 408.]

B. God Forgives (v. 5b)

5b. And thou forgavest the iniquity of my sin. Selah.

A sign outside a church read, "God is in the forgiveness business." What a great message for a community to see! We confess our sins. Jesus pleads our case before the Father. The Father is faithful to forgive us.

David painted a powerful picture of God. He is not some tolerant old uncle who sees our sins, then winks and grins. He is not a sadistic ogre who cannot wait to throw people into the pit of Hell. He is a just God who takes *sin* seriously. He is also a loving Father who desperately wants us to spend eternity with Him. We must acknowledge our sin to Him. He, being more gracious and loving than we can imagine, is eager to hear our confession and to forgive us.

Jesus told a parable about a loving father who waited anxiously to receive his son back from a life of sin (Luke 15:11-32). The son came home and confessed his sins to his father, and his father was so overjoyed at his return that he immediately reinstated his son and threw a big party to welcome him home. The father in that parable represents God. He wants us to come home.

CAN YOU SAY, "I'M SORRY"?

Judges are facing criminals these days who show no remorse for their crimes. Many of these felons are young first offenders. A teenage girl doesn't shed a tear as she hears her sentence for clubbing her mother to death with a bat. A young man, charged with multiple counts of kidnapping and rape, hardly blinks an eye in the courtroom.

What has happened to conscience and penitent sorrow? One would think these social predators would at least be sorry that they were caught in their wrongdoing. David could be thankful for the "heavy hand of God" that produced the godly sorrow that brought him to repentance. For when he finally confessed his sin with genuine remorse, he experienced the forgiveness that gives spiritual peace.

Judges are more inclined to soften a sentence when the convict demonstrates a contrite spirit. As David wrote, "A broken and a contrite heart, O God, thou wilt not despise" (Psalm 51:17).

How to Say It

AUGUSTINE. *Aw*-gus-*teen* (strong accent on *Aw*) or Aw-*gus*-tin.

BATHSHEBA. Bath-*she*-buh.

NATHAN. *Nay*-thun (*th* as in *thin*).

SELAH (Hebrew). *See*-luh.

URIAH. Yu-*rye*-uh.

Is there unconfessed sin in your life? Are you able to say, "I'm sorry"—and mean it? "If we confess our sins, he is faithful and just to forgive us our sins" (1 John 1:9). —R. W. B.

IV. The One Who Trusts in the Lord (Psalm 32:6-11)

A. Finds a Hiding Place (vv. 6, 7)

6. For this shall every one that is godly pray unto thee in a time when thou mayest be found: surely in the floods of great waters they shall not come nigh unto him.

David wrote of danger and safety. There is a danger in waiting too long to acknowledge sin and seek forgiveness. Three centuries after David penned Psalm 32, the prophet Isaiah warned the people of Judah: "Seek ye the Lord while he may *be found,* call ye upon him while he is near" (Isaiah 55:6). The message here is simple. God is sovereign. He can turn away from us at any moment He chooses. Do not place a false trust in the hope that God will forever keep open the door of salvation. There will come a day when He will call all people to be judged. If forgiveness has not been appropriated by then, it will be too late.

7. Thou art my hiding place; thou shalt preserve me from trouble; thou shalt compass me about with songs of deliverance. Selah.

Augustus M. Toplady (1740–1778) wrote the famous hymn "Rock of Ages." The words echo David's instruction: "Rock of Ages, cleft for me; let me hide myself in thee." In the swirling storms of life, God is our *hiding place,* our refuge, our safe harbor. If verses 3, 4 of our lesson text describe David hiding *from* God; then verse 7 describes David hiding *in* God.

Those who truly follow the Lord experience a certain sense of safety. Part of that safety is in avoiding certain practices that we know would displease the Lord and that can also be very dangerous and harmful. Alcoholism, drug addiction, premarital sex, and homosexual acts are potent examples. [See question #5, page 408.]

God surrounds us *with songs of deliverance.* The Israelites sang a song of deliverance after they crossed the Red Sea (Exodus 15:1-21). They escaped the perils of drowning and of capture by the Egyptian army. They had a lot to sing about! Those who are delivered from captivity to sin and its guilt have much to sing about, too.

B. Learns From the Lord (vv. 8, 9)

8. I will instruct thee and teach thee in the way which thou shalt go: I will guide thee with mine eye.

David was compelled to teach others the difficult lesson he had learned about trying to hide sin. He had promised God that he would teach others His ways (Psalm 51:13). It has been said that "experience" is what you learn from your own mistakes, while "wisdom" is what you learn from someone else's! Certainly the old saw "Experience is the best teacher" cannot be true, because it requires that someone take "the test" before it provides "the lesson."

David is one who learned about unconfessed sin by his own experience, but he certainly did not want others to repeat it. If the reader will accept God's instruction, he or she will not have to learn the hard way by experience.

God uses many avenues of communication to *instruct* or *teach* us. We have His written Word to enrich us (2 Timothy 3:16, 17). God also expects us to learn from Him by learning from others with more experience, maturity, and discernment (2 Timothy 2:2). Every parent wants to teach his or her children to make wise decisions and thus avoid some of the bumps and bruises of life. Parents have the responsibility of teaching their children to know and love the Lord (Ephesians 6:4). Those who trust the Lord have learned that life is a continuing spiritual adventure. The older generation is to pass on its knowledge and experience in trusting the Lord to those who are not as spiritually mature (Titus 2:3-5).

9. Be ye not as the horse, or as the mule, which have no understanding: whose mouth must be held in with bit and bridle, lest they come near to thee.

David issued a warning about pride and stubbornness. Learning demands humility and a willingness to be led. David had earned a Ph.D. in humility. At one time in his life he had arrogantly disobeyed God's commands about murder and adultery, and it cost him dearly. He did not want others to pay such a penalty. David had been like an animal out of control. Arrogance causes people to act like wild beasts, trying not to be accountable to anyone but themselves. Hosea 4:16 compares the rebellious Israelites to "a stubborn heifer" *(New International Version).*

C. Is Surrounded by Love (v. 10)

10. Many sorrows shall be to the wicked: but he that trusteth in the LORD, mercy shall compass him about.

Sometimes it seems that good people suffer and *the wicked* prosper, and that may be true on occasion (cf. Ecclesiastes 8:14). Those who observe the human condition would, however, generally conclude that wicked people most often get their just reward. For instance, many wicked people have become wealthy, but their wickedness has kept them from having true friends or people who genuinely love them. People who live sexually immoral lives may appear to be having more "fun" than others, but they also usually suffer from more disease, etc.

But the person who trusts in the Lord finds himself or herself surrounded by love and *mercy.* That person does not feel an occasional twinge of love. Such a person is overwhelmed and inundated by love! God's love and mercy keep coming like the ocean waves lapping onto the sandy shore. There is no end. It just keeps coming and coming and coming.

D. Is Filled With Praise (v. 11)

11. Be glad in the LORD, and rejoice, ye righteous: and shout for joy, all ye that are upright in heart.

David had experienced the heights and the depths of a relationship with God. When he had been victorious over his enemies, he danced before the Lord (2 Samuel 6:14). When David's child died, he was in such despair that his servants thought he might do something desperate (2 Samuel 12:18). Exactly when this psalm was written in relation to those two incidents, we do not know. But the one declared by God to be after His "own heart" (Acts 13:22) would certainly be one to know what it meant to be *upright in heart.*

The result is *joy.* One key to this joy is never to permit Satan to assail you with your past. The person who has accepted God's remedy for sin in Jesus is new in Christ. The old has gone; the new has come (2 Corinthians 5:17).

HAPPY ARE THE FORGIVEN

Rejoice, ye pure in heart;
    Rejoice, give thanks and sing.
Your festal banner wave on high,
    The cross of Christ your King.
        —Edward H. Plumptre (1821–1891)

Home Daily Bible Readings

Monday, July 15—Our Ancestors' Sins and Ours (Psalm 106:1-12)

Tuesday, July 16—The Lord Heals and Forgives (Psalm 103:1-14)

Wednesday, July 17—Restore Us Again, O God (Psalm 85)

Thursday, July 18—But There Is Forgiveness . . . (Psalm 130)

Friday, July 19—Blot Out My Transgressions (Psalm 51:1-9)

Saturday, July 20—New and Right Spirit Within (Psalm 51:10-19)

Sunday, July 21—Happy Are Those Who Are Forgiven (Psalm 32)

David found happiness ("blessedness") in seeking and finding God's forgiveness. Guilt had gone; peace had come. What a relief and release when he became accountable to God! Freedom from pangs of conscience, freedom from fear of punishment, freedom from personal shame—those were reasons for his uninhibited rejoicing.

Even so, David's forgiveness was "old covenant" forgiveness. It looked forward to Jesus Christ, whom he didn't know. This would be the One to be "the mediator of a better covenant, which was established upon better promises" (Hebrews 8:6). Christ promised, "I will be merciful . . . and their sins and their iniquities will I remember no more" (Hebrews 8:12).

We have a personal Savior who made a superior and permanent sacrifice, and who continues to intercede for us (Hebrews 7:25). Is that good news? "Happiness is the Lord!"   —R. W. B.

Conclusion

A. Lifesaving News

Many years ago a teenage girl was being swept to the brink of Niagara Falls. She was in the grip of certain death. Some people on Goat Island saw her and leaned through a protective railing to grab hold of her arm just before she was carried over the edge by the strong current. They pulled her to shore and saved her life.

Every day we see people whose lives are in immediate peril. Their sin has crushed them. They have given up on themselves, thinking they are beyond hope. They need to hear the joyous words of a forgiven sinner. They need to hear Psalm 32. Share David's testimony. Share the message of the cross and forgiveness of sin. Share God's love and yours. Snatch them from the brink of hopelessness. Share God's longing to forgive them. As Fanny Crosby (1820-1915) put it in one of her hymns, "Tell them of Jesus the mighty to save."

B. Prayer

Our Loving Heavenly Father, we thank You for being in the forgiveness business. May our lives be filled with praise because of Your power to remove our sin by means of the cross of Christ, and Your mercy in not counting that sin against us. Help us to tell others of Your love and Your desire to forgive them. In Jesus' mighty name, amen.

C. Thought to Remember

God is in the forgiveness business. No one else can do what He can do!

Learning by Doing

This page contains an alternate lesson plan emphasizing learning activities. Classes desiring such student involvement will find these suggestions helpful.

Learning Goals

After participating in this lesson, each student will be able to:

1. Summarize what David says in Psalm 32 about the blessing of confessing sin, experiencing God's forgiveness, and seeking God's counsel.

2. Contrast the condition of one who is forgiven with the miserable state of the one who tries to hide his or her sin.

3. Specify someone who needs to hear the message of forgiveness, and tell that person what God has done in Jesus.

Into the Lesson

CHOICE: *Agree-Disagree.* Read each of the following statements and ask your class to indicate whether they agree or disagree. Any who agree should raise a hand, pointing to the ceiling with the index finger. Any who disagree should raise a hand with five fingers spread. Tell them you will read each statement twice, count to three, and then they should raise their signs without checking friends' responses first. (This activity is included in *Adult Bible Class.)*

1. Many adults suffer from guilt.
2. Living with guilt damages one's health.
3. Some adults refuse to accept forgiveness.
4. Some have trouble forgiving themselves.
5. Most adults rejoice in their forgiveness.
6. Adults tend to cover up what they do wrong.
7. God will always forgive our sins.

Make the transition to the Bible study by saying, "These statements have raised some questions about forgiveness. Let's see if our text today answers any of our questions."

CHOICE: *Discussion Starters.* Reproduce the four Discussion Starters below for your class members. (This is included in *Adult Bible Class.)*

(1) By your personal standards, which of the following is the grossest sin: cheating on income tax; having premarital/extramarital sex; selling pornography; cutting shady business deals; child abuse?

(2) Whom would you have most trouble forgiving: a crooked politician; an adulterer; a Nazi war criminal; a drug dealer; a rapist?

(3) Why do more people confess their sins to a bartender than to anyone else? It's easier to talk when you're drinking; bartenders are more understanding; people are more at home in a bar;

bartenders never judge their confessors; everyone in a bar has failed. (My other explanation: _____.)

(4) What do you do when you fail: crawl in a hole; try to be extra good; confess it to God and move on; talk to a minister about it; shrug it off?

Into the Word

CHOICE: *Circle Response.* Use a circle response as a means of guiding the discussion of Psalm 32:1-11. Have each verse read, and then ask each person to make a short statement about the verse. Seat your class in circles of four to eight people. Go around the circle and each person speaks once before anyone speaks a second time. This will help to draw out quieter folks.

CHOICE: *Guest Lecturers.* Ask four class members to prepare mini-lectures on a part of today's text. Provide them with help and support so they can have a good experience and develop as teachers themselves. Break the passage into these sections: vv. 1, 2; vv. 3-5; vv. 6, 7; vv. 8-11.

Into Life

CHOICE: *Write a Witnessing Letter.* Provide paper and pens for your class members to write a witnessing letter to someone who needs to know God's forgiveness. Prepare for the writing by using these directions:

Name three people whom you know who need to experience God's forgiveness.

Which one would be most responsive to a letter from you about forgiveness?

What should be the tone of your letter?

What ideas or verses from today's text should be included?

Provide everything necessary, so that the project can be completed and ready for mailing by the end of the class. (This is included in *Adult Bible Class.)*

CHOICE: *Personal Testimony.* Ask class members to prepare their personal testimonies about their experience of God's forgiveness, beginning by explaining the negative results of sin in their lives. Tell them to focus on its negative impact on their lives—the guilt, anxiety, fear, and confusion. Then have them describe how they came to be aware of the availability of forgiveness. What events led up to "the change"? Conclude by sharing the joy and peace of full forgiveness in Christ. (This is included in *Adult Bible Class.)*

Let's Talk It Over

The questions on this page are designed to encourage review of the lesson Scriptures and to promote discussion of the lesson by the class. The answers provided are only discussion starters. Let your class talk it over from there.

1. Being "blessed" results in a sense of well-being and happiness. If David is right that the person whose sins are forgiven is the truly happy person, then why isn't forgiveness what most people are seeking in their "pursuit of happiness"?

One reason may be that many people have a limited understanding of the nature of true happiness. We often equate happiness with good fortune, success, pleasurable experiences, personal gratification, or comforts and conveniences. Even in our relationships, the focus is often on what another may do for me that "makes me happy." True happiness must be more than any or all of these.

Another reason may be that so few today seem to believe they need forgiveness for anything. The thinking today is, "I am free to do whatever I want, and no one should be offended or consider my conduct unacceptable. Certainly not God, who made me this way!"

2. If God's part in our forgiveness is not counting our sins against us, what is our part, if anything?

Our part is not to think we can somehow "earn" God's forgiveness or "work off" our sins through human effort. Our part, rather, is first to be honest with God and with ourselves. We must admit the truth that we "all have sinned" and fall "short of the glory of God" (Romans 3:23). Our part then is to "repent, and be baptized" (Acts 2:38). Genuine repentance will result in a changed attitude and conduct (Acts 26:20).

Admitting the reality of personal sin is not always easy to do, since a post-Christian culture no longer even recognizes the reality of sin. One day a Christian friend was attempting to share the gospel with a well-educated lady. In the course of explaining that we have all sinned, the lady responded, "Well, I'm really not sure what you mean by sin, although I do bite my nails some." Remember that God gave the commandments "in order that sin might be recognized as sin" (Romans 7:13, *New International Version*).

3. In addition to the failure to receive God's forgiveness, what are some of the other consequences of unconfessed sin?

Frequently (but not always) there can be significant *physical* consequences. They may include headaches, indigestion, high blood pressure, extreme fatigue, loss of appetite, sleeplessness, etc. Also common are *emotional* consequences, and they can be quite severe. These may include worry and anxiety, uncontrolled anger, difficulty concentrating, depression, withdrawal, and even suicidal tendencies.

Of course, the most tragic are the *spiritual* consequences. Sin that is unconfessed and covered up causes us to push away from God rather than draw near to Him. The person who refuses to acknowledge personal sin fights against God because of a misguided self-assurance—one that supposes that he or she is answerable only to self. The ultimate result of this attitude is eternal punishment in Hell (Revelation 21:8).

4. Since God demands repentance/confession in granting forgiveness, can we withhold our forgiveness of one who has wronged us unless that person first repents? Why or why not?

In the course of this discussion, someone will surely point out the obvious: we are not God! Only God can forgive sin absolutely, for only God in infinite. Our forgiveness is limited because we are limited. We can be wronged, but we ourselves have wronged others (and God), and so the "offense" against us is not as serious as offenses against God, who is perfectly holy.

What does it mean, then, for us to forgive someone? Romans 12:17-21 addresses this issue. To forgive another person is to release that person to the Lord. It is to release our right to vengeance. It is to seek peace. Must we wait for an apology to do that?

5. Why do you think it is important for us to think of God as our "hiding place" and the only One who can really protect us from "continuing in sin" (Romans 6:1).

Some who have known God's forgiveness mistakenly assume that they are now beyond the possibility of temptation and sin. Paul recognized this fallacy and so must we (Romans 7:21-25). Remember the continuing deceitfulness of Satan, who lures us by being "transformed into an angel of light" (2 Corinthians 11:14).

Even after we become a Christian, we continue to be vulnerable. We absolutely must find our protection and refuge in the Father's arms (Psalm 73:28).

Let All Peoples Praise God

DEVOTIONAL READING: Psalm 97:6-12.

BACKGROUND SCRIPTURE: Psalms 67; 96.

PRINTED TEXT: Psalms 67:1-5; 96:1-9.

Psalm 67:1-5

1 God be merciful unto us, and bless us; and cause his face to shine upon us; Selah.

2 That thy way may be known upon earth, thy saving health among all nations.

3 Let the people praise thee, O God; let all the people praise thee.

4 O let the nations be glad and sing for joy: for thou shalt judge the people righteously, and govern the nations upon earth. Selah.

5 Let the people praise thee, O God; let all the people praise thee.

Psalm 96:1-9

1 O sing unto the LORD a new song: sing unto the LORD, all the earth.

2 Sing unto the LORD, bless his name; show forth his salvation from day to day.

3 Declare his glory among the heathen, his wonders among all people.

4 For the LORD is great, and greatly to be praised: he is to be feared above all gods.

5 For all the gods of the nations are idols: but the LORD made the heavens.

6 Honor and majesty are before him: strength and beauty are in his sanctuary.

7 Give unto the LORD, O ye kindreds of the people, give unto the LORD glory and strength.

8 Give unto the LORD the glory due unto his name: bring an offering, and come into his courts.

9 O worship the LORD in the beauty of holiness: fear before him, all the earth.

Jul 28

GOLDEN TEXT: Let the people praise thee, O God; let all the people praise thee.
—Psalm 67:3.

Worship and Wisdom for Living
Unit 2: Praise the Creator and Redeemer
(Lessons 6-9)

Lesson Aims

After participating in this lesson, each student will be able to:

1. Tell what these Psalms say about the need for the entire world to praise God.

2. Explain how meeting this need is an important part of the church's mission.

3. Memorize a verse of praise from today's text.

Lesson Outline

INTRODUCTION
    A. Special Privilege, Special Responsibility
    B. Lesson Background
  I. PRAISE GOD FOR WHAT HE HAS DONE AND WILL DO (Psalm 67:1-5)
    A. God Has Shown Himself to All People (vv. 1-3)
    B. God Will Rule All People Righteously (vv. 4, 5)
 II. PRAISE GOD FOR WHO HE IS (Psalm 96:1-6)
    A. He Is the Source of Salvation (vv. 1, 2)
      No Bucket to Carry My Tune!
    B. He Is the Worker of Wonders (v. 3)
    C. He Is the One True God (vv. 4-6)
      Beautiful Sanctuaries
III. GIVE GOD WHAT IS DUE HIM (Psalm 96:7-9)
    A. Praise for His Power (v. 7)
    B. Offerings for His Glory (v. 8)
    C. Reverence for His Majesty (v. 9)
CONCLUSION
    A. "I Have a Cure for Cancer"
    B. Prayer
    C. Thought to Remember

Introduction

A. Special Privilege, Special Responsibility

Children seldom recognize the link between privilege and responsibility. As we mature, however, we learn just how strong that link becomes. The privilege of being married and sharing life with the one we love comes with the awesome responsibility of sacrificial love. Some wedding vows express that commitment "in joy and in sorrow, in prosperity and in adversity."

In employment, bosses have greater privileges, but they also bear more responsibility.

Even children can learn this important lesson. The privilege of having a pet brings the responsibility of feeding, walking, and grooming that pet. The privilege of driving an automobile brings the responsibility of obeying traffic laws.

The Jews were a people chosen for a special privilege. Their forefather, Abraham, had been very special to God, and He chose to bless all of Abraham's progeny because of his faith (Genesis 17:1-8). Specifically, God had said to Abraham, "I will establish my covenant between me and thee and thy seed after thee in their generations, for an everlasting covenant, to be a God unto thee and to thy seed after thee" (v. 7). God had firmly reestablished that covenant relationship after the Hebrew children were led out of bondage in Egypt. During their sojourn in the desert, God told Moses to tell the people, "If ye will obey my voice indeed, and keep my covenant, then ye shall be a peculiar treasure unto me above all people: for all the earth is mine: and ye shall be unto me a kingdom of priests, and a holy nation" (Exodus 19:5, 6; cf. 1 Peter 2:4, 5).

What a privilege to be a "peculiar treasure" unto God! But along with this special privilege came a special responsibility: they were to be a "kingdom of priests." A priest is someone who represents God to the people and represents the people to God—a mediator or "go-between," if you will. Sadly, the Israelites focused solely on being God's *peculiar treasure.* In so doing, they failed to understand that they were to usher in His Messiah who would, in turn, commission His disciples to be His emissaries to *all* the nations of the earth, not just the Israelites (Isaiah 42:6; 49:6; Matthew 28:19, 20; Acts 13:47).

B. Lesson Background

One significant difference between the Old and New Testaments is a distinction in missionary emphasis. The New Testament requires Christians to take the gospel to "all nations," but there is no similar command for Old Testament Israel. In fact, just the opposite seems to be true when we note that the ancient Israelites were not to mix with foreign peoples at all (Leviticus 20:24-26; Deuteronomy 7:3; 1 Kings 11:2; Nehemiah 13:23-27; etc.). Indeed, the idea of Israelite separation occurs about 260 times in the Old Testament. We see this "separation attitude" in the first-century disciples, who seem quite surprised that God had extended the offer of salvation to the Gentiles (Acts 11:18). The occasion of a foreigner converting to Judaism seems to have been relatively rare (cf. 1 Kings 8:41-43).

Even so, today's texts stress over and over that it is *all* nations and *all* peoples who are to praise the Lord. Other Old Testament texts stress this idea as well. In several contexts, we see this as ungodly nations that have no choice but to acknowledge that some miracle or wonder could have come from the one true God only, however grudging such an admission might be (e.g., Exodus 7:5; 14:4, 18; Leviticus 26:45; 1 Samuel 17:46; Ezekiel 20:41; 28:25; 36:23). In other contexts, this praise from "all nations" is a prediction of an ideal, future state of affairs that is not likely actually to occur until the second coming of Christ (Psalms 22:27; 47:9; 57:5; 64:9; 65:8; 66:1-7; 86:9; 98:2, 3; 99:2, 3; 102:15; Habakkuk 2:14).

The frequent references to praise from all nations and peoples in today's texts also reflect this ideal, as-yet-unrealized future. God wants all peoples to know Him, love Him, and praise Him for who He is and what He has done.

I. Praise God for What He Has Done and Will Do (Psalm 67:1-5)

A. God Has Shown Himself to All People (vv. 1-3)

1. God be merciful unto us, and bless us; and cause his face to shine upon us. Selah.

The Psalm begins with a familiar prayer. During the Exodus, God had told Moses to tell his brother Aaron, who would become the great high priest of Israel, to pronounce a blessing upon the people: "The Lord *bless* thee, and keep thee: the Lord make his face shine upon thee, and be gracious unto thee: the Lord lift up his countenance upon thee, and give thee peace" (Numbers 6:24-26). This blessing was thus very familiar to the Israelites. It is also quoted, in part, in Psalms 4:6; 29:11; 31:16; and 80:3, 7, 19.

On the other hand, there are also numerous times in the Old Testament when God is said to have hidden His face from the people (e.g., Psalm 13:1; 30:7; Isaiah 59:2). When God "hides His face," he is not playing "hide 'n' seek" games. The people of God knew when they were disobedient to God. That disobedience produced feelings of alienation and estrangement from Him. He seemed to be "hiding" from them.

The desire to have God shine His face upon them reflects the ancient idea that the facial expression of a king revealed that king's pleasure or displeasure, approval or disapproval. As such, this phrase did not necessarily express a desire for God to bless them in any material sense. It was the simple expression of a desire to have God's approval, and to feel close to Him again. [See question #1, page 416.]

2. That thy way may be known upon earth, thy saving health among all nations.

The psalmist got it right. The Israelites were not to be blessed because they deserved the blessings of God. They were to be blessed so that God's *saving health* would be demonstrated *among all nations.* The particular Hebrew word translated as *saving health* is very profound. It deals with not just with "deliverance" or "victory," but also, in a broader sense, with God's sovereign kingship. God wanted to reveal Himself to all the people of the world through His special relationship with the Hebrew people, His sovereignty and His kingship. The Israelites were to model for the world the kind of life that has the one true God at its center. God's blessings to and through the Israelites were to be so obvious that the whole world would notice (Psalm 46:10). These blessings would find ultimate expression in the Messiah, who would come to all peoples through the Israelite nation. [See question #2, page 416.]

3. Let the people praise thee, O God; let all the people praise thee.

When people see how great God is, *praise* is the natural response! God did not desire the praise of the Jews only. He desired the praise of *all the people* of all the nations of the earth. In the Old Testament, God chose to bless the Jews so that they could express His greatness to all people. Through Israel would come "a light to the Gentiles" so that all people could come to know God and be saved by Him (Isaiah 49:6; cf. Acts 13:47).

B. God Will Rule All People Righteously (vv. 4, 5)

4. O let the nations be glad and sing for joy: for thou shalt judge the people righteously, and govern the nations upon earth. Selah.

When people see how wonderfully God rules and reigns, they will praise Him. Sadly, many people in our day have a very secular view of God. They either see Him as a Santa in the sky who is there to bless us without asking anything from us, or they see Him as some vengeful, vicious, vindictive ogre who cannot wait to send people to eternal damnation. But both ideas are wrong. [See question #3, page 416.]

When God is enthroned on the human heart, He rules with wisdom, power, and compassion. A central concept of the Christian life is that because of God's grace through the death of Christ, we do

---

How to Say It

Abinadab. Uh-*bin*-uh-dab.
ABRAHAM. *Ay*-bruh-ham.
Kirjath-jearim. Keer-jath-*jeer*-um.

not get what we actually deserve (namely, Hell), and we *do* get what we do not deserve (namely, Heaven)! People have a choice to make in how they want to relate to God as their king. Those without Christ relate to Him as the Holy Lawgiver, who will punish them justly in His wrath. Those with Christ, on the other hand, relate to Him as a God of grace and love. Such people are quick to offer generous praise to Him, and they look forward to the time when Jesus will rule *the nations* fully and finally (Psalm 2:9; Revelation 19:15).

5. Let the people praise thee, O God; let all the people praise thee.

This is a repetition of verse 3. The repetition highlights the importance of the thought. God's righteous reign should cause all who know Him to *praise* Him. This does not mean that absolutely every person from every nation will actually praise God—at least, not in this life. But that fact does not stop the psalmist from *desiring* that all praise God. The apostle Paul affirms that in the judgment, "every knee shall bow" and "every tongue shall give praise to God" (Romans 14:10, 11, *New American Standard Bible*).

II. Praise God for Who He Is
(Psalm 96:1-6)

A. He Is the Source of Salvation (vv. 1, 2)

1. O sing unto the LORD a new song: sing unto the LORD, all the earth.

Psalm 96 is formed, in part, from 1 Chronicles 16. That text includes the joyous *song* of David on a festive occasion in Israel's history. The ark of the covenant, having been captured by the Philistines, was returned and held by the family of Abinadab in Kirjath-jearim (1 Samuel 6:21; 7:1). When it was ultimately returned to Jerusalem, David broke forth in praise to God (1 Chronicles 16:7-36). The middle verses of David's song (vv. 23-30) are recorded in Psalm 96:1-6. Other portions of David's song are repeated in Psalms 105 and 106.

The emphasis of David's Psalm is in singing praise to God. The imperative *sing* is repeated, signifying its importance. All the *earth* is to sing. Praise to God is not to be limited to one locale or one nation; neither is praise to be expressed merely through the familiar old songs we grew up with. We are to sing *a new song* because every day we recognize new facets to the wonder and majesty of God.

NO BUCKET TO CARRY MY TUNE!

Not everyone is blessed with a singing voice. Some can't "carry a tune in a bucket." A few don't even have a bucket! Inability to sing is a serious handicap in a worship assembly. Repeated admonitions in Scripture teach us to make vocal music in praise to God. What's the tone-deaf worshiper to do? Usually we tell such a person simply to make a "joyful noise." But the people seated next to that person in church may not find much joy in that noise!

Those who cannot sing can hum quietly, only mouth the words, or just read the lyrics silently as the congregation sings. Better yet, the church can offer basic singing classes to benefit even the tone-deaf.

But what about those who have no song in their hearts? That makes worship much more difficult. If you have no gratitude, joy, or hope to move you to sing in worship, there is hardly any way for you to participate with integrity.

On the other hand, your mood and your motives don't change the purpose of the worship assembly. Your despondency does not alter the truths that are being celebrated. Your joylessness cannot evict God's presence from praise.

When you don't feel like singing, sing anyway. The very action of participation can cheer your soul. Expression makes an impression. And God can make your worship real—even something you feel. —R. W. B.

2. Sing unto the LORD, bless his name; show forth his salvation from day to day.

The imperative *sing* is again repeated, but this time praise is linked to proclamation. The exact nature of *his salvation* in this context is uncertain, but it may be intended to include God's acts of creation as well as redemption (cf. vv. 11-13; Psalm 136:4-25).

To *show forth* is also an important concept in the New Testament. For instance, through our observance of the Lord's Supper we "*show* the Lord's death till he come" (1 Corinthians 11:26). Paul later says to the Corinthians that as a result of his ministry they "*show* that [they] are a letter from Christ" (2 Corinthians 3:3, *New International Version*). Just a bit later, his encouragement to them is that they have a "treasure in jars of clay to *show* that this all-surpassing power is from God" (4:7, *New International Version*). Such "showing" demonstrates that our witness is not hidden (cf. Matthew 5:14-16).

B. He Is the Worker of Wonders (v. 3)

3. Declare his glory among the heathen, his wonders among all people.

All people should glorify God once they recognize the *wonders* He has performed. The Jews could give many examples to *the heathen* (Gentile) people of the miracles that God had performed on their behalf. He had divided the Red Sea, made the seabed dry so that they could

Let
the
people
praise
thee, O God;
let all the people
praise thee. —Psalm 67:3

Visual for lesson 9. *Use this poster to illustrate Psalm 67:3. It shows people singing to praise God. Ask the class to suggest other ways to praise Him.*

cross, and then destroyed the pursuing Egyptian army. He had miraculously provided the Jews with food (manna) during their long sojourn in the desert. God had stopped the flooding Jordan River so that His people could cross into the land He had promised them. Miraculous victory was given at Jericho. The Israelites certainly were not lacking in examples of God's ability to work wonders on their behalf. Miracles cause us to recognize God (John 20:30, 31). They also cause us to praise God (Mark 2:12).

C. He Is the One True God (vv. 4-6)

4. For the LORD is great, and greatly to be praised: he is to be feared above all gods.

The one true God *is great* and deserves great praise from all people. He should be *feared* more than any other *gods*. Why? As we will learn in the next verse, the other "gods" are idols—mere statues people have made with their hands. They are a fiction; they do not represent any real supernatural being.

Some people have a problem with the concept of "fearing" God. Moses had instructed the Hebrew people to fear God (Deuteronomy 6:13; 10:12; 31:12). Fearing God is the beginning of wisdom (Psalm 111:10; Proverbs 9:10), and teaches wisdom (Proverbs 15:33). Fearing God causes us to avoid evil (Proverbs 16:6). Fearing God leads to life (Proverbs 19:23). Isaiah prophesied that even the Messiah would fear the Lord (Isaiah 11:3). The word *fear* includes the concepts of respect and reverence, but we should not dilute the significance of fear too much. Remember what Jesus said: "Be not afraid of them that kill the body, and after that have no more that they can do. But . . . Fear him, which . . . hath power to cast into hell; yea, I say unto you, Fear him" (Luke 12:4, 5).

5. For all the gods of the nations are idols: but the LORD made the heavens.

There are no other *gods* in the sense of actual, supernatural beings (Jeremiah 2:11). People made *idols* to worship. They were carved wood or chiseled stone. The only real God had commanded that no such images be worshiped (Exodus 20:4, 5). These were the products of human hands. Isaiah mocked the idea of a person worshiping something he had made with his own hands (Isaiah 44:9-20). [See question #4, page 416.]

6. Honor and majesty are before him: strength and beauty are in his sanctuary.

The psalmist considered certain attributes of God. Since no other gods were real, the Lord alone is worthy of *honor*. God's acts of creation (v. 5) mean that as Creator, He alone is splendid and majestic (Psalm 104:1-3).

In western culture, such an exclusive view of God is not politically correct. We are encouraged to believe that all religions contain truth (relative to the believers of each religion) and should be accepted as true, as long as the adherents of those religions are "sincere." We are encouraged to embrace religious diversity as a strength of modern civilization. To believe the Bible's exclusive statements about Jesus—that He is the only way to God (John 14:6)—is to be intolerant and narrow-minded (cf. Luke 13:24). Those who are vocal in their belief that Jesus' name is the only name by which we can be saved (Acts 4:12) can find themselves accused of bigotry and even hatred. Few people seem to be interested in the truth of the claim. But the claim is, indeed, true, and the disciple of Jesus must not be ashamed to believe and declare it (Mark 8:38).

BEAUTIFUL SANCTUARIES

Have you seen the Crystal Cathedral? Even on television it is awesome! Famous churches usually have beautiful sanctuaries. The design and decor of a worship center can impose considerable influence on the mood and expressions of worshipers.

Some of the largest churches, however, have rather plain and practical buildings, with conservative decorating and furnishings. They depend on lighting, sound, and programming to beautify their worship. Verse 6 of our text says the "strength and beauty" of God's sanctuary are reflected by His "honor and majesty."

What makes a sanctuary? Isn't it the presence of God and the praise of His people? Thousands of Christians in Africa and India worship in the open air. Those outdoor spaces become beautiful sanctuaries, as sincere songs are sung, as holy Communion is observed, and as the inspired Word is proclaimed.

The usually small chapels in hospitals can become unusually beautiful sanctuaries as the effectual, fervent (often desperate) prayers of worried "waiters" are offered there. People sometimes gather in gymnasiums, stadiums, campgrounds, or amphitheaters for worship. And wherever authentic worship happens, those places are transformed into beautiful sanctuaries.   —R. W. B.

III. Give God What is Due Him (Psalm 96:7-9)

A. Praise for His Power (v. 7)

7. Give unto the LORD, O ye kindreds of the people, give unto the LORD glory and strength.

All *people* are called to recognize the *glory* and power *(strength)* of God. Interestingly, Psalm 29:1 calls for the angels (the "mighty" ones) to offer the same acclamation.

B. Offerings for His Glory (v. 8)

8. Give unto the LORD the glory due unto his name: bring an offering, and come into his courts.

We don't come before God with silent lips; neither should we come before Him with empty hands. The psalmist encouraged the people to praise God with appropriate offerings. The Old Testament system included many types of offerings that the Israelites were to *give* to God. Today we often think of *offering* as a time in the worship service when we give our proportionate and sacrificial gifts of money to God. For the New Testament era, however, this concept of "offering" is far too limited. Romans 12:1, 2 describes the main offering God desires of us: He wants us to offer ourselves as living sacrifices to Him.

C. Reverence for His Majesty (v. 9)

9. O worship the LORD in the beauty of holiness: fear before him, all the earth.

When we *worship* God, we should do so with great humility and reverence. When we worship, we should be offering God our best. Sadly, many of the world's most blessed people seem to take God for granted. We do not tremble in the presence of God. Many people do not even manage to stay awake during a church service! We have lost our sense of awe. We may sing "How Majestic Is Thy Name," but end up mouthing mere words (cf. Isaiah 29:13). [See question #5, page 416.]

Often it is people in "less advanced" cultures who seem to offer more genuine praise to God. Perhaps they are not embarrassed to be believers. Maybe they are simply more sensitive to their own frailty. Perhaps they are not so overawed with their own accomplishments that they still have room in their lives for awe for God. A heightened sense of self destroys the ability to

recognize and appreciate the wonder and majesty of God.

The blindness of the Jews to the wonder and majesty of God caused many of them to reject Jesus as the Messiah (cf. Matthew 23:16-22). He did not fit their preconceived notions of what the Messiah would be. Even when performing the miracle of a resurrection right before their very eyes some would not believe (John 11:45). They failed to recognize that God was calling all people to Himself through His Son. He wanted to offer salvation to all people, and He wanted all people to worship Him (cf. John 20:28-31).

Conclusion

A. "I Have a Cure for Cancer"

Imagine that you had found a cure for cancer: would you keep that news to yourself? Would you offer your cure only to family and close friends? Of course not! You would share your cure with anyone who had cancer.

God has a cure for man's longing for fellowship with Him. He chose the Hebrew people to be His conduit to the world. They shared a special privilege and bore a special responsibility (Romans 3:1, 2). Sadly, they failed to understand their unique position. They failed to grasp the message (Acts 13:46). God loves all people. He wants all people to be saved (2 Peter 3:9). He wants all people to praise Him!

B. Prayer

Father, help us to be humble. Help us remember that You love all people. Compel us to share Your love with others. In Jesus' name. Amen.

C. Thought to Remember

God loves all people and desires their praise.

Learning by Doing

This page contains an alternate lesson plan emphasizing learning activities. Classes desiring such student involvement will find these suggestions helpful.

Learning Goals

After participating in this lesson, each student will be able to:

1. Tell what these Psalms say about the need for the entire world to praise God.

2. Explain how meeting this need is an important part of the church's mission.

3. Memorize a verse of praise from today's text.

Into the Lesson

CHOICE: *Hymn Study*. The lesson writer gives three reasons why God should be praised: for what He has done and will do; for who He is; and because it is due to Him. Bring hymn books for each class member to look for hymns that develop each of the three ideas. For example, the verses of "How Great Thou Art" praise God for what He has done, while the chorus exalts God for who He is; "Majesty" gives God the praise He is due. Display a transparency or poster containing these three ideas so that all class members can see it.

CHOICE: *Make an Acrostic*. Have your class make an acrostic about worship using words that are in the text, such as, *sanctuary, majesty*, or *holiness*. Write the words vertically; then have the learners work individually or in small groups to cite other worship words, using each letter of the acrostics to begin one of the new words.

Selah	Marvelous	Homage
Ascribe	Adoration	Obeisance
Name	Jesus	Lord
Courts	Exalt	Invoke
Tremble	Sing	Natural
Ubiquitous	Tremble	Elohim
Adoration	Yahweh	Shekinah
Reverence		Selah
Yahweh		

Into the Word

CHOICE: *Rewrite a Psalm*. Psalm 67 begins speaking to people, then addresses God, and finally addresses the worshipers again. Psalm 96 is addressed to other people, encouraging them to worship. Ask the class to rewrite Psalm 96 so that it addresses God. For example,

Lord, I sing to You a new song;

I join the whole earth in singing to You.

I sing to You, Lord, and praise Your name.

I proclaim every day that You have saved me.

I declare Your glory among the nations

And Your marvelous deeds among all peoples.

Provide pens and paper. Ask members to share their psalms with the class. Lead a brief discussion on why the whole world should praise the Lord. (Directions for this activity are in *Adult Bible Class.*)

CHOICE: *Choral Reading*. Today's text begs to be read dramatically. In preparation for this choral reading, read and discuss each verse of Psalm 67:1-5 and Psalm 96:1-9. Decide as a class whether it should be read by a male, female, or mixed voices, and assign parts. Should one person, a duet, trio, or the entire class read it?

Into Life

CHOICE: *Plan a Worship Hour*. Both of today's Psalms are "calls to worship," encouraging people to worship God. Using the text, ask your class to plan a worship hour for your church.

For example, Psalm 96:1-3 suggests a robust song service with a new song being introduced. Verses 4-6 could lead to a sermon on the character and attributes of God. Verses 7, 8 imply a testimony time sharing what God has done. An offering is mentioned in verse 8. The service might close with a time of prayer, and Psalm 67 prayed as a benediction. Submit your results to whoever plans the worship hour at your church. (This activity is included in *Adult Bible Class.*)

CHOICE: *Write a Letter*. Psalms 67 and 96 encourage people to worship. Every church has some members and acquaintances who are away from home for school, military service, or work. Be ready with addresses, envelopes, stationery, and stamps. Ask your class to use these chapters as a basis for encouraging someone to worship and praise God. This simple Bible school activity could become God's means for keeping a young believer on the high road of worship!

CHOICE: *Memorize a Verse*. Challenge your class members to memorize a verse that would be helpful in preparing for worship. Any verse from Psalm 96 would be a good choice. One group technique is to have the class sit in a circle and read through it two or three times in unison. Then go around the circle and have each person read one word. Have both the first and last person give the reference for the verse.

(Directions for this activity are included in *Adult Bible Class.*)

Let's Talk It Over

The questions on this page are designed to encourage review of the lesson Scriptures and to promote discussion of the lesson by the class. The answers provided are only discussion starters. Let your class talk it over from there.

1. There are moments in life when God seems to be distant. His face doesn't seem to be shining on us. What are some possible reasons we may have these times of doubt and uncertainty?

One reason may be that we tend to connect good fortune, prosperity, good health, and general well-being with God's favor. When we experience loss of any kind, it is easy to begin to question God's personal concern and graciousness. Yet we know that He has not changed in His love and care for us simply because our circumstances may have changed.

A similar reason might be that we can easily take His daily blessings for granted. We assume that He should bless us—He should bestow His favor upon us despite our failure to give Him priority and to remain faithful in all things. This attitude usually begins with, "If God is really a God of love, He would (or wouldn't) . . . ." The truth is, His love for us causes Him to relate to us in ways that are in our best interest, even though we may not realize it. Isaiah reminds us of this, "In returning and rest shall ye be saved; in quietness and in confidence shall be your strength: and ye would not" (Isaiah 30:15). "Therefore will the Lord wait, that he may be gracious unto you, and therefore will he be exalted, that he may have mercy upon you: for the Lord is a God of judgment: blessed are all they that wait for him" (Isaiah 30:18).

2. Why do you think God's people so often fail to understand the purpose of His blessings?

It is clear in these two Psalms that God blessed Israel so that they would ultimately be the people through whom all nations could know His love and grace. Yet, they missed it. They focused on the gift rather than the Giver. They counted their blessing rather than considering the responsibility this placed upon them.

Has this not been true of the church at times? Have we not been so drawn in upon ourselves that we have lost our passion for anything beyond our own perimeters? All too often the result is an inward-drawn, privatized religion that is described by Os Guinness "privately engaging" but "socially irrelevant."

3. What is the greatest danger for any people or nation who have been abundantly blessed by God?

The greatest danger that lies dormant in all earthly good fortune is our tendency to be absorbed in its enjoyment and, in doing so, to neglect the responsibilities that God has attached to these good things: gratitude, generosity, goodwill, compassion, humility, joy, and love. It is only when we look beyond the temporal to the eternal that we are truly blessed.

As we thank God for our blessings, we should also be asking Him to guide us in their use. We should be seeking opportunities to help make His ways known to the nations of the world where His ways are unknown.

4. In comparing the "gods of the nations" with the Lord, the psalmist identifies them as "idols" while he affirms that "the Lord made the heavens." What kind of "idols" are men and nations still worshiping today?

One "god" that many are trusting today is the god of human reason. This god is the product of the eighteenth-century Enlightenment. Its creed has been that the only reliable knowledge is that which is achieved through reason guided by the scientific method. There can be no revealed truth (such as the Bible).

5. In what way can we worship in order to fulfill the psalmist's call to worship the Lord in the beauty or splendor of holiness?

Much of our worship today is designed to appeal to our personal tastes and preferences rather than to humbly acknowledge God's holiness. Some seek to be entertained rather than "ascribing to the Lord the glory due his name." All too often it is repetition without reverence and performance without participation.

But true worship is an attitude that brings us into the presence of God with awe and adoration. In true worship, our praises are expressions of sincere gratitude for His holiness, majesty, and salvation. There is a genuine sense of reverent trembling before the Holy One. We can approach the throne of grace with confidence because we know that we "may obtain mercy, and find grace to help in time of need" (Hebrews 4:16). Take a few moments to reflect on the elements of a typical worship service and to consider how these elements may enable you to "give unto the Lord the glory due unto his name."

Embrace Wisdom

Proverbs 4:1-9

1 Hear, ye children, the instruction of a father, and attend to know understanding.

2 For I give you good doctrine, forsake ye not my law.

3 For I was my father's son, tender and only beloved in the sight of my mother.

4 He taught me also, and said unto me, Let thine heart retain my words: keep my commandments, and live.

5 Get wisdom, get understanding: forget it not; neither decline from the words of my mouth.

6 Forsake her not, and she shall preserve thee: love her, and she shall keep thee.

7 Wisdom is the principal thing; therefore get wisdom: and with all thy getting get understanding.

8 Exalt her, and she shall promote thee: she shall bring thee to honor, when thou dost embrace her.

9 She shall give to thine head an ornament of grace: a crown of glory shall she deliver to thee.

DEVOTIONAL READING: Proverbs 3:1-8.

BACKGROUND SCRIPTURE: Proverbs 3, 4.

PRINTED TEXT: Proverbs 3:13-18; 4:1-9.

Proverbs 3:13-18

13 Happy is the man that findeth wisdom, and the man that getteth understanding:

14 For the merchandise of it is better than the merchandise of silver, and the gain thereof than fine gold.

15 She is more precious than rubies: and all the things thou canst desire are not to be compared unto her.

16 Length of days is in her right hand; and in her left hand riches and honor.

17 Her ways are ways of pleasantness, and all her paths are peace.

18 She is a tree of life to them that lay hold upon her: and happy is every one that retaineth her.

Aug 4

GOLDEN TEXT: Happy is the man that findeth wisdom, and the man that getteth understanding.—Proverbs 3:13.

Worship and Wisdom for Living
Unit 3: Words for the Wise
(Lessons 10-13)

Lesson Aims

After this lesson, each student will be able to:
1. Describe the value and importance of getting wisdom and of passing it on.
2. Contrast God's wisdom with that of the world.
3. Suggest an area of one's relationship with God where His wisdom needs to be applied more consistently.

Lesson Outline

INTRODUCTION
  A. Finding Wisdom
  B. Lesson Background
I. THE VALUE OF WISDOM (Proverbs 3:13-18)
  A. For Its Inherent Qualities (vv. 13-15)
    Wisdom or Knowledge
  B. For the Blessings It Brings (vv. 16-18)
II. OUR ATTITUDE TOWARD WISDOM (Proverbs 4:1-9)
  A. Wisdom Received (vv. 1-3)
    Pass It Along
  B. Wisdom Retained (vv. 4-6)
  C. Wisdom Exalted (vv. 7-9)
CONCLUSION
  A. Wisdom for What?
  B. Wisdom Is Intergenerational
  C. Prayer
  D. Thought to Remember

Introduction

A. Finding Wisdom

Diogenes, a Greek philosopher who lived from about 412 to 323 B.C., led a simple life and often resorted to bizarre behavior to gain attention. Alexander the Great tolerated his eccentricities and learned to respect the old man.

On one occasion, Alexander saw Diogenes carefully examining a large pile of human bones. Having come to expect such curious behavior, Alexander retained his composure and asked Diogenes why in the world he was doing this.

"Sir, I am searching for the bones of your father," came the reply, "but I can't distinguish those of your father from those of his slaves." Diogenes seems to have realized that the "paths of glory lead but to the grave" and that wisdom is

"better than the merchandise of silver, and the gain thereof than fine gold" (Proverbs 3:14).

B. Lesson Background

Scholars refer to certain portions of the Old Testament as "Wisdom Literature." Although wisdom literature may be found at various places in the Old Testament, most of it is centered in the books of Job, Psalms, Proverbs, and Ecclesiastes. The main emphasis of wisdom literature is to impart moral values and provide information that will allow a person to live a godly life.

Solomon, for example, prayed at the beginning of his reign for "an understanding heart" that he might rule his people justly and prudently (1 Kings 3:9). God granted Solomon his desire, and before long he had gained a reputation for his wisdom. The life of Solomon also shows that wisdom is not necessarily a permanent endowment, for later in his life he made decisions that were anything but wise. The book of Proverbs is attributed to "Solomon the son of David, king of Israel" (Proverbs 1:1). While Solomon may have written some of the individual proverbs, most scholars believe that the book as we know it today is a collection of wise sayings that was assembled over a long period of time.

As for literary form, Proverbs is cast as poetry. Poetry takes various sub-forms. *Epic* poetry, such as the *Iliad* and the *Odyssey*, tells of heroes and legends. *Lyric* poetry is intended to be sung, and the book of Psalms offers good examples of this. *Didactic* poetry is designed to teach, and that is what we find in the book of Proverbs.

I. The Value of Wisdom (Proverbs 3:13-18)

A. For Its Inherent Qualities (vv. 13-15)

13. Happy is the man that findeth wisdom, and the man that getteth understanding.

The setting for the third chapter is a father making an appeal to heed parental advice (cf. 3:1). The first verse in our printed text depicts one who is actively seeking *wisdom*. Wisdom is not usually acquired by accident, nor is it gained without some effort. We may note also that it does not come suddenly. Even for our Lord it was a developmental process. Luke 2:52 notes that "Jesus increased in wisdom and stature." [See question #1, page 424.]

In this verse we are not told how or where the person should seek for wisdom, but common sense tells us that some activities and some places are more likely than others to prove fruitful in this quest. One is not likely, for example, to find wisdom when most of his or her energy is directed toward seeking pleasure. Nor is one likely to find wisdom in a place notorious for carnal or intemperate living.

Although the demands in the search for wisdom are rigorous, the result is worth the effort, for it brings happiness. This suggests Jesus' parables of the lost sheep, lost coin, and lost son. When they were found, great rejoicing resulted. In this verse wisdom and *understanding* are practically synonymous.

But remember that the mere gaining of knowledge does not necessarily lead to wisdom. Learning how to understand factual information and how to use it appropriately leads to the wisdom that is desired.

14. For the merchandise of it is better than the merchandise of silver, and the gain thereof than fine gold.

The merchandise of it refers to the profit one gains in a business transaction. The profit that results from gaining wisdom is far better than the profit one might realize by gaining only *silver* and *gold*. In the mythical story of King Midas everything the king touched turned to gold. It seemed like a dream come true; but when he touched his daughter and she turned to gold, the king learned how worthless that yellow metal really was. King Solomon himself learned a similar lesson. He accumulated large stores of silver and gold, but concluded with the dismal lament that it was all "vanity and vexation of spirit" (Ecclesiastes 2:11).

WISDOM OR KNOWLEDGE

A few years ago Caroline Sutton wrote a book entitled, *How Do They Do That?* The book answers all sorts of questions, such as "How do homing pigeons find their way home?" "How do they get the lead into a pencil?" "How do they make pictures big enough to put on billboards?" And, of course, "How do astronauts relieve themselves in outer space?"

It's amazing that there really are people who know the answers to questions like these. Maybe you're one of them.

The world is filled with smart people who have accumulated knowledge. Ours is the most educated generation in history. According to the *PrayerNet Newsletter* of July 18, 1997, the sum total of all human knowledge doubles about every twenty-two months. *Executive Book Summaries* reports more information was generated in the last thirty years than in the previous five thousand. More than four thousand books are published every day. The *New York Times* includes more information in a single day than a resident of seventeenth-century London was likely to encounter in a lifetime.

We're pretty smart, but are we wise? There is a difference between knowledge and wisdom. It's possible to accumulate tons of information about the world, but to know nothing about living. That's the reason wisdom is so valuable. Wisdom helps us use what we know. Wisdom guides us to a successful life, not just one filled with facts.
—J. A. M.

15. She is more precious than rubies: and all the things thou canst desire are not to be compared unto her.

In poetry of this period it was a common practice to personify qualities and attributes. Here wisdom is personified as a woman, a technique used in other places in Proverbs. *Rubies* may refer to the well-known gemstone or it may refer to a rare and valuable form of red coral. Either way, the point is that wisdom is more valuable than these items used in jewelry. In some of the mines, slaves were used to do the actual work of mining. If a slave found a precious stone of a certain size, he would be granted his freedom. Certainly few things could be more valuable or desired than freedom. Yet even this did not compare with the value of wisdom.

B. For the Blessings It Brings (vv. 16-18)

16. Length of days is in her right hand; and in her left hand riches and honor.

Every culture has a set of values by which it determines what things are most important. In ancient Israel, belief in a life after death was not so widely or firmly held as it is among Christians today. As a result, the Israelites thought a long life to be greatly desired. One thing wisdom promised was *length of days*. We can readily understand this. Even in those ancient days when little was known about medicine, wisdom would lead one to realize that a lifestyle based on carousing and excessive drinking would shorten one's life. Further, wisdom would lead one to avoid situations that were needlessly dangerous and to avoid personal confrontations that could lead to violence. Today a wise person would take advantage of all the advances made in medical science. We now know that proper diet, exercise, and regular physical checkups can prolong life. [See question #2, page 424.]

In addition to length of days, wisdom offers *riches and honor*. One who manages personal resources wisely is more likely to provide adequately for family needs and eventual retirement.

How to Say It

DIOGENES. Die-*ah*-jin-ees.
ECCLESIASTES. Ik-*leez*-ee-*as*-teez (strong accent on *as*).

One who, like the prodigal son, wastes resources in "riotous living" is not likely to be able to do either. When wisdom leads one to follow a life committed to honesty and humble service, that person will be honored even without seeking recognition.

As Solomon began his reign, he asked God for wisdom to rule wisely. God granted this prayer and then went far beyond it, promising "riches and honor" as well. God also promised to lengthen his days if he kept God's statutes and commandments (1 Kings 3:13, 14).

17. Her ways are ways of pleasantness, and all her paths are peace.

We should not understand this to mean that one who lives wisely will avoid all suffering and hardships. Indeed, in verses 11 and 12, just preceding our lesson text, we are told not to despise the "chastening of the Lord; neither be weary of his correction: for whom the Lord loveth he correcteth." As Christians we recognize that the road of life may be rough at times, but we also know that the destination is worth whatever we have to endure to get there.

One example is marriage. Even with wisdom on the part of both partners, the best of marriages is not always characterized by *ways of pleasantness* or *paths of peace*. But how much worse would that marriage be when one or both partners act unwisely!

18. She is a tree of life to them that lay hold upon her: and happy is every one that retaineth her.

The expression *tree of life* is used metaphorically to refer to the pleasures and satisfactions of life. But we cannot avoid the larger implications of this expression found in Genesis 2:9; 3:22; and Revelation 22:2, 14, where this phrase clearly refers to eternal life. The reader is encouraged to *lay hold upon* the tree of life, which represents wisdom. This must be an ongoing experience, for they must retain *her*. In other words, gaining wisdom is not a once-and-for-all experience; it must be a continuous process throughout life.

II. Our Attitude Toward Wisdom (Proverbs 4:1-9)

A. Wisdom Received (vv. 1-3)

1. Hear, ye children, the instruction of a father, and attend to know understanding.

In ancient Israel the *father* bore the major responsibility for the spiritual training of the children. Without any formal schools, this training took place in the home and in the daily work in the fields and pastures (Deuteronomy 6:3-9).

While the father had the responsibility for bringing his children up in the way they should walk, he, along with the mother, deserved the respect of the children. The Fifth Commandment required children to honor their parents, and the penalty was severe for those who openly rebelled against their parents—death by stoning (Deuteronomy 21:18-21). Thus, when the *children* (translated *sons* in most modern translations) are told to *hear* the *instruction* of a father, this admonition was not to be taken lightly.

2. For I give you good doctrine, forsake ye not my law.

Doctrine in the Bible is often synonymous with "teaching." The teaching is good first of all because it came originally from God. The Ten Commandments given to Moses on Mount Sinai and supplemented by later revelations formed the basis for all doctrine.

3. For I was my father's son, tender and only beloved in the sight of my mother.

The teacher reflects on his own childhood when he learned from his own father the teachings he now wishes to pass on to his son. Combined with *tender* love and care from his *mother*, one sees here the solid framework of love that always should surround parental teaching. An authoritarian stance by parents that lacks love is almost certain to lead to rebellion on the part of the child. On the other hand, this does not mean giving in to the child's every whim. This is not really love at all. Sometimes parents have to display "tough love" that makes demands and expects obedience. To do otherwise is to cheat the child out of the proper training that he or she deserves.

PASS IT ALONG

Proverbs 4:1 makes it clear that sharing wisdom is an intergenerational responsibility. Wisdom is to be passed along from parent to child. The late actor Jimmy Stewart used to tell how his father helped him connect with the wisdom and strength of the Bible.

When the United States entered World War II, Stewart enlisted in the Army Air Corps. When he deployed overseas, Stewart's father, Alex, wanted to encourage his son but was overcome with emotion. Instead he wrote a note. Jimmy later read the words his father had been unable to say aloud. He passed along this wisdom:

"My dear Jim boy. Soon after you read this letter, you will be on your way to the worst sort of danger. Jim, I'm banking on the enclosed copy of the 91st Psalm. The thing that takes the place of fear and worry is the promise of these words. I am staking my faith in these words. I feel sure that God will lead you through this mad experience. I can say no more. I only continue to pray. Goodbye, my dear. God bless you and keep you. I love you more than I can tell you. Dad."

Alex Stewart was a veteran of the Spanish-American War. He knew from experience the comforting power of Psalm 91:3-5: "Surely he shall deliver thee from the snare of the fowler . . . under his wings shalt thou trust. . . . Thou shalt not be afraid for the terror by night; nor for the arrow that flieth by day."

Jimmy Stewart returned home a decorated hero of twenty combat missions. He learned from his father the wisdom of trusting the God whom Psalm 91:1, 2 describes as a refuge and fortress.

—J. A. M.

B. Wisdom Retained (vv. 4-6)

4. He taught me also, and said unto me, Let thine heart retain my words: keep my commandments, and live.

When a baby enters the world, his or her mind is, except for a few rudimentary things, a blank. Immediately, however, the mind begins to absorb and respond to the stimuli that affect it. What happens to the child as he or she grows and matures depends upon the kind of stimuli received. Psychologists who work with children are unanimous in their belief that the "zero to three" years are crucial in forming a child's character and personality. (That is one good reason a church should be very concerned about the quality of programs it has in its nursery and preschool departments.)

In this verse, the writer is reflecting on his own learning experience as a child. In his own case, it seems obvious that his father had taken his responsibilities seriously. It is not enough for the father to be a good teacher, however. The student must also *retain* that which is *taught*. To help his son retain his teaching, the father undoubtedly drew upon his own experiences, telling how obedience to God's *commandments* had brought happiness. But at the same time it is likely that he shared with his son some of his misdeeds that led to painful consequences. These anecdotes would help the son remember the lessons the father taught.

5. Get wisdom, get understanding: forget it not; neither decline from the words of my mouth.

Learning is not a passive activity in which the teacher does all the work and the student sits through it like an inert lump. The imperative to *get wisdom* implies activity—seeking or buying—that involves a cost to the student. The same idea is expressed later in Proverbs 23:23: "Buy the truth, and sell it not; also wisdom, and instruction, and understanding."

The teacher is experienced enough to know that sometimes the student rebels against the truth, thus the warning to *neither decline from the words of my mouth*. Sometimes the rebellion

occurs because the ideas are new or strange to the one being taught, or because the ideas require the student to do something he or she doesn't want to do (or to avoid something he or she does want to do). A wise teacher will anticipate such reactions and be prepared for them.

6. Forsake her not, and she shall preserve thee: love her, and she shall keep thee.

This verse is a good example of "synonymous parallelism," a literary device common to Hebrew poetry. In this device the truth stated in the first line is then repeated in different words in the second line. In addition to its poetic value, the repetition reinforces the stated truth.

C. Wisdom Exalted (vv. 7-9)

7. Wisdom is the principal thing; therefore get wisdom: and with all thy getting get understanding.

Most of us, consciously or not, have a list of priorities that divides important things from those of lesser importance. This verse illustrates just such a list and at the top of it is *wisdom*, which is the *principal thing*. No matter how many other things a person may become involved in, getting *understanding* ought to be at the top of the list. In fact, one who gains wisdom and understanding is more likely to be able to gain the other things he or she seeks. [See question #3, page 424.]

8. Exalt her, and she shall promote thee: she shall bring thee to honor, when thou dost embrace her.

Not only are the children to seek wisdom and cling to it, they are to *exalt* it. Some young people sneer at learning, and if one of their number excels academically, he or she may be rejected as a "nerd." But this verse rejects such an attitude.

Visual for lesson 10

This poster illustrates Proverbs 4:7. Contrast the wisdom found in these settings with godly wisdom.

One who exalts wisdom will in turn be exalted. [See question #4, page 424.]

9. She shall give to thine head an ornament of grace: a crown of glory shall she deliver to thee.

The reward of an *ornament of grace* does not necessarily mean a *crown* such as a king might wear, but rather refers figuratively to any honor or blessing that comes as a result of pursuing wisdom. (Crown of glory, or "crown" in the New Testament, is used to designate eternal life; however, that does not seem to be the point here.) [See question #5, page 424.]

Conclusion

A. Wisdom for What?

The advantages of wisdom are many and varied. Employers prize the wisdom of a worker that goes beyond the skills needed to perform a job. Teachers appreciate the student whose wisdom carries him or her beyond the pages of the textbook. Churches earnestly seek wise leaders who can guide the congregation in the many decisions it must make.

But as important as wisdom is in all these areas, the wisdom that leads us to God is most important. While the book of Proverbs deals with many everyday forms of wisdom, its central emphasis is upon the wisdom that brings us to God and helps us to grow in our spiritual stature.

The psalmist writes, "The fear of the Lord is the beginning of wisdom" (111:10), and Proverbs 9:10 echoes this idea. Thus our concern must be to acquire not just wisdom, but wisdom that leads us to God (cf. 1 Corinthians 1:18-25).

B. Wisdom Is Intergenerational

In secular as well as Christian education, we hear a great deal about the important part that

Home Daily Bible Readings

Monday, July 29—Learning About Wisdom (Proverbs 1:1-7)
Tuesday, July 30—Listen to Wisdom for Security (Proverbs 1:20-33)
Wednesday, July 31—Accept God's Words (Proverbs 2:1-15)
Thursday, Aug. 1—Trust God, Not Your Own Insight (Proverbs 3:1-12)
Friday, Aug. 2—Keep Sound Wisdom and Prudence (Proverbs 3:21-26)
Saturday, Aug. 3—Hold On to Instruction (Proverbs 4:10-17)
Sunday, Aug. 4—Take Knowledge, Not Gold (Proverbs 8:1-12)

parents play in the education of their children. But even as we voice this emphasis, we should not overlook the part that grandparents can play in helping their grandchildren gain wisdom (cf. 2 Timothy 1:5). Grandparents are good for many things. If they live nearby, they are convenient baby-sitters. Then at Christmastime and at birthdays they can be generous givers. Of course, sometimes they may spoil the grandchildren, but that is a reasonable price to pay for all the help and wisdom they can bring.

I was fortunate to live in a three-generation household. When my grandfather died, we moved in with grandmother. When it became necessary for my mother to work outside the home, my grandmother watched over us during our growing-up years. In her quiet, humble, pious way she made a lasting impression on me, my siblings, and our cousins. One of the lasting images that we have is of her falling asleep each night in her favorite rocking chair as she read her Bible. In good times or bad, her usual response was to quote a Bible verse or a wise old saying. Today I find myself doing the same thing for my own children and grandchildren. Grandmother did not live to see the full impact of the wisdom she passed on to succeeding generations. Today six of her grandchildren and great-grandchildren are engaged in "full-time Christian service," and several others are involved actively in local churches.

This lesson emphasizes embracing wisdom. For one to embrace wisdom, he or she must come into contact with it. That is not as simple or as easy as it was in previous generations. For one thing, teaching Biblical wisdom is rarely possible in public schools. Further, many parents are not equipped for this task. And many have not come to realize how important it is to begin this teaching while our children are infants. Another serious obstacle to this kind of teaching is that we are immersed in a media sea that offers all kinds of alternatives to Biblical wisdom. All this means that we as parents, grandparents, and young people must embrace wisdom, and share with others the joys and blessings of following God's wisdom.

C. Prayer

Father God, Author of all true wisdom, we pray that You will give us the strength and determination to seek Your wisdom and the burning desire to share that wisdom with others. In Jesus' name we pray. Amen.

D. Thought to Remember

"The fear of the Lord is the beginning of wisdom."

Learning by Doing

This page contains an alternate lesson plan emphasizing learning activities. Classes desiring such student involvement will find these suggestions helpful.

Learning Goals

After participating in this lesson, each student will be able to:

1. Describe the value and importance of getting wisdom and of passing it on.

2. Contrast God's wisdom with that of the world.

3. Suggest an area of one's relationship with God where His wisdom needs to be applied more consistently.

Into the Lesson

CHOICE: *Sentence Completion*. Write "Wisdom is . . ." on the board or on a poster. Go around the class and have each person complete the sentence. Then make the transition to the Bible study by saying, "We have heard some good ideas about what wisdom is. How will our answers measure up with what the Bible teaches? Today's lesson will help us do that!"

CHOICE: *Video Interview*. Every church has someone interested in and knowledgeable about video equipment. Ask such a person or a group to prepare a man-on-the-street video to introduce this lesson. They should ask people to complete the two sentences "Wisdom is . . . " and "Understanding is . . . ." They could interview people after church or go to a mall or busy street corner to get a sampling.

Into the Word

CHOICE: *Chart*. Have class members complete a chart showing blessings and benefits from gaining wisdom and understanding. The chart could be duplicated for each student or you could do this as a class by drawing the chart on the board or a transparency. Results might look like this:

BLESSINGS AND BENEFITS OF WISDOM

3:13	Happiness
3:14	Gain, better than silver or gold
3:15	Value beyond that of rubies
3:16	Length of days, riches, and honor
3:17	Pleasantness and peace
3:18	Tree of life
4:4	Life
4:6	Being preserved and kept
4:8	Being promoted and honored
4:9	An ornament of grace and a crown of glory

CHOICE: *Write a Biblical Definition*. Challenge your class to write a Biblical definition for *wisdom*. Bring several concordances to class and have your students look up references to the words *wisdom* and *wise* in Proverbs and other Bible books to help them define the words.

CHOICE: *Marginal Markings*. Ask your class members to read through Proverbs 3:13-18 and 4:1-9 and make a mark in the margin beside each verse according to these guidelines. Write "Ouch!" beside any verse that convicts you of a sin or shortcoming. Put a PTL! for "Praise the Lord" beside any verse that makes you want to praise God. Put an "Amen!" beside any verse that preaches to you with corrective instructions. Put a question mark beside any verse that raises a question you would like to have discussed. You may want to reproduce the text on a handout for each class member.

After class members have completed their markings, ask, "What verse did you mark with a question mark?" Discuss the verse and then ask for another. Then ask for verses marked with other marks. (The instructions for this activity are included in *Adult Bible Class.*)

Into Life

CHOICE: *Plan a Speech*. Many adult classes have grandparents vitally concerned about passing wisdom and understanding on to their progeny. Young adults could look ahead to what they would want to say to grandchildren about wisdom and understanding. Make this a discussion activity rather than writing out the speech. What definitions would be important to include? What verses would you want them to memorize? What false ideas should they avoid? If they do not have Biblical wisdom and understanding, what results? What rewards should they anticipate?

(Directions for this activity are included in *Adult Bible Class.*)

Choice: *Write an Article*. Parents of young children have a staggering responsibility. Write a letter of encouragement to parents of young children for your church newsletter or bulletin. What ideas from today's text should you include? Is there a verse parents should memorize for motivation and mission? Conclude with a call for prayer on behalf of parents.

Some class members may prefer to personalize this article in the form of a letter to a specific parent or set of parents. If you take this direction, provide stationery and envelopes.

Let's Talk It Over

The questions on this page are designed to encourage review of the lesson Scriptures and to promote discussion of the lesson by the class. The answers provided are only discussion starters. Let your class talk it over from there.

1. If wisdom is of such great value, why is it not the primary pursuit of every person?

The most obvious answer is that many people have not made the logical connection that the writer of Proverbs makes, namely, that from wisdom flows the qualities and characteristics of life that bring lasting happiness. Instead, many have bought into the notion that it is prosperity, popularity, and power that result in true satisfaction.

Also, many believe that if they know "how" they don't need to ask "why?" Thus, pursuit of knowledge is more along pragmatic and utilitarian lines, rather than on gaining understanding for life. Mere accumulation of information can result in a failure to move from "'what' and 'how much' we know" to what we should actually *do* with what we know to help us live lives that are pleasing to God.

2. It would seem that length of years would inevitably result in greater wisdom, but this doesn't always seem to be the case. Why?

There are many reasons. One is laziness. Another is that as we experience life, we may not be asking the right questions about those experiences. It is not unusual to hear the observation, "He just never seems to learn." That's because the person fails to ask, "What should I have learned from that experience?" or "What might God be wanting me to learn?"

A further reason is that we simply assume we have grown wiser because we have grown older. This assumption produces a person who "has all the answers" and therefore ceases to learn. Such self-proclaimed experts usually have little to offer us. They are trapped within the confines of their own "expert" advice. They are not "lifelong learners" like the ninety-two-year-old man who, when asked what was the most important thing he had learned about life, said, "I've learned that I still have a lot to learn."

3. What do you think should be the primary purpose of education, whether Christian or secular?

One's philosophy of education is extremely important here. The inclusion of values and life application in this philosophy will determine what we think should be taught, and how we evaluate teachers and measure results. In any case, the purpose of either secular or Christian education must be more than mere "transmission of information."

The role of the parent in this process includes lifestyle modeling and interpretation. In the home, the child's question "why?" is important because it provides an opportunity to give a reason. Children, of course, also use "why?" simply because they want to argue! When that happens, the wise parent knows the difference between giving a child a *reason* and attempting to *reason with* the child.

4. Why is wisdom not highly esteemed and eagerly embraced by society today?

Contemporary culture places higher values on political correctness, inclusion, and tolerance than on wisdom and truth. The view today is that since all truth is relative, there is no morality that is absolute and no philosophical or religious teaching that is superior to any other (cf. Daniel 8:12). Individualism reigns supreme. Therefore, whatever lifestyle I may choose, whatever moral practices I may prefer, whatever religious beliefs I may hold must be respected and accepted as of equal value to any other. What I choose is the important thing, not the wisdom of that choice.

When this perspective prevails, then there is no reason to listen to and learn from the instruction of a godly parent or teacher, or to esteem godly wisdom and embrace it.

5. While we may desire wise leaders in the church, it seems that we don't easily recognize wisdom in others. How would you identify a "wise" person when selecting church leaders?

Our tendency is to develop a list of behavioral "do's and don'ts," and then measure possible leaders against this list. While this may identify some of the characteristics of a wise person, it may just as easily identify a person whose attitude is one of superiority and self-righteousness.

To behavioral characteristics and knowledge of Scripture must be added loving humility and servanthood. Such a person has learned wisdom from Jesus Himself, the ultimate Servant (Mark 9:35; 10:43-45). Mere knowledge without love and humility destroys (1 Corinthians 8:1, 11). True wisdom does quite the opposite (James 3:17)!

Run From Evil

DEVOTIONAL READING: Proverbs 6:6-15.

BACKGROUND SCRIPTURE: Proverbs 6.

PRINTED TEXT: Proverbs 6:16-28.

Proverbs 6:16-28

16 These six things doth the LORD hate; yea, seven are an abomination unto him:

17 A proud look, a lying tongue, and hands that shed innocent blood,

18 A heart that deviseth wicked imaginations, feet that be swift in running to mischief,

19 A false witness that speaketh lies, and he that soweth discord among brethren.

20 My son, keep thy father's commandment, and forsake not the law of thy mother:

21 Bind them continually upon thine heart, and tie them about thy neck.

22 When thou goest, it shall lead thee; when thou sleepest, it shall keep thee; and when thou awakest, it shall talk with thee.

23 For the commandment is a lamp; and the law is light; and reproofs of instruction are the way of life:

24 To keep thee from the evil woman, from the flattery of the tongue of a strange woman.

25 Lust not after her beauty in thine heart; neither let her take thee with her eyelids.

26 For by means of a whorish woman a man is brought to a piece of bread: and the adulteress will hunt for the precious life.

27 Can a man take fire in his bosom, and his clothes not be burned?

28 Can one go upon hot coals, and his feet not be burned?

Aug 11

GOLDEN TEXT: My son, keep thy father's commandment, and forsake not the law of thy mother: bind them continually upon thine heart, and tie them about thy neck.—Proverbs 6:20, 21.

Worship and Wisdom for Living
Unit 3: Words for the Wise
(Lessons 10-13)

Lesson Aims

After participating in this lesson, each student will be able to:

1. List the warnings about evil that are found in today's text.

2. Tell why the warnings against the specific sins mentioned in the text are especially necessary today.

3. Develop a strategy for dealing with one or more of the temptations cited in today's text.

Lesson Outline

INTRODUCTION
  A. Turning the Decrees to the Wall
  B. Lesson Background
 I. CATALOG OF ABOMINATIONS (Proverbs 6:16-19)
  A. Pride, Lying, Violence (vv. 16, 17)
  B. A Wicked Heart, Eagerness to Sin (v. 18)
  C. False Witness, Sower of Discord (v. 19)
    Have We Lost Our Sense?
 II. KEEPING PARENTAL COMMANDMENTS (Proverbs 6:20-23)
  A. Keep Them Continually (vv. 20, 21)
  B. Keep Them Wherever You Go (v. 22)
  C. Keep Them to Bring Light and Life (v. 23)
III. WARNING AGAINST ADULTERY (Proverbs 6:24-28)
  A. Avoid Evil Women (v. 24)
  B. Avoid Lust (v. 25)
    Eye Control
  C. Avoid the Consequences (vv. 26-28)
CONCLUSION
  A. On Your Mark! Get Set! Go!
  B. Is There Hope?
  C. Prayer
  D. Thought to Remember

Introduction

A. Turning the Decrees to the Wall

Under their great leader Pericles (495–429 B.C.), ancient Athens built an extensive empire around the Aegean Sea. To govern other cities that had become a part of this empire, Pericles from time to time issued decrees, which were inscribed on plaques and displayed in a prominent place in each city. On one occasion an ambassador came to Pericles asking that a certain decree be changed and the plaque be removed.

"I am sorry," replied Pericles, "but I cannot do that. We have a law that once a decree has been posted, the plaque carrying the decree cannot be removed."

"But," argued the ambassador, "we are not asking for you to remove the plaque. Just turn it around to face the wall so that we won't have to see it."

That sounds very much like the attitudes many today take toward sin. Although we've retained God's laws, those laws are "turned around" so that one is no longer a criminal or even a sinner, but is merely "socially maladjusted." A couple living in open adultery is demonstrating an "alternate lifestyle." Those who murder unborn babies talk about a woman's right to "privacy" or to "control her own body"; they are called "pro-choice," not "anti-life."

But the writer of the verses used as our lesson text would have none of these elusive euphemisms. He asserted that certain sins were "an abomination to the Lord." It may not be "politically correct" to use such forceful language, but it certainly is Biblically correct. There is no place in the Scriptures that allows us to turn divine decrees to the wall and thus ignore them.

B. Lesson Background

As in last week's lesson, the format today is that of a parent giving sound advice to his son. In the previous lesson the emphasis was on gaining wisdom as a means of avoiding sin and the troubles it brings. Today's lesson emphasizes the importance of guarding against certain sins. The lesson title, "Run From Evil," is appropriate for this kind of emphasis, and reminds us of Paul's advice to Timothy to "flee also youthful lusts" (2 Timothy 2:22).

I. Catalog of Abominations (Proverbs 6:16-19)

The list of sins found in the opening verses of the lesson text is not intended to be exhaustive, but it is representative of a wide range of sins that plagued society at the time these verses were written. During the Middle Ages the church had a list of "seven deadly sins"—pride, anger, envy, sexual impurity, gluttony, laziness, and greed. The sins listed in today's lesson could be called "Israel's seven deadly sins." If we were to draw up a list of sins that especially threaten our society, our list might be somewhat different, but all of the sins listed here are certainly prevalent today.

A. Pride, Lying, Violence (vv. 16, 17)

16. These six things doth the LORD hate; yea, seven are an abomination unto him.

The "numerical ladder" of *six things . . . yea seven* is a literary device used to attract attention (cf. Job 5:19). It hints that the list that is about to be set forth is not necessarily exhaustive—that is, there are not just seven things that God hates. Rather, the list is suggestive of the kind of things that God hates.

17. A proud look, a lying tongue, and hands that shed innocent blood.

Some scholars suggest that the writer mentions the sins of verses 17 and 18 in relation to parts of the human body, going from the head to the feet—eyes, *tongue, hands,* heart, and feet. Others have noted that the first five sins (vv. 17, 18) deal with general moral character, while the last two (v. 19) apply to a legal or judicial setting.

A proud look means "haughty eyes." A haughty look reveals a proud and arrogant heart. It shows disdain for others, but worst of all it shows an attitude of contempt toward God. Several Scriptures indicate that God deals severely with this sin. God will "bring down high looks" (Psalm 18:27); "God resisteth the proud, but giveth grace unto the humble" (James 4:6). Job requests God to "behold every one that is proud, and abase him" (Job 40:11). [See question #1, page 432.]

A lying tongue. Lying is the deliberate telling or withholding of information so as to misrepresent certain facts and thus deceive the listener. Lying is such a severe offense that Ananias and Sapphira were struck dead for misrepresenting their contribution to the church (Acts 5:1-11). "All liars" are subject to eternal punishment (Revelation 21:8).

Hands that shed innocent blood. We live in a violent society, making this warning against violence much needed. Psychologists, sociologists, legislators, and religious leaders have all addressed this issue with little to show for their efforts to date. Shedding innocent blood can occur in many contexts—in the home, in the schools, in the womb against the unborn, etc. Violence is widely portrayed and even glorified on our movie and television screens. Many remedies for reducing violence have been proposed, but no remedy is better than changing the anger and hatred that control many people's lives into love. That's what the gospel is designed to do.

B. A Wicked Heart, Eagerness to Sin (v. 18)

18. A heart that deviseth wicked imaginations, feet that be swift in running to mischief.

All of us at times struggle with *wicked imaginations* or evil thoughts. The condemnation in this verse is of those who nourish thoughts in their minds and plot wicked things. Martin Luther (1483–1536) once observed that while we

can't keep eagles from soaring above our heads, we can keep them from building nests in our hair. Those who devise "wicked imaginations" not only permit, but also encourage the eagles of sin to build nests in their hair.

Feet, for their part, also can be directed in a variety of ways. They can walk slowly, deliberately, and carefully; they can be *swift,* stumbling, and purposeless; or they can be some combination of these. The idea here is probably that of premeditated, rapid movement toward evil. The Lord considers such behavior an "abomination."

C. False Witness, Sower of Discord (v. 19)

19. A false witness that speaketh lies, and he that soweth discord among brethren.

Some scholars believe that the final two abominations have the tone of a judicial setting. Lying in the general sense already has been condemned in verse 17. Bearing *false witness* refers to lying in a court while under oath (cf. Exodus 20:16). Whether one is in court as the accused or as the accuser, lying under oath is destructive of the whole justice system. We refer to this as perjury, and our laws are designed to deal firmly with it (cf. 1 Timothy 1:10).

One who *soweth discord* subverts the harmony of a group or church, creating a hindrance to achieving goals. While some of the sins previously condemned affect only individuals, discord can disrupt the work of the entire group (Titus 1:11), which makes it a very dangerous sin, indeed. In the New Testament, church members are subject to discipline—even to the point of being disfellowshipped—for three reasons: doctrinal defection (e.g., 1 Timothy 1:3, 20), moral defection (e.g., 1 Corinthians 5:11), and divisiveness (e.g., Titus 3:10). Divisiveness is the

Visual for lesson 11. *This poster illustrates verses 16-19. Ask, "How can we be as aggressive in avoiding evil as runners are in keeping fit?"*

same as sowing discord. [See question #2, page 432.]

Most of us have heard the phrase that we are to "hate the sin, but love the sinner." That's good advice, especially since we are to reach out to those very sinners with the saving gospel of Jesus Christ. But the section of verses just studied is one of the clearest examples in the Bible of God actually *hating the sinner personally*. This speaks to the holiness of God.

HAVE WE LOST OUR SENSE?

Have we lost our good sense? Paul Harvey observed that "The world is jiving us. We call dirty pictures art. We build shrines to Elvis. We get our truth from tabloids and our religion from Shirley MacLaine."

Robert Welsh says, "The world is a giant insane asylum run by the worst of its inmates." We live in a world that needs, but often rejects, the wisdom of God.

When Sam Wyche was head coach of the Cincinnati Bengals, he once was fined thirty thousand dollars for not permitting a female reporter into the men's locker room. But when a player for the New England Patriots sexually exposed himself to a female reporter in his locker room, he was fined only twelve thousand dollars. Does that make sense?

It is illegal in Florida to gamble in a game of cards, but I've waited in line behind a man who spent one hundred dollars gambling on the state lottery at the local convenience store. Does that make sense?

A person can be heavily fined for cruelty to animals. But in each of the United States it is legal to destroy the life of an unborn human being. Does that make sense?

There are scores of examples of how we seem to have lost our good sense. Perhaps that would be interesting only if it were not dangerous. When wisdom is absent, society is threatened. We are called to be wise. Wisdom is the ability to see life from God's perspective. That means we learn to hate what God hates: the sinful behaviors that threaten our society.   —J. A. M.

II. Keeping Parental Commandments (Proverbs 6:20-23)

In this next section we move from the *what* to the *who*, *why*, and *how*.

A. Keep Them Continually (vv. 20, 21)

20. My son, keep thy father's commandment, and forsake not the law of thy mother:

The admonition is from the father to the *son* as at the beginning of chapter 6. In ancient Israel,

the father had the greatest responsibility for the proper upbringing of his children. But the law did not minimize the importance of the mothers in this duty. The children were required to obey the *mother* just as much as they were to obey the father (cf. Exodus 20:12). In fact, as our society is presently structured, mothers have a greater impact on the lives of their children than do most fathers (cf. 2 Timothy 1:5).

21. Bind them continually upon thine heart, and tie them about thy neck.

One cannot keep the commandments by just an occasional observance of them. They must be lodged permanently in one's mind and conscience. To ensure that this happens, we must discuss them with others, be involved in study groups, and listen to sermons regularly. Some may complain that they never hear anything new in lessons or in sermons, and in a sense they are right. The Lord's commandments are certainly not new, but we still need to hear them over and over again, lest Satan find a way to dislodge them from our hearts.

The phrase *tie them about thy neck* recalls Deuteronomy 6:8 and 11:18. The idea is surely a figure of speech, and the Pharisees got it wrong when they thought that a literal application of such passages would win God's favor (cf. Matthew 23:5). [See question #3, page 432.]

B. Keep Them Wherever You Go (v. 22)

22. When thou goest, it shall lead thee; when thou sleepest, it shall keep thee; and when thou awakest, it shall talk with thee.

This same order—going, sleeping, and awaking—is found in Deuteronomy 6:7. Keeping the Lord's commandments is not a part-time, one-day-a-week task. It is a "24/7/365" job. In our busy lives, we may find it difficult to stop in order to go through some ritualistic activities to ensure that we are keeping the Lord's commandments. That's really not the point of this verse. The important thing is that in all our thoughts and our relations with others we demonstrate that we understand how God wants us to behave.

C. Keep Them to Bring Light and Life (v. 23)

23. For the commandment is a lamp; and the law is light; and reproofs of instruction are the way of life.

Most of us have had the experience of walking through a room at night with all the lights out. Even a familiar room may be hazardous because of toys or clothing left on the floor. Yet some people try to make their way through the rooms of *life* without any spiritual *light* at all. To make the situation even more dangerous, they often have to travel through strange rooms where they have never been before. How much safer they would be if they just allowed the light of God's laws to light their way. "Thy word is a lamp unto my feet, and a light unto my path" (Psalm 119:105).

III. Warning Against Adultery (Proverbs 6:24-28)

Now the writer combines a *what* with a *why* concerning one of the most devastating of all sins.

A. Avoid Evil Women (v. 24)

24. To keep thee from the evil woman, from the flattery of the tongue of a strange woman.

This specific warning logically follows the teachings of the previous verses that urge the son to keep the commandments of the father and mother. The warning against adultery or other forms of illicit sex are found in other places in the book of Proverbs (5:3-23; 7:6-27). We may conclude from these and other passages that sexual sins were a common problem in ancient Israel. We know that they are a serious problem in modern times as well. The *strange woman* in other places in Proverbs may describe a prostitute; here it also can refer to a married woman who seeks to entice a man other than her husband in order to engage in adultery.

One obvious way to escape sexual temptations is to steer clear of people and situations where such temptations are likely to arise. "Bad company corrupts good character" (1 Corinthians 15:33, *New International Version*). If feet are to run swiftly (Proverbs 6:18), then let them be used to flee such a temptation (1 Corinthians 6:18)!

B. Avoid Lust (vv. 25)

25. Lust not after her beauty in thine heart; neither let her take thee with her eyelids.

Before *lust* results in the actual act of adultery, it grows in the *heart*. Modern culture crassly flaunts sexuality for commercial reasons, intending to plant certain desires within the person—desires that result in reaching for one's wallet. We see this technique used to sell everything from automobiles to clothing to food to jewelry to cosmetics. Pornography itself is readily available on the Internet and on newsstands.

With all of these temptations surrounding us, it is more difficult than ever to protect ourselves from the unhealthy lusts that arise from natural

How to Say It

ABOMINATION. A-bom-ih-*nay*-shun.
AEGEAN. *A*-jee-un.
PERICLES. *Pair*-ih-kleez.

human desires. But unless we do protect ourselves, we will not be able to view the people who are the objects of our lusts as being created in the image of God and in need of eternal life. They will simply be objects to be used and cast aside. Jesus cautioned against the lust of the eyes and heart (Matthew 5:28).

EYE CONTROL

In 1 John 2:16, the apostle John describes the power of the lust of the eyes. We must manage what we see. Job said, "I made a covenant with my eyes not to look lustfully at a girl. . . . If my heart has been led by my eyes, . . . then may others eat what I have sown, and may my crops be uprooted" (Job 31:1, 7, 8, *New International Version*). Job recognized in his day that the heart follows the eyes; the same holds true today. One key to conquering lust is to make a covenant with your eyes. Job determined *in advance* to guard himself in the area of sexual temptation by making a pact with his eyes not to gaze at a woman who might tempt him.

A study by Michigan State University reported that teenage girls will witness fifteen hundred hours of sexual acts before graduating. (Teenage boys will see one hundred hours less because they don't watch soap operas.) Approximately 94 percent of all sex acts on television are between people who are not married.

In 1998, Americans rented 686 million sexually explicit, hard-core videos. (That's about two-and-one-half for each and every American citizen!) The U.S. adult cable and satellite industries are a multi-billion dollar business. *On Command Corporation* and *LodgeNet Entertainment Corporation* provide movies for over 1.5 million hotel rooms. More than half of their pay-per-view business comes from pornography. Such temptations were not available to Job!

Our eyes are under attack. If you are serious about this area of your life, you're going to have to monitor your media intake. David declares, "I will set before my eyes no vile thing" (Psalm 101:3; *New International Version*). Are you exercising eye control?   —J. A. M.

C. Avoid the Consequences (vv. 26-28)

26. For by means of a whorish woman a man is brought to a piece of bread: and the adulteress will hunt for the precious life.

The phrase *a man is brought to a piece of bread* suggests that one who engages in adultery may be reduced to poverty (cf. Luke 15:13). While this may not always be literally true in the monetary sense, we all know cases where it was true in other ways—situations where adultery shattered families, destroyed marriages, and ruined ministries. The penalties for adultery are not limited to the physical *life*, but extend to eternal life as well (1 Corinthians 6:9, 10; Revelation 21:8). [See question #4, page 432.]

27, 28. Can a man take fire in his bosom, and his clothes not be burned? Can one go upon hot coals, and his feet not be burned?

To clinch his argument against adultery, the writer asks two rhetorical questions. The answer to both is obvious and inescapable.

A few years ago, a segment on the television news magazine *20/20* demonstrated how easy it was to tread on hot coals and actually *not* be burned. But the test subjects were moving quite fast across those hot coals! They weren't merely out for a stroll, as this text implies (see the translation "walk" in the *New International Version*). Both of the experiences depicted in this verse would be extremely painful, even life-threatening in some circumstances—just as adultery will be. [See question #5, page 432.]

Conclusion

A. On Your Mark! Get Set! Go!

These are the words that a runner hears at the start of a footrace. But one will not hear these words in the most important race of all: the race to escape evil. There are some interesting parallels between a footrace and the race of life. A person who wants to run a successful footrace must spend a great deal of time and energy training for the event. In the same way, if we are to escape evil, we must train by learning the Scriptures and learning how to apply them to life situations.

In a footrace a runner wears only the clothing and equipment that will aid in the run. To carry any extra weight will slow the runner down. The writer of Hebrews expresses a similar idea: "Let us lay aside every weight, and the sin which doth so easily beset us" (12:1). In the race of life we dare not allow the weight of sin to encumber and distract us. We run in order to get the prize of eternal life (1 Corinthians 9:24).

But as we attempt to escape from evil, we often need places of refuge and protection. We can find that shelter in God: "For thou hast been a shelter for me, and a strong tower from the enemy" (Psalm 61:3). We can also find in the church help and support from fellow Christians, who are also involved in the race of life. Fleeing *from* sin is not enough. After Paul warns Timothy to "flee also youthful lusts," he adds that he must move *toward* "righteousness, faith, charity, peace"; young Timothy will find these things "with them that call on the Lord out of a pure heart" (2 Timothy 2:22). We also find those noble things in God and in His church.

B. Is There Hope?

All of us at one time or another have failed to heed the good counsel of parents or teachers. Is there any hope for us when we have made a mess or our lives? Is it possible for God to take a life shattered by sin and put the pieces back together again? Thank the Lord, there is hope. All of us have been wounded by sin, but God can apply the healing "balm of Gilead" that can restore us. Even though the scars may remain, we can still be used by Him.

Where it is possible, we must make restitution for our misdeeds. If we have hurt others, we need to try to repair the damage. If we have rejected the good counsel of parents and teachers, it would be helpful to go to them and thank them for the help they tried to give and admit our mistake for not heeding it (cf. Matthew 5:23, 24).

In the parable of the prodigal son (Luke 15:11-23), Jesus gave us a wonderful picture of the attitude to have when we come to ourselves as the prodigal did. He also showed us the loving Father, standing and waiting, ready to receive us with open arms.

C. Prayer

Heavenly Father, we thank You for the wonderful help and direction You have given us through the Scriptures. We thank You also for Your love—a love that receives us back when we sin, sets our feet on the right path, and shows us the way we should go. In the Savior's name we pray. Amen.

D. Thought to Remember

"Fear God, and keep his commandments: for this is the whole duty of man."
—Ecclesiastes 12:13.

Home Daily Bible Readings

Monday, Aug. 5—Avoid Sinful Companions (Proverbs 1:8-19)

Tuesday, Aug. 6—Walk in Integrity (Proverbs 10:1-12)

Wednesday, Aug. 7—Righteousness Leads to Life (Proverbs 10:13-25)

Thursday, Aug. 8—Wicked Expectations Come to Nothing (Proverbs 10:27-32)

Friday, Aug. 9—The Wicked Fall by Wickedness (Proverbs 11:1-8)

Saturday, Aug. 10—Avoid Evil by Fearing the Lord (Proverbs 16:1-9)

Sunday, Aug. 11—Do Not Envy the Wicked (Proverbs 24:1-9)

Learning by Doing

This page contains an alternate lesson plan emphasizing learning activities.
Classes desiring such student involvement will find these suggestions helpful.

Learning Goals

After participating in this lesson, each student will be able to:

1. List the warnings about evil that are found in today's text.

2. Tell why the warnings against the specific sins mentioned in the text are especially necessary today.

3. Develop a strategy for dealing with one or more of the temptations cited in today's text.

Into the Lesson

Lead your class in a brainstorming session to list the most offensive sins—from God's perspective. The purpose of this activity is to prepare your class to look at the Bible for the answers. Make the list without lengthy discussion.

Write this phrase on the chalkboard: "The Most Despicable Sins." As class members enter, ask them to help you make a list. When you have an extensive list, ask them which ones you should put a star beside because they are worse than the others. Finally, ask which one you should underline because it is the worst of all. (Directions for this activity are included in *Adult Bible Class.)*

CHOICE: *Collage.* Bring a stack of old catalogs and magazines to class. Ask class members to tear or cut out pictures of things they would like to have. Use part of your stack of old magazines to ask class members to tear out or cut out pictures that would represent sins they would like to avoid.

Have your class members arrange their pictures on a poster with a vertical line dividing it into two parts: "Things I Would Like to Have" and "Things I Would Like to Avoid."

Into the Word

CHOICE: *Compare and Contrast.* Compare and contrast the list of sins in today's text with lists of sins in other places in Scripture. A catalog of sins is found in these three New Testament passages: Romans 1:29-31; Galatians 5:19-21; and 1 Corinthians 6:9, 10. List these sins in parallel columns on a board or transparency. What terms appear in all three lists? Circle those. Are there any that appear only here? Underline those. Is there significance to the order of the listings? (The directions for this activity are included in *Adult Bible Class.)*

CHOICE: *Research.* Many class members have Bibles with a center reference column, but some do not know how to use it. Others may not have them in their Bible because they do not realize how helpful they can be. Bring several Bibles to class that have a center reference column. Check your church library, ask your preacher for help, or call class members and ask them to bring center reference column Bibles to class.

Introduce the activity by saying, "Today's text has a list of sins to avoid. The words will not be hard to understand, but it will be hard to put the principles into practice. Sometimes looking at other passages that use the same terms or ideas can help us to understand and apply the truth we are studying. Let's read each verse; then we will look up all of the references in the center reference column and summarize what we find."

Into Life

CHOICE: *Evaluation and Confession.* Ask your class to list the sins that appear in today's text. Provide paper and pens. Then ask them to place a mark beside each sin. Give them these instructions: "Put an 'F' beside each verse that names a sin where you have **F**allen short and need forgiveness. Put an 'S' beside any verse that names a sin where you are struggling and need the Lord's **S**trength. Put a 'V' beside any verse where you are walking in the Lord's **V**ictory."

Ask your class to form prayer partners. Encourage members to confess to their prayer partner any sin for which they need forgiveness. Then their prayer partner should read 1 John 1:9 and assure them of God's forgiveness. Finally, they should pray for each other in those areas where they are struggling. (The directions for this activity are included in *Adult Bible Class.)*

CHOICE: *A Call for Sexual Purity.* Proverbs 6:25-28 gives a strong warning against sexual immorality. Have your class write a call for sexual purity based on the warnings in other Scriptures that may come to mind. For example, "Today I take a public stand for sexual purity. The Bible is clear in warning about the dangers of sexual sins and I pledge myself to purity before God. I will stay away from any woman (man) who would compromise my stand. I will be wary of anyone who flatters me. I will guard my eyes from looking lustfully at any woman (man)." (Directions for this are in *Adult Bible Class.)*

Let's Talk It Over

The questions on this page are designed to encourage review of the lesson Scriptures and to promote discussion of the lesson by the class. The answers provided are only discussion starters. Let your class talk it over from there.

1. Certain Scriptures seem actually to approve of pride (e.g., Galatians 6:4; 2 Corinthians 5:12; James 1:9, 10; *New International Version*). How can we reconcile these passages with the type of pride that God hates?

Is it appropriate for a parent to say to a child who has accomplished something worthwhile through diligence and discipline, "I'm proud of you"? Is it acceptable to feel a sense of pride in one's self for having broken a bad habit, completed a task well, or maintained a discipline that was needed to accomplish a goal? Is there a kind of pride that can be equated with self-respect that is a positive quality? (See Romans 12:3-8.)

Perhaps the kind of pride that these passages refer to is not contempt for others, but a sense of satisfaction for having applied God's wisdom to life. There is no need to compare ourselves with others, but there is value in comparing oneself to God's principles for living and recognizing when those principles are honored.

2. What might be the underlying motivations of one who "soweth discord" among fellow Christians?

There are many possibilities, but the primary motive seems to be self-interest. At least this is what Paul identifies in Romans 16:17, 18. In Titus 3:11, his evaluation is even more severe, describing this kind of person as one who is "warped and sinful" *(New International Version)*.

Whatever the specific motive, the general perspective of this kind of person is that his or her interests are of such importance that the destruction of relationships and even the division of the body of Christ are acceptable, if those interests can be served in the process.

3. Why is there value in the admonition in verses 20-22 to do those things that will continually keep God's commandments before us?

Charles Colson refers to the distinction that Aristotle makes between "intellectual virtue" and "moral virtue." Intellectual virtue is the understanding we have of virtuous living and its value. But moral virtue is the result of the habitual practice of those character qualities that are virtuous. Quoting Edmund Burke, Colson notes that, "A man's habits become his virtue," and argues that the only two institutions in society that can really

cultivate moral virtue are the family and the church. Government can't do it. Secular education with its value-neutral position can't do it. The media certainly can't do it. The failure of the family and the church to pass on this heritage of moral virtue, which we find in God's Word, will inevitably result in a degenerate society. History proves this!

4. Why do you think that persons who get involved in the kind of immoral behavior the writer identifies in verses 24-26 so often fail to take account of the consequences?

In some cases it might be that we overestimate our own ability to resist the temptations. There is usually a slow progression that takes place when we are tempted. James describes it in 1:14, 15. It's deadly! This is why Paul urges us to "flee from sexual immorality" at the first sight (1 Corinthians 6:18, *New International Version*).

Another reason might be that we aren't aware that our moral conscience is being anesthetized. By the time we have yielded to the temptation, we have partially lost our sense of sin. We have been justifying our interest and attraction to the degree that personal responsibility is minimized.

Another possibility might be that we have convinced ourselves that we can actually be two selves—a Christian person and a sinning person. James says this is really self-deceit (James 1:26).

5. Why is the battle against sin the one we so often lose?

The primary reason is that we often rely on our own strength too much. This is not a battle that anyone can win by resolve or personal discipline alone, although both are necessary. It is not just a matter of human will-power, although that, too, is important. This is a spiritual battle, and only when we have the Holy Spirit's enabling can we expect to win (Ephesians 6:10-18).

Alone, we are no match for Satan's deceptions— but we have within us the Spirit who is. "Life in the Spirit" is the key to resisting all sin (Romans 8:1-27). While defending his ministry in 2 Corinthians 10, Paul emphasizes that those arguments that seem so persuasive to us at times and lead us into sin are easily revealed to be no-brainers when they are put up against the "knowledge of God" (10:5).

Watch What You Say

August 18
Lesson 12

DEVOTIONAL READING: Proverbs 16:16-30.

BACKGROUND SCRIPTURE: Proverbs 15–17.

PRINTED TEXT: Proverbs 15:1-4, 7, 8; 17:4-10.

Proverbs 15:1-4, 7, 8

1 A soft answer turneth away wrath: but grievous words stir up anger.

2 The tongue of the wise useth knowledge aright: but the mouth of fools poureth out foolishness.

3 The eyes of the LORD are in every place, beholding the evil and the good.

4 A wholesome tongue is a tree of life: but perverseness therein is a breach in the spirit.
. . . .
7 The lips of the wise disperse knowledge: but the heart of the foolish doeth not so.

8 The sacrifice of the wicked is an abomination to the LORD: but the prayer of the upright is his delight.

Proverbs 17:4-10

4 A wicked doer giveth heed to false lips; and a liar giveth ear to a naughty tongue.

5 Whoso mocketh the poor reproacheth his Maker: and he that is glad at calamities shall not be unpunished.

6 Children's children are the crown of old men; and the glory of children are their fathers.

7 Excellent speech becometh not a fool: much less do lying lips a prince.

8 A gift is as a precious stone in the eyes of him that hath it: whithersoever it turneth, it prospereth.

9 He that covereth a transgression seeketh love; but he that repeateth a matter separateth very friends.

10 A reproof entereth more into a wise man than a hundred stripes into a fool.

Aug 18

GOLDEN TEXT: A soft answer turneth away wrath: but grievous words stir up anger.
—Proverbs 15:1.

Worship and Wisdom for Living
Unit 3: Words for the Wise
(Lessons 10-13)

Lesson Aims

After participating in this lesson, each student will be able to:

1. Summarize the benefits of wise speech and the dangers of foolish speech.

2. Tell what makes wise speech wise and foolish speech foolish.

3. Suggest some specific means of keeping one's speech wise and helpful.

Lesson Outline

INTRODUCTION
  A. Pearls
  B. Lesson Background
  I. CONTROLLING OUR SPEECH (Proverbs 15:1-4)
   A. Soft Speech (v. 1)
     Words Have Power
   B. Wise Speech (v. 2)
   C. Watched Speech (v. 3)
   D. Wholesome Speech (v. 4)
 II. VIRTUES AND VICES OF THE TONGUE (Proverbs 15:7, 8)
   A. Speech of the Wise and the Foolish (v. 7)
   B. Speech of the Wicked and the Upright (v. 8)
III. SUNDRY ADVICE (Proverbs 17:4-10)
   A. Listening to Liars (v. 4)
     Integrity
   B. The Hard-hearted (v. 5)
   C. The Joy of Children (v. 6)
   D. Speech Reveals Character (v. 7)
   E. The Value of "Gifts" (v. 8)
   F. Forgiving and Revealing Speech (v. 9)
   G. Speech That Corrects (v. 10)
CONCLUSION
  A. Before You Say It
  B. Prayer
  C. Thought to Remember

Introduction

A. Pearls

People respond differently to good counsel. In the Sermon on the Mount, Jesus spoke of the danger of casting pearls before swine. When swine see a person throwing something out before them, they come expecting to be fed. But if one should throw pearls to them rather than the corn

they are expecting, they will "trample them under their feet, and turn again and rend you" (Matthew 7:6). Of course, Jesus was not giving information about hog farming. He was talking about using discretion in instructing people. Some people will not only reject godly counsel, but will also turn on the one who offers it to them.

On another occasion, Jesus told a parable about the kingdom of Heaven involving a man who discovered a valuable pearl. Once he realized the value of his discovery, he sold all that he had to buy the pearl (Matthew 13:46). But not all will realize the value of what they have found. Even today, some people are like this man while some are not.

In these two situations, the offer/discovery of the pearls results in surprisingly different reactions. The differing responses reveal the differing characters of the hearers.

B. Lesson Background

The first nine chapters of Proverbs are made up of discourses on vices and virtues. These discourses are laid out rather logically. However, with chapter 10 there begins what one scholar calls "a collection of pithy sayings seemingly without editorial arrangement." That seems to be the case with the texts for today's lesson. While several of these sayings deal with the use or abuse of the tongue, other sayings are interspersed with them in a way that seems to depart from this pattern.

Proverbs 10:1 begins, "The proverbs of Solomon. A wise son maketh a glad father." Here we have a picture of a father offering advice to his son. Sessions between parents and children often do not follow any logical pattern and may even seem rambling and disconnected. But that's the way it happens in real life. If we understand that and put ourselves into the situation, what follows makes a lot of sense. Above all else, today's lesson conveys a great deal of good advice—for both children and parents.

I. Controlling Our Speech (Proverbs 15:1-4)

A. Soft Speech (v. 1)

1. A soft answer turneth away wrath: but grievous words stir up anger.

Perhaps no verse of Scripture has been so often underused as this one. Jesus' teaching embodied the same idea when He advised us to turn the other cheek when someone strikes us (Luke 6:29). We might speak of holding our tongue as a certain way of turning the other cheek. Even though we don't always heed this good advice, we know that it works. All of us have seen or been involved in heated controversy and watched as *a soft answer* acts as a fire extinguisher to put out the flames of anger.

We know just as certainly that *grievous words stir up anger.* How often domestic arguments turn into anger and even violence just because each party wants to get in the last angry word or insult. Even as I write this, a football star sits in jail charged with murder. A discussion following the Super Bowl led to heated words and then to violence. The result was two men lying on the pavement, stabbed to death. In the Chicago area in the mid-1990s, an off-duty sheriff's deputy and an off-duty Chicago police officer were providing security for a social event. During a conversation, both pulled their handguns and emptied them into each other at very close range.

The issues that all these folks were arguing about just couldn't have been that important! At any point short of violence, a soft answer could have prevented these tragedies.

James tells us that the tongue is a hard member to control. "For every kind of beasts . . . is tamed, . . . but the tongue can no man tame" (James 3:7, 8). Even if we didn't have this Scriptural warning about how difficult the tongue is to tame, we would know this from experience. All of us on occasion have said things, sometimes thoughtlessly, sometimes angrily, that we wished we could take back. [See question #1, page 440.]

WORDS HAVE POWER

The book of Proverbs makes it clear that words have power. Life and death is in our speech. With our words we bless and curse, build and destroy. As surely as God's spoken Word created reality, our words shape our environment.

In an article in *U.S. News & World Report,* July 21, 1994, Joannie Schroff pointed out that the way newlyweds speak to one another is one important predictive factor of their marital success. One study found that newlyweds who ended up staying married would be critical about each other in only five comments out of one hundred times they spoke to each other. Among those who later divorced, ten of every one hundred remarks was a put-down. By the time ten years of marriage had rolled by, the pairs who were headed for divorce were insulting each other five times more often than the other couples.

For a marriage to survive, husbands and wives should learn to keep their negativity under control, to use words to keep the conflict manageable. Otherwise, the hostility escalates to the point that their mental state and physiological condition make it impossible to process any new information. Efforts to communicate then become futile.

God's ancient wisdom says, "a soft answer turneth away wrath; but grievous words stir up anger." That's true at home and every other place people talk to one another.   —J. A. M.

B. Wise Speech (v. 2)

2. The tongue of the wise useth knowledge aright: but the mouth of fools poureth out foolishness.

Elsewhere in Proverbs the writer has pointed out the difference between *knowledge* and wisdom. In our modern electronic culture, knowledge is readily available to almost anyone who turns on a computer. But having information available is not the same as understanding what this information means or how it should be used. Wisdom is the ability to employ knowledge in a useful way that will help others and please God.

Fools are not necessarily those who are ignorant. Indeed, a fool may be well educated and score very high on an IQ test. Yet such a one *poureth out foolishness* if his or her intellectual prowess is not put to good purposes. A few years ago, we were shocked by the exploits of the "Unabomber." Although he probably had the IQ of a genius, he lacked wisdom, using his intelligence to maim and kill the innocent. The person who says there is no God is a fool no matter what his or her IQ, or how many degrees he or she may hold (Psalm 14:1). [See question #2, page 440.]

C. Watched Speech (v. 3)

3. The eyes of the LORD are in every place, beholding the evil and the good.

Since we are talking about speech, we might expect the writer to speak of the "ears of the Lord," but here he is stressing God's omnipresence. What God can see, He can certainly hear.

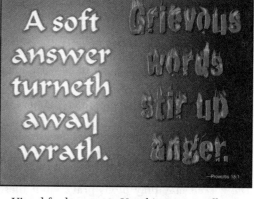

Visual for lesson 12. *Use this poster to illustrate Proverbs 15:1. Ask learners to tell of times they have seen the truth of this verse demonstrated.*

No corner is so remote nor whisper so quiet that God does not see and hear. What God sees and hears He also judges. "Every idle word that men shall speak, they shall give account thereof in the day of judgment" (Matthew 12:36).

D. Wholesome Speech (v. 4)

4. A wholesome tongue is a tree of life: but perverseness therein is a breach in the spirit.

A wholesome tongue brings words of praise to God and words of joy and healing to others. Lives that are enhanced by such words will be more useful in the Lord's kingdom.

A perverse tongue, on the other hand, is destructive of the spirits of others. Today on television and in the movies we hear language that was once confined to the gutter and would never be heard in polite society, much less in a Christian gathering. "Sitcoms" are filled with the kind of slashing sarcasm that creates humor by demeaning and dehumanizing others. Even the kidding and teasing we do with others is often painful to its victims. [See question #3, page 440.]

II. Virtues and Vices of the Tongue (Proverbs 15:7, 8)

A. Speech of the Wise and the Foolish (v. 7)

7. The lips of the wise disperse knowledge: but the heart of the foolish doeth not so.

The *wise* are respected, not because they have *knowledge,* but because they know how to use it wisely. A wise person is also respected for not being a know-it-all who displays knowledge to bolster an ego. The wise person is respected for knowing when to speak and when to remain silent (cf. Ecclesiastes 3:7). An old Quaker proverb cautions "Do not speak unless you can improve on silence."

But *the heart of the foolish* leads a person to a very different kind of speech. Those whose hearts are full of envy and pride will be betrayed by their tongues. Deceitful people may fool others for a time, but sooner or later their own tongues will trap themselves. Following the foolish counsel of foolish people can be devastating (1 Kings 12:13-15).

B. Speech of the Wicked and the Upright (v. 8)

8. The sacrifice of the wicked is an abomination to the LORD: but the prayer of the upright is his delight.

In this context, *sacrifice* refers not just to offerings made in formal worship, but also to prayers. *The wicked* may pray pious prayers but these prayers are *an abomination to the Lord.* The King in Shakespeare's *Hamlet* (Act III, Scene III), expresses the idea well:

My words fly up, my thoughts remain below.
Words without thoughts never to heaven go.

God "hears" every prayer, but He doesn't necessarily "listen" to every prayer (Isaiah 1:15; Lamentations 3:44). He views the prayers of the the hypocrite to be just that. Jesus dealt with this problem when He contrasted the prayers of the Pharisee and the publican (Luke 18:9-14).

On the other hand, God delights in *the prayer of the upright* (cf. James 5:16). Some prayers are uttered in public, others in private. The most sincere prayers of all are those that are offered from the depths of our hearts. [See question #4, page 440.]

III. Sundry Advice (Proverbs 17:4-10)

A. Listening to Liars (v. 4)

4. A wicked doer giveth heed to false lips; and a liar giveth ear to a naughty tongue.

The author now moves to other topics that in one way or another involve speech. We all know that good people sometimes are misled by those who are evil. Indeed, good people tend to be more trusting of others and thus often fall victim to the schemes of con men. But that is not the point the writer is making in this verse.

The thrust of the message here is captured in the axiom, "Birds of a feather flock together." People who are bent on doing wicked deeds will listen to liars and will themselves turn to lying to further their own evil schemes. Further, they will lie to escape their guilt when they are challenged.

This is another example of Hebrew parallelism. To give *heed to false lips* is synonymous with giving *ear to a naughty tongue* (or, in the *New International Version,* a "malicious" tongue). This may refer to the gossip that many people engage in. The *liar* often makes the gossip worse by "enhancing" the stories as he or she repeats them. [See question #5, page 440.]

INTEGRITY

Years ago, the old TV game show *Truth or Consequences* challenged people to tell the truth or face the consequences. The results were often funny. Centuries ago Jesus called the church at Pergamum (also known as "Pergamos") to be true or face the consequences (Revelation 2:12-16). Christ's call is no game. The results of compromise are never funny. Jesus expects us to put away lying and be true, to live with Christlike integrity in every circumstance.

Integrity, even in the face of adversity, is not all that common. A recent U.S. president tarnished his presidency by his poor choices and subsequent lies. For him, false lips became an art form, and many around him seemed intent on helping him cover up his lies. And while it seemed that most people considered the matter a minor one, not worthy of severe reprimand, his party's next presidential candidate blamed him and the scandals associated with him for his own inability to win the election.

A few years ago a man went to a large Christian bookstore looking to find any books written on living a life of integrity and honesty, free from lies. He found a few scattered references, but no entire book addressing the topic. Finally, he asked the clerk for help and indicated that he couldn't find any books on how to live a life of integrity or how to be a person known for truth. She said, "That's strange, we have a whole wall of them." She smiled and pointed to a wall of Bibles.

The wholeness, the integrity, we seek is found in God's truth. So, will we look to the words of Jesus and live them, or will we face the consequences instead?   —J. A. M.

B. The Hard-hearted (v. 5)

5. Whoso mocketh the poor reproacheth his Maker: and he that is glad at calamities shall not be unpunished.

Poverty has been a curse of every civilization in history. Poverty has many causes—crop failure, ill health, political oppression, bad decisions, ignorance, laziness, etc. Though many solutions to poverty have been suggested and tried, no society has yet been able to eliminate poverty. Even as the United States now enjoys the greatest prosperity any nation in history has ever known, it still has pockets of extreme poverty (cf. Mark 14:7).

This verse does not suggest any solutions to the problems of poverty. Rather, it deals with the attitudes of those who are not poor. The reason for the condemnation of one who *mocketh the poor* is that every person, regardless of financial status, is created in the image of God and deserves to be respected.

It is hard to imagine anyone so perverse as to rejoice in the *calamities* that others suffer. Perhaps such a one is motivated by envy, or is so bitter and miserable himself that he wants others to share his suffering. God will deal with such a one; he *shall not be unpunished.*

C. The Joy of Children (v. 6)

6. Children's children are the crown of old men; and the glory of children are their fathers.

In ancient Israel, a family that included many children and grandchildren was considered a blessing (cf. Psalm 127:3-5). In an age that didn't have such things as Social Security, a large family

ensured that older people would be cared for in their advanced years. But, just as important, a large family made for stability in society and within the family itself. Grandchildren are *the crown of old men;* that is, they are a source of joy and honor. For older people few joys are greater than that of watching their grandchildren mature into responsible citizens.

In the same way, parents become a source of joy and honor for their children and grandchildren. Unfortunately, modern society is missing out on much of this. In the United States, the old "extended family" has long since given way to the "nuclear family." A highly mobile society and changing values have helped undermine these wonderful relationships, and modern civilization suffers as a result.

D. Speech Reveals Character (v. 7)

7. Excellent speech becometh not a fool: much less do lying lips a prince.

Every culture develops a system of classes. In some it is a vague recognition of a poor class, middle class, and upper class. In others it is a more complicated and rigid arrangement, such as India's caste system. Each class is likely to develop its own distinctive dress, speech, and behavioral patterns. Each class is expected to conform to its own patterns. In the writer's day *a fool* was not expected to converse with *excellent speech.* This may have involved such things as grammar, accents, and content of the speech. For example, we would not expect a common laborer to talk intelligently about nuclear physics.

In the same way, certain speech and behaviors were expected of rulers. *A prince* was not expected to speak with *lying lips.* It is unfortunate that we don't have the same high standards for our rulers today. The truth is, we have come to expect politicians to lie to us. This in turn may say something about our own values.

E. The Value of "Gifts" (v. 8)

8. A gift is as a precious stone in the eyes of him that hath it: whithersoever it turneth, it prospereth.

In the *New International Version* and other modern versions, *gift* is translated "bribe," which makes more sense in this context because a bribe is a form of speech (compare the *King James Version* with the *New International Version* at Exodus 23:8 and Deuteronomy 16:19). The latter

---

How to Say It

PERGAMOS. *Per*-guh-muss.
PERGAMUM. *Per*-guh-mum.

part of this verse is satire, in that the giver of bribes *prospereth* in the sense that such a person receives favors in return for the bribe. Bribery has been a problem in every culture, and, unfortunately, is still an accepted practice in many places today. Even where bribery is illegal, giving and receiving gifts and favors often become a "legal" way to effect the same result.

F. Forgiving and Revealing Speech (v. 9)

9. He that covereth a transgression seeketh love; but he that repeateth a matter separateth very friends.

He that covereth a transgression is not the one who is guilty of wrongdoing and is trying to cover the matter to avoid detection. This phrase describes one who is willing to forgive and forget a wrong that has been done by another person. The transgression may be something done against this one personally or against someone else. Either way, this person is seeking or promoting love by working to minimize the offense and to bring about reconciliation.

He that repeateth a matter is a gossip. This one will not cover the transgression, but will broadcast and embellish it. As a result, a minor oversight may be portrayed as a deliberate snub. Close *friends* are divided when they might have been able to work out their differences.

G. Speech That Corrects (v. 10)

10. A reproof entereth more into a wise man than a hundred stripes into a fool.

One way to distinguish between a *wise* person and *a fool* is to note how one responds to *reproof*. A wise person will accept criticism and change accordingly. A fool stubbornly refuses to change behavior even when beaten severely—*a hundred stripes*. None of us enjoys being corrected, especially in public. Our egos become involved, and when that happens, we are likely to become defensive, even when the criticism is justified. And we have to recognize that at times criticism is not always fair, and even when it is fair it may be stated unkindly and harshly. But the wise person will learn to deal with even this kind of criticism.

Conclusion

A. Before You Say It

Among other things, humans are superior to animals in the fact that we can *talk*. (Although animals do have rudimentary ways of communicating with one another, they cannot carry on conversations.) Our ability to communicate is increasingly enhanced by all kinds of electronic gadgets, whether for good or for evil.

This means that we must be more careful than ever about what we say (and write). Here are a few suggestions that may help us use our speech—whether by tongue or by E-mail—more effectively for the Lord.

1. Don't talk too much. If we do, sooner or later we are likely to say some things that are stupid, false, or hurtful to others. Even God doesn't like to hear someone babble on and on (Matthew 6:7).

2. Don't put your tongue in motion until your brain is in gear (cf. Proverbs 13:3). This is usually easier for introverts than for extroverts!

3. Don't speak hastily when you are filled with anger or hatred (Proverbs 15:1). Try counting to ten—or a hundred—first.

4. Don't be a gossip (Proverbs 11:13; 18:8).

5. Don't use foul language or "trash talk" that seems so popular in many circles today. This is specifically condemned in Ephesians 5:4.

6. Speak to edify (Proverbs 25:11), especially with the saving message of the gospel.

7. Be an encourager. A few kind words can lift a discouraged person. Think of Barnabas, whose name means "Son of Encouragement" (Acts 4:36, *New International Version*).

8. Carry on every conversation as if Jesus were listening—which He is.

B. Prayer

Almighty God, we thank You for the wonderful blessing of speech. Teach us how to use that gift in such a way that Your name will be honored and that those to whom we speak will be blessed. In Jesus' name. Amen.

C. Thought to Remember

"Let the words of my mouth, and the meditation of my heart, be acceptable in thy sight."

—Psalm 19:14

Home Daily Bible Readings

Monday, Aug. 12—Mouths That Destroy Neighbors (Proverbs 11:9-14)

Tuesday, Aug. 13—Transgressions of the Lips (Proverbs 12:13-22)

Wednesday, Aug. 14—Foolish and Gracious Words (Proverbs 15:12-14, 23-30)

Thursday, Aug. 15—Pleasant Words Are Like a Honeycomb (Proverbs 16:21-29)

Friday, Aug. 16—Stop Before Quarreling Begins (Proverbs 17:14-20)

Saturday, Aug. 17—Tongue's Power: Life and Death (Proverbs 18:6-8, 19-21)

Sunday, Aug. 18—Lips Informed by Knowledge (Proverbs 20:15-22)

Learning by Doing

This page contains an alternate lesson plan emphasizing learning activities.
Classes desiring such student involvement will find these suggestions helpful.

Learning Goals

After participating in this lesson, each student will be able to:

1. Summarize the benefits of wise speech and the dangers of foolish speech.

2. Tell what makes wise speech wise and foolish speech foolish.

3. Suggest some specific means of keeping one's speech wise and helpful.

Into the Lesson

CHOICE: *Sentence Completion.* Today's text has much to say about the misuse of tongue and words. Reproduce sentences to be completed without looking at Proverbs. (This activity is included in *Adult Bible Class.)*

A soft answer turneth away _____ (15:1).
Grievous words stir up _____ (15:1).
The mouth of fools poureth out _____ (15:2).
A wholesome tongue is a _____ (15:4).
Whoso mocketh the poor reproacheth _ (17:5).
He that covereth a transgression _____ (17:9).

CHOICE: *Skit.* Ask members of your class to prepare a skit featuring concerned parents giving their final words of advice to a young adult leaving home for college, the military, or a job in another city. Set the tone of the conversation rather than spelling out specific lines. Both parents are deeply concerned for their adult child. They can hardly wait for their partner to finish a sentence before they jump in with another admonition. The young adult leaving home could vacillate between "Yes, Mom. I know Mom. Okay, Mom," and "Can I still bring laundry home?"

Make the transition to the Bible study by saying, "Concerned parents are eager to give their final words of advice to a young adult leaving home. Such sessions usually are not well organized, rehearsed speeches, but rambling shots at a variety of topics. This section of Proverbs is like that. Where earlier sections dealt with connected thoughts or a logical progression of ideas, today's text lacks any cohesive unity. It is random bits of good advice and warnings."

Into the Word

CHOICE: *Small Group Study.* Divide your class into six small groups for study and discussion. Assign each group one of these sets of verses: Proverbs 15:1, 2; Proverbs 15:3, 8; Proverbs 15:4, 7; Proverbs 17:4, 5; Proverbs 17:6, 7;

Proverbs 17:8-10. Each group should assign a recorder to write down their insights and report to the rest of the class. They should read their verses three times before discussion begins. Then each person must make at least one comment before anyone can make a second comment. Have commentaries available, if necessary.

CHOICE: *Translation Study.* Bring a variety of translations of the Old Testament for your class members to use in studying today's text. Try to get a sampling of the spectrum of translations and paraphrases. Start the discussion of each verse by having a student read a translation or paraphrase.

CHOICE: *Draw Cartoons.* Many turn to the comics when they open the newspaper. A cartoon can be useful in illustrating Biblical truth. Ask your class to draw cartoons that will explain and illustrate each verse in today's text. For example, Proverbs 17:6 almost begs to show grandparents gloating with pride over their grandchildren and youngsters boasting of their father's strength. Or Proverbs 17:10 depicts a young man listening intently while his father shakes a correcting finger at him. The adjacent frame could portray a man bent over receiving a beating but all the while covering his ears so he cannot hear the correcting advice. (The directions for this activity are included in *Adult Bible Class.)*

Into Life

CHOICE: *Write a Letter.* Most churches have young adults away from home temporarily for college, the military, or work. Encourage your class members to write letters including the advice from today's text. Discuss the tone of the letter, the topics to be addressed, and how personal it is to be.

Provide all that is needed, so that the good advice from these verses gets to the young adults who desperately need it. (The directions for this activity are included in *Adult Bible Class.)*

CHOICE: *Tongue Tamers.* Today's text is filled with verses that warn about the misuse of the tongue and words. Select three verses that could be used as "tongue tamers" to memorize and meditate upon. For example, Proverbs 15:1, 2, and 4 would make a fine trio of "tongue tamers." (The directions for this activity are included in *Adult Bible Class.)*

Let's Talk It Over

The questions on this page are designed to encourage review of the lesson Scriptures and to promote discussion of the lesson by the class. The answers provided are only discussion starters. Let your class talk it over from there.

1. Many people seem to have an extremely short fuse. The slightest thing can set them off—an inconsiderate driver, a spilled drink, or a delay at the checkout counter. What are some ways you have been able to get control before speaking in anger?

Because we are emotionally driven in moments of anger, it is necessary to take some specific action to allow reason to regain control. We speak before we think, but what we want is to think before we speak. Often a simple physical action can give us a moment to gain control. It may be taking a deep breath, or in the right situation, just closing the eyes for a moment. Devices that allow us to pause long enough to consider what we are about to say are helpful.

If words of anger spoken in haste are a problem for you, try putting the words, "Think First," or, "A Gentle Answer," from this proverb on small cards in places where you will see them regularly. These reminders will help you retrain yourself to speak more thoughtfully.

2. The words we speak carry tremendous potential for either good or ill. How can we be sure that our words have a positive rather than a negative effect in the lives of others?

We have no control, of course, over what others do with what they hear, but we do have control over what we say and how we say it. One way to assure that what we say has a more positive effect is to think of our words as deeds. For example, we would never think of throwing a bucket of paint on another person, but we will thoughtlessly gossip or spread a rumor that may be untrue and which may smear another's reputation. Our words *do* things—either good or ill.

Also consider the number of words you may use in criticizing others as compared to the number you use to encourage or commend others. Words of criticism rarely bring about positive change in others, but they do have the potential to destroy. Words really are deeds in symbolic form. This is why Jesus placed such emphasis on this in His discussion of murder (Matthew 5:21, 22). We can destroy people with our words.

3. People value freedom of speech. Can you think of ways in which this freedom is sometimes misused and abused?

The assumption is that we should be free to say anything we want to say, in any place, at any time, using any words we choose to use. Thus, vulgarity, profanity, defamation of character, and innuendo are defended on the basis of "freedom of speech." The viewpoint is that if what I say is offensive to you, then you are the one with the problem. Today's lesson, however, demonstrates God's displeasure with this type of "freedom."

4. Proverbs 15:7, 8 identifies the connection between character and communication. How can the words we use be an indicator of our character?

Most of us want to judge others by their words, while we want to be judged only by our actions. We say, "I didn't really mean that," or, "I just wasn't thinking," or, "I didn't really intend to hurt you," etc. That's just not good enough.

Jesus said, "For out of the abundance of the heart the mouth speaketh" (Matthew 12:34). It's true that we may speak before we think and we may not intentionally want to hurt another, but we cannot deny that our words do more than communicate what we want to say to others. They also say something about us, about our character, and what they say is not always flattering. The words we speak are a reflection of what we have been thinking, and the content of our thought life is the real indicator of our true character, that is, the person we really are.

5. It's interesting how people tend to gravitate to their own "kind." Why do you think this is true?

Remember the old cliché, "Birds of a feather flock together"? When you meet a person who enjoys telling dirty jokes, you can be pretty sure that most of his friends do the same. A person who gossips spends time with other gossips, etc.

One of the reasons for this may be that we find ourselves more comfortable and accepted in the circle of those who share our weaknesses. In this environment there is no challenge to change or to grow. The obvious choice for one who wants to grow in godly character is to spend time in the company of godly people. But we must not do so to the point of trying to withdraw totally from those to whom God calls us to witness (cf. 1 Corinthians 5:9, 10).

Care for the Poor

DEVOTIONAL READING: Proverbs 19:1-8.

BACKGROUND SCRIPTURE: Proverbs 19:17;
22:1-4, 8, 9, 16, 22, 23; 23:10, 11.

PRINTED TEXT: Proverbs 19:17; 22:1-4, 8, 9,
16, 22, 23; 23:10, 11.

Proverbs 19:17

17 He that hath pity upon the poor lendeth
unto the LORD; and that which he hath given
will he pay him again.

Proverbs 22:1-4, 8, 9, 16, 22, 23

1 A good name is rather to be chosen than
great riches, and loving favor rather than silver and gold.

2 The rich and poor meet together: the
LORD is the maker of them all.

3 A prudent man foreseeth the evil, and
hideth himself: but the simple pass on, and
are punished.

4 By humility and the fear of the LORD are
riches, and honor, and life.

. . . .

8 He that soweth iniquity shall reap vanity:
and the rod of his anger shall fail.

9 He that hath a bountiful eye shall be
blessed; for he giveth of his bread to the
poor.

. . . .

16 He that oppresseth the poor to increase
his riches, and he that giveth to the rich, shall
surely come to want.

. . . .

22 Rob not the poor, because he is poor:
neither oppress the afflicted in the gate:

23 For the LORD will plead their cause, and
spoil the soul of those that spoiled them.

Proverbs 23:10, 11

10 Remove not the old landmark; and
enter not into the fields of the fatherless:

11 For their Redeemer is mighty; he shall
plead their cause with thee.

GOLDEN TEXT: He that hath pity upon the poor lendeth unto the LORD; and that which
he hath given will he pay him again.—Proverbs 19:17.

Worship and Wisdom for Living
Unit 3: Words for the Wise
(Lessons 10-13)

Lesson Aims

After participating in this lesson, each student will be able to:

1. Give several reasons, both practical and theological, that the believer should help those who are poor.

2. List reasons that Christians sometimes give for not helping the poor, and examine each in light of today's Scriptures.

3. Get involved in some effort, either individually or with others, to provide tangible relief to those who are disadvantaged in some way.

Lesson Outline

Introduction

A. God Loves the Poor

Every society in the history of the world has had its share of poverty. Even today, one can find very definite pockets of poverty within the borders of the world's most affluent nations. Thus far no society has found a way to solve this problem.

But this failure is not for lack of effort. On March 16, 1964, U.S. President Lyndon B. Johnson introduced to the U.S. Congress his "Proposal for a Nationwide War on the Sources of Poverty," which led to a massive effort to reduce or even eliminate poverty. The U.S. spent billions of dollars on this "war" with little positive results to show for the effort. Instead, the country created a bureaucracy that institutionalized the very problem it was trying to eliminate, creating a dependency class in the process. By general consent, both major political parties in the U.S. agree that the effort was a failure. So now what?

Today's lesson emphasizes the Christian's personal responsibility in response to poverty. One problem is that those of us who live in affluent suburbs are safely insulated from the poor and rarely see a poor person unless we are accosted by a beggar in the central city; this results in an "out of sight, out of mind" mentality. Another problem is that many Christians are very cautious about "doing more harm than good" while in the process of feeding and clothing the poor (cf. 2 Thessalonians 3:10).

If we are to help the poor, most of us, as a first order of business, will have to get out of our "comfort zones" and go to where the poor are. Perhaps your church already has a program that works with the poor. Some churches cooperate with other churches in such programs. Either way, these programs almost always need volunteers. If your congregation is not presently involved in a program that addresses some of the problems of poverty, perhaps you and your class could investigate some opportunities to do so.

B. Lesson Background

Today's lesson is the final one in this unit that deals with wisdom from Proverbs. All of these lessons have emphasized various aspects of Christian living rather than theological issues. These studies may encourage you and your students to do further study in this helpful book. Such a study will not necessarily reveal any new truths, but these truths are often couched in catchy language that make them easier to remember and to share with others.

I. God's Concern for the Poor (Proverbs 19:17; 22:1-4)

A. Kindness to the Poor (v. 17)

17. He that hath pity upon the poor lendeth unto the LORD; and that which he hath given will he pay him again.

The economy of ancient Israel was largely agricultural, but the nation was not blessed with an abundance of rich soil. Further, the rainfall in good years was just barely enough to grow a crop. If the land did get enough rain for a good crop, it could be devoured by an invasion of locusts. Most of the farmers had only a small plot of ground to till, and even if they had a good crop year, few of them had adequate facilities to store the crops over a two- or three-year period. In addition, they sometimes faced the danger of foreign invaders who would steal their crops (cf. Judges 6:3, 4).

All this adds up to a rather pessimistic picture for the typical Israelite. When bad times hit for whatever reason, the ancient Jew had to turn to friends and other family members for help. An appeal might be made to wealthier neighbors for a loan because there were no lending agencies or a benevolent government to help. While the Old Testament laws prohibited the charging of interest on loans to fellow Israelites (Exodus 22:25; Leviticus 25:35-37), unscrupulous people found ways around these laws. As a result, people who did not repay their loans ended up losing their land (cf. Mark 12:40), and, in extreme cases, even their freedom.

The situation of the poor did not have to be so desperate, however. The wealthy were encouraged to take *pity upon the poor*—extending kindness in the form of a loan or an outright gift. They were to look upon this act of kindness as if it were extended *unto the Lord*. The Lord would then *pay him again*. The suggestion is that the Lord's favor would be more valuable than any money actually lent. [See question #1, page 448.]

B. A Good Name and Riches (v. 1)

1. A good name is rather to be chosen than great riches, and loving favor rather than silver and gold.

This verse is another good example of Hebrew parallelism, the poetic device that makes a statement in the first part of the verse and then repeats the idea in different words in the second part. While the word *good* is not in the Hebrew text, it is clearly implied in the context and most translations include it.

One who hoards wealth does not have a *good name;* a miser will probably have no pity on the poor (19:17). *Riches* may buy luxuries and pleasures, but they cannot obtain what a good name offers. *Silver and gold* may buy companions, but they can never win real friends. This verse does not oppose wealth as such, but when a person sells his or her good name for riches, the price is always too high.

Some people have done such evil in their lives that their very names have become synonymous with evil. (Judas and Hitler are two examples.) A

few years ago, the History Channel® noted the case of a baby boy who, at the insistence of his grandfather, was given at birth the same name as the notorious outlaw Jesse James. As the child moved into adulthood, he lived up to (or, rather, "down to") his namesake—he became a hardened criminal, noting that his name had caused him nothing but trouble.

On the other hand, some people have the good fortune of having been born into a family that has established a good name for itself across two or three generations. A person born into such a family has a responsibility to maintain this noble family reputation. All of us, and especially young people, need to be reminded that one bad decision, one misstep, can destroy a good name, and it may take years to recover what has been lost.

C. God Made the Rich and Poor (v. 2)

2. The rich and poor meet together: the LORD is the maker of them all.

The distinctions we make because of externals such as *rich and poor* are ultimately artificial. Those who have forfeited their good names or who have taken advantage of the poor to gain wealth are reminded that all of us are created by the Lord. The rich and the poor do not live in two separate worlds, but *meet together* in the common pursuits of life. And when this life is over, the grave erases all the artificial distinctions we create. Thomas Gray reminds us that the "paths of glory lead but to the grave."

D. Actions of the Prudent (v. 3)

3. A prudent man foreseeth the evil, and hideth himself: but the simple pass on, and are punished.

The *prudent man* is one who anticipates problems and avoids them. When this type of person sees a storm approaching, taking cover becomes a priority. This type of person may have gained wisdom from painful experience, or may have gained it from observing others (which is usually the better way).

The simple (that is, the foolish) always seem to learn the hard way—if they learn at all. They may ignorantly pursue an unwise financial

---

How to Say It

AHAB. *Ay*-hab.
CEAUSESCU (Romanian). Chow-*chess*-cue.
NABOTH. *Nay*-bawth.
HOSEA. Ho-*zay*-uh.
ISAIAH. Eye-*zay*-uh.
JEREMIAH. Jair-uh-*my*-uh.
JEZEBEL. *Jez*-uh-bel.

course, such as pursuing "can't lose" investments, and end up being part of the poor we just talked about. Or they may reject good advice and arrogantly plunge into situations that are dangerous. Family and society may attempt to erect "foolproof" barriers that will protect the simple, but such folk often find ways around or over these restrictions. Decisions and actions have consequences, and those who make unwise decisions will be *punished*. Sometimes they are punished by the laws of nature, such as when they drive an automobile recklessly. At other times they are punished by the legal system—ours or God's—when they are involved in criminal or sinful activity. [See question #2, page 448.]

E. Two Graces and Their Reward (v. 4)

4. By humility and the fear of the LORD are riches, and honor, and life.

Humility is frequently extolled in the Scriptures as a virtue, but it is rare indeed in a modern, self-centered culture. *Humility and the fear of the Lord* are logically expressed together. A humble person readily acknowledges personal weaknesses and thus turns to the Lord. At the same time, one who fears the Lord also recognizes such weaknesses and does not dare attempt to stand on his or her own strength (cf. James 4:10).

The rewards for such behavior *are riches, and honor, and life*. We should not take this to mean that the humble person will always enjoy material wealth. Indeed, a humble person may walk the paths of poverty. But humility enables one to appreciate what little he or she does have and thus, in a very real sense, be rich (cf. Luke 6:20). [See question #3, page 448.]

HUMILITY

A chief executive officer (CEO) of a Fortune 500 company visited his doctor. The news wasn't good—the businessman had a terminal disease. Knowing that his time on earth was coming to an end, he started thinking, "What is the most important principle I can teach my associates?" He really cared about those who worked closely with him.

He called together his vice presidents for a special luncheon meeting to brief them on his health and the future of the company. Before he started the meeting, a disagreement arose among them as to which man carried the most weight. To them, authority was equated with position.

The CEO now knew what he needed to teach the men. He interrupted the discussion and told them about his health, and how he expected the company to be run after his death.

Then he did a very strange thing. He sent for a shoeshine kit that he kept in his office and proceeded to shine their shoes! The room was silent—no one knew what to say. When he came to the man most likely to succeed him, that man refused the shine, saying it was beneath the dignity of the CEO to do such a thing.

The CEO replied, "If you won't let me shine your shoes, then clean out your desk—you're outta here." Because the man greatly respected his boss, he told him to do whatever he wanted.

The wise CEO passed on an invaluable life lesson: "When you stoop to serve, you raise your level of authority" (cf. John 13:1-17).   —J. A. M.

II. Sowing and Reaping (Proverbs 22:8, 9)

A. Sowing Iniquity (v. 8)

8. He that soweth iniquity shall reap vanity: and the rod of his anger shall fail.

Both in the physical world and in the moral realm, the law of the harvest is absolute. If one plants corn in a garden, a corn crop will grow. But if thistles are planted, the result is a crop of thistles.

In the same way, God rewards those who live lives pleasing to Him. A person who sows *iniquity*, however, will reap *vanity* (or "trouble," as in the *New International Version*). Some commentators see *the rod of his anger* as God's wrath on the evildoer. But since this rod will *fail*, it is much more likely that it refers to the evildoer's persecution of others. The rod will fail in the sense that his persecution of others will ultimately cease.

GARDEN-VARIETY WISDOM

I grew up where farming was the predominant activity and where every family had a garden. Every summer day found me helping my mother in the garden. For years I thought my mother was growing tomatoes, corn, and green beans. Only later did I realize my mother's primary crop was me. In the garden I discovered the laws of the harvest.

Harvest principle #1: You reap what you sow. This is the principle of *investment*. Proverbs 22:8, 9 makes this clear: Sow evil and reap a harvest of trouble. Sow blessings and you will reap blessings as surely as one who plants tomatoes reaps tomatoes.

Harvest principle #2: You reap after you sow. This is the principle of *interval*. The productive farmer is patient. The crop that is planted today does not yield its fruit tomorrow. Neither evildoers nor the righteous reap the harvest of their behavior at the end of every day, but harvest day will come.

Harvest principle #3: You reap more than you sow. This is the principle of *increase*. Every gardener understands this. A farmer who plants two bushels of wheat can anticipate reaping sixty-seven bushels, a 33:1 return! Three bushels of oats usually produce seventy-nine bushels at harvest time, an increase of 2,630 percent. Plant seven and a-half pounds of corn, and you can expect an average yield of one hundred twenty bushels at harvest. A farmer in Illinois regularly receives back seven hundred grains of corn for every grain he plants. What an amazing return!

God calls us to be wise and understand these harvest principles. Evaluate your life. What are you sowing? Is this wise? What kind of harvest can you expect?   —J. A. M.

B. Blessings of the Generous (v. 9)

9. He that hath a bountiful eye shall be blessed; for he giveth of his bread to the poor.

The person with *a bountiful eye* contrasts sharply with the person having an evil eye (Proverbs 23:6; 28:22). The former looks for opportunities to share blessings with others, going out of his or her way to find those who need help. In ancient Israel, *bread* was a basic necessity of life. This verse suggests that the generous person provides this staple food even when it means taking from his or her own supply.

III. God Protects His People
(Proverbs 22:16, 22, 23; 23:10, 11)

A. From Oppressors (v. 16)

16. He that oppresseth the poor to increase his riches, and he that giveth to the rich, shall surely come to want.

Every society has oppressors who take advantage of others to enrich themselves. This is just as true today as it was in ancient times—maybe even more so. Oppressors come in many sizes and shapes. Some may be military dictators, who seize power by force and squeeze everything they can from the people they rule in order to support their lavish lifestyles.

More familiar to most of us are those who sell shoddy goods or overcharge their customers. When a natural disaster strikes, we see such "vultures" swarm into the disaster area, taking advantage of people who have been left destitute by hurricanes or floods. And what about companies that import goods from countries that use child labor to produce products that we gladly buy because they are less expensive than goods produced here at home? The list could go on, but we can see that this verse is just as applicable today as when it was written. We have our share of oppressors today; the only difference is that they are more sophisticated than they were in Bible times.

The oppressors may seem to prosper for a time. But justice will be done. The twentieth

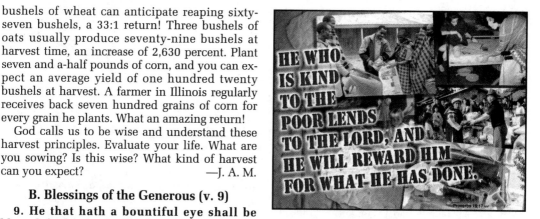

Visual for lesson 13. *The* Adult Visuals *packet contains this real-life illustration of the message of verse 17.*

century has seen the violent end of some brutal dictators—Hitler, Mussolini, and Ceausescu are examples. But those who are able to avoid justice in this life eventually will stand before the Eternal Judge, where complete justice will be meted out.

God has promised to protect *the poor* from oppressors. But how would you answer an unbeliever who says, "Why isn't your God rescuing such-and-such people from their grinding poverty?" Gideon asked a similar question in Judges 6:13, and the answer in the very next verse was "Go . . . and save Israel. . . . Am I not sending you?" *(New International Version).*

B. From Robbers (vv. 22, 23)

22, 23. Rob not the poor, because he is poor: neither oppress the afflicted in the gate: for the LORD will plead their cause, and spoil the soul of those that spoiled them.

The opening lines of these two verses hearken back to verse 16. *The poor,* with what little they do have, are ready targets for robbers because their poverty leaves them in a weakened condition, both socially and physically. The poor are usually not very well organized. The rich ignore them and their problems and, in fact, may even contribute to their problems by oppressing them and charging interest on loans. Governments frequently ignore their pleas for help because the poor don't have many friends in high places and don't make many campaign contributions. These same conditions exist today in the slum areas of large cities. [See question #4, page 448.]

The poor could appeal for justice from judges presiding at the city *gate,* since this was the place court was ordinarily held in ancient times. But justice here was not always fair. When King

Ahab wanted Naboth's vineyard, the powerful Jezebel arranged with the elders and nobles to bring false witness against Naboth. He was condemned, taken outside the city, and stoned (1 Kings 21:1-14). [See question #5, page 448.]

C. From Land Grabbers (vv. 10, 11)

10, 11. Remove not the old landmark; and enter not into the fields of the fatherless: for their Redeemer is mighty; he shall plead their cause with thee.

Fertile soil was scarce in ancient Israel, and it was important for a family to hold on to whatever land it had. In a day when accurate surveying tools and precise records of land ownership did not exist, people had to depend on identifiable landmarks to indicate boundary lines, such as large rocks, outcroppings of stone, or trees. Some of these could be moved or changed in such a way that one could steal land from a neighbor. *The fatherless* (orphans)—especially young children—would be quite vulnerable to this kind of activity. With no older person around to remember where the landmarks originally had been, an evil person could readily take advantage.

But their situation was not hopeless. Even though they had no defenders, *their Redeemer* was *mighty*. This Redeemer, of course, was God. One important instance when He ended up pleading *their cause* was the punishment meted out in the form of exile (Isaiah 1:23-25; 10:1-4; Jeremiah 5:27-29; Hosea 5:10).

Conclusion

A. The Poor Are Still With Us

When we were children, we were urged to clean our plates at mealtime because the "starving children in India" had no food at all, let alone any food to waste. There are still starving children in India and many other places in the world. The problem is getting worse, not better, and because of the media we are made more aware of them. Perhaps forty thousand children die of starvation every day worldwide.

There are many reasons for world hunger. Some things, such as floods, hurricanes, and drought, are beyond human control. Insects, which eat a very large percentage of the world's food supply each year, are only partially within our control. In other situations, political and military upheavals have created starvation and poverty in areas that could support themselves. Some governments intentionally use hunger as a "weapon" against factions of their own populations. Sometimes starvation and malnutrition occur because people do not know how to use the resources they have available. The extent of the need is so great that frequently only governmental and large private relief agencies, such as the International Disaster Emergency Service (IDES), can be of real help. We rejoice that such agencies are in place and that we can contribute to them financially.

But we don't have to travel overseas to find the needy. They are all about us, especially in our larger cities. Many churches support missions in the inner cities to feed, clothe, and teach the homeless. These missions always need contributions of food, clothing, and money. But they especially need volunteers. It is not easy work, and at times it is even frightening, but God gives a special blessing to those who do this task.

Remember: you don't have to get a passport, a visa, and learn a foreign language to help. The needy are all about us. For example, one man serves as a financial counselor with a group that shows people how to manage their money so that they can escape poverty. A woman serves with an agency that counsels unwed pregnant women, helping them arrange for their babies to be adopted or for the mothers to become responsible single mothers. Yes, the impoverished "Lazarus" may be at your gate. Don't be "the rich man" who ignored him!

B. Prayer

Father, we pray for the sick, the hungry, and the helpless of the world. But we also pray for ourselves that we may open our hearts to them. Save us from "compassion fatigue," which results in our doing nothing. In Jesus' name, amen.

C. Thought to Remember

"Blessed are the merciful: for they shall obtain mercy" (Matthew 5:7).

Home Daily Bible Readings

Monday, Aug. 19—Plight of the Poor (Proverbs 19:1-8)
Tuesday, Aug. 20—The Lord Pleads the Poor's Case (Proverbs 22:7-9, 16, 22, 23)
Wednesday, Aug. 21—Give to the Poor (Proverbs 28:20-27)
Thursday, Aug. 22—Defend Rights of the Poor (Proverbs 31:4-9)
Friday, Aug. 23—Do Not Withhold Good (Proverbs 3:27-35)
Saturday, Aug. 24—Generous Persons Will Be Enriched (Proverbs 11:17, 18, 24-28)
Sunday, Aug. 25—Happiness: Kindness to the Poor (Proverbs 14:20-22, 31-34)

Learning by Doing

This page contains an alternate lesson plan emphasizing learning activities.
Classes desiring such student involvement will find these suggestions helpful.

Learning Goals

After participating in this lesson, each student will be able to:

1. Give several reasons, both practical and theological, why the believer should help those who are poor.

2. List reasons that Christians sometimes give for not helping the poor, and examine each in light of today's Scriptures.

3. Get involved in some effort, either individually or with others, to provide tangible relief to some who are disadvantaged in some way.

Into the Lesson

CHOICE: *Debate.* Early in the week, ask two people from your class to debate the resolution: "The poor are poor because they are the victims of the greed and callousness of the rich." Allow each person two to three minutes to present his case. Then make the transition to the Bible study by saying, "Our debaters have raised some interesting and controversial points about poverty. Let's look to the Word of God to get God's perspective on the poor."

CHOICE: *Agree-Disagree Quiz.* Begin your class today with this Agree-Disagree Quiz. The statements are designed to be somewhat controversial. The purpose is to get people to say, "But the Bible says . . . ." When people ask you for the "right" answers, turn the question back with, "What do you think?" (The directions for this activity are included in *Adult Bible Class.*)

1. People are usually poor because of their own laziness, foolishness, or inability to handle money.

2. God has a special concern for the poor.

3. The church has an obligation to meet the needs of the poor.

4. The government has a responsibility to meet the needs of the poor.

5. Neither the church nor the government can solve the problem of poverty.

Use a transition statement like the one in the first choice above to move to the Bible study portion of the lesson.

Into the Word

CHOICE: *Personalized Paraphrase.* Guide your class in writing a personalized paraphrase of today's text. Personalize the passage by inserting personal pronouns, such as *I*, *me*, and *my*. Paraphrase by putting the ideas of the text in your own words.

For example, Proverbs 19:17 might be personalized and paraphrased to read, "When I show pity by giving to the poor, I am actually lending my money to the Lord; and He will no doubt pay back my loan!"

CHOICE: *True-False Quiz.* Have your class write a true-false quiz about God's view of poverty and the poor. Each verse could easily generate several questions. For example, Proverbs 19:17 suggests these affirmations:

1. If I give money to a beggar, God will give back to me whatever I give to the poor.

2. One cannot show pity without a financial involvement.

3. Giving money indiscriminately to the poor is not wise or godly.

4. Having pity on the poor means giving them money.

5. Giving money to the poor is wasting your money.

(Directions for this activity are in *Adult Bible Class.*)

CHOICE: *Make a Poster.* Each verse in today's lesson could stand alone and make good sense. Therefore, each would make a good poster to decorate your classroom or provide a focal center for the "Into Life" section of the lesson. Provide poster board and brightly-colored markers. Ask class members to carefully letter posters to present the truths of today's text graphically.

Into Life

CHOICE: *Partner With a City Congregation.* Probably someone in your class is acquainted with an urban congregation in need of help that your class could provide. Ask for volunteers to look for an urban church involved with serving the poor that you could become a partner with in providing prayer support, funds, equipment, and short-term workers. (The directions for this activity are included in *Adult Bible Class.*)

CHOICE: *Sponsor a Child.* Many Sunday school classes have the resources to sponsor a third-world child through some missionary benevolent agency. Ask for volunteers to form a search committee to gather information. Start by checking with missionaries whom your church supports. (The directions for this activity are included in *Adult Bible Class.*)

Let's Talk It Over

The questions on this page are designed to encourage review of the lesson Scriptures and to promote discussion of the lesson by the class. The answers provided are only discussion starters. Let your class talk it over from there.

1. What are some of the reasons Christians need to be more concerned and helpful with regard to the needs of the poor?

The most significant reason is the dignity and worth of all humans as created in the image of God (cf. Genesis 1:27, 28; Proverbs 22:2). This means that we have a responsibility to one another that transcends our physical and material circumstances. The actions a government may take against another nation for political or economic purposes must not affect the decisions we make as Christians to relieve the consequent suffering of innocent people.

Another reason is that most of us live in a social environment in which the choices of others can affect us dramatically. The decisions of businesses and large companies have often left significant numbers of people out of work and in near poverty conditions. Once-indispensable skills are no longer needed. Prior qualifications no longer qualify. In these instances, the church needs to seek ways to help these people through the difficult times.

2. Why are some Christians reluctant to be involved in a significant ministry to the poor?

It is easy to assume that the poor are simply victims of their own bad choices, that they have not been "prudent" as suggested in 22:3. Sometimes this is true. The culture of the U.S. values "rugged individualism"; this causes us to look skeptically at the person who has not been successful. Therefore, we are sometimes unsure about what help is best to provide, if any.

Another reason may be that since the government has various "safety nets," we think that there is no need for us to take personal responsibility. "After all, the government uses the taxes I pay to provide for the poor, and that's enough!"

Furthermore, some are concerned about the tendency of "theological liberalism" to substitute "social action" programs for the real mission of the church: taking the gospel to the lost. However, we should remember that to Jesus this was not an either/or choice. We must do both.

3. The poor often seem to be significantly disadvantaged when faced with legal concerns, whether civil or criminal. What can we do to help them at these times?

First, Christian attorneys can and should offer equal quality in representation to all clients. Second, the church can provide a referral service that identifies those individuals and firms with high ethical standards and a reputation for equal representation. The Christian Legal Society provides a national directory for this purpose. Finally, if a family with limited resources is faced with what appears to be legal oppression, then we could assist them in managing family needs so that they are not "crushed."

4. These proverbs speak of the benefit that comes to those who are humble, reverent, and generous. What is there about these qualities that blesses us?

These qualities seem to enable a person to see life with clarity. We can think of ourselves "soberly" (Romans 12:3). We do not compare ourselves with others in a proud way or take too much credit for our good fortune (Galatians 6:3, 4). Rather, we seek for opportunities to share what we have and to lift others up who have experienced misfortune (Galatians 6:2). Compare Philippians 2:3, 4.

The result is that we live with such a clear understanding of who we are in God's grand design that regardless of our circumstances, we are blessed. We have learned to be "content" (Philippians 4:11, 12). It then becomes easy to help others who are in need (cf. 1 John 3:17).

5. What are some specific ways that your local church or you personally might "care for the poor" of other needy persons?

One possibility is to start with the *IDEA* acronym. The *I* stands for "*i*dentify the need." Some needs, such as food, are valid. Specific requests for certain types of food, however, may be questionable.

The *D* stands for "*d*etermine the priorities," while *E* stands for "*e*valuate the resources." Taken together, these two concepts recognize that a church's resources can only be stretched so far, and discretion is called for in deciding where the church can and cannot help out.

The *A* stands for "*a*pply the process." This means that your church has to have a process, such as a benevolence ministry, in place and ready to help out at any time of day or night.